Handbook of

Gender
& Work

Dedicated to *Tony Butterfield*—
my great mentor, collaborator, colleague, and friend

Handbook of
Gender
& Work

Gary N. Powell
Editor

SAGE Publications
International Educational and Professional Publisher
Thousand Oaks   London   New Delhi

For information:

SAGE Publications, Inc.
2455 Teller Road
Thousand Oaks, California 91320
E-mail: order@sagepub.com

SAGE Publications Ltd.
6 Bonhill Street
London EC2A 4PU
United Kingdom

SAGE Publications India Pvt. Ltd.
M-32 Market
Greater Kailash I
New Delhi 110 048 India

Printed in the United States of America

Library of Congress Cataloging-in-Publication Data

Main entry under title:

Handbook of gender and work / edited by Gary N. Powell.
    p. cm.
  Includes index.
  ISBN 0-7619-1355-6 (alk. paper)
  1. Leadership in women. 2. Women executives. 3. Sex role in the
work environment. 4. Leadership. 5. Women—Employment.
I. Powell, Gary N.
  HQ1233.H33 1999
  306.3′615—dc21   99-6394

99 00 01 02 03 10 9 8 7 6 5 4 3 2 1

Acquiring Editor:	Marquita Flemming
Editorial Assistant:	MaryAnn Vail
Production Editor:	Diana E. Axelsen
Editorial Assistant:	Nevair Kabakian
Typesetter/Designer:	Janelle LeMaster
Indexer:	Mary Mortensen
Cover Designer:	Candice Harman

Contents

Part I. Gender and Other Identities

Part II. The Economic and Societal Context

Part III. Organizational, Group, and Interpersonal Processes

Part IV. Careers and the Quality of Life

Part V. Organizational Initiatives

Part VI. Conducting Future Research

Acknowledgments

I wish to express my appreciation and sincere thanks to a number of people for their contributions to the preparation of this book:

Marquita Flemming at Sage Publications, for suggesting the book and helping a novice editor to bring it to fruition.

Diane Adams and Julie Tamarkin, for an excellent job of editing the various chapters.

Tiger the Cat, for her loving, affectionate, playful, and stress-relieving presence in my life.

Laura Graves, my wife, favorite colleague, and a chapter author, for encouraging, supporting, and standing by me all the way.

The many contributors of individual chapters, who have shared their expertise and commitment to examining the intersection of gender and work on these pages. Without their efforts, this book would not have been possible.

Introduction

Examining the Intersection of Gender and Work

Gary N. Powell

The role of women in the workplace has been expanding steadily in recent years in most countries. For example, in the United States, the labor force participation rate for women (i.e., the proportion of all adult women who were employed or seeking employment) increased from 43% in 1970 to 60% in 1998 (U.S. Department of Labor, 1998a, 1998b). However, during the same period of time, the labor force participation rate for men decreased from 80% to 74%. As a result, the proportion of women in the labor force (i.e., the proportion of all adults employed or seeking employment who were women) increased from 38% in 1970 to 46% in 1998. In addition, the proportion of women executives, administrators, and managers in nonfarm occupations (called simply *managers* from this point on) almost tripled between 1970 and 1998, increasing from 16% to 44%.

Similar trends have been exhibited in other countries. As Table I.1 indicates, the proportion of women in the labor force increased between 1985 and 1995 by 2% to 9% in countries as diverse as Australia, Botswana, Brazil, Egypt, France, India, Ireland, Israel, Singapore, and Swaziland (International Labour Office, 1986, 1996). Although the proportion of women in the labor

TABLE I.1   Proportion of Women in the Labor Force

Country	1985 (%)	1995 (%)
Australia	34	43
Bermuda	46	50
Botswana	29	36
Brazil	33	39
Canada	42	45
Chile	30	32
Egypt	17	20
France	41	44
India	13	15
Ireland	31	38
Israel	38	42
Italy	33	35
Mauritius	32	36
New Zealand	36	44
Norway	43	46
Panama	29	32
Singapore	36	39
Spain	29	34
Swaziland	27	30
United Kingdom	42	46
Venezuela	28	32

SOURCE: 1985: International Labour Office (1986, pp. 295-306, Table 3A); 1995: International Labour Office (1996, pp. 73-84, Table 2A).

force in the countries listed in Table I.1 varied widely (from 15% to 50% in 1995), the trend in all countries was in the same direction, favoring the increased employment of women.

Furthermore, between 1985 and 1991, the proportion of women in management positions increased in 39 of 41 countries for which statistics were available (International Labour Office, 1993). The proportion of women in management in these countries varied widely due to national differences in culture and in definitions of the term *manager,* from 1% in Bangladesh to 41% in Australia in 1991. However, the trend in almost all countries was in the same direction, favoring the increased representation of women in the managerial ranks.

Despite these trends, the economic status of women in the workplace remains lower than that of men. For example, the average female full-time worker continues to be paid less than the average male full-time worker, and recent evidence suggests that the gender gap in earnings is increasing after a period of decline (see Chapter 6 by Roos and Gatta). This gap is partly due to workers in female-dominated occupations being paid lower average wages than workers in male-dominated occupations. However, it is also due to women being paid less than men in the same occupation.

The international labor force also remains sharply segregated on the basis of gender. In recent years, women have shown more interest in entering male-dominated occupations than men have shown in entering female-dominated occupations, which is not surprising because workers in male-dominated occupations are the higher paid. However, women continue to be crowded into a narrower and lower-paying set of occupations than men (see Chapter 7 by Jacobs).

Furthermore, within all countries, the proportion of women decreases at progressively higher levels in managerial hierarchies (Parker & Fagenson, 1994). Although definitions of what constitutes *top management* vary from company to company, the proportion of women in top management was only 11% in a recent survey of large American corporations (Catalyst, 1998a) and has consistently been reported as less than 5% in other countries (e.g., Adler & Izraeli, 1994; Davidson & Cooper, 1993a).

Thus, the influence of gender in the global workplace appears to be in flux in some directions and stable in others. The shifting and variable nature of this influence calls for our attention.

Purpose of the *Handbook*

The purpose of *Handbook of Gender and Work* is to increase our understanding of the intersection of gender and work. It examines how gender, alone and with other factors, influences

1. the conduct of work itself;
2. the encouragement, selection, development, and choices of people to perform some roles in the workplace and not others; and
3. the experiences of employees as they contribute to the conduct of work in organizational settings.

One way to consider what *Handbook of Gender and Work* is intended to accomplish is to evaluate how well it fits various definitions of the term *handbook*. My trusty dictionary (Random House, 1987, p. 866) offers four definitions of the term:

1. *"A book of instruction or guidance, as for an occupation; manual."* The purpose of this book is less to serve as a "how-to" manual and more to increase awareness of gender-related issues in the workplace. However, it does provide some guidance for dealing with specific situations that arise as a result of the influence of gender on individuals' work experiences.
2. *"A guidebook for travelers."* The purpose of the book is not to suggest itineraries and maps for exploring the world of work as in a conventional guidebook. This book describes various gender-related phenomena that occur in the workplace and suggests how to navigate

through occupational and organizational minefields, past hazards and obstacles, to achieve personal goals.

3. *"A reference book in a particular field."* This definition describes the primary purpose of the book. It is intended to provide definitive chapters on a comprehensive set of topics related to the intersection of gender and work. It may be used as a reference book by scholars to examine such issues as well as by readers with a general interest in the subject.

4. *"A scholarly book on a specific subject, often consisting of separate essays or articles."* This definition describes the basic design of the book. If the book is successful at meeting this definition of handbook, it will at least partially meet the first two definitions and fully meet the third definition. That is, it will provide useful guidance and navigational assistance to fellow travelers in the world of work as well as serve as a valuable reference book on the subject.

To accomplish these goals, *Handbook of Gender and Work* provides a forum for presentation of reviews of theory and research on a wide range of topics pertaining to the intersection of gender and work. These reviews both summarize the state of knowledge and identify useful directions for future theory and research.

In their chapters, authors were asked to address two basic questions regarding their topics: (1) What do we know, or think we know? (or, What have we learned so far?) and (2) What else do we need to know? (or, What else would we gain from learning?). They were asked to acknowledge controversies, debates, or disagreements over the state of knowledge on particular issues. They were also told that they need not reference every piece of work that has ever been conducted on their topics, an impossible task given the page constraints of book chapters. However, they were asked to make the reader aware of the most important pieces of work on their topics.

The authors represent a multidisciplinary and multinational group of scholars who are experts on their chosen topics. Each author was asked to incorporate a global or multicultural perspective on his or her topic. There are no chapters that have been included solely to provide an "international perspective." Indeed, most of the topics apply to the conduct of work and experiences of workers in many countries, although issues pertaining to gender and work are manifested differently in specific cultural contexts.

Chapter Topics

The first two chapters examine the meaning and significance of gender in relation to other influences on the world of work. Karen Korabik discusses the importance of distinguishing between the terms *sex* and *gender* and considers how researchers have used (and misused) these terms. Sex refers to a biological property of individuals. Gender, although the term has been used in many different and sometimes confusing ways, refers in general to the psychological and social ramifications of being biologically male or female. Korabik describes the evolution in conceptualizations of sex and gender over the past century. In addition, she examines the effect of such conceptualizations on the conduct of research into gender dynamics in the workplace.

However, sex is not the only personal characteristic that affects how people interact with the workplace. Bernardo Ferdman discusses the importance of considering other personal characteristics that may influence an individual's sense of identity, especially race, ethnicity, and the culture of the groups with which one identifies. The influence of sex and gender in the workplace is not the same for individuals from different races, ethnic groups, or cultures; similarly, the influence of race, ethnicity, and culture on work experiences is not the same for women and men. Ferdman recommends that researchers interested in gender dynamics in the workplace simultaneously examine dynamics pertaining to race, ethnicity, and culture.

The next five chapters examine the influence of the economic and societal context on the intersection of gender and work. Cary Cooper and Suzan Lewis describe the evolution in the nature of work over the past half century. They focus on four trends in particular: increased use of flexible or part-time workers, decreased levels of job security, increased expectations for hours spent on the job, and the advent of "virtual organizations" in which the traditional boundary between work and nonwork has become blurred. Cooper and Lewis consider the implications of each of these trends for gender roles in the family and in the workplace of the 21st century.

There has also been an evolution over time toward a global economy that is based more on the delivery of services than on farming or the manufacture of tangible products. Barbara Gutek, Bennett Cherry, and Markus Groth explore the implications of this shift. More women than men hold service jobs, and women are the primary consumers of services. When the work environment is dominated by members of one sex, as Gutek has noted in earlier work (e.g., Gutek, 1985), it tends to become gendered as gender roles spill over into work roles. As a result, service work often takes on the characteristics that are traditionally associated with being female, with an expectation for behavior that is pleasant ("Have a nice day!"), agreeable, patient, sensitive to the needs of others, and nurturing.

In contrast, Mark Maier examines the many ways in which traditional societal and industrial (i.e., bureaucratic) norms are embodied in the nature of work organizations. He argues that formal organizations promote a gendered work environment by embodying characteristics that are traditionally associated with being male. Organizations tend to expect employees to exhibit behavior that is rational, autonomous, competitive, action oriented, and hierarchical. Maier describes how such expectations shackle both men and women in organizational settings. He clearly articulates a feminist alternative to the "masculinist" practices and norms that have prevailed in organizations.

Patricia Roos and Mary Gatta describe how gender is associated with compensation for work. Most countries display a gender gap in earnings, although the size of this gap varies considerably across countries. The gender gap in earnings has been persistent over time with some fluctuations, despite the expanded role of women in the workplace in the global economy. Roos and Gatta examine how the gender gap in earnings varies according to variables such as race, age, and education. They also evaluate the merits and supporting evidence for various theories that purport to explain the gender gap in earnings.

Gender is also associated with the occupations in which individuals work. Jerry Jacobs examines the sex segregation of occupations, or the unequal distribution of women and men across the different types of jobs and occupations that collectively comprise the workplace. Within the United States, sex segregation was essentially stable during the 1990s and at a much higher level than popularly believed. Jacobs concludes that a system of sex segregation of occupations is maintained in most countries, even those with a small gender gap in earnings, by a combination of social and cultural forces.

The next eight chapters examine specific organizational, group, and interpersonal processes that influence as well as reflect the intersection of gender and work. The process by which organizations decide which new employees to hire may contribute to the sex segregation of occupations. Laura Graves examines gender effects in the initial employment interview, which is typically the first face-to-face meeting between the job applicant and a representative or representatives of the hiring organization. Because employment interviewers have little information about applicants prior to the interview, biases based on applicant sex or other applicant characteristics may have a considerable influence on how they conduct the interview and evaluate applicants' performance during the interview. Graves systematically addresses the questions of whether gender bias occurs in interviewers' judgments about job applicants, when it occurs, and how it occurs.

Once individuals join organizations, they are subject to formal or informal performance evaluations for almost everything that they do. As Kathryn Bartol points out, any gender biases in performance evaluations are likely to have indirect effects on subsequent career-related decisions about individuals such as assignments to training and development programs, salary increases, and promotion decisions. Thus, the overall effect of gender on individuals' work experiences through their performance evaluations can be considerable. Bartol reviews research on the influence of rater sex, ratee sex, rater-ratee similarity, individuals' self-ratings, and contextual variables such as the sex type of the task or job (i.e., the sex with which the task or job is most associated) on performance evaluations.

Gender dynamics may be examined within work and task-oriented groups. Pamela Tolbert, Mary Graham, and Alice Andrews examine the effects of the gender composition of work groups on relations within the group. They consider effects of group gender composition ranging from self-oriented attitudes such as satisfaction with the group and intentions to remain a member to attitudes and behaviors toward same-sex and opposite-sex group members. They review research evidence regarding these effects through five theoretical perspectives: similarity-attraction, social contact, group competition, social identity, and relative deprivation. Based on their review, Tolbert, Graham, and Andrews offer recommendations for future theory and research regarding the effects of the gender composition of work groups.

Linda Carli and Alice Eagly consider the influence of gender on group relations from a somewhat different perspective. Drawing on social role theory and status characteristics theory, they examine men's and women's influence over others and tendency to emerge as informal leaders in task-oriented groups, which include but are not limited to formal work groups. They review research on determinants of gender differences in social influence and emergent leadership such as perceptions of men's and women's competence, roles played in group interactions, communication styles, and the sex type of the group's task. Carli and Eagly conclude that differences in the status and roles of women and men in society lead to patterns of interactions in mixed-sex task-oriented groups that place women at a disadvantage.

The linkage between gender and leadership is also exhibited by individuals who occupy formal leader roles. Anthony Butterfield and James Grinnell focus on leadership exhibited below the top level of work organizations. They review research on evaluations of male and female leaders' style, behavior, and effectiveness; the impact of leader sex and style on subordinate satisfaction; and stereotypes of leaders as compared with gender stereotypes. Butterfield and Grinnell conclude that the considerable volume of research evidence regarding gender and leadership has offered mixed results. As do other authors in this book regarding their respective topics, they suggest that the context in which leadership takes place influences the extent to which gender differences in leadership may be observed.

Nancy Adler offers a unique point of view on the topic of gender and leadership by examining women who have acted as global leaders, as either chief executives of large multinational companies or heads of state. She distinguishes between global leadership and leadership from a more narrow or "domestic" perspective. In addition, she describes the backgrounds, motivation, visions, sources of power, and paths to power of numerous women global leaders. Adler suggests that women global leaders, due to their novelty as well as approaches to leadership, act as powerful symbols for change and unity in their companies and nations.

Issues pertaining to the expression of sexuality also arise within organizations. Lynn Bowes-Sperry and Jasmine Tata examine the pervasive phenomenon of sexual harassment, or the directing of unwelcome sexual attention by one member in an organizational setting toward another. Sexual harassment is examined from an individual or subjective perspective, a conceptual or behavioral perspective, and a legal perspective. Bowes-Sperry and Tata review the antecedents and consequences of sexual harassment from each perspective, considering the influence of gender and other personal characteristics such as race, ethnicity, and sexual orientation. In addition, they review responses to sexual harassment by individuals (e.g., targets and observers) and organizations, as well as organizational actions to prevent harassment.

Sharon Foley and I examine the also-pervasive phenomenon of workplace romances, or the sharing of welcome sexual attention by two people in an organizational setting. Unlike other dyadic relationships between organizational members, workplace romances have no organizational purpose and are intended to meet personal needs outside of work roles; thus, organizations prefer to ignore workplace romances. However, workplace romances, particularly those in which one participant directly reports to the other or is motivated primarily by job-related concerns (e.g., the desire for advancement), may disrupt the conduct of work. We review the antecedents, dynamics, and consequences of workplace romances. In addition, we review managerial actions, including policies about workplace romance in general and decisions about whether to intervene in specific relationships.

The next six chapters consider the influence of gender on careers and the quality of life. Linda Stroh and Anne Reilly present an overview of career issues faced by managers and professionals. They examine differences attributable to sex or gender in key issues such as the development of attitudes toward work and career, the role of education in career choice, and the paths and patterns of careers. They compare career issues that emerge for individuals early, in the middle, and near the end of their careers, thereby identifying differences that lead to conflicts among individuals at different career stages. According to Stroh and Reilly, the increasingly turbulent work environment has led to less linear career patterns and questions the very meaning of career.

In my chapter, I examine recent trends in statistics regarding the status of women in management, particularly the proportions of women in management overall and in top management (however *top management* is defined). In most countries, these trends reflect both good and bad news. The overall proportion of women in management has increased considerably. However, the proportion of women in top management is still small, suggesting that the glass ceiling remains firmly in place. I offer explanations for the news, good and bad, and describe the forces most likely to influence the future status of women in management, overall and in the executive ranks.

Belle Rose Ragins examines the most important developmental relationship that individuals may experience in organizations: mentorship by a senior. Mentored individuals (protégés) experience greater career success in objective terms than those without mentors; they also experience greater satisfaction and commitment to their jobs, careers, and organizations. According to Ragins, although mentoring relationships are important for all organizational members, they are essential for women. Mentors can protect women from discrimination and help them learn what the "old boys' network" teaches men about how to navigate past obstacles to career success. Ragins reviews the effect of protégé gender, mentor gender, and the gender composition of the mentoring relationship on mentoring functions and outcomes.

When people are frustrated by obstacles to their career success in organizations run by others, or when they simply feel like working for themselves, they are increasingly likely to forsake the corporate world to run their own businesses. Dorothy Moore reports that women-owned businesses represent the fastest-growing segment of small businesses. Similar to research on many other topics, early research on entrepreneurship focused primarily on the characteristics, experiences, and performance of male entrepreneurs. Moore reviews more recent research that has examined women entrepreneurs as a distinct group, examining issues such as personal traits, prior business experiences, motivation for going into business for themselves, support networks, and performance as business owners.

Most people, whether they work for themselves or others, are not solely concerned with being successful in the workplace; they also want to have rewarding lives outside of work. Jeffrey Greenhaus and Saroj Parasuraman review the influence of gender on the linkages between individuals' work and family lives. Work and family are often seen in conflict because they invoke simultaneous and mutually incompatible role pressures. However, there may also be mutually beneficial effects of work and family roles. Greenhaus and Parasuraman identify three key mechanisms—role experiences, role involvement, and role attitudes—that, in conjunction with gender, explain both positive and negative linkages between work and family roles for women and men.

While receiving tangible and intangible benefits from their careers, many people also experience high levels of stress. Marilyn Davidson and Sandra Fielden examine sources, coping strategies, and outcomes of stress, focusing on women's experiences in male-dominated work environments. They suggest that women in such environments, especially racial or ethnic minorities, experience unique work stressors not faced by their male counterparts. In addition, working women, especially those with children at home, experience greater stress from their family roles than their male counterparts because they bear greater family responsibilities. Furthermore, men tend to adopt problem-focused coping strategies that address the roots of stress, whereas women prefer emotional-focused coping strategies that address feelings raised by stress, a difference arising from early socialization that reinforces independence in males and dependence in females. As a result, working women exhibit significantly higher stress levels than do working men.

The next two chapters consider organizational initiatives that influence the intersection of gender and work. Alison Konrad and Frank Linnehan examine affirmative action programs that are intended to increase the numerical representation of historically excluded groups in organizations, including women and racial minorities. In many countries, organizations are required to implement affirmative action programs to comply with equal opportunity laws and policies. Konrad and Linnehan review the history and effects (economic, social, and psychological) of affirmative action programs and individuals' attitudes toward affirmative action. They conclude that affirmative action programs have had positive economic effects for their intended beneficiaries and remain an important societal and organizational tool for promoting equal opportunity.

Affirmative action programs contribute to quantitative changes in the composition of the workforce in organizations. In contrast, diversity and work-life (also known as work-family) programs contribute to qualitative changes in organizations by enhancing employees' relationships with people of diverse backgrounds and lifestyles while improving their family lives. Sharon Lobel describes a variety of such programs, their objectives, and indicators of program success. However, the success of many diversity and work-life programs is supported only by testimonials from organizational representatives and unsubstantiated by research. Lobel reviews research on the effects of diversity and work-life initiatives on attitudes, individual and team performance, human resource management indicators, and organizational strategic goals.

Finally, because this book reviews research on a variety of topics regarding the intersection of gender and work, it is useful to consider methodological issues pertaining to the conduct of such research. In the final chapter, Elizabeth Cooper and Susan Bosco discuss issues that are consciously (or unconsciously) faced by researchers in this area. They distinguish between two ideologies or general schools of thought regarding research on gender in organizations: positivism and feminism. Cooper and Bosco examine the influence of research ideology on the choice of research question, setting, sample, design, method of data collection, and analysis. They categorize recent research on gender in organizations according to methodology and discuss the implications of researchers' ideologies and ensuing methodological choices for what they learn (or think they learn) about the intersection of gender and work.

Overview

I have grouped the chapters into sections roughly according to the topics they address. The individual chapters of *Handbook of Gender and Work,* however, are not easily categorized. Gender-related influences on the world of work are interrelated and occur simultaneously at many levels. As the various chapters demonstrate, the influences of gender may be exhibited at the societal, industry, occupational, organizational, work group, interpersonal, family, and individual levels. Gender also interacts with other variables, both personal and situational, to influence workplace phenomena.

At the societal level, conceptualizations of sex and gender influence beliefs about the roles that women and men should play in society (Korabik). Gender influences are seen in the nature of work (C. Cooper and Lewis), including work in service industries (Gutek, Cherry, and Groth) as well as other types of work, and in the nature of work organizations (Maier). When women serve as elected heads of state and multinational corporations, they are often viewed in different terms than male heads of state or corporate leaders and may take advantage of what women's holding of such positions symbolizes for others (Adler).

At the occupational level, gender influences how men and women are compensated for their work, even when they work in the same occupation and hold the same type of job (Roos and Gatta). Gender also influences who is interested in entering various occupations and who actually does (Jacobs).

At the organizational level, gender influences are seen at the entry stage in judgments made about job applicants (Graves). Once individuals join organizations, gender influences how they are evaluated (Bartol) and developed (Ragins). Gender also influences the career tracks and paths that are available for organizational members to follow (Stroh and Reilly), the barriers that they face if they aspire to top management positions (Powell), and the motivations that drive them to quit organizations run by other people and launch their own organizations (Moore). Organizational initiatives such as affirmative action programs (Konrad and Linnehan) and work-life programs and other diversity initiatives (Lobel) represent a response to societal laws and regulations regarding gender as well as to the needs of employees that may differ according to gender. In addition, organizational policies and norms influence the extent to which sexual-related phenomena such as sexual harassment (Bowes-Sperry and Tata) and workplace romances (Powell and Foley) occur in the work environment and what, if anything, happens to the involved parties.

At the work group level, the roles that group members play and the influence that they exert over each other are affected by the gender composition of the group (Tolbert, Graham, and Andrews) and by the relative status and proscribed roles of women and men in society (Carli and Eagly). In addition, gender influences may be seen in stereotypes of leaders, leadership styles, and subordinates' responses to and expectations of leaders (Butterfield and Grinnell; Adler).

At the interpersonal level, gender influences many types of relationships between members of work environments, including those between employees and customers (Gutek, Cherry, & Groth), managers and subordinates

(Butterfield and Grinnell), mentors and protégés (Ragins), perpetrators of sexual harassment and their victims (Bowes-Sperry and Tata), and participants in workplace romances (Powell and Foley).

At the family level, life is influenced by the nature of both work (C. Cooper and Lewis; Gutek, Cherry, and Groth) and work organizations (Maier) and by organizational initiatives such as work-life programs (Lobel). These influences are seen in the division of responsibilities among family members, the quality of family relationships, and the presence of harmony or conflict between work and family in men's and women's lives (Greenhaus and Parasuraman).

At the individual level, gender has many influences. It influences the roles that children are socialized to play in society, the roles that adults aspire to and are selected to play in the workplace, and the success that they experience in these roles (Jacobs; Graves; Stroh and Reilly; Powell). It influences the stress levels of organizational members and the coping strategies that they use to deal with stress (Davidson and Fielden). It influences whether people seek to become self-employed (Moore). Overall, gender simultaneously influences individuals' aspirations, expectations, and experiences as members of society, the labor force, industries, occupations, organizations, work groups, dyadic work relationships, and families.

In addition, other variables influence the intersection of gender and work. First, sex interacts with other personal characteristics of individuals that have psychological and social ramifications such as their race, ethnicity, and culture in exerting all of the above influences (Ferdman). Second, as several chapters suggest (e.g., Graves; Bartol; Carli and Eagly; Butterfield and Grinnell; Roos and Gatta), contextual factors influence the extent to which gender effects are present or absent in particular situations. Thus, researchers are presented with enormous challenges in designing and conducting studies that investigate the influence of gender in combination with other personal and situational variables on what transpires in the workplace (E. Cooper and Bosco).

In conclusion, gender, alone and with other factors, influences the conduct of work, the roles that people play in the workplace, and the experiences that people have as they are working and otherwise living their lives. The various chapters identify theories at different levels of analysis that may be used to explain the multifaceted influences of gender on work, including theories drawn from the fields of psychology, sociology, economics, management, history, education, communications, anthropology, and gender studies. In addition, they review many research studies using a wide range of methodologies. The purpose of *Handbook of Gender and Work* is to increase our understanding of these influences in their full complexity and to suggest useful directions for future theory and research.

Part I

Gender and Other Identities

Chapter 1

Sex and Gender in the New Millennium

Karen Korabik

Ever since the Garden of Eden, issues of sex and gender have affected the life of every human being on our planet. Only relatively recently, however, have these topics become the focus of systematic investigation by researchers. This chapter examines the changes that have occurred in our thinking about sex and gender during the 20th century, discusses the effect that this has had on organizations and organizational research, and identifies the issues needing attention in the new millennium.

The Doctrine of Separate Spheres

At the start of the 20th century, the accepted notion of gender roles in Western culture was based on the doctrine of separate spheres (Hunter College Women's Studies Collective [hereafter Hunter College], 1983). According to this ideology, because men and women have different natures, the roles they play in society should be radically different. Thus, it was viewed as natural for men to immerse themselves in business and commerce, whereas women concerned themselves with domestic pursuits (Hunter College, 1983).

The belief that men and women should occupy different social roles was grounded in the fact that most women's lives were dominated by their capacity to bear children. During the 20th century, however, the industrial and technological development of Western society freed women from the reproductive constraints of the past (Hunter College, 1983). Also, work was restructured to be less dependent on men's superior physical strength (Cook, 1985). Thus, as the century advanced, North American women spent less of their lives rearing children and more in paid employment (Powell, 1993).

Yet, despite the sweeping societal changes that were taking place, the doctrine of separate spheres remained (Hunter College, 1983). It was so predominant that North American society was organized according to its underlying assumptions, much like the flat earth theory once dictated thinking about the universe. It has only been during the latter part of the century that the assumptions underlying this ideology have been questioned and new conceptualizations of sex and gender have been put forth. Accompanying this have been dramatic changes in societal gender-role prescriptions as well as in the composition of the workforce. These have occurred in such a short period that, not surprisingly, they have resulted in a variety of adjustment problems for organizations and researchers as well as for society.

The Evolution of 20th-Century Models of Gender

Unidimensional Models

Unidimensional conceptualizations of gender are dictated by separate spheres ideology and are bipolar in nature (see Figure 1.1). Thus, masculinity and femininity are placed at opposite ends of a continuum, with masculinity and men at one end and femininity and women at the other.

Assumptions. Unidimensional theories of gender incorporate the notion of biological essentialism (i.e., that men and women have inherently different natures) (Bem, 1993). Biological sex (whether one is male or female) is used as the determinant of psychosocial gender (one's masculinity or femininity). Thus, such theories presume biopsychological equivalence; gender is automatically assumed to be congruent with an individual's sex. Such theories also embrace the notion of gender polarization (i.e., that these supposed sex differences should be an organizing principle for both individual identity and social relationships) (Bem, 1993). Moreover, the assumption is made that the various components of gender are congruent with one another. Thus, psychologically adjusted men and women are expected to have sex-congruent (i.e., masculine for men and feminine for women) personality traits, attitudes, values, and behavioral preferences (Ashmore, 1993).

Implications. Because individuals who deviate from these norms are considered to be maladapted (Bem, 1993), those who subscribe to the unidimensional view prescribe a high degree of gender-role conformity for men and women. They also believe in the rigid adherence to stereotyped gender roles by children and the imposition of severe social sanctions for the failure to act like a "real" man or a "real" woman, beliefs that perpetuate separate social roles for men and women and serve to maintain the status quo (Bem, 1993). One consequence of

The Unidimensional Model

Men   Women
Masculinity   Femininity

The Bidimensional Balance Model

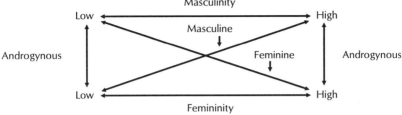

The Bidimensional Additive Model

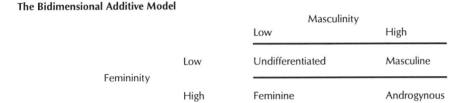

Figure 1.1. Unidimensional and Bidimensional Models of Gender

such thinking has been the persistence of occupational sex segregation in the North American workforce (see Chapter 7 by Jacobs in this book).

Limitations. Unfortunately, however, the types of jobs that are held by men and women are not only separate, but far from equal because the status quo is characterized by a high degree of androcentrism (Bem, 1993). Under this belief system, men are used as the normative group, and the patriarchal attitude that men are superior to women prevails. Because of this, women are generally relegated to roles and positions that are lower in prestige, power, and income than those thought to be appropriate for men (Ridgeway, 1992). Thus, even when women do gain entry into male-dominated occupations, they often find themselves relegated to low-status "pink ghettos" (Betz & Fitzgerald, 1987).

Between the 1940s and the 1960s, challenges arose to this way of organizing society. For example, in the United States, many women who had taken men's jobs during World War II became disenchanted when they were expected to return to full-time homemaking in the postwar era (Powell, 1993). They rebelled against the necessity of conforming to what Betty Friedan (1963) labeled the "feminine mystique." The women's liberation movement also raised consciousness about the extent of gender-based discrimination that was present in North American society.

Around this time, researchers started to question the assumptions underlying the unidimensional model of gender (Block, 1973; Constantinople, 1973). Anthropologists produced evidence that gender roles were not universal across different cultures (Hunter College, 1983). Historians pointed out that except for those who were White and middle class, few women actually conformed to the "happy homemaker" stereotype. Upper-class women often delegated their domestic and child care responsibilities to others, whereas most lower-class women worked outside the home throughout their lives out of economic necessity (Hunter College, 1983). Psychologists demonstrated that there were few actual differences between the sexes (Maccoby & Jacklin, 1974) and that the personalities of men and women often differed significantly from societal gender-role stereotypes (i.e., men were not as masculine nor were women as feminine as stereotypes suggested) (Rosenkrantz, Vogel, Bee, Broverman, & Broverman, 1968).

Bidimensional Models

A dramatic shift occurred in the way that gender was conceptualized when bidimensional theories of gender were proposed (Bem, 1974; Spence, Helmreich, & Stapp, 1975). Unlike the unidimensional view, no assumptions of biological essentialism, biopsychological equivalence, or gender polarization were made. Gender was viewed as consisting of two conceptually independent (i.e., orthogonal) dimensions, masculinity (M) and femininity (F), that were independent of biological sex.

This new way of looking at gender had wide-ranging implications. Because gender was now viewed as being distinct from sex, the two concepts needed to be clearly distinguished from one another. Unger (1979) proposed that the term *sex* be reserved for processes that were essentially biological in nature and that the term *gender* be employed when referring to the multitude of psychosocial ramifications associated with biological maleness or femaleness. (See Appendix for additional definitions.)

These early theories focused on only one aspect of gender: gender-role identity or one's sense of oneself as a man or a woman. Furthermore, this was most often operationalized in terms of gender-role orientation or the degree to which a person had internalized masculine or feminine personality traits. To describe those individuals who had both masculine and feminine characteristics in their personalities, Bem (1974) used the word *androgynous* (a combination of the Greek words for man and woman). She originally defined androgyny as consisting of (1) equal amounts or a balance between M and F and (2) a high degree of both M and F. Over time, two competing bidimensional gender-role models were proposed. Bem's (1974) balance theory emphasized the first part of this definition, whereas Spence et al.'s (1975) additive model stressed the second (see Figure 1.1).

The balance model. Bem (1974) operationalized androgyny in terms of the difference between the M and F subscale scores on the Bem Sex Role Inventory

(BSRI). Individuals were categorized as masculine or feminine in their gender-role orientation if there was a large difference between their M and F scores and as androgynous if the difference was nonsignificant (see Figure 1.1, middle). Thus, Bem assumed that those who were not balanced in M and F were conceptually distinct from those who were balanced.

The additive model. Instead of focusing on whether M and F were balanced, Spence et al.'s (1975) model of gender-role orientation concentrated on the magnitude or absolute amount of M and F that an individual possessed, using median splits to divide individuals into four categories (see Figure 1.1, bottom). Thus, they distinguished between those who were balanced and high on both M and F (i.e., the androgynous) and those who were balanced but low on both M and F (i.e., undifferentiated). Their model is additive in that outcomes are assumed to be a sum of the amounts of M and F an individual possesses (Cook, 1985).

Strong support exists for the additive model (Cook, 1985). For example, numerous studies demonstrate that vast differences exist between androgynous and undifferentiated individuals, with the androgynous demonstrating better outcomes in many areas (Cook, 1985). Moreover, research documenting the presence of significant main effects for both M and F on a multitude of dependent variables has verified the assertion that both M and F contribute positively and uniquely to different outcomes and that more of each is better (Cook, 1985). Support for the additive model also comes from studies on the cognitive processing of gender-related information. Self-schema theory (Markus, Crane, Bernstein, & Siladi, 1982), which postulates separate cognitive schemas for M and F, appears to have greater validity than Bem's (1981b) gender schema approach, where some people are seen as gender schematic (i.e., they use gender cues to process information across a variety of domains) and others as aschematic for gender. Moreover, most of the assumptions underlying bidimensional models have been extensively validated by research (Cook, 1985). In particular, a large body of evidence over the past 20 years has demonstrated that the unidimensional model's assumptions of biological essentialism and biopsychological equivalence are unfounded. Studies that have examined the separate effects of sex and gender-role orientation typically find that gender-role orientation accounts for a larger proportion of variance in an individual's personality, attitudes, and behavior than sex does (Cook, 1985). Research also suggests that M and F predict actions in the instrumental and expressive domains (Ashmore, 1993). For example, studies clearly indicate that gender-role orientation is a better predictor of leadership style and behavior than is sex, with M being related to task-oriented leadership and F to person-oriented leadership for both men and women (Korabik, 1996).

Limitations. Factor analytic studies, by demonstrating that M and F are multidimensional constructs, indicate that the bidimensional approach may not be sufficient to capture the essence of gender (Cook, 1985). Although the bidimensional view acknowledges different components of gender (e.g., schemas, traits, attitudes, and behaviors), there is still an underlying assumption that these components are congruent with one another; however, this often is not the case (Cook, 1985). Most research employing the bidimensional approach has not only been confined to examining one particular aspect of gender (gender-role orientation), but it has also concentrated only on positive or socially desirable M and F traits.

Multidimensional Models

As the end of the millennium approaches, there is an increasing appreciation that gender is not only multidimensional and multifactorial but also context dependent, multiply determined, and confounded with other variables (Ashmore, 1993; Cook, 1985; Deaux & Major, 1987). Consequently, models of gender have become increasingly sophisticated and complex. For example, current theories propose that gender schemas are multidimensional (Spence, 1985) and that separate schemas exist for attitudes, sexual orientation, gender identity, and personality traits (Bem, 1993).

There is also an increasing awareness that the labels M and F are too narrow and have sex-linked connotations. Various alternatives have been proposed including instrumentality versus expressivity, agency (self-focus, self-assertion, self-expansion) versus communion (other-focus, being one with others), and task-orientation versus person-orientation or socioemotionality (Cook, 1985). Such gender-neutral terminology can be particularly useful when one wishes to avoid making prescriptions about men's and women's behavior. The labels M and F, however, continue to be descriptive of the present situation. For example, women managers are seldom criticized for being too instrumental or overly agentic. Instead, they are perceived as too masculine or not feminine enough (Korabik, 1997). The judicious use of gender-specific terminology, therefore, may help researchers to draw attention to such conditions. (It is for this reason that a mixture of gender-neutral and gender-specific terminology is used in this chapter.)

During the past two decades, there has also been an increasing realization that both additive and balance model considerations are important. In response, emergent properties and interactive androgyny models have been proposed (Cook, 1985). Researchers have recognized the need to examine the separate main effects of sex, M, and F, as well as all of the resulting interactions, either through ANOVA or regression-based approaches (Cook, 1985). Furthermore, there is a growing awareness that it is essential to consider the social, societal, developmental, and cultural contexts in which gender is enacted (Ashmore, 1993).

In recent years, several specific multidimensional models have been developed, each of which attempts to explicate a different aspect of gender. In this section, some models that are particularly applicable to organizational research are presented.

The differentiated additive androgyny model. Research using bidimensional models of gender-role orientation has sometimes indicated that more positive outcomes are associated with M than with F (Cook, 1985). This "masculine supremacy effect" is most likely a reflection of societal androcentrism, which influences researchers to adopt practices that produce findings biased in favor of M (Cook, 1985). Such artificial results are particularly likely when global or subjective outcome measures are used or if there is a focus on task-oriented outcomes, rather than interpersonal ones (Marsh & Byrne, 1991). Marsh's (1987) differentiated additive androgyny model postulates that M and F have differential effects, with M affecting competency-related outcomes and F affecting relationship-oriented ones. He contends that to get an accurate picture of the effects of both M and F, one must assure content validity by sampling an adequate number of dependent variables from both areas.

Although this model has been applied primarily to the study of the self-concept, it is relevant to a number of organizational issues. A similar masculine supremacy effect is apparent in much organizational research. For example, although both task and interpersonal skills have been deemed essential for leadership effectiveness, the schema of a good manager is a masculine one (Powell, 1993). Consequently, both men and women managers tend to be highly masculine, with task-oriented skills generally perceived as more important for managerial success than person-oriented ones (Korabik, 1990). Research on leadership effectiveness often reflects this bias by relying primarily on global judgments or only on dependent variables in the task-oriented domain, and not surprisingly, such research demonstrates a link between M and effectiveness. When dependent variables from both domains are included, however, it becomes apparent that person-oriented outcomes are a function of F rather than of M. Moreover, when numerous criteria from both domains are sampled, research clearly demonstrates that the most effective leaders are those who are high in both M and F (i.e., androgynous) (Korabik, 1996).

The differentiated multidimensional gender-role model. Another problem with bidimensional conceptualizations of gender is that they have been focused solely on the socially desirable aspects of masculinity and femininity (M+ and F+) (Marsh & Byrne, 1991). McCreary and Korabik's (1994) model (see Figure 1.2) addresses this limitation by expanding the concept of gender to include negative as well as positive attributes. According to this theory, either too little or too much M or F can be undesirable. The notions of too little agency (M–) and communion (F–) are derived from Wiggins's (1979) circumplex model of interpersonal traits. Two of its major orthogonal dimensions are masculinity, with endpoints at M+ (ambitious-dominant) and M– (lazy-submissive), and femininity, with endpoints at F+ (warm-agreeable) and F– (cold-quarrelsome) (McCreary & Korabik, 1994). By contrast, Spence, Helmreich, and Holahan (1979) have referred to too much agency or communion (in conjunction with

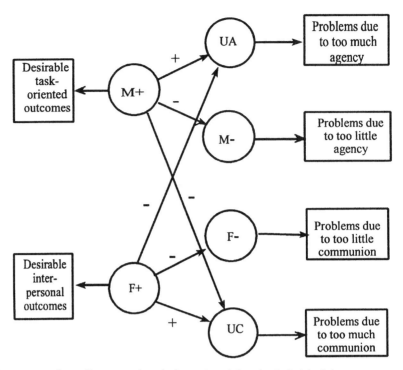

Figure 1.2. The Differentiated Multidimensional Gender-Role Model
NOTE: M+ = desirable agency; F+ = desirable communion; M– = too little agency; F– = too little communion; UA = unmigitated agency; UC = unmigitated communion.

too little of the other gender-role domain) as unmitigated agency (UA) and unmitigated communion (UC), respectively. Individuals high in UA are autocratic and domineering, whereas those high in UC are overly expressive and overly accommodating.

The differentiated multidimensional gender-role model is particularly relevant when examining the relationship of gender to negative organizational outcomes. In such instances, ignoring the undesirable gender-role constructs and focussing solely on M+ and F+ may produce artificial results. Because M+ and F+ are correlated with UA, UC, M–, and F– (see Figure 1.2), outcomes that are actually due to the undesirable constructs may easily be misattributed to the desirable ones. For example, one might conclude that managerial ineffectiveness is a function of socially desirable masculinity (M+) or femininity (F+), when the real culprits are either too little agency (M–), which results in managers being overly passive and submissive; too much agency (UA), which results in their being overly competitive; too little communion (F–), which results in their being overly cold; or too much communion (UC), which results in their being overly exploitable.

Research supporting this viewpoint (Bowen-Willer & Korabik, 1997; Kirso & Korabik, 1996; Korabik & McCreary, 1995) shows that the desirable and undesirable gender-role constructs have different outcomes. For example, leaders high in UA lack consideration and manage conflicts by dominance, whereas those high in UC lack task-orientation and are overly obliging when managing conflicts. Leaders who lack both agency (M–) and communion (F–) manage conflicts by avoidance. By contrast, those high in both M+ and F+ (i.e., androgynous) are high in both initiating structure and consideration leadership; they use integrating or win-win conflict management strategies (Korabik, 1996).

Multilevel models. Bidimensional models also fail to take into account the fact that gender may be enacted at a variety of levels. Rosen and Rekers (1980) have proposed a taxonomic framework that differentiates sex and gender at three levels: physical, intrapsychic or intrapersonal, and psychosocial or interpersonal.

According to their conceptualization, at the physical level sex refers to the genetic, hormonal, and anatomical aspects that make a person physiologically a male or a female. In terms of intrapersonal processes, sex refers to one's sexual identity (e.g., homosexual, bisexual, or heterosexual), whereas for interpersonal processes the appropriate focus is on sexual behavior (i.e., sexual orientation).

At the physical level, gender refers to one's gender assignment as a man or woman. It is operationalized in terms of biological sex and is assumed to be dichotomous. Intrapersonally gender encompasses such things as gender schema; gender identity; and gender-role traits, attitudes, and values, whereas at the interpersonal level it includes gender-role behaviors. At the intra- and interpersonal levels, Rosen and Rekers consider gender to be bidimensional (consisting of M and F).

Unger and Crawford (1996) also identify three levels at which gender can be studied: individual, interpersonal, and social structural. The individual level consists of M and F and is similar to Rosen and Rekers's intrapersonal level. However, at this level Unger and Crawford do not focus solely on internalized personality traits in the M and F domains, as has been the tendency in androgyny research. Instead they adopt a broader perspective that includes other aspects of gender typing (e.g., how and why women internalize their devaluation and subordination). Moreover, unlike Rosen and Rekers, Unger and Crawford view gender at the interpersonal level as being inextricably intertwined with sex. Thus, they feel that in our interpersonal interactions we use perceived sex (what Rosen and Rekers call gender assignment) as a cue for gender and gender as a cue for sex.

Unger and Crawford also propose a level that is not included in Rosen and Rekers's taxonomy. It is the social structural level in which gender is seen as a system of social classification that influences access to power and resources. A number of theories (e.g., expectation states theory, status characteristics theory, and social role theory) are particularly useful in explicating those aspects of gender dynamics that result from the structural inequality in our society (Ridgeway, 1992). The emphasis in these theories is on sex as an ascribed status characteristic; therefore, as in Rosen and Rekers's physical level, gender is operationalized in terms of biological sex.

The interpersonal interaction model. Deaux and Major's (1987) model expands on these concepts by focusing on the fact that gender is enacted within the context of dynamic, socially constructed interpersonal interactions. They argue that our own and others' behavior is a function of gender-related beliefs and expectations about the self (schemas) and others (stereotypes) that we hold and the manner in which such beliefs are conveyed. For example, research shows that individuals tend to choose careers that are consistent with their self-schemas, with masculine sex-typed men and women choosing to work in male-dominated areas like management and feminine sex-typed men and women choosing to work in female-dominated occupations like nursing (Betz & Fitzgerald, 1987). Individuals' career choices, however, also are influenced by the sex-stereotypic expectations and attitudes that are conveyed to them by others (e.g., their parents, teachers, guidance counselors, the media, and those in charge of selection decisions) (Betz & Fitzgerald, 1987).

Deaux and Major (1987) contend that the above factors interact with situational cues that may make gender more or less salient. For example, gender schemas can be primed by recent events, by personal attributes like dress or gestures, or by sex-linked tasks or situations (e.g., skewed sex ratios). The nature of the resulting interactions also depends on the degree to which a target's self-conceptions, a perceiver's expectancies, and the situational context are congruent with one another. Furthermore, moderating factors, such as the degree to which beliefs and behaviors are socially desirable or rewarded and whether cues are clear or ambiguous, also play a role. This model is relevant to a wide variety of organizational issues including career choice, selection, and performance appraisal.

Issues for the New Millennium

As we stand on the threshold of the new millennium, researchers, organizations, and individuals confront a variety of challenges. The recent loosening of societal gender-role prescriptions has meant that individuals are faced with problems arising from a vastly expanded realm of behavioral possibilities. As a result, organizations have had to cope with the difficulties associated with accommodating increased diversity. As organizational researchers, we can help them to meet these challenges. However, to do so, a number of issues must first be confronted.

Clarification of the Distinction Between Sex and Gender

Over the past 20 years, there have been sweeping changes in our conceptualization of sex and gender. A voluminous body of research has demonstrated that, at the intrapersonal level, they are orthogonal constructs.

However, although sex and gender are theoretically independent, the sex-linked gender-role socialization that is still commonplace in Western culture means that empirically they often are not. Consequently, the idea of bio-psychological equivalence still pervades much of today's research and thinking. For example, a content analysis of the literature (Korabik & Whiltshire, 1993) indicates that even those researchers who publish in journals specializing in gender-related issues often confuse sex and gender. They frequently operationalize gender inappropriately by using biological sex as a proxy variable when studying gender as an intrapersonal phenomenon.

Moreover, due to the prevalence of androcentrism in our culture, biological sex is confounded with a number of variables including authority, power, experience, and organizational level; as a result many apparent sex differences are actually due to situational context (Ridgeway, 1992). For example, sex differences in variables such as job satisfaction, organizational commitment, and propensity to quit disappear once differences in age and experience between men and women managers are controlled (Rosin & Korabik, 1995). If such confounds are not controlled, it may appear that women are less satisfied with and committed to their jobs and more likely to leave them than are men, when actually it is the younger and less experienced employees (who are primarily women) who are susceptible to greater dissatisfaction and attrition.

Researchers who fail to make a clear distinction between sex and gender, therefore, leave their findings open to misinterpretation. Results that are viewed as sex differences rather than as gender differences, for example, can be used to justify a status quo in which women and men are seen as being naturally suited to different roles and as deserving of differential treatment. Such thinking can have serious consequences, influencing organizational decisions about selection, promotion, and compensation (Korabik, 1997).

Greater Reliance on Theory

Due to the rapid transformation of thinking about gender during the latter part of the 20th century, today's researchers are faced with a bewildering assortment of theories and methods (Sherif, 1982). Even the experts disagree about which are most appropriate (Deaux, 1993; Gentile, 1993; Ridgeway, 1992; Unger & Crawford, 1993). One way to circumvent problems is to specify whether sex, gender, or situational context is the causal mechanism that is being postulated. In practice, however, most researchers have not articulated their underlying assumptions; consequently, most research on sex and gender has been atheoretical in nature (Wallston, 1987). Because of this, the literature is "replete with inconsequential, accidental, and incidental findings of 'sex' differences" (Grady, 1981, p. 632).

Greater reliance on theories, like the ones presented above, will aid researchers in determining what aspects of gender they are interested in and the level at which they should be studied. For example, at the individual or intrapersonal level, the focus is on a person's own perceptions, motivations, values, personality traits, and attitudes. As these are more likely to be a function of socialization than of biology, the appropriate operationalization is in terms of the individual's gender-identity, gender-schema, or gender-role traits or attitudes.

By contrast, biological sex is an appropriate operationalization when studying gender at the physical level (i.e., for studies of gender assignment) or at the social structural level. In this case, research examines issues such as others' perceptions, attributions, attitudes, or behaviors toward a target person (e.g., stereotyping, sexism, and tokenism). In such instances, sex is a more salient and overt cue than gender role; therefore, perceivers' judgments and actions will more likely be influenced by the sex of the target person (i.e., their status or their attributed gender assignment as a man or a woman) than by the target person's gender identity or gender-role traits or attitudes.

At the interpersonal level, complex interactions between the sex and gender of the target person and that of the perceiver are likely. For example, some men (e.g., those who are highly masculine or who have high status) may be more prone to sexually harass women, whereas some women (e.g., those who are very feminine or who have low status) may be more prone to suffer harassment. Therefore, more complex research designs that examine interactions between the sex and gender role of the perceiver, the sex and gender role of the target, and the situational context in which interpersonal interactions occur are often warranted (Deaux & Major, 1987).

Reliance on theory will also help identify which measuring instruments should be used. For example, if gender-role traits are the focus, the BSRI or Extended Personal Attributes Questionnaire can be employed, with measures of the undesirable gender-role constructs (i.e., UA, UC, M–, and F–) added if applicable. Several excellent measures of gender-role attitudes (Frieze & McHugh, 1997) and gender-role behaviors (Cook, 1985) also are available. To further enhance the validity of their findings, researchers should ensure that they have included an adequate range of dependent variables from both the task-oriented and interpersonal domains.

Greater Integration of Theoretical Perspectives

No one theory incorporates all that we presently know about gender. More complex and comprehensive theories need to be developed, particularly ones that integrate the various levels and domains across which gender is manifested. There should be a greater appreciation of gender as a dynamic construct and a focus on understanding the personality by situation interactions through which it is enacted. Instead of pitting the intrapersonal and social structural viewpoints against one another, the new millennium will, it is hoped, fully bring with it a much needed theoretical synthesis of the intrapersonal, interpersonal, and social structural determinants of gender.

One way to accomplish this is by understanding gender as a process of acculturation. Bem (1993) has endeavored to explicate the intrapersonal mechanisms through which individuals in our society become acculturated with respect to gender. Korabik and Ayman (Korabik, 1993) have employed John Berry's acculturation theory to explain gender dynamics in organizational settings, whereby organizations are viewed as gendered subcultures that inculcate a set of norms and values determined by the dominant group. According to Berry (1983), newcomers from a minority group may adjust to such contexts either by separation, assimilation, marginalization, or integration. The particular mode of acculturation will be a function of intrapersonal (e.g., gender-role identity, attitudes, and values), interpersonal (e.g., relationships with coworkers, supervisors, and subordinates), and structural (e.g., reward systems) factors.

Thus, by working in female-dominated occupations, some women may opt for separation. They may be willing to accept lower status and pay because they view such jobs as more socially acceptable, as more compatible with their feminine gender-role identity and values, as offering a more hospitable climate, or as providing a greater opportunity to combine work and family life. Some women who enter male-dominated fields may try to assimilate (fit in by acting like the men in the in-group), whereas others may experience marginalization (feel isolated and like out-group members). Both of these options can result in a number of undesirable consequences (Korabik, 1997). Women also can acculturate through integration, that is, taking on some of the values and characteristics of the in-group (i.e., task orientation) while inducing those in the majority to change by adopting some of the characteristics and values traditionally associated with women. More research using this type of approach is needed to understand how the various aspects of an individual's gender interact with the gendered nature of organizational contexts over time.

Greater Awareness of Cultural Differences

Related to this is the need to understand gender in an international context. Cross-cultural studies suggest that, at least with respect to the intrapersonal level, notions about gender roles do not necessarily generalize across different cultures. Asian cultures, for example, are more communal than Western ones (Adler & Izraeli, 1994). Greater generalizability, however, may exist at the social structural level. Androcentrism and patriarchy still prevail in most present-day societies (i.e., whatever is associated with men is viewed as more valuable than whatever is associated with women) (Hunter College, 1983). Consequently, women are underrepresented in positions of power and authority throughout the world (Adler & Izraeli, 1994). Still, there are wide variations in the way that women and men enact their occupational and domestic roles in different cultures. More cross-cultural research, such as that reported by Hofstede (1998), is desirable. Not only is etic (between culture) research on gender in organizations important, but emic (within culture) studies are also necessary. Furthermore, given the increasing focus on diversity issues in today's business environments, research that incorporates issues related to race, class, and ethnicity (see, e.g., Higginbotham & Romero, 1997) is also imperative.

Conclusion

Conceptualizations of sex and gender have shifted dramatically during the 20th century and are still undergoing a process of rapid evolution as we enter the new millennium. This presents a tremendous challenge for researchers attempting to contend with increasingly complex models and theories regarding the nature of gender. It is essential to have a thorough appreciation of what gender is before a comprehensive understanding of how gender dynamics operate in the workplace can be achieved. Such knowledge is important because gender-related processes continually affect the life of every working person. As a result of such processes, individuals are often judged in terms of inaccurate negative stereotypes and subjected to prejudice and discrimination in the form of sexism and gender bias (Korabik, 1997). In addition to acting as barriers to career advancement, the psychological consequences of such processes are considerable and can include problems with work stress and cultural adaptation, maintaining a positive sense of identity, and feelings of marginalization and isolation (Korabik, 1997). It is incumbent on organizational researchers to strive to alleviate these problems by providing individuals and organizations with information about how to best combat them.

Appendix: Glossary of Terms	
Gender identity	One's sense of oneself as a man or woman
Gender schema	One's cognitive representations of gender
Gender-role attitudes	Attitudes about men's and women's roles in society
Gender-role orientation (also called *sex-role orientation*)	A classification system whereby individuals are categorized as masculine, feminine, androgynous, or undifferentiated as a function of the degree to which they have internalized masculine and feminine personality characteristics
Gender-role stereotypes	Beliefs about the differences between men and women
Gender-role traits	Personality characteristics in the masculine (or instrumental) and feminine (or expressive) domains

Chapter 2

The Color and Culture of Gender in Organizations

Attending to Race and Ethnicity

Bernardo M. Ferdman

Growing numbers of theorists and researchers (e.g., Bell, Denton, & Nkomo, 1993; Cox & Nkomo, 1990; Holvino, 1994; St. Jean & Feagin, 1997) have called for increased attention to race and ethnicity as key variables in the study of gender in organizations, pointing out the limitations of a color- and culture-blind approach. Others seek more explicit consideration of gender when the focus is race or ethnicity. Hurtado (1997), for example, decries the separation of ethnic and gender studies and points out that research on group differences has not sufficiently addressed individuals' multiple group identifications and their relationships to psychological outcomes.

The same can be said with respect to most theory and research on gender in organizations. Much of this literature ignores or makes only cursory

AUTHOR'S NOTE: I am grateful to Cláudio Vaz Torres, Arianne Weiner, Lydia Hang-I Leong, and Kasey Corbett, who provided valuable and extensive assistance in the preparation of this chapter by locating, selecting, organizing, abstracting, and joining in conversations about many of the articles, books, and chapters reviewed here. The first two were especially supportive in developing this project. Raquel Hicks, SchuyLer Gordon, Stella Nkomo, and Gary Powell provided useful and thoughtful comments on an earlier draft.

mention of race, ethnicity, and culture. One reviewer (Ely, 1991) found that in four major journals over a five-year period in the late 1980s only 9 of 48 studies focusing on gender and organizational behavior addressed issues of race. Three of these considered both race and gender in the analyses, and just one looked at their interaction. In contrast, the interconnections of gender, race, ethnicity, and culture have been increasingly explored by many scholars in the broader social science literature (e.g., Collins, 1998; Weber, 1998). This is only a more recent and less developed trend in work on gender in organizations. Bell et al. (1993) point out that much of the theory and research on women in management typically has focused on the experiences of White women and has overlooked the perspectives, roles, and experiences of women of color. Work focusing more broadly on gender differences or similarities also has not attended to race, ethnicity, and culture and so has been implicitly centered on dominant group perspectives and experiences.

Although some of the literature on gender in organizations occasionally mentions racial and ethnic dimensions of identity, this is typically done in separate and usually short subsections, or in asides or end remarks reminding readers to consider these issues in the future. This approach reinforces the notion of gender as an identity dimension quite distinct from race and ethnicity. Other work, especially that focusing on racial and ethnic variables, often considers each dimension independently, such that when gender is discussed, race or ethnicity is ignored, and when race or ethnicity is discussed, gender is neglected. For example, many researchers report the demographic composition of their samples in terms of gender and race, without reporting the two-way frequencies. Others, in focusing on ethnicity or race, control statistically for gender, thus precluding consideration of interactions. In one such study (Sánchez & Brock, 1996), focusing on perceived discrimination among Latinos/as, the authors viewed the likelihood that women would perceive gender discrimination as a potential confound. Rather than exploring the possibility that gender and ethnicity could interact or combine in perceptions of discrimination, the authors assumed that the two identities could be separated and so controlled for gender as the first step in hierarchical regression analyses. This approach, however, made it impossible to see if their assumption was valid, because they did not test for or even discuss the possibility of interactions.

We are often reminded, however, that individuals cannot separate gender from race, ethnicity, or culture. As Collins (1998) remarks,

> I am frequently asked, "Which has been most oppressive to you, your status as a Black person or your status as a woman?" What I am really being asked to do is divide myself into little boxes and rank my various statuses. If I experience oppression as a both/and phenomenon, why should I analyze it any differently? (p. 481)

Every person has both gender and ethnic or racial identities, which together with a range of other group memberships make up the individual's social identity (Deaux, 1996; Ferdman, 1995; Nkomo & Cox, 1996).

This multiplicity of group-based identities is not always or even typically acknowledged, especially among dominant racial or ethnic groups. Alderfer (1991) indicates the problems with a commonly used term, *women and minorities.* In his view, this usage simply differentiates between White men and everyone else and obscures other important differences and dynamics, including, in the case of Black-White relations, all combinations of relationships among Black and White men and women. In the context of multiracial and multiethnic populations, such as that of the United States (Reed, 1997), dynamics are even more complex. In Alderfer's view, usage of the term women and minorities can be defensive, in that it permits avoiding consideration of who specifically is in the minority in an actual setting and reduces the complexity of investigations and conversations about race and gender dynamics, ultimately preserving the racial status quo.

Similarly, the often unacknowledged focus on White women and men in gender research and theory may not be simply a passive oversight, but a way of maintaining a particular racial and ethnic order. As Hurtado (1996) points out, "The powerful have the privilege to ignore and therefore to make invisible those with less power" (p. 129). She explains how "naturalizing whiteness" is a key component in its maintenance at the "center of the universe":

> For whiteness to be the "center of the universe" it has to be considered a "natural" unmarked racial category. Indeed, the recurrent finding in the study of whiteness is the fact that white respondents do not consider their "whiteness" as an identity or a marker of group membership per se. Most feminist theorists also assume whiteness is the norm. . . . [W]hiteness is a natural identity because it has not been problematic and therefore salient to most respondents in these studies or to most feminist theoreticians. (p. 137)

Hurtado cites duCille: "Feminist [critics] continue to see whiteness as so natural, normative, and unproblematic that racial identity is a property only of the nonwhite. . . . '[A]s a woman' in mainstream feminist discourse all too often continues to mean 'as a white woman' " (duCille, 1994, p. 607, in Hurtado, 1996, p. 137).

There is insufficient work focusing on how gender, race, ethnicity, and culture combine to affect how people behave, interact, and perceive themselves and others in the workplace. There is however, a growing stream of theory and research that is specific about some gender and ethnic or racial combinations, focusing, for example, on the experiences of African American women (e.g., Blake, 1999; Davidson, 1997; Denton, 1990; Dumas, 1979; Parker & ogilvie, 1996) or other women of color (e.g., Bento, 1997; Karambayya, 1997; Mighty, 1997; Muller, 1998; Ontiveros, 1998) in organizations. This work has typically focused on the "marked" groups. Scholarship on White women still gets framed simply as work about women, whereas scholarship on men is often framed simply as work on (generic) people. Considering race and ethnicity in the study of gender is not only about including those "others." It also means examining whiteness (Fine, 1997; Jacques, 1997) and the ways in which gender studies have not traditionally done so (Hurtado & Stewart, 1997). "Doing gender" (West & Zimmerman, 1998) is not now nor has ever been culture free or color-blind.

Framing Gender in the Context of Race, Ethnicity, and Culture

Why is it important to consider gender simultaneously with other aspects of identity, particularly race and ethnicity? What do we know at this point about how gender in the workplace is framed in the context of race, ethnicity, and culture? In this section, I review these constructs and then insert them into gender and gender processes. My primary thesis is that the significance and experience of gender are colored and given shared (i.e., cultural) meaning by race and ethnicity.

Race

Scholarship focused on race in recent years emphasizes the socially constructed aspects of this system of classification (Appiah, 1996; Banton, 1988; Ferrante & Brown, 1998; Nkomo, 1992; Oquendo, 1998; Zack, 1998). Responses on the U.S. census and other surveys, as well as reports from those not easily classified into whatever system happens to be in use, highlight how racial categories are not biologically fixed or meaningful. In the United States, categories used to classify individuals by race have shifted over time (Lee, 1993). Although physical markers combined with ancestry are used as the primary bases for assigning individuals to racial categories, scientists have concluded that "there is no scientific basis for our idea of race as a human biological difference. Race . . . is a social overlay on actual physical traits" (Zack, 1998, p. 4).

Nkomo (1992) points out how much of the work purporting to explore the dynamics of race in organizations has instead reified the concept in ways that tell us less, rather than more, because the focus has been on people in essentialized categories, instead of on race relations in which " 'race' is not a stable category" (p. 507). Others (e.g., Fishman, 1989) emphasize that the primary function of racial classification systems is to maintain racial hierarchies and racism. Jones (1997) elucidates the multiple levels—interpersonal, institutional, and cultural—at which racism can operate.

Many scholars have begun to focus on racial identity as an individual-level variable (e.g., Helms, 1995; Thompson & Carter, 1997), constituted by how persons deal with the way they are categorized within the society. Helms (1996) distinguishes racial and ethnic identity models, suggesting that those primarily related to intergroup relations of domination and oppression should be considered "racial," whereas those focused on the acquisition and maintenance of cultural characteristics should be considered "ethnic." Within this racial identity approach, growing heed is being paid to White identity (e.g., Fine, Weis, Powell, & Mun Wong, 1997) and biracial or multiracial identity (e.g., Kerwin & Ponterotto, 1995).

Privilege and oppression have been key themes in the consideration of race and racial dynamics. McIntosh (1988), for example, in a widely distributed essay, focuses on her own blindness to the privileges she carries as a White person in a White-dominated society. In her struggle for women's rights, this unearned privilege had become particularly obscured to her. Maier (1997b) and Jacques (1997) consider similar issues as White men.

Gender in the Context of Race

In the United States, both at present and historically, race has been intertwined with gender in the workplace and in the production and maintenance of gender ideologies, stereotypes, and processes. I review theory and research on these intersections in this section.

Data on earnings and other social indicators show that race and gender are both important in predicting wages, occupation, and other opportunities (e.g., Barnum, Liden, & DiTomaso, 1995; Durden & Gaynor, 1998; Farley & Allen, 1989; Landrine, Klonoff, Alcaraz, Scott, & Wilkins, 1995; U.S. Department of Labor, 1997a). Higginbotham (1997) describes how the increase in the number and proportion of working mothers is primarily a White phenomenon, because large numbers of Black women have always worked outside of the home. Robles (1997) documents the broad racial diversity among women on a variety of socioeconomic indicators, including age distribution, family arrangements, educational attainment, labor force participation, occupation, income, and poverty.

Hurtado (1997) critiques the common practice of aggregating statistics across all women for the purpose of comparisons with men, because this hides the large differences among women from different groups. Such differences are also present among men of different groups. The magnitude of the gender differences also often varies by group, indicating an interaction of race and gender. As Robles (1997) shows, gender differences in median income in the United States are greatest among Whites. Even though men in all groups had higher median incomes than women (in 1992), the within-group ratio of women's to men's income was lowest (0.70) among non-Hispanic Whites. Among Asians, Hispanics, and African Americans it was 0.78, 0.85, and 0.89, respectively. Median income among White women was more than for any of the other groups of women, except Asian Americans. Essentially, being White *and* male was disproportionately associated with having a higher income. Stated differently, the advantage of being male was not as evident for men of color. Similarly, U.S. Department of Labor (1997a) statistics show that, in 1996, 15.3% of employed White men in the United States were in executive, administrative, or managerial occupations. The corresponding proportions of employed White women, Black men, and Black women were 13.9%, 8.3%, and 9.6%, respectively. Not only were Whites employed in such occupations proportionately more than Blacks, but also White men had an advantage relative to White women, whereas the opposite gender pattern was found among Blacks. The gender difference was even larger for Hispanics, among whom 6.6% of employed men and 8.5% of employed women were in such managerial occupations. Comparisons of these data to those for 1988 and 1995 show that although the difference between White men and White women has diminished, that between Black women and Black men has increased. Among Hispanics, the difference has both increased and shifted in the opposite direction.

Hurtado (1996), following Sojourner Truth and other feminists of color, argues that the critical distinction between women of color and White women has been their relationships to White men in a system focused on maintaining White privilege:

> White men need white women in a way that they do not need women of Color because women of Color cannot fulfill white men's need for racially pure offspring. This fact creates differences in the relational position of the groups—distance from and access to the source of privilege, white men. Thus, white women, as a group, are subordinated through seduction, women of Color, as a group, through rejection. (p. 12)

In Hurtado's view, this has resulted in a "dual construction of woman-hood . . . [in which] the definition of *woman* is constructed differently for white women and for women of Color" (p. 13).

Sidanius and Pratto (in press), in their social dominance theory, argue that men in subordinated racial groups are likely to experience greater discrimination than women in the same groups. As does Hurtado, they use an argument based on sexuality and reproductive strategies to claim that discrimination by dominant men against both dominant and subordinated women is motivated by the desire to control rather than to weaken or to harm. In contrast, they see discrimination against out-group males as more aggressive and designed to debilitate, implying that dominant men view subordinated men as threats and rivals in reproduction.

■ Racism and Sexism

Reid (1988) and others (e.g., Garcia, 1997; Sterba, 1997) explored the similarities and differences between racism and sexism. Although finding parallels, in that both are ideologies and systems of exclusion of some groups and privileging of others, Reid also found important distinctions between the two concepts. Similarly, Glick and Fiske's (1996) notion of ambivalent sexism, although in some ways similar to ambivalent racism (Katz & Hass, 1988), is in essence different. Using the case of Black women, Reid looked at the interactive and additive effects of race and sex prejudice. In doing so, she highlighted that Black men and Black women historically have been treated quite differently by Whites, whereas women have been treated differently on the basis of race. Concurrently, Black women have been the targets of sexism on the part of Black men and racism on the part of White women. This, according to Reid, has put Black women in a double bind and disadvantaged them compared with other groups defined by race and sex.

In her work on racism, Essed (1991) explores its forms that may be unique to the experiences of Black women and considers the interactions of racism with other ideologies of domination. She argues that because sexism and racism "narrowly intertwine and combine under certain conditions into one, hybrid phenomenon . . . it is useful to speak of *gendered racism* to refer to the racial oppression of Black women as structured by racist and ethnicist perceptions of gender roles" (p. 31). Such constructions of gender roles can also greatly affect Black men, for example, via certain stereotypes, but Essed does not explore these in any detail.

Historically, Black women in the United States have had to do many types of jobs, often at the bottom of the labor market and including many arduous ones that most White women did not have to do. Harley (1997) points out how "the middle-class gender norms that were the guiding principles of the 19th-century 'cult of domesticity' were unattainable for enslaved and most free (and newly freed) African American women and men" (p. 31). These dominant norms also contrasted with attitudes about women's work and reproductive roles rooted in Africa and with African American women's realities. It was only after the civil rights movement that Black women were able to get jobs that were traditionally female (and White), such as clerical positions, but typically only the lowest paying of these.

Essed (1991) describes how racialized notions of femininity and sexuality, especially White standards of female beauty, served to rationalize continued abuse:

> Contrary to the patriarchal image of White, middle-class women as weak, dependent, passive, and monogamous, Black women were thought of as hardworking, strong, dominant, and sexually promiscuous. . . . The "Aunt Jemima" stereotype epitomized the sexist/racist/classist stereotype of Black

women. . . . These images . . . rationalized the violation of the role of Black
women as mothers and the control of Black women through rape and sexual
exploitation. (pp. 32-33)

Via such stereotypes, features seen as positive in White men were and are
viewed as negative in Black women. Thus, to advance, Black women have to
be better than both Black and White men, but they "have to conform to the
ideal of White femininity, which means that they cannot afford to appear
threatening" (Essed, 1991, p. 35). Gendered racism, then, works by marginalizing, culturally problematizing, and blocking social mobility of Black
women (Essed, 1991). Consistent with Essed's analysis, Deaux and LaFrance
(1998) point out that racial and ethnic groups in the United States have
different gender stereotypes and are also stereotyped differently. Similarly,
they point out how "people's gender stereotypes exist at varying levels of
specificity and include beliefs about particular types of women and men, each
with its own defining features" (Deaux & LaFrance, 1998, p. 796). It is likely
that such subtypes are systematically associated with different ethnic or racial
categories.

Other work has approached race relations and gendered processes of
domination from the perspective of White men, also documenting how racism
is directly connected to and intertwined with gender and sexism. Fine, Weis,
Addelston, and Marusza (1997), for example, studied the views of other
groups and themselves held by urban poor and working-class men and high
school boys. On the basis of their research, the authors argue that "white
working-class male identity is parasitically coproduced as these men name and
mark others, largely African American and white women. Their identity
would not exist in its present form (and perhaps not at all) if these simultaneous productions were not taking place" (pp. 55-56). The White high school
boys, for example, view themselves as having "entitled access to white
women" (p. 57), whom they protect from a supposedly aberrant African
American male sexuality. Expressions of racism in this context become ways
of subordinating both Blacks and White women, thus becoming intertwined
with sexism. As the authors point out, these young White men "treat Black
women far worse than they say Black men treat white women" (p. 58). The
parallel study of working-class young adults shows how "the target site for
this white male critique shifts from sexuality to work but remains grounded
against men of color" (p. 60).

In related research highlighting the importance of attending to gender in
studies of racism, and vice versa, Stack (1997) compared the views of White
men and women with regard to race-targeted interventions in the workplace
(such as affirmative action). Data from a 1990 national survey of adults in the
United States showed that, overall, White men were more opposed to
race-targeted interventions. White women who were against income inequality or who thought White-Black differences are not due to discrimination were

also more likely to be opposed, whereas these relationships were not present for the men. Stack concluded that this was consistent with predictions derived from social dominance theory (Sidanius & Pratto, in press). In a study also using U.S. national survey data, Gay and Tate (1998) found that most Black women strongly identified on the basis of both race and gender and that the two were positively correlated. However, the researchers found that, overall, Black women's political attitudes were better predicted by racial than by gender identification, a possible explanation of why Black and White women often view gender issues differently. Aries et al. (1998) found that group racial composition affected college students' awareness of their own gender; for men their gender was most salient when they were in the racial minority, whereas for women it was more salient when they were in the racial majority.

■ Double Jeopardy or Double Advantage?
  Exploring Interactions of Race and Gender

Bell et al. (1993) and others (e.g., Landrine et al., 1995) review evidence related to the combined impact of race and gender for Black women and other women of color relative to White men and women, Black men, and other men of color. Such combinations, according to Landrine et al., may have (1) only additive effects, such that gender and race function independently to affect outcomes; (2) only interactive effects, such that neither gender nor race alone is sufficient to predict outcomes; or (3) both additive and interactive effects, such that, for some groups, effects are stronger (or weaker) than would be predicted simply by summing the effects of race and gender. Building on Ransford's (1980) work, Landrine et al. (1995) advance a double jeopardy-advantage hypothesis, which "predicts that (1) people who occupy a subordinate (low-status) position in more than one hierarchy will be found to be doubly disadvantaged, whereas (2) those who occupy a ruling (high-status) position in more than one hierarchy will be found to be doubly advantaged" (p. 186). According to this hypothesis, Black women and other women of color should be especially disadvantaged, whereas White men should be especially advantaged, relative to White women and to men of color. Bell et al. (1993) point to an alternative version of the double advantage hypothesis, based on claims of benefits to the race-gender combination experienced by Black women:

> The double advantage (colloquially referred to as "twofer") hypothesis holds that the sum effect of race *and* gender is positive and black women enjoy a preferred status in organizations compared with other groups including black males. (p. 111, italics in original)

Bell et al.'s review of some empirical evidence related to both hypotheses as applied to Black women points to little or no research supportive of the "twofer" prediction and suggests the need for more complexity in considering the double jeopardy perspective. In exploring predictions of multiple jeopardy and advantage, Landrine et al. (1995) review a variety of evidence, including salary data and empirical investigations of interpersonal discrimination. They conclude that, although evidence does point to the presence of either double advantage or double jeopardy in a range of settings, it is important to develop hypotheses that are "more specific regarding the nature of the interaction among specific status positions with respect to specific discriminatory behaviors" (p. 221). They also warn against approaches that treat all low-status positions as socially equivalent.

In a more recent study of perceived discrimination among African American, Latino/a, and White men and women at the University of California, Los Angeles, Levin, Sinclair, Veniegas, and Taylor (1998) explored both additive and interactive double jeopardy hypotheses, as well as a new prediction they designate the *transfer hypothesis*. This hypothesis predicts that perceptions of discrimination in one domain influence those in another for women of color, but not other groups. Thus, among women of color, experiences or perceptions of gender discrimination should result in increased perceptions of racial or ethnic discrimination, and vice versa. Levin et al. propose that this transfer may occur, first, because women of color may have a greater recall of incidents and misattribute them to the other domain, and second, because women of color may have increased sensitivity to one type of discrimination as a function of their experiences with the other. This prediction is supported by findings that women of color, compared to White women, report experiencing more sexism (Klonoff & Landrine, 1995; Weber & Higginbotham, 1997) and that Mexican American high school girls see sexism as a greater problem than their White counterparts (McWhirter, 1997). Regarding the transfer from sexism to racism, three studies reviewed by Levin et al. showed that, in contrast to their prediction, men of color see more ethnic discrimination than do women of color, and two other studies found no gender differences.

Levin et al. (1998) found that, consistent with the additive double jeopardy hypothesis, African Americans and Latinos reported more ethnic and general discrimination than did Whites, whereas women perceived greater amounts of gender and general discrimination than did men. This was consistent with Weber and Higginbotham (1997), who found that 42% of Black women professionals in their study reported unfair treatment as "Black women," compared to 25% of White women professionals reporting unfair treatment as "White women." At the same time, in contrast to an interactive double jeopardy prediction, Levin et al. found no difference between women and men of color in perceptions of general discrimination. However, White women saw themselves as worse off than White men. In line with the transfer hypothesis, women of color who perceived ethnic discrimination were more likely to perceive gender discrimination, and this correlation was greater among women of color than among White women. However, men and women of color saw about the same amount of ethnic discrimination. Also, perceptions of gender discrimination varied as a function of group among women, but not for men, such that there was no main effect of ethnicity in perceived gender discrimination. Finally, there was a greater difference in perceived general discrimination (both personal and social) between White women and White men than between African American and Latino men and women.

Powell and Butterfield (1997), in a study of the effects of race on promotions in a government agency, also considered the possibility of interactions with gender. Although the results suggested the presence of such an interaction, the small number of women of color in their sample did not permit formal statistical tests. Nevertheless, they saw the data as possibly, though not reliably, indicating double advantage for women of color. One interpretation they did not consider, however, is that the extremely small and disproportional number of women of color in managerial ranks was itself an indication of double jeopardy.

Ethnicity and Culture

Introducing ethnicity, and with it culture, adds even greater complexity to the consideration of interactions of gender with other identities. Before discussing these interactions, I explore the construct of ethnicity.

Some authors use the terms *ethnicity* and *race* interchangeably or even blend them into one construct. Cox (1993), for example, uses the term *racioethnicity,* defining it as "racially and/or ethnically distinctive within the same nationality group" (p. 6), and Phinney (1996) uses the term *ethnicity* "to refer to broad groupings of Americans on the basis of both race and culture of origin" (p. 919). Similarly, because of common usage and for convenience, investigators often request research participants in organizations and elsewhere to identify themselves on questionnaires in terms of "racial/ethnic" categories.

I believe it is important and useful to distinguish between race and ethnicity in spite of the associations of these two concepts. Conflating race and ethnicity makes it more difficult to consider their socially constructed yet different components and applications, including the ways their use varies at different times and in different places. Some authors base their work in part on the distinction between race and ethnicity. Landrine and Klonoff (1996), for example, see race as a problematic basis for distinguishing among people in part because it blends together and blurs the differences between a variety of ethnic groups, ignores cultural differences, and harms society, groups, and individuals.

Ethnicity, in contrast to race, can have both positive and negative associations. Fishman (1989), for example, describes how the notion of *ethnos* was historically viewed in both of these manners. In a widely used definition, Schermerhorn (1996) framed the construct as follows:

An ethnic group is defined here as a collectivity within a larger society having real or putative common ancestry, memories of a shared historical past, and a cultural focus on one or more symbolic elements defined as the epitome of their peoplehood. Examples of such symbolic elements are: kinship patterns, physical contiguity (as in localism or sectionalism), religious affiliation, language or dialect forms, tribal affiliation, nationality, phenotypical features, or any combination of these. A necessary accompaniment is some consciousness of kind among members of the group. (p. 17)

Hutchinson and Smith (1996), building on this definition but making it less restrictive, offer the following construction of ethnic group:

A named human population with myths of common ancestry, shared historical memories, one or more elements of common culture, a link with a homeland, and a sense of solidarity among at least some of its members. (p. 6)

Similarly, Nash (1996) sees the focus of ethnic inquiry as "cultural categories with social and group referents" (p. 24) and identifies both the most common markers of ethnic boundaries as well as the elements of ethnicity as "blood, substance, and cult" (p. 25). Eriksen (1996) points out that ethnicity, in social anthropology, "refers to aspects of relationships between groups which consider themselves, and are regarded by others, as being culturally distinctive" (p. 28). He goes on to note that, even though the focus in ethnicity discourse is often on subgroups or minorities, "majorities and dominant peoples are no less 'ethnic' than minorities" (p. 28).

Ethnicity, then, involves both identity and culture (Ferdman, 1990, 1992) and is a characteristic of all people. In terms of identity, ethnic groups are distinguished by socially meaningful labels that distinguish between *us* and *them,* capturing a sense of shared ancestry and continuity with the past. This boundary typically also incorporates a shared style (Royce, 1982) or distinguishing cultural features—patterns of behaviors, values and beliefs. In addition to individual- and group-level aspects, ethnicity also incorporates intergroup elements (Ferdman, 1992). It is for this reason that ethnicity is typically more salient among members of minority groups, those groups in the society with less power than the dominant group; such groups are usually somewhere below the top in the social stratification ladder. In this sense, ethnic minorities and their members are "marked," such that their differences from the dominant group are considered to reside in them, instead of in their relationship to the dominant group; their ethnic identity is seen as added to or combined with the larger national identity. In the United States, for example, one often hears talk of "diverse" people when what is meant is people who are not White. Similarly, the generic "American" is used for citizens of White European descent, whereas other citizens are referred to in ethnic terms, such as

Latino, African American, and Chinese American. Members of the dominant group are seen as the standard. When no mention is made of ethnic group membership in the United States, it is typically assumed that the reference is to a White person. As defined here, however, ethnicity is a feature of all groups, including those with power. Thus, attending to ethnicity permits noting the cultural diversity within groups broadly categorized in racial terms, such as Whites, that include a variety of ethnic groups. Power differentials, however, are an important component of ethnic dynamics and experience.

In addition to boundaries and identity, culture is a key component of ethnicity. Although a group's culture and its expression by individuals is continually in flux (Ferdman & Horenczyk, in press; Nagel, 1994), at the group level and from a psychological perspective it can be seen to consist of shared lenses for perceiving, believing, evaluating, communicating, and acting (Triandis, 1996). It is useful to consider culture not only in terms of those features prevalent for the group in general but also as it is constructed or represented for each individual group member. I describe elsewhere (Ferdman, 1990, 1995; Ferdman & Horenczyk, in press) the construct of *cultural identity* as referring to one's individual images of the cultural features characteristic of one's group together with both one's feelings about those features and one's understanding of their location in oneself.

Gender in the Context of Ethnicity and Culture

As a primary culture-bearing grouping, ethnicity gives memory and reality to gender. A growing literature (e.g., Cheng, 1996b; Das Gupta, 1997; Doss & Hopkins, 1998; Hurtado, 1997; Levant, Majors, & Kelley, 1998; Tay & Gibbons, 1998; Vazquez-Nuttall, Romero-Garcia, & De Leon, 1987; Watkins et al., 1998; Williams & Best, 1994) documents how the meaning and experience of gender is culturally defined in the context of particular societies, social settings, and ethnicities. Given that gender is constructed and lived in an ethnocultural context, gendered experiences and interactions may not be the same for members of different ethnic groups, and gender in organizations may be better illuminated when ethnicity is explicitly considered. As Muller (1998) points out, "Group distinctiveness is reflected in culturally specific understandings of gender and gender differences" (p. 6).

Fundamentally, gender, as a set of beliefs and practices for structuring human experience, is relatively meaningless outside of a particular cultural context. There is no such thing as "just" a man or a woman, without reference to culture. All men and women belong to or participate in social groupings and interactions that shape the meaning and experience of their genders. To the extent that these groups and their interactions are ethnic, gender interacts with ethnicity and culture. Individuals may often think of themselves solely in gender terms, but this may in part be a result of belonging to the privileged group (McIntosh, 1988). At the individual level, people of all groups can vary in the degree to which they think about or incorporate ethnic identity in their self-concept (Phinney, 1996). For those with weaker ethnic identities, one might speak of gender operating by itself at the individual level, but this is logically problematic from the group or intergroup level. The fact that ethnic identity has not been elaborated or does not play a conscious role for the individual can itself be evidence of the ways that ethnic group membership affects the person and group.

Various studies have documented how gender interacts with culture. Watkins et al. (1998), in their study of self-concepts in 14 nations, expected that women would place greater emphasis than men on "family values" and "social relationships" as a basis for self-esteem. They found, however, that this difference was only present in individualist countries. Williams and Best (1994), in contrast, did not find culturally based differences in masculinity and femininity, and they found that across countries, stereotypes of men tended to be stronger and more active than those of women. They did find variation in the degree of differentiation of the stereotypes for men and women and in their self-concepts across cultures. Moreover, there were great disparities in the sex-role ideologies expressed in different countries; in some countries, such as the Netherlands, Germany, and Finland, more egalitarian views were expressed, whereas in others, such as Nigeria, Pakistan, and India, views tended to be more male dominant. Finally, and most relevant here, although, on average, women in all countries expressed more egalitarian sex-role ideologies than men, this sex difference varied by country. On average, however, these differences were smaller than the between-country differences, suggesting that culture contributes to sex-role ideology more strongly than gender.

In two U.S. studies, Gaines et al. (1997) compared cultural values across race and ethnic groups and found that although people of color scored higher than Anglos on collectivism and familism in Study 1, this was replicated only for men and not women in Study 2. Vazquez-Nuttall et al. (1987) reviewed literature on sex roles among Latinas, documenting their differences from sex roles in other ethnic groups as well as their variations as a function of both subgroup and acculturation. Similarly, Das Gupta (1997), Muller (1998), Cheng (1996b), Levant et al. (1998), and others explore variations in gender roles and ideology as a function of culture and ethnicity.

A common theme in this body of work is that many members of ethnic minority groups experience cultural transitions in part through shifts in expected and received gender roles. Among Dominican immigrants in New York, for example, women tended to assume new roles in their family as they increased their labor force participation and became the primary wage earner (Pessar, 1987).[1] Thus, gender can become a key locus for experiencing cultural transitions and transformations (Hurtado, 1997). Women who are not of the dominant culture must switch between two worlds, part of which involves dealing with gender relations in their own group. Thus, attending to culture and ethnicity highlights the problems inherent in generalizing about all women and men.

In the organizational context, Parker and ogilvie (1996) describe a model of African American women executives' leadership strategies as culturally distinct. They criticize the predominant practice of describing "female" models of leadership as contrasting with Anglo-American male hierarchical models, and they suggest that African American women display a distinctive style influenced by both culture and gender. Filardo (1996) conducted a related study of social interaction patterns in mixed-gender, same-race groups. On the basis of social role theory (Eagly, 1987), she predicted that men and women differ in social behaviors because they occupy different roles in society, and she cites Williams and Best (1990b) to point out that gender stereotypes and behaviors vary cross-culturally as a function of the proportion of women working outside of the home. Filardo also cites evidence of greater gender equality among African Americans than Whites in their mixed-gender social interactions. The results of her study of eighth graders in the northeast United States, matched for socioeconomic status and reading achievement, showed that although White boys displayed greater activity, more influence attempts and fewer incomplete, interrupted utterances than White girls, African American groups showed no such gender differences. On two speech form measures, action opportunities and mitigated performance outputs, among African Americans, girls were higher than boys, but there was no difference for Whites. Overall, White girls were less powerful and less assertive, and displayed speech that was more tentative, conciliatory, and polite. Filardo inferred that the equality among African Americans was due to assertiveness by African American girls, rather than facilitation by African American boys. The implication, then, is that White males may experience African American females as unfeminine and aggressive and that this could create ambivalence for African American females as they try to "fit in" to largely White contexts. The results also fit well with a social role theory account.

Implications for Future Theory and Research

This review raises a variety of important issues for the study of gender in organizations. Key themes, summarized in Figure 2.1, may be illuminated and better addressed by simultaneously attending to gender, race, ethnicity, and culture. This section builds on these themes and considers implications for future theory and research.

As illustrated earlier, experiences of discrimination in the workplace can be better understood when both gender and racial or ethnic identities are considered. The research by Levin et al. (1998), Landrine et al. (1995), Weber and Higginbotham (1997), and others shows that gender by itself is insufficient to illuminate perceptions of sex, race, or general discrimination. Similarly, DiTomaso (1989) found differences in how Black women as opposed to

Sexism and racism are intertwined in their history and expression. Although distinct, they cannot be fully separated either in individual or collective experience.

Gender stereotypes are neither color- nor culture-blind.

Experiences of discrimination in the workplace can vary as a function of both gender *and* race or ethnicity. Gender by itself is insufficient to illuminate perceptions of sex, race, ethnic, or general discrimination.

Identity is complex, and incorporates multiple components, which intersect and interact to affect the subjective experience of individuals and their treatment by others (Ferdman, 1995). Interactive and complex views of identity can help to move us away from essentialism and permit greater understanding of how identity is shaped by situational factors.

Gender roles in the workplace can be better and more fully understood in their ethnocultural and racial context. Predominant norms in U.S. organizations have often been those of White men (Maier, 1997c), not those of men in general.

The nature and dynamics of power, privilege, and oppression can be better illuminated and understood if gender is considered in combination with other identities, especially race and ethnicity, but also class, sexual orientation, and other bases of social stratification (see Ferree & Hall, 1996).

Gendered processes such as mentoring and networking may be more clearly understood when race, ethnicity, and culture are also considered and addressed (see, e.g., Ensher & Murphy, 1997; Ibarra, 1993; Pugliesi & Shook, 1998; Ragins, 1997b).

The relationships of work, family, and other life domains, which are often addressed only in terms of gender, may be better illuminated to the extent that multiple cultural constructions of work, family, and other life concerns are considered (see, e.g., Watanabe, Takahashi, & Minami, 1997). This includes variant views of the nature and permeability of the boundaries between work and home.

The study of organizational socialization of women and men may benefit from incorporating constructs of acculturation, more often used in the literature on cultural transitions.

Planned change processes in organizations geared toward increasing inclusion, such as diversity initiatives (Ferdman & Brody, 1996), may be more effective to the extent that they address the full complexity of identity and pluralism and simultaneously attend to a variety of differences and similarities. For example, programs directed at "Women" are likely to be more meaningful and have a greater impact to the extent that they consider the diversity among women.

Figure 2.1. Key Themes Highlighted by Considering Gender in Organizations in Combination With Race, Ethnicity, and Culture

White or Hispanic women experienced discrimination, and Yoder and Aniakudo (1997) documented the unique patterns of subordination lived by African American women firefighters.

Because the expression of sexism can be colored by racism, consideration of race and gender interactions should lead to a clearer understanding of both of these ideologies of oppression. Most researchers and theorists continue to sustain the guiding (usually unstated) assumption that gender and racial or ethnic discrimination processes are distinguishable and separate. It may be very difficult if not impossible, however, to know definitively if a particular incident is an instance of gender discrimination and not of racial or ethnic discrimination, or vice versa. When the target is a woman of color, making such a determination is especially problematic. If a White man treats a woman of color poorly, the two dimensions clearly may be involved. But when a Black man treats a Black woman in a sexist manner, the history of race relations in the United States is also playing a background role in the interaction. Similarly, racism against Blacks on the part of White men (and White women) has always included a component of sexism, affecting not only Blacks but also White women. Thus, the two processes of racism and sexism are inextricably linked.

Explorations of the interactions of race and ethnicity with gender pose both empirical and conceptual challenges. Empirically, it is often problematic to find appropriate samples of sufficient size and diversity to test hypotheses. Moreover, it is not always clear what is the appropriate group in which to test predictions, and whether the measures used appropriately capture the domain of interest. Conceptually, it is important to consider the full range of possibilities in exploring what the interaction of race and gender might look like. The interactive position would simply say that, either, (a) gender effects and gender dynamics will be different across racial groups, or (b) race or ethnic effects will be different for men and women. A complete set of predictions would specify which specific patterns will be present under what conditions and why.

Complex interactions are also the case when the focus is identity. Individual identities cannot be easily (if at all) disentangled into separate components. Certainly, attempts to do so should address the potential implications and influences of one type of identity on the others. Here, I have presented the view that it is only in a social system that takes one racial or ethnic identity, such as White, as normative, that gender can be considered apart from its ethnic or racial context and that doing so can be a way of perpetuating that social system. By considering gender in the context of other identities, the ways in which individuals simultaneously carry multiple identities that together constitute a whole is highlighted. An individual's identities intersect and interact to affect the person's subjective experience and treatment by others (Ferdman, 1995). Elsass and Graves (1997) take such an approach in developing a model for interactions and experiences in a diverse work group. Such strategies can help us resist essentialism and shed light on the reciprocal effects of identity and situations, as well as on the simultaneous reality of both between- and within-group diversity.

Interactive perspectives are also important in the study of gender roles in organizations. Much literature focuses on gender roles in the context of work, as well as on what women versus men bring to the workplace. By considering gender roles in their cultural, ethnic, and racial context, we should be able to get a better understanding of their subtlety and complexity. Traditional theory and research considers the ways in which gender shapes people's behavior patterns, as well as expectations by and of individuals. This can have implications for systemic differences, for example, in power. Maier's (1997c; also Chapter 5, this volume) work on masculinity in organizations is quite sensitive to this, in that he focuses on normativeness in organizations as mostly akin to White maleness, not to maleness in general. Similarly, Cheng (1996b) shows how Asian and Asian American men are not considered "hegemonically masculine." He found, for example, that being an Asian American man meant a loss of male privilege. Black men and Latinos can also be denied such privilege, although in different ways. Popular depictions and stereotypes, for example, often show Black men as hypermasculine. Latino men must likewise contend with a stereotype of machismo.

Hofstede (1980a) has documented notable cross-national differences in the degree of distinction made between genders and in the "softness" of the society's culture. Thus, in the international arena, the interaction of gender roles and culture also becomes an issue, for example, as women expatriates seek to work effectively in host societies with expectations and norms different from those to which they are accustomed (see, e.g., Caligiuri & Cascio, in press). The experience of women heads of state, diplomats, and many executives working in societies that are very restrictive of women's roles is that they are sometimes treated as honorary males (e.g., Adler, 1987; also Chapter 13, this volume).

Romero (1997) reminds us that

> recognizing that a woman cannot be a woman without race, ethnicity, and social class allows us to begin examining both the range of diversity and the kinds of commonalities that make up the gendered work experience. (p. 236)

Certainly, this is true both for women and men. A focus on ethnicity and race highlights the cultural, ethnic, and racial specificity of gendered interactions. Theorists and researchers interested in gender must be more precise about the ethnic, racial, and cultural context for their work and the identities of their participants. I believe that the time has come for the study of gender in organizations to fully incorporate and attend to race, ethnicity, and culture.

Note

1. Related to this, Schoeni (1998) documents how different groups of immigrant women participate in and assimilate into the labor force at different rates. Whereas Filipinas had the highest labor force participation (80% in 1990), Mexican women were the least likely to be working outside the home. Also, Japanese, Korean, and Chinese immigrant women were found to have the highest probability of working in the first 10 years after immigration.

Part II

The Economic and
Societal Context

Chapter 3

Gender and the Changing Nature of Work

Cary L. Cooper and Suzan Lewis

The past half century has seen enormous changes in the nature of society and of the workplace in particular (Cooper, 1998). The 1960s epitomized the limitless possibilities of change. It was an era that embraced new technology, with British Prime Minister Harold Wilson proclaiming that the "white heat of technology" was about to transform our lives, producing a leisure age of 20-hour working weeks. A period of industrial strife, conflict, and retrenchment followed in the 1970s, highlighted by Terkel (1972), who wrote of the daily humiliations in the workplace and argued that merely to survive the working day was a triumph for most of the workforce. Out of the turmoil of the 1970s came the "enterprise culture" of the 1980s, a decade of mergers and acquisitions, strategic alliances, joint ventures, process reengineering, and the like, transforming workplaces into free market hothouse cultures. It was a period of increased competitiveness and a time when stress and burnout became concepts in the everyday vocabulary of many working people.

But the most profound changes in the workplace since the Industrial Revolution began to take place in the 1990s. The early years of the 1990s were dominated by the effects of recession and globalization, as organizations downsized, delayered, flattened or right sized. Whatever the euphemism, the hard reality experienced by many was job loss and constant change. There were fewer people, doing more work and feeling more job insecure. The rapid expansion of information technology also meant the added burden of information overload and accelerated pace of work, with people demanding more information, quicker and quicker. At the same time, the number of women in the workplace continued to expand, pushing, but certainly not shattering, the glass ceiling further upward. The changing role of men and women at work and at home has added another dimension to the enormous changes taking place in offices, factories, and technocultures of the world of work.

This chapter considers some of the changes that have been taking place in the nature of work and explores some of the implications for gender in organizations and beyond. We first examine some of the trends and their general consequences, using the situation in the United Kingdom as an example. We then explore some future gender scenarios that might arise out of four aspects of the changing nature of work, "flexibilization" and its effects in terms of careers, job insecurity, long working hours, and distributed work in virtual organizations. We highlight some of the many challenges and opportunities for change as well as the barriers to change in the gender order.

Changing Workplaces

The downsizing and the rapidity of change has certainly taken its toll. In the United Kingdom where the restructuring of industry has outpaced other European states, levels of employee satisfaction have declined much more dramatically than elsewhere in Europe while absence due to illness has risen during the past decade (International Survey Research, 1995). These changes have had effects on families as more and more dual-earner and single-parent families emerged in a climate that, it could be argued, was anything but family-friendly. In particular, the long-working-hours culture makes family life difficult to sustain (Demos, 1995; Lewis, 1997a). The trend toward a short-term contract and freelance culture has led to what employers euphemistically refer to as the "flexible workforce," although in family-friendly terms it is anything but flexible. The psychological contract between employers and employees in terms of reasonably permanent employment for work well done is being undermined as more and more workers do not regard their work as secure and growing numbers engage in part-time work. There may be nothing inherently wrong with these trends, but the recent Quality of Working Life Survey (Worrall & Cooper, 1997) found some disturbing results among British managers. First, organizations at the end of the 1990s were found to be in a state of constant change, with 61% of the national sample of managers having undergone a major restructuring over the past 12 months. The consequences of this change, even among a group supposedly in control of events, were increased job insecurity, lowered morale, and the erosion of motivation and loyalty. Poor communications and concerns about their future employability were some of the reasons for managers' insecurity. Sixty percent felt they were in the dark about their organizations' future strategies, and 48% said their biggest worry was financial security and employability in the wider labor market. The workplace of the future appears destined to be one where most organizations have only a small core of full-time permanent employees, working from a conventional office, and where most skills are brought in on a contract basis, either working from home or hired for specific projects (Cooper & Jackson, 1997).

Below we explore some possible gender-related consequences of these changes.

The Flexible Workforce: Changing Notions of Careers

With employers increasingly looking for and recruiting flexible workers, will women be the preferred workers given their history of flexibility? For example, there are currently five times as many women as men working part-time in Britain, and although twice as many men are now working part-time than a decade ago, women everywhere are historically more experienced at discontinuous career patterns, flowing in and out of the labor market, working part-time and on short-term contracts. Of course, it can be argued that employers have always preferred women for certain jobs, particularly those with relatively low pay, poor conditions, and few opportunities for advancement. Part-time and discontinuous employees have traditionally been regarded as second-class workers, not fully committed or serious workers (Lewis, 1997a; Raabe, 1996). The argument has been that despite the lack of opportunities attached to these jobs, women with family responsibilities preferred to work in this way. Indeed, even though full-time, inflexible jobs were the norm, in the absence of good child care facilities or men's sharing of child care, many women had few alternatives.

But if more pluralistic ways of working (Raabe, 1996) become the norm, all this may change. Women may be preferred for their flexibility rather than their exploitability. There is already evidence that this may be beginning to happen in some contexts. For example, in Britain, where there is a high rate of part-time work and where only one employee in three works what used to be regarded as a "normal" working week (full-time, 9 until 5, with regular hours (Hewitt, 1991), unemployment is much higher among men than women. Young women in particular seem to be adapting relatively effortlessly, forging ahead in education and striving to emulate successful, can-do role models (R. Katz, 1997). Meanwhile, young men are more likely to drop out of education and achievement than are young women, particularly those who subscribe to the emerging "laddish" culture of pride in nonachievement, sexism, poor communication, and irresponsibility, an image encapsulated in what has become a highly popular British television sitcom, *Men Behaving Badly*. One commentator on recruitment trends asks, "Is there a trend where the lad culture that encourages and even applauds underachievement is producing not just an underqualified male workforce but an increasingly unemployable one too?" (Howard, 1998).

Could this culture be understood as a reaction to the demise of traditional male gender roles as breadwinners, with the security of jobs for life? Men who resist changes in gendered family roles may be the least willing to adapt to changes in the nature of work. A cross-national qualitative study of orientations to work and family among young people (under the age of 30) in five European countries suggests that it is blue-collar or working-class men who are finding it most difficult to adapt to shifts in the nature of work and also to changes in family roles and relationships (Lewis et al., 1998). In this study, most of the women in all social groups in each country hoped to be financially independent, be in egalitarian relationships, and have satisfying careers, predominantly defined as a series of jobs, usually fitting around family obligations at some stage. The men in the white-collar and professional groups in this study talked in similar terms. They acknowledged the demise of jobs for life and the need to sustain employability, and many also said they hoped to be able to be involved fathers when the time came. Recognition of the need to be adaptable, flexible, and self-reliant and to develop their own careers was reflected in the discourses of the women and the more educated men. Some of the blue-collar or less highly educated men also recognized the need to keep up their skills through lifelong learning. However, it was these less educated men in all five countries who were most likely to be left behind, sticking to traditional expectations of work and of gender, rather than adapting to new realities.

We have argued that women may increasingly be the preferred recruits for employment. But is it possible that women not only may be recruited in greater numbers but may also become the more promotable than men and better represented in management positions?

The underrepresentation of women in management and the glass ceiling are debated with both individual and structural arguments. Both approaches, however, suggest the potential for women to benefit from changes in the nature of work. Structural explanations have included the prevalence of the male model of work (Cook, 1992; Pleck, 1977), that is, the assumption that ideal employees are those who work continuously from the end of education to retirement, often working long rigid hours, not allowing family or other concerns to interfere with work. Related to this is the traditional notion of career as a series of advancements within hierarchical organizations (White, Cox, & Cooper, 1992). It has long been argued that the male model of work and traditional notions of career need to be challenged to promote gender equality (Cook, 1992; Lewis & Cooper, 1988, 1996). It now appears that economic conditions and organizational trends have achieved what decades of equal opportunities initiatives could not do. The male models of work and careers are giving way to a postmodern pluralism. The discontinuous careers that are replacing jobs for life and the shift from careers of advancement to careers of achievement (Zabusky & Barley, 1997) may be congruent with women's needs but could be more difficult for men to adapt to.

Even if individual rather than structural explanations of gender differences in organizational advancement are proposed (implying gender-neutral models of organization and leadership), the potential exists for a change in favor of women. Individual explanations have referred to gender differences in education, in career aspirations, and in management style. Differences in level of education are declining everywhere, and in many countries women are more highly educated than men (European Commission, 1997). Differences in aspirations have been conceptualized within patriarchal, hierarchical organizations. That is, women have been characterized as lacking in aspirations for success in comparison with men because they are more likely to focus on performance and satisfaction within a job and less likely to put themselves forward for promotion (White et al., 1992). Women are less likely to equate success with climbing organizational ladders than with developing expertise. This is often interpreted as a lack of self-esteem but has also been constructed as a reaction against male-defined career structures and careers of advancement (Marshall, 1995). Again, careers of achievement in flat organizations may be much more congruent with women's needs as well as being more in line with the needs of employers in the contemporary context.

Another individual explanation of gender differences in achievement relates to management style. This proposes that men's greater competitiveness and a macho style are necessary to get to the top. Women have been regarded as less suitable workers and especially managers, precisely because they lack "male" qualities (Marshall, 1995; Morgan, 1986). But being a good manager in the 1990s and beyond is less about competitiveness, aggression, and task orientation and more about good communication, coaching and people skills, and being intuitive and flexible, all more typically or at least stereotypically associated with women. In a climate of corporate change, effective communication is essential. There is evidence that women leaders tend to be more open, approachable, and encouraging to others (Gibson, 1995; Rosener, 1990) and to be more likely to display transformational leadership (Bass, Avolio, & Atwater, 1996) and encourage an atmosphere of participative safety in teams (Atkins & Dunning, 1998), all essential skills in rapidly changing workplaces.

If women's skills may be more in keeping with employers' needs, this raises a number of possibilities for the future of gender versus role in organizations. Will organizational structures change? Will there be more women in senior positions? Or will men try to develop more "feminine" skills? Will men need special support to adapt, to be more flexible? Will they be taught to adopt new styles of management? Will men model themselves on successful women? If basic beliefs and values change, we may see even greater shifts in organizational cultures.

But perhaps this is the optimistic scenario. There is also evidence to support alternative views. For example, Woodhall, Edwards, and Welchman (1997) demonstrate in a case study of three large U.K. organizations that organizational restructuring, far from enhancing gender equality, can exacerbate women's disadvantage in a number of ways: making it more difficult to monitor gender balance; affecting management functions where women are predominant more than other areas of management; reducing line management support for women and increasing the importance of informal organizational networks from which women are often excluded. Furthermore, there is some debate about whether career paths may in fact regress back to the traditional pattern in the new, transformed organizations (Guest & Mackenzie-Davies, 1996), heralding a return to the status quo and perpetuating women's disadvantage. And of course, men remain at the top of most organizations and are unlikely to relinquish their greater power willingly.

Job Insecurity

In the past, many white-collar and professional workers have expected high levels of job security. Even many blue-collar workers who were laid off in heavy manufacturing industries of the past were reemployed when times got better. What will happen to the pervasive gendered division of paid and unpaid work as paid work becomes increasingly uncertain, and how will that affect organizations? Men's family provider roles are already being challenged as women participate more in the labor force and men can no longer count on secure lifelong incomes. Nevertheless, gendered family roles remain remarkably resilient. Despite the greater family involvement of many men, women continue to carry most domestic responsibilities, and many expect to continue to do so (Lewis et al., 1998; Major, 1993). What does appear to make a difference, however, is the extent to which women define themselves as sole providers or coproviders. Women who think of themselves as providing economic support for families on an equal basis are much more likely to expect partners to pull their weight at home and to have partners who do so (Potuchek, 1992). One possibility, then, is that as nonpermanent jobs become the norm, it will no longer be possible to prioritize one partner's job. Most women will perceive themselves as sole providers or coproviders. We may see more egalitarian gender roles in the family. If men as well as women demand and take advantage of working time flexibility, the issues of supporting employees in reconciling work and family demands may become mainstreamed as a strategic business issue, rather than being marginalized as a women's issue (Gonyea & Googins, 1996; Lewis, 1997a). In some cases, the perceived threat to gender identities of both men and women may cause some to reassert their traditional gender roles by playing down women's economic support for families and men's family work, and regarding these activities as temporary. But the demise of jobs for life and long-term job insecurity may ultimately force many families to reassess gender identities and roles in relation to family and work.

Job loss is a stressful experience. Both men and women are likely to be stressed if they do lose their jobs, even if their partners' continuing employment cushions them from the worst financial outcomes. However, there is some evidence that women are more affected by their partners' job-loss-related stress than vice versa, which has implications for future male and female roles. A longitudinal study of male managers during redundancy and reintegration into a new position revealed high levels of stress during the period of unemployment but a return to stability after reentering work for the men, whereas their wives, even if they were themselves in high-powered careers, were not only stressed during their husbands' unemployment but continued to manifest high levels of distress after the men were in their new jobs (Johnson & Jackson, 1998). The authors of this study suggest that women may act as shock absorbers, taking on men's stress and protecting them. Although this study did not look at female managers and the responses of their partners, other evidence supports the view that women may be more affected by partners' stress than are men. For example, occupational stress can cross over to affect the well-being of female partners at home, whereas men are less likely to be affected by wives' occupational stress (Jones & Fletcher, 1993). Male distress appears to be more contagious than women's distress. If this is the case, higher unemployment among men than women may create stress for partners and indeed whole families. As long as women continue to do the emotional work for men without reciprocal support, some women may be less able to benefit from opportunities and challenges if men have high levels of unemployment.

Long Working Hours

One consequence of job insecurity has been that employees feel they must be visible in the workplace for long hours to display commitment and not to jeopardize their jobs. Traditionally, it has been less legitimate for women to work long hours when they have young children than it was for fathers. But increasingly, mothers as well as fathers appear to be working long hours. This is not only because of job insecurity, nor is it always involuntary. Hochschild's (1997a) interviews with executives and clerical and factory workers in a *Fortune* 500 company demonstrated how parents began by putting in more hours of work to succeed in their careers, creating more stress at home, causing them to spend more time at work to escape from the tensions at home. If women as well as men opt out of home life while children are young, what will be the impact on families? And because family stress spills over to affect work (Crouter, 1984), what would be the consequences for organizations if this trend intensifies?

Indeed, what will families of the future look like in the context of long working hours and job insecurity? Will young workers decide not to have children when work and family balance becomes so difficult to sustain? There is already evidence of a dramatic decline in the birth rate across Europe (Eurostat, 1997). This is raising concerns in countries with the lowest birth rates about whether there will be enough young people to work and to ensure the future competitive success of these countries and to pay taxes and support the older generations. In France, for example, the government has implemented a number of social policies to encourage women to have more children, indirectly encouraging women back into the home (Fagnani, 1998). Will these concerns become more widespread if men and women compete to put in more hours of work and combining work and parenting becomes unsustainable?

Will the lengthening of working hours set us on a course to self-destruction, or will the workers of the future, themselves often the children of parents caught up in the long-hours culture, reject this course? Younger men and women in Europe say they value quality of life and are not prepared to put in long hours of work for employers whose commitment to them is limited (Lewis et al., 1998). Rather, they talk about a new psychological contract whereby they do not expect jobs for life but do expect working time flexibility and time for a life outside work. This suggests a possible convergence of gender expectations, with both men and women seeking a better work-life balance.

Virtual Organizations

As more and more men and women work from home, whether full-time or part-time, on short-term contracts or self-employed, we will increasingly be creating virtual organizations. The boundaries between work and nonwork are already becoming increasingly blurred as technology is used to enable people to work not only in their homes but on planes, trains, at the gym, and on vacation. With two out of three families dual earner or dual career, how will working from home or other distributed work (Wikstrom, Palm Linden, & Michelson, 1997) affect the delicate balance between home and work and the shifting roles of women and men?

There are two models of the potential impact on gender of home-based work and virtual organizations. One model proposes that these changes will lead to a reallocation of unpaid work and equalizing of gender roles in the home. This is based on the belief that virtual organizations will provide greater flexibility for combining work and family, provide opportunities for those with caretaker commitments to engage in paid work, and have a liberating effect for men as well as women, allowing more time for family (Dooley, 1996; Hill, Hawkins, & Miller, 1996). Distributed work may facilitate a reintegration of work and family, which have been separated since the Industrial

Revolution (Daly, 1996), particularly as the younger generation of men and women actively seeks more equitable relationships and balanced lives (Lewis et al., 1998). In addition, relocation of one partner will cause fewer difficulties for spouses and families as work of either partner can be performed at a distance (Cooper, 1996).

The alternative model argues that rather than providing benefits, home-based working will perpetuate gender inequalities both in the workforce and at home (Haddon & Silverstone, 1993), because employers will provide poorer benefits for home-based workers, women will use flexibility to integrate paid and unpaid work, and men will maintain boundaries between the two domains.

The evidence for these two views is mixed. Certainly, home-based work, performed by men and women, can be associated with a more egalitarian division of domestic labor and even role reversal in some cases, but this is by no means inevitable (Huws et al., 1996). For men, working from home can be a feminizing experience, and this may liberate them to spend more time with family but can also threaten gender identity and cause them to cling to traditional behaviors (Huws et al., 1996). Outcomes appear to depend primarily on previous division of labor and sexual politics within families (Haddon & Silverstone, 1993; Hill et al., 1996; Huws et al., 1996; Silver, 1993; Sullivan & Lewis, 1998), rather than on the effects of distributed working per se.

As boundaries between work and nonwork become blurred, some workers become workaholics. Without clear boundaries, work spills over more easily into family and leisure time. Others use flexibility to perform work and nonwork tasks simultaneously. Although both men and women may experience either scenario, the evidence suggests that men are more likely to let work spill into family time and women more likely to multitask (Sullivan & Lewis, 1998). Virtual organizations thus have the potential to revamp gender roles, but the impact of new ways of working is not independent of wider social processes. Greater social change may take more time. Meanwhile, perpetuation of gender roles may mediate the potential advantages of working from home unless the need to challenge these roles is articulated and specifically pursued.

Conclusions

Despite women's achievements in the workplace and men's greater involvement in family life, the glass ceiling remains firmly in place in most organizations and organizational culture still reflects predominantly male values while women retain the major responsibility for home and family. We have argued that enormous changes in the nature of work provide challenges and opportunities for shifts in gender experiences, roles, and relationships, although it is far from certain that such shifts will occur. The opportunities for change arise because deep-seated assumptions underpinning gendered organization cultures, such as the male model of work, the ideal of continuous full-time careers, and the notion that work and family should be physically and psychologically separated, are all being challenged. Employers want "flexible" workers and value career patterns with which women are more comfortable than men. The primacy of traditionally male styles of management is also being challenged and more "feminine" styles are becoming appropriate for the contemporary context. There are also opportunities for changes in gender roles and relationships within families. Job insecurity is forcing couples to rethink strategies of prioritizing one partner's career, and there is some indication that younger men and women are questioning the viability of the long-hours culture. The increase in distributed work, in the home or at other sites, also offers the potential for convergence of male and female roles.

On the negative side, men still retain the greatest power in most organizations and are unlikely to relinquish this, or their power in the home, without a struggle. Processes that contribute to the reproduction of gender in the workplace and the home will take time to dismantle and may prove resistant to fundamental change. But the turbulence in the world of work may yet be reflected in even greater changes in the construction of gender.

Chapter 4

Gender and Service Delivery

Barbara A. Gutek, Bennett Cherry, and Markus Groth

In his forecast about the postindustrial society, Daniel Bell (1976) provides a brief historical summary of the nature of work. When the United States was an agrarian society, farmers struggled against the physical environment. As manufacturing replaced farming in the industrial era, people wrestled with and mastered machines to produce goods. In the postindustrial (service) society that Bell predicted, he noted that people would simply have to deal with each other rather than with the land or with machines. That postindustrial society based on services rather than manufacturing or farming is now upon us.

Service is a broad category covering work that does not produce either a tangible durable product or foodstuffs. It ranges from professional activities such as law, medicine, and higher education to fast food, insurance, banking, and retail operations to domestic labor. In addition, many manufacturing firms and agribusiness ventures also have service components to them.

Over 70% of the U.S. labor force now works in service jobs (Appelbaum & Batt, 1994). Americans also spend more time than ever using (and purchasing) services. For example, consumers paid approximately $3.3 trillion for services in 1997 (U.S. Department of Commerce, 1998). The payroll for service industries is about 1.5 times the payroll for goods-producing industries (Bureau of Economic Analysis, 1998b), and although the United States has a trade deficit for goods, it has a trade surplus for services (Bureau of Economic Analysis, 1998a). Because the importance of services will probably not diminish anytime in the foreseeable future, much attention has been directed toward understanding this growing segment of the economy and how people experience service in the marketplace.

This chapter explores the topic of gender and service delivery. Both sexes work in service jobs, and both sexes purchase services. There is evidence, however, that a higher proportion of women than men work in service jobs (Hochschild, 1983) and that women do more buying than men (i.e., women purchase goods and services for their household, family, and spouse more than men do) (Katz & Katz, 1997). Prior to the introduction of equal opportunity legislation in the 1960s, part of the male sex role was to be the breadwinner for the family and part of the female sex role was to act as chief consumer for the household. As more women have moved into the labor force, these roles have blurred, with both sexes earning money and spending it. Furthermore, households are likely to consume more services than ever, purchasing some of the services formerly provided by the housewife/mother. In turn, many of those wives and mothers are today employees who are engaged in providing services to others for pay.

Our analysis of gender and service delivery is organized around the service provider, the customer, and the environment in which they interact. First, we review the key concepts for studying service delivery and the key concepts for studying the gendered nature of service, then we discuss the research as it relates to gender and service providers, to gender and customers, and to gender and the service environment. Finally, we discuss the different ways in which this research is conducted and draw some conclusions. In this way, we expect to address two questions: (1) What do we know about gender and service delivery? and (2) What else do we need to know?

Key Concepts

We begin by discussing four concepts of interest: the service transaction, the service provider, the customer, and the service environment.

The Service Transaction

Service interactions constitute a subset of all human interactions that take place between two parties. In a typical service transaction, a customer (service seeker) desires a product (service) that is usually offered by multiple parties (service providers) in the marketplace. Often, the customer identifies the most desirable service provider, communicates the desire to receive some service, and the service provider responds. After receiving the service, the customer typically offers money in exchange for the service rendered and departs the service environment. Many variants exist, however. In the case of government services, there is typically only one agency providing service. Sometimes the customer pays a set periodic fee in exchange for an unspecified amount of service (e.g., membership in a club, professional association, or health maintenance organization [HMO]). Service transactions may occur over the telephone rather than face-to-face, and they can even occur without a human provider. For instance, automatic teller machines (ATMs) and voice mail instructions are increasingly available to provide service to customers.

In purchasing a good (e.g., a car or a TV), a customer will usually determine its satisfaction and utility by assessing the purchased good itself. However, the customer's assessment of the utility of a service purchase is dependent on his or her experience in the interaction with the service provider. In fact, the social interaction between the recipient and the provider is to a large extent the service rendered. Those who study services often point out that services are produced and consumed simultaneously to separate them from goods in which production and consumption are separate processes (Grönroos, 1983, 1990; Schneider & Bowen, 1985, p. 423).

Service interactions can take place between two people who know each other or between two strangers (Gutek, 1995; Gutek, Bhappu, Liao-Troth, & Cherry, in press). Service *relationships* occur when a customer has repeated contact with a particular provider. Customer and provider can get to know each other as role occupants and sometimes as acquaintances or even friends. *Encounters,* on the other hand, typically consist of a single interaction between a particular customer and provider; neither expects to interact with the other in the future. Most research on service providers focuses on encounters.

The Service Provider

Service providers deliver intangible goods to paying customers, usually face-to-face or over the phone. Employees who actually deliver the service and interact directly with customers are called frontline service personnel (Hochschild, 1983; MacDonald & Sirianni, 1996) because, in most cases, they are pseudo-ambassadors for the organization, living representations of the organization to the customer. According to Bulan, Erickson, and Wharton (1997), "The primary tasks of such [frontline] workers is not to produce material goods, but to produce speech, action, and emotion that symbolize one's willingness to 'do for' the client or customer" (p. 235). As organizations become more aware of the impact these representatives have on their customers' perception of the service interaction, they try to manage employees' behavior and emotions such that the service interaction is deemed satisfactory by the customers.

Customers who value expertise are likely to have relationships with providers they seek out based on reputation. This is true not only of highly educated professional service providers such as attorneys, physicians, and stockbrokers, but also of hairstylists, auto mechanics, nannies, and travel agents (Gutek, 1995). Providers who deliver service in encounters, on the other hand, are likely to be evaluated by their delivery style, especially if all providers deliver the same service (e.g., same quality hamburger and fries) or if the customer is not able to evaluate the provider's expertise (Gutek, 1995; Iacobucci, Grayson, & Ostrom, 1994).

The Customer

Customers purchase goods or services for which they or someone else typically pays, making them valuable assets because they ultimately assure profits and revenues that determine a service organization's success. Knowing who their customers are and understanding their customers is often viewed as a competitive advantage for service providers. Customers, who often witness the process of service delivery firsthand, usually measure the success of a service transaction by comparing the *actual* service quality with their *expected* service quality. Because customer satisfaction may determine the willingness to repeat a service delivery, service providers strive to know what does not satisfy people consuming their services. At times, when customers actively participate in the service transaction (e.g., using an ATM or filling out an order form before approaching a service counter), they are engaging in coproduction, so-called because of their participation in the production as well as the consumption of the service (Bowen & Jones, 1986; Mills, Chase, & Margulies, 1983).

Customers are typically treated differently in relationships and encounters. They may receive customized service from a provider they know and trust in a service relationship, whereas in an encounter, customers are typically subject to standardized treatment by a provider who is a stranger to them (including learning the provider's first name, e.g., "Hello, my name is Gary. I will be your server tonight!"). Although more frequent and better-paying customers may get priority over others in relationships, encounters usually are egalitarian (i.e., all customers are treated the same and are typically served on a first-come, first-served basis).

The Service Environment

The physical environment (Bitner, 1992) and the social environment (Baker, 1987) in which services are performed have long been the focus of research in the service literature. Bitner provides a framework that focuses on objective physical elements (the *servicescape*), such as ambient conditions, spatial layout and functionality, as well as signs, symbols, and artifacts. Bitner argues for the importance of considering the impact of physical surroundings on the behaviors of customers and employees. However, she excludes components of the social environment. Interpersonal issues between customers and service providers as well as gender issues have been considered by others (e.g., Baker, 1987) interested in either broadening the concept of servicescape or simply understanding the environment in which service interactions take place.

The Gendered Nature of Service

Because gender is a basic cognitive category by which we classify people (e.g., Bem, 1981b; Laws, 1979) and because of its visibility, it is plausible to think that the gender of both participants will affect their experiences in service interactions and their evaluation of those experiences. Gender can affect the consumption and delivery of service in several ways. First, we can consider provider gender and/or customer gender. Because work is sex segregated, men are more likely to hold some provider jobs and women are more likely to hold other provider jobs. Although not as well documented or discussed, it is also probable that men are more likely to be customers in certain kinds of situations (e.g., buying tires, getting a haircut at a barber shop), whereas women are more likely to be customers in other situations (e.g., purchasing children's clothing or household items). Thus, we can consider the provider gender, customer gender, the gender role associated with the provider, and the gender role associated with the customer. A provider role is either congruent with (or "fits") one's gender or incongruent with gender. Similarly, a customer role is either congruent with (or "fits") one's gender or is incongruent with gender. Thus, one could be a female provider congruent with the provider role (e.g., a female waitperson), a female provider incongruent with the provider role (e.g., a female surgeon), a male provider congruent with the provider role (e.g., a male mechanic), or a male provider incongruent with the provider role (e.g., a male hairstylist). Similarly, one could be a female customer congruent with the customer role (e.g., getting a manicure), a female customer incongruent with the customer role (e.g., purchasing a tire for her motorcycle), a male customer congruent with customer role (e.g., purchasing sports equipment), or a male customer incongruent with customer role (e.g., getting a manicure). In this chapter, we use the term *congruency* or congruent to refer to the association between gender and role. We consider the term *fit* as a synonym for congruency.

Although we recognize that some provider roles and some customer roles may not be associated with one gender or the other, we expect that (1) these situations are relatively uncommon, (2) they are more common of the customer role than the provider role, and (3) whether a particular provider or customer role is associated with one gender or the other changes over time. For example, the roles of residential real estate salesperson and bartender have relatively recently changed from being male dominated to female dominated (Reskin & Roos, 1990). The role of clinical psychologist, which today is relatively sex integrated, may in 10 or 20 years become female dominated, because jobs rarely stay sex integrated but tend to become either male dominated or female dominated over time. Today, both sexes do grocery shopping, whereas that was a customer role associated more with women in the past. In the past, men purchased cars much more often than women, but today both sexes do so.

Gender can affect service delivery in yet other ways. Regardless of the provider or customer role, gender can be expected to have an effect. Sex-role spillover operates in service delivery such that women are expected to exhibit certain kinds of behaviors (whether they are in a congruent role or not) and so are men (Gutek & Morasch, 1982; Nieva & Gutek, 1981). Sex-role spillover is the carryover of gender-role expectations to the provider role and/or the customer role. For example, women providers and customers, regardless of the sex composition of the occupation they hold, may be expected to smile more, to be nicer or more accommodating than men in the same position. More than women, men may be expected to act as an authority or be waited on quickly. Thus, sex-role stereotyping may affect both provider and customers and may influence how both respond to the service interaction. Furthermore, sex-role spillover may be stronger when providers are in jobs that are sex-role congruent, where the job itself takes on aspects of gender role (Gutek & Morasch, 1982; Sheffey & Tindale, 1992).

One aspect of sex-role spillover that has been examined in several studies is emotional labor. Hochschild (1983) defined emotional labor as the "management of feeling to create a publicly observable facial and bodily display" (p. 7). Women may be expected to engage in more emotional labor than men, that is, to create a publicly observable facial and bodily display more than men are expected to do so. In addition, men may be expected to engage in a different kind of emotional labor (e.g., to be demanding or authoritative when selling insurance or collecting debts) than women (who, more often, may be expected to create a friendly, ingratiating, or perky emotional display). Although the concept of emotional labor has generated considerable interest among researchers (e.g., James, 1989; Rafaeli, 1989a, 1989b; Sutton & Rafaeli, 1988), relatively little has focused on gender as our review below shows.

Gender can be considered in yet another way in the study of service delivery because service delivery takes place between two people, each of whom is either a man or a woman.[1] A study may focus on the gender of the provider but ignore (or not study) the gender of the customer. Alternately, a study may focus on the gender of the customer but ignore (or not study) the gender of the provider. A study may also focus on both the gender of the provider and the gender of the customer. Figure 4.1 shows a 2×2 matrix that allows one to classify research on service delivery into one of four cells. The majority of the research on service delivery falls into Cell I, in which the gender of provider and gender of customer are both ignored (or not studied). In contrast, as will be clear in our review of the literature that follows, relatively few studies fall into the other three cells.

Gender of Provider

		Ignored	Observed
Gender of Customer	Ignored	Gutek, Bhappu, Liao-Troth, and Cherry (1999) **I**	**II** Rind and Bordia (1996)
	Observed	**IV** Iacobucci and Ostrom (1993)	**III** Kulik and Holbrook (1998)

Figure 4.1. Categorization of Research Studies Taking Into Account Ignoring or Observing the Impact of Gender on the Service Experience

Cell III is particularly relevant to researchers interested in the study of gender and services because they can consider not only whether both customer and provider are congruent or incongruent with gender role but also whether provider and customer are the same gender or a different gender. That is, we can consider the gender composition of the provider-customer dyad. We use the term *gender matching* to refer to those instances in which provider and customer are the same gender. Where customer and provider are different genders, gender is not "matched." Note that one can have gender matching (provider and customer are same gender) but one or both parties may be incongruent with gender role. For example, there is a gender match when a female patient has a female surgeon although that female surgeon is gender incongruent because surgery is a male-dominated field. There is a gender match when a male customer sees a male loan officer at a bank; in addition, both customer and provider are congruent with their respective roles. Men are expected to seek bank loans more than women, and traditionally more loan officers are male than female (Kulik & Holbrook, 1998).

In sum, in examining gender and service delivery, one can examine the gender of provider and/or customer, the congruency between the provider and customer roles and gender of the provider and customer, the spillover of gender role to both the provider and customer role, and the effects of having provider and customer the same or different genders. Despite the myriad ways in which gender can affect service delivery, the available research, reviewed below, is scanty. It shows that very few of the many possibilities have been explored.

Gender and Service Providers

We now turn to a review of the research on gender and service delivery, starting with research on service providers.

Depending on the industry, the majority of service providers can be male or female or the work can be gender integrated. The traditional women's professions, nursing (94.5% female in 1990), elementary school teaching (85.2% female in 1990), librarianship (83.3% female in 1990), and social work (68.2% female in 1990, see Williams, 1995, p. 3), are all service jobs; not surprisingly, women occupy a majority of the service jobs in the United States (U.S. Bureau of the Census, 1996). Hochschild (1983, Table 4, pp. 240-241) estimated that in 1970 approximately 4.4 million women and 3.6 million men worked in service occupations excluding private household workers (a very high proportion of whom are women). According to Adkins (1995, p. 8), 81% of all employed women in Britain work in service occupations and more than 70% of women's employment in nine of the member states of the European Community is concentrated in the service sector. It is therefore not surprising that service jobs tend to be sex segregated, with women dominating some areas (e.g., manicurists, baby-sitters, flight attendants, and dental hygienists) and men dominating others (e.g., police officers, insurance salespersons, bill collectors, and physicians). As Leidner (1991) notes, the "gender segregation of service jobs contributes to the general perception that differences in men and women's social positions are straightforward reflections of differences in their natures and capabilities" (p. 175).

Research on service providers tends to focus on several service domains including industrial selling, banking, hospitals, restaurants, dental services, and insurance sales. In general, there is relatively little research on gender and service providers; what exists tends to focus on a somewhat disparate set of topics. We divide the research into two broad topics: the delivery of services by male and female providers and customers' reactions to male and female providers. Within each of these topics, we review research relevant to each of the gender concepts reviewed above. Much of the research focuses on sex-role spillover (i.e., the carryover of gender-based expectations to the workplace). This is discussed as "doing gender" and as creating "gender scripts." In addition, there is some research on emotional labor, including the extent to which men versus women are expected to engage in emotional labor and how emotional labor affects them and their job satisfaction. Surprisingly little research focuses on the effects of being in a gender-incongruent job, but some research focuses on gender matching (i.e., differences in behavior when provider and customer are either the same sex or different sexes).

Delivery of Services by Male and Female Providers

Siguaw and Honeycutt (1995) investigated gender differences in selling behaviors and job attitudes of industrial salespersons who sell high-cost products, typically including high-quality service and expertise, to the buyer. Their results support previous findings that saleswomen have higher customer-oriented selling behaviors (Busch & Bush, 1978; Gibson & Swan, 1981) and are more considerate of their customers (Rhey, Rustogi, & Watson, 1992). Responses to a self-report questionnaire by members of a sales association yielded a response rate of only 16.4%, and of those responding, only 10.4% were women. Although the authors argue that the low representation of females is consistent with the male-dominated industrial sales industry, both the low response rate and the low representation of women raise concerns about the validity of the results.

Many other studies show that sex-role spillover is common in service delivery. For example, it has been posited that organizations create gendered scripts of behavior for employees to use while on the job, requiring workers to display their gender as an integral part of their job tasks and duties (Hall, 1993). A female provider is doing gender if she presents herself as a caring nurturer, a motherlike figure providing for her child, or a sex object (Hall, 1993). From the data yielded in the case study, Hall (1993) concluded that restaurants create gendering processes by embedding gender into prescribed work performance; specifically, they "frame service work as women's work . . . construct and legitimate a gendered image of a deferential servant . . . and structure interactions of women servers as sexual objects" (pp. 455-456). For example, restaurants tend to hire women who display social and domestic skills needed to perform good service. Hall also reveals that managers are sometimes "pleased when customers make sexual advances" toward their servers (p. 457).

In another case study, Leidner (1991) investigated two highly routinized interactive service jobs: fast food counter workers and insurance sales.

Leidner (1991) noted that both McDonald's counter workers and insurance salespersons have to "take on the role of interactive inferior, adjusting themselves to the styles and apparent preferences of their customers and paste on smiles when they did not feel like smiling and to behave cheerfully and deferentially to people of every status and with every attitude" (p. 171). However, managers, customers, and employees generally interpret these tasks in different ways depending on the structure of the environment, the incumbents, and the perception of control or subservience in the service context, which encourages sex-role spillover. The standardization of many service interactions encourages "repeat performances" of socially congruent gendered behaviors. As an example, trainers and agents view insurance sales job as demanding masculine attributes like determination, aggressiveness, and persistence. By continually reinforcing these attributes, through training and organizational literature, the "manly" nature of the sales job is understood.

It is not only jobs or organizational practices that encourage sex-role spillover but also service workers' behavior. In a sense, the service provider affirms his or her own gender identity when he or she works in a way that matches the socially constructed stereotype of male or female. As Leidner (1991) suggests, "Workers in all kinds of jobs need to consider how their work relates to their own identities, including their gender identities" (p. 157). Thus, service providers might be more comfortable in their jobs when they behave in a manner consistent with gender-role expectations. If that were the case, one might expect that service providers in gender-incongruent jobs would experience more negative job outcomes than those who are in jobs that are traditionally held by their sex. But the scant research available suggests that this is not necessarily the case. For example, Siguaw and Honeycutt (1995) found that industrial saleswomen have lower levels of role conflict and role ambiguity than their male counterparts.

Because an important aspect of service work is attentiveness to customers' needs and expectations, many organizations are creating prescriptions of behavior for frontline employees to follow. For instance, some service personnel are expected to smile and greet each customer as if they were really glad to see them. These performance expectations create an additional type of employee cost (in excess of physical or mental work), which has been termed emotional labor (Hochschild, 1983). Albrecht and Zemke (1985) described the emotion management task: "The service person must deliberately involve his or her feelings in the situation. He or she may not particularly feel like being cordial and becoming a one-minute friend to the next customer who approaches, but that is indeed what frontline work entails" (p. 114). This presentation of self used to be a private issue; now it is often controlled by an organization (Hochschild, 1983; Wharton, 1993). Emotional labor may produce a workforce of people faking their feelings to increase profit share (Hochschild, 1983; Leidner, 1991).

In her pioneering study, Hochschild (1983) examined two service occupations, flight attendants and bill collectors. Although both are "frontline" service workers, they are expected to display very different emotions. Whereas flight attendants are expected to be cheerful, nurturing, and subservient, bill collectors are expected to be suspicious and sometimes exude bad will (Hochschild, 1983, p. 137).

Hochschild (1983) concluded that emotional labor has costs for workers. Workers can identify wholeheartedly with the job and risk burnout, or they can separate themselves from the job and feel they are "fakes, just acting" (p. 187). Although both sexes are expected to engage in emotional labor, Hochschild contends that men and women experience it differently. In particular, she argues that (1) women more than men are expected to be emotional managers and (2) men have a "status shield" that protects them against poorer treatment of their feelings. She notes that female flight attendants are "the company's main shock absorbers against 'mishandled' passengers" and that "their own feelings are more frequently subjected to rough treatment" (p. 175).

Although Hochschild's innovative notion of emotional labor has fostered a substantial amount of research, not everyone agrees that emotional labor is exclusively a cost. Being good at emotional labor might be a source of accomplishment and satisfaction. As Bulan et al. (1997) suggest and Wharton (1993, p. 218) states, "It may be that previous researchers have overstated the psychological costs and understated the psychological rewards of emotional labor, relative to other types of work."

Richmond (1997) explored Hochschild's suggestion that emotional labor is associated with negative job outcomes by studying 203 fast-food workers at one of 14 locations of a chain of stores in Tucson, Arizona. Contrary to expectations, she found that employees who engaged in more emotional labor reported greater job satisfaction, more job commitment, and less job stress than service providers who did not.

A number of researchers have extended Hochschild's (1983) work by doing in-depth case studies of service work, focusing specifically on gender and emotional labor. For examples, see Adkins (1995) on the tourism industry in Britain, Pierce (1995) on law firms in the San Francisco area, and Tyler and Taylor (1998) on the airline industry in the United Kingdom. Others have used survey research to study gender and emotional labor. For example, Wharton (1993) examined the social-psychological consequences, both positive and negative, of emotional labor for a sample of men and women service providers. She hypothesized that women are more likely to be involved in emotional labor jobs than men and will suffer more negative effects of emotional labor because their feelings on the job are less protected than those of men.

Wharton found that men and women were equally unlikely to experience emotional exhaustion from emotional labor but, in direct contrast to the hypothesized relationship, the women who engaged in emotional labor were more satisfied with their jobs than their male counterparts (p. 225). Bulan et al. (1997) claim that women may be less negatively affected by emotional labor because of their satisfaction in interacting with other people.

Bulan et al. (1997) were interested in understanding the impact of organizationally imposed rules of facial and bodily display on employees' feelings of inauthenticity at work. They operationalized inauthenticity as the employees' inability to be themselves at work and how often they had to "fake how they really felt when they were at work" (p. 240). Results showed that service providers who spent more time interacting with other employees had lower levels of inauthenticity, whereas "handling people" was related to higher levels of inauthenticity:

> Most [women] experience the most inauthenticity when they were highly involved in their jobs and did not spend much time interacting with other workers. In contrast, men felt most inauthentic when they were *not* very involved in their jobs and did not spend much time interacting with others. (Bulan et al., 1997, p. 252)

Most of the research on emotional labor focuses on service encounters where providers are interacting with customers whom they have neither previously met nor expect to meet again in the future. Because the customer is a stranger, the provider typically has no prior feelings about him or her and therefore manufactures the appropriate emotion as part of the job. The effects of service relationships on emotional labor, however, may be quite different (Gutek, 1995, pp. 80-83). In relationships, the provider not only displays appropriate emotions but also, over time, develops real feelings about the customer, and vice versa. Although in some cases the emotions may be strong, both customer and provider are expected to refrain from displaying their felt emotions. For them, emotional labor means putting aside real feelings and displaying less intense, blander emotions, whether positive or negative. Service providers cannot let a client know they think he or she is boring or obnoxious. Repeated interaction can lead to one person developing strong bonds of affection, physical attraction, or love, which may not be reciprocated by the other. At the very least, strong emotions can complicate the service relationship. In contrast to the burgeoning research on emotional labor and emotional expression in encounters, these phenomena have not been studied in service relationships.

Reactions to Male and Female Service Providers

It is probable that customers facilitate sex-role spillover when they react to male and female providers differently because of the gender stereotypes they hold. These gender stereotypes can affect a provider's behavior in a number of ways. One possibility is that some behavior may be more effective for a female than a male provider in the same job, and vice versa. An interesting example comes from a series of studies on tipping behavior in restaurants.

Research has shown that certain provider behaviors (e.g., smiling) can generate increased restaurant tips given by customers (Tidd & Lockard, 1978). Rind and Bordia (1995) found that writing "thank you" on the back of the check resulted in positive tipping behavior. In a later study, they examined the effect of drawing a happy face on the back of the check. Using both male and female servers allowed them to ascertain whether the gender of the server combined with the drawing had any effect on tipping behavior. To test this, two servers (one male, one female) provided service at an upscale restaurant during the lunch hour throughout a 3-day period. To achieve randomization, each server was given 50 3 × 5 cards, half with a happy face, the other half blank. At the end of the meal, the server randomly selected a card. If a happy face was drawn, the server drew a happy face on the back of the meal check, if a card was blank, the server simply delivered the check.

Rind and Bordia (1996) hypothesized that drawing a happy face on the check would be effective for the female server but not for the male server (the happy face would be considered "perfectly natural" for a woman to draw, but not for a man). They thought that the drawing would create a negative impression of the man and would likely negate any positive "friendliness" effect of the drawing on tipping behavior. On the other hand, the woman would be responding to sex-role spillover or doing gender by drawing a happy face because women are believed to be more emotionally expressive than men (Allen & Haccoun, 1976; Broverman, Vogel, Broverman, Clarkson, & Rosenkrantz, 1972). A woman would engage in sex-role spillover when she drew a happy face, a man when he did not draw a happy face. Results show that the happy face significantly increased tips for women but not for men.

Under some circumstances, the gender of the service provider may be less important than whether the service dyad is same sex or other sex. For example, an other-sex customer might elicit different behavior in a provider than a same-sex customer. Hall (1993) found that food servers were friendlier to customers of the other gender (e.g., male servers were most apt to flirt with a party composed of women, and female servers were most likely to flirt with a male-dominated group). As well, she found that although flirting occurred at high-prestige restaurants, job flirts and sexual bantering by waitresses were more likely to occur at low-prestige restaurants than in elite restaurants. Finally, Hall found that control clashes were more likely to occur when the customer and provider were of the same gender. As one waiter remarked about his interactions with male customers, "[They] tend to talk a little harshly to the waiter . . . 'Hey, get me this' . . . and the waiter takes offense . . . 'I'm not a dog . . . I'm not below you' " (Hall, 1993, p. 463).

Gender and Customers

We all play the role of customer many times a week, but there is evidence that women play that role more often than men. In fact, the amount of goods and services purchased by American women is staggering. By one estimate, women in the United States have "more purchasing power than the total economic output of any other country, including Japan" (Katz & Katz, 1997, p. 4). Katz and Katz argue that women can put this purchasing power to work in a variety of ways by supporting companies that are woman-friendly. To help women in this endeavor, they rate companies, states, and countries on a variety of criteria, including number of women on the board, number of female top officers, the company's benefits program, and pay disparities. Although it is generally acknowledged that gender is important, there is a paucity of research on how gender affects the experiences or evaluation of customers. "Gender colors what we customers expect as good service" (Hall, 1993, p. 452). Our real-world experiences as customers of service establishments help to bolster our feelings that one gender often does a better job in one service area than in others.

We divide the research on gender and customers into two areas: treatment of male and female customers and male and female customers' evaluation of services. Within these two areas, we examine the extent to which gender congruency, sex-role spillover, and gender matching are studied. In the case of research on customers, gender matching sometimes assumes an in-group bias (i.e., that customers prefer a service provider of their own sex).

Treatment of Male and Female Customers

Although the effects of customers' gender during the delivery of services have not been subject to much research, speculations about gender differences naturally lead to the question of whether a customer's sex affects the service that the customer receives. Zinkhan and Stoiadin (1984) attempted to determine if men receive service priority over women in department stores. They defined priority as the order of service when two customers arrive at a department store counter simultaneously. Even though service priority does not directly measure service quality, service length, or interpersonal treatment, it is nevertheless considered to be an important service dimension.

In the study, pairs of one female and one male customer simultaneously approached a counter in various department stores; observers recorded which one (the male, the female, or neither) received service first. Results show that men receive service priority over women. Men were served first 63% of the time and women 23.5% of the time; 13.5% of the time service priority was considered neutral. The male advantage was homogeneous across several factors such as price of merchandise (high, moderate, low) and type of merchandise ("male," "female," "neutral"). Furthermore, the sex of the clerk also did not significantly affect the results. The only exception was that female customers who shopped in department stores offering primarily "male" products received especially poor service.

Beliefs about male and female customers appeared to influence the results in Zinkhan and Stoiadin's (1984) study. Qualitative data, obtained through interviews with clerks after observations of service priority, suggest that women are perceived to shop around more, that they need less help than men, that men are more serious buyers, and that men are easier to deal with.

In a similar field study, Stead and Zinkhan (1986) examined whether certain customer characteristics, such as sex and dress, affect service priority. Again, a male and a female customer arrived simultaneously at a counter in a department store and observations were made as to who received service first. Results were similar to Zinkhan and Stoiadin's (1984) study. Overall, men were served first 61% of the time and women 32% of the time; in 7% of the cases service priority was neutral. Customer dress also showed a significant effect. Men in business dress were served first 67.3% of the time, whereas those in casual dress were served first only 54.7% of the time. Service promptness was especially low, however, for women in business dress (29.3%) relative to those in casual dress (34.7%). No other main effects or interactions were observed. Neither the sex of the clerk nor the type of department store (selling either "female," "male," or "neutral" products) was significant.

Evaluation of Services by Male and Female Customers

Iacobucci and Ostrom (1993) studied the role of customers' sex in the delivery of services by drawing on the literature on gender differences in information processing as well as Fiedler's (1967) work on leadership, suggesting that some people are more task oriented and others are more relationship oriented. Iacobucci and Ostrom cite several studies (Eagly, Makhijani, & Klonsky, 1992; Inderlied & Powell, 1979) as further evidence that under certain circumstances, men may be more goal oriented and women more relationship oriented.

Applying these findings to the service setting, Iacobucci and Ostrom (1993) predicted that the two sexes will attend differently to two components of the service experience that have been identified in the marketing literature: the core service (e.g., a haircut or a dinner) and the relationship component (e.g., the interpersonal interaction between the service provider and the customer as well as the delivery of the service itself) (L. Berry, 1983). Using written scenarios describing hypothetical short-run and long-run service experiences, Iacobucci and Ostrom expected that in the short run, men will attend more to the core service and women to the relationship component. In the long run, one expects these differences to disappear because if one of the two components is not satisfactory in repeated interactions, the customer is likely to be dissatisfied with the service overall and is less likely to return to the provider in the future.

Overall, the results suggest that there are indeed differences between men and women in the evaluation of services. However, the data did not clearly support the initial hypotheses and are somewhat complicated and contradictory. For example, women seem to attend to both aspects (core service and relationship component) in the short run as well as in the long run. Men, on the other hand, attend more to the core service in the short run and attend to both components in the long run, suggesting that men and women attend to different aspects of service in service encounters but not in service relationships. More specifically, in service encounters women attend more than men to service delivery, whereas in relationships both sexes attend to both service and service delivery.

Mohr and Henson (1996) examined whether customers care about the gender of a service provider and whether there is a general bias in favor of one gender over the other. They explored congruency bias (i.e., customers preferring men in male-dominated jobs and women in female-dominated jobs) and in-group bias (i.e., customers preferring providers of their own sex).[2]

The results of responses to written scenarios of hypothetical service encounters in which one expects either mostly male or mostly female employees show that customers generally preferred employees whose gender is congruent with the gender type of the job (e.g., a male auto mechanic or a female nurse). Some evidence (though not very strong) of in-group bias existed in that male and female customers generally seemed to prefer same-sex providers.

Overall, it appears that the gender of providers had far less of an effect than service quality on the evaluation of customer satisfaction. Customers rate providers more favorably if their sex is congruent with their expectation, but overall service quality plays a more important role than the gender of the service provider.

Another study suggests that in the field of psychotherapy, there have been some changes in clients' expectations. Stamler, Christiansen, Staley, and Macagno-Shang (1991) cited an earlier study by Fuller (1964), who found that both male and female clients indicated a preference for male counselors, presumably because males were viewed as more competent. In their study of 495 clients who participated in an intake interview for individual therapy at a large university during 1987, Stamler et al. (1991) asked, "Do you have a preference for a male or female therapist?" They found that 57% of women and 37% of men expressed a preference; of those who did, a majority of both sexes (90% of women and 69% of men) said they preferred a female therapist. Perhaps women, or women therapists more specifically, were viewed in 1987 as more competent than they were in 1964 or perhaps factors other than competence influenced the choice of clients. Therapy has changed over the years from being a male-dominated field to being a gender-neutral or even female-dominated area. Thus, in 1964 male therapists were gender congruent, whereas by 1987 it was female therapists, at least in the minds of some clients.

Finally, in her in-depth interview study of 76 men working in the traditionally female professions of nursing, elementary school teaching, librarianship, and social work, Williams (1995) found that customers expected these service workers to be women. Men, she concludes, face discrimination and prejudice from "clients, who often react negatively to male nurses, teachers, and to a lesser extent, librarians. Many people assume that the men are sexually suspect if they are employed in these 'feminine' occupations either because they do or they do not conform to stereotypical masculine characteristics" (Williams, 1995, p. 108). Men who conform to masculine stereotypes are viewed as potential sexual predators who might exploit their access to vulnerable populations like children or patients, whereas those who do not are suspected of homosexuality.

Gender matching assumes that customers prefer a same-sex service provider. Kulik and Holbrook (1998) recently conducted an interesting study that examined the effects of gender and race matching between customers and service providers. Kulik and Holbrook surveyed 119 people who had applied for a loan from a large bank. The respondent pool included multiple races and both sexes (57% were male). (For the purposes of this chapter, the race effects are not discussed.) The researchers expected that gender-matched customers would not respond any differently to unfavorable outcomes than would gender-unmatched customers; results, however, were contrary to the hypothesis. In fact, gender-matched customers responded most negatively to unfavorable outcomes. They reasoned that this result is based on the customers' trust in the service provider, citing organizational research that suggests that lower levels of trust are sometimes observed in female gender-matched relationships.

For this study in particular, the gender-matching effect suggests that female customers may respond negatively to unfavorable outcomes because they perceive that the female loan officer has limited ability to provide a more favorable outcome. Male gender typing of the loan officer job may fuel expectations by customers that female loan officers will provide inferior outcomes. Drawing conclusions from these results may be a bit premature, however, in that only one service area was investigated and results were not easily explained. Perhaps men and women prefer interacting with members of the other sex in applying for loans just as wait staff and their customers seem to (Hall, 1993). Additional research is needed to more fully understand gender matching between service provider and customer.

Gender and the Service Environment

A number of researchers have examined the way customers respond to the service environment. Building on Bitner's (1992) concept of the servicescape, Fischer, Gainer, and Bristor (1998) explore what makes servicescapes feel more or less gendered. Fischer et al. presented participants with hypothetical service scenarios (e.g., auto repair shops, hardware stores, fabric stores, and aerobic classes). They collected qualitative data by asking open-ended questions about reactions to particular service settings that were not clearly labeled as male or female, about elements that participants perceived as contributing to the gendering of the servicescape, and about suggestions of how a new hair studio or auto repair facility should be designed to target the other sex (e.g., layout and design). As one would expect, results suggest that people perceive some service settings to be gendered. However, the cues in the environment that seem to be responsible for these perceptions are not all physical. It appears that people perceive the sex of the provider, the sex of the people who will be in the service setting, and which sex will buy or use the product or service to be most important in influencing the perception of gendered servicescapes. Interestingly, people seem to "construct" servicescapes in their own minds. Even though they had never actually been in the hypothetical service settings that were described, the study's participants nevertheless formed a clear representation of what the servicescape would be like.

The most common reactions to gendered spaces by the "other gender" are confusion and mystery, as well as fear and feeling unwelcome and alien (Fischer et al., 1998). When they are in men's spaces, women report lack of information and lack of control as a common fear, whereas men in women's spaces fear a contamination of their masculinity. Schmidt and Sapsford (1995) reported similar findings in a study that examined females' reactions to being in public bars in the United Kingdom, a service environment that appears to be traditionally male. Focus groups and in-depth interviews with women between 26 and 47 years of age revealed that, from the moment they walk in the bar and feel the stares of male customers, to bartenders' behavior that appears to be preferential toward males, to sitting alone at a table and feeling vulnerable, female customers often feel uncomfortable and intimidated and perceive the servicescape to be highly gendered.

Fischer et al.'s (1998) conclusion that the sex of service providers and the sex of customers are the most salient in the perception of gendered servicescapes has also been supported by Stern, Gould, and Tewari (1993). Stern et al. found that service-related variables (those pertaining to service context) were more important in determining sex-typed service images than self-related variables (those pertaining to the customer). Although many services have sex-typed images based on masculinity or femininity ratings, the sex of the customer only partially influences the sex typing of services. Furthermore, study respondents tended to predict that the sex of the "typical customer" and the "typical provider" will be congruent with the sex-typed images (e.g., typical customers and providers of a feminine service [jewelry store] are likely to be women).

Methods of Studying Gender and Service Delivery

Research Design

In studying gender and service providers, researchers have mainly used self-report questionnaires and large-scale surveys directed toward frontline service providers (Bulan et al., 1997; Klose & Finkle, 1995; Siguaw & Honeycutt, 1995; Wharton, 1993) or their customers (Klose & Finkle), or they conduct case studies. In general, whereas questionnaires ask frontline service personnel about the requirements and the consequences of service work, the case studies investigate sex-role spillover or the "gendering" of jobs (Adkins, 1995; Hall, 1993; Leidner, 1991; Pierce, 1995; Tyler & Taylor, 1998; Williams, 1995) including the emotional requirements of frontline service employees (Hochschild, 1983; Pierce, 1995). Illustrative information about real employees in real service jobs has been obtained by conducting interviews with employees and engaging in participant observation of actual work. In many qualitative studies, researchers rely on multiple methods of obtaining information (e.g., participant observation, content analysis of documents, structured or unstructured interviews) (Leidner, 1993; Tyler & Taylor, 1998). Multiple sites are frequently studied (Hall, 1993; Pierce, 1995). In some cases, researchers have attended training or worked in the job of service provider to gain information about the work (Adkins, 1995; Hochschild,

1983; Pierce, 1995). For example, to learn about service jobs at McDonald's, Leidner (1991, 1993) attended classes at Hamburger University (McDonald's training center), participated in orientation and "window crew" training, and actually worked as a food order taker. To learn about insurance sales jobs, she went through a two-week training program for life insurance agents, interviewed agents, and worked with a team in the field.

In studying gender issues from the customer's viewpoint, a common approach is to use written scenarios that describe a particular hypothetical service experience (Fischer, Gainer, & Bristor, 1997, 1998; Iacobucci & Ostrom, 1993; Mohr & Henson, 1996). Participants (students in most cases) read a hypothetical scenario and then rated the quality of service and service satisfaction, as well as other aspects regarding the service experience. Using written scenarios in the laboratory allows for tight control over independent variables such as characteristics of the customer and the provider, and the physical and social aspects of the service environment. In one study (Fischer et al., 1997), participants were shown black-and-white line drawings to elicit visual perceptions about the service environment. Although these methods are effective in controlling the environment being explored, they lack realism and may not be very effective in collecting data about actual reactions from real customers.

Despite some of the methodological challenges, field studies are very effective in overcoming some of the shortcomings of laboratory studies. Most important, actual behavior can be observed, rather than asking people how they would behave or feel in a hypothetical situation. A few researchers (Rind & Bordia, 1996; Stead & Zinkhan, 1986; Zinkhan & Stoiadin, 1984) have designed field studies to investigate gender effects in the real world. Even though most such studies are limited to service encounters within a particular domain (e.g., department stores), the results are nevertheless interesting and suggest the need for further research using field experiments.

Service Domains

Domains studied in the research on gender and the delivery of services have typically been service settings that are commonly perceived to be dominated by one gender—for example, beauty salons and barber shops (Fischer et al., 1998), auto repair (Mohr & Henson, 1996), banking (Bulan et al., 1997; Wharton, 1993), health care (Bulan et al., 1997; Mohr & Henson, 1996), and industrial selling (Siguaw & Honeycutt, 1995). Even though one would expect these service environments to differ in certain physical attributes, Fischer et al.'s (1998) hypothetical examples of hardware stores, fabric stores, auto repair shops, and aerobics studios suggest that gendered servicescapes are mainly socially constructed rather than physically constructed.

Service Usage and Duration

In the past, it appears that researchers limited their investigations to frequent customer usage environments (e.g., barber shops). Gutek et al. (in press), on the other hand, investigate both frequent and infrequent service interaction environments to gain a better understanding of the complexity of all types of service interactions. Extant research has mainly investigated service interactions that occur over a short duration or are one-time interactions (Gutek, 1995). In most cases, the service interaction took place between strangers (i.e., encounters), not between individuals known to each other (i.e., relationships). Additionally, most research conducted thus far on service and gender reflects occupations that are staffed by nonprofessionals (e.g., food servers), possibly because of researchers' accessibility to these occupations.

As researchers continue examining gender effects in service interactions, they should pay careful attention to the duration of the interaction, the type of interaction (encounter or relationship), and whether the service provider is considered a professional (e.g., lawyer, accountant, physician). We reason that the effects of gender will be different or maybe nonexistent in certain kinds of service interactions. Because some professional jobs are stereotyped as either male or female, gender may play a part in the customer's evaluation of service quality. Williams (1995) found, for example, that some customers are suspicious of the motives of men in the female-dominated professions of nursing, elementary school teaching, and social work. However, the certification or licensing of service providers may help to calm customers' fears about the expertise (of female providers) or the motivations (of male providers), thus making gender less important. On the other hand, the gender of the provider may be a ready attribution if the service outcome is unfavorable (e.g., "I knew I shouldn't have trusted a woman to sell industrial equipment"), but may be irrelevant for favorable outcomes (Kulik & Holbrook, 1998).

Similarly, gender effects might differ depending on whether the provider and customer have a service relationship or a one-time encounter (see Gutek, 1995, pp. 253-257). Encounters are universalistic and egalitarian in that everyone, at least in theory, is treated the same and given equal access to treatment; providers who discriminate against any class of customer could be charged with discrimination. The one-time nature of encounters invites stereotyping because neither customer nor provider has any prior experience with the other. Because gender is so noticeable, it is easy to attribute behavior to gender when it fits a gender stereotype (e.g., "She took forever to make up her mind" and "Men buy on impulse"). Although it is relatively difficult to discriminate in encounters, it is easier to do so in relationships where, generally, men and women can select same-sex providers if they choose. Thus, we might expect to see more gender matching in relationships than in encounters. Relationships do not facilitate stereotyping, however, because customer and provider build up a history of interaction against which they can interpret any specific behavior (e.g., "She took a long time to make up her mind because she was distracted by family problems" and "He was late for work so he did the shopping quickly"). In short, we would expect to see more discriminatory treatment in relationships and more stereotyping in encounters.

Conclusions

Although it is clear that services are increasingly important and a dominant force in the United States and the global economy, we know relatively little about how gender affects the service delivery process. It appears that the old dichotomy of men earning money and women spending it is breaking down, yet we seem to have relatively little information in the research literature (perhaps much more in marketing research) about the extent to which men versus women provide and purchase services. (For an exception, see Katz & Katz, 1997.)

Service jobs, occupations, and industries seem to be as sex segregated as those in the non-service sector, and sex-role spillover appears to play a role in the delivery of service. Stereotypes appear to affect men and women who are in nontraditional service jobs, much as they affect any other nontraditional worker. Sex-role spillover occurs, however, as much or more in traditionally female jobs, where it appears that the job takes on some of the characteristics that are associated with being female (e.g., being patient and nurturing). Presumably, sex-role spillover occurs in traditionally male jobs as well, but most of the research focuses on women in traditional jobs (e.g., flight attendants, wait staff). Williams's (1995) research is an exception.

One difference between service jobs and other jobs is that providers are affected by stereotypes held by customers as well as those held by managers and coworkers. Furthermore, service providers also engage in sex-role spillover; they seem to expect male customers in some situations and females in others, apparently based on history or institutionalization (i.e., whichever sex has filled the role in the past seems to be viewed as the appropriate one to fill the role in the present). Being stereotyped is a particular concern for encounter providers and customers. Because each interacts only once with the other in encounters, providers and customers do not even have the opportunity to counteract stereotyping the way a provider can with a coworker or manager, or the way both provider and customer can with the "regular" customers or provider in a service relationship.

Although there is some evidence that providers and customers of the "wrong" sex are penalized or punished (Williams, 1995), the results are not always consistent (Siguaw & Honeycutt, 1995), nor is it clear how they attempt to compensate, successfully or unsuccessfully, for their disadvantage. Finally, service environments are gendered to the extent that the people in them (providers and customers) are one sex or the other. People, not physical cues, make a service environment gendered.

In contrast to gender congruency and sex-role spillover, we find less support for gender matching. It is not clear that gender matching of customer and provider systematically yields either positive or negative results. In some situations, such as in restaurants, being waited on (or waiting on) someone of the other sex seems to be desirable, but there is little support for the notion that across the board people prefer to interact with either the same sex or the other sex. The relative paucity of research on gender matching gives us little on which to base a conclusion. Examining the differences between, for example, the therapy situation (where a majority of women clients seem to prefer a female therapist) and restaurant dining (where both sexes might prefer the other sex as a waitperson or customer) might provide some clues about how gender matching works. Finally, we think it is important to place gender effects in context. Research is insufficient to determine the magnitude of gender effects, but even where gender is significant, it is not clear that the effect is all that strong. As the amount of research grows, it is important to report effect sizes so that we can compare the effects of gender with other factors. After all, don't we really just want good service?

Notes

1. The exception occurs when a customer interacts with a machine (e.g., ATM, voice mail) rather than a human service provider (see Gutek, 1995, chaps. 3, 8, and 9).

2. Their study fits under the general concept of a *service gap* (as summarized by Klose & Finkle, 1995). A service quality gap occurs when the actual service received fails to meet the consumer's expectations of the service experience. A particular example of this failed expectation can come as a result of a customer expecting a service provider of one gender and receiving the other gender instead.

Chapter 5

On the Gendered Substructure of Organization

Dimensions and Dilemmas of Corporate Masculinity

Mark Maier

The modern world continues to spawn organizations which . . . make total claims on their members and which attempt to encompass within their circle the whole personality. These might be called *greedy institutions,* insofar as they seek exclusive and undivided loyalty and they attempt to reduce the claims of competing roles and status positions on those they wish to encompass within their boundaries. Their demands on the person are omnivorous.

—Lewis Coser (1974, p. 4)

The world we have created is a product of our way of thinking. It cannot be changed without changing the way that we think.

—Albert Einstein

The egalitarian bias [regarding male-female equality] assumes that women want to be like men or that men are worth emulating; that women be allowed to participate in society as we know it without questioning whether that society is worth participating in.

—Jo Freeman (1979, p. 572)

If I had known what it would be like to have it all, maybe I would have settled for less.

—Lily Tomlin

When I was completing my graduate training in 1986, "gender" was used widely as a euphemistic reference for woman/female. Back then, I was investigating the dimensions of egalitarianism in male-female family (marriage) relationships. When I first became involved in management (and later, leadership) education and scholarship, the same bias prevailed. Women, as women, had become a legitimate object of inquiry. The idea of naming, much less studying, men as men had not yet appeared on the organizational scholarship radar screen, although the nascent interest in men's studies would eventually make up for that (Brod, 1987; Cheng, 1996a; Collinson & Hearn, 1994; Franklin, 1984; Kimmel, 1993; Kimmel & Messner, 1989; Morgan, 1992; Tolson, 1977). Approaches to gender equality stressed the movement of women into the public sphere (Kanter, 1977c). The notion of equal opportunity implied opening up work domains previously dominated by (White) men to women (and people of color).

Although the force of the current began to receive notice (the external manifestations of male-female inequality), the direction of the flow—that is, the presumed neutrality and legitimacy of organizational norms that demanded a near-monastic commitment to organizations (Kanter, 1977c; Maier, 1994; Rifkin, 1987), blindly overlooked the very real interdependence between work and nonwork life domains, and promoted a particular orientation toward appropriate managerial attitudes and behavior (e.g., regarding career advancement, power, motivation, leadership)—was rarely up for contention. Yet it is precisely these unquestioned norms—the underlying substructure of organization—that comprised the wellspring of external manifestations of gender, in which maleness and masculinity are distinguished from femaleness and femininity and in which the latter is consistently (historically and cross-culturally) subordinated to the former.

This chapter examines and challenges some of the underlying gender-based norms that continue to pervade organizational life, managerial practice, and organizational scholarship. When we refer to a practice as *gendered,* what we mean, of course, is that it embodies values, characteristics, and qualities more commonly associated with one sex than the other at a particular place and point in time. We use gender in this context to refer to "patterned, socially produced distinctions between male and female, masculine and feminine" (Acker, 1992, p. 250). It is socially constructed; it is not something people

AUTHOR'S NOTE: I express my gratitude to the following for their contributions to the writing of this chapter: Joan Acker, for inspiring the concept of the "gendered substructure"; Marta Calás and Linda Smircich for mentoring my early development as a pro-feminist scholar, including my participation in the 1989 National Science Foundation-sponsored Conference on the Relationship of Feminist Theory to Ethical and Value Issues in Organization Science, and for their incisive writing over the years regarding the transformative potential of feminism in organizational life; Roy Jacques and Pushkala Prasad, for a decade of friendship, numerous insights, and their keen sense of perspective regarding gender issues in organizations; Kathy Ferguson, who contributed to an earlier (unpublished) collaboration that found application here, along with Gary Powell, for his patience and confidence in this effort; and Diane Adams for her incisive and helpful review of this chapter.

are, it is something they *do:* at work, in the community, and in families. Gendered processes or practices therefore both reflect and reinforce prevailing conceptions of masculinity and femininity. For some organizational types (e.g., the military, police departments), the prevalence of masculinity may be even more pronounced. And though there are multiple masculinities at work in organizations (Cheng, 1996a; Collinson & Hearn, 1994, 1996), the archetype described here is dominant (Connell, 1987, 1995; Kerfoot & Knights, 1993; Kilduff & Mehra, 1996) at this point in time. For the purposes of this review, we borrow from Kerfoot and Knights's (1993) description of masculinism as "the ideology that naturalizes and justifies men's domination over women; and patriarchy is the structure of unequal power relations sustained by this ideology" (p. 661).

It is also true, however, as Acker (1992) perceptively recognizes, that "gender may be deeply hidden in organizational processes and decisions that appear to have nothing to do with gender" (pp. 251-252); it is "embedded in and recreated daily in organizational activities, most of which do not appear on the surface to be gendered" (p. 255). These deeply hidden and embedded aspects of gender—what Acker names the "masculine substructure of organization" and that I call corporate masculinity (Maier, 1992, 1994, 1997c)—comprise the principal focus of this chapter. Although increasing numbers of scholars are questioning the presumed inevitability and efficacy of corporate masculinity (e.g., Jacques, 1996; Kimmel, 1993; Maier, 1997a; Mills, 1989, 1997; Prasad, 1997), this reappraisal is not arrived at without resistance: "Men in organizations often seem extraordinarily unaware of, ignorant about, or even antagonistic to any critical appraisal of the gendered nature of their actions and their consequences" (Collinson & Hearn, 1994, p. 3).

Rather than examining the institutional impediments to gender equality, we focus on more basic, deep-rooted cultural impediments (Cockburn, 1991). Central to this analysis is an appreciation for the way work organizations dominate employees' lives "greedily," as total institutions (Coser, 1974). In what Chris Argyris (1993) calls Model I approaches, we accept existing constraints as given, and we seek ways to enhance our performance or condition within those given constraints from within, and consistent with, that worldview; Model II approaches allow us to call the existing worldview itself into question. However, as Markus (1987) notes, "It is only through changing the dominant definition of success, through challenging the externally prescribed and uniform model of life-careers, that women *can* 'succeed' " (p. 107, emphasis in original); that men might live fuller, more realistically integrated lives; that they can succeed in a life beyond, but inclusive of, work too, only if they are freed from the ideological shackles of corporate masculinity.

Consistent with critical theory (Prasad & Caproni, 1997), Model II thinking, and reflective practice (Schön, 1983), we shall analyze the masculine-gendered substructure of organization (i.e., corporate masculinity), tak-

TABLE 5.1 The Gendered Foundations of Classic Managerial Paradigms, 1900–Present

		Implicit Gendered Dimension(s)	
Management Approach	Developer (paradigm)	Masculine	Feminine
Scientific management	Frederick Taylor (1911)	Productivity, efficiency, standardization of tasks[a]	–
Human relations approach	Hawthorne studies (ca. 1927-1945)	–	Attention to people, informal relations[a]
Behavioral approaches	Douglas McGregor (1960)	Theory X–directive productive side: Control	Theory Y–participative human side: Growth and development[a]
	Rensis Likert (1967)	System 1, exploitative-authoritative	System 4, participative-democratic[a]
	Ohio State studies (Stogdill, 1974)	"Initiating structure"[a]	"Consideration structure"[a]
	Managerial grid (Blake & Mouton, 1978)	"Concern for production"[a]	"Concern for people"[a]
Contingency approaches	Contingency theory (Fiedler, 1967)	"Task motivated"	"Relationship motivated"
	Vroom and Yetton (1973)	"Autocratic"	"Consultative, group"
	Situational leadership (Hersey & Blanchard, 1988)	"Task behavior"	"Relationship behavior"

SOURCE: Maier (1992, p. 33). Used by permission.
a. Indicates dimension(s) advocated by developer.

ing into account some of the dilemmas it creates for the men it ostensibly benefits. We shall close with a cursory glance at several prominent models of organization that embrace alternatives to the corporate masculinity paradigm, based largely on feminist critiques of management and organization (Calás & Smircich, 1996; Ferguson, 1991; Helgesen, 1995; Koen, 1984; Martin, 1993; Rothschild, 1992).

"Engendering Management": A 20th-Century Overview

Feminist critics (Acker, 1990; Calás & Smircich, 1992; Martin, 1990a, 1990b; Mills, 1989) point out how the existing body of organization and management theory "implicitly assumes that managers and workers are male, with male-stereotypic powers, attitudes, and obligations" (Acker, 1992, p. 255). Table 5.1 articulates the gendered foundations of the dominant theoretical traditions pertaining to management during the 20th century.

There has been a long-standing tradition for managers (and management scholars) to describe (and often proscribe) managerial roles generally as configured around the two central (some would argue "polar") dimensions of "task" and/or "people." Whereas some researchers assume the oppositional incompatibilities of these two dimensions, others argue for their integration, and still others emphasize the importance of situational factors in determining which managerial approach is appropriate. Examples of the first approach include (1) Frederick Taylor's (1911) focus on task, embodied in *Scientific Management*'s emphasis on efficiency, productivity, and standardization versus the human relations approach, which grew out of the Hawthorne studies and emphasized the essentiality of "people" factors; (2) Douglas McGregor's (1960) commitment to "the human side of the enterprise," embedded in his advocacy of Theory Y/participative management over a Theory X/directive style; and (3) Rensis Likert's (1967) preference for System 4 ("participative") over System 1 ("exploitative") management.

Classic examples of the second approach include (1) the Ohio State studies' emphasis on the importance of "initiation structure" and "consideration" (Stogdill, 1974), and (2) Blake and Mouton's (1978) "9,9–managerial grid" ideal of "high concern for production" combined with "high concern for people." Finally, although the contingency theories that have dominated managerial paradigms for the past 25 years do not advocate one best approach to management, the critical dimensions underlying these theories maintain close ties to the (simplistic) "people/task" distinctions made by their predecessors. Thus, for example, Fred Fiedler (1967) describes "task-motivated" versus "relationship-motivated" managers, Vroom and Yetton (1973) speak of "autocratic" or "consultative" behaviors, and Hersey and Blanchard (1988) stress "task" as well as "relationship" behaviors.

Although the proponents of these theories do not consciously consider the gendered perspective that underlies them, it is nonetheless implicit, as Table 5.1 reveals: Concern for "task/production/initiation" and their corollaries (e.g., efficiency) is something that is more closely associated with masculinity in most global cultures (Cann & Siegfried, 1990; Eisler, 1993; Gilligan, 1982; Mills, 1989; Morgan, 1996; Waring, 1988), whereas concern for "people/relationships/consideration" and their corollaries (e.g., caring) are more closely aligned with femininity (Fondas, 1993; Gordon, 1990; Hearn, Sheppard, Tancred-Sheriff, & Burrell, 1989; Kimmel, 1993; Martin, 1993, 1996; Sargent, 1981, 1983). Because gender is central to our theoretical conceptions of management, any attempt to understand either management or organizational transformation must take gender into account.

How might an understanding of gender help workers (including managers) integrate their artificially bifurcated organizational and extraorganizational commitments (Kanter, 1977c; McKenna, 1997; Morris, 1995, 1997, 1998; Pleck, 1977, 1985; Prasad, 1997; Rifkin, 1987), bifurcation promoted by the power, pervasiveness, and persistence of masculine substructures? To answer this question, we will identify how many of the taken-for-granted assumptions and practices in organizations, particularly as they relate to managerial employees in complex, large-scale organizations, are inherently gendered, noting specifically how they reflect the primacy of corporate masculinity (Maier, 1992, 1994; Prasad, 1997).

"Guise" and Dolls: Confronting the Masculine Substructure of Organization

A lasting consequence of the industrialization of society (and the related sex segregation of human activity) has been the creation of a bureaucratic social order grounded in norms conventionally ascribed to men. Or, as David Morgan (1996) concludes, "The more an organization conforms to the key dimensions of Weber's ideal type [bureaucracy], the more the organization will be masculinist in its composition and guiding assumptions" (p. 47). In a world that accords higher status to men and what men do, women and what they do indeed often "counts for nothing" (Waring, 1988). As Jacques (1996) puts it, to be valued in a market-driven economy means that women have had to enter the world of men "on its own terms, [resulting in] a sort of occupational cross-dressing. . . . In the masculinized world of the industrial society, women and men can be equalized *only by giving both the status of men* [and which thus] produces two masculine role players" (p. 85, emphasis in original). The male lifeworld masquerades under the guise of "humanity," purporting to apply equally to both men and women. In this implied masculinist order, men are, as Spender (1984a) observed, the "hidden referent": "Women can only aspire to be as good as a man; there is no point in trying to be as good as a woman" (p. 201).

In a society that differentiates sharply between males and females from birth and that accords greater status and worth to males, the dominant understandings of selfhood and society—and their consequences for one's relationship to others; for one's images of leadership, organization, and power; and one's view of social relations, basis for reasoning, key influence strategies, ethical frameworks, decisional guides, and so forth—tend to differ along gendered lines. Some of the more noteworthy differences, catalogued and described below, are summarized in Tables 5.2, 5.3, and 5.4.

Intrapersonal Dimensions of Corporate Masculinity

A cursory glance at the dimensions enumerated in Tables 5.2-5.4 reveals how the experiences and perspectives of women as a group are distinguished from, and usually subordinated to, those of men as a group (Ferguson, 1984, 1991; Martin, 1990a, 1990b; Martin, 1993; Morgan, 1996; Prasad, 1997). "Masculine" and "feminine" ways of attending, being, and relating may function as metaphors for quite different—basically gendered—ways of

TABLE 5.2 Intrapersonal Dimensions of Gendered Organizational Substructures

	Masculinist	*Feminine/Feminist*
View of self	Autonomous, separate: Independent.	Relational, contextual: Connected (interdependent).
Presumed ultimate motivators (individual)	"Self-actualization"; me-first; success.	"Actualization of others"; team first; service.
Individual view of success	Advancing in occupations. Distancing from those lower in the hierarchy; competing successfully *against* those at the same level; emulating (and eventually joining) those placed "above." In short: "Winning."	Maintaining balance in life activities (and relationships). Actions that allow maintenance of relations and/or advance others and the self are more highly valued than those that advance the self at the expense of others. Mentoring and vicarious achievement are prized.
View of organizational commitment and extraorganizational roles	Other life activities and commitments are subordinated to priority of career advancement:	Active balancing of career obligations with extraorganizational needs. Life-work integration priority:
	Work and one's employer/work organization expected to be one's central life focus: "Act as though" you have no competing loyalties; "if I do well . . . we do well."	Work and one's employer are assumed to comprise but a subset of one's life purpose. Acknowledge the reality of multiple commitments; "if we do well . . . I do well."
Basis of reasoning and "knowing"/(decisional guides)	Formal, abstract, linear: Stresses deductive logic and technical rationality supported by measurable, quantifiable factors that count as "hard" evidence.	Personal, contextual, reciprocal: Stresses intuition and feeling. "Situated objectivity," grounded in personal experience, yields important insights that are difficult to quantify.
	"Knowing" occurs through dispassionate distancing of the self from one's object of inquiry, that is, rational "objectivity":	"Knowing" through wholehearted connection and identification with one's object of inquiry, that is, rational "subjectivity":
	"Separate knowing" (decide with the head).	"Connected knowing" (decide with head and heart).

understanding and acting upon the world. In many instances, and certainly in many occupations, men may find themselves *only* in the presence of other men. Most men are subordinate to other men in organizational hierarchies, and are, therefore, likely to find themselves perceived and acting "like women," just as women can come to act "like men" (Cheng, 1996a; Ferguson, 1991). (Within this discussion, *feminine* processes refer to female-patterned ways of operating within the broader masculine-dominated order, whereas *feminist* processes refer to female-centered ways of operating that pose a direct challenge to that order.)

Thus, organizational practices that are inherently masculine gendered provide graphic evidence of how men's organizational experience is pro-

TABLE 5.3   Interpersonal Dimensions of Gendered Organizational Substructures

	Masculinist	*Feminine/Feminist*
Primary orientation of self to others	Competitive, winning:	Collaborative, compromising:
	Exclusion—ranking	Inclusion—linking
Practices and purpose of communication	"Fix" or "solve"	"Listen" and "respond"
	To establish status	To establish connection
	To signal independence	To signal intimacy
	Argument (convince)	Dialogue (understand)
View of power	Zero-sum, win-lose notion of power: Stand firm (or tall) or be seen as "wishy-washy."	Synergistic, expansive notion of power: Power shared is power enhanced, therefore:
	Use of power *over* others, to control (through aggression and violence, if necessary)	Use of power *with* others, to get things done; compromise; integrative solutions
Approaches to conflict and view of organizational politics	Respect for authority:	Respect for participation:
	Suppression of conflict under the assumption that it poses a problematic threat to the group or organization.	Expression of conflict as symptomatic of underlying problem: Opportunity to expose and resolve issues; stimulus for inclusion of diverse perspectives.
	Silence the opposition:	Give "voice" to opposition:
	Dissent = disloyalty	Dissent = loyal opposition
Guiding ethics for resolving conflict	Impartiality; respect universal procedures: Equal treatment, due process, and equal protection for all, regardless of their place in the social (or organizational) order.	Case-by-case responsiveness to particular circumstance or individual. Decisions should be context dependent, with a need to appreciate the particularities of time, place, and circumstance.
	General: "Ethic of rights"	Concrete: "Ethic of caring"
	Consistency: Maintain rules	Flexibility: Maintain relationships and/or purpose
	"Might makes right": Authority or majority rule	"All for one and one for all": Participation and consensus

foundly influenced by their need to conform to inherently masculinist prescriptions. My analysis of the 1986 Space Shuttle *Challenger* disaster (Maier, 1997a, 1997c) demonstrates that conformity should be scrutinized for the

TABLE 5.4 Implications of Gendered Organizational Substructures for Images of Leadership and Organization

	Masculinist	*Feminine/Feminist*
Summary of selected structural symbols and organizational metaphors	Pyramids, ladders, channels, chains, boxes, units, divisions, teams (external: us vs. them)	Circles, networks, webs, bubbles, communities, gardens, teams (internal: us and we)
Images of leadership/vertical division of labor	At the top, at the helm	At the center; at/on your side
	Head: Provides "push"	Heart, soul: Provides "spirit"
	Director, commander, master: "Makes it all happen"	Servant, coach, colleague; "Allows and/or enables others to co-make it happen"
	Standing at the top, telling others what to do. Managers "think" (set strategy); workers "do" (carry it out). Positional authority, determined by location in hierarchy and status	Standing at the center (or side), marshaling collective energies for codeveloping and implementing a shared vision. Personal authority, determined by competence and expertise; exercised by communication
Leadership objectives	"Get the job done" (ends); action focus; results focus; "do"	Inclusion of all (means); reflecting-in-action focus; process focus; "be"
	To direct	To serve, inspire, and/or follow
Primary source of influence/ approaches relied on by organizational authorities	Fear: Command and control, intimidate, force, coerce; aggression, manipulation	Love: Facilitate and empower, embrace common vision; empathy, responsiveness
Reactions to leadership and authority (from "below")	Awareness of, and especially respect for, one's place (and that of others) in the organizational "chain of command"	Empowered to challenge authority; commitment to confront others (including "superiors") who have a corresponding obligation to listen to and be responsive to one's concerns
	Compliance: Ingratiation to those with power (please the boss)	Commitment
Summary of core organizational and leadership values	Hierarchy; individualism	Egalitarianism; community
	Competition, conformity	Collaboration, diversity
	Command and control— dominance, "play hard"	Empowerment of others— partnership, "play fair"
	Task (and cost-) efficiency, aggressiveness, independence, achievement, success, consistency	Relationship, inclusiveness, gentleness, intimacy, serving, caring, responsiveness

ways in which it can contribute to individual, interpersonal, and even organizational dysfunction (see also Luthans, 1988, for a discussion of how effective managers are not necessarily the successful ones in organizations, in spite of meritocratic claims to the contrary). Using women's experience metaphorically, a substantially different approach to the understandings of self, of relations with others, and of approaches to leadership becomes possible. How might these worldviews be characterized and distinguished, keeping in mind that they are gender *related*, not gender *specific* (Belenky, Clinchy, Goldberger, & Tarule, 1986)?

View of self, presumed ultimate motivators, and individual view of success. Drawing from Table 5.2, one can see how men's lifeworlds typically conceive of individuals as separate, autonomous beings who value independent achievement and eschew commitments that might hinder success in competitive endeavors (Cheng, 1996a; Collinson & Hearn, 1994, 1996; Connell, 1987, 1995). The female system, in contrast, typically requires its participants to maintain relationships, attend to the needs of others, and care for bodies as well as minds and spirits. Women generally learn to see themselves and others as embedded in relations, as interdependent with others and responsible for their collective well-being (Benhabib, 1987; Eisler, 1987, 1993; Ferguson, 1984; Gilligan, 1982; Tannen, 1990). As Deborah Tannen (1990) found in her ground-breaking study of male-female interaction patterns, "Independence is key [in the masculine life world], because a primary means of establishing status is to tell others what to do, and taking orders is a marker of low status. Though all humans need both intimacy and independence, women tend to focus on the first, and men on the second" (p. 26). One rarely notices the irony that men can appear "autonomous" in one arena of their life, their occupational sphere, for example, only as a direct consequence of their dependence on others: Self-reliant men typically have wives to keep their households running and raise their children, secretaries to support functions at work, competent colleagues, and "subordinates" to delegate responsibilities to who "get the job done" whatever that job happens to be (see Hare-Mustin & Marecek, 1986, and our discussion of the "act-as-though principle," below).

Most industrialized societies define success as maximizing one's career potential (i.e., occupational achievement and advancement). As Pleck (1977) indicates, "As the paid work role has evolved in modern society, it has come to call for full-time, continuous work from the end of one's education to retirement, desire to actualize one's [occupational] potential to the fullest, and subordination of other roles to work" (p. 425). He points out, however, that this is in effect a *male* model of work, under the guise of a gender-neutral model of work: It is mostly men who can conform to the conventional rules, arrangements, and assumptions embedded within organization because women frequently are subject to family and reproduction obligations assumed (or imposed on them) by society and/or their husbands (Ford Foundation, 1989; Harris, 1995; Lewis, 1996; Markus, 1987), a point echoed by Acker (1992):

The gendered substructure lies in the spatial and temporal arrangements of work, in the rules prescribing workplace behavior, and in the relations linking workplaces to living places. These practices and relations, encoded in arrangements and rules, are supported by assumptions that work is separate from the rest of life and that it has first claim on the worker. Many people, particularly women, have difficulty making their daily lives fit these expectations and assumptions. (p. 255)

To achieve this success in the masculine lifeworld requires distancing oneself from those lower in the hierarchy, competing successfully with those positioned similarly, and emulating (and eventually joining) those placed above, to "win" (Ferguson, 1984; Franklin, 1984; Kimmel & Messner, 1989). In the feminine lifeworld, however, actions that allow the maintenance of relations (e.g., mentoring, vicarious achievement) are more highly valued than those that advance the individual but leave others behind (Barrentine, 1993; Helgesen, 1990; Loden, 1985; Martin, 1993; Rogers, 1988), thus raising the issue of motivation.

The concept of motivation is imbued with deep-rooted notions of gender (Glazer, 1997; Harriman, 1985; Powell, 1993). The dominant worldview seems to accept on faith Maslow's (1943, 1954) "hierarchy of needs" theory, which places self-actualization above social needs at the apex of human motivation, along with such derivatives as Alderfer's (1972) "existence-relatedness-growth" theory. Similarly, McClelland's (McClelland, Atkinson, Clark, & Lowell, 1953; McClelland, 1984) influential work proffers long-since taken-for-granted distinctions between "achievement," "affiliation," and "power" needs. Lawler's (1977) reward system, like Maslow's and Alderfer's, is also predicated on a hierarchy of needs, where "individual quality-of-worklife issues related to equity and satisfaction of basic security needs are subordinate to organizational effectiveness concerns related to individual performance, reward distribution patterns, and organizational membership" (p. 172, cited in Glazer, 1997, p. 41). As Glazer emphasizes, "Implicit in Lawler's model of an equitable reward system is the assumption that good performance leads to valued rewards" (p. 41). Taken together, this body of literature assumes, in other words, that the principal motivation guiding human action (i.e., men's and women's alike) is, ultimately, self-interest. It turns out to be an erroneous assumption.

Recent feminist conceptualizations of human motivation stress the interconnectedness among these presumably disparate needs. Inspired by the manner in which women's experiences did not seem to mesh with the generic (human) motivation theories expounded by previous experts (nearly all of whom based their models on research conducted exclusively on men), feminist researchers discovered that for women (as a group), achievement, affiliation, and power were generally linked as "mutually reinforcing motives . . . [which] contradicts need theorists in the Maslow tradition who view affiliation and achievement needs as midway points in a hierarchy of lower- and higher-order needs and who emphasize the importance of individuation-differentiation as evidence of self-actualization and personal growth" (Glazer, 1997, p. 45). Thus, McClelland's empirical research isolating motivational determinants of behavior from other aspects of human thought and actions (e.g., values, beliefs, attitudes, skills) was untenable. Cultural (or "self-in-relation") feminists assert that "women are repositories of qualities of affiliativeness, relatedness, empathy, and nurturance, [qualities that] are devalued and distorted in male-dominant culture and by men" (Chodorow, 1993, p. 120, cited in Glazer, 1997, p. 45). Feminist studies of motivation attempt to move beyond dualisms of person/society, dependence/independence, and separation/individuation to a model, as Glazer (1997) explains, based on "relationship-differentiation" (p. 45).

In this paradigm, women's self-development occurs through relationships and relational competencies that contribute to personal growth (that of the self and the "other"), not through the hierarchical sequence of defined separations implicit in androcentric models. Motivation and empowerment are achieved through "mutual intersubjectivity" (Jordan, 1991), in which the self takes an active interest in, attunes to, and is responsive to the "other" at both a cognitive and affective level (and vice versa). This position, as Glazer (1997) notes, finds profound support in the pioneering works of Carol Gilligan (1982), who has extensively documented the importance of relationships throughout women's lives, and Mary Belenky and her colleagues (1986), who find that "personal growth and intellectual development move [women] toward connected learning, mutual empathy, and self-understanding" (Surrey, 1991, p. 171).

View of organizational commitment and extraorganizational roles. In his book *Greedy Institutions,* Lewis Coser (1974) warns of the "omnivorous" demands of modern organizations to "seek exclusive and undivided loyalty" from those they "wish to encompass within their boundaries" (p. 4), ultimately expressed by one's willingness and ability to put in substantial amounts of overtime, which in a strict sense managerial workers are exempt from. For managers, 12- to 16-hour days are not uncommon, especially when electronic capabilities are factored in. The threat of being "eaten alive" by one's work is all the more pronounced in an era of technological innovation where ubiquitous e-mail, voice mail, faxes, and cell phones make workers accessible to their "boundaryless" organizations 24 hours a day: Like the fabled sorcerer's apprentice in Walt Disney's animated classic *Fantasia,* managers are powerless to stem the tide of incessant demands and rising expectations. If Coser is right, then the voracious appetite of organizations is whetted all the more by the expanded "menu" enabled by these so-called technological breakthroughs, particularly for organizational managers.

As Kanter (1977c) suggests, organizations are incapable of eliminating family as a workplace issue, so they attempt to push it aside, dictating to members, "While you are here, you will *act as though* you have no other loyalties, no other life" (p. 15, emphasis in original). This "act-as-though principle" is one of the cornerstones of modern organization and of corporate masculinity: Acting as though family claims do not exist is an option (requirement?) extended seriously only to employed fathers; employed mothers, in deference to those fathers' careers, engage in what economists call the "convenient social virtue" of shouldering primary responsibility for family life to enable the work of their husbands. Thus, married men's ability to conform to workaholic notions of loyalty is predicated on their wives' enactment of the "family support role" (Jacques, 1996, 1997; Kanter, 1977c; Morris, 1998; Papanek, 1973; Prasad, 1997; Schwartz, 1992b). With notable exceptions (e.g., Fassel, 1990; Frost, Mitchell, & Nord, 1997; Hewlett & West, 1998; McKenna, 1997; Rifkin, 1987), the costs of such commitments to work—to men, to women, to families, and to organizations—have gone largely unexamined or are rarely laid at the doorstep of organizations, particularly their impact on organizational members' ability to fulfill other equally, if not more important, life roles.

This creates a dilemma particularly pronounced for managerial men because they are more likely to be married and have children than their female counterparts (Baderschneider, 1989; Maier, 1994, 1997b; Morris, 1995, 1997; "Motherhood," 1998; Ragins, Townsend, & Mattis, 1998; Schwartz, 1992b; Shellenbarger, 1998b): Estimates for male senior managers who fit this description range from 85% to 95%, whereas executive women are overwhelmingly more likely to be divorced or never married (one estimate puts it at 44.5% vs. 3.6% of male executives). Among the 40% or so of managerial women who are married, most do not have children (Chow & Berheide, 1988; "Gender and Management," 1996; "The Mommy Track," 1989; Morris, 1995, 1997; "Motherhood," 1998; "Women Close the Gap," 1997). Initiating policies such as flex-time, flex-place, on-site child care, and the like represents Model I attempts to allow women to succeed as "surrogate men"; that is, they try to remove barriers to success within the current system rather than questioning the appropriateness of that system and structure itself. "The male bias in organizational cultures, which are based around traditional male lifestyles" (Lewis, 1996, p. 7), characterized in particular by the support of a stay-at-home spouse, is overlooked. Allowing women to put in long hours of work and to act as though they have no primary responsibilities for family does nothing to challenge the beliefs and values about traditional ways of working or recognize the reality of the interdependence between work and personal lives, a point forcefully voiced by critics of the so-called mommy track ("The Mommy Track," 1989; Schwartz, 1992b; "The Stigma," 1989; F. Wohl, personal communication at the Organizational Flexibility, Productivity and the Work-Family Interface symposium in Washington, DC, August 1989).

The blind acceptance of corporate masculinity as a requisite norm for both genders, focusing narrowly only on organizational issues, ignores the interdependence between work and family as a tightly coupled system, reinforcing what Kanter (1977c) refers to as the "myth of separate worlds" (p. 8). Work and family systems are not only tightly coupled, they are both gendered, albeit in asymmetrical ways (Pleck, 1977): Men's paid work role is expected to spill over and may legitimately interfere with family responsibilities (they may fulfill work and family responsibilities simultaneously, i.e., through the enactment of their economic provider role), whereas women's family responsibilities are expected to take precedence over their economic role (they fulfill one at the expense of the other). It would be a mistake to conclude that this represents a woman's autonomous choice, because the allocation of household roles is negotiated between two parties. A woman's greater family role involvement may therefore have more to do with her husband's preferences than her own, although her (usually male) supervisor will assume the reverse!

If the rules of corporate masculinity are not challenged, individual managerial women may permeate (but not crack!) the glass ceiling to the extent that they are prepared, as Schwartz (1989, 1992b) implies, to forgo either marriage, child rearing, or both. On the other hand, as Faith Wohl (personal communication, August 1989), former employee relations manager at E. I. DuPont de Nemours, expressed it, "I'm not sure we should honor lack of family as a criterion and value women who are willing to put it aside." Given the current gendered bias of organizational (man's work) and family (woman's work) life, in the aggregate, men and women can never be equal to one another in the world of work until and unless they are equal outside it (Lewis, 1996; "Motherhood," 1998; Parasuraman & Greenhaus, 1993). Workplaces must recognize and accept diverse constraints on people's working lives imposed by family commitments (Shellenbarger, 1998a); the family is entitled, as Kanter (1977c) argues, to "fight back."[1]

Bases of reasoning and knowing and decisional guides. Rosabeth Kanter (1977a) notes that management as a profession was infused from its very inception with a particularly "masculine ethic" (p. 20), which "elevates the traits assumed to belong to some men to necessities for effective management: a tough-minded approach to problems; analytic abilities to abstract and plan; a capacity to set aside personal, emotional considerations in the interests of task accomplishment; and a cognitive superiority in problem-solving and decision-making" (p. 22), a legacy that persists to this day (Burrell, 1992; Cann & Siegfried, 1990; Collinson & Hearn, 1994, 1996; Helgesen, 1990; Jacques, 1996, 1997; Kimmel, 1993; Loden, 1985; Maier, 1992; Morgan, 1996). The dominant masculine-based managerial decision stance stresses instrumental rationality, orderliness, conformity to the requirements of authority, and respect for the chain of command. The pursuit of "objectivity" implicit in this stance promotes a "separate" way of knowing (Belenky et al., 1986), in which one distances oneself from the object of inquiry and truth emerges from impartial, universal, and impersonal procedures (Harding, 1986). Reason and logic are narrowly construed, referring mainly to quantifiable factors that count as evidence in a linear process of sensing, thinking, and deduction. Rational discourse, in the masculine lifeworld, is reflected in a propensity to intimidate, challenge, and argue. In the resulting "doubting game," the listener is perceived as a potentially hostile judge, not as a potential ally in conversation. As Belenky et al. (1986) note, the "objectivity" demanded by this perspective "means to exclude all feelings, including those of the adversary, examining the issue from a strictly pragmatic, strategic point of view" (p. 109).

Women's worldviews, in contrast, tend to value those kinds of insights that are difficult to quantify because they come from feeling and from intuition (Benhabib & Cornell, 1987). From a feminine perspective, truth is discovered subjectively, through connection and direct personal experience (Belenky et al., 1986; Chodorow, 1993; Hartsock, 1983). Where doubting and judgment occupy center stage in masculine discourse (Tannen, 1990), trust and understanding predominate in its feminine counterpart; where masculine discourse derives its moral legitimacy from impersonal procedures, feminine discourse stakes its moral claim in caring (Harding, 1986); where masculine discourse aims for generalities, feminine discourse focuses on particularities (Benhabib, 1987); and where masculine discourse stresses agency and action, separation and control, feminine discourse strives for community, acceptance, and fusion (Belenky et al., 1986).

Interpersonal Dimensions of Corporate Masculinity

Primary orientation of self to others, practices and purpose of communication, views of power. Because most females have emulated and imitated the prevailing (i.e., masculine) norms for management (e.g., Cockburn, 1991; Collinson & Hearn, 1994; Jacques, 1997; Kerfoot & Knights, 1993; Konrad & Cummings, 1997; Powell, 1990; Rothwell, 1985), male managers are generally oblivious to how their gender identity as men might be influencing their behavior and relationships in the organizations in which they spend a majority of their waking hours, whether women are present or not. Male managerial behavior has been unconsciously accepted as the norm that all managers aspiring to the top must adopt, including male managers (Cheng, 1996a; Hearn et al., 1989; Kerfoot & Knights, 1993). Adapting to the implicit demands of this culture comes so easily to men that they are unconscious of its power, influence, and privilege. But adopting the masculine ethic not only keeps males from realizing how they are advantaged at the expense of others, it blinds them to its potential limitations,

limitations that become visible when we consider the feminine or feminist alternatives to masculinist substructures in Tables 5.2-5.4.

As Table 5.3 reveals, the masculinist substructure of organization reinforces a competitive, zero-sum view of power, in which being ranked over others and beating them (winning) takes precedence (Belenky et al., 1986; Eisler, 1993; Gilligan, 1982; Glazer, 1997). Men (generally) find hierarchical relations comfortable, and look to such arrangements to legitimate the process of exclusion as well as to mediate the conflicting rights of autonomous selves (Eisler, 1987, 1993; Loden, 1985; Smith & Smits, 1994). Women, on the other hand, tend to find greater comfort in inclusive relations, to value their links to others (Eisler, 1987). The feminine worldview is thus more likely to be grounded in an ethic of care (Eisler, 1993; Gilligan, 1982; Lewis, 1996), in which rules are regarded as inherently context dependent and exceptions legitimized by attention to circumstance. Power, in such a framework, is used to give voice to the conventionally silent, as a basis for empowering others, and as a resource to be continuously shared (Josefowitz, 1983; see our earlier discussion on the presumed ultimate motivators for men and women). "Intimacy is key," Deborah Tannen (1990) writes of women, "in a world of connection where individuals negotiate complex networks of friendship, minimize differences, try to reach consensus, and avoid the appearance of superiority which would highlight differences" (p. 26).

Using communication to signal status or to establish connections are both ways of demonstrating involvement with others. But, as Tannen's (1990) research reveals, men often use communication to "focus on the jockeying for status in conversation: Is the other person trying to be one up or put me down? Is he trying to establish a dominant position by getting me to do his bidding?" (p. 38), that is, to use language as "a form of masculine ceremonial combat" (p. 110).

The predominant communication pattern practiced in most organizations tends to be premised on male-associated characteristics (Pearson, 1985; Rakow, 1986), particularly the masculine bias reflected in the prevalence of "sex/war/games" imagery (Rothstein, 1984)—much of it violent—used conversationally to describe organizational practices and phenomena (e.g., "knock them dead," "we got screwed," "attaboys," "take the ball and run with it," "the top brass," "the troops in the trenches") as well as the preoccupation with following and discussing the escapades and records of professional athletes and sports teams.

Communication by women is more often "attuned to the negotiation of connections: Is the other person trying to get closer or pull away?" (Tannen, 1990, p. 110). It is significant that men's use of communication to affix status and assert independence is accompanied by an overriding mentality to "solve the problem" or "fix the conflict." In contrast, women use communication to develop intimacy and connectivity, reflected by a preoccupation with listening to others for understanding, with wanting to be heard and acknowledged. Or, as Joan Acker (1992) put it, "Today, organizations are lean, mean, aggressive, goal-oriented, efficient, and competitive, but rarely empathetic, supportive, kind and caring" (p. 253).

View of politics, approaches to conflict, and guiding ethics for resolving conflicts. Kohlberg's (1981) original research underscored that masculine discourse typically projects faith in authority, that is, the rule of position and the rule of law (policy). Men base their moral decisions on notions of fairness and justice, women on fairness and care (Belenky et al., 1986; Benhabib, 1987; Gilligan, 1982; Rothstein, 1984). For men, treating specific cases "fairly" means treating them alike (identically): "What is right, is right." In other words, the highest form of morality is the ability to apply an abstract principle universally (Kohlberg, 1981, 1984). Conflicts erupting from the masculinist substructure are resolved by relying both on an ethic of rights (Kohlberg, 1981), which emphasizes consistency, impartiality, and objective evaluations of competing claims, and on due process and equal treatment for all individuals, regardless of their place in the social order (see also Harding, 1986).

Feminine notions of justice, on the other hand, tend to call for the avoidance of harm to others, for an active (and contextual) response to others' needs (Belenky et al., 1986; Gilligan, 1982; Glazer, 1997). Where masculinist politics are instrumental, suppressing dissent frequently to the point of violence, feminine politics aim for cooperation, compromise, and allowance for difference (Chodorow, 1993; Ferguson, 1984, 1991; Gilligan, 1982; Hartsock, 1983; Ruddick, 1989). Colloquially, from a masculine worldview, "Might makes right," with "might" residing either in the one with more power, the side with greater numbers, or the side of justice (i.e., objective policy, impartially dispensed and universally applied). In contrast, the feminine worldview is attuned to context, allowing for flexible responses to situations that only appear on the surface to be identical (Benhabib & Cornell, 1987). In the feminine lifeworld, the stance is "All for one and one for all."

Implications of Corporate Masculinity for Images of Leadership and Organization

Selected symbols of organization, images of leadership, and the vertical division of labor. As Table 5.4 reveals, the masculine manager-leader stands at the top of an exclusionary pyramid; the feminine manager in the center of a web of inclusiveness (Helgesen, 1995; Loden, 1985; Rogers, 1988; Smith & Smits, 1994). The masculinist bias toward hierarchy and ranking expresses itself here in references to leaders as the "heads" of units or organizations; the ones at the top who set the vision, chart the course, and make it all happen. Consistent with broader cultural conceptions of masculinity stressing agency and control (e.g., Cheng, 1996a; Collinson & Hearn, 1996; Franklin, 1984; Jacques, 1997; Kimmel, 1993; Kimmel & Messner, 1989; Maier, 1997c; Prasad, 1997; Tolson,

1977), this view reinforces a classic separation of thinking from doing, with "superiors" responsible for the former and "subordinates" for the latter. The relative authority to influence and shape decisions and direction varies in direct proportion to one's vertical position in the organizational hierarchy. As Helgesen (1995) reports,

> Since hierarchies are pyramidal, information must travel up and down a strictly defined vertical chain of command, which discourages direct communication across levels. The adherence to channels accentuates the importance of rank within the organization. . . . The insistence on restricted access serves the purpose of exclusion: the focus is on who, by virtue of rank, will *not* be invited to this meeting, who has *no* right to that information, who may *not* communicate directly with whom, [which] strengthen[s] the power and dominance of the organization's top leaders, creating a kind of caste system that isolates people who are not in top positions rather than broadly involving them in the overall process. . . . The overriding message on leadership sends a message to those at the bottom that they are relatively unimportant to the overall functioning of the organization . . . less valuable, weaker. (pp. 21-22, emphasis in original)

The language of "teams" is invoked most frequently in masculine discourse either to induce conformity to group norms (as in "get with the team," "be a team player") or to emphasize the importance of solidarity in the face of an external threat (as in "beat the other team") (Barrentine, 1993; Jacques, 1996; Rothstein, 1984). Given the assumption of autonomy, it is no surprise that the masculinist substructure engenders an image of leadership that is attached to individuals (i.e., the leader). Prevailing models of leadership are thus premised on male notions and characteristics (Calás, 1993; Helgesen, 1990; Rogers, 1988; Smith & Smits, 1994), or, as Collinson and Hearn (1996) observe, views of what constitutes effective management are "imbued with particular notions of masculinity" (p. 4). We should not be surprised, therefore, when researchers continue to discover that perceptions of the good (successful/effective) manager (i.e., the one who fits our existing stereotype of managers) is masculine (Cann & Siegfried, 1990; Donnell & Hall, 1980; Konrad & Cummings, 1997; Powell, 1990, 1993; Powell & Butterfield, 1989).

Compare and contrast masculinist images of organizational leaders with the vision of organization and leadership that emerges from the alternative feminine or feminist paradigms. Such leaders see themselves at the center of organizations (O'Toole, 1995), or on the side, more as colleagues and servants (Barrentine, 1993; Smith & Smits, 1994; Spears, 1998); their authority resides not in the positions they hold, but the positions they take. Leadership from a feminine worldview is seen more as a process that emerges from the collective, with the reciprocal roles of leader and follower in a state of perpetual motion (see Rost, 1991, and Maier, 1998, for elaboration on the distinctions between leaders and managers). From a feminine perspective, organizations are nearly always described in ways antithetical to the exclusionary foundations of pyramids: as circles (Eisler, 1993; Kuchler, 1997; Smith & Smits, 1994), networks and webs (Helgesen, 1990, 1995), bubbles (Hesselbein, Goldsmith, & Beckhard, 1996), communities, and even gardens (Keating, 1993). Where action, doing, and "performativity" define corporate masculinity, reflection-in-action (self-awareness), being, and connectivity are the focus in the feminine lifeworld (Cashman, 1998; Prasad, 1997; Rosener, 1990). The feminine worldview sees teams from the vantage point of community, as in "we are all on the same team together," a team whose composition might include organizational outsiders such as clients, customers, even competitors (Barrentine, 1993; Spears, 1998). Finally, notice how the "web of inclusion" structure described by Helgesen (1995) meshes with a more feminine worldview (as reflected in Table 5.4):

> Since web structures are circular rather than pyramidal, those who emerge in them as leaders tend to be people who feel comfortable being in the center of things rather than at the top, who prefer building consensus to issuing orders, and who place a low value on the kind of symbolic perks and marks of distinction that define success in the hierarchy. (p. 20)

Women, by virtue of a predominant socialization emphasis on caring, tend to approach conflict and problem solving in a more subjective manner as well (Belenky et al., 1986; Fondas, 1993; Gilligan, 1982; Helgesen, 1990; Rosener, 1990). Under assimilation to corporate masculinity, however, these alternative approaches become devalued; logic and objectivity (rationality) are prized above intuition and subjectivity (feeling). To value diversity in organizations, however, implies supporting, nurturing, and embracing differences as sources of strength (Ferdman, 1997; Fondas, 1993; Nelton, 1991; Smith & Smits, 1994). One stream of scholarship finds that differences between the sexes do in fact exist, but that they favor women and validate a "woman's way" of leading. Seeing "female" approaches to leadership as sources of strength rather than weakness (Cohen, 1989; Fondas, 1993; Grant, 1988; Helgesen, 1990, 1995; Rosener, 1990), however, has the unintended consequence of reifying existing gender stereotypes and challenges neither the masculine-biased ends of organization nor the mythical independence of work and family domains: It simply harnesses masculine and feminine means toward existing (Model I) masculine ends.

Leadership objectives, primary influence strategies, and reactions to leadership. The expectation that men and women must both adopt a masculine standard of managerial leadership, although constricting to men's effectiveness, is particularly problematic for women. Women frequently encounter hostility because of the cognitive conflicts they create between people's stereotypes of managers, on the one hand, and women, on the other (Cann & Siegfried, 1990; Gordon, 1990; Konrad & Cummings, 1997; Maier, 1994; Ragins et al., 1998; Sargent, 1981; Tharenou, Latimer, & Conroy, 1994; Vinnicombe, 1985), invoking a "damned if we do and damned if we don't" dilemma. To the extent that women succeed at imitating and incorporating corporate masculinity, they typically experience differential evaluations (Haccoun, Haccoun, & Sallay, 1978; Josefowitz, 1983; Maier, 1997b; Schein, Mueller, & Jacobson, 1989; Schwartz, 1989, 1992b; Vinnicombe, 1985).

Where masculine leaders often rely on force and intimidation (expressed or implied) to get the job done or to extract compliance from others, feminine and/or feminist leaders are responsive and focused on the process by which common objectives are defined and pursued, often by consensus (Eisler, 1993; Helgesen, 1990, 1995; Rogers, 1988). Top managers are typically described as "strong, decisive, rational, and forceful" (Acker, 1992, p. 253). The pyramid's top-down emphasis on power and privilege ensures, according to Helgesen (1995), that "the kind of people who emerge as leaders in traditional hierarchies are those who enjoy exercising power from a distance, and feel comfortable with the lack of collegiality that pervades their organizations" (p. 22) (i.e., typically men, or at least those men and women who can best assimilate to corporate masculinity). In the masculinist substructure, participants, given the type of organization (top-down, controlling) and leaders (directors, masters) they must contend with, tend to be particularly aware of their place in the organizational pecking order, and the appropriate channels to follow in their chain of command. Because career advancement, the sine qua non of motivation within this worldview, is contingent on one's ability to please one's boss (Block, 1991, 1993), "manipulative (unauthentic) tactics" (Block, 1991, p. 21) result, with subordinates ingratiating themselves to those who have power and complying with them to curry their favor (Messerschmidt, 1995).

This stands in marked contrast to more feminine-based objectives and strategies anchored not in fear, but love (i.e., genuine caring and intimacy), the empowerment of others, and service (Marcic, 1997). Helgesen (1995) points out that this preference on the part of web style leaders "infuses their organizations with a collegial atmosphere, which . . . enables people to focus on *what* needs to be done rather than *who* has the authority to do it" (p. 21, emphasis in original). The importance of rank is systematically and deliberately de-emphasized, resulting in greater access and communication across divisions. The great contribution of Helgesen's work is the reminder that individual actions require structural supports. Thus, there is an essential integrity between the values of masculinity and those of management and organization (as currently practiced in the masculine-gendered substructure of organization), on the one hand, and the values of femininity, feminism, and circular, weblike organizations, on the other (Barrentine, 1993; Calás & Smircich, 1991a, 1992).

Toward the Future: Closing Reflections on the Gender Prism

When organizational (particularly bureaucratic) imperatives clash with gender difference, the organization usually wins (Ferguson, 1991). Men and women recruited into positions of dominance within organizations tend to internalize the requirements of their position, becoming like men. Subordinates tend, correspondingly, to become like women in their attention to the requirements of others, their need to please their superiors, their reluctance to assert themselves, and so on. In complex ways, therefore, masculine dominance and feminine subordination are reproduced and reinforced, and gender becomes a metaphor for power (Ferguson, 1984, 1991).

As David Morgan (1996) put it, the culture and ethos of organization itself conform largely to "hegemonic forms of masculinity present in the wider society" (p. 47) that value competition over cooperation, focus more on rights than on needs, internalize the requirements of a narrow technical rationality, and so on. To elaborate and summarize, Schaef (1981) identifies five central pillars of the masculinist substructure of organization, what she calls the White Male System: (1) "one-up; one-down" relations (vs. egalitarian/peer relations typical of the female system); (2) self and work (doing) as one's center of focus (as opposed to self-awareness or relations with others); (3) a zero-sum/scarcity model of power (in contrast to a synergistic orientation, which assumes that power, life, love, or knowledge is enhanced by sharing it); (4) a vision of leading anchored in commanding or directing others (vs. facilitating or enabling); and (5) differences are seen as competitive threats that must be reduced, assimilated, or eliminated, instead of being seen as opportunities to learn, grow, and change collaboratively.

What does this analysis reveal? First, worldviews are likely to vary according to one's gender. Second, there is a world of difference between these masculine and feminine/feminist vantage points. Third, organizations implicitly, extensively, and consistently favor the masculine worldview, whether they realize it or not, rewarding those who conform to it and marginalizing or subordinating those women and men alike who don't (Cheng, 1996a); that is, men's worldviews mesh neatly with the social order of organization, whereas those of women tend to clash with it. Fourth, perhaps most fundamentally, one's perception of why this matters changes as one moves progressively further away from a masculine-bounded view of organization, so that such questions as "Should women managers have to act like men?" (Korabik & Ayman, 1989) are reframed (Bolman & Deal, 1997): "Act like men in order to . . . get ahead (like men)? . . . to be accepted as leaders (like men)? . . . to advance the organization's interests (like men)?"

Such reframing allows us to recognize not only the privileges available to members of the dominant group but also the costs men have incurred to acquire and maintain those privileges, chief among which, as Frye (1983) argues, is a certain unconsciousness (i.e., when you pass for "normal" in any given social environment, you don't even think about it, need to think about it, or get to think about it. For a fuller elaboration on the invisible privileges enjoyed by White males in organizations, see Maier, 1997b). Examining the gendered foundations of taken-for-granted practices allows us to view organizational life from a fresh perspective that permits new ways of managing, leading, and organizing based on that awareness; new ways of being in organizations that allow participants to live fuller, richer, more integrated, and even more spiritual lives (Bolman & Deal, 1995; Cockburn, 1991; Fassel, 1990; Ferdman, 1997; Frost et al., 1997; Marcic, 1997; "Motherhood," 1998; Schaef & Fassel, 1988; Schwartz, 1992b; Whyte, 1994). This requires a shift in thinking, from Model I ("single loop") to Model II ("double loop") learning (Argyris, 1993; Argyris & Schön, 1992). As we make this transition, something more important than performance or advancement may emerge as the top (or central?) life value and priority. As Albert Einstein reminds us, "The world we have created . . . cannot be changed without changing the way that we think."

When that happens, new models of organization materialize. This review has taken a transformative, "critical" perspective on the implications of gender for organizations in general and management in particular. A summary of some of the more prominent (and promising) alternatives to the masculine-gendered substructure of organization proposed in the feminist and/or critical literature is provided in Table 5.5 (readers might want to consult Calás & Smircich, 1996, for background, especially pp. 227-229 and 243-245).

These alternative frameworks allow us to question why we take for granted that women (or even men, for that matter) want to be "like men." Are men (or at least how we construe men socially) worth emulating, as Jo Freeman (1979) asks? When both men and women acquiesce to the masculinist substructure of organization, that system is allowed to reproduce itself without regard for its dysfunctional consequences for women, men, and organizations. The lens of gender allows us to shift our attention away from the traits of the individuals making decisions in organizations and toward the characteristics of the masculine-encoded structures and processes within which men and women are required to operate. These structures and processes are gendered in ways that elevate typically male experiences to the level of unquestioned norm while dismissing that which appears feminine as irrational, illogical, unsubstantiated, or irrelevant; that is, "normal" managers are masculine.

TABLE 5.5   Toward a Feminist Organizational Epistemology: Selected Alternatives to Masculinist (Sub)structures and Practices

Features and Design Principles of "Feminist Workplaces" (Koen, 1984)	Characteristics of "Feminist Organizational Structures" (Ferguson, 1991)	Characteristics of a "Feminine Model of Organization" (Rothschild, 1992)	Practices of "Feminist Management" (Martin, 1993)	Characteristics of Women-Led "Web" Type Organizations (Helgesen, 1995)
Participatory decision making	Democratic authority	Value members as individual human beings Commitment to employee growth	Promotes democracy and participation; promotes subordinate empowerment: Views power as obligation (to help employees grow)	Circular structures (not pyramidal); create lasting networks that redistribute power; Consensus building (vs. "order giving")
System of rotating leadership	Leaders as coordinators and facilitators	Power sharing	Uses feminist practical reasoning (e.g., responsive to diverse circumstances; contextualizes issues vs. statically imposing existing rules and norms)	Leaders operate from the "center" (not from the "top")
Flexible, interactive job designs	Equality and sharing of labor; connection of mental and manual labor			Distinction between conception ("thinking") and execution ("doing") is blurred
Equitable system of income distribution	Egalitarian division of reward			De-emphasize importance of rank and marks of distinction
Interpersonal and political accountability	Roles and events integrated and connected; governed by relations and communication Sharing of knowledge and skills	Nonopportunistic and nonexploitative relationships are valued Creation of a caring community	Collaborative, interactive consciousness-raising; through ongoing dialogue Asks "the woman-question" (e.g., challenging claims that male-normative practices and values are necessary or correct) Promotes community and cooperation Promotes nurturance and caring	Open communication across levels (vs. one-way; "proper channel"; chain of command) Embrace world outside the organization; blurring lines between "insiders" and "outsiders"; involve outsiders as collaborators
	Recognition of politics and of more than one legitimate solution; acknowledges opposition	Careers are defined in terms of service to others	Strives for "transformational outcomes" for: (a) individual women, (b) women collectively, (c) men, and (d) the organization	Serve as vehicle for continuous improvement; constant reorganization (adaptable structure) Evolve through trial and error: Experiment-learn-modify

SOURCE: This table is inspired by Calás and Smircich (1996, p. 228).

All of which leads to this rather self-evident conclusion: Organizations cannot ameliorate masculinist biases simply by hiring more women. Explication of the masculine-gendered substructure of organization makes compelling arguments for alternatives to that worldview, particularly as it affects the prevailing assimilationist bias in promoting male-female equality in organizations. The foregoing analysis demonstrates how corporate masculinity advantages men in relation to women (in the aggregate) in the competition for promotions while it undermines their ability and that of any women who follow in their footsteps to lead in different, perhaps more effective, ways, and certainly live more balanced, less work-obsessed, lives. Reframing organizational change through the lenses of Model II/double-loop learning (Argyris, 1993), critical theory and feminist epistemology strips away the veneer of neutrality associated with "the *normative masculinity* of management" (Martin, 1993, p. 277; emphasis in original).

Critical theory allows us to reflect on and illuminate such formerly unconsidered questions as "What is the current organizational reality promoted in this culture? What ends are served and not served by this version of reality? What are the processes through which this reality is produced, reinforced, and revised over time? Are there alternative realities that may better serve individuals, organizations, and society?" (Prasad & Caproni, 1997, p. 294). Examining the dimensions of corporate masculinity provides significant insights into the reality promoted by the masculine-gendered substructure, of the ends served by that version of reality, and most vividly, into our awareness of the processes through which this reality is produced, reinforced, and revised. And, in the articulation of the feminine and feminist counterparts to that worldview, along with an accompanying summary of some of the more prominent examples of organizational structures and practices, we have discovered potential and viable alternative realities that may better serve individuals, organizations, and society. By carefully excavating the ideologically masculine foundations of modern management, we find a more integrative and realistic approach to promoting gender equity in organizations (Ferdman, 1997; Lewis, 1996; Thomas & Ely, 1996).

Thus, we are left with a final and paradoxical dilemma: The more we succeed in transforming the gendered substructure of organizations so that men and women of all races can break the glass ceiling and advance to the top, the less important and desirable that objective may appear. After all, a preoccupation with occupational success is itself a hallmark of the masculinist substructure we have sought here to expose and to challenge. As Lily Tomlin quips, "If I had known what it would be like to have it all, maybe I would have settled for less." The Zen tradition teaches us that grasping for what we don't have creates a source of endless anxiety. Thus, and consistent with the Model II change strategies advocated in this chapter, we close with the wisdom of the old adage: "There are two ways to be rich: One is to have more. The other is to want less." The ultimate paradox then becomes evident once the way we think changes: Less *is* more.

Note

1. Two brief examples from my experience illustrate this point. First, my former institution had an (unpaid) parental leave policy—open to men and women—that had been on the books for seven years. At the time I applied for it (shortly after our first child was born), not a single faculty member, male or female, throughout the entire state university system of multiple sites, had taken advantage of it. My dean's initial reaction to the request may help explain why: "You know, you're coming up for tenure soon, and if you take 'time off' for a parental leave, however minimal, your colleagues are going to expect more productivity out of you" (this from a dean who was a mother and grandmother herself). The request, which was subsequently granted, took on perhaps greater symbolic significance than I realized. Dana was born on March 4, 1992. The following December, the dean refused to support my bid for tenure and I left. To this day, I am convinced her actions were related to other matters, but at the Academy of Management meetings in Boston in 1997, I ran into a colleague from my former institution who wanted to know what had happened. When I told her what I thought was the real story, she said, "Oh. Well, that's not what I heard. I heard you were denied tenure because you took a parental leave."

Second, shortly after Dana was born, I was invited to deliver an address at Cornell University. I asked the organizers for $30 to cover the cost of child care while I was absent from home for the few hours the seminar would require, including driving time. "You wouldn't believe the stir you've caused around here," the symposium organizer told me. Recalling that I had declined an invitation to dinner because of my child care commitment, she explained, "A hundred dollars to take a speaker to dinner? *No* problem at all! But money for *child care?* That's a *different* story!" (The money was eventually cleared, and I was able to proceed with the seminar as scheduled.)

Chapter 6

The Gender Gap in Earnings

Trends, Explanations, and Prospects

Patricia A. Roos and Mary Lizabeth Gatta

It is a social truism that women earn less than men. This gender gap in earnings existed in 1955, when the United States first began to track systematically the female to male earnings ratio, and remains as we near the century's end.[1] This "cost of being female" (Reskin & Padavic, 1994, p. 101) persists regardless of how you define earnings (e.g., annual vs. weekly, mean vs. median), in all race/ethnic groups, across educational categories, over the life cycle, within detailed occupational categories, and across cultures.[2]

Despite its ubiquity, the gender earnings ratio—as a measure of the gender gap—has varied over time. Published data show two distinct time periods since 1955. From 1955 until 1981, the earnings ratio remained essentially constant, and even declined slightly: The median annual earnings of women who worked year-round, full-time was 64% that of comparable men in 1955 and 59% in 1981 (Goldin, 1990, Table 3.1). After 1981, the earnings ratio rose steadily, from 59% in 1981 to 71% in 1995 (Institute for Women's Policy Research [IWPR], 1996, Table 1). Focusing on weekly earnings yields slightly higher ratios: 75% in 1995.[3] Recent Bureau of Labor Statistics data (IWPR,

AUTHORS' NOTE: We are indebted to our editors Gary Powell and Julie Tamarkin for excellent advice, and to Barbara Reskin, Leslie McCall, Lee Clarke, Paula England, Judith Gerson, and Margaret Mooney Marini for excellent comments on an earlier draft.

1996; see also Lewin, 1997) suggest a third pattern may be emerging: After reaching a high of 77% in 1993, the median weekly earnings ratio began to decline, dropping below 75% in 1997. Although it is too early to determine whether this new pattern will reverse women's earnings gains, it is clear that it is a "slowdown, a plateau, a consolidation after a period of rapid social change" (Francine Blau, quoted in Lewin, 1997, p. 1).

In this chapter, we examine the literature on the earnings gap between men and women.[4] We begin descriptively by reviewing historical trends in the female-male earnings ratio and variation in the earnings ratio across various demographic groups, detailed occupations, and cultures. We then assess proposed explanations for, and ongoing debates about, the persistence of the earnings gap. We conclude by speculating on future trends. Although reviewing trends in the gender earnings ratio is intrinsically interesting, the implication of our review is farther reaching. As Spalter-Roth and Hartmann (1992, p. 395) noted, women's expanded economic responsibility for their families and children in recent years, coupled with increases in the number of women and children living in poverty and declines in men's real wages, underscores the need for policies that significantly enhance working mothers' earnings. Moreover, changes in welfare law in the late 1990s may exacerbate the recent declines in the earnings ratios, as more low-skill women workers flood the labor market (Lewin, 1997).

Variations in the Earnings Ratio

How does the female-male earnings ratio vary across time, and how do variables such as race, age, and education affect it? Answers to these questions—posed by numerous sociologists and economists over the past few decades—vary based on the sample chosen and how earnings variables are measured (Spain & Bianchi, 1996). Other factors—such as the age range of workers, the degree of error in measurement, and whether wages are from all jobs (Marini, 1989)—also affect estimates. Regardless of measurement, all studies demonstrate that women consistently earn less than men across numerous demographic variables. In this section we use existing data, as well as census microdata for 1970, 1980, and 1990,[5] to examine the following:

1. How the gender earnings ratio varies over time for all workers, and year-round/full-time workers, by race;

2. How the gender earnings ratio varies over men's and women's life cycles and across educational levels, for year-round/full-time workers in 1990, by race;

3. How the gender earnings ratio differs for detailed occupational groups, for year-round/full-time workers in 1990; and

4. How the gender earnings ratio varies cross-culturally.

We chose to measure the gender gap in earnings by calculating the ratio of the median earnings of women to the median earnings of men, and presenting it as a percentage. It is important to bear in mind that change over time in this measure—conventional in the field—can be the consequence of change in either the numerator or denominator. Thus, increases in women's earnings relative to men's can be attributed to either increases in the real earnings of women, declines in the earnings of men, or both operating simultaneously.[6]

Historical Trends in Earnings Ratios

Consistent with previous research, Figure 6.1 and Table 6.1 demonstrate that, overall, the ratio comparing men's and women's median earnings remained relatively constant from 1955 to 1980, but increased notably in the 1980s. The IWPR (1996) used data from the U.S. Bureau of Labor Statistics (BLS) to summarize trends in the earnings ratio. These data—the larger solid black line in Figure 6.1—indicate that full-time/year-round women workers in 1955 earned 64% of men's salaries, 59% by 1975, and 71% by 1995. This increase in the earnings ratio accompanied a dramatic increase in women's labor force participation during the same time period (Marini, 1989; Smith & Ward, 1984; Spain & Bianchi, 1996).

The census results are similar to the BLS data, showing the same basic pattern during the 1970 to 1990 period for which we have data.[7] Using the census data, however, enables us to make finer distinctions than did the BLS, specifically in examining race, age, educational, and occupational differences. Most notable in Figure 6.1 are the dramatic differences in over-time patterns for full-time White and Black workers. For Whites, the gender earnings ratio declined slightly between 1970 and 1980, rebounding notably between 1980 and 1990. For Blacks, the earnings ratio was significantly higher than Whites for each census year and increased monotonically between 1970 and 1990. Thus, by 1990, White women were earning 64% of their male counterparts' earnings, compared to 81% for Black women.

Table 6.1 presents the census data used to produce the trend lines for all workers and for the year-round/full-time workers presented in Figure 6.1. We focus here on the latter. The data show that, overall, women who worked year-round/full-time increased their earnings relative to men by 5.3 percentage points between 1970 and 1990. The comparable figures for Whites and Blacks were 5.4% and 14.1%, respectively. Perhaps not surprisingly given their lower starting points, Black women improved their earnings relative to Black men over twice the equivalent figure for White women.[8]

Table 6.2 shows that White men still outearn all other race/sex groups, and that this is true both for all workers and for year-round/full-time workers. Black men working year-round/full-time in 1990 were least disadvantaged relative to White men, earning about 72% of comparable White men's

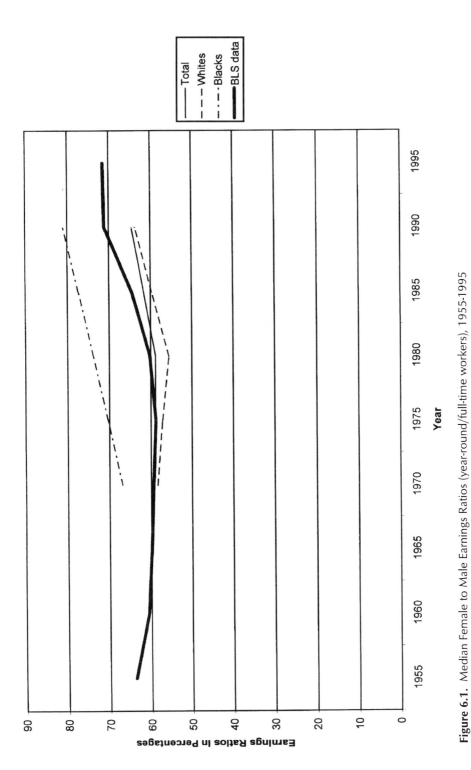

Figure 6.1. Median Female to Male Earnings Ratios (year-round/full-time workers), 1955-1995

SOURCE: Census data—U.S. census microdata, 1970, 1980, and 1990 (U.S. Bureau of the Census, 1972, 1983, 1993); Bureau of Labor Statistics (BLS) data—Institute for Women's Policy Research (1996).

NOTE: To make the comparison between the BLS and census data, we included values in five-year increments for the BLS data (e.g., 1955, 1960, and so on, to 1995). For the census data, we calculated 1975 and 1985 data points by averaging the terminal points (e.g., the average of 1980 and 1990 for the 1985 estimate). Data refer to annual earnings ratios.

TABLE 6.1 Women's Median Annual Earnings as a Percentage of Men's, by Race, 1970, 1980, and 1990[a]

	All Workers			Year-Round/Full-Time Workers		
	Total[b] (F/M)	Whites (F/M)	Blacks (F/M)	Total[b] (F/M)	Whites (F/M)	Blacks (F/M)
1970	47.7	45.2	58.4	59.3	58.4	66.9
1980	49.9	46.7	70.0	58.8	55.6	73.8
1990	56.5	54.2	81.2	64.6	63.8	81.0
Change: 1970-1990	8.8	9.0	22.8	5.3	5.4	14.1

SOURCE: U.S. census microdata, 1970, 1980, and 1990 (U.S. Bureau of the Census, 1972, 1983, 1993).
a. Data are expressed as percentages within race groups [(women's median annual earnings/men's median annual earnings) × 100].
b. Includes other races, in addition to Whites and Blacks.

TABLE 6.2 Median Annual Earnings Ratios for Sex and Race/Sex Groups (Relative to White Men), 1970, 1980, and 1990[a]

	All Workers				Year-Round/Full-Time Workers			
	Whites		Blacks		Whites		Blacks	
	M	F	M	F	M	F	M	F
1970	100	45.2	64.3	37.6	100	58.4	69.9	46.8
1980	100	46.7	66.7	46.7	100	55.6	70.2	51.8
1990	100	54.2	66.7	54.2	100	63.8	72.4	58.6
Change: 1970-1990	—	9.0	2.4	16.6	—	5.4	2.5	11.8

SOURCE: U.S. census microdata, 1970, 1980, and 1990 (U.S. Bureau of the Census, 1972, 1983, 1993).
a. Data are expressed as a percentage of White men [e.g., (Black women's median annual earnings/White men's median annual earnings) × 100].

income. It is notable that they have shown little improvement in their relative earnings potential since 1970 (only 2.5%). Full-time White women earned 64% of the White male wage in 1990, up from 58% in 1970. The comparable percentage for Black women was 59%, up nearly 12% from 1970. Despite this dramatic gain, Black women remained furthest behind White men in 1990 in their relative earnings.

Earnings, by Age and Education

Table 6.3 demonstrates how men's and women's earnings vary across the life cycle. Consistent with the literature on age and earnings, overall, the earnings ratio in 1990 was highest among younger workers, gradually decreasing with age, and then increasing slightly around retirement. For example, women who are 16 to 24 years old earned nearly 87% of what comparably aged men earned, whereas women 35 to 39 years old earned 67%, and women 50 to 54 years old earned 58%. The earning ratio increased slightly at re-

TABLE 6.3 Median Annual Earnings and Earnings Ratios, by Race and Age, Year-Round/Full-Time Workers, 1990

Age	Total			Whites			Blacks		
	F (in $)	M (in $)	F/M Ratio	F (in $)	M (in $)	F/M Ratio	F (in $)	M (in $)	F/M Ratio
16-24	13,000	15,000	86.7	13,000	15,000	86.7	12,200	13,000	93.8
25-29	18,000	22,000	81.8	18,000	23,000	78.3	16,000	18,000	88.9
30-34	19,439	27,000	72.0	20,000	28,000	71.4	17,000	20,000	85.0
35-39	20,000	30,000	66.7	20,000	31,000	64.5	19,000	24,000	79.2
40-44	20,000	33,000	60.6	20,000	34,000	58.8	20,000	25,485	78.5
45-49	20,000	34,625	57.8	20,000	35,000	57.1	19,000	26,000	73.1
50-54	19,000	33,000	57.6	19,000	34,000	55.9	18,000	25,000	72.0
55-59	18,000	31,103	57.9	18,200	32,000	56.9	17,000	24,000	70.8
60-64	18,000	30,000	60.0	18,000	30,000	60.0	15,600	21,802	71.6
65+	16,000	24,000	66.7	16,220	25,000	64.9	14,573	18,000	81.0

SOURCE: U.S. census microdata, 1970, 1980, and 1990 (U.S. Bureau of the Census, 1972, 1983, 1993).

tirement age, with women 65 and older earning 67% of the male wage. This slight increase is attributable primarily to increased male retirements and declines in men's earnings with age.

With respect to race, the same basic pattern of decreasing ratios occurred for both Whites and Blacks. White women in the prime of their working lives (ages 45 to 49) earned $15,000 less than (or 57% of) their White male counterparts. Black women of the same age fared somewhat better relative to Black men, earning $7,000 less than (or 73% of) their Black male counterparts. Of course, each race/sex group earned notably less than the $35,000 White men aged 45 to 49 averaged.

As England (1997) noted, these findings on age could reflect one or more different age effects. First, the data could reflect cohort changes. Put simply, if cohort effects are operative all those born in a given year will keep the same sex ratio with respect to earnings as they age (p. 75). This fairly optimistic interpretation suggests that as older cohorts—those with the highest wage gap—retire, the overall earnings ratio will increase. Second, variations in the earnings ratio may reflect, in part, social changes over the life cycle. In this case, the earnings ratio would continue to decrease with age, regardless of birth cohort, because women are segregated into jobs with low pay and low mobility. Third, period effects—such as declining levels of discrimination, or federal legislation—may also be operating, shifting the ratios up or down, depending on the effect (England, 1997). Fortunately, Spain and Bianchi (1996, Table 5.3) provided data that enable us to adjudicate among these possible explanations. They found that female-male earnings ratios do tend to improve in succeeding cohorts, especially in early career: Women born in 1956-1965 earned 74% of men's earnings at ages 25 to 34, compared with a figure of 59% for women born in 1926-1935. However, these higher earnings ratios do not persist, suggesting that cohort effects are moderated by social changes over a woman's lifetime.

TABLE 6.4   Median Annual Earnings and Earnings Ratios, by Race and Education, Year-Round/Full-Time Workers, 1990

Educational Level	Total			Whites			Blacks		
	F (in $)	M (in $)	F/M Ratio	F (in $)	M (in $)	F/M Ratio	F (in $)	M (in $)	F/M Ratio
No school	12,000	15,000	80.0	13,000	17,000	76.5	12,645	15,000	84.3
Some grammar school	12,000	18,000	66.7	12,000	19,000	63.2	11,427	16,000	71.4
Some high school	13,000	20,000	65.0	13,444	21,000	64.0	12,999	17,000	76.5
High school	16,000	24,000	66.7	16,000	25,000	64.0	15,000	19,000	78.9
Some college	19,000	28,887	65.8	19,025	29,587	64.3	18,888	24,000	78.7
College	25,000	37,172	67.3	25,292	38,000	66.6	25,000	30,000	83.3
Graduate school	32,000	50,000	64.0	32,000	50,000	64.0	32,000	40,000	80.0

SOURCE: U.S. census microdata, 1970, 1980, and 1990 (U.S. Bureau of the Census, 1972, 1983, 1993).

As demonstrated in Table 6.4, education has a strong positive effect on earnings for both men and women. However, education yields greater economic returns for men than women. Within each educational level, male workers consistently outearned women. For example, in 1990, college-educated women earned $25,000, an income comparable to that of high school-educated men. College-educated women earned only $5,000 more than a male high school dropout ($25,000 to $20,000). The most highly educated women (those with advanced graduate degrees) had the lowest earnings ratio relative to men (64%). In contrast, those with the least amount of education (no schooling) had the highest ratio (80%), attributable in large measure to the very low earnings of men with no schooling. Women with graduate degrees earned $32,000 in 1990, compared to $50,000 for comparable men. On the other hand, women with no schooling earned only $3,000 less. This finding reflects the significant existing inequality in men's earnings: Men without education earned particularly low salaries, in contrast to the very high pay of men with postgraduate degrees.

These educational effects on earnings persisted within categories of race. In all education groups except no schooling (where the earnings ratio was 77%), White women earned between 63% and 67% of White men's salaries, whereas Black women's equivalent salaries ranged from 71% to 84% that of Black men. Much of this higher percentage among Blacks is attributable to the lower relative salaries of Black men as demonstrated in Table 6.2. Recalculated as a percentage of White men's salaries (data not included in table), the figures for Black women approximated those of White women: Black women with no schooling earned 74% of White men's income and between 60% to 66% as much in the other educational categories.

The overall findings in Table 6.4 demonstrate that simply increasing the education of individual women will not increase the female-to-male earnings ratio and eradicate the wage gap. Although education does raise women's pay, it does so less for women than for men.

Earnings, by Occupation

Many theorists have critiqued the earnings gap literature as not attending sufficiently to the role of occupation and, specifically, for not comparing men and women doing similar jobs (see Spain & Bianchi, 1996, pp. 123-129 for an extended discussion of this critique). Men and women are segregated into different occupations, industries, and jobs (Bielby & Baron, 1986; Blau & Ferber, 1986; Reskin & Roos, 1990). One implication is that much of the earnings gap is attributable to sex differences in occupational location and if we compare the earnings of men and women in similar work, their earnings would be more comparable. The census data allow us to compare male and female earnings within detailed occupation codes.

As Table 6.5 demonstrates, among full-time/year-round workers in 1990 the sex gap in earnings persists within both majority male and majority female occupations. We chose for inclusion in Table 6.5 a broad selection of occupations representing each of the 11 aggregated census groupings, ranging from higher-paying, higher-prestige managerial occupations to the lower-paying, lower-prestige unskilled occupations. We also included female occupations (e.g., nurses, secretaries, private household child care workers) and male occupations (e.g., lawyers, physicians, firefighters). One obvious conclusion to draw from Table 6.5 is that occupations varied widely in their earnings ratios, from a low of 44.9 for farmers to 93.3 for mail carriers.

Perhaps not surprisingly, in male occupations women earned less than their male counterparts. For example, female air traffic controllers earn 67% of the earnings of their male counterparts, and female physicians only 52%. In both of these occupations, women made up less than 25% of the labor force. The pay gap also existed in predominantly female occupations. Among dental hygienists (98% female), women earned 79% of men's salaries; among licensed practical nurses (94% female), women earned 87%.

The situation is similar in occupations with a more equitable distribution of men and women. Female real estate agents, who represented half of all agents, earned 72% of male agents' salaries. Among accountants and auditors (53% of whom were women), women earned 66% of men's salaries. In none of the occupations we selected for Table 6.5 did women earn more than men. In only 13 of the 497 detailed occupations available for 1990 was the earnings ratio equal to or greater than 1.0 (e.g., sociology teachers, social science teachers, waiters/waitresses' assistants, baggage porters/bell hops, brickmason and stonemason apprentices, carpenter apprentices). Our data thus illustrate a common finding in the literature: Earnings differences exist both within as well as across occupations.

Earnings Ratios Cross-Culturally

Much of the research investigating the gender gap in earnings has consistently focused on the United States, leaving it unclear to what extent

TABLE 6.5 Percentage Female and Median Earnings Ratios for Selected Occupations, Year-Round/Full-Time Workers, 1990

1980 Occupational Title (code)	% Female	Year-Round/Full-Time Median Earnings Ratio
Executive, Administrative and Managerial Occupations		
Financial Managers (007)	46.0	58.5
Personnel and Labor Relations Managers (008)	49.2	68.8
Managers, Marketing, Advertising and Public Relations (013)	31.8	60.0
Accountants and Auditors (023)	52.6	65.5
Personnel, Training and Labor Relations Specialists (027)	57.3	71.3
Professional Specialty Occupations		
Computer Systems Analysts and Scientists (064)	30.8	82.8
Physicians (084)	20.7	51.5
Registered Nurses (095)	94.4	88.2
Pharmacists (096)	36.3	87.5
Teachers, Elementary School (156)	78.4	79.9
Librarians (164)	80.3	81.3
Social Workers (174)	68.8	84.6
Clergy (176)	10.1	86.6
Lawyers (178)	24.2	66.9
Editors and Reporters (195)	51.0	78.1
Public Relations Specialists (197)	58.5	68.8
Technical Occupations		
Dental Hygienists (204)	98.3	79.1
Licensed Practical Nurses (207)	93.6	87.1
Electrical and Electronic Technicians (213)	14.5	79.4
Air Traffic Controllers (227)	22.6	66.7
Computer Programmers (229)	32.4	83.3
Legal Assistants (234)	76.6	83.0
Sales Occupations		
Insurance Sales Occupations (253)	35.1	56.7
Real Estate Sales Occupations (254)	50.4	71.7
Sales Workers—Apparel (264)	81.2	60.0
Sales Workers—Radio, TV, Hi-Fi, and Appliances (267)	28.5	79.7
Cashiers (276)	78.5	67.3
Administrative Support Occupations		
Computer Operators (308)	60.9	69.2
Secretaries (313)	98.7	90.0
Telephone Operators (348)	87.0	75.0
Mail Carriers, Postal Service (355)	26.5	93.3
Insurance Adjusters, Examiners and Investigators (375)	70.9	66.7
Bank Tellers (383)	90.0	81.5
Private Household and Protective Service Occupations		
Child Care, Private Household (406)	97.2	90.0
Firefighting Occupations (417)	2.5	75.0
Police and Detectives, Public Service (418)	11.8	84.0
Other Service Occupations		
Bartenders (434)	48.9	73.3
Waiters and Waitresses (435)	80.0	66.7
Cooks, including Short Order (436/437)	47.5	74.1
Janitors and Cleaners (453)	30.7	68.8

(continued)

TABLE 6.5   Continued

1980 Occupational Title (code)	% Female	Year-Round/Full-Time Median Earnings Ratio
Farming		
Farmers, Except Horticultural (473)	12.9	44.9
Farm Workers (479)	18.5	71.3
Fishers (498)	5.9	63.9
Precision Production, Craft and Repair Occupations		
Automobile Mechanics, Except Apprentices (505)	1.9	90.0
Electricians, Except Apprentices (575)	2.6	74.6
Plumbers, Pipefitters and Steamfitters, Except Apprentices (585)	1.4	88.5
Cabinet Makers and Bench Carpenters (657)	6.1	76.9
Dressmakers (666)	93.3	71.4
Bakers (687)	45.3	67.3
Operators, Fabricators and Laborers		
Typesetters and Compositors (736)	69.2	67.3
Textile Sewing Machine Operators (744)	88.1	68.8
Truck Drivers–Heavy and Light (804/805)	5.8	66.7
Bus Drivers (808)	47.9	62.5
Handlers, Equipment Cleaners, Helpers and Laborers		
Garbage Collectors (875)	3.4	78.9
Stock Handlers and Baggers (877)	29.5	76.5
Laborers, Except Construction (889)	21.6	72.1

SOURCE: U.S. census microdata, 1970, 1980, and 1990 (U.S. Bureau of the Census, 1972, 1983, 1993).

the patterns we have noted are more generally true of other societies (Treiman & Roos, 1983, p. 613). Although the evidence shows that in industrial societies men always earn more than women, the size of the earnings ratio varies considerably across countries (Blau & Ferber, 1986, p. 324).

Blau (1996, p. 10) argued that, although American women have higher work qualifications with respect to education, experience, and other human capital factors relative to women in other countries, the United States has one of the lowest earnings ratios worldwide. Throughout the 1980s, the United States saw a ratio of women's to men's *hourly* earnings in manufacturing of 71%, whereas several other countries experienced much higher earnings ratios, including Sweden (90%), Denmark (85%), Norway (83%), and Australia (83%) (see Blau & Ferber, 1986, Table 10.2). These findings have been supported by other sociological work in this area (Blau & Kahn, 1992; Rosenfeld & Kalleberg, 1990; Treiman & Roos, 1983). A nation's wage and labor force structures, occupational sex segregation, degree of modernization, and gender ideology all have been linked to the diversity of the earnings gap cross-culturally (e.g., Blau & Kahn, 1992, 1996).

We supplemented Blau and Ferber's (1986) data with trend data published by the International Labour Office (see Table 6.6). To calculate male-female earning ratios, we could choose only those countries that published

TABLE 6.6 Women's Earnings as a Percentage of Men's, in Manufacturing and Nonagricultural Activities, in Selected Countries, 1975-1994

Country (currency)[a]	1975		1985		1990-1994	
	Nonagriculture	*Manufacturing*	*Nonagriculture*	*Manufacturing*	*Nonagriculture*	*Manufacturing*
Australia (dollar)	83.7	78.5	87.2	79.4	89.9	84.8
Belgium (franc)	71.2	71.3	74.6	74.3	75.3	74.5
Denmark (kroner)	83.2	84.3	88.8	85.6	83.4	84.8
Egypt (pound)	67.7	67.8	84.4	73.3	84.8	75.0
France (franc)	78.7	76.4	81.4	79.1	80.8	79.1
Germany (mark)[b]	72.3	72.1	72.8	72.7	74.2	73.6
Japan (yen)	55.8	47.9	51.8	42.1	50.8	42.9
Korea (won)	47.0	47.4	47.9	47.0	54.5	50.8
Netherlands (guilder)	79.5	74.7	76.4	77.7	78.9	78.8
New Zealand (dollar)	73.8	65.6	77.4	70.2	80.6	77.5
Switzerland (franc)	66.7	68.0	67.5	67.2	66.6	68.7
United Kingdom (pound)	67.6	66.5	69.5	67.7	71.2	68.9

SOURCE: International Labour Office (1985, 1995).
a. Earnings ratios are calculated from earnings per hour, except for Egypt (earnings per week), and for Japan and Korea (earnings per month).
b. Federal Republic of Germany in 1975; Germany thereafter.

data separately for both men and women; for example, the United States provided only aggregate data. Within that constraint we chose countries to represent different regions of the world. Interestingly, Table 6.6 does not show dramatic change over time, but, consistent with Blau and Ferber, it does show cross-cultural differences. By the early 1990s, the earnings ratios, in at least one of the economic sectors, were at least 80% in Australia, Denmark, Egypt, France, and New Zealand. Another group—Belgium, Germany, the Netherlands, Switzerland, and the United Kingdom—hovered in the 66% to 79% range. Only the two Asian countries—Japan and Korea—were substantially lower, in the 50% to 55% range.

Although a full evaluation of these cross-cultural differences is beyond the scope of our chapter, it is interesting to note that the highest hourly earnings ratios were in Australia, where women earned 90% as much as men in nonagricultural sectors, and 85% as much in manufacturing. As Gregory, Anstie, Daly, and Ho (1989, p. 229) noted, since 1969 a network of government tribunals has set Australian wage rates for all occupations, in both the private and public sectors. Prior to 1969, wage-setting boards explicitly reduced wages in female jobs to 75% of what the wages would have been had the occupation been predominantly male. Eliminating this bias dramatically increased women's wages relative to men's. At the other end of the spectrum, Japanese women earned about half of men's wages in nonagricultural work, and less than that in manufacturing jobs. As Brinton (1993) pointed out, this substantial earnings gap is attributable in large measure to a highly segregated labor market, supported by differing societal expectations by sex and work-place-based occupational sorting by sex. These processes lead to sex differences in educational preparation, job assignment, and levels of experience, which in turn reduce the gender earnings ratio.

Explaining the Earnings Gap

Sociologists and economists have proposed a variety of theories to explain why women continue to earn less than men. Typically, theorists frame the debate either as explanations of individual choice or institutional/structural constraint (e.g., Coverman, 1988; Ferree & McQuillan, 1998; Marini, 1989; Stevenson, 1988; see also Reskin, 1993). Although economists traditionally favor individualist explanations and sociologists institutionalist explanations, there are economists and sociologists in both camps. In this section, we evaluate the efficacy of these theories in explaining the earnings gap (and its narrowing), summarizing the current state of knowledge in the field.

Individualist Theories

Some theorists argue that women earn less than men because they possess attitudes, preferences, or qualifications that make them less productive in a presumably open, fully competitive labor market. Adherents to this individual-choice model thus focus on the characteristics of those who supply themselves to the market, arguing that market forces both determine wages and operate to reduce any discrimination that may emerge from the possible prejudice of labor market actors. Thus, the earnings gap between the sexes simply reflects sex differences in the value of the human capital men and women bring to, and expend in, the marketplace. Concomitantly, these theorists de-emphasize institutionalized mechanisms that may restrict the competitiveness of the labor market or impinge on individual free choice.

Neoclassical theory. Neoclassical human capital theory best exemplifies the individualist approach (Blau & Ferber, 1986; Madden, 1985; Stevenson, 1988). The human capital perspective focuses most on sex differences in education, work experience, on-the-job training, expectations, the allocation of time between work and home, and the amount of effort on the job (Becker, 1985). According to this theory, men and women presumably freely choose how much, and what types of, education they achieve, the number of years they spend in the labor force, the amount of time they allocate to job training both prior to and on the job, whether to work full- or part-time, and the effort they expend on the job. Mincer and Polachek (1974) go further, arguing that human capital will atrophy with time spent out of the labor market. According to the neoclassical view, then, sex differences that favor men on a variety of factors lead inevitably to a more productive, and hence better-paid, male labor force.

Status attainment. Among sociologists, it was status attainment researchers who took up the individualist banner (for reviews, see Coverman, 1988; Marini, 1989). Status attainment researchers also assumed a competitive labor market, although "new structuralist" stratification researchers later relaxed this assumption, taking into account the effects of labor market characteristics.[9] The central goals of this research tradition were to investigate the *process* whereby individuals achieved various statuses, such as education, occupation, earnings, and the extent to which ascribed (e.g., race, sex, social class) versus achieved (e.g., education, experience) characteristics led to occupational or earnings attainment.

Within the neoclassical and status attainment paradigms, researchers have also investigated the effects of an additional set of explanatory factors, such as parents' status, marital status, number of children, academic performance, intellectual ability, occupational aspirations, and socialization (Coverman, 1988; Marini, 1989; Marini & Fan, 1997). Some of these variables allowed researchers to acknowledge that pre-labor market discrimination existed, through class inheritance, or socialization through families and schools. However, according to the individualist perspective, factors such as length and type of education completed, years of labor force attachment, and extent of on-the-job training affect workers through the *choices* they make prior to their entry to their current, although not necessarily first, job. Accordingly, these researchers play down the likelihood of labor market discrimination, assuming instead that market forces make long-term labor market discrimination unlikely.

Evidence on individualist theories. Human capital and status attainment theorists focus attention on sex differences in individual characteristics as the primary explanation for the earnings gap, and reductions in these sex differences as the major explanation for the narrowing gap. Recent estimates suggest that between 30% and 50% of the decline in the earnings gap is attributable to narrowing sex differences in a variety of human capital variables, changes that have occurred primarily because of women's increased labor force participation and because better educated and more experienced cohorts have replaced those less educated and less experienced (O'Neill & Polachek, 1993; see also Madden, 1985; Smith & Ward, 1984).

O'Neill and Polachek (1993) found that increases in women's *schooling and experience* contributed to the convergence in wages between men and women (see also Corcoran & Duncan, 1979; O'Neill, 1985; Smith & Ward, 1984). Researchers agree that the narrowing sex gap in experience may be the primary explanation of the declining earnings gap, at least for individual-level data. Using data permitting direct measurement of experience (NLS and PSID[10] data), O'Neill and Polachek (1993, p. 212) found that between 1977 and 1987 women's cumulative experience increased notably relative to men's, especially among the most recent cohorts: Women with 15 or fewer years of "potential experience" worked 83% of the years since leaving school in 1987, compared with 75% 10 years earlier. The comparable percentages for men were 92% versus 94%.

Some researchers also point to the declining sex gap in education as a determinant of the reduced earnings gap: Using Current Population Survey data, O'Neill and Polachek (p. 219) found narrowing sex differences in average years of schooling and in the proportion of college grads between 1977 and 1989. Interestingly, this may be a more recent phenomenon. O'Neill and Polachek (p. 209) noted that in the 1950s, working women were actually better educated than working men, an advantage that eroded by the mid-1960s as less educated women entered the labor force (see also England, 1997, p. 77). Most researchers attribute little explanatory value to education because data from this period (roughly the mid-1960s to the early 1980s) show women's average years of education as nearly identical to those of men (e.g., Marini, 1989, p. 349).

Using PSID data for Whites, Wellington (1994) similarly found that reductions in sex differences for several experience variables (including years of experience prior to current employer, total years employed full-time, and years with current employer prior to current position) contributed significantly to reducing the sex gap in earnings. In addition to increases in the *amount* of women's experience and education relative to men's, O'Neill and Polachek (1993, pp. 218, 221) found that a narrowing of sex differences in the rates of returns to education and experience over time (e.g., coefficients) also helped to reduce the earnings gap.[11] As Wellington (1994, p. 847) noted, however, even with women's increased human capital characteristics the sex gap in earnings remains large; in her 1985 data over 50% of the wage gap between White men and women remained unexplained by such variables.

Human capital theorists also point to sex differences in *on-the-job training* as an important explanation for the earnings gap. Using PSID data, Corcoran and Duncan (1979, pp. 10-11) found that White men had completed twice as much current job training as their female or Black male or female counterparts. These training gaps explained 11% of the wage gap between White men and women, and 8% and 15% of the gap between White men and Black women and Black men, respectively. Examining change over time using more recent PSID data on Whites, Wellington (1994, pp. 843-845) found that sex gaps in training persisted, although at a reduced level: The gap in years of training in current position between White men and women declined from 1.0 to 0.8 year between 1976 and 1985. This training difference explained 9.2% of the male-female wage gap in 1976, and 10.6% in 1985. Barron, Black, and Loewenstein's (1982) data also showed that because of occupational sex segregation, the duration of training varied by sex, as did the cost of the capital workers used: Men's training was twice women's (28 to 14 weeks) and men worked with substantially more expensive machinery

($42,900 vs. $13,600), factors that helped to explain the sex gap in earnings (Barron et al., 1993, Table 1).

There are two components to Becker's (1985) argument regarding *work effort*. Given the presumption that women and men anticipate differing levels of attachment to the workforce, men are expected to allocate more time than women to work, and to allocate significantly more "physical and mental energy" to their jobs (see also Marini, 1989; Stevenson, 1988, p. 91). With respect to full- versus part-time work, Wellington (1994, Table 1) demonstrated that White women continued to work part-time more often than White men: 12% versus 2% in 1985, down from 17% versus 2% in 1976. Net of a set of labor market history variables including experience, current part-time employment accounted for 2.5% of the wage gap in 1985 (Wellington, 1994, Table 2). Contrary to claims of sex differences in effort, Bielby and Bielby (1988) documented that two-thirds or more of women reported that they allocated more effort to work than did similar men (p. 1056; see also Marini, 1989, p. 351; Reskin & Padavic, 1994, pp. 112-113). Of course, to the extent that occupational aspirations and premarket socialization reduce the amount of time women devote to the labor market, these factors indirectly affect women's earnings relative to men's. These findings imply that, once on the job, women and men allocate equivalent effort to work.

If Becker's argument were correct, we should also observe similar differences *among* women, specifically between those with and without family responsibilities. Waldfogel's (1997, p. 211) findings are mixed in this regard: After controlling for labor market experience, being married or divorced earned women a wage premium relative to single women, similar to what has traditionally been true for men. Although this finding is consistent with the work effort argument for men, for women it is inconsistent.[12] More in line with expectation, however, is her finding that having children (especially two or more children) significantly reduced women's earnings. Waldfogel reported a penalty of 13% for those women with two or more children (pp. 212, 215), although this is attributable in large measure to the indirect effect of being employed part-time in a market that penalizes such work.

Finally, Corcoran and Duncan (1979) found no evidence for another aspect of the human capital argument, Mincer and Polachek's (1974) argument that skills atrophy during time out of the labor market. England (1984, p. 727) defined *skill atrophy* as a worker's receiving lower real wages after returning to the job than when he or she left. Corcoran and Duncan found little support for the skill atrophy argument. Indeed, the only significant, negative coefficient was for White women and even that coefficient was relatively small (one-half of 1% for each year out of the labor force). These data suggest that although labor force withdrawals do reduce women's earnings, there is no additional penalty attributable to skill depreciation per se.

England (1984) tested a related individualist claim: that men and women optimize their lifetime earnings by choosing occupations traditional for their sex. Assumed to have intermittent labor force participation, women choose female occupations because they should have low depreciation rates for years out of the labor force. In an analogous way, men who tend to be employed continuously choose male occupations without regard to depreciation rates. Contrary to this expectation, England found that rates of depreciation do not vary by occupational sex composition. Indeed, women maximized their lifetime earnings by working in male, not female, occupations precisely because they earned more in such jobs. The evidence is clear that women pay a net wage penalty for their overrepresentation in women's occupations (p. 742).

Policy. As a vocal advocate of the individualist approach, Polachek (1987, p. 49) argued that earnings inequality occurs as a consequence of individual choice. Hence, he argued that relying on governmental intervention to fix the process of pay allocation would lead to tremendous macroeconomic inefficiencies. Proponents of individualist theories give primacy to explanations for the earnings gap that are based on male-female differences in a variety of human capital factors relevant to earnings. The policy implication that flows from such arguments is to increase women's productivity vis-à-vis men, through, for example, increasing women's labor force attachment, their lifetime levels of experience, the time spent in on-the-job training, allocation to full-time work, effort on the job, and so forth. And, according to the argument, these changes require altering individual attitudes and behavior, not governmental intervention.

Institutionalist Theories

Whereas individualists view labor market participants as exercising choice within an open, fully competitive labor market, institutionalists focus on those moments when, and sectors of the economy where, the competitive market breaks down, producing constraints and rigidities that limit choice (Stevenson, 1988, p. 92). Rather than an unfettered market's operating to reduce the effects of discrimination arising from individual-level prejudice, institutionalists argue that structural arrangements develop and perpetuate a "taste for discrimination" (e.g., from employers, employees, customers; Madden, 1985, p. 91). In this section, we turn to explanations and evidence for the earnings gap that focus on institutionalized mechanisms that reduce the competitiveness of the labor market and restrict individual choice. Rather than the characteristics and choices of individuals driving supply, the focus is on how the characteristics of labor market location affect the *demand* for workers. For many who espouse the institutionalist perspective, the debate is not whether structural arrangements replace choice, but rather how structural arrangements over which individuals have little or no control constrain individual choice. The institutionalist theories we review point to the importance of a variety of structural factors that affect earnings. The evidence to date from empirical evaluations of these theories makes it clear that structural factors play a major role in reproducing the gender gap in earnings.

Labor market segmentation theories. Segmented labor market theories have deep roots in economic theory (e.g., Doeringer & Piore, 1971; Madden, 1985; Piore, 1971; Stevenson, 1988), as well as in sociology (e.g., Althauser & Kalleberg, 1981; Baron & Bielby, 1984; Beck, Horan, & Tolbert, 1978; Wallace & Kalleberg, 1981). These theories recognize that the process of earnings determination—a major part of labor market experience—depends on the labor market sector of a job. Depending on the author, "sector" or "segment" is operationalized by jobs, industries, or firms.

According to *internal labor market theory* (ILM theory) (Althauser & Kalleberg, 1981, pp. 121-123), markets are structured institutionally in ways that affect subsequent occupational access and earnings. An "external" market operates much like the traditional neoclassical competitive market, in the sense that wages are set via supply and demand. But for some job clusters, this external market operates at only a few "ports of entry." Once employees are hired, "internal" markets govern promotion and earnings determination, with precedence given to those already employed in the firm. Elaborating on ILM theory, Doeringer and Piore hypothesized the existence of dual labor market sectors: a "primary labor market" whose job clusters are structured as ILMs and a "secondary labor market" that includes a mixture of ILMs and external sector jobs (Doeringer & Piore, 1971; Piore, 1971, 1975). Jobs in the former sector theoretically enjoy high wages, good working conditions, job stability, and due process, whereas those in the latter sector are characterized by low wages, poor working conditions, little opportunity for mobility, and severe and arbitrary discipline (see also Althauser & Kalleberg, 1981, p. 123).[13]

Althauser and Kalleberg's description of multiple ILMs within a given firm (e.g., craft, managerial ILMs) makes it clear that the earnings consequences of these structural arrangements for the individual can be quite long-lasting. Employees internal to the market are protected from competition from those outside the ILM, in effect creating labor market shelters, whereas those restricted to non-ILM sectors are hindered from transferring to better-paid sectors. Moreover, those in the more competitive, external market develop work behaviors and attitudes, such as job instability and malingering, that limit upward mobility and earnings.

Segmentation has also been investigated through *dual economy theory.* Referring both to the economic organization of *firms* and the distribution of technical systems of production within *industries,* dual economy theory evaluates the uneven nature of the capital accumulation process (Wallace & Kalleberg, 1981, p. 77). The "core" sector consists of large, high-production, high-profit, heavily unionized, capital-intensive industries; the "peripheral" sector includes small, labor-intensive, low-profit, and low-production industries (Coverman, 1988, p. 105). To the extent that men predominate in the core and women in the periphery, sectoral location will affect earnings potential and the male-female earnings gap. Typically, theorists operationalize dual economy's two sectors as a dichotomous measure of industry location, although this model has been criticized as simplistic (Wallace & Kalleberg, 1981; Zucker & Rosenstein, 1981).

In reviewing the empirical evidence on segmentation theory, it is useful to distinguish two relevant issues: (1) to what extent dual segments overlap occupational segregation by sex, and (2) the use of segmentation theory to explain the gender earnings gap. Segmentation theory was originally developed to understand the plight of marginal workers, with attention initially focused on race differences in opportunities and earnings. Coverman (1986, p. 142) argued that segmentation typologies do not sufficiently tap the positional inequality that exists in the labor market, at least among women. Specifically, theoretical descriptions of the upper or lower primary sectors refer mainly to traditionally male jobs, such as accountants, physicians in the upper primary, and union-production jobs in the lower primary sectors, respectively. The characteristics of traditionally female jobs that fall into the lower primary sector, in contrast, are not consistent with theoretical predictions: Such jobs typically lack job security, opportunities for advancement, and high pay. Indeed, women's primary sector jobs more closely resemble men's secondary sector jobs. Using data from the 1977 Quality of Employment Survey, Coverman found that women were more likely than men to be employed in secondary sector occupations (26% vs. 13%; p. 152). However, sex differences in women's reward structure across labor market segments were not as strong as segmented labor market theory would predict. Only education effects fit theoretical expectation; there was almost no theoretical fit for women in the lower primary sector (pp. 154, 159).

Similarly, Taylor, Gwartney-Gibbs, and Farley (1986, p. 129) found White men overrepresented in core industries, White women and Blacks overrepresented in peripheral industries, and reward structures varying by race and sex. Others have shown other segment effects. Hodson and England (1986), for example, found women's lower representation in heavily unionized or heavily capitalized industries an important explanation for their lower earnings vis-à-vis men. Finally, Marini and Fan (1997, p. 602) found segmentation into sex-specific labor markets at career entry to be an important determinant of the gender earnings gap. Women were steered to traditionally female jobs by employers and by job information gained through informal social networks (see also Roos & Reskin, 1984).

Segmentation can be expanded to include a variety of formal and informal arrangements that structure opportunity. Thus, unions can seek labor market shelters for workers (e.g., by requiring lengthy apprenticeship programs), government agencies can establish policies favoring one class of workers over others (e.g., preferences for veterans), and employers can establish entrance requirements that inhibit women's entry (e.g., height/strength requirements not relevant to job performance). As Roos and Reskin (1984) noted, such institutionalized practices can perpetuate occupational sex segregation (and, hence, sex differences in earnings), a topic to which we now turn.

Occupational/job segregation. Expanding on the dual labor market idea of "primary/good" versus "secondary/bad" jobs, theorists have broadened the idea of segmentation to other forms of positional inequality, including occupational or, preferably, job segregation by sex. Many institutional theorists view job segregation as the major mechanism for perpetuating discriminatory wage differences (Stevenson, 1988, p. 93). Ideally, of course, we would like to measure positional inequality at the job level, although such detail is seldom available. With few studies having job-level data, researchers typically measure sex segregation at the *detailed* occupational level. Although those using detailed occupations can explain a larger portion of the male-female earnings gap than can be had in dual-sector models, measurement at the specific job or establishment level can nearly close the earnings gap. Such findings indicate that estimates of the effect of sex segregation on the earnings gap vary notably by the level of aggregation: The more refined the occupational classification, the greater portion of the gap explained (Bielby & Baron, 1986; Marini, 1989, p. 367; Petersen & Morgan, 1995).

Jobs and occupations vary according to their sex composition, occupational earnings, cognitive skill, occupation-specific training, and physical skill. Viewing occupations as distinct labor markets, Parcel (1989) argued that occupations differ in job content (a productivity-related dimension), but also in nonproductivity-related, or what she called "social organization," dimensions (see also Huffman & Velasco, 1997; Stolzenberg, 1975). Parcel's examples of the latter include occupational unemployment rate, occupational size, extent of government employment, female concentration, racial concentration, unionization, and marital status (pp. 136-137, 148).

The empirical evidence makes it clear that positional inequality at the detailed occupational level, and especially at the job or establishment level, plays a major role in reproducing the earnings gap. Reviewing results from a variety of studies, Marini (1989, p. 367) reported a range of 35% to 40% for occupational studies. Cotter, DeFiore, Hermsen, Kowalewski, and Vanneman (1995, pp. 440, 453), citing Goldin, put the figure closer to 19%, and Sorensen (1989, 1990, p. 78) estimated 20% to 23%. Our reading of Goldin's (1990, chap. 3) data, however, suggests that her estimate of occupational segregation was a lower-bound estimate of the effect of occupation per se, because significant sex differences in wages persist *within* occupations. Indeed, employing BLS industry wage data for 1974-1983, Petersen and Morgan (1995, p. 361 and Table 4) estimated that occupation-establishment location explained 89% of the wage gap between men and women, with segregation indexes ranging from 62.6 to 97.0 for the 17 industries examined. Similarly, in their study of job titles in 290 California workplaces, Bielby and Baron (1986, p. 777) found that 96% of women would need to change job titles to equalize their distribution with men (see also Bielby & Baron, 1984; Tomaskovic-Devey, 1993).

Findings such as Petersen and Morgan's (1995) and Bielby and Baron's (1984)—that controlling for occupation-establishment location accounts for nearly the entire sex gap in earnings—require a shift in analysis to factors that produce occupational sex segregation in the first place. Fortunately, other scholars have usefully reviewed that literature (e.g., Reskin, 1993; see also Reskin & Hartmann, 1986; Roos, 1985). Explanations for occupational sex segregation have relied on many of the same theories proposed for the earnings gap, including individualist theories that focus on individual choice and institutional theories that address structural constraints. Thus, Reskin (1993) pointed to both supply explanations such as gender-role socialization, human-capital explanations, labor supply, and worker values, and demand explanations such as employers' preferences, demand for workers, and discrimination to explain why occupations are segregated by sex.

Another fruitful area of inquiry focuses on how and why such segregation began to decline after 1970, after persisting throughout most of the century (e.g., Reskin & Roos, 1990). This work directed researchers' attention to the need to integrate individualist and institutional explanations in explaining women's entry into selected traditionally male occupations. Reskin and Roos's queuing perspective theorized, and found evidence, that occupational sex composition shifts as a consequence of the operation of two distinct queuing processes: (1) employers rank groups of potential workers into *labor queues* according to their attractiveness, and (2) workers similarly rank potential jobs in *job queues*.

Presenting data for a set of 14 case studies, Reskin and Roos (1990) found evidence that employers chose men first and then moved down the labor queue as necessary until their hiring needs were met. High levels of sex segregation produce gendered labor queues. As crowding theory recognized, the gendering of labor queues is further exacerbated by employers' steering women away from the full range of occupational opportunities, and crowding them into a smaller number of traditionally female occupations, driving down wages (Blau & Ferber, 1986, p. 255; Sorensen, 1990).[14] Reskin and Roos (1990, chap. 2) found a variety of factors important to explaining changing occupational sex composition, including labor shortages; occupational growth; declining occupational earnings, security, or prestige; and reduced male interest. In some occupations, changing societal expectations, changing skill mixes, declining discrimination, and reduced male resistance to women increased women's ranking in the labor queue. Some of these same factors also increased selected occupations in women's job queues. Reskin and Roos (chap. 3) found that women's movement into male occupations did not translate for the most part into higher earnings for them. Instead, women remained ghettoized in selected job specialties, or the occupation resegregated as female. By the time women integrated male occupations, the occupations had lost much of their attraction for men. Such processes do not hold much promise for increasing women's real earnings relative to men's.

Occupational sex segregation and the earnings gap. Reflecting the substantial amount of sex segregation in occupations and jobs is the long-standing negative association between occupation percentage female and earnings (e.g., Macpherson & Hirsch, 1995, p. 427; Roos, 1981, p. 198). One approach to explaining this negative association is compensating differentials theory, which recognizes the existence of occupational sex segregation but argues that it occurs by choice. Women theoretically trade off wages to avoid physical or nonphysical "disamenities" associated with some occupations. Additionally, women theoretically choose female occupations because of better working conditions, higher starting wages, and lower wage depreciation (England, Farkas, Kilbourne, & Dou, 1988, p. 546; Filer, 1989; Jacobs & Steinberg, 1995; Kilbourne, England, Farkas, Beron, & Weir, 1994, p. 692; Tam, 1997). Compensating differentials theory dates back at least to Adam Smith and recognizes the principle that employers must pay a wage premium for jobs with unpleasant working conditions. The newest theorists to adopt this approach are those most sympathetic to neoclassical economics.

In evaluating the compensating differentials approach, Filer (1989) found that the gender earnings gap can best be explained by reference to occupational differences in effort, responsibility, working conditions, or other productivity-relevant factors. Using data from the 1980 census, Filer found that controlling for 225 "compensable job characteristics" reduces the sex composition-wages effect to nonsignificance.[15] Contradicting Filer's results, England and colleagues (1988) and Kilbourne and colleagues (1994) found little support for the expectation that female occupations have advantages that compensate for lower earnings. In the latter study, for example, the authors (p. 708) documented that occupational controls for cognitive skills, physical skills, and physical disamenities explained little of the gender earnings gap. Similarly, Jacobs and Steinberg (1995) found that variation in working conditions was not responsible for the earnings gap. Huffman and Velasco (1997, p. 214) demonstrated that the earnings penalty for female representation existed over a variety of organizational types, suggesting that the negative effects of female representation persist in spite of organizational attempts to ameliorate them (e.g., through government regulation or employment formalization). Finally, Tam (1997) found little support for the devaluation hypothesis claim of wage discrimination against female occupations per se. Instead, sex composition effects are in large measure explained away by occupation-specific training (the *Dictionary of Occupational Titles'* Specific Vocational Preparation [SVP] measure) and industrial mix (see also Macpherson & Hirsch, 1995). As Tam and Macpherson and Hirsch noted, this finding does not "explain away" sex differences in earnings, because it does not address how women and men get allocated to occupations with such different levels of SVP in the first place.

Statistical discrimination. Recent scholarship has focused more attention on processes internal to organizations to explain persistent male-female earnings differences. A major theme of such work has been statistical discrimination, or discrimination against a particular class of persons because of group, rather than individual, characteristics (Reskin, 1993, p. 254). An important component in statistical discrimination theory is the role of employer beliefs and perceptions. Consistent with their role of ranking workers in labor queues (Reskin & Roos, 1990), employers are the labor market actors responsible for allocating workers to jobs and setting wage rates. To the extent that employers use sex as a screen to steer comparable men and women to sex-typical jobs, they are engaging in statistical discrimination. Similarly, when employers pay men more than comparable women, or set pay rates for male jobs higher than those of equivalent female jobs, they are engaged in statistical discrimination. To the extent that statistical discrimination by sex affects employers' initial job allocation decisions, institutionalized processes such as internal labor markets can limit women's subsequent mobility and earnings opportunities.

The evidence on this issue is clear: Employers' beliefs and perceptions can and do affect women's and men's occupational access. Bielby and Baron (1986, pp. 787-788) documented that even women and men in sex-integrated occupations work in very different locations, both within and across organizations and even within detailed occupations. Men were in larger organizations, were in unionized workplaces, did more complex tasks, had jobs requiring more training, and had jobs with greater physical demands. Such blatant and persistent sex segregation is inconsistent with expectations of an efficient market model, and quite consistent with employer statistical discrimination. Baron, Mittman, and Newman (1991, p. 1394) found, for the California State government jobs they examined, that other organizational actors—most notably unions—also hindered integration. Gender integration occurred most often in younger and smaller organizations, less mired down by vested interests and internal politics, and in those organizations with key internal and external constituencies promoting integration. Baron and Newman (1989, p. 125) showed how much *prescribed* pay rate—a measure of job worth—varied by women's integration: Even among jobs requiring similar duties and requirements, the net wage penalties for female jobs were severe. Such devaluation was not inevitable, however, because women and minorities were able to benefit monetarily from economic expansion (p. 126).

Employing data from a Washington State government pay system, Bridges and Nelson (1989, p. 654) demonstrated that intraorganizational decision making with respect to wage setting was also sheltered from market forces. Organizational processes operated to foster pay inequity by honoring customary wage expectations of both workers and managers, maintaining relative wage rates among jobs, and allowing the union an insider's role in pay-setting decisions. The absence of women's groups within the organization meant that there was no organized group to lobby for women's interests, and historical disadvantages reflected in wage-setting practices persisted.

Structure. Researchers have linked broader, macro-level changes in the economy to changes in the earnings gap, specifically by examining how economic restructuring affects wage structures. Blau (1996) described "wage structure" as a measure of wage inequality that summarizes the effects of individual-level differences in labor market skills and the market return to those skills. Wage structures emerge as a consequence of the supply of labor at various skill levels, the demand for labor, technology, and wage-setting entities (Blau, 1996, p. 8). A focus on restructuring enables researchers to take into account more explicitly the effects of declining male earnings and increasing wage inequality on earnings ratios (Bernhardt, Morris, & Handcock, 1995, p. 305; see also Blau & Kahn, 1997; Levy & Murnane, 1992). As Blau and Kahn (1994, p. 23) pointed out, increased wage inequality—interpretable as "high returns to skill"—exacts a large penalty for being below average in the wage distribution.

A focus on restructuring has also shifted researchers' attention to industrial and regional restructuring and to the dramatic growth of externalized—or contingent—work arrangements. McCall (1998a, 1998b) has examined similar questions in her work linking economic restructuring to men's economic losses: She tackled the issue of spatial variation in inequality by examining how variation across regional labor markets with different economic conditions produced gender, class, and racial inequality.

The evidence regarding structural explanations has grown notably in recent years, as researchers focused their attention on the effects of growing wage inequality and economic restructuring on earnings. Bernhardt et al. (1995) argued that understanding shifts in wage inequality is critical to understanding past and future changes in the gender earnings gap (see also Cotter, DeFiore, Hermsen, Kowalewski, & Vanneman's 1997 critique and Bernhardt, Morris, & Handcock's 1997 response). Bernhardt and her colleagues demonstrated that a major reason for women's relative earnings gains was the dramatic increases in wage inequality among men. Focusing on the relative earnings *distributions* as opposed to *median* earnings ratios, Bernhardt et al. (pp. 314, 324) found that increasing wage inequality among men pushed women out of the lower rungs of the earnings distribution. Few women gained entry into the highest ranks of the distribution, although the increasing polarization of women's wages suggests that some women moved into the higher-paying men's jobs. It is striking that, even by 1987, over 80% of women earned less than the median male worker (p. 314). Contrary to the impression of across-the-board improvement for women given by an increasing earnings ratio, a distributional analysis revealed a more stubborn and persistent inequality in the American labor market.

In related work, Blau and Kahn have written a series of articles investigating the effects of "wage structures" on the gender earnings gap (Blau, 1996; Blau & Kahn, 1994, 1996, 1997). Using this approach, Blau and Kahn (1994, p. 28) found a "gender twist" with respect to the demand for skills: Changing demands benefited women relative to men at the lower end of the skill distribution, but benefited men at the top (see also Katz & Murphy, 1992). The implication of the gender twist—supported by their data—is that the earnings ratio increased more rapidly for those at the bottom of the wage hierarchy than those at the top, a finding consistent with Bernhardt et al.'s (1995) results. Blau (1996, p. 21) provided additional evidence, from international comparisons, of the usefulness of the "wage structure" construct: The bottom line is that without improvements in "gender-specific factors," such as improvements in qualifications and declines in labor market discrimination, increasing wage inequality would have widened the gender pay gap in recent years, not narrowed it (see also Blau & Kahn, 1996, 1997, for additional evidence, both cross-culturally and over time in the United States).

With respect to industrial and regional restructuring, broad industrial shifts from manufacturing to services, as well as deunionization and casualization within goods and service industries, have also increased inequality. Increases in service and high-technology jobs, for example, have not offset significant declines in well-paid and typically male manufacturing jobs in industries like steel and auto. The classic fast-food counter worker or other low-paid service work is the more likely alternative to high-paying manufacturing jobs for the average American worker. Regional shifts in the location of work—from northeastern and midwestern to southern and western states, and from cities to suburbs—have also increased wage inequality by (1) widening the skills mismatch between urban residents and the local, available jobs, and (2) enlarging the spatial mismatch between urban residents and the newly suburban jobs that need labor (Kasarda, 1995; Wilson, 1987, 1996).

The growth of externalized—or contingent—work arrangements has restructured how work is organized, and increased wage inequality. By 1995, about 34.5 million workers—approximately 30% of the labor force—worked in non-full-time positions (Cassirer, 1997, p. 2). Cassirer included in her definition of externalized workers those in part-time, temporary, independent-contracting, self-employed, on-call, or day labor, and contract workers (see also Kalleberg, Reskin, & Hudson, in press). Cassirer (1997) documented how externalized work arrangements produce sex inequality in wages. Not only were White men substantially more likely than White women or non-Whites to be concentrated in full-time work, they were also better represented in higher-paid externalized work such as contract and independent-contract work (p. 171). Among Whites, men were also better compensated for the externalized work they did. As a consequence, such work accounted for approximately 25% of the wage gap between White men and women, with equivalent figures for White men and Black and Hispanic women of 11% and 15%, respectively (pp. 172-173). Similarly, Kalleberg et al. (in press) argued that working in jobs with nonstandard work arrangements increased wage inequality because these jobs were "bad": jobs that were contingent or insecure, lacked health insurance benefits, lacked pension benefits, and had low wages.

McCall's (1998a, 1998b) recent work on the effects of economic restructuring on inequality effectively linked economic conditions in labor markets to gender, class, and race inequality (see also Bluestone, 1994). Drawing insights from case study and macro-comparative methods, McCall demonstrated how these forms of inequality operate simultaneously to produce "configurations of inequality" within local U.S. markets. Thus, although men's declining wages were one reason for the increasing gender earnings ratio, this process was not uniform across class categories, nor across labor markets. Rather, class differences among men and among women also played a role, as did their interaction with economic conditions in regional labor markets.[16]

Policy. Contrary to policy implications that flow from individualist theories of the gender earnings gap, institutionalist theories promote (1) policies that enhance women's access to a fuller range of occupations and jobs and (2) pay equity policies intended to increase women's relative pay in traditionally female occupations through improved pay-setting practices (e.g., Filer, 1989, p. 156; Michael, Hartmann, & O'Farrell, 1989). Policymakers proposing either of these approaches typically justify calls for government intervention by pointing to the noncompetitive elements in the labor market that are producing macro-level inefficiencies. As Stevenson (1988, p. 92) argued, governmental intervention is sometimes necessary to correct the abuses of a malfunctioning private sector.

The more recent focus on macro-level, structural determinants of the earnings gap points to the complexities of implementing a comparable worth policy to equalize the wages of women in traditionally female occupations. McCall (1998a) warned that in an economy with increasing wage inequality, pegging definitions of success to men's salaries in traditionally male occupations is at least questionable. What such strategies typically fail to take into account is the confluence of economic decline, lower wages, and higher gender inequality among the most disadvantaged workers, which tends to occur for those in labor markets with high unemployment and large numbers of casual workers. Men's jobs are not always "good" job with high wages.

Conclusion

The gender gap in earnings is a long-standing attribute of the American economy. Women continue to earn less than men regardless of how you measure it, across time, throughout the life cycle, in all race and ethnic groups, within all education categories, within detailed occupations, and across cultures. The earnings gap has persisted for as long as records have been kept, and its deeply embedded nature suggests that it's not likely to disappear any time soon.

Sociologists and economists in particular have focused on two sets of explanations for the earnings gap: (1) individualist explanations that attempt to explain the earnings gap by reference to the exercise of choice within open, competitive labor markets (e.g., sex differences in attitudes, preferences, and qualifications); and (2) institutionalist explanations that focus on structural mechanisms that restrict the competitiveness of the labor market as well as individual choice. As discussed, each explanation has different implications for policy, with the former focusing on altering individual attitudes and behavior and the latter focusing on needed interventions to fix labor market imperfections that inhibit women's mobility and earnings attainment. As Bluestone (1994) outlined, intervention in the U.S. case might take the form of structural approaches to reducing wage inequality, such as progressive tax rates, income transfer programs, direct market regulation, increasing the minimum wage, and labor law reform to level the playing field for unions.

The prognosis for women's market mobility and earnings depends on the perspective one holds. Individualists are heartened by the progress women have achieved, especially since 1970. Upgrades in women's productivity-related characteristics such as education, experience, and on-the-job training have reduced the earnings gap between women and men. Proponents also point to significant declines in labor market discrimination, and they see signs for similar improvements in the future. Alternatively, institutionalists are more guarded, arguing that macro-level features of the economy—embedded inequality, wage inequality operating through increasingly polarized wage structures, a restructured economy—can substantially reduce women's relative earnings, even with beneficial changes in the characteristics and behaviors of women.

The ubiquity and intractable nature of the earnings gap suggests that we have a long way to go before we will be able to substantially reduce the gender gap in earnings. Future research on this topic would benefit from integrating individualist and institutionalist explanations, in particular, focusing on how institutionalized arrangements delimit occupational and earnings choices. We need to know more about macro-level factors embedded in organizational and labor market processes and how they structure both employer's and employee's behaviors. For example, given the critical importance of occupational sex segregation in the perpetuation of the earnings gap, we would benefit from knowing more about how statistical discrimination operates: how and why employers steer women and men to sex-typical jobs and how gender is used in the wage-setting process. Similarly, on the supply side we need to know more about how and why men and women continue to rank sex-typical jobs high in their job queues. Finally, we would also benefit from additional cross-cultural research on the earnings gap, research that focuses on how and why some countries have been more successful than others in reducing the gender gap in earnings.

Notes

1. Of course, the earnings gap also existed prior to 1955: Reskin and Padavic (1994, p. 101) noted that in 1313 Parisian women's taxable wealth was approximately two-thirds that of men. Similarly, Goldin (1990, Table 3.1) found that in 1850 women in manufacturing earned less than half that of men, and by 1900 they earned slightly more than half.

2. For an overview of U.S. data series, see Goldin (1990, Table 3.1), Institute for Women's Policy Research (1996, Table 1), and Spain and Bianchi (1996, Table 5.1). For an analysis of earnings ratios cross-culturally, see below and Treiman and Roos (1983).

3. One reason why earnings ratios are lower for annual relative to weekly earnings estimates is that the former includes bonuses and overtime, which tend to be higher for men (Lewin, 1997).

4. We build on a number of excellent overviews, including Smith and Ward (1984), Blau and Ferber (1986), Coverman (1988), Stevenson (1988), Marini (1989), Goldin (1990), Reskin and Padavic (1994), Spain and Bianchi (1996), and England (1997).

5. Our basic sample selection for the census data was for those persons 16 and older who worked the previous year (1969, 1979, 1989) and who also worked in the civilian labor force during the reference week. The 1980 and 1990 characteristics were aggregated from the 1980 and 1990 Public Use Microdata (A sample, 5%), respectively. The 1970 characteristics were aggregated from two 1% samples of the 1970 Public Use Microdata that contain imputed 1980 industry and occupation codes. We concatenated the two 1% samples (1% each from the original 5% and 15% samples) to create a 2% sample of the United States in 1970. Consult the codebooks for additional information (Roos & Reskin, 1996; U.S. Bureau of the Census, 1972, 1983, 1993).

6. Reskin and Roos (1990) described this explicitly: "Feminization between 1970 and 1980 could have increased women's earnings relative to men's if both men's and women's real earnings increased but women's did so at a faster rate; if both men's and women's real earnings decreased but women's did so at a slower rate; if women's real earnings increased while men's remained steady or declined; or if women's remained steady while men's declined" (pp. 79-80).

7. Our earnings ratios are calculated for those who work year-round/full-time, operationalized in 1980 and 1990 as those working 50 or more weeks in the previous year *and* usually working 35 or more hours per week in the previous year. For 1970, the comparable operationalization included those who worked 50 or more weeks in the previous year *and* 35 or more hours in the reference week. Unlike some previous estimates, ours were calculated for *all* civilian workers (e.g., private wage and salary workers, federal and state government workers, self-employed workers).

8. The 1970-1990 change in the *total* median earnings ratios (in the last row in Table 6.1) are unexpectedly lower than either Whites or Blacks. A clarification is in order because this figure should be within the White to Black range. The *total* figure represents all members of the sample, including Whites, Blacks, and all other races, and hence will not simply be the average of Whites and Blacks. We did a supplementary run for 1990 calculating the earnings ratios for the other race categories (all non-White, non-Black), and found results similar to those for Blacks. Thus *not* including other races in the calculation of the total figure would have attenuated the earnings ratio in 1990, further reducing the change figure. We believe that the explanation for the unexpectedly lower total figure is rounding error. As Tables 6.3 and 6.4 indicate, there are a large number of medians rounded to the nearest thousand, reflecting the tendency of census respondents to round their estimated earnings. Comparable means for the totals, as opposed to medians, were indeed within the expected range (data not shown).

9. As Margaret Mooney Marini pointed out (personal communication, 1998), this explicit focus on a competitive labor market occurred primarily among economists and not status attainment researchers. Status attainment paid little attention to how the labor market functioned, focusing instead on how individuals would seek socially valued rewards (e.g., occupational status and earnings). It was only when the new structuralists emerged that these issues were directly tackled.

10. National Longitudinal Surveys (NLS) and the Panel Study of Income Dynamics (PSID).

11. Corcoran and Duncan (1979, p. 13) found, however, that when they took into account different dimensions of work history, rates of return per year of experience within any particular dimension of experience were similar for all four race/sex groups. What varied across the groups was the amount of time spent in differently valued dimensions (e.g., completed training, preemployer experience). This is consistent with Wellington (1994, p. 847), who found that with the exception of education and part-time status the payoffs to most of the human capital variables were similar for men and women.

12. The findings of Hill (1979) and Roos (1983) also contradicted the human capital expectation. Roos's findings (p. 862) suggested that although marital status affected the kind of jobs women had, it did not translate into differences in wage rates. Similarly, Hill found no evidence of a detrimental wage effect of marriage (see also Marini & Fan, 1997).

13. In Piore's (1975) three-sector labor market taxonomy, the primary labor market is further divided into an upper and lower tier, marking differences in autonomy (see also Wallace & Kalleberg, 1981, p. 89).

14. Organizational gatekeepers use gender stereotypes in a segregative way when they crowd women into sex-typical occupations (Reskin & Padavic, 1994, p. 113). For similar reasons, gender ideologies also steer women and men into choosing sex-typical occupations.

15. Smith (1989) and Sorensen (1990) critiqued this approach, because the large number of variables created instability and difficulty in interpreting the independent effects.

16. McCall (1998a) operationalized *class* as college- versus non-college-educated workers.

Chapter 7

The Sex Segregation of Occupations

Prospects for the 21st Century

Jerry A. Jacobs

Men and women work in different jobs, and often do so in different organizations. The differing distribution of men and women across positions within the occupational structure may be referred to as the "sex segregation" of occupations. The term *segregation* may be more familiar in the context of residential segregation by race and ethnicity, but there are a number of analogies that may be made between residential segregation and occupational segregation. The same statistical measures are used in both cases, and some of the theoretical explanations of both phenomena resonate.

Sex segregation remains a defining element of the American occupational structure. It is pervasive, although it has declined somewhat in recent years. The composition of incumbents in a position, whether they are male or female, helps define choices for women and men. The concentration of women in low-paying, female-dominated occupations also contributes to the earnings gap between women and men.

This chapter outlines the multiple facets or dimensions of segregation. A simple example is presented along with the formulas used to calculate various measures of segregation so that interested readers can calculate these indexes for themselves. Issues of measurement are discussed, followed by a presentation of data on recent trends in segregation in the United States. Subsequent sections consider international comparisons, the gender gap in earnings, and the causes of sex segregation. The conclusion includes a discussion of the prospects for sex segregation in the 21st century.

Multiple Facets of Segregation

There are at least three distinct aspects of sex segregation (Jacobs, 1993; Massey & Denton, 1989). The principal dimension of segregation that is the focus of most research is the degree to which men and women are distributed unevenly across fields. This concept is typically measured with the index of dissimilarity (D), which indicates the proportion of women (or men) who would have to change fields to be distributed in the same manner as men (or women). As we will see, over half of women in the United States labor force would have to change occupations to match the occupational distribution of their male counterparts. The level of labor force sex segregation has declined during the 1970s and 1980s after remaining largely unchanged for most of the century (Jacobs, 1989a). However, new data presented below suggest that a new equilibrium level may be emerging during the 1990s. In other words, after two decades of slow but steady progress, women appear to be making few additional inroads into male-dominated fields in recent years.

The index of dissimilarity is often supplemented with a size-standardized measure of segregation, designated here as SSD. The size-standardized measure treats each occupation as having the same number of incumbents. This counterfactual approach can be useful for assessing change between two points in time. By holding the size of occupations constant, the size-standardized measure helps to answer the question "How much change is due to the changing size of occupations, and how much is due to the changing mix of men and women within occupations?"[1]

A second feature of sex segregation is the crowding of women into a limited number of fields. This aspect is not directly captured by the index of dissimilarity, and requires the use of specific indexes of concentration, designated C, for concentration or crowding.[2] I use the measure RC to describe the "relative crowding" of one group versus another.

Crowding is important for two reasons. First, crowding is an indication of the extent of opportunities for women. Although all occupations are now formally open to both men and women, some fields, such as engineering, remain de facto male preserves. The concentration of a great majority of women into a handful of fields would be one indication of the pervasiveness of social restrictions on women. For example, in 1960 almost half of women receiving bachelor's degrees did so in one field, namely, teaching. Over 75% of women received their degrees in one of six fields: English, fine arts, history, home economics, nursing, and teaching (J. A. Jacobs, 1995). (Friedan's 1963 discussion of the constraints on women college students during this period remains instructive.) Their male counterparts were more widely dispersed across the range of specialties, with no single field garnering as much as 20% of male degree recipients. At that time, women were crowded into a few fields, thus effectively limiting their range of choices.

A second reason to examine the dispersion of men and women across fields is that the financial potential of a field is influenced by the relationship between supply and demand. Edgeworth (1922) argued that women earned less than men in part because they were crowded into a limited number of fields. The issue of crowding is also discussed by Bergmann (1986) and Parcel (1989). Restricting women to a narrow set of jobs approved of as "women's work" can produce an excess supply of women for these occupations, thus limiting women's bargaining power and lowering their wages. The extent to which women are crowded into a few fields of study is one indication of the potential economic returns to their educations. The evidence provided by this measure is necessary, but not sufficient, proof of crowding, because it does not directly compare the number of degrees to the demand for talent in different fields.

A third aspect of segregation is the degree of intergroup contact, in other words, the chances of men and women sharing an occupation. This measure indicates the probability of interaction on the job. The intergroup contact index—designated P* by Lieberson (1980)—reflects both the level of segregation and the representation of each group. Moreover, women's chances of sharing an occupation with men differ from men's chances of sharing a field with women. One striking result of the growth in women's labor force participation is that women's chances of sharing an occupation with men has declined (as working women's numbers increase, women's chances of sharing an occupation with another woman increase) while men's chances of sharing an occupation with women has increased markedly. The two groups thus differ in how they experience the same changes, an aspect of segregation revealed by measures of intergroup contact.

Those interested in calculating these statistics may find Table 7.1 helpful. Table 7.1 provides a simple example of occupational segregation using hypothetical data. The formulas for the measures just described (see appendix) as well as results are provided, so that all who are interested can check the accuracy of their calculations and computer programs. In this hypothetical case, there are five occupations that range from 10% female to 100% female, and there are twice as many employed men as women. Just under half (45.0%) of women would have had to change occupations to be distributed in the same manner as men. Nursing is the most segregated occupation but also is the smallest. Thus, the size-standardized index of segregation measure is larger than the unadjusted one (52.81 vs. 45.00), because standardizing for size gives the case of nursing relatively more importance in the overall calculation. Men are quite likely to share their occupation with other men (P*MM = 74.66),

TABLE 7.1 Hypothetical Data

Occupation	No. of Men	No. of Women	M_i/M	W_i/W	% Female[a]	% Male[a]
Carpenters	90	10	45	10	10.0	90.0
Lawyers	60	20	30	20	25.0	75.0
High school teachers	40	40	20	40	50.0	50.0
Sociologists	10	20	5	20	66.7	33.3
Nurses	0	10	0	10	100.0	0.0
Total	200	100	100	100	251.0[b]	248.3[b]

D (index of dissimilarity)	45.00
SSD (size-standardized index of dissimilarity)	52.81
P*WW (women's chances of sharing an occupation with another woman)	49.33
P*MM (men's chances of sharing an ccupation with another man)	74.66
RC (relative crowding) (women – men)	–15.00

a. These columns represent PF_i and PM_i, respectively.
b. These figures represent the sum of PF_i and PM_i, respectively.

but women are almost equally likely to have male or female coworkers (P*WW = 49.33). That disparity results from the numerical predominance of men in the labor market. In this example, men are somewhat more crowded into a limited set of occupations than are women (RC = –15.0), because nearly half of men work in one field, namely, carpentry. Thus, we need to employ several complementary measures to understand the varied facets of occupational segregation.

Measuring Sex Segregation: The More Detail the Better

The degree of differentiation between men and women in the labor market is quite sensitive to the units of analysis across which segregation is measured. The more fine-grained the units, the more segregation is revealed. We may conceive of the occupational structure as 10 or so broad occupational groups arranged hierarchically. Although this representation is satisfactory for some purposes, it captures only a small portion of segregation by sex. That is because within each broad occupational strata, some occupations are female dominated and others are male dominated. For example, within the professions, some fields such as elementary and secondary education are typically occupied by women, whereas other fields, such as surveyors, airplane pilots. and clergy, are typically staffed by men. If one groups all of the professions together into a single occupational group, these distinctions will be lost, and the occupational system will seem more integrated than it really is.

The same criticism can be levied at more detailed occupational measures. The detailed occupational classification system of the U.S. census divides the

TABLE 7.2 Occupational Distributions of Men and Women, 1997, in 10 Major Occupational Groupings

	% of Workers		
Occupation	*Men*	*Women*	*% of Females*
Managerial	14.4	13.2	44.6
Professional and technical	15.1	20.3	54.2
Clerical	5.8	23.9	78.2
Sales	11.0	13.5	51.9
Craft	19.0	2.1	8.7
Operative	7.2	5.4	39.5
Transport	7.2	0.9	9.6
Service	10.1	18.1	61.1
Farm	4.1	1.0	17.2
Laborers	6.1	1.8	20.3
Total	100.0	100.2	46.7
D (index of dissimilarity)			33.65
SSD (size-standardized index of dissimilarity)			41.73
P*WW (women's chances of sharing an occupation with another woman)			59.35
P*MM (men's chances of sharing an occupation with another man)			59.27
RC (relative crowding) (women – men)			19.22

SOURCE: Data for the 10 occupational groupings are from the March 1997 Current Population Survey (U.S. Department of Commerce, 1997b).

labor force into over 500 different types of work. Yet even these 500 units lump together many disparate situations in which some jobs are performed by men and other jobs typically employ women. Since the early 1980s, it has been established that specific job titles within specific companies are more segregated by sex than are occupations, even when occupations are divided by industry. In an influential work, Bielby and Baron (1984) showed that when job-level data were scrutinized, many firms approached complete segregation by sex. For example, Reskin and Roos (1990) showed that the occupation "bakers" should be best thought of as representing several related types of work. Bakers who work for grocery stores are typically women who bake frozen sheets of dough to make store-fresh rolls, breads, and cakes. Specialty bake shops, which pay bakers more than do supermarket chains, are more likely to employ men to make more specialized pastries. Thus, the national statistic that 46% of bakers are men does not fully capture the true level of gender differentiation within this field.

The results presented in Tables 7.2 and 7.3 document the increase in segregation that can be seen with more precise occupational measures. These data are drawn from the March 1997 Current Population Survey (CPS), a large sample of the working population that provides the most consistent and reliable estimates of labor force trends available. The top panel of results

TABLE 7.3   Measures of Segregation, 1990-1997, Based on Detailed (3-Digit)
Occupational Classifications

Measure	1990	1997
D (index of dissimilarity)	56.4	53.9
SSD (size-standardized index of dissimilarity)	59.6	60.1
P*WW (women's chances of sharing an occupation with another woman)	69.1	67.8
P*MM (men's chances of sharing an occupation with another man)	71.5	70.4
RC (relative crowding) (women – men)	9.6	8.2

SOURCE: Current Population Survey, 1990 and 1997 (U.S. Department of Commerce, 1997b, and earlier versions
in the same series).

displays the percentage of men and women in each of 10 broad occupational
groupings. Some of these patterns are no doubt familiar: Women represent
the majority of workers in clerical and retail sales positions, whereas men
represent the majority of those employed in skilled craft and transportation
jobs. However, some may find it surprising that women represent the majority
(54.2%) of professionals and that women have nearly reached parity with men
in managerial positions. Women represent 44.6% of managers, which is just
short of their 46.7% representation in the labor force.

These results reveal two important facts about occupational segregation
by sex. The first, as we have already mentioned, is that more detailed measures
of occupations will produce higher levels of segregation than will more
aggregated units of analysis. The second is that occupational segregation is
not a simple matter of women being concentrated in low-status occupations.
There are female-dominated occupations among low-, middle-, and relatively
high-status occupations, although very few are at the highest echelons of the
status hierarchy. Rather, occupational segregation is better thought of as the
concentration of women in low-paying occupations within each broad occupational group.

If sex segregation is measured across the 10 broad groupings displayed
in Table 7.2, then just over one-third (33.7%) of women would have to change
occupations to match the pattern of men in the labor force. However, if we
increase our precision in occupational measurement to 505 categories, we
then see (in Table 7.3) that over half of women (53.9%) would have to change
occupations to be distributed in the same manner as men.

The 505 detailed occupations are about the smallest unit of analysis that
can be considered with the CPS data. However, some other data sources allow
us to look even more closely at this phenomenon. Tomaskovic-Devey (1995)
conducted a survey of employees in North Carolina that included information
about respondents' job titles and found that over two-thirds of women would
have had to change jobs to be distributed in the same manner as men. This
figure was similar to that found by Petersen and Morgan (1995), who analyzed
job-level data from Department of Labor surveys.

Recent Trends in Sex Segregation in the United States

In 1997, just over half of women would have had to change (U.S. census detailed) occupations to be distributed in the same manner as men (see Table 7.3). The index of segregation was 53.9 in 1997, which means that 53.9% of women would have had to relocate to match men's occupational patterns. This figure strikes many who are unfamiliar with research in this area as surprisingly high. There is a widespread sense that most fields are equally open to men and women. The entry of women into such high-profile jobs as television news anchors, physicians, and lawyers has heightened the popular sense of the changes in women's roles. And there has been change.

But change is slower than is popularly believed. There are many female fields employing large numbers of women that have experienced little change. Secretarial work, nursing, and waiting on tables are largely female fields and employ far more women than law or medicine. Occupations that are still dominated by men include some professions, such as engineers and clergy; protective service occupations, such as police and firefighters; many craft occupations, such as carpenters, electricians, and plumbers; and transport occupations, such as truck drivers and taxi drivers. Thus, despite all the attention paid to women's entry into a few, relatively small, high-profile fields, many large occupations remain dominated by one sex or the other.

A second important conclusion evident in Table 7.3 is that the size standardized index of segregation was virtually unchanged between 1990 and 1997. In other words, had there been no change in the size of occupations, there would have been no trend toward greater gender integration in the occupational structure. Another way of putting this point is that all of the decline in sex segregation during the 1990s can be attributed to a shift in the distribution of occupations, that is, a growth in the size of relatively integrated fields, rather than to changes in the sex composition of specific fields.

Which fields grew and which declined? The more integrated occupational groups—professionals, technical workers, managers, and sales occupations—grew while the more segregated occupational groups—clerical workers and craft workers—declined in size. These shifts were often quite small in size, but their cumulative effect was sufficient to account for the modest declines in sex segregation during the 1990s.

A reader might wonder which (D or SSD) is the "right" statistic, or the more meaningful measure. I would suggest that they are complementary indicators, in that each helps to answer an important but related question. The (unweighted) index of dissimilarity indicates that there has been a modest continuing trend toward greater gender integration in the labor market, although at a slower rate than during the 1970s or 1980s. The size-standardized measure, however, shows that the only remaining momentum is due to changes in the occupational structure. In other words, there has been no further mixing of men and women within occupations other than that

TABLE 7.4   Sex Segregation by Educational Level, Based on Detailed Occupational
              Classifications, 1971-1997

Educational Level	1971	1981	1997	1971-1997
Less than high school	68.7	62.7	56.9	−11.8
High school graduate	65.6	62.9	60.7	−4.9
Some college	68.2	59.9	57.3	−10.9
College graduate	64.9	49.7	44.9	−20.0
Some postgraduate	61.5	42.0	43.7	−17.8

SOURCE: Current Population Surveys, 1971, 1981, and 1997 (U.S. Department of Commerce, 1997b, and earlier versions in the same series).
NOTE: Measures reported are unstandardized indexes of dissimilarity (D). Changes in detailed occupational classification make the 1971 results not strictly comparable to later figures.

produced by the growth of relatively integrated industries such as services and the decline of relatively segregated sectors such as manufacturing.

Intergroup contact measures indicate that both men and women typically share their occupation with other members of the same sex. Despite the fact that women represent 46% of the labor force, the average man is employed in an occupation with 70% men (P*MM = 70.4). Women typically find themselves in occupations where two out of three coworkers are women (P*WW = 67.8). There were slight increases in contact between men and women at work as the levels of segregation declined during the 1990s.

Women remain crowded in a more limited set of occupations than men (RC = 8.2 in 1997). However, there are good reasons to be cautious about this conclusion because men's occupations tend to be reported in more detail than women's occupations. If that were the case, the difference in concentration could be an artifact of the categories employed in the CPS data, rather than a true reflection of the range of choices made by men and women.

Table 7.4 provides estimates of segregation by sex within educational groups over three decades.[3] As recently as 1971, sex segregation was essentially evenly distributed by educational levels. At that time, there was nearly as much segregation between men and women with similar educational levels as there was in the labor force as a whole. Indeed, one may understand the historical emergence of occupational segregation in part as a response to the high levels of education attained by women. Segregation between many groups in society is often accomplished via the ostensibly neutral criterion of education: By limiting access to individuals with specific educational credentials, many with limited educational credentials are shut out. But the problem with men using this strategy against women is that women have had high levels of educational credentials for decades. Thus, the sex typing of occupations is needed to supplement selection based on educational credentials.

Since the early 1970s, declines in sex segregation have occurred most rapidly in the professions and management. The index of dissimilarity declined 20.0 points for college graduates, compared with 11.8 points for those without a high school degree. This development in part reflects important changes that have occurred in higher education. In 1960, women pursued teaching above all other fields of study as undergraduates, and few women went on to graduate and professional school. By 1985, business was the leading field of study for women obtaining bachelor's degrees, and women entered law school and other professional schools in steadily increasing numbers (J. A. Jacobs, 1995). The entry of women into the professions and managerial positions in part stems from this transformation in the type of education women have obtained. Thus, there is a kernel of truth in the popular view that women have gained an important place in the nation's professions.

International Comparisons

Sex segregation is high in many countries throughout the world, but precise comparisons are difficult because it is hard to obtain data from different countries that use comparable, detailed occupational coding systems. Studies that have been done have typically relied on a high degree of aggregation in occupations, and consequently uncertainty remains about what the relative standing of different countries would be if detailed and comparable measures were available.

Some international studies have been cross-sectional, whereas others have conducted longitudinal analyses. Cross-sectional studies show variations across countries, but suffer from uncertainty about the comparability of occupational coding schemes across countries (Charles, 1992). Longitudinal analyses avoid much of these difficulties by focusing on change in individual countries (Jacobs & Lim, 1992).

Yet international comparisons may be instructive in many respects. Some have suggested that countries with low levels of sex segregation do not necessarily exhibit gender equality in wages and, conversely, that nations with high levels of segregation sometimes have a smaller gender gap in wages. Japan represents the first case. Measures of occupational segregation in Japan are lower than in many other industrial countries (Brinton & Ngo, 1993),[4] whereas the gender gap in wages is quite high. In Sweden, sex segregation is relatively high but the gender gap in wages is small.

Blau and Kahn (1992) explain this paradox by calling attention to the way the overall structure of wages affects the earnings gap between men and women. They suggest that countries with limited wage dispersion favor women. Because women tend to be concentrated at the lower end of the wage spectrum, those countries where the bottom tail of the wage curve is compressed tend to exhibit a smaller gender gap in wages. Blau and Kahn's thesis helps to explain why the gender gap in wages in Sweden is relatively low despite the high levels of occupational sex segregation in the labor market. The compressed wage distribution in these countries brings up women's wages relative to men's, and more than compensates for the high degree of occupational differentiation by sex. Blau and Kahn's analysis of the wage structure reminds us that we should not focus on the effects of occupational segregation in isolation. It also reminds us that the structure of the labor market may be as important to study as individual attributes associated with personal choices. New research on the impact of sex segregation on wages, discussed below, further reinforces this conclusion.

Gornick and Jacobs (1998) discuss the role of government employment as it influences opportunities for working women. In most industrial countries, women are overrepresented in government employment, yet the size of the public sector varies substantially from country to country. In some countries, such as Sweden, most women work in the public sector, whereas in other countries, such as the United States, government employment represents a modest fraction of the labor force. Cross-national analyses indicate marked variation across liberal, conservative, and social democratic welfare states in the size of the government sector and its impact on women workers, but reveal a number of uniformities as well. Gornick and Jacobs report that public sector workers earn more, on average, than those working in the private sector in most countries in their sample and that most of the public sector earnings advantages are concentrated in the lower end of the earnings distribution. Yet the effect of public employment on the overall gender gap in earnings is limited in most countries. This occurs because those countries where the government sector is the largest and thus has the most potential to affect the wages of women have the lowest public sector wages, relative to the private sector. There appears to be a trade-off between a small public sector with good wages and a large public sector with lower wages.

Sex Segregation and Earnings

Much of the interest in occupational sex segregation stems from the low wages paid in female-dominated occupations. Bianchi (1995), citing the work of Cotter, DeFiore, Hermsen, Kowalewski, and Vanneman (1995), concludes that the effect of occupational segregation on earnings in the United States has declined. She suggests that only 14% of the sex gap in wages is now due to occupational segregation by sex (Bianchi, 1995, p. 126).

But this is just one part of the story. Bianchi considered occupational segregation but not differences between women and men in industry. Sorensen (1989) showed that adding the effects of industrial segregation nearly doubled the effect of workplace segregation on wages. Sorensen estimated that 20% of the gender gap in wages was due to the sex segregation of occupations, and another 16% was due to the sex segregation of industries. The combined effect, 36%, was substantially higher than the effect of occupation alone.

But this too is an understatement of the effects of sex segregation in the workplace because of imprecise measurement. As noted above, occupational classifications, even detailed ones, typically lump together disparate types of work and mask much of the segregation of men and women on the job. Most studies do not fully capture these effects because the data are reported at the occupational level, rather than as a description of the particular conditions of an employee's job. Several studies have estimated the effects of job-level segregation on wages (Petersen & Morgan, 1995; Tomaskovic-Devey, 1995). This research shows that a very substantial proportion of the sex gap in wages is due to women's concentration in female-dominated occupations.

But even these job-level analyses understate the significance of occupational segregation by sex. A recent analysis by Cotter, DeFiore, Hermsen, Kowalewski, and Vanneman (1997a) showed that the concentration of women into female-dominated occupations affects the pay of all women, not just those in female-dominated fields. Consider an example of how women moving into male-dominated fields might indirectly help to increase the wages of women in a more traditional female-dominated profession. As women pursue business degrees instead of education degrees, they move into a traditionally male field and stand to earn higher wages. But, in doing so, they gradually reduce the pool of new teachers, thus driving up the wages of teachers. Thus, the earnings of women across the board may benefit from even a modest decline in occupational segregation by sex.

Why do female-dominated jobs pay less? Two explanations have been most influential: crowding and culture. The crowding view holds that restricting women from entering large numbers of occupations results in large numbers of women available for work in female-dominated fields such as child care, retail sales, and waiting on tables, thereby depressing wages in these fields (Bergmann, 1986; Edgeworth, 1922; Parcel, 1989). The analysis discussed above by Cotter et al. (1997a) suggests that restricting women to female-dominated occupations not only reduces wages in these occupations but reduces women's earnings in male-dominated fields as well.

A more recently developed view holds that our culture tends to devalue women's work. Much of the activity performed by women is invisible or is held to be of marginal value (Steinberg, 1990). Occupations that score high on such feminine values as nurturance are not accorded additional compensation but, instead, are devalued and are accorded low wages (England, Herbert, Kilbourne, Reid, & Medgal, 1994). It should be noted that these explanations persist after educational investments, which are emphasized by the human capital school of economics, are taken into account. It should also be noted that the crowding and cultural explanations are not mutually exclusive.

One explanation that has not held up under scrutiny is the compensating differential hypothesis. This view holds that female-dominated fields are paid less because they involve work that is more pleasant and less risky than that found in many male-dominated fields. The higher wages in men's positions, it is held, represent monetary compensation to offset the countervailing differences in working conditions. Hence, the wage difference represents a "compensating differential" that offsets the differential in working conditions.

There are two principal problems with this thesis. The first is that careful scrutiny reveals that many female-dominated occupations are associated with undesirable working conditions. Women's jobs are more likely to involve emotional stress and to require cleaning others' dirt, whereas men's jobs are more likely to involve working in hot or cold conditions and to require strenuous physical activity. People often assume that men's jobs involve more risk of injury, due to working with machinery, but some women's jobs, such as nursing, involve risk due to lifting heavy patients and exposure to potentially serious illness through needle sticks.

The second is that neither male-dominated nor female-dominated occupations necessarily receives a significant monetary bonus due to unfavorable working conditions. In a detailed study of working conditions, Jacobs and Steinberg (1990) found that unpleasant working conditions often lowered the wages associated with the job, rather than raising them as the compensating differentials thesis would predict.[5]

Explaining Sex Segregation

Why do men and women work in different occupations? Polachek (1979) offered an economic explanation. He suggested that occupational sex segregation reflects the rational choices of individual men and women seeking to maximize their lifetime earnings. Because women tend to interrupt their careers, they want to make as much as possible early in their careers to maximize their lifetime earnings. Given their expected pattern of discontinuous lifetime labor force participation, it would make sense to choose jobs that had higher initial wages but lower earnings trajectories than would men. The problem with this idea is that those working in female-dominated fields earn less at the outset than they would have if they pursued employment in a male-dominated field (England, 1982). Sex segregation thus produces low initial wages in female-dominated fields, which fall further and further behind wages in male-dominated fields as workers' experience grows. The sex segregation of occupations thus cannot be attributed to the rational choices of women seeking to maximize their lifetime earnings.

Perhaps the most common explanation for occupational sex segregation is that women choose different occupations because they are socialized to prefer different types of work from men. For example, girls play with baby dolls and learn to take care of others, becoming elementary school teachers and nurses, and boys play with trucks and building blocks, becoming truck drivers and engineers. There is much personal experience and statistical evidence to support this view. Most adults can recall instances in which they were encouraged as children to conform to prevailing norms of gender-appropriate behavior and to pursue gender-appropriate roles as adults. Statistical evidence is not hard to come by as well. For example, occupational aspirations of young men and women are roughly as segregated as the occupational structure (Jacobs, 1989b; Marini & Brinton, 1984). Thus, many believe that sex-role socialization plays a crucial role in the reproduction of gender inequality in the workplace.

One problem with this view is that aspirations are not as stable as assumed. Occupational choices shift frequently, and often cross sex-typed boundaries. In earlier research (Jacobs, 1989b), I explored the strength of the connection between sex-typed aspirations and subsequent occupational choices. The great majority of young women change the specific occupation to which they aspire, and among these changers, there was little connection between early aspirations, later aspirations, and subsequent occupational choices. Similar patterns of mobility were found among college students, who frequently shift between male-dominated and female-dominated majors, and in the labor force, where mobility between male-dominated and female-dominated occupations is surprisingly common. Subsequent research has confirmed these patterns in the United States (Levine & Zimmerman, 1995; Rosenfeld & Spenner, 1995), but research conducted in the United Kingdom and Germany reports much lower levels of mobility (Blossfeld, 1987; S. C. Jacobs, 1995).

A second problem with the socialization thesis is that it implies that change will occur only when a new generation reared in a more egalitarian manner replaces those currently in the labor force. Demographers call this process of change a "cohort replacement process," because a new generation (cohort) must gradually take the place of older individuals for change to occur. Yet change also occurs as individuals age, and not simply as a result of cohort replacement. Indeed, during the 1970s and 1980s there was about as much change in occupational sex segregation experienced by cohorts as there was in the labor market overall. In other words, groups of women (and men) remain more adaptable during their careers than the socialization perspective would imply. People's attitudes are not set in stone, but remain flexible in important respects. People appear to remain open to change as new opportunities arise.

Table 7.5 displays data on occupational sex segregation spanning the 1970s, 1980s, and 1990s by age group. It is evident from these results that there have been declines in sex segregation not just among new entrants to the labor force but for every age group through age 65, the typical retirement age. It is true that the changes have been largest for the youngest groups, but it is remarkable that there have been declines at the older ages as well.

These findings suggest that, at least in some respects, sex-role attitudes are not as firmly implanted in individuals' psyches as the socialization thesis assumes. As opportunities for women expanded, there were many women willing to take advantage of them. Thus, despite significant attrition of women

TABLE 7.5   Sex Segregation by Age Group, Based on Detailed Occupational
              Classifications

Age Group	1971	1981	1990	1997	1971-1997
16-24	67.4	59.4	57.5	54.2	−13.2
25-34	68.4	64.5	55.6	54.1	−14.3
35-44	66.9	62.7	57.4	56.8	−10.1
45-54	67.5	63.1	59.1	56.1	−11.4
54-64	68.2	64.1	62.6	59.6	−8.6
65+	64.1	63.2	68.0	64.1	0.0

SOURCE: Current Population Surveys, 1971, 1981, 1990, and 1997 (U.S. Department of Commerce, 1997b, and earlier versions in the same series).
NOTE: Measures reported are unstandardized indexes of dissimilarity (D). Changes in detailed occupational classification make the 1971 results not strictly comparable to later figures.

from male-dominated fields, over the past three decades there has been a net addition of women making midcareer moves into male-dominated fields.

Thus, socialization is not sufficient to account for sex segregation without taking into account discrimination by bosses and coworkers. I prefer to think of sex-role socialization as the early stages of the social controls that reinforce distinctions between men and women. Social pressures later in life, in school and at work, combine with socialization to form a lifelong system of social control. Continued pressure throughout the life course maintains gender distinctions in the labor force. When these pressures abate for a period of time, as they did in the 1970s and 1980s, evidence of change can be found throughout the life course.

Whereas most theories of sex segregation focus on one decisive life stage or causal factor, it seems to me that a multiplicity of forces contributes to the maintenance of sex segregation. I see sex segregation as a system of social control that endures from early childhood throughout individuals' careers. There are feedback loops from current to future segregation—it is hard for young individuals to see a sex-segregation system and not take that into account in forming their career plans. At the same time, the links between aspirations, education, and careers may be slippery and imperfect. However, in countries such as Germany, there are tight connections between the early life decisions of students, their subsequent education, and their ultimate occupational destinations. In the United States, there is room for shifting, shuffling, and resorting for those in the occupational systems as well as those about to enter it. At the same time, social pressure to conform to sex-appropriate norms does not end with early-life socialization but continues throughout people's lives. The result is a system of sex segregation with room for substantial individual mobility but that is nonetheless resilient enough to endure all but the most dramatic combination of social and cultural changes.

Prospects for the 21st Century

I expect significant levels of occupational segregation to persist in the early decades of the 21st century for several reasons. The rate of decline in occupational segregation appears to be slowing. During the 1990s, the principal declines resulted from shifts in the relative size of occupations, rather than an increased mixing of men and women within occupations. And after two decades of steep declines, the sex segregation of college majors has hit a plateau since the mid-1980s (J. A. Jacobs, 1995). As a result, I expect to see the rate of gender integration of the professions and management positions slow in coming years. Because the professions and management have been a major locus of gender integration in the labor force, this trend does not bode well for future gender integration. Finally, in recent years the gender gap in wages appears to be leveling off again. This pessimistic prediction reflects the fact that basic organizational changes in society are needed to facilitate further progress for gender equality in the labor market. We are currently in a period of political retrenchment, with bold new proposals unlikely to gain serious attention. It will take another wave of reforms like those initiated during the 1960s—changes that affect our political, cultural, social, and economic systems—to produce another major decline in occupational segregation.

Although the broad outlines of sex segregation remain clear, there is much additional room for research on the processes that produce and maintain sex segregation. Specifically, it would be useful to have more research on specific occupations, on comparative patterns across countries, on the reasons for the low pay of women's work, on the processes of occupational segregation and integration, and on the formation and change in occupational aspirations. Because sex segregation is likely to persist for many years, this topic will be of enduring interest to scholars interested in understanding gender inequality in the labor market.

Appendix: Formulas for Various Indexes of Segregation

1. The formula for D, the index of dissimilarity, is

$$D = \sum_{i=1}^{n} |(W_i/W) - (M_i/M)|/2,$$

where W_i is the number of women in occupation i, W is the sum of women in all occupations, M_i is the number of men in occupation i, and M is the sum of men in all occupations.

2. The formula for SSD, the size-standardized index of dissimilarity, is

$$SSD = \sum_{i=1}^{n} |(PF_i/\sum_{i=1}^{n} PF_i) - PM_i / \sum_{i=1}^{n} [PM_i]|/2,$$

where PF_i is the proportion female of occupation i, and PM_i is the proportion male of occupation i.

3. The formula for P*WW, women's chances of sharing an occupation with another woman, is

$$P*WW = \sum_{i=1}^{n} (W_i/W)(PF_i).$$

One can calculate the same measure for men's contact with other men, P*MM, by substituting M_i for W_i and M for W, and substituting PM for PF. Women's contact with men, P*WM, can be calculated by subtracting P*WW from 1, because P*WW and P*WM sum to 1. P*WM = 1 – P*WW. Similarly, men's contact with women, P*MW, can be obtained by subtracting P*MM from 1. P*MW = 1 – P*MM.

4. The formula for C, the index of concentration, is

$$C = \sum_{i=1}^{n} |(W_i/W) - (1/n)|/2.$$

This formula gives the concentration of women, relative to an equal distribution across occupations. One can calculate the same statistic for men, and then subtract the two, thus obtaining the relative concentration of women compared to men.

Notes

1. Another approach, decomposition, is designed to achieve the same objective. This technique divides changes into a component due to occupational shifts and a component due to changes in the level of integration within occupations. See Blau and Hendricks (1979) for an application.

2. Imagine one scenario in which women are crowded into a single occupation, whereas men are distributed across a range of other occupations. In a second scenario, it is men who are all crowded into a single occupation, and women are distributed across a range of jobs. In both cases, the index of dissimilarity would be at its maximum, 100, but these cases clearly differ in terms of their implications for gender equity. Measures of concentration or crowding help to distinguish these two cases.

3. These are unstandardized indexes of dissimilarity (D), not size-standardized measures (SSD).

4. I suspect that job-level segregation would be quite high in Japan and that the relatively low level of segregation stems in part from combining disparate jobs into occupational aggregates.

5. Ross and Mirowsky (1996) consider a different spin on the compensating differentials thesis. They explore whether women get more psychological gratification from relationships and less from money. They find that women do receive more interpersonal rewards than men and that there is negative correlation between interpersonal and financial rewards. However, they did not find that women prefer interpersonal rewards over money. They found no differences between men and women in the emotional gratification garnered from these two categories of job rewards.

Part III

Organizational, Group, and Interpersonal Processes

Chapter 8

Gender Bias in Interviewers' Evaluations of Applicants

When and How Does It Occur?

Laura M. Graves

During the past 25 years, researchers have devoted considerable attention to examining the effects of gender on employment decisions, resulting in a substantial body of evidence. Research on this topic began in the 1970s, galvanized by a growing interest in the psychology of sex differences (e.g., Maccoby & Jacklin, 1974), the development of a social psychological perspective on gender (e.g., Deaux, 1976), and government legislation forbidding gender discrimination in employment (e.g., the United States' Civil Rights Act of 1964, the United Kingdom's Sex Discrimination Act). Most research has focused on gender discrimination in the employment interview, perhaps because of the widespread use of the interview in the United States and Europe (Dipboye, 1992).

Several reviews of research on gender discrimination in the interview have been published. However, no substantive reviews have appeared since 1989 and much new research has been conducted. This chapter reviews research on gender bias in employment interviewers' evaluations of applicants. A brief summary of earlier reviews of the literature is provided, followed by a detailed review of recent research. Suggestions to guide future research are also offered.

Previous Reviews

Between 1979 and 1989, eight reviews of the effect of gender on interviewers' judgments were published. Richard Arvey and his colleagues catalogued the results of experimental and field studies in four different narrative reviews (Arvey, 1979; Arvey & Campion, 1982; Arvey & Faley, 1988; Campion & Arvey, 1989). Powell (1987) conducted a comprehensive narrative review of 34 experimental and field studies, and Harris (1989) reviewed (also narrative) 10 investigations conducted in the 1980s. In addition, Olian, Schwab, and Haberfeld (1988) and Tosi and Einbender (1985) used meta-analysis to quantitatively synthesize gender effects reported in experimental research.

Four key issues were addressed: (1) To what extent does gender bias occur? (2) What variables moderate the effect of applicant gender on interviewers' judgments? (3) What are the underlying processes by which gender discrimination in the interview occurs? and (4) How does research methodology affect the nature of research findings?

To What Extent Does Gender Bias Occur?

The eight reviews failed to provide a decisive answer concerning the extent to which gender bias occurs. Whereas Arvey (1979) suggests that females tend to receive lower evaluations than males, later narrative reviews (Arvey & Campion, 1982; Arvey & Faley, 1988; Campion & Arvey, 1989; Powell, 1987) are more tentative about the prevalence of bias. In fact, Harris (1989) concludes that studies conducted in the 1980s show little evidence of discrimination against women, perhaps due to the realistic settings and stimuli used in the particular studies he reviews, or to a decline in discrimination.

In contrast, Olian et al. (1988) found that applicant gender explained 4% of the variance in evaluations of applicants, with males receiving more positive evaluations than females. The mean effect of applicant gender on interviewers' evaluations was .41, corresponding to a correlation of .20 between gender and selection decisions. The discrepancy between these findings and the results of narrative reviews conducted during the same time period may be due, at least in part, to the fact that Olian et al.'s meta-analysis focused exclusively on experimental research, whereas the narrative reviews included both field and experimental studies.

What Variables Moderate the Effect of Applicant Gender on Interviewers' Judgments?

Previous reviews (Arvey & Campion, 1982; Arvey & Faley, 1988; Campion & Arvey, 1989) identified several characteristics of applicants, recruiters, and situations that may moderate the occurrence of sex bias in interviews.

Applicant characteristics. Two applicant characteristics, qualifications and physical attractiveness, received attention in early reviews (Arvey, 1979; Arvey & Faley, 1988). There was little support for the notion that highly qualified females, who may be threatening to males, are evaluated less favorably than highly qualified males. Investigations of whether physical attractiveness has differential effects for male and female applicants yielded mixed results. However, two studies found that attractiveness was detrimental when female applicants applied for jobs that were typically held by males (Cash, Gillen, & Burns, 1977; Heilman & Saruwatari, 1979).

Recruiter characteristics. Early reviews also considered the moderating effects of recruiter gender and personality. They offered little support for the idea that recruiter gender influences the occurrence of applicant gender effects (Arvey, 1979; Powell, 1987). Two studies found, however, that gender bias was most likely to occur when interviewers were authoritarian (Simas & McCarrey, 1979) or believed in traditional sex-role stereotypes (Sharp & Post, 1980).

Situational factors. One situational factor, the sex type of the job, received a great deal of attention in early reviews. Although numerous studies tested the notion that women who apply for male-typed jobs (i.e., jobs that are typically held by men) are more likely to be victims of discrimination than women who apply for female-typed jobs (i.e., jobs that are typically held by women), the reviews did not offer consistent conclusions about the results of these studies. Olian et al.'s (1988) statistical test of the moderating effect of sex type of job yielded nonsignificant results; however, the researchers note that the preponderance of male-typed jobs in the sample affected the test's validity. Powell (1987) notes that the results of studies that systematically varied the sex type of the job are mixed. In contrast, Arvey (1979) and Campion and Arvey (1989) conclude that interviewers seek a match between the sex type of the job and the sex of the applicant.

Only three studies focused on the effects of situational factors other than the sex type of the job. These studies found that bias against female applicants was most likely to occur when women comprised 25% or less of the applicant pool (Heilman, 1980) or when the prospective subordinates of a female candidate were male (Rose & Andiappan, 1978). Also, when organizations had strong equal opportunity policies, evaluators exhibited bias against females by recommending that they receive lower starting salaries than males (Rosen & Mericle, 1979). Generally, the reviewers note the need for more research in this area (e.g., Arvey, 1979; Arvey & Faley, 1988).

What Are the Underlying Processes by Which Gender Discrimination in the Interview Occurs?

As early as 1979, Arvey noted the need to examine the underlying processes by which gender discrimination in the interview occurs. By the time of Campion and Arvey's (1989) review, researchers had just begun to explore this topic. For instance, Binning, Goldstein, Garcia, and Scattaregia (1988) examined the effect of applicant gender on whether evaluators chose questioning strategies that were designed to confirm or disconfirm their initial impressions of applicants. Their findings indicated that student respondents preferred disconfirmatory questioning strategies when interviewing candidates of the opposite sex. In addition, Graves and Powell (1988) tested whether the applicant's similarity to the recruiter and likability mediated the effect of applicant gender on recruiters' evaluations of applicants. The results indicated that applicant gender did not affect recruiters' evaluations; however, perceived similarity and liking had large effects on evaluations of applicants.

How Does Research Methodology Affect the Nature of Research Findings?

Early reviews raised a number of concerns about the methodology used in research on gender bias in the interview. In particular, the reviews suggest that findings vary as a function of the amount of information study participants receive about applicants, the nature of the sample, the study design, and the realism of the stimulus materials.

Amount of information. Several of the reviews stressed the need for researchers to provide participants with a realistic amount of information about job applicants (Arvey, 1979; Arvey & Faley, 1988; Campion & Arvey, 1989; Powell, 1987; Tosi & Einbender, 1985). In real interview situations, interviewers have considerable information about candidates (e.g., application materials, cover letters, references, transcripts, and answers to interview questions). Yet, in most interview studies, participants are given limited information about hypothetical applicants. Because reliance on stereotypes and other cognitive shortcuts increases when information is limited, failing to provide participants with adequate information about applicants may lead to gender bias (Tosi & Einbender, 1985). In fact, Tosi and Einbender demonstrated that discrimination is less likely to occur when raters are given four or more pieces of information about the applicant as opposed to three or fewer pieces.

Nature of sample. Also of concern was whether the extensive use of student subjects limits the generalizability of research on gender bias in the interview (Arvey, 1979; Arvey & Campion, 1982; Olian et al., 1988; Powell, 1987). Although the reviews generally criticize the use of students, the meta-analysis conducted by Olian et al. suggests that the nature of the sample does not moderate the effect of applicant sex on raters' evaluations of applicants.

Study design. Examining the effect of study design, Arvey (1979) suggested that within-subjects designs, which allow subjects to evaluate and compare multiple applicants, may be more likely to yield applicant gender effects than between-subjects designs, which expose subjects to a single applicant. Furthermore, the fact that more degrees of freedom are available in within-subjects designs increases the likelihood of significant findings. The results of Olian et al.'s (1988) meta-analysis indicate that sex bias is more likely to occur in studies that use within-subjects designs. Because interviewers typically evaluate more than one applicant for a position, such designs mirror the real world.

Realism of stimulus materials. In many of the studies conducted prior to 1989, researchers asked candidates to evaluate "paper people" (e.g., bogus résumés or applications). The reviews note that paper-people techniques are not representative of real-world interview situations and may not yield meaningful results (Arvey, 1979; Campion & Arvey, 1989; Powell, 1987). Video-based studies and field research on real interviews are proposed as alternatives.

Summary

Past reviews have not provided a definitive answer concerning the extent of sex bias in interviewers' judgments of applicants, although several potential moderators, including the attractiveness of the applicant, the recruiter's personality, the sex type of the job, the sex composition of the applicant pool, and the nature of the organization's equal opportunity policies were identified. The reviews also note that researchers started to explore the processes that underlie sex bias in the interview.

Several methodological issues were raised in the reviews. For instance, the reviews suggest that raters who receive limited information about applicants are more likely to engage in discrimination. There also was some agreement that within-subjects designs, which mirror real employment decisions, are likely to evoke discrimination. In addition, overreliance on paper-people techniques and student subjects may limit the generalizability of research findings.

Recent Research

A great deal of new research has been conducted on the effect of applicant gender on employment interviewers' judgments. Table 8.1 identifies 23 recent studies that were not included in earlier reviews of the literature. Twenty of the studies were conducted in the United States, two were conducted in the Netherlands, and one was conducted in Australia. Sixteen of the studies were

TABLE 8.1   Summary of Recent Research on Gender Bias in the Employment Interview

Study	Design	Stimulus	Number of Applicants That Participants Evaluated	Nature of Sample	Key Findings
Atwater and Van Fleet (1997)	Experimental	Information packets containing detailed applicant descriptions	8	U.S. students	Female, rather than male, applicants were preferred for female-typed jobs.
Buttner and McEnally (1996)	Experimental	Résumés and interview scripts	1	U.S. corporate executives	Effectiveness of interview behaviors differed for male and female applicants.
Cable and Judge (1997)	Nonexperimental	Real applicants at campus placement facility	Not applicable	U.S. campus recruiters	Female applicants were more likely to be hired than male applicants.
Crow, Fok, and Hartman (1995)	Experimental	Case study describing applicants	8	U.S. full-time employees	Rankings of applicants were a function of gender, race, and sexual orientation.
Forsythe (1990)	Experimental	Soundless videotapes of applicants	4	U.S. managers and professionals	Female applicants who wore masculine clothing were viewed more favorably than those who did not.
Gallois, Callan, and Palmer (1992)	Experimental	Videotapes of interviews	6	Australian personnel officers	Assertive males and females were viewed as suitable for the job. Nonassertive females were favored over nonassertive males.
Glick, Zion, and Nelson (1988)	Experimental	Résumés	1	Predominantly male U.S. managers and professionals	Exposure to personal information about applicants reduced stereotyping, but discrimination still occurred.
Graves and Powell (1995)	Nonexperimental	Real applicants at college placement facility	Not applicable	U.S. campus recruiters	Gender similarity negatively affected female recruiters' evaluations of applicants.
Graves and Powell (1996)	Nonexperimental	Real applicants at college placement facility	Not applicable	U.S. campus recruiters	Gender similarity had a positive effect on female recruiters' ratings of applicants.

Author (year)	Design	Stimulus materials	n	Sample	Findings
Hitt and Barr (1989)	Experimental	Videotapes of interviews	16	U.S. managers	Managers used job-irrelevant demographic variables to evaluate applicants. Interactions played an important role in selection decisions.
Kacmar and Hochwarter (1995)	Nonexperimental	Mock interviews with student applicants	Not applicable	U.S. employees at a *Fortune* 500 organization	Interviewer and applicant gender did not affect behavioral interactions in the interview or outcomes.
Katz (1987)	Experimental	Completed applications	1	U.S. students	Organizational diversity climate affected evaluations of male and female applicants.
Konrad and Pfeffer (1991)	Nonexperimental	Not applicable	Not applicable	Data from the College and University Personnel Association's compensation surveys of U.S. universities	Women were selected when the position was typically held by a woman, the organization had a higher percentage of women administrators, and the previous jobholder was female.
Marlowe, Schneider, and Nelson (1996)	Experimental	Résumés and pictures	4	Supervisors and managers at a U.S. financial services company	Attractive candidates were preferred over unattractive candidates. Unattractive women were seen as less suitable than all other candidates.
McRae (1994)	Experimental	Résumés	1	Black managers in the United States	Black men were evaluated less favorably for a female-typed job than Black women.
Perry (1994), Studies 2 and 3	Experimental	Computerized applicant profiles	6	U.S. students	Applicants whose gender matched the sex type of the job were preferred, but only when they possessed job-related characteristics.
Pingitore, Dugoni, Tindale, and Spring (1994)	Experimental	Videotapes of interviews	1	U.S. students	Overweight women were evaluated less favorably than overweight men.

(continued)

151

TABLE 8.1 Continued

Study	Design	Stimulus	Number of Applicants That Participants Evaluated	Nature of Sample	Key Findings
Sheets and Bushardt (1994)	Experimental	Résumés	1 or 2	U.S. students	Participants did not seek a match between the gender of the applicant and the sex type of the job when the applicant was not qualified.
Van Vianen and Van Schie (1995)	Nonexperimental	Mock interviews of Dutch college students	Not applicable	Staff members at a Dutch university	Descriptions of ideal and accepted applicants were similar. Masculinity/femininity determined evaluations of female, but not male, applicants.
Van Vianen and Willemsen (1992)	Nonexperimental	Real applicants for academic and professional positions at a Dutch university	Not applicable	Members of selection boards at a Dutch University	Descriptions of ideal and accepted applicants were similar. Masculinity/femininity determined evaluations of female, but not male, applicants.
White and White (1994)	Experimental	Application forms and information from a phone reference check	1	U.S. students	No main or interaction effects involving applicant sex were found.
Williams, Radefeld, Binning, and Sudak (1993), Study 2	Experimental	Cover letters and résumés	1	U.S. college recruiters	No main or interaction effects involving applicant sex were found.
Zebrowitz, Tenenbaum, and Goldstein (1991), Studies 1 and 2	Experimental	Résumés and photographs	8	U.S. students	In Study 1, females were preferred for a male-typed job. In Study 2, males were preferred for a male-typed job and females were preferred for a female-typed job, especially when applicants were highly qualified.

experimental and seven were nonexperimental. Of the experimental studies, about half used professionals as participants, and the remaining half used students. Experimental studies continued to rely heavily on paper people; only 3 of the 15 studies used videotape methodology with sound to present applicants to the participants. Roughly half presented the participants with more than one applicant and half presented the participants with a single applicant. The seven nonexperimental studies included two studies of hiring decisions for academic or professional positions at universities, three studies of corporate recruiters' evaluations of applicants during campus interviews, and two studies based on mock interviews conducted in corporate or university settings.

Investigators addressed three of the issues raised in earlier reviews: (1) To what extent does gender bias occur? (2) What variables moderate the effect of applicant gender on interviewers' judgments? and (3) What are the underlying processes by which gender discrimination in the interview occurs?

To What Extent Does Gender Bias Occur?

As before, there is no definitive answer concerning the extent of sex bias in interviewers' judgments of applicants. The nonexperimental studies yielded mixed results. A study of applicants for faculty and staff positions at a Dutch university found discrimination against women (Van Vianen & Willemsen, 1992), whereas studies of campus recruiting in the United States revealed favoritism toward women by all recruiters (Cable & Judge, 1997), favoritism toward women by female recruiters (Graves & Powell, 1996), and favoritism toward men by female recruiters (Graves & Powell, 1995). Finally, a study of mock interviews at a corporation in the United States revealed no effect of applicant gender (Kacmar & Hochwarter, 1995), whereas one conducted at a Dutch university revealed favoritism toward women (Van Vianen & Van Schie, 1995).

The results of the 16 experimental studies were equally ambiguous. Although two revealed no main or interaction effects of applicant gender on interviewers' evaluations, most found complex interactions between gender and a variety of other variables, making it difficult to assess the extent of gender discrimination. In fact, Hitt and Barr (1989) note the important role that such interactions play in selection decisions by observing that "questions of discrimination in selection are not simple" (p. 58).

What Variables Moderate the Effect of Applicant Gender on Interviewers' Judgments?

The prevalence of complex interactions between applicant gender and other factors suggests that the critical issue is not whether gender bias occurs, but under what conditions it occurs. Recent research provides a wealth of information about the factors related to the applicant, recruiter, and situation that moderate the effect of gender on interviewers' evaluations of applicants.

Applicant characteristics and behaviors. Researchers continued to examine the effect of applicant qualifications and appearance and also began to look at the moderating effects of applicants' demographic characteristics and behavior. Generally, research evidence indicates that applicant qualifications do not moderate the effect of applicant gender on interviewers' evaluations. For instance, White and White (1994) found that gender bias did not vary as a function of whether the applicant's ability was proven or unproven.

Recent research explored whether several aspects of the applicant's appearance affected the occurrence of gender bias, including physical attractiveness, weight, and clothing. For instance, Marlowe, Schneider, and Nelson (1996), who examined managers' evaluations of the paper credentials and photographs of applicants for a management training program, found that men were preferred over women and attractive candidates were preferred over unattractive ones. However, unattractive women were routinely viewed as less suitable for hire and less promotable than were other candidates. This finding contradicted earlier research by Heilman and Saruwatari (1979), which indicated that unattractive women were preferred over attractive women for male-typed management positions.

In addition, Pingitore, Dugoni, Tindale, and Spring (1994) studied the effects of applicant gender, body weight, and the extent of client interaction required by the job on students' evaluations of applicants based on videotaped interviews and résumés. For normal-weight applicants, who were preferred to overweight ones, gender had no effect; however, overweight men were more likely to be selected than overweight women.

Finally, Forsythe (1990) examined the effect of clothing masculinity on evaluations of female applicants for management positions. Participants from the banking and retail industries evaluated four soundless videotapes, which varied the masculinity of the applicants' clothing. Masculine clothing led to more positive hiring recommendations and enhanced raters' perceptions of candidates' self-reliance, aggressiveness, dynamism, and forcefulness.

Taken together, these findings suggest that women who are unattractive, obese, or dressed in a feminine manner are likely to be evaluated unfavorably. Moreover, women who are unattractive or overweight are more likely to be victims of discrimination than are men who possess such characteristics.

One new issue that researchers began to address was the possibility that applicant gender interacts with other applicant demographic variables. In particular, Crow, Fok, and Hartman (1995) looked at raters' decisions about eight hypothetical candidates representing all the combinations of gender, race (Black, White), and sexual orientation. The most preferred candidate was the White heterosexual female, followed by the Black heterosexual female, the Black heterosexual male and the White heterosexual male (second), and the White gay male and the White gay female (third); the least preferred applicants were the Black gay male and the Black gay female. Although the interactions between the demographic variables were not tested formally, the results suggest that race, gender, and sexual orientation interacted to determine evaluations of applicants.

Researchers also examined whether applicants' job search or interview behaviors moderated the effect of gender on evaluations of applicants. A study by Williams, Radefeld, Binning, and Sudak (1993) that examined the effects of applicant availability (easy vs. hard to get), gender, and qualifications on college recruiters' evaluations of hypothetical applicants revealed no effects of applicant gender and no interactions between the applicant's gender and availability.

Also, Buttner and McEnally (1996) and Gallois, Callan, and Palmer (1992) studied the effects of applicant communication style and gender on professionals' reactions to hypothetical candidates. Buttner and McEnally found that males who used assertive influence tactics (e.g., demands, pressure) were more likely to be hired than those who used rational tactics (e.g., logic, detailed plans), whereas rational females are more likely to be hired than assertive females. In a somewhat different study, Gallois et al. found that although recruiters viewed assertive candidates of both sexes as being highly suitable for the job, nonassertive females were viewed as more suitable than nonassertive males. Although these mixed findings do not allow us to reach any definitive conclusions, they do provide support for the general notion that interviewers' reactions to applicants' behaviors vary as a function of applicant gender.

In sum, recent research suggests that the physical appearance of the applicant moderates the effect of applicant gender on interviewers' judgments. Also, applicants' demographic characteristics other than gender, as well as the extent of assertiveness, may interact with applicant gender to determine how applicants are evaluated.

Recruiter characteristics. Recent research focused on the effects of recruiter demographic characteristics and personality on the occurrence of sex bias. Spurred by research in the area of relational demography (e.g., Tsui & O'Reilly, 1989), researchers began to examine how the similarity between applicant and recruiter gender affects evaluations of applicants. Generally, the relational demography literature suggests that demographic similarity between interviewers and applicants should lead to favorable interview interactions and judgments.

Three studies provided evidence on the effects of gender similarity on evaluations of applicants. In a study of Australian recruiters, Gallois et al. (1992) found that gender similarity affected female, but not male, recruiters' perceptions of applicants. Although female recruiters saw themselves as more similar to female than male applicants, gender similarity did not affect hiring recommendations. Likewise, two field studies conducted by Graves and Powell (1995, 1996) indicate that gender similarity affects female, but not male, recruiters' perceptions of applicants. Surprisingly, in 1995, Graves and Powell found that female recruiters saw male applicants as more qualified than female applicants; however, the 1996 study showed that female recruiters preferred female to male applicants. Graves and Powell (1996) suggest that situational factors (e.g., organizational emphasis on managing diversity) might account for the difference in the results of the two studies. Thus, gender similarity effects may vary as a function of the recruiter's gender and the situation.

Researchers also explored how managerial experience affected the likelihood of gender bias in the interview, with mixed results. Crow et al. (1995) found no differences in managers' and nonmanagers' evaluations of applicants who varied in gender, race, and sexual orientation. Atwater and Van Fleet (1997) found that students with prior managerial experience engaged in *more* bias against male applicants for a female-typed job than those who did not have such experience. In contrast, Marlowe et al. (1996) found that experienced managers exhibited *less* bias against unattractive applicants than did inexperienced managers. However, even experienced managers rated the unattractive, female applicant as least suitable for the job. Clearly, these three studies do not provide sufficient information to form any conclusions about the moderating effect of managerial experience.

Researchers examined the effects of several personality variables on the tendency to exhibit bias. Katz's (1987) examination of the effect of the participant's need for approval on his or her evaluations of male and female applicants found no effect. Similarly, Sheets and Bushardt (1994) determined that self-monitoring, or the extent to which an individual's behavior is guided by external standards of appropriateness, did not influence respondents' hiring recommendations. However, self-monitoring did affect recommended starting salaries. High self-monitors exhibited bias by recommending lower starting salaries for qualified applicants applying for gender-incongruent jobs than for unqualified applicants applying for gender-congruent jobs.

In addition, Gallois et al. (1992), who examined the effect of raters' tendencies to endorse sex-role stereotypes on their evaluations of candidates, found that interviewers who engaged in moderate to high levels of stereotyping did not distinguish between male and female applicants, however, those who engaged in low levels of stereotyping preferred female over male applicants. This finding conflicts with Sharp and Post's (1980) earlier finding that individuals with a high propensity to stereotype discriminated against women.

Finally, in their 1995 study, Crow et al. examined whether liberalism versus conservatism affected participants' reactions to hypothetical applicants whose gender, race, and sexual orientation varied. Their findings indicated that conservatives always favored heterosexual candidates over gay candidates. In contrast, when the candidate was White and female, liberals favored gays.

In sum, recent research suggests that gender similarity between the interviewer and the applicant influences interviewers' evaluations, at least among female interviewers. Findings also indicate that the interviewer's managerial experience and personality probably influence the likelihood of applicant gender effects; however, research in these areas is quite limited and somewhat contradictory.

Situational factors. Research on the effects of situational factors on the occurrence of gender discrimination in the interview continued to focus on the sex type of the job. Studies show some support for the notion that interviewers prefer applicants whose gender matches the sex type of the job. For instance, Atwater and Van Fleet (1997) found that females were preferred over males for two female-typed social work positions. Glick, Zion, and Nelson (1988) found that business professionals preferred females for the female-typed job of receptionist/secretary in a dental office, but preferred males for the male-typed job of sales manager at a heavy machinery company. Zebrowitz, Tenenbaum, and Goldstein (1991) found that while females were preferred over males for a feminine job of day care center teacher, male and female applicants were evaluated similarly for the somewhat more masculine job of day care center director. Similarly, an examination (McRae, 1994) of Black managers' evaluations of hypothetical Black applicants revealed stereotypical applicant sex effects for the female-typed job of benefits officer but not for the male-typed job of finance officer.

Interviewers are most likely to match the gender of the applicant to the sex type of the job when applicants possess the desired job-related qualifications. For instance, Zebrowitz et al. (1991) found that when applicants were high achieving, females were preferred for the feminine job of loan counselor and males were preferred for the masculine job of loan officer. Similarly, Perry (1994) found that females were preferred for the feminine job of stenographer and males were preferred for the masculine job of firefighter, but only when applicants possessed many of the qualifications needed to do the job. Furthermore, Sheets and Bushardt (1994) demonstrated that no gender congruency preference existed when the job candidate was unqualified. In fact, participants preferred a qualified candidate whose gender was incongruent with the position over an unqualified candidate who was gender congruent. However, one study (Atwater & Van Fleet, 1997) found that participants preferred a moderately qualified candidate whose gender was congruent with the job rather than a highly qualified candidate who was gender incongruent.

Thus, interviewers generally prefer applicants whose gender is congruent with the sex type of the job. However, this preference may vary as a function of the particular job in question. Furthermore, interviewers do not seem to be willing to sacrifice decision quality simply to obtain gender congruency.

Matching the gender of the applicant to the sex type of the job appears to be important only when applicants are qualified for the position.

Researchers also examined how organizational diversity climate and gender composition patterns affected the occurrence of gender bias. Katz (1987) found an interaction between an organization's diversity climate and applicant gender such that male applicants were preferred over females when the climate was male dominated. However, in an egalitarian climate, male and female applicants were viewed as equally suitable. Konrad and Pfeffer's (1991) study of the selection of women for administrative positions at academic institutions indicated that women were more likely to be hired when the job was typically held by women across institutions, the particular institution had a higher percentage of women administrators, and the previous jobholder was female. Surprisingly, Atwater and Van Fleet (1997) found that hiring decisions for a female-typed job did not vary as a function of whether the prospective subordinates of a candidate were predominantly female or unspecified, perhaps because participants in both the predominantly female and unspecified conditions assumed that the subordinates were female. Generally, these findings suggest that applicant gender effects vary as a function of occupational and organizational gender composition patterns.

What Are the Underlying Processes by Which Gender Discrimination in the Interview Occurs?

In recent years, researchers have devoted considerable attention to examining the processes by which applicant gender effects occur. Several studies examined how interviewers' prototypes of the ideal applicant affected sex discrimination in the interview. Interviewers' prototypes of the ideal applicant are cognitive structures that define the traits and behaviors associated with the ideal candidate for a particular job (Graves, 1993). To the extent that these prototypes include gender or traits and behaviors stereotypically associated with gender, they may lead to differences in evaluations of male and female applicants (Perry, Davis-Blake, & Kulik, 1994).

Perry (1994) tested the notion that gender discrimination is likely to occur when gender is a central feature of the interviewer's ideal applicant prototype (e.g., a firefighter's job, a stenographer's job). Results indicated that participants preferred applicants who possessed the gender specified in the prototype, but only if these applicants also matched many other features of the prototype.

In addition, Van Vianen and Willemsen (1992) found that prototypes of the ideal applicant were important in determining evaluations of applicants for professional positions at a Dutch university. Interviewers' ratings of the ideal and accepted applicants were quite similar (i.e., both tended to be masculine and to possess positive attributes). Not surprisingly, female applicants were seen as more feminine than male applicants. Females also were less likely to be hired than were males. Moreover, interviewers' perceptions of applicants' masculinity/femininity affected their evaluations of female, but not male, candidates. Accepted and rejected females differed in masculinity/femininity, whereas accepted and rejected males did not.

Van Vianen and Van Schie (1995) extended this research by examining how ideal applicant prototypes and actual applicant behavior created gender effects in mock interviews at a Dutch university. Results indicated that interviewers' ratings of the ideal and accepted applicants were quite similar to one another (i.e., both were positive and gender neutral). Female candidates were rated as more feminine and male applicants were rated as more masculine than the ideal. Surprisingly, female candidates were preferred over male candidates.

As before, masculinity/femininity was used to distinguish between accepted and rejected females, but not accepted and rejected males. Analysis of videotapes of the interviews indicated that interviewers' ratings of applicants' masculinity/femininity were explained not only by applicant gender but also by differences in the extent to which applicants exhibited feminine (e.g., use of equivocal statements, smiling) or masculine (e.g., nodding, taking initiative) behaviors. Females who engaged in masculine behaviors were viewed as more masculine and more acceptable than females who did not.

Taken together, these studies suggest that gender and gender-linked attributes are embedded in interviewers' prototypes of the ideal applicant. Moreover, masculinity/femininity appears to be particularly important in determining interviewers' evaluations of women. To the extent that interviewers rely on gender and gender-related traits to evaluate applicants, they are likely to exhibit gender bias. Furthermore, the likelihood of discrimination against women increases if gender-linked traits such as masculinity/femininity are disproportionately used to evaluate female applicants. Under these circumstances, female applicants must meet a standard that is not applied to male applicants.

Another area of interest was the effect of interviewer exposure to personalized information about the applicant on gender discrimination in the interview. In particular, Glick et al. (1988) provided participants with information indicating that the applicant engaged in feminine, masculine, or gender-neutral activities. Exposure to this information changed participants' perceptions of applicants (i.e., participants' ratings of the masculinity/femininity of applicants mirrored the information that was provided, rather than applicant gender). However, participants still expected to interview applicants whose masculinity/femininity was congruent with the sex type of the job. Thus, despite the availability of personalized information about applicants, gender-related effects still occurred.

Investigators also began to examine whether behavioral interactions between interviewers and applicants create gender bias. Kacmar and Hochwarter (1995) found that applicant and interviewer gender had little effect on behavior in the interview or on interview outcomes. Of course, further research is needed to conclude that behavioral interactions do not play a role in gender effects in the interview.

Finally, two studies conducted by Graves and Powell (1995, 1996) explored the mediating processes that underlie the effects of gender similarity on interviewers' judgments. As noted earlier, both studies found that gender similarity affected female, but not male, recruiters' evaluations of applicants. In their 1995 study, Graves and Powell found that perceived similarity and interpersonal attraction mediated the effect of gender similarity on recruiters' evaluations. Surprisingly, female recruiters saw male applicants as more similar to themselves and more likable than female applicants, and therefore, rated male applicants as more qualified than female applicants. The 1996 study showed that the quality of the interview mediated the effect of gender similarity on interview outcomes. Female interviewers who met with female, rather than male, applicants believed that they had more positive interview interactions and, consequently, evaluated female applicants more highly than male applicants.

A growing body of evidence suggests that gender and gender-linked traits such as masculinity/femininity are embedded in interviewers' cognitive structures for evaluating applicants. As a result, interviewers may differentiate between male and female applicants. In contrast, there is little information about the behavioral processes that underlie applicant gender effects. With respect to gender similarity effects, preliminary research has identified several factors that may mediate the effect of gender similarity on evaluations of applicants, including the interviewer's similarity to and liking for the applicant and the quality of the interview.

Summary

Recent studies indicate that applicant gender influences interviewers' judgments. However, the likelihood of gender effects seems to be a function of factors in the applicant, recruiter, and situation. For applicants, physical appearance appears to be particularly important. Women who possess "undesirable" physical features are especially likely to be victims of discrimination. There is also some evidence that applicants' behaviors (e.g., assertiveness) and demographic characteristics (e.g., race, sexual orientation) affect the likelihood of gender discrimination, although further research on these effects is needed before definitive conclusions can be reached.

With respect to recruiter characteristics, recent research indicates that the interaction of recruiter and applicant gender is important in determining reactions to applicants, at least among female recruiters. Preliminary findings also suggest that the interviewers' managerial experience, tendency to engage in self-monitoring, propensity to engage in sex-role stereotyping, and liberalism versus conservatism may have moderating effects.

Research on the moderating effects of situational factors indicates that interviewers generally prefer applicants who apply for gender-congruent jobs. However, the preference for a match between the gender of the applicant and the sex type of the job is most likely to occur when applicants are highly qualified. In addition, organizational diversity climate and gender composition patterns are important determinants of gender bias in the hiring process.

Finally, a growing body of evidence suggests that gender and gender-related traits are primary components of interviewers' cognitive structures for evaluating applicants. The fact that gender is embedded in these cognitive structures increases the likelihood of gender discrimination. In addition, preliminary research suggests that gender similarity affects interviewers' judgments by influencing their similarity to and liking for applicants, as well as the quality of interview interactions.

Suggestions for Future Research

Although a substantial amount of research on the effect of applicant gender on employment interviewers' judgments has been conducted, a number of critical research issues still need to be addressed.

Methodological Issues

Generally, the methodology used in recent studies is of higher quality than the methodology used previously. For instance, researchers make greater use of field methodology and nonstudent samples. Yet many of the methodological issues raised by Arvey (1979) in his initial review of the literature still remain. In particular, experimental researchers continue to conduct a large number of paper-people studies, despite the fact that they do not mirror the richness of real-life interview situations. Research is needed to determine how different experimental methodologies (e.g., résumé, résumé plus photograph, résumé plus interview script, résumé plus videotape of interview) affect the occurrence of sex bias (Campion & Arvey, 1989). Such research will indicate whether the continued use of paper people in interview research is appropriate.

In addition, studies of real interviews, particularly in nonuniversity settings, are warranted (Campion & Arvey, 1989). When testing for applicant sex effects in real interviews, researchers should try to control for differences in candidates' actual qualifications to ensure that any applicant gender effects that are uncovered are due to interviewer bias, rather than preexisting gender differences in applicants' qualifications.

The Intersection of Applicant Gender and Other Social Identities

To date, most research has looked solely at the effects of applicant gender, without regard to other demographic characteristics of the applicant. Yet interviewers are likely to react to the applicant's complete social identity, not simply to gender. For instance, evaluations of White women will not necessarily be the same as ratings of women of color, nor may ratings of men of color and White men be identical (Cox & Nkomo, 1993). Researchers must recognize that applicants possess complex social identities that are based on multiple characteristics. (See Chapter 2 in this book for further discussion of the intersection of gender and other social identities.)

Relational Demography

Explorations of the effects of gender similarity on interviewers' judgments have just begun. In particular, researchers should examine (1) the nature of these effects, (2) the circumstances under which they occur, and (3) the mechanisms by which they operate. Existing demography research (e.g., Ely, 1995) suggests that it might be useful to analyze how interviewer gender, as well as organizational diversity climate and the gender composition of top management, influences the size and direction of gender similarity effects in the interview. In addition, examining the simultaneous effects of gender similarity on recruiters' perceptions of applicants (e.g., liking for applicants, perceptions of person-organization fit) and behavioral interactions in the interview could provide helpful information about the processes that underlie these effects.

Interviewer Personality Traits

Because past research has been haphazard, systematic study of the links between interviewers' traits and gender bias in the interview is needed. Researchers should use theory to identify personality traits that might be related to gender bias. Then, research should be conducted to determine which traits are actually associated with differential evaluations of male and female applicants. Such research could help organizations choose unbiased interviewers.

Contextual Factors

Noting the lack of attention to the effects of the interview context on the occurrence of gender bias, Perry et al. (1994) recently called for a systematic examination of the effects of contextual factors such as the gender of existing jobholders, applicants, and managers, as well as the organization's size and commitment to hiring and promoting persons of both genders. In addition, researchers should examine how the nature of the interview (e.g., demographic composition of the interview panel, interview structure) influences the occurrence of gender effects (Campion & Arvey, 1989). For instance, interviews that are based on job analysis, ask the same questions of all applicants, use anchored rating scales, involve multiple interviewers, and use behavior-based questions should reduce the likelihood of gender discrimination (Campion, Palmer, & Campion, 1997).

Furthermore, researchers should consider how the society within which the organization is embedded influences the occurrence of gender effects. Given the globalization of business, it would be particularly desirable to examine the effects of national culture (e.g., Hofstede, 1980a) on gender bias in the interview. One would expect gender effects to occur in cultures that have large distinctions between the accepted roles of women and men in society and offer few legal protections against gender discrimination.

Underlying Cognitive and Behavioral Processes

Researchers should continue to examine how interviewers' cognitive structures contribute to the occurrence of gender bias (Perry et al., 1994), especially whether gender or traits associated with gender pervade interviewers' prototypes for evaluating applicants across a variety of jobs. In addition, researchers should examine whether interviewers use different prototypes for evaluating male and female applicants, as suggested by recent research. Furthermore, researchers might test how the cognitive structures used by interviewers who exhibit gender bias differ from those used by interviewers who do not display such bias (Perry et al., 1994). It also would be helpful to determine whether interviewers' prototypes can be altered through training to reduce the occurrence of gender bias.

With respect to behavioral processes, it would be particularly useful to examine how the interplay between interviewers and applicants varies as a function of applicant and recruiter demographics (Campion & Arvey, 1989). Such research might increase our understanding of the mechanisms by which both applicant gender and gender similarity between the recruiter and the applicant affect interview evaluations.

Finally, researchers should explore how the interview context alters underlying cognitive and behavioral processes (Eder & Buckley, 1988; Perry et al., 1994). If interviewers' gender-based cognitions and behaviors change as the interview context changes, then it may be possible to reduce discriminatory cognitions and behaviors by manipulating the interview context.

Conclusions

To date, research on gender bias in the interview has examined whether it occurs, when it occurs, and how it occurs. The results of this research reinforce the notion that "questions of discrimination in selection are not simple" (Hitt & Barr, 1989, p. 58). Numerous factors in the applicant, recruiter, and the situation influence whether interviewers give differential evaluations of male and female applicants. Moreover, gender and gender-linked attributes appear to be embedded in the cognitive structures that interviewers use to evaluate applicants. New research is needed to more fully understand when and how applicant gender affects interviewers' judgments. Such research will answer what is unarguably the most important question about gender bias in the interview: How can differential evaluations of male and female applicants be prevented?

Chapter 9

Gender Influences on Performance Evaluations

Kathryn M. Bartol

The past three decades have witnessed a major increase in the number of women holding managerial positions. For example, in the United States, the proportion of women managers increased from 16% in 1970 to 44% in 1998 (see Chapter 17 by Powell in this book). Despite these changes, gender structuring of organizations persists (Bartol, 1978; Bartol & Martin, 1986; Jacobs, 1992; Perry, Davis-Blake, & Kulik, 1994; Stroh, Brett, & Reilly, 1992). Women are still greatly underrepresented in the higher levels of management (Powell, Chapter 17, this volume; Ragins & Sundstrom, 1989). Heilman (1995) argues that one cannot point to the pipeline as the problem, because research indicates that women who moved into management in the 1970s have not advanced as rapidly as males who entered management positions at around the same time. Thus, despite significant progress, women are still experiencing serious difficulties scaling the hierarchy.

One possible explanation for the persistent gender structuring of organizations is bias in performance evaluations. In an important early review, Nieva and Gutek (1980) found evidence that males tend to be favored in many evaluation situations. Such conditions can have serious implications for the upward mobility of women. Once individuals join organizations, formal (official) and informal performance evaluations influence virtually every major career-related decision made about them, including task assignments, training opportunities, developmental programs, salary increases, and promotions (Cleveland, Murphy, & Williams, 1989). If bias exists in many performance evaluation situations, the cumulative effect, through influencing a variety of decisions that ultimately affect upward mobility, could be devastating. Because performance evaluations constitute an important feedback mechanism (Cleveland et al., 1989), they also have the potential to boost or undermine self-efficacy, an important ingredient in subsequent performance (Bandura, 1997).

This chapter has two purposes. First, I review studies that are particularly relevant to assessing the extent to which gender issues affect performance evaluations in the workplace. Second, I outline major questions that need to be addressed to further our understanding of gender influences on performance evaluations in organizations.

Evaluations of Men and Women

Gender influences on performance evaluations can be considered from several major perspectives: the gender of the individuals doing the ratings (raters), the gender of the individuals being rated (ratees), and gender differences in how individuals rate their own performance (self-ratings). This latter issue is important not only because it provides insight into self-efficacy issues but also because self-ratings are becoming a more common component of formal performance appraisal processes in organizations (Atwater, 1998).

Gender of Rater

Findings from a variety of laboratory studies suggest little or no impact of rater gender on performance evaluations (Hall & Hall, 1976; Jacobson & Effertz, 1974; Lee & Alvares, 1977; London & Poplawski, 1976; London & Stumpf, 1983; Stumpf & London, 1981a). Although laboratory studies generally have been fairly consistent in finding few rater gender effects on performance evaluations, relatively few field studies have assessed such effects. A primary reason is that managers doing performance ratings are often predominantly male (Griffeth & Bedeian, 1989; Thompson & Thompson, 1985; Tsui & Gutek, 1984; Tsui & O'Reilly, 1989) or sometimes predominantly female (Yammarino & Dubinsky, 1988), precluding such tests.

In one of the few field studies, Pulakos, White, Oppler, and Borman (1989) analyzed the official ratings of more than 8,000 first-term Army enlisted personnel. They found main effects on two of three performance dimensions, indicating that females gave higher ratings than males. There were also significant interactions with ratee gender and/or rating source (peer or supervisor), but the researchers argued that the gender effects were minimal. Two other field studies have not found rater gender effects: Mobley (1982), in a study of official performance appraisal ratings for nonmanagerial and nonprofessional employees in a large supply distribution center, and Shore and Thornton (1986), in an analysis of performance ratings collected for research purposes for men and women doing assembly work.

The small number of field studies has been largely confined to ratings of incumbents in nonmanagerial positions. Although gender of rater effects should not be the sole subject of a major inquiry, it would be useful to have more studies, particularly field studies that address possible gender of rater differences as they apply to middle- and upper-managerial positions. As is discussed later in this chapter, issues of superior-subordinate similarity and gender makeup of work groups may actually prove to be more important factors than simply rater gender in affecting performance evaluations.

Gender of Ratee

A perhaps more important question relating to the upward mobility of women is whether there are systematic differences in the performance evaluations *received* by men and women. A related consideration is the extent to which similarity and task/job congruence issues influence ratings received.

▨ Ratings Received

Although several laboratory studies have suggested that the gender of the ratee has no influence on performance evaluations (e.g., Frank & Drucker, 1977; Giannantonio, Olian, & Carroll, 1995; Hall & Hall, 1976), others have pointed to significant gender effects. Some of these latter studies have favored women (e.g., Bigoness, 1976; Hamner, Kim, Baird, & Bigoness, 1974), whereas others have favored men (e.g., Pazy, 1986; Woehr & Roch, 1996).

Field studies of official performance evaluations received by men and women have also uncovered significant gender effects. For example, Mobley's (1982) study of nonmanagerial and nonprofessional employees working in a large supply distribution center found that women were rated higher than men. In opposite findings, Pulakos et al. (1989) found main effects indicating that males were rated higher than females on two of three performance dimensions, but there were interactions related to gender of rater and rating source (peer and supervisor).

In one of the few studies to investigate gender effects in performance appraisals of men and women in managerial positions, Powell and Butterfield (1994) examined the files of the applicant pool for senior executive service positions in an agency of the U.S. government. They found that during the most recent performance appraisal rating cycle, the women applicants had received higher ratings from their supervisors than had the male applicants, suggesting possibly that women who were better performers had chosen to apply. A review panel evaluated the candidates and chose those to be referred to the selecting official for further consideration. Women received higher panel evaluations and were significantly more likely to be referred than men. Aside from their higher performance appraisals, women were significantly more likely than the men to be employed in the hiring department, a factor that was positively related to panel evaluations. They also had significantly less work experience, but that factor was negatively related to panel evaluations. Thus, women fared better than men on evaluations from both their supervisors and the screening panel.

Tsui and Gutek (1984) also studied official performance appraisals at the managerial level. Their findings showed no ratee gender differences in formal performance appraisals among middle-level managers in a multicompany corporation.

Overall, there have been surprisingly few field studies that have considered ratee gender effects in official performance appraisals, and this is particularly true of studies at managerial levels. Those that have been conducted have produced somewhat inconsistent results, suggesting that more complex issues are involved.

Tsui and Gutek (1984) argue that if there is gender bias in evaluations, it is more likely to emerge in research ratings than in official ratings because supervisors are more likely to be honest about their opinions when they will be held confidential. Because their study also included ratings collected solely for research purposes, they were able to assess this possibility. Their findings showed no ratee gender differences associated with ratings done for research purposes or official ratings (as mentioned above). The lack of differences was somewhat surprising given that female managers were at lower grade levels, had received larger recent merit increases, and were being promoted at a faster rate than male managers. Moreover, they were younger and had less company tenure and management experience than their male counterparts. A second wave of data 18 months later indicated that, although company appraisal ratings were still equivalent and a similar proportion of male and female managers were receiving promotions, merit increases continued to be higher for females. In another study involving managers' performance ratings for research purposes, Pulakos and Wexley (1993) found that women received higher ratings than males on a performance scale, but there were no differences on several other dimensions, such as goal emphasis and general satisfactoriness.

Several other field studies involving first-line supervisors and nonsupervisory personnel have also found no significant differences in research-related performance evaluations of female and male ratees: Deaux's (1979) study of first-line managers in a telephone company and supervisors in a national retail chain store, Thompson and Thompson's (1985) study of blue-collar workers in a plastics plant, Shore and Thornton's (1986) study of assemblers, and Yammarino and Dubinsky's (1988) study of insurance and retail sales personnel. Whether supervisors are actually more honest when providing ratings for research purposes is an open question. Even though supervisors are promised confidentiality by researchers they may well be wary, particularly because the ratings are usually provided to researchers outside of the organization and also are likely to generate summary reports to upper management.

Several studies have focused on assessment centers, which typically provide evaluations of the performance of nonmanagerial and low-level supervisory personnel for purposes of identifying management potential. Presumably, assessment centers have the capacity to reduce bias because they assess individuals on the same tasks, incorporate relatively clear criteria, and pool evaluations from multiple assessors. On the other hand, the relatively short duration of interpersonal contact between the assessees and assessors and the lesser information available compared to ongoing work settings could make gender more salient (Pulakos et al., 1989; Wendelken & Inn, 1981). For the most part, studies of assessment center ratings have shown that men and women tend to be rated equivalently (Moses, 1973; Moses & Boehm, 1975; Ritchie & Moses, 1983; Schmitt & Hill, 1977).

Shore (1992), however, found evidence of a possible subtle bias at work in her study of female and male assessees at a large petroleum company. Although women scored significantly higher than men on one of the major dimensions (performance style) and equivalently to men on the other two dimensions (cognitive measures and interpersonal style), women's overall ratings were not significantly higher. Her study points up one of the dilemmas in attempting to evaluate the presence or absence of bias in performance evaluations: Equal ratings for males and females may not always be equitable.

The question of consistent interactions associated with the gender of the rater and the gender of the ratee have also been raised (Landy & Farr, 1980; Nieve & Gutek, 1980); however, there appears to be little support (Hall & Hall, 1976; Mobley, 1982). Studies to date suggest that neither males nor females give higher ratings to same gender ratees, nor do they consistently give higher or lower ratings to opposite-gender ratees.

■ Influence of Rater-Ratee Similarity

Another perspective from which to investigate potential gender bias in evaluations is through considering actual and perceived similarity (Turban & Jones, 1988). Noting that a number of research studies have considered one or two demographic characteristics in evaluating effects on performance evaluations, Tsui and O'Reilly (1989) argue that such approaches may not be sufficient to capture the simultaneous demographic differences between raters and ratees. In a study of middle managers and their superiors in a *Fortune* 500 multidivisional company, they measured actual differences between superior-subordinate pairs on six demographic variables (gender, age, race, education, job tenure, and company tenure). Based on the argument that performance ratings obtained for research purposes are more valid, they controlled for official performance ratings, as well as superior and subordinate demographics.

Overall results showed that demographic differences between a subordinate and a superior significantly affected performance evaluations (collected for the study) of the subordinate. Gender differences were a significant predictor, with specific results indicating that subordinates in opposite-gender dyads were rated as performing more poorly and were liked less well than subordinates in same-gender dyads. Further analysis of interactions indicated that female superiors gave female subordinates higher evaluations than male subordinates and indicated greater liking, but male superiors gave equivalent effectiveness ratings to female and male subordinates and indicated similar liking.

Given that other demographic variables also influenced outcomes, the researchers suggest that it might be prudent for managers to increase communication when they have subordinates who differ demographically. Tsui and O'Reilly (1989) use the term *relational demography* to refer to the study of comparative demographic characteristics of members of dyads or groups who hold positions in which there is a need or opportunity to engage in regular interactions (p. 403).

In related research focusing on a similar question, Liden, Wayne, and Stilwell (1993) conducted a study of leader-subordinate dyads in which subordinates were new hires into a wide range of positions at two major universities. No significant link was found between *demographic similarity* and performance ratings collected after the subordinate had spent two weeks on the job. A strong link existed, however, between the supervisor's *perceived similarity* with the subordinate and the supervisor's rating of the subordinate's performance. Thus, these findings suggest that supervisor perceptual similarity may be more important than demographic similarity.

This research may not have adequately tested the demographic similarity issue for at least three reasons. First, it used a composite measure of demographic similarity based on gender, race, education, and age that may have masked the gender effects isolated by Tsui and O'Reilly (1989). Second, the two-week time frame may have been too short to assess a demographic similarity and performance evaluation linkage. Third, it is likely that the supervisors had considerable input into hiring decisions and, therefore, had hired individuals with whom they felt reasonably comfortable. Nevertheless, Liden et al.'s (1993) study helps to highlight the association between perceived similarity and performance ratings and suggests a need to continue to investigate both demographic and perceptual similarity issues. Turban and Jones (1988) contend that similarity issues are important not only because of direct bias but also because perceived similarity positively influences the nature of ongoing supervisor-subordinate interactions.

Pulakos and Wexley (1983), in their study of manager-subordinate dyads from a variety of organizations, found that a fairly sizable proportion of variance in performance ratings was associated with perceptual similarity. Also, there was a gender interaction related to perceptual similarity and ratings of dependability. When subordinates perceived themselves as similar to their managers, female subordinates received significantly higher dependability ratings than did males; when perceptions were dissimilar, both males and females were rated uniformly lower on dependability.

Others have addressed the similarity issue by studying the proportions of men and women in a work unit (Kanter, 1977b). For example, to validate a measure to be used for career counseling, Sackett, DuBois, and Noe (1991) evaluated gender and performance evaluations in 486 work groups consisting mainly of blue-collar and clerical jobs developed by the U.S. Employment Service. Women received lower performance evaluations when the proportion of women in the work group was small, a finding consistent with Kanter's work on tokenism. Thus, the gender proportions approach may warrant further study.

▓ Influence of Task/Job Congruence

Many tasks and jobs are gender typed in the sense that they tend to be viewed as primarily "man's work" or "woman's work" (Dipboye, 1985). Freedman and Phillips (1988) argue that gender of the ratee may interact with the gender type of the job in leading to gender bias in performance evaluations. Thus, a critical factor may be whether the gender of the ratee is compatible or congruent with the role that appears to be required by the job (based on its gender type; Knight & Saal, 1984; Nieva & Gutek, 1980). There is some empirical support for the gender-congruence notion.

For example, in a laboratory study, Robbins and DeNisi (1993) found that raters deflated performance ratings in the gender-incongruent situations (male in secretarial job or female in carpenter job) as compared to the gender-congruent situations (female in secretarial job or male in carpenter job). Interestingly, these effects occurred only when there was more than one individual in the work group whose gender was incongruent with the job. The researchers suggested that raters may be more likely to use stereotypes in such situations because the gender issue is less salient and, therefore, raters may not be cued to take precautions to avoid gender bias in ratings. These results, coupled with those of Sackett et al. (1991) in which the females received lower performance evaluations when the proportion of women in the work group was small, suggest that it may be useful to pursue further research integrating both the gender-congruence and tokenism issues.

In a related laboratory study supporting the value of the gender-congruence notion, Barnes-Farrell, L'Heureux-Barrett, and Conway (1991) found that the gender of the worker himself or herself (executive secretary and contracts administrator) did not affect the accuracy of the performance ratings. However, the gender type of the task interacting with the gender type of the job did have an effect. Specifically, worker behaviors from male-typed (female-typed) tasks were evaluated more accurately when presented in the context of male-typed (female-typed) jobs. These results also are consonant with suggestions from social cognition theory that situations or categories more closely related to commonly held stereotypes should be easier to judge because they can be more readily recognized and matched with cognitively available information (Taylor & Crocker, 1981; Taylor, Fiske, Etcoff, & Ruderman, 1978; see also Bartol & Martin, 1986).

Some researchers have argued that the perceived gender characteristics of an individual (i.e., masculinity vs. femininity) may be more important than their actual gender in assessing how performance will be evaluated in gender-typed jobs. For example, Maurer and Taylor (1994) investigated the issue of congruence between the gender type of the job and the perceived masculinity/femininity of the ratee by asking university students from psychology classes to rate their instructors. Results indicated that ratings of female instructors were higher when they were described with increasing emphasis on masculinity by raters. Positive attitudes toward women as instructors were also related to higher ratings for female instructors, but had a negative effect on ratings for male instructors when they were perceived as highly masculine. Thus, not only the perceived gender characteristics of the ratee but also attitudes toward women in the male-typed job influenced performance evaluations of both men and women. Other evidence supports the idea that perceived masculine characteristics are positively associated with higher performance evaluations, at least in male-typed job contexts (Harman, Griffeth, Crino, & Harris, 1991; Moore, 1984).

Self-Ratings

Self-ratings have also been subject to several investigations. They are important not only because they provide insight into issues of self-efficacy and self-esteem but also because self-ratings are being increasingly used within performance appraisal systems in organizations. Therefore, gender-related differences in self-ratings could ultimately affect the ratings that individuals receive from their supervisors.

In an early study, Deaux (1979) found that male heads of department stores in a retail store chain viewed themselves as performing significantly better overall and having greater ability, higher intelligence, more difficult jobs, and better relationships with the supervisor than did their female counterparts, and as receiving relatively more approval for their work than did their female counterparts.

More recent studies, though, indicate a trend toward equivalent or even higher self-ratings by women. For example, Tsui and Gutek's (1984) study of middle managers in a multicompany corporation showed that female manager self-ratings of performance effectiveness were significantly higher than those of male managers. There were no significant differences in the first wave of data collected; however, 18 months later, female self-ratings had risen, whereas those of male managers had declined, creating the significant difference. Given that merit increases and promotion rates were higher for women during the first period of the study and merit increases continued to be higher in the second part, the decrement in male manager self-evaluations seemed to match the realities of the situation—at least as signaled by the reward system. In another study focusing on managers, Wohlers, Hall, and London (1993) concluded that male and female managers from a variety of organizations did not differ in self-ratings.

Several studies of nonmanagerial personnel suggest that women sometimes, but not always, rate their performance higher than do males. For example, Weeks and Nantel (1995) showed that female salespeople in a large industrial sales force organization reported higher self-evaluations than did their male counterparts, with the major area of difference being perceived performance in the area of customer interaction. In their study of insurance and retail sales personnel, Yammarino and Dubinsky (1988) found that women rated themselves higher than did their male colleagues on job congruence (i.e., the degree to which each salesperson performed his or her job congruently with the supervisor's preference), but self-ratings of performance were the same. Among blue-collar workers, female assemblers rated themselves the same as male assemblers, and both groups rated themselves higher than did their supervisors (Shore & Thornton, 1986).

Thus, there is little evidence in these studies that female self-ratings are lower than those of males. In fact, the few available studies of gender effects in self-ratings suggest a tendency toward higher self-ratings for women. At this point, however, we know very little about the conditions under which women are likely to rate their performance higher than men in organizations.

Research Issues

The limited data that exist on the link between gender of rater or gender of ratee and performance evaluations in real and simulated workplaces suggest that simply using gender as a predictor does not capture the complexities of the area of inquiry. Although the data suggest few differences associated simply with gender, this tentative conclusion must be tempered by several factors. For one, the number of studies conducted in field settings has been small. For another, the available field studies have largely concentrated on positions near the bottom of the hierarchy where women have experienced more success in being promoted. Still another factor is that it has been frequently necessary to include a broad mix of positions to acquire adequate sample sizes. However, without adequate controls (e.g., organizational level, functional area, tenure, pay) the analyses may produce spurious results or mask important relationships (Lefkowitz, 1994).

On the other hand, studies related to similarity and task/job congruence issues suggest that contextual variables may be of critical importance in understanding gender-related influences on performance evaluations. Hence additional studies are needed involving these variables. In addition to areas requiring future research that have already been mentioned, many other questions, such as the following, remain to be answered.

Are there gender differences in the degree to which performance evaluations reflect actual performance? Even in situations in which the performance evaluations of men and women are equivalent, bias is still possible because the performance evaluations may not adequately reflect performance differences. For instance, as mentioned earlier, Shore (1992) found in her study of assessment centers that higher ratings for women on a major dimension did not translate over to higher overall ratings for women.

Conversely, evaluations could differ when performance is actually equivalent. In a pair of laboratory studies that incorporated an objective work sample (stacking cans in a grocery store), Hamner et al. (1974) and Bigoness (1976) found that the high-performing female received higher performance ratings than the high-performing male, even though both had exhibited the very same objective performance. The researchers speculated that women might be evaluated more favorably in lower-level nontraditional positions (i.e., stock person) but experience greater evaluation difficulties in professional and managerial positions.

Few studies of gender effects on performance evaluations have attempted to match performance evaluations with objective indicators of performance. Although such studies can be particularly difficult in field settings, they would be useful additions to literature attempting to understand gender differences in performance evaluations and the circumstances under which bias is likely to occur.

What types of information are most important in reducing gender bias? Based on a meta-analysis of studies related to personnel selection, Tosi and Einbender (1985) argue that individuals make more stereotypical judgments when information is limited than when more extensive information regarding competence and job qualifications is available. Yet we still do not know what types of information would be best to provide to reduce the likelihood of gender stereotyping (Foschi, 1996; Ragins & Sundstrom, 1989). On the other hand, it is possible that stereotypes also may be engendered when there is an information overload, but this question has not been adequately addressed (Stumpf & London, 1981a). Various researchers stress the importance of developing appropriate standards and criteria to help specify what information is relevant and how it should be used in making performance evaluation judgments (Bobko & Colella, 1994; Murphy & Cleveland, 1991; Stumpf & London, 1981b). The effectiveness of these approaches in reducing the potential for gender bias needs to be evaluated, particularly within the context of different types of gender-typed tasks and jobs.

What role do rater goals play with respect to gender bias in evaluations? Longenecker, Gioia, and Sims (1987) present evidence suggesting that executives are more concerned with how to use the evaluation process to motivate and retain subordinates than with accuracy of ratings. Along similar lines, managers sometimes face situations in which it is particularly important to retain certain employees for strategic and/or operational reasons. Based on resource dependency theory, Bartol and Martin (1988, 1989, 1990) have shown that when there are threats to retention under these types of circumstances, managers are prone to award larger raises than might be warranted from a strict pay-for-performance point of view. Such issues are likely to affect performance evaluations as well, but little research has addressed the extent to which resource dependency issues, such as reward systems, political connections, and the need for important expertise, might moderate tendencies toward gender bias (Fiske & Neuberg, 1990; Rudman, 1998).

Does accountability influence the performance evaluations received by men and women? A number of field studies that have found equal or higher performance ratings for women as compared to men have mentioned the possible impact of equal employment programs and pressures in the organization (Powell & Butterfield, 1994; Thacker & Wayne, 1995). However, the influence of this potentially important context factor has not been systematically studied (Powell & Butterfield, 1994).

Based on the results of a laboratory study, Foschi (1996) suggests that accountability (i.e., the extent to which individuals anticipate having to justify their actions) may decrease the use of stereotypical responses in evaluating performance. Apparently, participants in the study paid greater attention to the information when they knew that they would have to justify their actions. The lack of accountability may possibly account for studies indicating that female college professors tend to be rated lower than male professors (Dobbins, Cardy, & Truxillo, 1988; Sidanius & Crane, 1989).

Are there gender implications to instituting 360-degree performance appraisal systems? An increasing number of organizations are instituting some form of multisource performance assessments, often referred to as 360-degree feedback (Atwater & Waldman, 1998). Such systems typically incorporate performance evaluation feedback from a variety of sources, including supervisors, subordinates, peers, and even customers. Relatively little is known, however, regarding gender effects related to evaluations provided by sources other than supervisors, particularly within the framework of a 360-degree feedback system. A study by Pulakos et al. (1989) found some evidence of significant gender effects related to peer ratings, in which females were rated lower than males on two out of three performance dimensions. Research by London and Wohlers (1991) indicated greater profile agreement (the correlation between self-ratings and average subordinates' ratings across a number of feedback items) for female than male managers. Wexley and Pulakos (1983) demonstrated that perceptual congruence (the extent to which subordinates accurately perceived their managers' work-related attitudes) was likely to be stronger in same-gender dyads and was associated with higher ratings of managers' performance by subordinates. Thus, the potential exists for gender effects in multisource feedback environments.

Are there gender differences in responsiveness to evaluative feedback in the workplace and, if so, what are the implications? In a variety of laboratory situations, most of which involved feedback from an experimenter or a peer, Roberts and Nolen-Hoeksema (1989, 1994) found that gender differences exist in responsiveness to evaluative feedback in achievement-oriented situations. Females seem to modify their self-evaluations more than males do when evaluated by others, apparently because they view such feedback as having more informational value than do males.

The potentially important implications of gender differences in evaluative responsiveness indicate a need for further replicative laboratory research in settings more closely akin to the workplace and also for extensions of this research to field settings. Roberts (1991) speculates that males may be more responsive to evaluative feedback from individuals who are clearly their superiors than they were in the studies conducted by her and Nolen-Hoeksema (1989, 1994). Moreover, she points out that how females and males adapt may be heavily dependent on the situation. For example, being open to feedback during a learning phase may be useful, whereas being too reactive to negative feedback while presenting a project plan to one's superiors may undermine one's confidence and lead to poor performance. At this point, we know very little about these issues as they apply to gender differences.

Are women managers less willing to provide needed negative feedback? After studying records for more than 1,900 employees of a southeastern state government, Feild and Holley (1977) found no differences related to gender of rater in the rater's voluntary decision to discuss the results of an official performance rating with the ratee. Raters tended to discuss ratings with employees when the ratings were low.

In contrast, a laboratory study by Benedict and Levine (1988) showed that female raters took longer to do performance appraisals and to schedule feedback sessions with a subordinate (a White male confederate). Females also more positively distorted ratings than did male raters, particularly when rating lower performers. Possible explanations are that females exhibit lower confidence when rating male subordinates or that they take greater care in preparing their ratings and show greater concern for the impact of the rating on the subordinate. Of course, given the rater-ratee similarity issues mentioned earlier, woman participants may have been at a disadvantage in this situation because they were rating an opposite-gender subordinate whereas male participants were rating a same-gender subordinate.

In another study suggesting gender differences in providing feedback, Brewer, Socha, and Potter's (1996) laboratory study showed that male supervisors are more likely to provide specific negative feedback to poorly performing subordinates. There were no interactions due to subordinate gender, although such effects have been found in related studies by Dobbins (1986) and Dobbins, Pence, Orban, and Sgro (1983). Future studies, particularly field studies, are needed to assess the willingness of female and male managers to provide both positive and negative feedback and their actual effectiveness in terms of impact on subordinate productivity and related affective outcomes.

Do women register lower self-ratings of their prospects for performance on unfamiliar tasks and, if so, is less confidence the reason? Whether or not women are less confident than men in unfamiliar achievement situations has been the subject of considerable inquiry (Maccoby & Jacklin, 1974). Based on an extensive literature review, Lenney (1977) suggests that gender differences in self-confidence are less likely to occur when individuals can obtain objective or clear information regarding their task-specific ability. Further study indicates that women tend to state lower expectations than men only for tasks on which they had not received prior performance feedback (Lenney, Browning, & Mitchell, 1980; Shore & Thornton, 1986). Unfortunately, managers, particularly high-level ones, typically are confronted with many unprogrammed situations in which they must take action. As discussed earlier, women do not appear to devalue their current performance; however, there are little data on how women managers view their prospects for future performance, especially in unfamiliar situations.

Are there gender differences in impression management and, if so, do they influence performance evaluations? Considerable evidence suggests that impression management can positively influence performance evaluations, pay raises, and other important individual outcomes (Dreher, Dougherty, & Whitely, 1989; Wayne & Kacmar, 1991). Moreover, Kipnis and Schmidt (1988) found that the gender of the ingratiator can influence the effectiveness of various impression management styles on evaluation judgments. For example, the highest performance evaluations were awarded to male managers who tended to use logic and reason and to female managers who used either ingratiation or bystander (i.e., little influence) tactics. Rudman (1998) has noted the dilemma confronting women because, although self-promotion may be important to establishing a competent impression, it violates female gender norms of modestly and may engender negative social reactions. Wayne, Liden, and Sparrowe (1994) contend that many questions endure concerning gender effects on impression management, including possible gender differences related to frequency of use of upward influence techniques, general effectiveness, susceptibility to upward influence, effectiveness in opposite-gender dyads, and appropriateness in traditionally female versus traditionally male jobs. Further research is needed on the modesty issue as well (Daubman, Heatherington, & Ahn, 1992; Heatherington et al., 1993; Kacmar & Carlson, 1994).

How do differences in cultural context influence links between gender and performance evaluations? Although studies have explored gender issues and performance evaluation in the context of specific countries, such as Canada (Kirchmeyer, 1995) and Israel (Pazy, 1986), little cross-cultural research appears to have been conducted on gender influences on performance evaluations. Yet, as Davis (1998) points out, many organizations are competing in a global environment and face considerable challenges in making performance management and measurement systems work across borders. Given ample evidence of differences in the status of women around the globe, cross-cultural research regarding gender influences on performance evaluations is sorely needed.

Conclusions

Of course, these 10 questions are by no means exhaustive. However, progress in these areas and the others mentioned in this review would make important contributions to an enhanced understanding of gender issues related to performance evaluations. Such issues are critical because direct gender influences on performance evaluations also are likely to have subsequent indirect effects (through the performance evaluations) on other important outcomes in which performance appraisals play a significant role, such as compensation, training, and promotion decisions (Cleveland et al., 1989; Powell & Butterfield, 1994).

Chapter 10

Group Gender Composition and Work Group Relations

Theories, Evidence, and Issues

Pamela S. Tolbert, Mary E. Graham,
and Alice O. Andrews

Prior to the publication of Kanter's seminal *Men and Women of the Corporation* in 1977, the field of organizational studies exhibited a striking degree of oblivion to the effect of gender relations on work group dynamics (Acker & Van Houten, 1974). This neglect may have been due, in part, to the relatively small proportion of women in the labor force in the first half of the 20th century,[1] as well as to high levels of occupational and job segregation, which helped conceal the influence of group gender composition on individual and group behavior. In the postwar years, however, women's rate of entry into the labor force nearly doubled that of the preceding three decades, and women began to occupy many jobs and occupations that had been the near-exclusive province of men. In this context, Kanter's provocative analysis of the impact of work group gender composition on group relations served as the impetus for an outpouring of both theoretical and empirical work.

Studies following Kanter's have explored the effects of gender composition on a wide range of outcomes, based on a variety of theoretical perspectives. In this chapter, we review five major theoretical paradigms that, singly or in combination, have provided the underpinning for most empirical studies, then review the findings from empirical work, focusing on the degree to which they provide support for each perspective. In concluding, we identify several avenues that merit greater attention in future research and theorizing.

Theoretical Perspectives on the Gender Composition of Work Groups

Empirical work on the effects of group gender composition has drawn on an array of sociological, social psychological, and psychological theoretical traditions, most of which were developed to explain phenomena other than gender-based social relations. As a consequence, their application to the study of the gender composition of work groups has, at times, required an expansion of the original theoretical logic. Here we focus on five general perspectives: similarity-attraction, social contact, group competition, social identity, and relative deprivation.

A number of key dimensions may be used in comparing these perspectives. One is whether they are aimed primarily at explaining social relations or individuals' subjective states, a distinction reflected in differences in central outcome measures implied by theoretical foci—attitudes and behaviors toward others versus the internally oriented attitudes and behaviors resulting from an individual's perception of the social setting (e.g., job satisfaction, propensity to leave a group). A second dimension is whether social competition for collective status and resources is treated as a driving force in the formation and evolution of intergroup relations. And a third dimension is whether the perspective provides an account of potential differences in the effects of composition on women and men. Our comparison of the perspectives highlights differences among them along these dimensions.

Similarity-Attraction Perspective

A well-established explanatory framework often used in studies of gender composition is similarity-based interpersonal attraction. This psychological tradition traces its roots to early sociometric studies conducted by Moreno (1943) and to research by Newcomb (1943) on interaction and friendship patterns of students at Bennington College during the Depression years. The original studies aimed at explaining interpersonal attraction and the effects of such attraction and interaction on attitudinal change. The core logic of this approach suggests that individuals are attracted to others from whom they expect to gain positive outcomes as a result of interaction. What leads people to expect, a priori, more or less rewarding interactions? One documented basis for such expectations is perceived similarity between self and others in terms of attitudes, values, and activity preferences (Byrne, 1971). Individuals who are similar in these respects presumably are more likely to provide positive, affirming feedback on opinions, abilities, and ideas, which enhances self-esteem. Prior interaction with a particular person may not be necessary for individuals to form expectations of attitudinal similarity; rather, similarity may be inferred on the basis of characteristics that are believed to serve as indicators of certain attitudes and values.

Thus, researchers have argued that easily visible demographic characteristics, such as age, sex, and race, are commonly used as indexes of similarity (Tsui & O'Reilly, 1989). Insofar as individuals are more attracted to and psychologically more comfortable with those they view as similar to themselves, the gender composition of a group should affect both subjective states (e.g., satisfaction) and behavioral predispositions (e.g., intentions to leave a group). This perspective implies that as the proportion of women in a work group increases, women are more likely to be satisfied with their jobs and less likely to leave; as the proportion of women decreases, the reverse should be true. Conversely, men should be less satisfied as the proportion of women in their work group increases and the proportion of men decreases.

This perspective emphasizes internally focused subjective states and, as developed, offers no specific insights into the effects of group proportions on social attitudes and behaviors (i.e., positive or negative attitudes toward others). This issue is addressed, however, by a related perspective, social contact.

Social Contact Perspective

Studies of group gender composition that reflect a social contact perspective often draw on two key analyses published in 1977, by Rosabeth Moss Kanter (1997a) and by Peter Blau (1977a, 1977b). Tracing their arguments to work by Simmel (1908) on the impact of group size on inter- and intragroup relations, both analyses rest on two assumptions: that increased rates of social interaction among individuals will lead to the formation of affective ties to members of a given social group, and that such ties affect individuals' attitudes toward the group as a whole.[2]

Based on a case study she conducted of a large industrial firm, Kanter (1997a) developed her theory to explain her observations of interactions between men and women, both within and across different subunits. Her analysis emphasizes the way in which the proportion of individuals in a work group with a particular, visible characteristic affects that characteristic's salience within the group. In groups containing a very small proportion of members with a given characteristic (*skewed groups,* in her terminology), the majority often becomes sensitized to the characteristic as defining social boundaries within the work group, and inclined to act in ways that promote interaction among majority members and minimize their contact with minority members.

Kanter identified a number of social behaviors exhibited by majority members: increased solidarity in response to the heightened salience of their common group membership; intense awareness and close scrutiny of the behavior and performance of individual minority members due to the visibility of the latter within the group; and cross-group interactions characterized by the role-casting of minorities in ways consistent with common cultural stereotypes. She hypothesized that, in response, minority members would experience a general sense of social isolation, intense performance pressure, and unusually strong social constraints on their behavior in social interactions.

Although Kanter's arguments are both provocative and intuitively plausible, her proposed theoretical framework has a number of logical limitations, as subsequent analysts have pointed out. A common criticism of her analysis is its exclusive focus on the impact of numerical proportions on work group dynamics, and its neglect of the potential mediating impact of general social prestige and status accorded to different groups in society (Martin, 1985; Yoder, 1991); that is, the social status of the minority group provides an important, unspecified scope condition for her theory. Moreover, she focuses almost entirely on the impact of group proportions on the attitudes and behaviors of majority members toward the minority, offering few specifics on the impact of group proportions on relations among members of the minority group, or on their attitudes and behavior toward the majority.

Blau's (1977a, 1977b) theory, proposed as a generic theory of relative group size and group relations, addresses some of these issues. He distinguishes between two key aspects of social differentiation: (1) the relative sizes of categorically defined social groups and (2) hierarchically arranged status divisions, including levels of wealth, education, and power. He argues that status-graded as well as categorical group distinctions discourage social interaction across divisions and encourage interaction within divisions, presumably as a consequence of the sorts of social psychological processes postulated by the similarity-attraction perspective.

Blau's approach is distinguished from Kanter's (1977a) approach by its emphasis on how the proportionate size of a given subgroup within a larger group affects an individual's chances of interacting with members of her own subgroup (the in-group) and members of other subgroups (out-groups). He argues that the rate of out-group associations between members of two subgroups necessarily will be greater for the smaller of the two.[3] Although he does not elaborate on the social psychology involved in cross-group contacts to the extent that Kanter does, he does note that the

> social experience of associating with persons with different backgrounds undoubtedly affects attitudes and conduct. It may well broaden people's horizons, promote tolerance, and stimulate intellectual endeavors. . . . The structurally generated differences in intergroup experience between small minorities and a large majority would lead one to expect these characteristics to be more prevalent among the minorities. (Blau, 1977b, p. 36)

Blau's quote suggests that in work situations characterized by a relatively large majority group, and a much smaller minority group, the lack of out-group contacts by majority members increases the likelihood that they will sustain prejudices against minority members and engage in discriminatory behavior. Increases in the proportionate size of the minority should, ceteris paribus, promote more out-group contacts among the majority and thus reduce negative attitudes and behavior. (Note the assumption that individuals have relatively few chances to leave the group; otherwise, increases in the minority could conceivably cause the majority simply to leave.[4]) On the other hand, because members of small minority groups have relatively few opportunities for in-group interactions and greater chances for out-group interactions, they might be expected to have, on average, a relatively high tolerance for (if not positive attraction to) out-group members. Paradoxically, an increase in the proportionate size of the minority group, by decreasing the probabilities of out-group interaction among minority members, may result in more negative attitudes toward the majority. Such an increase also enhances the likelihood that members of the minority will have more interaction with each other; this could be expected to reinforce initial attraction and propensities to provide support to in-group members.

Although a social contact perspective makes some of the same assumptions as a similarity-attraction perspective, it emphasizes the impact of group demography as an independent influence on the formation of social ties and focuses on individuals' attitudes and behaviors toward in-group and out-group members rather than on internal subjective states. It suggests that the higher the proportion of women in a work group, the more women will exhibit supportive attitudes and behaviors toward other women and the less they will show supportive attitudes and behaviors toward men. Although Blau explicitly recognizes the role of status as an influence on interaction patterns, he does not specify how the relation between group size and interaction patterns may differ for high- and low-status groups. As noted, Kanter does not consider the effects of status at all; the consequences of membership in a small minority group are presumably the same for men as for women.

Blau's framework does not give much attention to the impact of group proportions on individuals' internal subjective states. Kanter does, however, suggest that women in skewed groups suffer feelings of psychological discomfort and stress, largely as an outcome of the negative social environment created by the majority's attitudes and behaviors. Furthermore, she proposes that such feelings should decrease as the proportion of women increases and group dynamics shift. She does not address the impact of increases in the proportion of women on the psychological states of male work group members, nor whether men in small subgroups experience the same negative psychological outcomes as do women. If the group dynamics are the same when women are in a majority, as Kanter's and Blau's silence on this point might suggest, then it is reasonable to expect that when men are a minority in a skewed group, they will experience psychological discomfort created by social isolation, heightened performance pressures, and so on.

Group Competition Perspective

Another perspective that focuses on the impact of group proportions on social relations but offers predictions very different from those of a social contact perspective is the group competition perspective. This approach, which originated in studies of racial and ethnic relations, assumes that individuals typically identify themselves in terms of membership in a social group and are inclined to protect and advance their group's interests vis-à-vis other groups (even at their own expense).

Blalock (1967) has offered one theoretical framework in this tradition on which a number of empirical studies have been based; thus, we will concentrate on his arguments here. Blalock's theorizing reflects his empirical work, which focused on expressions of prejudice and discrimination by Whites against Blacks.[5] In consequence, like Kanter (1977a), he does not explicitly distinguish between the effects of numerical and social dominance, nor does he consider the impact of relative group size on the attitudes and behavior of socially subordinate groups. He uses the term *minority* only in reference to socially subordinate groups; because we use that term to refer to the smaller of two groups, we substitute *socially subordinate group* for Blalock's *minority*.

His analysis is predicated on the notion that the outcomes of competition between social groups for collective control of resources are importantly influenced by the relative sizes of competing groups. Thus, as a socially subordinate group increases in size, so does its perceived level of threat to the dominant group, which leads to increased hostility among members of the latter toward the former and to discriminatory acts to protect the dominant group's control of resources.

Blalock distinguished between competition for economic resources (e.g., jobs) and social resources (e.g., power). In the case of economic resources, he theorized a positive, declining curvilinear relationship between subordinate group size and discrimination by the dominant group, based on the assumption that threats to economic resources would quickly generate strong discriminatory activity by the dominant group, generally aimed at confining subordinates to selected areas of economic activity (see Figure 10.1). If successful, such activity would largely eliminate the subordinate group's competitive threat, regardless of increases in size, and thus stabilize the level of economic discrimination by the dominants. The potential applicability of this analysis to gender-based occupational and job segregation is evident (see, e.g., Reskin & Roos, 1990; see also Chapter 7 by Jacobs in this book).

In the case of political power resources, Blalock postulated a positive, exponential relationship between discrimination by dominant group members and increases in the size of the subordinate group based on the assumptions

Level of Discrimination

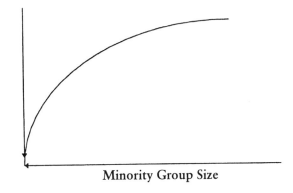

Minority Group Size

Figure 10.1. Relationship Between Subordinate Group Size and Discrimination by Dominant Group, by Type of Competition: Competition for Economic Resources

Level of Discrimination

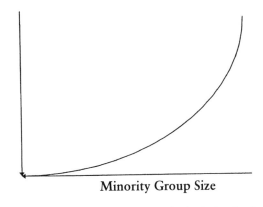

Minority Group Size

Figure 10.2. Relationship Between Subordinate Group Size and Discrimination by Dominant Group, by Type of Competition: Competition for Political Resources

that no comparable segregating tactics could allay competition for political power resources and that growth of the subordinate group would thus represent a progressively greater threat to the dominant group's control of political resources (see Figure 10.2). This argument may have particular relevance for analyses of the effects of increases in the number of women in management and decision-making positions.

Thus, in contrast to a social contact perspective, which predicts more positive attitudes and behaviors by a dominant majority toward an increasing subordinate minority (due to the increased rates of out-group contacts by the former group), a competition perspective predicts the opposite. Specifically, this perspective predicts that as the proportion of women in a work group increases, men will exhibit more negative attitudes toward them and engage more in economic and political discrimination. Because women are not a socially dominant group in contemporary American society (e.g., Ridgeway,

1997), whether they, as a majority group, would be similarly threatened by an increase in the proportion of men, and thus respond with more out-group antagonism, is unclear.

This perspective is largely silent on questions concerning the impact of group composition on internally oriented subjective states, as is a social contact perspective. Following Kanter's (1977a) arguments, negative social environments for women (presumed to be associated with increases in their relative group size) may lead to greater psychological discomfort and lower levels of attachment to the larger group. This might be reduced, however, once women reached a critical mass that allowed them to counter discrimination by the majority effectively. Insofar as economic and power threats entail uncomfortable psychological states, a competition perspective implies that the increasing representation of women in a work group will affect men's attitudes negatively (e.g., decrease work group satisfaction, increase willingness to leave the group).

The literature on social identity theory, on which studies of group gender composition have frequently drawn, shares some key assumptions with a group competition perspective. However, social identity theory provides a somewhat different view of the effects of increasing minority group size on individuals' psychological states.

Social Identity Perspective

Social identity theorists assume that much, if not most, social behavior is driven by individuals' needs to protect and enhance their self-esteem or self-image (Tajfel, 1978, 1982; Tajfel & Turner, 1985; Turner & Giles, 1981). An individual's self-image reflects both a personal component, based on characteristics that are unique (e.g., personality, intellectual and physical capabilities), and a social component that is based on identification with various social groups and their perceived social status. The latter component entails self-categorization, the cognitive processes of developing contrasting categories of group membership, and assigning oneself to one or more of these categories.

The need to enhance self-esteem leads individuals to seek to maximize the status of groups with which they identify by attributing favorable qualities to members of those groups (and thus, themselves), and negative qualities to individuals who are *not* members of those groups. Because group social status is normally aligned with control of material resources and power, a social identity perspective implies that individuals will be motivated to maximize control of resources by group members and to prevent outsiders from having access. Thus, self-categorization processes enhance behavioral as well as attitudinal in-group solidarity and promote hostility and discrimination toward out-groups (Brewer & Miller, 1996).

Because individuals typically identify with an array of groups (status, occupational, religious, political, etc.), what determines the salience of a given identity at any point in time is a critical theoretical and empirical question. Research within this tradition has suggested a number of conditions that may influence salience, including the degree to which the group a person identifies with is perceived to be threatened by another (Ashforth & Mael, 1989; van Knippenberg, 1984). Insofar as increases in a subordinate group threaten control of power and resources by a dominant group, as Blalock suggests, this condition should heighten the salience of dominant group membership for individuals. In-group support and out-group hostility should increase among members of a dominant group when the subordinate group expands. Likewise, when a subordinate group is very small, in-group/out-group distinctions should be less salient to members of the dominant group, and they should show relatively little support for other in-group members or hostility toward out-group members.

Social identity theory elaborates the arguments of the group competition perspective by specifying effects of group size for members of lower-status minority groups. Social identity theorists have argued that identification with a group that is clearly accorded lower status in society may be threatening to an individual's self-esteem. If raising the status of the group does not appear to be viable, individuals may respond by distinguishing themselves from their group as being exceptional or uncharacteristically superior. Under these circumstances, the drive to promote positive self-identity may undermine in-group solidarity among members of subordinate groups and encourage more positive attitudes and behaviors toward members of out-groups than toward the in-group (Williams & Giles, 1978; see also Graves & Powell, 1995).

Insofar as increases in the size of a lower-status group lead to perceptions of greater power (and potentially higher group status), as small, socially subordinate groups increase in relative size, members could be expected to have more supportive attitudes and behaviors toward in-group members and more hostile attitudes and behaviors toward out-group members. In addition, individuals might be expected to be less satisfied in situations where the social identity that is activated threatens their self-esteem. The perception of increasing power and status of groups in which individuals have vested their social identities should alleviate stress created by unfavorable group status, and thus positively affect individuals' subjective psychological states (Wharton, 1992).

The application of these arguments to analyses of gender relations suggests that when the proportion of women in a work group is smaller, women are more likely to hold negative attitudes toward other women in the group and positive attitudes toward men. Once the proportion of women reaches a level that makes it possible (in actuality or perception) to exercise collective influence, women should show higher levels of in-group support and less favorable out-group attitudes with further increases in proportional representation. In addition, women should experience more positive internally oriented psychological states as the number of women in a work group increases.

Because men hold higher status in society, they could be expected to exhibit positive attitudes and supportive behavior toward other men, as members of their in-group, even when they constitute a numerical minority. In fact, insofar as being in a minority enhances the salience of their gender group membership, they may show an even stronger commitment to other men in the work group than when they are in a majority. The impact of minority status on men's subjective states is more ambiguous theoretically, but it seems likely that the lower power associated with being in a small minority will reduce the normally positive effects on self-esteem of having membership in a socially dominant group. Status ambiguity is a key element in the final perspective that we consider: relative deprivation.

Relative Deprivation Perspective

The term *relative deprivation* was first applied in research on American soldiers in World War II (Stouffer, Suchman, DeVinney, Starr, & Williams, 1949) that found that men in units with high rates of promotion reported significantly lower morale and more negative attitudes than those in units with much lower rates. The general explanation of this phenomenon, that individuals' expectations, based on social comparisons, determine levels of contentment regardless of their objective situation, was soon adopted by researchers interested in explaining variations in individuals' political discontent and susceptibility to political protest activity (Gurr, 1970; Runciman, 1966).

Crosby (1982) was among the first to apply the concept of relative deprivation in the context of gender studies to explain the common finding of that women and men have comparable levels of job satisfaction, despite women's lower earnings and less favorable working conditions. She suggested that, because of job and occupational segregation, women typically use other women as their social comparison group and, consequently, have lower expectations for work rewards than do men. Building on Crosby's work, Major (1994) argued that women feel less entitled to job rewards than men, and that is key to women's greater job satisfaction. Women's sense of entitlement is likely to be affected by their acceptance of gender-based inequality in job rewards and conditions.

Research using a relative deprivation perspective has not explicitly addressed the issue of how changes in a group's gender composition may affect women's choices for self-comparisons or their level of job satisfaction. However, Crosby cites job and occupational segregation in explaining why women compare themselves to other women, and her data (1982) indicate that women in occupations with low prestige are much less likely to compare themselves to men than women in high-prestige occupations (which are more likely to be male dominated). This suggests that whether women compare themselves to men or other women depends on the gender composition of the groups to which they belong. Women in male-dominated groups should be more likely to adopt men as a comparison group; conversely, women in female-dominated groups should be more likely to compare themselves to other women. Because men tend to receive greater job rewards than women, women's work satisfaction should be lower in groups with a smaller proportion of women (Graham & Welbourne, in press).[6]

Most of the research on job satisfaction that draws on a relative deprivation perspective has focused on women; how relative deprivation processes might affect men's work attitudes has been almost completely neglected. If men take other men as their reference group, their overall level of job satisfaction could be expected to be negatively related to the proportion of women in their group, because female-dominated occupations and jobs typically provide low levels of rewards (Pfeffer & Davis-Blake, 1987). Crosby's (1982) research suggests that men rarely use women as a comparison group.

However, based on assumptions of theoretical consistency, because women's choice of comparative others is presumed to be affected by the gender composition of groups, we infer that men's choices of comparison others should also be affected by the composition. Small-groups research (see Walker & Fennell, 1986; Walker, Ilardi, McMahon, & Fennell, 1996) indicates that men in gender-mixed or female-dominated groups often enjoy greater nonmaterial rewards, such as opportunities for participation and influence, than in all-male groups. These advantages could conceivably result in *higher* levels of satisfaction for men as the proportion of women in their group increased. And if men in groups with a high proportion of women take their female coworkers as a reference group, they should have relatively high levels of job satisfaction compared with men in groups with a higher proportion of males, because men often receive higher rewards than women coworkers (Blau & Ferber, 1992).

Empirical Research on Group Gender Composition

The predictions from each of these perspectives are depicted schematically in Table 10.1. As the table and our review imply, different theories address three possible outcomes of an increase in the proportion of women in a work group: changes in subjective attitudes toward the social setting (e.g., job satisfaction or propensity to change jobs), changes in attitudes and behaviors toward other members of an in-group, and changes in attitudes and behaviors toward members of out-groups. Most studies consider only one of these potential outcomes, and none explicitly addresses all three. We group studies according to the outcome they examine and then assess the degree to which empirical

TABLE 10.1 Predicted Effects of Increases in the Proportion of Women in a Work Group, by Sex

Theoretical Perspectives

Predicted Outcomes	Similarity-Attraction		Social Contact		Group Competition		Social Identity		Relative Deprivation	
	Women	*Men*	*Women*	*Men*	*Women*	*Men*	*Women*	*Men*	*Women*	*Men*
Subjective states	Positive	Negative	Positive	Negative	Negative to positive	Negative	Positive	Negative	Positive	Positive
Responses to in-group members	Unspecified	Unspecified	Positive	Negative	Unspecified	Unspecified	Positive	Positive	Unspecified	Unspecified
Responses to out-group members	Unspecified	Unspecified	Negative	Positive	Unspecified	Negative	Negative	Negative	Unspecified	Unspecified

support exists for different, relevant theoretical frameworks. We focus first on work that has examined the impact of group gender composition on individuals' attitudes toward their work and the social setting (which constitutes the largest stream of research in this area), then turn to studies focused on in-group relations, and finally examine work on out-group relations.

Consequences for Internally Oriented Work Attitudes and Behavior

Much, if not most, of the research on group gender composition has focused on women's satisfaction with work and group relations, intentions to leave a group, and other similarly self-oriented attitudes and behavior. As Table 10.1 indicates, similarity-attraction, social contact, social identity, and relative deprivation perspectives all predict that increases in the proportion of women in a group will have positive effects on such outcomes, although each perspective suggests slightly different mechanisms through which such effects are produced. A group competition perspective, on the other hand, implies at least an initial decline in women's satisfaction with their work and the social setting as their representation in a group increases, presumably occasioned by the decreased support and negative treatment of women by men in such groups.

With a few notable exceptions, empirical research has generally supported predictions that increases in the proportion of women in a work group have positive effects on women's subjective states. One exception to this conclusion is represented by Wharton and Baron's (1991) analysis of data from the 1973 Quality of Employment Survey. They found a curvilinear, rather than a linear, relationship: Women in occupations that had a more balanced proportion of women exhibited lower job satisfaction compared with women in occupations that had *either* a high proportion of men or a high proportion of women. This is at least partially consistent with predictions of a positive effect of increases in the proportion of women in a group on women's psychological states. In contrast, Fields and Blum (1997), using data from a randomly drawn survey of workers in 1992, found that both men's and women's job satisfaction was significantly lower in more homogeneous groups; they argue that these results are consistent with a social contact perspective.[7]

The bulk of research, however, suggests a positive linear relationship between the proportion of women in a group and the degree to which a favorable psychological environment exists for women. Thus, for example, Spangler, Gordon, and Pipkin (1978), following Kanter's (1977a) arguments, found that women in a law school with a small proportion of women scored significantly higher on measures of performance pressure and social isolation than women in a school with a more balanced gender composition. Some behavioral support for this is provided in an analysis by Alexander and Thoits

(1985) of gender differences in the academic achievements of students, which indicated that the proportion of women in a department had a positive impact on women's grades; men's grades were not affected by the demographic composition of departments. Both of these analyses are consistent with research by Stover (1994), Tolbert and Oberfield (1991), and Tidball (1986) indicating a positive relation between the proportion of women faculty in a school or department and the proportion of women students. Similarly, Izraeli's (1983) study of local union officers in Israel showed that women on committees with relatively few women were significantly more likely to feel constrained by gendered role expectations than women on committees with greater gender balance. Izraeli's study also showed that the self-reported efficacy of women on the committees with a small proportion of women was significantly lower than that of their male colleagues. This was not the case in committees with more women.

Studies have also found the proportion of women in a work group to affect women's perceptions of their own efficacy and performance. Mellor's (1995) study of local unions showed that women in locals with a small proportion of women officers evaluated their own competence and ability to participate significantly lower than did those in locals with more women officers. Likewise, Ely (1995) found that women associates in law firms with few women partners were significantly more likely to perceive differences in the attributes of successful lawyers and their own attributes than did women in firms with higher proportions of women partners. These results are compatible with the findings of experimental research by Eskilson and Wiley (1976) that indicated that women in charge of two men were less likely to exhibit leadership behaviors than those in charge of two women, or one woman and one man.

Relatedly, research has indicated that women in groups with relatively few women are less satisfied than women in more gender-balanced groups. For example, Konrad, Winter, and Gutek's (1992) study of white-collar work groups found that the fewer women in a group, the greater women's social isolation and the lower their job satisfaction. This effect was particularly pronounced in groups where women held positions of higher authority. Martin and Harkreader's (1993) study of a military depot indicated that having a higher proportion of women in a work group significantly increased women's overall level of job satisfaction as well as their satisfaction with coworkers. Consistent with these findings, Loscocco and Spitze (1991) found that both women's and men's pay satisfaction was enhanced when they worked in factories with higher proportions of women. Similarly, Graham and Welbourne (in press) found that in a highly gender-segregated workplace, women exhibited higher pay satisfaction than men.

In addition, several studies have shown that the lower the proportion of women in a work group, the more likely women are to contemplate leaving the organization. Burke and McKeen (1996), in a study of professional and managerial women, found that women in organizations with lower propor-tions of women indicated greater job dissatisfaction and were more likely to express intentions to quit. Popielarz and McPherson (1995) found that both women and men in voluntary organizations who were in a distinct gender minority had higher rates of dropout than did those in organizations with more favorable (from the respondents' standpoint) gender ratios.

This last study raises the question of whether the impact of group gender composition on subjective states is the same for men and women (Gutek, 1985). Research on the relationship between the proportion of men in a work group and men's self-related attitudes has produced much more mixed results than that focusing on women. As noted, Fields and Blum (1997) found no difference between men and women in the effects of gender composition on job satisfaction. Their research indicated that both groups exhibited the highest level of satisfaction in more heterogeneous, gender-balanced groups. These results are in sharp contrast to those from Wharton and Baron's (1987) analysis of male respondents in the 1973 Quality of Employment Survey. Their research indicated that for men, as for women, job satisfaction was significantly higher in positions that were typified as *either* all male *or* predominantly female than positions in mixed-sex settings. Martin and Harkreader's (1993) study indicated that men's job satisfaction was unrelated to the proportion of women in their department; this is in contrast to the positive relation found among women. However, the proportion of women in the same *job ladder* did have a positive impact for male respondents on four of the five measures, including a measure of satisfaction with coworkers.

One possible interpretation of the latter finding, as well as of Wharton and Baron's finding that men had relatively high levels of satisfaction in female-dominated work settings, is that men perceive greater opportunities for promotion when there are more women on the job ladder. This is consistent with Williams's (1992) findings from research on the advantages enjoyed by men in traditionally female occupations. Thus, these results are compatible with a relative deprivation perspective, suggesting that men's satisfaction is the result of their gender-based expectations for promotion and advancement being more than met in female-dominated occupations and career ladders. We know of no research, however, that shows whether men's rate of advancement is indeed greater in female-dominated settings than in balanced or male-dominated settings.

Other research, however, indicates that men become increasingly satisfied as the proportion of men in their group rises. Pelled's (1996) research on blue-collar work groups indicated that both men and women experienced less emotional conflict as the proportion of group members of the same gender increased. Likewise, studies by Tsui, Egan, and O'Reilly (1992) and Allmend-inger and Hackman (1995) found that being in groups with fewer members of their gender decreased satisfaction and lowered group attachment among men significantly more than among women. This is consistent with McPherson and Smith-Lovin's (1986) finding of high levels of sex segregation in voluntary organizations.

Although the range of findings in research on men makes drawing general conclusions about the impact of gender composition on men's attitudes problematic, it does suggest that the psychological impact of being a member of a gender minority may differ for men and women. A similar conclusion emerges from research focused on in-group relations.

Consequences for In-Group Relations

Relatively little research has been devoted to exploring the effects of gender composition on either in-group or out-group relations. Studies by Ely (1994, 1995), South, Markham, Bonjean, and Corder (1987), South, Bonjean, Markham, and Corder (1982), and Izraeli (1983) investigated the impact of increases in the proportion of women on women's attitudes toward other women. In Izraeli's study of local unions in Israel, women respondents in locals whose membership contained less than 20% women were significantly less likely to view women as possessing necessary leadership skills than women in locals with a greater proportion of women. Ely (1994) found very similar results in a notably different context: women lawyers in corporate law firms in the United States. Women associates in firms with relatively few women in partnership positions were significantly less likely to perceive relationships with same-gender peers as supportive, and they were also less likely to perceive women partners as suitable role models. Further analysis (Ely, 1995) indicated that women in firms with fewer women were more likely to characterize women as "flirtatious" and "sexually involved with coworkers" compared with women in firms with a greater number of women; the latter were more likely to characterize women in more high-power terms such as "aggressive" and "able to promote oneself."

In a study of six departments in a federal agency, South et al. (1982) found that the greater the proportion of women in a department, the higher the rate of reported social contacts among women. As this rate increased, women perceived greater encouragement for advancement from other women. Surprisingly, though, controlling for the effects of social contact, the higher the proportion of women in a department, the *less* women perceived that other women provided encouragement for advancement. A second study by South et al. (1987), exploring this issue in more detail, found that men and women did not differ in the amount of encouragement they perceived women coworkers as providing. Men did perceive significantly more encouragement from male coworkers than women did; moreover, the amount of encouragement men received from other men was positively related to the proportion of women in the work group.

This finding is compatible with Williams's (1992) research on men in four female-dominated occupations: nursing, librarianship, elementary school teaching, and social work. Based on in-depth interviews with men and women in these occupations, she concluded that men were commonly on a "glass escalator" to higher-level administrative positions within the occupation, often under the mentorship of male supervisors. Similarly, Izraeli's (1983) analysis indicated that men in local unions with a higher proportion of women were more likely to perceive men as having greater leadership skills than women, compared with men in locals with fewer women (although this difference did not attain significance). Regardless of group gender composition, men were significantly more likely to attribute such qualities to men than were women.

Schmitt and Hill's (1977) research on the composition of assessment center groups on assessment center ratings is the only study that suggests a negative relation between the proportion of women in a group and the level of support for men by men. In this study, the proportion of men in an assessment group was found to be positively related to ratings of male applicants on both oral and written communication skills. The correlation between the number of men and overall ratings of male applicants, however, was not significant.

Thus, the limited research on the impact of gender composition on in-group relations suggests that the impact may vary for men and women. Men appear to be more inclined to support other men than women are to support other women, and when men are part of a numerical minority this propensity may intensify. For women, being in a group with relatively few women is likely to be detrimental to in-group relations.

Consequences for Out-Group Relations

The research on the impact of gender composition on out-group relations is even more limited than that on in-group relations. The lack of research on this topic stands in marked contrast to the literature on racial and ethnic relations, in which studies of the consequences of group proportions on prejudice and discrimination constitute a major stream of research. This neglect is surprising in light of Kanter's (1977a) emphasis on the role of men's reactions to female "tokens" as a driving force in the dynamics she observed.

The studies by Ely (1995) and Izraeli (1983) support the argument that women's attitudes toward male group members will be most favorable when there are few women in a group and will become less favorable as the proportion of women increases. Ely showed that women lawyers in firms with few women were significantly more likely to see men as possessing attributes of successful lawyers than were women in firms with a higher proportion of women. Likewise, Izraeli found that women in locals with fewer women were more likely to characterize men as having necessary leadership qualities than were women in locals with more women.

However, Williams's (1992) interviews of women in traditionally female occupations yielded no evidence of negative or hostile attitudes toward male colleagues. Thus, conditions that foster less favorable in-group relations for women appear to foster more favorable out-group relations, but even in groups where men represent a distinct minority, women's attitudes and behaviors toward male colleagues are not overtly hostile. Perhaps a curvilinear relationship exists between the proportion of women in a work group and the amount of support provided by women to male colleagues; this remains to be explored in empirical work.

There is only indirect evidence on the impact of increases in the proportion of women on men's out-group attitudes and behavior. Although Kanter reported that, in her study, a lower representation of women was associated with more negative attitudes toward women by men, she did not offer a systematic comparison of men in work groups with few women and those with many women. The women respondents in the study by South et al. (1987), contrary to Kanter's (and Blau's) arguments, reported significantly less support from male coworkers and supervisors as the proportion of women in a department increased. Similarly, Tolbert, Simons, Andrews, and Rhee (1995), studying turnover of women in academic departments, found a positive relation between the rate of turnover and the proportion of women in a department, which they interpreted as the result of more conflict with male colleagues in departments with more women.[8]

Bhatnagar and Swamy (1995) examined the impact of frequent interactions with female bank managers on male managers' attitudes toward female colleagues. Their results indicate no relationship between the frequency of interaction and holding favorable attitudes, which directly contradicts social contact arguments. This null result held when they considered male managers' rates of interactions with female bank clerks. An experimental study of the impact of group composition on patterns of social interaction by Smith-Lovin and Brody (1989), however, found that although men systematically interrupted women more than other men, this pattern was not affected by the proportion of women in the group. Thus, although the evidence is relatively limited, existing data suggest that increases in the number of women in a group have a negative rather than a positive impact on men's attitudes and behaviors toward women.

Assessing Empirical Support for the Theoretical Perspectives

We return to the five theoretical perspectives described at the outset to assess how well these empirical results support their predictions. The majority of studies suggest a positive effect of increases in the proportion of women in a group on women's job satisfaction and attachment to the group, as four of the theoretical perspectives, similarity-attraction, social contact, relative deprivation, and social identity, predict. A similarity-attraction approach explains such results in terms of the satisfaction of desires to interact with others who are perceived to be similar and suggests that men should exhibit complementary attitudes: Their attitudes toward their job should become progressively less positive with increases in the proportion of women. There is some evidence to support this (Tsui et al., 1992), although other evidence suggests that the relationship may be curvilinear (Wharton & Baron, 1987; Williams, 1992); "token" men may be happier than men in settings where the gender balance is more even. This finding is difficult to explain strictly from a similarity-attraction approach. Because this approach also fails to offer any substantial insights into the impact of work group gender proportions on either men's or women's in-group and out-group relations, its theoretical limitations seem to make it less useful to research on gender composition than the other approaches.

Social contact theory, which draws attention to out-group as well as in-group connections, also suggests that women should experience more favorable subjective states as the proportion of women increases, because of greater opportunities to satisfy desires to associate with other women. Male colleagues should show more positive attitudes and behaviors toward women as their relative proportion increases, as a consequence of men's higher rates of interaction with women. Although evidence does suggest that the proportion of women in a group enhances women's attitudes toward their work, the predicted positive effect of frequent interaction with women on men's attitudes and behaviors toward women is not supported in research (Bhatnagar & Swamy, 1995; Smith-Lovin & Brody, 1989). Some studies even suggest a negative relation between the proportion of women in a work group and the amount of support men provide to women colleagues (South et al., 1987; Tolbert et al., 1995). Moreover, little evidence exists to support the implication of a social contact perspective that men's attitudes and behaviors toward other men will become less positive as the proportion of women in a group increases, as a function of fewer opportunities for in-group interaction. If anything, men's support for other men appears to increase with increases in the proportion of women (South et al., 1987; Williams, 1992).

As a social contact perspective predicts, however, increases in the proportion of women in a group are generally associated with more positive in-group relations among women (Ely, 1994; South et al., 1982; South et al., 1987) and less favorable attitudes and behaviors toward men (Ely, 1995; Izraeli, 1983). These patterns are also consistent with predictions from group competition and social identity perspectives. On the balance, support for the predictions derived from a social contact perspective is mixed, and the predictions pertaining to men's attitudes and behavior appear especially problematic.

Although a competition perspective suggests that increases in the number of women will lead to greater power for women ultimately and thus to women's increased satisfaction, it predicts that before the threshold is reached, such increases will result in more hostile relations with male coworkers and thus negatively affect women's satisfaction. This implies a curvilinear impact of the proportion of women on women's subjective outcomes, with increases in the proportion of women in a group leading first to a decline in women's satisfaction, then to an increase once the number of women is sufficient to affect power relations. There is some evidence that a curvilinear relationship may exist, such that women have the most positive attitudes when there is either a high *or* very low proportion of women in a group (Wharton & Baron, 1987, 1991). Unfortunately, the possibility of nonlinear effects has been explored in only a limited number of studies, perhaps because gender and job-level sex segregation make it difficult to find settings in which the proportion of women in a given type of work group varies substantially. Insofar as most research suggests a positive, linear effect of increases in women's representation in a group on women's subjective states, however, the prediction of curvilinearity from a competition perspective is not borne out.

A group competition perspective offers few insights into the effects of changes in gender composition on women's attitudes towards either in-group or out-group members. It does suggest that increases in the proportion of women may create an environment in which men's collective control of resources and power are threatened, leading men to be more dissatisfied and to experience other negative psychological states. This prediction is supported by a number of studies (Allmendinger & Hackman, 1995; Tolbert et al., 1995; Tsui et al., 1992). Thus, although some predictions derived from a competition perspective are consistent with empirical research, others are called into question. And like other perspectives, the utility of a competition approach for research on the effects of group gender composition is limited by its lack of theoretical specificity in a number of respects.

Research findings indicating positive effects of increasing numbers of women on women's psychological states are generally consistent with a social identity perspective.[9] In contrast to either similarity-attraction or social contact perspectives, this approach explains such findings in terms of the greater collective power and status that members of low-status groups may receive as a consequence of increasing group size. It also yields predictions about these effects of group gender composition on women's in-group and out-group relations, ones that are consistent with the findings that increases in women's representation in work groups have a positive impact on women's in-group attitudes (Ely, 1994, 1995; Izraeli, 1983; South et al., 1982) and a negative impact on women's out-group attitudes (Ely, 1995; Izraeli, 1983). It also suggests that proportionate increases among women will have a positive impact on men's in-group relations, consistent with research by South et al. (1987) and Williams (1992), and a negative impact on men's out-group relations, supported by South et al. (1987), Izraeli (1983), and Tolbert et al. (1995). In addition, there is some support for social identity's prediction that the potential group power loss associated with increases in the proportion of women in a group will have offset the generally positive psychological outcomes for men of membership in a high-status group (Allmendinger & Hackman, 1995; Tsui et al., 1992). Thus, there is a relatively high level of support for predictions derived from social identity theory.

Research findings of a positive relation between the proportion of women in a group and levels of satisfaction are consistent with relative deprivation claims that women are more likely to compare themselves to other women, and that such comparisons should not produce relative deprivation. We infer from the logic of relative deprivation research that men should also be more likely to use female coworkers for social comparisons when the proportion of women in a group increases. Because such comparisons are likely to be favorable for men, their satisfaction should be higher in groups with more women. This prediction is supported by several studies (Martin & Harkreader, 1993; Wharton & Baron, 1987; Williams, 1992) that suggest men perceive greater advancement opportunities in female-dominated groups than in male-dominated groups. Other research suggests that men who work with women may experience greater satisfaction because they realize that they are substantially better off than their female coworkers (Graham & Welbourne, in press; Major, 1994).

Although the concept of fraternal, or group-based, deprivation from relative deprivation theory implies in-group and out-group distinctions, how fraternal deprivation may be related to changes in minority and majority group proportions, and hence to in-group/out-group attitudes and behaviors, is not specified. Although we have drawn some inferences about the effects of group proportions on individuals' sense of relative deprivation, we should emphasize that most work in this tradition does not explicitly specify how individuals choose referent comparisons, or how changes in these comparisons may occur. This lack of theoretical specificity limits the utility of a relative deprivation approach for current studies of the impact of group gender composition.

Based on our review of empirical research, then, we conclude that a social identity approach provides predictions most compatible with findings from existing research. However, limits in research as well as in the theoretical frameworks themselves require a good deal of caution in drawing strong conclusions along these lines. It is to such limits that we turn in our concluding section.

Directions for Future Theorizing and Research

Despite the growing accumulation over the past 20 years of empirical research on group gender composition, there are some striking lacunae in this research, due at least in part to the limits of extant theoretical perspectives. A completely developed theory of gender composition would specify how variations in the relative numbers of men and women in a group affect the attitudes and actions of members of the numerical majority toward members of their in-group, out-group members, and their social setting (in terms of internally oriented subjective states such as job satisfaction, sense of competence, efforts to participate, etc.). It would also explain the impact of gender composition on the attitudes and actions of members of the numerical minority toward their in-group, their out-group, and their social setting. Such a theory would specify other variables that mediate the effect of group proportions on outcome variables, such as differences in the relative social status of men and women or the degree to which a given context is defined as gender appropriate, and so on (see Yoder, 1991, 1994).

Most theoretical perspectives currently used in research on work group gender demography address a fairly narrow subset of potential consequences of variations in gender composition: psychological states of comfort or discomfort, attitudes and behaviors of men toward women colleagues, or women colleagues toward other women. Insofar as gender composition affects a variety of relationships that interact to produce group outcomes, predicting such outcomes requires theoretical and empirical consideration of all these relationships.

Several specific issues deserve more attention. One is how variations in the proportion of women in a group affect men's and women's in-group and out-group attitudes and behaviors, and whether any such effects are monotonic or curvilinear. The issue of curvilinear effects has been suggested by several studies, and such effects seem intuitively plausible, although not considered in extant theoretical perspectives. Current levels of sex segregation in jobs and occupations may pose some problems for examining curvilinear relationships, although research could compare several similar occupations or jobs (e.g., comparable in level of education, pay, etc.) that differ in terms of gender composition. Surveying both men and women in such occupations could provide some insights into the relationship between gender composition and our major outcome variables: subjective perceptions of the social setting, in-group attitudes and behaviors, and out-group attitudes and behavior.

Researchers also need to recognize that different measures of the demographic composition of groups severely hinders comparison of results. Whereas similarity/attraction and social identity approaches typically rely on measures of "fit" between the gender of a given individual and that of other persons in the group, social contact, group competition, and relative deprivation approaches commonly use the proportion of women as their measure. Although these two general approaches yield important information on the effects of gender composition, they do not produce identical measures for a given group and they may lead to differing conclusions concerning the effects of group gender composition.

Even within the two general measurement approaches, the nature of measures that are used varies. Some studies treat the percentage of women in a work group as a continuous variable, whereas others create categorical variables (e.g., 0 to 25%, 26% to 50%, etc.). These categories are rarely derived from theory and do not contribute to the theoretical or empirical development of the notion of "tipping points" at which gender composition effects may occur. Similarly, studies focusing on the fit between an individual's gender and that of other group members use a variety of measures of fit. We note that a number of fit measures commonly employed in gender composition studies may not be measuring the "fit" construct adequately (see Edwards, 1994, for a complete discussion of this issue).

More theoretical and empirical attention should be given to the issue of whether variations in proportions have differing effects on men and women, and what conditions are associated with such differential effects. Differences in men's and women's social status in contemporary society, social definitions of different types of work as appropriate for men or for women, and cross-hierarchical relations could all produce differences in responses of men and women to variations in gender composition—these confounding factors are generally ignored in current theoretical perspectives, and this neglect is, not surprisingly, echoed by empirical work (see Yoder, 1994).

Finally, researchers should give more consideration to comparing the effects of gender composition and racial/ethnic composition of work units. For example, although both women and minority workers may experience dominant group hostility, the contexts in which this hostility occurs may differ. Likewise, the effects of group proportions on such hostility may vary by race and by gender.

We are encouraged by the progress made to date in understanding the potential effects of gender composition on organizational groups, but clearly many topics still demand research attention. The growth in the number of women in the work force, reductions in gender-based occupational segregation, and changes in the representation of women at higher levels of organizational hierarchy increase the need for better understanding gender composition effects to develop effective organizational and social policies.

Notes

1. The proportion of the labor force constituted by women rose from 20% in 1920 to 27% by 1950; thus, women remained a small (but hardly negligible) fraction of workers up through midcentury (Deldycke, 1968). This proportion increased to 32% in 1960 and 37% by 1970; thus, the rate of increase during these two decades was nearly double that of the three earlier decades. By 1990, women made up just under half (45%) of the labor force (U.S. Bureau of the Census, 1997).

2. In addition to Simmel's (1908) influence, each work reflects, at least implicitly, conclusions drawn from post-World War II research on the effect of cross-group interaction on racial prejudice and discrimination. This research suggested that increased social interaction among members of two different social groups tended to decrease individuals' propensity to subscribe to stereotypes and prejudicial attitudes toward the other group's members, and hence to reduce discriminatory behavior. (See

Allport, 1954, for a classic statement of this research, and Hewstone & Brown, 1986, for a more contemporary summary.)

3. This is inherent in the computation of rates of in-group and out-group associations. For any two groups, the number of contacts with the other group will be identical. Thus, the numerator used in calculating the rate of association will be the same for both groups, whereas the denominator is based on the size of the group. Smaller groups will have a smaller denominator and thus a higher rate of out-group contacts. This proposed measure does not, of course, take into account the proportion of members within a group that have out-group contacts. In practice, such contacts could be concentrated in just a few members or widely distributed among members. How the concentration of out-group associations within a group might affect the typical attitudes and behaviors by members toward the out-group is not made clear in Blau's arguments.

4. As suggested by the editor, Blau's argument also assumes the work group is a self-contained entity and ignores the possibility that people may learn from their contacts with others outside the group.

5. Other sociological studies that also have contributed to this perspective have similarly focused on changes in the racial composition of communities and have emphasized the role of the dominant majority group—Whites—as the key force in shaping intergroup relations (e.g., Bonacich, 1972; Beck & Tolnay, 1990; Brown & Fuguitt, 1972).

6. If women compare themselves to other women, they may become even more satisfied with their situation when there are more men in their group, because women in male-dominated jobs and occupations may receive higher rewards than those in female-dominated ones (Loscocco & Spitze, 1991). However, Tolbert's (1986) research, indicating that differences in the average salary of women faculty in large, research-oriented, male-dominated institutions and in smaller, less prestigious, female-dominated institutions were comparatively small, suggests that employment in male-dominated work settings may bring women fewer rewards than expected.

7. We disagree with their interpretation that a social contact approach, and Blau's work in particular, necessarily implies that women will experience more negative social relations as the proportion of women in a group exceeds a balanced threshold. Our reading suggests that women will experience out-group relations (i.e., those with men) as more unpleasant in this condition, as the result of fewer affiliation-building contacts, but their in-group relations will be increasingly positive, and because they will have more opportunities for interacting with other women, the net psychological effects should be positive.

8. Thanks go to the editor for suggesting another interpretation on these findings: that an increase in women faculty may result in a more cohesive and supportive work group, such that women gain the confidence to leave voluntarily for better jobs.

9. A social identity perspective could also be taken to imply a threshold-level effect, as does a competition perspective, but it does not suggest a negative relation between the proportion of women in a group and women's satisfaction prior to that point, as a competition perspective does.

Chapter 11

Gender Effects on Social Influence and Emergent Leadership

Linda L. Carli and Alice H. Eagly

Research on women's status in organizations reveals that even though women possess 50% of bachelor's degrees and 42% of advanced degrees (U.S. Bureau of the Census, 1997) and constitute 46% of all workers (U.S. Department of Labor, 1998c), women continue to experience workplace discrimination. Compared with men, women are concentrated in a relatively small number of occupations (Dunn, 1996), are underrepresented in the most powerful positions in business (holding less than 5% of upper-management and executive positions), and earn lower salaries than men (Federal Glass Ceiling Commission, 1995). Even when women attain executive positions, they still experience lower levels of compensation, mobility, and authority (Lyness & Thompson, 1997). One interpretation of women's lack of advancement at work commensurate with their educational accomplishments and amount of

AUTHORS' NOTE: Work on this chapter was facilitated by Alice Eagly's research grant, SBR-9729449, from the National Science Foundation. Also important is the support of the Murray Research Center of Radcliffe College, where Alice Eagly was Visiting Scholar when she completed work on the chapter. We would like to thank Michael Dorsey for his comments on previous drafts.

workforce participation is that women face a glass ceiling of discriminatory barriers (Morrison & Von Glinow, 1990). We first outline theoretical explanations for this resistance and then review empirical research that documents sex differences in influence, styles of interaction, and emergent leadership. The general domain of the chapter is task-oriented interaction, defined as social interaction that is oriented toward attaining goals. This is the type of interaction that people carry out as work, although not necessarily as paid work. Groups in the workplace thus engage in task-oriented interaction, but so do community groups, sports teams, classrooms of students, and boards and committees in many contexts.

Aiding interpretation of resistance to women's influence and leadership are two of the most prominent and well-developed theoretical explanations for sex differences in social influence: *status characteristics theory* (Berger, Fisek, Norman, & Zelditch, 1977) and *social role theory* (Eagly, 1987, 1997). Both of these theories focus on social structural factors contributing to sex differences in behavior rather than on biological or learned dispositional differences between men and women. These two theories emphasize that the sexes differ in their social position (i.e., status and roles) and that these structural differences are the root cause of sex differences in behavior. In contrast, biological, evolutionary, and socialization explanations for sex differences consider these differences to be intrinsic to human personality. Such theories generally view sex differences as relatively stable and constant across individuals, situations, and historical periods (Buss, 1995; Hines, 1993; Jacklin & Reynolds, 1993). Because status characteristics and social role theories emphasize social structural factors that produce expectations about female and male behavior, they can better account for variability in sex differences that results from variation in the social position of men and women across cultures, subcultures, historical periods, and individual life histories. In addition, situational variation in the sex differentiation of behavior depends on the salience of gender norms and the influence of social roles that compete with gender roles.

Theoretical Explanations for Gender Effects in Social Influence

Status Characteristics Theory

According to status characteristics theory (Berger et al., 1977), which is one aspect of a broader approach known as *expectation states theory* (Berger, Wagner, & Zelditch, 1985), members of task-oriented groups form expectations about how other members will perform. These expectations can be based on specific information about an individual's past performance or inferred from *diffuse status characteristics,* which are general characteristics such as sex, race, education, occupation, or physical attractiveness that are correlated with status and perceived competence in society. For example, as a general rule, people tend to have more social status if they are male rather than female, White rather than Black, more educated rather than less educated, in prestigious occupations rather than less prestigious ones, and physically attractive rather than unattractive. For a diffuse status characteristic to operate, it must be activated or made salient in some way (e.g., by composing a group of members who differ with respect to that characteristic). If the characteristic is salient, members will assume that high-status individuals are more competent at the task, unless there is evidence to the contrary (Wagner & Berger, 1997).

According to status characteristics theory, gender acts as a diffuse status characteristic in our culture because more respect, honor, and importance are attached to men than women (Berger et al., 1977; Carli, 1991; Meeker & Weitzel-O'Neill, 1985; Ridgeway & Diekema, 1992; Wagner & Berger, 1997). Therefore, men are thought to be more competent than women in many domains. According to this argument, sex operates as a diffuse status characteristic by affecting performance expectations whenever men and women are in the same task-oriented group, even when tasks are not gender typed, although the impact of the characteristic would be stronger for a traditionally masculine task.

In general, individuals who have high diffuse status receive more opportunities to make contributions to the group task, receive higher evaluations for their contributions, and exert greater influence over the behaviors and opinions of others in the group (Berger et al., 1977). Performance expectations are often self-fulfilling because individuals who are expected to perform well have more opportunity to participate and therefore actually do make more task contributions, thereby enhancing their perceived status and competence (Ridgeway, 1978; Wood & Karten, 1986) and increasing their chances of emerging as group leaders (Hawkins, 1995; Stein & Heller, 1979). Based on this theory, then, men should make more contributions to groups (particularly task contributions), exert more influence over group decisions, and be selected as leaders more often than women.

Status theorists maintain that individuals' diffuse status affects not only their perceived competence and expectations about their future performance but also their expectations about what constitutes appropriate behavior in the group. In essence, low-status individuals lack sufficient *legitimacy* to act as leaders or influence agents in groups (Meeker & Weitzel-O'Neill, 1985; Ridgeway & Berger, 1986). In groups whose members have equal diffuse status, individuals who are talkative, confident, and assertive are typically perceived as especially competent and therefore become persuasive and emerge as group leaders. When group members have unequal diffuse status, low-status individuals who are talkative, confident, and assertive are typically not perceived as especially competent because the competence potentially conveyed by such behaviors contradicts group members' expectations

(Ridgeway & Berger, 1986). Therefore, gains in persuasiveness and leadership do not routinely accrue to low-status individuals who manifest especially competent behavior.

According to this legitimacy argument, group members expect and accept that individuals with high diffuse status will behave in the competent, confident manner that asserts status. However, group members do not expect low-status individuals to behave in this manner, and they tend to view such behavior as an illegitimate attempt to attain leadership or influence in the group. Consequently, low-status individuals find that their contributions are ignored or rejected, causing their status to drop even more over time (Meeker & Weitzel-O'Neill, 1985). These tendencies suggest that status-asserting behavior is less acceptable in women than in men and that women may rely more on subtle and indirect forms of influence than men. In addition, women should be able to overcome some of the resistance to their contributions by portraying their status-asserting behavior as especially group oriented and cooperative, perhaps by demonstrating strong commitment to the group and its goals, or by expressing higher levels of socially facilitative behavior and interpersonal warmth than men do (Ridgeway & Diekema, 1992).

Social Role Theory

Social role theory posits that sex differences in social influence and other behaviors derive from the societal division of labor between the sexes—specifically, from the different norms and expectations associated with the social roles that men and women generally hold (Eagly, 1987). According to this approach, women typically possess very different roles than men, roles that tend to demand different behavior. Women and men seek to adjust to sex-typical roles by acquiring the specific skills and resources linked to successful role performance and by adapting their social behavior to role requirements.

A variety of sex-specific skills and behavioral styles arise from men's and women's typical family and economic roles, which in many societies can be described as breadwinner and homemaker. Examples of adjustment are women learning domestic skills such as cooking and men learning skills that are marketable in the paid economy. According to the typical division of labor, women are more likely than men to be primary caretakers of children, a role requiring nurturance, sensitivity, and interpersonal warmth. Women's greater involvement in domestic roles, such as caretaker, results in a greater need for them to display traditional feminine behaviors (Eagly & Steffen, 1984), characterized as *communal* (i.e., reflecting concern for others and selflessness) (Bakan, 1966; Wiggins, 1992). Men, in contrast, typically are more involved in occupational roles, not only because they are somewhat more likely to be employed but also because they are less likely to be employed part-time or part-year (Shelton, 1992). Moreover, the occupational roles that men occupy tend to be different from those occupied by women, in an economy characterized by widespread gender segregation of the labor force (Tomaskovic-Devey, 1995). For example, higher-level managers tend to be male, and administrative assistants tend to be female. The role of manager requires more independence and directiveness than that of administrative assistant. In general, men's roles can be characterized as *agentic,* reflecting self-assertion and a desire for achievement (Bakan, 1966; Wiggins, 1992). Consistent with this reasoning, empirical research has established that men are concentrated in occupations thought to require agentic personality characteristics for successful performance, whereas women are concentrated in occupations thought to require communal personality characteristics (Cejka & Eagly, 1999; Glick, 1991).

In agreement with status characteristics theory, social role theory also acknowledges the greater power and status that tends to be associated with many especially male-dominated roles. Women's adaptations to roles with lesser power and status in society produce a greater need to display behaviors that might be described as subordinate, and men's adaptations to greater power and status produce a greater need to display dominant behaviors. Subordinate behavior is more compliant to social influence, less overtly aggressive, and more cooperative and conciliatory. Dominant behavior is controlling, assertive, relatively directive and autocratic.

Although social role theory treats the differing assignments of women and men to social roles as the basic underlying cause of sex-differentiated social behavior, their impact on behavior is held to be mediated by psychological and social processes. The tendency of men and women to occupy different roles, which require somewhat different behaviors, fosters gender roles by which people expect each sex to have characteristics that equip it for its sex-typical roles. Yet, like other social roles, gender roles describe not only expectations about how men and women are likely to behave but also beliefs about how they should behave. In Cialdini and Trost's (1998) terminology, these roles consist of both *descriptive norms* (i.e., expectations derived from observations of what people do) and *injunctive norms* (i.e., expectations about what people should do). This "oughtness" associated with gender roles enhances the ability to foster behaviors consistent with sex-typical work roles. Because gender-stereotypic behaviors become not just expected but demanded, violations of these expectations can lead to negative sanctions.

In summary, gender roles emerge from the productive work of the sexes; the characteristics embodied in these roles become stereotypic of women or men. To the extent that women more than men occupy roles that demand communal behaviors, domestic behaviors, or subordinate behaviors for successful role performance, such tendencies become stereotypic of women and are incorporated into a female gender role. To the extent that men more than women occupy roles that demand agentic behaviors, resource acquisition behaviors, or dominant behaviors for successful role performance, such tendencies become stereotypic of men and are incorporated into a male gender role.

To the extent that these normative expectations about behavior appropriate to women and men become internalized as part of individuals' self-concepts and personalities, people form dispositions or traits that are consistent with gender roles (Feingold, 1994; Wood, Christensen, Hebl, & Rothgerber, 1997). Yet people may also behave consistently with their gender roles without necessarily acquiring dispositions that foster such behavior. Congruent with empirical research on the behavioral confirmation of stereotypes and other expectancies (Olson, Roese, & Zanna, 1996) in social interactions, people communicate their gender-stereotypic expectations about how others should behave and thereby directly induce those individuals to behave in a manner consistent with those expectations (Skrypnek & Snyder, 1982; Wood & Karten, 1986).[1]

Sex Differences in Expectations, Behavior, and Influence

Both social role theory and status characteristics theory predict that men should exert greater influence over others than women do. In interactions between men and women, men resist influence by women more than women resist influence by men, even when the group task is not gender typed (Pugh & Wahrman, 1983; Ridgeway, 1982; Wagner, Ford, & Ford, 1986). More generally, Lockheed's (1985) meta-analysis of 64 data sets from 29 studies of power and influence in mixed-sex groups found that men, in fact, do exert more influence than women. For example, Propp (1995) studied four-person simulated juries, in which specific case information was either given to all members of the group, given to two members, or given to only one member. Participants then discussed and reached consensus on the case. Results showed that even though men and women were equally likely to introduce the specific information they had received and this information did not differ between the sexes, the information was more likely to be used by the group in forming its decision when the information was presented by a man. This trend was most pronounced when the information was known to only one person; in that condition, group members used the information 72.0% of the time when it was presented by a man but only 12.5% of the time when it was presented by a woman.

Status characteristics theory and social role theory attribute women's lesser degree of influence to a variety of factors. First, they both predict that sex should be associated with perceived competence. Status characteristics theory asserts that sex, like all diffuse status characteristics, affects performance expectations (i.e., group members expect men to outperform women). Social role theory asserts that the male gender role conveys self-efficacy and mastery, leading to the expectation that men should exhibit higher competence than women in contexts in which such qualities would enhance performance. Second, in addition, according to both theories, competent and confident behavior is less acceptable in women than in men, except in traditionally feminine domains such as child care. According to status theorists, status-asserting behaviors, including displays of competence, are less legitimate in individuals who have low diffuse status (e.g., women or African Americans) than in those who have higher diffuse status, whereas social role theorists assert that behavior that contradicts traditional gender roles, including behavior conveying task competence, violates norms dictating appropriate behavior for women.

According to status characteristics theory, the gender difference in social influence is associated with gender differences in behavior; men and other high-status individuals exhibit a variety of behaviors that convey their high status, whereas women and other low-status individuals exhibit behaviors that convey low status (Berger, Webster, Ridgeway, & Rosenholtz, 1986). Among the behaviors that convey status are eye contact and direct versus indirect forms of speech (Carli, 1991). Similarly, social role theory predicts that both men and women should exhibit behavior consistent with their respective gender roles (i.e., men should be more agentic and dominant and women more communal and subordinate). Consequently, both theories predict that, in task-oriented groups, men should generally participate more, contribute more task behaviors, and express more disagreement than women, whereas women should contribute more positive social behaviors and express more agreement than men. In addition, men's verbal and nonverbal language should convey greater power and authority than women's language, which should convey more deference and warmth.

Perceptions of Male and Female Competence

Are women assumed to be less competent than men? Research on gender stereotypes reveals that people consider men to have more agentic qualities (e.g., more assertive, independent, competitive, daring, and courageous) and women more communal qualities (e.g., more gentle, kind, supportive, expressive, affectionate, and tactful) (Broverman, Vogel, Broverman, Clarkson, & Rosenkrantz, 1972; Deaux & Kite, 1993; Ruble, 1983; Williams & Best, 1990a). These stereotypes extend to cognitive characteristics as well, with men perceived as more analytical, exact, and better at abstractions, reasoning, and problem solving and women as more imaginative, intuitive, perceptive, verbally skilled, and creative (Cejka & Eagly, 1999; Williams & Best, 1990a). Therefore, for many kinds of tasks, especially those involving analysis and reasoning, group members consider men to be more competent than women, unless group members are presented with evidence of female superiority at a group task (Carli, 1991; Wood & Karten, 1986).

These findings demonstrating higher perceived competence of men than women in task-oriented groups should not be taken to imply that men are evaluated generally more favorably than women or that men are thought to constitute a social group that is generally superior to women. On the contrary, in research on U.S. and Canadian university students, Eagly and her colleagues (Eagly & Mladinic, 1989, 1994; Eagly, Mladinic, & Otto, 1991) have demonstrated that attitudes toward women appear to be more positive than attitudes toward men. Also, the evaluative content of the female stereotype is more favorable than that of the male stereotype, a tendency the researchers call the "women are wonderful" effect. This especially positive evaluation of women may derive primarily from the ascription to women of communal characteristics—that is, niceness, kindness, and nurturance—which people think are excellent human qualities.

These communal qualities are not thought to be highly relevant to outstanding performance in task-oriented groups. Instead, such qualities may contribute to socially facilitative group behavior and, in natural settings, are thought to qualify individuals for the domestic role (Eagly & Steffen, 1984) as well as for female-dominated occupations (Cejka & Eagly, 1999). This point is aptly noted by Jackman (1994), based on her survey research assessing Americans' beliefs about women and men: "Women are warmly congratulated for their distinctiveness in personal traits that are appropriate to the tasks and behaviors assigned to them and to which men have no aspirations" (p. 347). Therefore, the women-are-wonderful effect is not incompatible with men's generally higher status in society, which stems from their greater occupancy of social roles that have more power attached to them and that are accorded more importance in society.

The impact of the gender typing of behavioral domains on evaluations of women and men was established by Swim, Borgida, Maruyama, and Myers's (1989) meta-analysis of 123 experiments in the "Goldberg paradigm" (Goldberg, 1968), in which the sex of target persons was varied and participants evaluated a behavior or product produced by the target person. The small overall tendency to rate women's behaviors and products less favorably than men's disappeared when the work evaluated was in a traditionally feminine domain, but remained intact in a neutral or masculine domain. Also, on the basis of a narrative review of this same research literature, Top (1991) concluded that because task-oriented groups are typically in a masculine domain, men have an advantage in such contexts.

Self-evaluations of women and men are also affected in task-oriented groups. When making predictions about future performance, men expect to perform better than women expect to perform, even under conditions when women ultimately end up equaling or exceeding the performance of men (Ryujin & Herrold, 1989). Of greater interest, however, is evidence that self-evaluations depend on the gender composition of groups. In two studies, independent raters found no sex differences in the quality or quantity of ideas expressed in group interactions of either mixed-sex or same-sex dyads (Carli, 1997). However, sex differences in self-evaluation occurred in the mixed-sex dyads, where men evaluated themselves more favorably than women evaluated themselves. Although no sex differences occurred between same-sex pairs, both men and women made more gender-stereotypic self-evaluations after mixed-sex interactions than same-sex ones: This finding shows that the presence of the other sex fostered gender-stereotypic self-construals. In addition, both men and women felt they had performed better after interacting with a woman than a man. These findings are consistent with the claim of status characteristics theory and social role theory that people expect greater task competency in men than in women. Moreover, the findings show that participants' evaluations of their own past behavior tend to confirm these expectations.

This gender bias in the evaluation of performance in task-oriented groups is reflected not only in the perception of greater male competence but also in the different standards that are applied to evaluate the performance of men and women. In fact, a double standard exists: What constitutes a high level of competence is higher for women than for men. This phenomenon means that women must perform better to be considered equally competent, regardless of whether group members evaluate themselves (Foddy & Graham, 1987, cited in Foschi, 1992; Foschi, 1996) or other group members (Foschi, 1996). Although people appear to set lower minimum standards of competence for women than men, presumably because they believe that women are less competent, they require more evidence from women than men to infer high ability (Biernat & Kobrynowicz, 1997).

Because people generally are more influential when they are perceived to be competent, the perception that men are more competent than women and the double standard of evaluation makes it more difficult for women to exert influence. The double standard probably also creates a disadvantage for women in hiring and promotion, especially when women are being evaluated by men. One study revealed, for example, that men preferred hiring a man or not hiring anyone at all to hiring a woman whose performance was somewhat superior to that of a male candidate (Foschi, Lai, & Sigerson, 1991). On the other hand, when participants were informed explicitly that women performed better or when participants observed that women's performance was clearly superior to that of the best-performing men, women were recognized as having higher levels of competence (Shackelford, Wood, & Worchel, 1996; Wagner et al., 1986; Wood & Karten, 1986). Evidently, women's superiority must be very clear and explicit to overcome the double standard.

When women are perceived to be competent, is their influence enhanced? Even though it may seem logical that highly competent women would be more influential than less competent women, this consequence does not always follow, particularly when women are attempting to influence men. Women, it appears, can be too competent. For example, Carli (1990) found that women who conveyed uncertainty and tentativeness were more influential with a male audience than women who conveyed confidence and assertiveness, even though the men considered the tentative women to be less competent, intelligent, and knowledgeable than the assertive women. Men thus resisted the influence of a highly competent woman, finding her less likable and trustworthy than her less competent counterpart. In subsequent research, competence was found to be highly predictive of influence, except when women were influencing men (Carli, LaFleur, & Loeber, 1995). For this group, likableness predicted influence, and women who were highly task oriented and competent were also not well liked. This is not to say that competent women cannot influence men. In fact, when receiving good information is important to men—for example, if they stand to gain money or some other reward from making a well-informed decision—men are more influenced by highly competent than less competent women (Shackelford et al., 1996). Nevertheless, research indicates that women experience a double bind when it comes to their perceived competence: Either it is questioned, or it is acknowledged but at the cost of losing likability and influence.

Reactions to Women's
Confidence and Assertiveness

Given the double bind women experience in terms of their competence, should they work more aggressively to promote themselves and to ensure that their competence is visible, especially in contexts where it can benefit their group or organization? Self-promotion generally enhances the extent to which a person is perceived as competent (Jones & Pittman, 1982) and has been shown to increase a person's attractiveness as a job candidate (Stevens & Kristof, 1995). In groups and organizations where outcomes depend on a high-quality group product, competence should be desirable in women. Nevertheless, there is good evidence that self-promotion can backfire for women. Women receive greater recognition for their successes when they are modest, whereas men receive greater recognition when they are somewhat self-promoting (Giacolone & Riordan, 1990; Wosinska, Dabul, Whetstone-Dion, & Cialdini, 1996).

Illustrating some of the difficulties that women can experience from self-promotion, Rudman (1998) conducted a series of studies examining a variety of reactions to men and women who described themselves in either a self-effacing or self-promoting manner. Participants were told they would be evaluating the job-interviewing skills of a target individual and then later playing a computerized game of *Jeopardy* on a team with this individual. Some of the participants thought that they would have an opportunity to win money if their team performed well, whereas others did not have any potential to win money. Results revealed that self-promoting targets, who spoke directly and highlighted their accomplishments, received higher competence ratings than self-effacing targets who spoke indirectly and modestly. Among participants who could win money and for whom identifying a competent partner therefore had personal relevance, self-effacing targets were rated as more competent if these targets were male compared with female. Again, as found in the research on perceived competence, unless there was very clear evidence of female competence, men were presumed to be more competent. Although these results on perceived competence suggest that self-promotion might be advantageous to women, Rudman found that there were costs of self-promotion for women. First, when male participants had nothing to gain from having a competent partner, they liked the self-promoting woman less and considered her less hirable than a self-effacing woman. Moreover, female participants considered the self-promoting woman less likable and hirable than the self-effacing woman, regardless of condition. On the other hand, in no condition were male self-promoters perceived to be less likable or hirable than self-effacing men. Hence, although a woman who self-promotes may be perceived as more competent than one who is modest, women find the self-promoting woman unattractive, and men accept such a woman only when they can directly benefit from her competence. Self-promotion thus presents another double bind for women.

Contributions to Group Interactions

Both social role theory and status characteristics theory predict that, in task-oriented groups, men should generally make more contributions and also display more task behavior than women, whereas women should display more positive social behavior that facilitates social interaction and avoids conflict. On the whole, men contribute more to task interactions in mixed-sex groups than women do (James & Drakitch, 1993). Studies comparing sex differences in participation in mixed- and same-sex groups have revealed that men talk more and women talk less when interacting with the other sex than when interacting with their own (e.g., Lee, 1991; Smith-Lovin, Skvoretz, & Hudson, 1986). Nonetheless, sex differences in amount of participation vary depending on the social context. Specifically, James and Drakitch's (1993) review showed that the male predominance in talking is most pronounced in formally structured situations that call for task-oriented contributions (e.g., mock juries, committee meetings), somewhat weaker in situations that call for informal task-oriented interactions (e.g., participation in college classrooms), and weakest in situations that are not formally task oriented (e.g., persons getting to know one another). These findings are consistent with the interpretation that casual conversations foster more facilitative contributions that are oriented to maintaining pleasant social interactions. Because women tend to specialize in this type of behavior, the amount of their contribution increases in situations that favor it. In general, when men and women are together, especially in formally structured task-oriented situations, men take a more active role in the group than women do.

To assess sex differences in the way that men and women interact, studies examining contributions to groups frequently distinguished between two forms of group behavior: *task activity,* defined by direct contribution to the group's task, and *social activity,* defined by contribution to the maintenance of satisfactory morale and interpersonal relations among the group members. Operationally, within Bales's (1950) interaction process analysis and related methods, task activity has generally been defined in terms of behaviors coded as attempted answers or problem-solving attempts, which include giving suggestions, opinions, and information, whereas social activity has generally been defined as showing solidarity, releasing tension, and agreeing with other group members.

In a meta-analytic review, including 21 studies using Bales-type categories, Carli (1981) found moderate-size sex differences: In task-oriented groups, men exhibited more task behavior than women, and women exhibited more social behavior than men, except when the task favored female expertise or interests (see also Anderson & Blanchard, 1982). Subsequent research has continued to reveal these sex differences (e.g., Carli, 1989; Craig & Sherif, 1986; Mabry, 1985; Wood & Karten, 1986); Wheelan and Verdi's (1992) review also confirmed this overall pattern of findings. These sex differences in the context of interaction are not confined to mixed-sex groups, but are fully intact, or even somewhat larger, when all-female groups are compared with all-male groups (Hutson-Comeaux & Kelly, 1996; Piliavin & Martin, 1978). Men also express more direct disagreement than women, and women express more agreement than men (Carli, 1989; Johnson, Clay-Warner, & Funk, 1996; Piliavin & Martin, 1978). Moreover, women tend to reciprocate positive social behaviors more than men and men tend to reciprocate negative social behaviors, such as disagreements (Rhodes & Wood, 1990, cited in Wood & Rhodes, 1992). Overall, then, men engage in relatively more task behavior and disagreement, and women in more positive social behavior and agreement.

How does group interaction affect influence? Research indicates that individuals' leadership and influence are positively associated with the amount that they participate in groups. Mullen, Salas, and Driskell's (1989) meta-analysis of 33 tests of this hypothesis showed that the overall relation between amount of participation and leadership is large—specifically, a correlation of .55. Other evidence suggests that although the relation of leadership to amount of task contribution is substantial (Morris & Hackman, 1969), its relation to amount of socially oriented behavior is much weaker (Hawkins, 1995; Ridgeway, 1978; Stein & Heller, 1979). However, because making many task contributions is unexpected and illegitimate in women, the relation between social influence and task behavior should be clearer for men than for women. Moreover, women may have to convey selflessness and group orientation before their group will accept their task contributions (Lockheed & Hall, 1976; Meeker & Weitzel-O'Neill, 1985). If this is so, the use of positive social behaviors, such as agreement, should enhance women's influence. Also, because direct disagreement violates sex-role norms for women, women who disagree should be negatively sanctioned more than men who do so.

Research does indicate that the relation of task contributions to influence is stronger for men than for women. Men who are judged by their group to be competent exert greater influence, but women who are judged to be competent exert no more influence than women perceived to be not as competent (Walker, Ilardi, McMahon, & Fennell, 1996). Women's task contributions are more likely to be ignored or to evoke negative reactions from others than men's contributions (Altemeyer & Jones, 1974; Ridgeway, 1982). As Butler and Geis (1990) showed, these negative reactions can be relatively subtle, involving, for example, more facial expressions conveying disapproval and fewer conveying approval.

Although task behaviors may have limited effects on women's influence, other behaviors appear to be consequential. In particular, accompanying task-oriented influence attempts with positive social behaviors increases women's influence (Ridgeway, 1982; Shackelford et al., 1996). In Carli's (1998) study, each participant was paired with a male or female confederate who exhibited agreement or disagreement in the interaction. Men were equally influential and likable whether they agreed or disagreed with participants. In contrast, women were more influential and likable when they agreed with participants. In fact, participants responded to the disagreements of a woman by increasing their disagreement, as well as their negative social behaviors (e.g., showing tension or antagonism). These results correspond to the findings on sex differences in self-promotion and perceived competence. Women are more constrained than men in the kinds of behaviors that they can engage in and still be influential.

Despite the evidence that we have cited, generalizations about sex differences in the contributions that men and women make to social interaction are incomplete at this point because this research is based primarily on experiments carried out with student participants. The question of whether task-oriented behavior remains sex differentiated in the workplace needs to be addressed by field and organizational studies that obtain detailed measures of interaction. In a rare example of such a study, Moskowitz, Suh, and Desaulniers (1994) examined the simultaneous influence of gender roles and workplace roles in organizational settings. They used an experience-sampling method that produced separate measures of agentic and communal workplace behaviors. In general, agentic behavior was controlled by the relative status of the interactants; participants behaved most agentically with a supervisee and least agentically with a boss. In contrast, communal behavior was influenced by the sex of participants; women behaved more communally, especially in interactions with other women.

Style of Verbal and Nonverbal Communication

Within the very large research literature on sex differences in language and communication (Canary & Dindia, 1998; Crawford, 1995; Tannen, 1993), the behaviors of relevance to our analysis are those that are predicted by status characteristics and social role theories—specifically, behaviors conveying either power and authority or deference and warmth that have been linked to social influence. Although the results of studies examining sex differences for such behaviors have been mixed, overall, women's nonverbal and verbal communications tend to be more deferent and warm and those of men more powerful and authoritative (Carli, 1991; Mulac, 1998). For gender-neutral tasks, women speak more tentatively (Carli, 1990; Crosby & Nyquist, 1977; Mulac, Lundell, & Bradac, 1986), report using more indirect influence strategies (Howard, Blumstein, & Schwartz, 1986; Offerman & Kearney, 1988; Steil & Weltman, 1992), and show more nonverbal warmth than men (Hall, 1984). Women also show less visual dominance than men; that is, women maintain more eye contact while listening and less while talking than men do (Dovidio, Brown, Heltman, Ellyson, & Keating, 1988; Dovidio, Ellyson, Keating, Heltman, & Brown, 1988) particularly in mixed-sex interactions (Ellyson, Dovidio, & Brown, 1992). Based on status characteristics and social role theories, women should be less influential than men when using direct and powerful language, and their influence should increase when their language is less direct and powerful.

Confirming these predictions about sex differences in the effectiveness of more and less dominant styles of influence, research on the effects of visual dominance indicates that, in mixed-sex interactions, visual dominance is associated with effective influence for men but not for women (Mehta, Dovidio, Gibbs, Miller, Huray, Ellyson, & Brown, 1989, cited in Ellyson et al., 1992). Women who display high levels of visual dominance exert less influence than women who display low levels. Also, as mentioned earlier, Carli (1990) reported that women exert greater influence over a male audience when they use somewhat tentative rather than direct speech, whereas men are equally influential with a male and a female audience regardless of whether they speak assertively or tentatively. These results demonstrate not only that directness in language is less acceptable in women but also that men can exhibit a wider range of behavior and still be influential.

In a follow-up study, Carli et al. (1995) examined the effect of nonverbal behavior on influence, by having participants view a videotape of either a male or a female speaker who disagreed with them while displaying one of four nonverbal styles: mere competence, warmth plus competence, dominance plus competence, or submissiveness. In general, participants were less influenced by the dominant and submissive compared with the competent and warm styles. Participants considered the submissive speakers to be highly incompetent and the dominant speakers to be threatening and not very likable. More important, although women were equally influenced by the competent man and the competent woman, men were less influenced by the competent woman, judging her to be less likable and more threatening than her male counterpart. Again, women received negative sanctions for being direct, but men were able to exhibit a wider range of behaviors and still remain influential.

Carli et al.'s (1995) study also tested the prediction that warm language should enhance women's ability to influence men because it helps convey a group orientation in much the same way that positive social interaction does. As expected, men liked the warm and competent female speaker more and were more influenced by her than by the female speaker who was merely competent; they also considered the warm woman to be as competent as the competent one. It seems that a woman, particularly when interacting with men, can combine competence with warmth to overcome resistance to her influence.

Also suggesting the necessity for women to leaven their influence efforts with friendly, nice behavior are findings from a study of male and female middle managers' efforts to influence their superiors in organizational hierarchies (Lauterbach & Weiner, 1996). Female managers, more than male managers, reported that they acted more out of organizational interest rather than self-interest, considered others' viewpoints, and focused on the interpersonal aspects as well as the task aspects of the influence episode. More generally, Eagly and Johnson's (1990) meta-analysis of 162 studies comparing the leadership style of women and men found a tendency for women who were managers in organizations as well as leaders in laboratory small-group experiments to lead in a more democratic and participative style than men. Eagly, Makhijani, and Klonsky's (1992) meta-analysis of 61 experiments on leader evaluation suggests that this stylistic difference may stem from the resistance to female assertiveness and influence that we have noted. These studies, designed to hold constant the characteristics of leaders other than their sex, revealed that a small overall tendency for men to be evaluated more favorably than women was exaggerated when leadership was carried out in stereotypically masculine styles, particularly when this style was autocratic or directive. Subsequent research has continued to confirm that autocratic or dominating leadership behavior is less well received from female than from male leaders (Copeland, Driskell, & Salas, 1995).

Sex Differences in Leader Emergence

Many of the findings that we have described suggest that men should be more likely than women to emerge as leaders in groups. Not only do men tend to talk more than women in task-oriented groups, but men also show dispropor-tionate specialization in the strictly task-oriented behavior that moves the group toward its explicit goals. In general, as we noted earlier, group members emerge as leaders to the extent that they participate more, especially if that participation is task oriented (Mullen et al., 1989; Stein & Heller, 1979); men therefore have a leadership advantage on these grounds. Moreover, as we have argued, women's task-oriented behaviors may not result in acknowledgment of their competence, because such contributions by women are perceived as less legitimate, especially if they are delivered in a style that is confident and self-promoting.

Another trend to take into account in thinking about emergent leadership is women's disproportionate specialization in socially facilitative behaviors. In typical task-oriented groups, such behavior would not contribute to overall leadership (Stein & Heller, 1979). However, if facilitative behaviors become especially important to a group's success (e.g., because the group must engage in negotiation and cooperation to achieve its goals), women might emerge as leaders somewhat more often than in other circumstances because of their greater attention to group morale and delivery of positive interpersonal behavior. Also, in a wide variety of circumstances, such behavior might lead to being identified as a social facilitator or, to use the term favored by Bales and his collaborators (Parsons & Bales, 1955; Parsons, Bales, & Shils, 1953), as a social-emotional leader.

To determine whether the predicted tendencies for men to emerge as leaders and for women to emerge as social facilitators are empirically robust, Eagly and Karau (1991) quantitatively synthesized the results of 58 studies. Most of these studies were laboratory experiments in which small groups of undergraduate students were asked to discuss a particular topic or to solve a particular problem. Leadership was assessed by group members' responses to questionnaire measures of leadership contribution or by researchers' coding of members' verbal behavior. Other, more naturalistic studies of emergent leadership examined groups composed of students from a university course who generally met for most of a semester to work on projects. Leadership was typically assessed toward the end of the semester by group members' responses to questionnaire measures of leadership contribution.

Eagly and Karau (1991) found a small- to moderate-sized tendency for men to emerge as leaders more than women on measures of general, overall leadership as well as on measures that assessed strictly task-oriented contri-butions. Although the small tendency for women to emerge as social facilita-tors was based on only the 15 studies that examined social leadership, these meta-analytic findings are strikingly consistent with the results noted earlier in this chapter pertaining to the relative specialization of men versus women in task-oriented versus socially facilitative behavior.

This meta-analysis found very close correspondence between measures of leadership based on behavior and those based on perceptions of leadership.

The fact that the sex differences were equally strong in each case suggests that men and women not only are perceived differently in group settings but also behave differently. Therefore, the tendency for men to emerge as leaders should not be interpreted as a biased tendency to choose men over women, despite behavioral equivalence of the sexes. Instead, the preference for men may primarily reflect a tendency to define leadership in terms of strictly task-oriented contributions, which men deliver somewhat more than women do, at least in part because of resistance to high levels of task-oriented contributions from women.

Eagly and Karau's (1991) synthesis also established that several theoretically relevant attributes of these leadership studies moderate the relation between gender and the emergence of leaders. Especially interesting is the tendency for men's greater emergent leadership to decrease for tasks requiring relatively complex social interaction and increase for tasks that do not require such interaction. Presumably, women's positive social contributions become relevant to leadership for tasks requiring negotiation and extensive sharing of ideas (Wood, 1987; Wood, Polek, & Aiken, 1985), allowing women a more equal chance of achieving leadership.

Another predictor of leader emergence was the amount of social interaction that had transpired before leadership was assessed: The longer the interaction, the weaker was the tendency for men to emerge. This trend could reflect the lesser influence of gender as group members obtain more individuating information about one another. Another possibility is that cohesion and social concerns become more important for groups that must maintain themselves over time, and women's greater contribution to this aspect of group process becomes more important.

Gender typing of the group's task was also important. Men emerged strongly when groups had distinctively masculine tasks and much less strongly when the tasks were distinctively feminine, reflecting the importance of task-relevant competence. Yet men's general advantage in being perceived as competent in task-oriented groups is suggested by the fact that the sex difference did not reverse—that is, women did not emerge more than men— with tasks that were clearly feminine. Instead, there was a weak tendency for men to emerge. Moreover, under no circumstances identified by Eagly and Karau's (1991) meta-analysis did women show more task or general leadership than men. Only on measures of social leadership did women's leadership exceed men's.

Research on leader emergence in task-oriented groups thus replicated the societal tendency for men to assume leadership roles. The importance of examining leader emergence in small groups is underscored by research showing that men gain leadership roles at least in part because they engage in certain types of leadership behaviors more than women do. Although the de facto association between men and leadership in organizational settings is clear-cut, other potential causes of this association have little to do with performance of leadership behavior. For example, men may be thought to be less burdened by family obligations or to possess greater resources in the form of money and influential friends. In organizations, the belief that men possess such advantages rather than men's behavior may be responsible for their selection for leadership roles. Because men emerge more than women even in initially leaderless small groups that are composed of students and that are not formally linked to larger organizations, the causes of men's emergence that we have emphasized in this chapter—in particular, sex differences in participation, interaction style, and perception of competence—become plausible explanations of women's lack of advancement in organizational hierarchies.

In summary, Eagly and Karau's (1991) findings suggest that men's greater participation and their specialization in strictly task-oriented behaviors is one key to their emergence as group leaders. Women, more attentive to interpersonal relations and group harmony, achieve some recognition as social facilitators, but less recognition as leaders. In general, the tendency that this meta-analysis revealed for men to become leaders no doubt reflects the importance that group members assign to task-oriented behaviors as components of leadership and their lesser appreciation of socially facilitative behaviors. Women would probably emerge more often than observed in the meta-analysis if members of task-oriented groups regarded the social aspects of leadership as more important than they have in the past.

The sex differences in emergent leadership that Eagly and Karau (1991) demonstrated may well carry over to organizational settings, where there are many chances for informal leadership. People who are perceived as informal leaders are more likely to be promoted to higher managerial roles, because they have demonstrated leadership ability. To the extent that women informally take on the role of social facilitator and not the role of task leader, they may be less likely to rise in organizations.

Cultural Variation in Sex Differences in Influence and Leadership

The research discussed in this chapter was conducted with participants who are predominantly White, middle-class, and young citizens of the United States. This lack of diversity raises the issue of whether different findings would be obtained from participants who represent other cultural groups. Both social role theory and status characteristics theory suggest that findings should vary, depending on the gender relations prevailing in particular cultural contexts. According to social role theory, in cultures or subcultures in which greater gender equality prevails, gender stereotypes and roles should be less traditional and more egalitarian. Similarly, status characteristics theory suggests that if men do not have higher status than women in a culture or subculture, they should not exhibit the pattern of more dominant and influential behaviors. Although it is typical in world societies for men to have greater power and status than women, some societies can be characterized as relatively egalitarian (Whyte, 1978).

Unfortunately, little research has compared the patterns of sex-differentiated social interaction between cultures and subcultures. Within the United States, comparisons of African American and European American subcultures would be particularly interesting, in view of the historically greater workforce participation and economic independence of African American women (Farley & Allen, 1987) and their greater equality to men in family decision making compared with European American women (King, 1975). Consistent with these racial differences in the social position of women and men, the gender stereotypes and ideologies of children and adolescents are more egalitarian among Blacks than Whites (e.g., Albert & Porter, 1988; Kleinke & Nicholson, 1979), and Black adults express more disapproval of gender inequality than White adults, especially White men (Dugger, 1996; Kane, 1992). Consequently, social interaction should be less differentiated by sex among African Americans.

In an exceptional study, Filardo (1996) compared sex differences in social interaction patterns in mixed-sex groups of African American and European American adolescents who were given a cooperative problem-solving task. Among the European Americans, most of the sex differences we have emphasized in this chapter were intact; namely, the males showed more participation, more influence attempts, fewer utterances that were interrupted and incomplete, and fewer socially facilitative behaviors than the females. In contrast, none of these sex differences were significant among the African Americans, suggesting greater gender equality in this subculture. These findings support the principle, consistent with social role theory and status characteristics theory, that sex differences in social interaction reflect gender arrangements in the larger society. In fact, Filardo's study provides a powerful demonstration that sex differences in interaction style and influence stem from the social position of women and men rather than the kinds of intrinsic factors emphasized by scholars who give biological and evolutionary interpretations to male dominance (Goldberg, 1993).

Conclusion

In this chapter, we have provided one part of the explanation of why most leadership roles are male dominated, especially at the highest levels of organizations, despite the educational parity of women and men and the entry of greatly increased numbers of women into managerial and most professional careers in the past 30 years. Although conventional explanations have assumed that the number of qualified women is insufficient to produce much change in historic sex ratios, a far more adequate explanation lies at the intersection of the macro approaches of sociologists, who emphasize economic and social structural factors, and the micro approaches of those psychologists who emphasize individual characteristics and processes. Consistent with our blending of micro and macro variables, we have examined how the division of labor in society and the gender hierarchy that accompanies it affect the behavior of women and men in groups, people's reactions to these behaviors, and the possibility of exerting influence and claiming leadership. As we have demonstrated, the normative patterns of interaction that develop in groups tend to place women at a disadvantage. Women's task contributions are seen as less legitimate than men's, and status-asserting, dominant, and self-promoting behavior especially challenges people's ideas of how women ought to behave. The resulting tendencies of women to participate less in mixed-sex groups and to specialize less than men in strictly task-oriented behaviors compromise women's chances to exert leadership.

Because these tendencies in turn reflect the social position of women and men in society, change in these patterns should reflect the movement of societies toward gender equality. There are many signs of such a shift in the United States and other postindustrial societies. For example, Twenge (1997) meta-analytically demonstrated a general shift toward more egalitarian definitions of women's rights and responsibilities between 1970 and 1995. This change in attitudes corresponds to changes in the division of labor between the sexes: For example, the percentages of women and men in the labor force in 1950 were 34% and 86%, respectively, whereas these percentages in 1996 were 59% and 75% (U.S. Department of Labor, 1997b). With such shifts, the sex differences in social interaction we have noted in this chapter should be eroding and should erode more profoundly as greater equality between the sexes is achieved.

Note

1. Status characteristics theory and social role theory make very similar predictions for the sex differences in influence and emergent leadership that we review in this chapter. Yet status characteristics theory emphasizes status differentiation and its implications for perceived competence, whereas social role theory emphasizes not only status differentiation but also the sexual division of labor between domestic work and paid labor. Social role theory thus suggests that a broader range of sex-differentiated expectations than those relating to task competence follow from the positioning of women and men in the social structure. These additional expectations pertain to the skills and interaction competencies associated with the domestic role and female-dominated occupations. For a comparative discussion of predictions of the theories, see Ridgeway and Diekema (1992).

"Re-Viewing" Gender, Leadership, and Managerial Behavior

Do Three Decades of Research Tell Us Anything?

D. Anthony Butterfield and James P. Grinnell

The topic of gender, leadership, and managerial behavior encompasses a wide domain.[1] Given the scope of this book, we have limited our analysis because some topics are discussed in greater detail by other contributing authors. For example, Karen Korabik covers sex and gender roles, Jerry Jacobs discusses sex segregation of occupations, Linda Carli and Alice Eagly evaluate issues of gender and emergent leadership, and Alison Konrad and Frank Linnehan address affirmative action. In some respects our work will overlap with these contributors, but our goal is not to provide an exhaustive literature review. Rather, we seek to evaluate where research in this area has been, where it currently stands, and where it might go.

AUTHORS' NOTE: We wish to thank Alice Eagly for her helpful comments and suggestions on the meta-analysis portion of this chapter.

Synthesizing research on gender, leadership, and managerial behavior is a difficult task. Several reviews have been done, with each scholar organizing the literature differently (for examples, see Bartol, 1978; Bartol & Martin, 1986; Klenke, 1996; Nieva & Gutek, 1981; Riger & Galligan, 1980; Terborg, 1977). In this chapter, we organize our review in terms of three broad questions: Are male and female leaders evaluated differently in terms of styles, behaviors, and effectiveness? Do leader styles and sex influence subordinate satisfaction? And, is leadership conceived in masculine, feminine, or androgynous terms?

Research on Gender, Leadership, and Managerial Behavior

Are Male and Female Leaders Evaluated Differently in Terms of Styles, Behaviors, and Effectiveness?

Studies evaluating leader styles and sex have been extremely popular during the past three decades (Nieva & Gutek, 1981), primarily because much of the previous literature was based on male leaders (Lee & Alvares, 1977). In fact, women leaders were often excluded from early studies because they were considered anomalies (Powell, 1993). Given the exclusionary nature of these early studies, much of the research on leader style and gender since the 1970s has sought to determine whether male and female leaders are different, typically in terms of consideration and initiating structure (Bartol & Martin, 1986). Put differently, given the same style(s), are males and females evaluated differently?

Some of the first indications of sex differences were noted by Bartol and Butterfield (1976), who found that high-consideration females were evaluated more favorably than their male counterparts. Conversely, males were viewed more positively than females on the initiating structure dimension. Bartol and Butterfield note that the prevailing prescriptions for success, which emphasize a "high/high" leadership style, might not apply when leader sex is taken into account: "Our research suggests that females who become more structuring and males who become more considerate, at least when compared with opposite sex managers using the same style, may actually be perceived as less effective" (p. 453). Similarly, Jago and Vroom (1982), noting that females were expected to demonstrate a participative style, pointed out that autocratic females were unfavorably evaluated: "Apparently, male managers have substantially greater freedom than do female managers to engage in either autocratic or participative practices without arousing negative evaluations" (p. 782). In general, research indicating sex differences tends to show that males are evaluated more favorably when they adopted a structuring/directive style, whereas females are rated higher on consideration (Bartol & Martin, 1986).

Other researchers found less conclusive support for sex differences. In a replication of their earlier study, Butterfield and Bartol (1977) found no sex effects. (This result may have been due to sampling, because the earlier study used undergraduate students whereas the latter included professional MBA students.) Butterfield and Powell (1981) concluded that males and females were comparably evaluated when they adopted similar styles and that group performance was the most important determinant of leader evaluations. Chapman (1975) found that although male and female leadership behaviors may be different in certain respects, there were no significant differences in terms of fostering positive interpersonal relationships; that is, female leaders did not overcompensate by creating a positive relationship with subordinates, and males did not express more task-oriented behavior. Lee and Alvares (1977) likewise concluded, "The predominant finding of the present study was that there were no sex differences in the descriptions and evaluations of supervisory behavior" (p. 408).

Leader effectiveness and performance have also been studied extensively, though most of the studies were laboratory based and therefore did not obtain objective, "real world" performance data (Bartol & Martin, 1986). Although numerous studies have shown sex differences in effectiveness and performance (Bartol & Butterfield, 1976; Korabik, Baril, & Watson, 1993), others found little, if any, sex effects (Adams, Rice, & Instone, 1984; Day & Stogdill, 1972). For example, Rosen and Jerdee (1973) concluded that males were regarded as more effective than females when they adopted a reward style, though this finding was subsequently contradicted by Petty and Lee (1975). Haccoun, Haccoun, and Sallay (1978) found that directive females were evaluated as poor performers, whereas Luthar (1996) concluded otherwise. Overall, this area of inquiry has been hotly contested. Table 12.1 summarizes representative studies of male/female leader differences with respect to leader styles, behavior, and effectiveness.

Do Leader Styles and Sex Influence Subordinate Satisfaction?

During the same time that some researchers were attempting to determine whether males and females were evaluated differently, other researchers were beginning to concentrate on subordinate satisfaction. For instance, Bartol (1974) evaluated the effects of leader dominance on subordinate satisfaction. Male groups displayed higher satisfaction with high-dominance male leaders than did mixed groups, suggesting "that high need for dominance male leaders may have a detrimental effect on female follower satisfaction with task structure" (Bartol, 1974, p. 232). Interestingly, Bartol found that high-dominance females did not have a negative impact on subordinate satisfaction, although low-need-for-dominance females were evaluated more harshly by males.

TABLE 12.1   Representative Studies: Are Male and Female Leaders Different?

Study	Methodology	Research Question(s)/Key Findings
Day and Stogdill (1972)	Field study involving civilian Air Force personnel	*How do males and females perform in leadership roles?*
		Male and female supervisors demonstrated similar leadership styles.
Chapman (1975)	Field study involving one military and one civilian organization	*How do situational and biographical variables influence styles of male and female leaders?*
		There were no significant differences between male and female leaders in regard to managerial style.
Haccoun, Haccoun, and Sallay (1978)	Experiment involving Canadian blue-collar workers	*How are male and female leaders evaluated when displaying different leadership styles?*
		In general, male supervisors were evaluated more favorably than female supervisors.
		Male subordinates were least supportive of female superiors who demonstrated an authoritarian style.
Butterfield and Powell (1981)	Experiment involving undergraduates	*Do group performance and leader/rater sex affect evaluations of leader behavior?*
		There was no difference in evaluations of male and female leaders when they used the same style.
		Group performance was more important than leader sex in determining evaluations of leaders.
		Rater sex had a slight effect on evaluations, with females providing higher ratings on both consideration and initiating structure.
Jago and Vroom (1982)	Multiple experiments using working professionals	*Do male and female leaders use different styles?*
		Females were more apt to display a participative style than men.
		Males were evaluated favorably when they demonstrated an autocratic style, whereas females were evaluated negatively.
Adams, Rice, and Instone (1984)	Study involving undergraduates at a military academy	*Do attitudes toward women affect evaluations of leaders?*
		Negative attitudes toward women did not affect evaluations of leader success.

Study	Methodology	Research Question(s)/Key Findings
Korabik, Baril, and Watson (1993)	Experiment using MBA students	*Do male and female leaders handle conflict differently?*
		There were no differences in conflict management styles for individuals with managerial experience.
		Are male and female leaders evaluated differently when demonstrating different conflict resolution styles?
		Females using dominating style were evaluated less favorably than males using the same style. Females were evaluated more favorably than males when using an obliging style.
		Overall, male and female supervisors were evaluated less favorably when they demonstrated a style that was not congruent with their respective sex roles.
Denmark and Diggory (1966)	Study involving respondents with varied work experience	*How are male and female leaders evaluated with respect to empowering styles?*
		Authoritarian behavior was associated more often with males than females.
		Male and female leaders were not evaluated differently with respect to empowering behavior.
		Females evaluated female supervisors as demonstrating lower levels of empowerment.
		Males evaluated female leaders as possessing higher leadership ability than did females.
Luthar (1996)	Experiment involving undergraduates	*How do evaluations of leader performance vary with respect to leader and follower sex?*
		Females gave higher performance ratings than males for female leaders.

Other satisfaction studies showed slight, if any, differences. Osborn and Vicars (1976) published one of the earliest and most influential studies that indicated that male and female leaders had the same impact on subordinate satisfaction: "Leader sex does not appear to have a consistent influence on either leader behavior or subordinate satisfaction, either by itself or in interaction with leader demographics, subordinate demographics, leader behavior, and subordinate sex" (p. 447). In a similar fashion, Sitt, Schmidt, Price, and Kipnis (1983) concluded that male and female leaders elicited similar levels of satisfaction, although females typically had a stronger reaction to different leader styles. Kushell and Newton (1986) found a general level of dissatisfaction when leaders, regardless of sex, acted autocratically. Autocratic female leaders, ironically, elicited more dissatisfaction from females than from males. Kushell and Newton concluded that leader style was a more important determinant of subordinate satisfaction than leader sex. Representative studies relating to subordinate outcomes are summarized in Table 12.2.

Is Leadership Conceived as Masculine, Feminine, or Androgynous?

Much of the previous research on gender and leadership focused on biological sex. Because these studies presented an incomplete and often contradictory picture (Korabik, 1990), some researchers began emphasizing sex roles. For example, Bem (1974) posited that individuals are simultaneously masculine and feminine, although males are socialized to be more masculine and females more feminine. Bem (1986) clearly separates sex from sex roles by asking, "How does the culture transform male and female infants into masculine and feminine adults? How does it create the many gender differences in behavior, motivation, and self-concept that transcend the dictates of biology?" (p. 304). She refers to individuals who are high on both masculinity and femininity as androgynous, whereas those low on these dimensions are referred to as undifferentiated. According to Bem, androgynous individuals are characterized by a higher level of psychological health.

Assuming that psychological health was related to managerial success and that effective managers were both instrumental and expressive, Powell and Butterfield (1979) hypothesized that a prototypical "good manager" was androgynous as opposed to masculine. Contrary to expectations, however, they found that the prototypical good manager was firmly conceived as masculine. In a later study, Powell and Butterfield (1984) questioned how prototypical "bad managers" would be evaluated. Findings in this study indicated that the bad manager was seen as undifferentiated: They were low on both the masculine and feminine dimensions. Powell and Butterfield (1989) revisited the issue of how the good manager is evaluated at the end of the 1980s, this time using the revised Bem Sex Role Inventory (BSRI; Bem, 1981a). The original BSRI contained 20 masculine items, 20 feminine items, and 20 filler items. The revised BSRI cut the number of items for each dimension down to 10 because several of the original feminine items were considered highly undesirable. Powell and Butterfield reasoned that the negative nature of these feminine items may have lowered the overall feminine scores, thereby reducing the likelihood of finding an androgynous style. Analyzing new data and reanalyzing their original data based on the revised items, Powell and Butterfield still found not only a predominantly masculine

TABLE 12.2 Representative Studies: Subordinate Outcomes

Study	Methodology	Research Question(s)/Key Findings
Bartol (1974)	Experiment involving undergraduates	*How does leader need for dominance affect subordinate satisfaction?*
		High-dominance females do not have a negative impact on subordinate satisfaction.
		Male respondents were more satisfied with high-need-for-dominance females than with low need for dominance females.
		High-need-for-dominance males were more favorably evaluated by all male groups than they were by mixed-sex groups.
Petty and Lee (1975)	Study involving non-academic employees of a state university	*What is the relationship between supervisor behavior and subordinate satisfaction?*
		Satisfaction was higher for females when they demonstrated a consideration style.
		Leadership style and leader/follower sex were not related to subordinate effectiveness.
		Overall, for both male and female leaders, consideration was positively correlated with satisfaction, whereas initiating structure was uncorrelated.
Osborn and Vicars (1976)	Study of two mental health organizations	*Do male and female leaders demonstrate different behaviors and, if so, how does this affect subordinate satisfaction?*
		Leaders sex did not have an impact on either subordinate satisfaction or leader behavior.
Lee and Alvares (1977)	Experiment involving undergraduate students	*Does the sex of the supervisor and subordinates affect evaluations of supervisory behavior?*
		No significant differences were found in evaluations of supervisors.
Sitt, Schmidt, Price, and Kipnis (1983)	Experimental design using undergraduates	*What impact does leader sex have on leader behavior, group productivity, and subordinate satisfaction?*
		Male and female leaders were equally likely to display autocratic and democratic behaviors.
		Leader sex had a small effect on leader behavior, whereas subordinate sex had no effect.
		Subordinate satisfaction was unaffected by leader sex.
		Females had more extreme responses to different leadership styles.
Kushell and Newton (1986)	Experimental design using undergraduates	*How does leader sex and style affect subordinate satisfaction?*
		Participants were dissatisfied when leader demonstrated an authoritarian style.
		Leadership style was more important than sex in determining satisfaction.
		Males were less harsh in assessments than females.

view of a good manager but one that was more strongly held than in their previous study.

Arkkelin and Simmons (1985) built on the work of Powell and Butterfield. Instead of using the entire BSRI, the scale was winnowed down to favorable and unfavorable masculine, feminine, and androgynous pairs. Overall, masculine traits were favored, although several qualifications were noted. First, although respondents did not offer androgynous traits when asked to describe a good manager, they evaluated androgynous traits as favorably as masculine traits when they were presented with both sets of traits. Arkkelin and Simmons (1985) elaborate: "Thus, while respondents apparently do not *offer* androgynous characteristics of the good manager when asked to describe one, at least they sometimes respond equally favorably to managers *described to them* in androgynous terms as in masculine terms" (p. 1195). Second, female likable traits were clearly favored over similar male traits, though the opposite was not the case for unlikable traits. Arkkelin and Simmons conclude, "This analysis could imply a rather ironic twist on the good manager notion: If a manager exhibits unlikable traits, it would be better that they be masculine—or at least androgynous combinations—rather than feminine traits!" (p. 1196). Although there was limited support for an androgynous view, the overall conclusion of the study was that the masculine bias prevailed.

Cann and Siegfried (1987) questioned whether sex typing was different when evaluating a superior or subordinate manager. They found that respondents favored a masculine view of subordinate managers, whereas the opposite was true for superior managers. Nevertheless, Cann and Siegfried offered some support for an androgynous view. Their findings, along with others (Arkkelin & O'Connor, 1992; Gurman & Long, 1992; Kapalka & Lachenmeyer, 1988; Kolb, 1997; Korabik, 1990; Moss & Kent, 1994, 1996), gave renewed life to an androgynous view. Yet the case for androgyny was dealt a blow by Baril, Elbert, Mahar-Potter, and Reavy (1989), who found that androgynous individuals were evaluated less favorably than either masculine or feminine individuals. Noting that the research on androgyny had produced inconclusive results, Baril et al. (1989) called for a "moratorium on the discussion of androgyny . . . until more research evidence is available" (p. 246).

Although the concept of androgyny has received mixed support, one aspect of sex-role research has been clear: Leadership is generally conceived in masculine terms (Goktepe & Schneier, 1988; Kruse & Wintermantel, 1986). Thus, some research suggests that females should adopt a masculine style to become more accepted as leaders (Sapp, Harrod, & Zhao, 1996). In support of this suggestion, females in upper-management positions have been shown to be more masculine (Fagenson, 1990; Wong, Kettlewell, & Sproule, 1985). Yet this prescription is not as straightforward as it might seem. For one thing, research has indicated that masculine females demonstrate lower performance (Watson, 1988). Furthermore, females opting for such a strategy often experience role conflict (Geis, 1993; Heilman, Block, & Martell, 1995; Nieva & Gutek, 1981). It seems that with regard to sex roles, adopting a contingency approach wherein the individual adjusts his or her masculine and feminine behavior as each situation warrants might be the best approach (Baril et al., 1989). Table 12.3 summarizes representative studies in this area.

What Can We Conclude From Three Decades of Work?

Where does the literature stand at the end of three decades of work? On the one hand, by the end of the 1970s research indicating sex differences was expanding (e.g., Haccoun et al., 1978; Petty & Lee, 1975). On the other hand, there was considerable literature indicating that male and female leaders were similar (e.g., Chapman, 1975; Cullen & Perrewe, 1981; Day & Stogdill, 1972; Osborn & Vicars, 1976). As the 1970s came to a close, the literature was proliferating, but scholars were finding more questions than answers. During the 1980s, researchers attempted to rectify the limitations of previous research through more rigorous research designs. In general, studies proliferated, designs became more comprehensive, and methods increased in sophistication, unfortunately to little avail.

As a result of the expansion of research, scholars sought to determine whether previous results stood the test of time. Several researchers evaluated the status of the field through literature reviews (Bartol, 1978; Bartol & Martin, 1986; Nieva & Gutek, 1981; Powell & Butterfield, 1982; Riger & Galligan, 1980). Others replicated previous studies. Finally, meta-analytic studies began to appear.

Replications

Brenner, Tomkiewicz, and Schein (1989) replicated Schein's (1973) classic study by comparing the sex-role attitudes of managers in the late 1980s to attitudes held in the early 1970s. In the 1989 study, females viewed male and female leaders as being equally likely to possess managerial characteristics. Male attitudes, however, did not change. Brenner et al. (1989) elaborate: "It appears that female middle managers no longer sex-type the job of manager. Unlike her male counterpart, today's female manager would be expected to treat men and women equally in selection, promotion, and placement decisions" (p. 668). A related study by Schein, Mueller, and Jacobson (1989) provided complementary results. These two studies, along with others (Deal & Stevenson, 1998; Russell, Rush, & Herd, 1988; Welch, 1979), indicated that females were not quite as likely to sex-type female leaders. Schein (1994) confirmed this finding, but cautioned that male attitudes had not changed. Nevertheless, other researchers (Cooper, 1997; Frank, 1988) were finding that females engaged in sex-role stereotyping behavior.

TABLE 12.3   Representative Studies: Sex-Role Stereotyping

Study	Methodology	Research Question(s)/Key Findings
Schein (1973)	Study involving middle managers	*Do individuals sex-role stereotype managerial positions?*
		Successful managers were sex-typed according to masculine stereotypes.
Powell and Butterfield (1979)	Study involving undergraduates and MBA students	*Is a prototypical "good manager" androgynous as opposed to masculine?*
		The good manager was not viewed as androgynous, but, rather, was viewed in masculine terms.
Powell and Butterfield (1984)	Study involving undergraduates	*If the prototypical "good manager" is viewed as masculine, how is a "bad manager" viewed?*
		The "bad managers" were viewed as undifferentiated, meaning that they were low on both masculinity and femininity.
Arkkelin and Simmons (1985)	Multiple experiments using undergraduates	*How do sex roles influence evaluations of leader desirability?*
		Masculinity was preferred over femininity when evaluating managers; androgyny was evaluated as favorably as masculinity.
		Unlikable masculine and androgynous traits were evaluated more favorably than unlikable feminine traits.
		Likable feminine and androgynous traits were preferred over likable masculine traits.
Wong, Kettlewell, and Sproule (1985)	Study involving working women	*How does sex-role identity affect career achievement?*
		Masculinity was an important predictor of success for females.
		Masculine females were more apt to attribute ability and effort as the reason for career success.
Cann and Siegfried (1987)	Study using undergraduates	*Do individuals apply different sex-role stereotypes to their superiors and subordinates?*
		Masculine traits were preferred in subordinates, whereas feminine traits were preferred in superiors.
Schein, Mueller, and Jacobson (1989)	Experiment using undergraduates	*Do students still sex-type managers?*
		Female management students no longer sex-typed managerial positions.
		Male attitudes had not changed from the attitudes held in the 1970s.
		How do the attitudes of managers and students compare?
		The sex-typing attitudes of managers and students were similar.

Study	Methodology	Research Question(s)/Key Findings
Baril, Elbert, Mahar-Potter, and Reavy (1989)	Field study involving first-line supervisors	*Is there a relationship between androgyny and leader effectiveness?* High-masculinity females with moderate femininity scores were evaluated more favorably than low-masculinity females. Androgynous and undifferentiated supervisors were considered to be the least effective.
Powell and Butterfield (1989)	Study involving undergraduates and MBA students	*Had the evaluations of a prototypical "good manager" changed?* The "good manager" was still viewed as masculine. *Did the original and revised Bem Sex Role Inventories (BSRI) produce similar results?* The original BSRI produced lower scores on femininity.
Arkkelin and O'Connor (1992)	Multiple experiments using undergraduates	*Does sex typing occur in both sex-typed and non-sex-typed occupations?* Unlikable masculine traits in male sex-typed occupations (e.g., lawyer and manager) resulted in favorable evaluations. Conversely, unlikable feminine and androgynous traits were evaluated negatively when the occupation was either female sex-typed or neutral. *What impact do likable/unlikable masculine and feminine traits have on sex typing?* Replicated earlier findings (Arrkelin & Simmons, 1985) that female likable traits were favored over male likable traits. When masculinity and femininity levels were manipulated (and likableness was controlled), androgynous traits were preferred across occupations.

Heilman, Block, Martell, and Simon (1989) replicated and extended Schein's (1973) work by evaluating whether context information, such as level of success, would mitigate sex-role stereotyping (the importance of context is discussed later in this section). Results indicated that contextual information reduced sex typing somewhat, though this may not be as positive as it seems. For one thing, when women were described as "managers" or "successful managers" they were likely to be evaluated with negative stereotypes. As Heilman et al. (1989) elaborate: "The attributes which were ascribed to them as distinct from men and from successful managers are hardly pleasant ones. They are notable for their negative qualities, such as bitter, quarrelsome, and selfish, and they imply unbridled ambition for power and achievement" (p. 941).

TABLE 12.4   Representative Meta-Analytic Studies

Study	Types of Studies Included in Meta-Analysis	Key Findings
Dobbins and Platz (1986)	Studies involving leader behavior, subordinate satisfaction, and leader effectiveness	Ratings of leaders on initiating structure and consideration did not differ according to the sex of the leader.
		Leader sex did not affect subordinate satisfaction.
		Male leaders were viewed as more effective in laboratory studies, although this finding did not hold up in field studies.
Eagly and Johnson (1990)	Studies involving leader style	Sex differences in task-oriented and interpersonally oriented styles were less stereotypic in field studies than in laboratory studies.
		In laboratory studies, leaders who emerged behaved more stereotypically than leaders who were selected.
		Female leaders adopted a more democratic or participative style and a less autocratic or directive style than did men in field as well as laboratory studies.
Eagly, Makhijani, and Klonsky (1992)	Studies of leader desirability	Overall, female leaders were evaluated more negatively than males.
		More negative evaluations of female than male leaders were especially strong when women demonstrated masculine styles, particularly autocratic and directive styles. However, men were not penalized relative to women for adopting feminine styles.
Eagly, Karau, and Makhijani (1995)	Studies of leader effectiveness	Aggregated over all studies, male and female leaders were equally effective.
		Men were more effective than women in roles that were defined in more masculine terms, and women were more effective than men in roles that were defined in less masculine terms.

Meta-Analytical Studies

The findings on gender, leadership, and managerial behavior were also tested by several meta-analytic studies (summarized in Table 12.4). Dobbins and Platz (1986), in one of the earliest of these studies, evaluated the state of research in three areas: leader behavior (specifically initiating structure and consideration), subordinate satisfaction, and leader effectiveness. They reported no differences with respect to leader behavior, nor did they find significant effects for subordinate satisfaction. The only significant effects were found for leader effectiveness, where males were rated higher. Separating their data into laboratory and field studies, they found that males were rated higher in the former, whereas there were no sex effects in the latter. Overall, Dobbins and Platz (1986) concluded, "The present meta-analytic review does not support the proposition that leader sex exerts a significant influence on leader behavior or subordinate satisfaction. Male and female leaders differed only on the criteria of effectiveness, and then . . . only when the study was conducted in a laboratory setting" (p. 125).

In a series of carefully designed and exhaustive meta-analyses, Eagly and her colleagues have examined several different aspects of gender and leadership behavior issues. These studies were an important contribution to the literature in that the researchers meticulously coded the constituent studies based on such factors as methodologies, research questions, and sample types. In contrast, Dobbins and Platz essentially pooled a wide variety of studies, thereby ignoring the influence of contextual variables except differences between lab and field settings.

Evaluating studies involving leader styles, Eagly and Johnson (1990) found, as did Dobbins and Platz, that laboratory results were different from studies using organizational samples. With respect to leader styles, an important finding across all settings was that there was a tendency for females to adopt a democratic, participative style, whereas men were more apt to display an autocratic, directive style. Nevertheless, Eagly and Johnson (1990) point out that both sexes favor a task-oriented style when in a gender-congruent context: "Our findings suggest that leaders of each sex emphasized task accomplishment when they were in a leadership role regarded as congruent with their gender" (p. 248). Put differently, men were more task oriented than women in masculine contexts, and females were more task oriented than men in feminine contexts. It would seem that the style displayed by both male and female leaders is a function of the gendered nature of the leadership role.

Eagly, Makhijani, and Klonsky (1992) tested research on leader evaluations in experimental studies where leader behaviors were equated for males and females. They found, overall, that there was a slight tendency to evaluate female leaders negatively. This finding was most pronounced when the leader style was masculine and when females were evaluated by males. Although masculine females were evaluated unfavorably, feminine males were not. Eagly et al. (1992) note, "It appears that all other factors being equal, men have greater freedom than women to lead in a range of styles without encountering negative reactions" (p. 16). Another interesting finding was that females were evaluated as more task oriented than males, which seems to contradict prevailing sex-role stereotypes.

In a subsequent meta-analysis, Eagly, Karau, and Makhijani (1995) assessed leader effectiveness research, concluding that male and female leaders did not differ. However, they note that their findings were not universal: "In general, leaders of each sex were particularly effective when they were in a leadership role regarded as congruent with their gender. These findings suggest that being 'out of role' in gender-defined terms may produce a decline in the leaders' actual or perceived effectiveness" (pp. 137-138). Eagly et al. also evaluated the impact of the type of organization on evaluations. The most pronounced differences occurred in studies involving military organizations, where males were evaluated more favorably. There were classes of organizations in which females were more effective than males—namely, education, government and social services, and to a lesser degree, business. Finally, they looked at how organizational level affected evaluations of effectiveness. Males were evaluated as more effective at the supervisory level, whereas females were evaluated more favorably at the middle-management level. Looking at the supervisory and middle-management levels, Eagly et al. (1995) make the following provocative assertion: "Consistent with research suggesting that women are, on average, more socially skilled than men, women may tend to be particularly suited for middle managerial roles" (p. 138). It is important to point out that Eagly et al. did not have data for upper-level managerial positions; therefore, no conclusions can be drawn regarding differences between men and women at higher levels of management.

Context, Context, Context!

After all the work that has been done on this topic, one is left questioning why the results are so discrepant. One explanation is that context is extremely important in mitigating sex effects (Heilman et al., 1995; Ragins, 1991; Rosen & Jerdee, 1973; Terborg & Ilgen, 1975). For example, when females are portrayed as successful, individuals are less likely to invoke sex-role stereotypes (Dodge, Gilroy, & Fenzel; 1995; Jacobson & Effertz, 1974; Pheterson, Kiesler, & Goldberg, 1971). Discrepancies in findings can also be partially explained by the duration of interaction (Aries, 1996; Canary & Hause, 1993; Reskin & Hartmann, 1986; Shimanoff & Jenkins, 1991). In laboratory studies that involved a single encounter, males typically assumed leadership roles (Porter, Geis, & Walstedt, 1983), though such was not the case when interactions lasted for a longer period of time. Findings also vary based on the task being studied (Carbonell, 1984; Megargee, 1969; Nyquist & Spence, 1986). For example, when tasks were male oriented (e.g., assembling mechanical components), males were more likely to become leaders. Ragins (1991) found that power-related variables can also confound results. Finally, Lord, Phillips, and Rush (1980) asserted that leader personality affects results.

After reviewing three decades of work on the topic of gender, leadership, and managerial behavior, it appears that we have not provided conclusive answers. Few areas of inquiry could have endured as long with such a mixed record, yet leadership and gender have remained a central area of exploration throughout the 1990s. As we move toward the next millennium, we are left questioning whether research in this area will continue.

As noted previously, the meta-analytic studies by Eagly and her colleagues provide some encouragement insofar as the studies point out that the apparent inconsistency in results is actually somewhat orderly when contextual variables are taken into account. Accordingly, we challenge researchers to "re-view" the literature on gender, leadership, and managerial behavior. Researchers' efforts have not been futile—collectively, they have produced a remarkably rich body of literature. However, researchers should critically evaluate the limitations of past research as they develop their own studies. Clearly, contextual variables need to be scrutinized more closely.

As we close the 1990s, we look toward new frontiers. One important area for future scholarship involves addressing gender, leadership, and managerial behavior from an international perspective. In recent years, a number of studies have evaluated the glass ceiling from an international perspective (for reviews, see Adler & Izraeli, 1994; Anat & Izraeli, 1993; Black, Stephens, & Rosener, 1992). There has also been a growing body of literature on leadership and managerial behavior in an international context. For example, Schein and Mueller (1992) replicated Schein's (1973) study using German and British student participants. In this study, male participants in these two nations demonstrated similar sex-typing behavior as American males. Contrary to the findings with American samples, females in both Germany and Great Britain sex typed managerial positions. In a follow-up study using Japanese and Chinese students, Schein, Mueller, Lituchy, and Liu (1996) found a similar pattern. Powell and Kido (1994) likewise studied the attitudes of Japanese students, comparing the findings with American students. Japanese students were found to prefer femininity over masculinity when evaluating a prototypical manager. Rojahn and Willemsen (1994) evaluated how Dutch students evaluate leaders when the leaders demonstrate gender-role-incongruent behavior. Findings indicated that male participants provided lower evaluations of leader effectiveness when the leader demonstrated gender-incongruent behavior.[2]

Additionally, given the trend in other social science disciplines, it seems likely that postmodern scholarship will expand in the leadership area. According to postmodernists, knowledge is an amalgam of discursive practices that privileges some individuals while excluding others (Burrell, 1988; Cooper, 1989; Culler, 1982; Flax, 1987; Hassard, 1993; Parker, 1989; Townley,

1993). To topple the subjective nature of these discursive practices, many postmodernists employ the technique of deconstruction. This method seeks to show alternative versions of knowledge to expose the exclusionary function of discourse (Hassard, 1993; Martin, 1990a). To date, there has been little postmodern leadership scholarship, with the exception of Calás (1993) and Calás and Smircich (1991b). Although postmodernism stands outside the quantitative, empirical research presented in this chapter, it likely will become more widespread in the coming years.

As noted earlier, most of the studies of leadership style have revolved around consideration and initiating structure; therefore, other areas could be explored. Transformational leadership, which has become increasingly popular in recent years, offers one avenue for additional research. In one of the few studies in this area, Mahar (1997) found a clear distinction in how male and female participants evaluate leaders on the transformation dimension. Females provided higher transformation ratings for hypothetical female leaders than did males for male leaders. This finding confirmed an earlier finding by Druskat (1994), but contradicted the evidence provided by Komives (1991).

Finally, it seems that there is an opportunity for more qualitative research, whether it be hypothesis driven or interpretive. For instance, Apfelbaum (1993), using semistructured interviews, examined how French and Norwegian women construct narratives of leadership. Based on the interviews, Apfelbaum compared and contrasted the French and Norwegians with respect to personal qualities, experiences with role models, and cultural/contextual differences.

In conclusion, the search for the keys to effective leadership, for men and women alike, will surely continue. Some studies will break new ground, whereas others will provide support for what has come before. Whatever the case, it is important that researchers continue to explore this important dynamic of organizational life.

Notes

1. Although sharp conceptual distinction could be made, for this review we use the terms *leadership* and *managerial behavior* somewhat interchangeably by defining leadership as the behaviors and qualities of persons in formally designated leadership positions.

2. Indeed, cultural contexts themselves vary on masculinity and femininity (Hofstede, 1998), thereby potentially influencing ratings of managerial behaviors.

Global Leaders

Women of Influence

Nancy J. Adler

We have a responsibility in our time, as others have had in theirs, not to be prisoners
of history, but to shape history.

—U.S. Secretary of State Madeleine K. Albright[1]

Global Leadership: 21st-Century Challenges

Vaclav Havel (1994), president of the Czech Republic, eloquently explains,

> There are good reasons for suggesting that the modern age has ended. Many
> things indicate that we are going through a transitional period, when it seems
> that something is on the way out and something else is painfully being born.
> It is as if something were crumbling, decaying and exhausting itself, while
> something else, still indistinct, were arising from the rubble. (p. A27)

Havel's appreciation of the transition that the world is experiencing is
certainly important to each of us as human beings. None of us can claim that
the 20th century is exiting on an impressive note, on a note imbued with

AUTHOR'S NOTE: I would like to thank Soraya Hassenelli for her research support and insight
on this chapter, and the Social Sciences and Humanities Research Council of Canada for their
support of her research on all aspects of globalization and human resource systems, including
global leadership. This chapter is based on Nancy J. Adler's article "Global Leadership: Women
Leaders," in *Management International Review*, 37(1) [Special issue], pp. 135-143, 1997b. Used
with permission.

wisdom. As we ask ourselves which of the 20th century's legacies we wish to pass on to the children of the 21st century, we are humbled into shameful silence. Yes, we have advanced science and technology, but at the price of a world torn asunder by a polluted environment, by cities infested with social chaos and physical decay, by an increasingly skewed income distribution that condemns large proportions of the population to poverty (including people living in the world's most affluent societies), and by rampant physical violence continuing to kill people in titularly limited wars and seemingly random acts of violence. No, we do not exit the 20th century with pride. Unless we collectively learn to treat each other and our planet in a more civilized way, will it not become blasphemy to consider ourselves a civilization (Rechtschaffen, 1996)?[2]

The dynamics of the 21st century will not resemble those of the 20th century. To survive as a civilization, 21st-century society must not resemble the 20th century. The world needs a new style of leadership. Where will society find wise leaders to guide it toward a civilization that differs so markedly from that of the 20th century? Although many people continue to review men's patterns of historic success in search of models for 21st-century global leadership, few have begun to appreciate the equivalent patterns of historic and potential contributions of women leaders (Adler, 1996). My personal search for leaders who are outside of traditional 20th-century paradigms has led me to review the voice of the world's women leaders. This chapter looks at the nature of global leadership and the role that women are beginning to play at the most senior levels of world leadership.

Leadership: The Concept's Long History

To lead comes from the Latin verb *agere,* meaning to set into motion (Jennings, 1960). The Anglo-Saxon origins of the verb *to lead* come from *laedere,* meaning people on a journey (Bolman & Deal, 1995). Today's meaning of the word *leader,* therefore, connotes someone who sets ideas, people, organizations, and societies in motion—someone who takes the worlds of ideas, people, organizations, and societies on a journey. To lead such a journey requires vision, courage, and influence.

According to U.S. Senator Barbara Mikulski, leadership involves "creating a state of mind in others" (Cantor & Bernay, 1992, p. 59). Leaders, therefore, are "individuals who significantly influence the thoughts, behaviors, and/or feelings of others" (Gardner, 1995, p. 6). Beyond strictly focusing on the role of the leader himself or herself, leadership is increasingly thought of today as being interactive: Leadership is seen as "an influence relationship among leaders and followers who intend real changes . . . [reflecting] their mutual purposes" (Rost, 1991, p. 102). To emphasize the inherent mutuality, Eisler (1987) labels this influence relationship as a partnership approach. She contrasts the interactive partnership approach with the more hierarchical, single-person-focused dominator approach; an approach that, historically, has most often been associated with recognized leaders.

According to Bolman and Deal (1995), true leadership also includes a spiritual dimension:

> Two images dominate in concepts of leadership: one of the heroic champion with extraordinary stature and vision, the other of the policy wonk, the skilled analyst who solves pressing problems with information, programs, and policies. Both images miss the essence of leadership. Both emphasize the hands and heads of leaders, neglecting deeper and more enduring elements of courage, spirit, and hope. (p. 5)

The end of the 20th century has brought a plethora of books and articles emphasizing the spiritual dimension to leadership (e.g., Briskin, 1998; Conger, 1994; Greenleaf, 1998; Jaworski, 1996; Manz, 1998; Vaill, 1998).

As Warren Bennis aptly observed, leaders do the right thing, whereas managers do things right (Bennis & Nanus, 1985). Leadership must therefore be viewed as something more than just role and process—something more than the style with which a particular leader uses influence and power. To fully appreciate leadership, we must ask the ends to which a particular leader's behavior is directed. What is his or her vision? With this combined process and outcome perspective, leaders become people whose vision, courage, and influence move people, ideas, organizations, and societies toward their betterment.

Although comprehensive, this definition of leadership cannot be considered historically agreed on; indeed, no such agreed-on definition of leadership exists. After reviewing more than 5,000 published works on leadership, neither Stogdill (1974) in the 1970s nor Bass (1991) in the present decade succeeded in identifying a commonly agreed-on definition of leadership. As Bennis and Nanus (1985) concluded,

> Decades of academic analysis have given us more than 350 definitions of leadership. Literally thousands of empirical investigations of leaders have been conducted in the last 75 years alone, but no clear and unequivocal understanding exists as to what distinguishes leaders from non-leaders and, perhaps more important, what distinguishes effective leaders from ineffective leaders. (p. 4)

Rather than adding to the already overabundance of leadership definitions, this chapter simply introduces two dimensions to the historical definitions of leadership. The first dimension is a global perspective, and the second is the inclusion of women leaders in a field that has heretofore focused almost exclusively on men.[3]

Global Leadership: Global Leaders

Global leadership involves the ability to inspire and to influence the thoughts, attitudes, and behavior of people around the world. From an interactive process and outcome perspective, global leadership is the "process by which members of . . . [the world community] are empowered to work together synergistically toward a common vision and common goals . . . [resulting in an] improve[ment in] the quality of life" on and for the planet (based on Astin & Leland, 1991, p. 8; Hollander, 1985). Global leaders are those people who most strongly influence the process of global leadership.

Whereas there are hundreds of definitions of leadership, there are no global leadership theories. Most leadership theories, although failing to state so explicitly, are domestic theories masquerading as universal theories (Boyacigiller & Adler, 1991, 1996). Most commonly, they describe the behavior of leaders in one particular country, the United States (and, as discussed later, of one particular gender, male). This is particularly unfortunate for understanding global leadership because "Americans' extreme individualism combined with their highly participative managerial climate may render U.S. management practices [including leadership] unique; that is, differentiated from the approaches in most areas of the world" (Dorfman, 1996, p. 292; see also Dorfman & Ronen, 1991; Dorfman & Howell, 1988; Hofstede, 1991).

Recent research on leadership supports this conclusion in finding that the United States is unique in several respects among all Eastern and Western cultures that have been studied (Howell, Dorfman, Hibino, Lee, & Tate, 1994). For example, based on 221 definitions of leadership from the 20th century, Rost (1991) concluded that leadership has most frequently been described as rational, management oriented, male, technocratic, quantitative, cost-driven, hierarchical, short term, pragmatic, and materialistic. Not surprisingly, many of these descriptors reflect core values of American culture. For instance, relative to people from most other cultures, Americans tend to have a more short-term orientation, as highlighted by Americans' disproportionate use of the current quarter's results and daily-reported share prices to measure managerial effectiveness and organizational success. Similarly, Americans tend to hold more materialistic views than do most of their colleagues from other countries, as exemplified by the fact that 40% of American managers still think that "the bottom line" is *the* criterion for corporate health, whereas less than 30% of managers in other countries hold a similar view (Hampden-Turner, 1994). Likewise, Americans tend to have a more quantitative orientation than most of their global counterparts, as illustrated by their emphasis on measurable contributions and measurable results rather than reliance on less easily quantified qualities such as successful long-term relationship building.[4]

Of those leadership studies and theories that are not based on the United States, most still tend to be domestic, with the only difference being that their cultural focus reflects the values and context of a country other than the United States, such as descriptions of Israeli leaders in Israel (e.g., Vardi, Shrom, & Jacobson, 1980) or Indian leaders in India (e.g., Kakar, 1971). The fundamental global leadership question is not "Do American leadership theories apply abroad?" (Hofstede, 1980b), nor is it the comparative question inherent in attempts to determine which behaviors of leaders in one culture replicate those of leaders in other cultures.[5] Both questions frame leadership within a domestic context. The only difference is that the former focuses on a single country (descriptive domestic theories), whereas the latter focuses on multiple countries (comparative multidomestic theories) (see Boyacigiller & Adler, 1991, 1996).

Global leaders, unlike their domestic counterparts, address people worldwide. Global leadership theory, unlike its domestic counterpart, concerns itself with the interaction of people and ideas among cultures. It does not concern itself with either the efficacy of particular leadership styles within the leader's home country or with comparisons among leadership approaches from various countries—each of whose individual domain is limited to issues and people within one country's domestic environment. A fundamental distinction between prior leadership theories and global leadership is that global leadership is neither domestic nor multidomestic: Global leadership focuses on multinational interaction rather than on either single-country description or multicountry comparison. For example, as a global leader, the secretary general of the United Nations cannot change his message for each of the UN's more than 100 member states. Similarly, the CEO of a global company cannot change her vision statement for each of the countries and cultures in which her company operates.

As we move toward the 21st century, the domain of influence of leadership is shifting from circumscribed geographies to globally encompassing geographies, from a part of the world—for example, a nation or domestic economy—to the whole world. Historically, leadership "that goes beyond the nation-state and seeks to address all human beings" has been "the most important, but rarest and most elusive, variety of leadership" (Gardner, 1995, p. 20). The essence of such transnational leadership, however, was expressed already centuries ago by Diogenes when he asserted to his fellow Athenians, "I am not an Athenian or a Greek but a citizen of the world" (as quoted in Gardner, 1995, p. 51). It was captured more recently by Virginia Woolf (1938), one of the 20th century's intellectual leaders:

As a woman, I have no country.
As a woman, I want no country.
As a woman, the whole world is my country.

Within this emerging cross-culturally interactive context, global leaders must articulate a vision that is global. They articulate the meaning within which other people around the world work and live. According to Britain's Anita Roddick (1991), founder and CEO of the highly successful global firm The Body Shop,

> Leaders in the business world should aspire to be true planetary citizens. They have global responsibilities since their decisions affect not just the world of business, but world problems of poverty, national security, and the environment. Many, sad to say, duck these responsibilities, because their vision is material rather than moral. (p. 226)

Roddick's view of global leaders as "true planetary citizens" echoes Bolman and Deal's (1995, p. 5) observation that strictly emphasizing the hands and the head of leaders misses the essence of leadership by neglecting the deeper and more enduring elements of courage, spirit, and hope. The vision of a global leader, by definition, must be broader than the particular organization or country that he or she leads.

Beyond having a worthy vision, global leaders must communicate their vision in a compelling manner to people around the world. According to leadership expert Howard Gardner (1995), "Leaders achieve their effectiveness chiefly through the stories they relate" (pp. 8-9), both by communicating the stories and by embodying them. "Nearly all leaders are eloquent in voice," with many being "eloquent in writing as well. . . . [As leaders,] "they do not merely have a promising story; they can [also] tell it persuasively" (Gardner, 1995, p. 34).

Gardner (1995, p. 11) goes on to distinguish between leaders of a domain and leaders of a society. Leaders of a domain address an audience that "is already sophisticated in the stories, the images, and the other embodiments of that domain. To put it simply, one is communicating with experts"—such as when a medical doctor addresses other physicians. Leaders of a society "must be able to address a public in terms of the common-sense and commonplace notions that an ordinary inhabitant absorbs simply by virtue of living for some years within a society" (Gardner, 1995, p. 12). Ireland's former president, Mary Robinson (1996, as quoted in Pond, 1996), reflects her less hierarchical leadership and communication approach in explaining that

> a woman leader often has a distinctive approach as the country's chief "storyteller, [personifying] a sense of nationhood and [telling] a story that also [helps] shape people's sense of their own identity." This is leadership by "influencing [and] inspiring" rather than by commanding. (p. 59)

As society goes global, the audience of a leader also goes global. Members of a global audience have in common that which is most fundamentally human to each individual. Global leaders, more than their domestic counterparts, must communicate in terms of what is common sense and commonplace for people worldwide; they must communicate in the most fundamental terms of humanity. Global leaders no longer enjoy the simplified reality that their domestic predecessors enjoyed of speaking primarily to people from one culture, one country, one organization, or one discipline.

Global Leadership: Women Leaders

The feminization of leaders and of leadership is a significant development in our understanding and the governance of global political, economic, and societal structures.[6] As we approach the end of the 20th century, the number of women in the most senior global leadership positions is increasing, and at the same time, the style of domestic and global leadership is increasingly incorporating approaches frequently labeled as feminine. It appears that "the economic exigenc[ies] of global competition . . . [are making] feminine characteristics admirable in both men and women" (Calás & Smircich, 1993).

This chapter focuses on women with positional power, women in the most senior leadership roles in major global companies and nations. The focus goes beyond the assumption that scholarship on women leaders must be limited to women's historical and traditional role—that of influencing, primarily from behind the scenes, the men who hold society's elite positions of power while the women themselves hold no positional power. Contemporary discussions of the influence of American first ladies on their presidential husbands, including the more than 50 books published on Hillary Rodham Clinton and the extensive literature on Eleanor Roosevelt (Goodwin, 1995), underscore the pervasive history of viewing women's power as influence without position.

The feminist literature has tended to champion the nonhierarchical notion of broadly dispersed leadership—that is, the empowerment of many leaders within society (among many others, see Astin & Leland, 1991). It contrasts this broadly based leadership with the traditional, role-based, hierarchical, and more exclusive notions of leadership historically associated with men. This chapter attempts to bring together the notions of women's influence and their positional power. What will the nature of senior elite role leadership, as exhibited by women, be in the organizationally flattened world of the 21st century?

Whereas political and business leadership are certainly not identical, both have clearly delineated, elite role-based senior leadership positions that increasingly affect societal well-being and success. This chapter discusses both global political leaders—presidents and prime ministers of countries—and global business leaders—chairs of the board, chief executive officers, and presidents of major global companies. Given the increasingly global, border-crossing nature of world business, and its growing impact on the well-being of people worldwide, it is imperative that a study of global leadership include the economic domain. Similarly, given the mandate of the political sphere to provide for society's well-being, one cannot ignore political leadership. It is important, however, to recognize that the paths to power and the organizational structures of political leaders and business leaders vary. Political leaders are responsible to a constituency that either elects them personally for a specific term in office or elects others who then appoint them. The ability to get reelected or reappointed is often directly related to constituent popularity and may or may not be related to efficacy in office. In contrast, business is not a democracy and leaders are not selected by the popular acclaim of their constituents. The CEO of a company is generally appointed by a board of directors for an indeterminate period of time. Efficacy, as measured by financial performance, is easier to assess for business leaders than for political leaders. Likewise, business leaders often have greater discretion in hiring, firing, promoting, and rewarding employees than do political leaders, whose influence relative to their volunteer organizations and the civil service is often more limited. Given that countries remain geographically defined, whereas multinational companies now span multiple geographies, business leaders are increasingly more international and powerful than their political counterparts. The problem inherent in this shifting power base from countries to companies is that countries—political leaders—have traditionally been responsible for societal well-being. As world problems increasingly become transnational, and yet government structures remain national, the crucial 21st-century question becomes "Who will take care of the world?" Will business leaders take on the mandate that political leaders once held? Will business and political leaders work together in new ways that were unnecessary until this era of globalization? These problems and their solutions will define the very nature of society in the 21st century.[7]

Women Leaders: Numbers Increasing

The "feminization of an occupation or a job refers to women's disproportionate entry into a customarily male occupation" (Fondas, 1997, p. 258, based on Cohn, 1985; Reskin & Roos, 1990). Thus, the feminization of global leadership would refer to the disproportionate entry of women into the most senior political and business leadership roles in the world. Is there reason to believe that we will see the feminization of global leadership in the 21st century? The answer is yes. Although rarely recognized or reported in the media, one inescapable trend is that the number of the most senior women political leaders—presidents and prime ministers of countries—is rapidly increasing, albeit from a negligible starting point. As shown in Figure 13.1, no women presidents or prime ministers came to office in the 1950s, only 3 came to office in the 1960s, 5 in the 1970s, 8 in the 1980s, and to date in the 1990s, 26 have come to office. More than half of all women who have ever

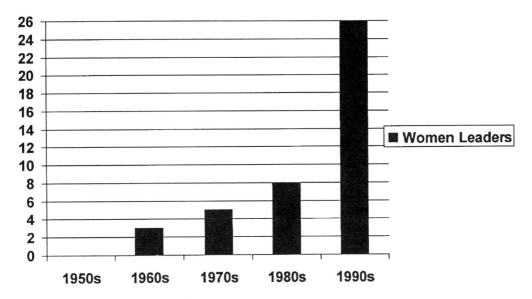

Figure 13.1. Women Political Leaders: Numbers Increasing
SOURCE: © 1999 Nancy J. Adler.

served as political leaders—26 of 42—have come to office since 1990. At the current rate of increase, more than twice as many women may be expected to become presidents and prime ministers in this decade as have ever served before. As shown in Table 13.1, countries as dissimilar as Sri Lanka, Ireland, and Rwanda all have had women lead them.[8]

Are there similar increases in the number of women leading major companies? Although the pattern among global business leaders is not yet clear, initial surveys suggest that there are not yet many women CEOs.[9] According to a 1995 United Nations report, *The World's Women,* there are no women running the world's largest corporations (as reported in Kelly, 1996, p. 21). Catalyst reports that only 2.4% of the chairmen and CEOs of *Fortune* 500 firms are women (Wellington, 1996, as reported in Himelstein, 1996). Moreover, not until 1997 did Britain gain its first woman chief executive of a *Financial Times* (FT-SE) 100 firm, Marjorie Scardino at Pearson Plc (Pogrebin, 1996). Women's ascendancy into global leadership roles in major companies appears to lag behind their gaining their countries' highest political leadership positions.

However, contrary to popular belief, women's scarcity in leading major corporations does not mean that they are absent as leaders of global companies. Unlike their male counterparts, most women chief executives have either created their own businesses or assumed the leadership of a family business. A disproportionate number of women have founded and are now leading entrepreneurial enterprises. According to the Small Business Administration,

TABLE 13.1   Women Political Leaders: A Chronology

Country	Name	Office	Date
Sri Lanka	Sirimavo Bandaranaike[a]	Prime minister	1960-1965, 1970-1977, 1994-
India	(Indira Gandhi)	Prime minister	1966-1977, 1980-1984
Israel	(Golda Meir)	Prime minister	1969-1975
Argentina	(Maria Estela [Isabel] Martínez de Perón)	President	1974-1976
Central African Republic	Elizabeth Domitien	Prime minister	1975-1976
Portugal	Maria de Lourdes Pintasilgo	Prime minister	1979
Bolivia	Lidia Gveiler Tejada	Interim president	1979-1980
Great Britain	Margaret Thatcher	Prime minister	1979-1990
Dominica	Mary Eugenia Charles	Prime minister	1980-1995
Iceland	Vigdís Finnbógadottir	President	1980-1996
Norway	Gro Harlem Brundtland	Prime minister	1981, 1986-1989, 1990-1996
Yugoslavia	Milka Planinc	Prime minister	1982-1986
Malta	Agatha Barbara	President	1982-1987
Netherland-Antilles	Mary Liberia-Peters	Prime minister	1984, 1989-1994
The Philippines	Corazon Aquino	President	1986-1992
Pakistan	Benazir Bhutto	Prime minister	1988-1990, 1993-1996
Lithuania	Kazimiera-Danute Prunskiene	Prime minister	1990-1991
Haiti	Ertha Pascal-Trouillot	President	1990-1991
Myanmar (Burma)	Aung San Suu Kyi[b]	Opposition leader[c]	1990-
East Germany	Sabine Bergmann-Pohl	President of the Parliament	1990
Ireland	Mary Robinson	President	1990-1997
Nicaragua	Violeta Barrios de Chamorro	President	1990-1996
Bangladesh	Khaleda Zia	Prime minister	1991-1996
France	Edith Cresson	Prime minister	1991-1992
Poland	Hanna Suchocka	Prime minister	1992-1993
Canada	Kim Campbell	Prime minister	1993
Burundi	Sylvia Kinigi	Prime minister	1993-1994
Rwanda	(Agatha Uwilingiyimana)	Prime minister	1993-1994
Turkey	Tansu Çiller	Prime minister	1993-1996
Bulgaria	Reneta Indzhova	Interim prime minister	1994-1995
Sri Lanka	Chandrika Bandaranaike Kumaratunga[a]	Executive president and former prime minister	1994-
Haiti	Claudette Werleigh	Prime minister	1995-1996
Bangladesh	Hasina Wajed[a]	Prime minister	1996-
Liberia	Ruth Perry[a]	Chair, Ruling Council	1996-
Ecuador	Rosalia Artega	President	1997
Bermuda	Pamela Gordon	Premier	1997-1998
Bosnian Serb Republic	Biljana Plavsic[a]	President	1997-
Ireland	Mary McAleese[a]	Prime minister	1997-
New Zealand	Jenny Shipley[a]	Prime minister	1997-
Guyana	Janet Jagan[a]	Prime minister, president	1997-
Bermuda	Jennifer Smith[a]	Premier	1998-
Switzerland	Ruth Dreyfuss[a]	President	1999-

SOURCE: Updated and adapted from Nancy J. Adler's "Global Women Political Leaders: An Invisible History,, an Increasingly Important Future," *Leadership Quarterly, 7*(1), p. 136, 1996. © 1999 Nancy J. Adler.
NOTE: Name in parentheses = no longer living.
a. Currently in office.
b. Nobel Prize laureate.
c. Party won 1990 election but Suu Kyi was prevented by military from taking office.

for example, women currently own one-third of all American businesses. These women-owned businesses in the United States employ more people than the entire *Fortune 500* list of America's largest companies combined (Aburdene & Naisbitt, 1992). As the list of women business leaders in Table 13.2 attests, the reality is that women from around the world are leading major companies. Moreover, these global women business leaders do not come only from the West (see Adler, 1997a, 1997b).

There is, of course, a fallacy in assuming that because global women leaders are few in number that they are not important (Bunch, 1991, pp. xi-xii). In fact, as Charlotte Bunch (1991), director of the Center for Global Issues and Women's Leadership, suggests, perhaps the most important question is "why so little attention has been paid to the women who have become [global] leaders and why the styles of leading more often exhibited by women are particularly useful at this critical moment in history" (p. xii).

The Feminization of Global Leadership

In addition to the increasing numbers, feminization also refers to "the spread of traits or qualities that are traditionally associated with . . . [women to people and processes] not usually described that way" (Fondas, 1997, p. 258, based on Douglas, 1977, and Ferguson, 1984). Hence, the feminization of global leadership—beyond referring strictly to the increasing numbers of women who are global leaders—refers to the spread of traits and qualities generally associated with women to the process of leading organizations with worldwide influence. Whereas this certainly has not been true of traditional 20th-century leadership models that have primarily reflected American men and their norms, it appears that 21st-century global leadership is increasingly being described in terms that reflect neither the masculine ideal nor the American ethos.

What is a feminine style of leadership? "Feminine is a word that refers to the characteristics of females" (Fondas, 1997, p. 260). Many authors argue that "there are character traits, interaction styles, and patterns of reasoning, speaking, and communicating that are culturally ascribed as feminine attributes" (Fondas, 1997, p. 260). Although theorists debate whether these traits are biologically inherited or socially constructed, most researchers credit a disproportional number of women with many, if not all, of the following qualities:

> empathy, helpfulness, caring, and nurturance; interpersonal sensitivity, attentiveness to and acceptance of others, responsiveness to their needs and motivations; an orientation toward the collective interest and toward integrative goals such as group cohesiveness and stability; a preference for open, egalitarian, and cooperative relationships, rather than hierarchical ones; and an interest in actualizing values and relationships of great importance to

TABLE 13.2   Global Women Business Leaders

How many of us recognize the names of the world's women business leaders? All of the women included on the following list lead or have led companies with current revenues over U.S. $1 billion, or for banks, with assets over U.S. $1 billion:

Ernestina Herrera de Noble, Argentina, $1.2 billion: President and editorial director of Grupo Clarin.

Francine Wachsstock, Belgium, $2.25 billion: President of the board of administrators, La Poste, Belgium's state-owned post office and largest employer.

Beatriz Larragoiti, Brazil, $2.9 billion: Vice president (and owner) of Brazil's largest insurance company, Sul America S.A.

Maureen Kempston Darkes, Canada, $18.3 billion: President and CEO of General Motors of Canada.

Ellen R. Schneider-Lenne, Germany, $458 billion in assets: Former member of the Board of Managing Directors, Deutsch Bank AG, responsible for operations in the United Kingdom (deceased).

Nina Wang, Hong Kong, $1-$2 billion in assets: Chairlady of Chinachem Group, property development.

Tarjani Vakil, India, $1.1 billion in assets: Former chairperson and managing director, Export-Import Bank of India, highest-ranking female banking official in Asia.

Margaret Heffernan, Ireland, $1.6 billion: Chairman, Dunnes Stores Holding Company, largest retailing company in Ireland.

Galia Maor, Israel, $35.6 billion in assets: CEO of Bank Leumi le-Israel.

Gloria Delores Knight, Jamaica, $1.86 billion in assets: Former president and managing director, the Jamaica Mutual Life Assurance Society, largest financial conglomerate in English-speaking Caribbean (deceased).

Sawako Noma, Japan, $2 billion: President of Kodansha Ltd., largest publishing house in Japan.

Harumi Sakamoto, Japan, $13 billion: Senior managing director, The Seiyu, Ltd., a supermarket and shopping center operator expanding throughout Asia.

Khatijah Ahmad, Malaysia, $5 billion: Chairman and managing director, KAF Group of Companies, financial services group.

Merce Sala i Schnorkowski, Spain, $1.1 billion: CEO of Renfe, Spain's national railway system, currently helping to privatize Colombian and Bolivian rail and selling trains to Germany.

Antonia Ax:son Johnson, Sweden, $6 billion: Chair, Axel Johnson Group, retailing and distribution, more than 200 companies.

Elisabeth Salina Amorini, Switzerland, $2.8 billion: Chairman of the board, managing director, and chairman of the group executive board, Société Generale de Surveillance Holding S.A., the world's largest inspection and quality control organization, testing imports and exports in more than 140 countries.

Emilia Roxas, Taiwan, $5 billion: CEO, Asiaworld Internationale Groupe, multinational conglomerate.

Ellen Hancock, United States, $2.4 billion: Executive vice president and co-chief operating officer, National Semiconductor Corp.

The list includes most other countries of the world when companies are included with revenues over U.S. $250 million, including such women business leaders as

Donatella Zingone Dini, Costa Rica, $300 million: Zeta Group, fifth-largest business in Central America, conglomerate.

Nawal Abdel Moneim El Tatawy, Egypt, $357 million in assets: Former chairman, Arab Investment Bank.

Colette Lewiner, France, $800 million: Chairman and CEO, SGN-Eurisys Group, world's largest nuclear fuels re-processing company.

Jannie Tay, Singapore, $289 million: Managing director, The Hour Glass Limited, high-end retailer of watches.

Aida Geffen, South Africa, $355 million: Chairman and managing director, Aida Holdings Ltd., residential commercial real estate firm.

Ann Gloag, United Kingdom, $520 million: Stagecoach Holdings Plc; Europe's largest bus company.

Linda Joy Wachner, United States, $1.1 billion (combined); chairman of Warnaco Group ($789 million) and Authentic Fitness Corporation ($266 million).

Liz Chitiga, Zimbabwe, $400 million: Former general manager and CEO, Minerals Marketing Corporation of Zimbabwe; in foreign-currency terms, the biggest business in Zimbabwe.

SOURCE: Adapted from Kelly, Caitlin (1996). "50 World-Class Executives," *Worldbusiness, 2*(2), pp. 20-31.

community (Belenky, Clinchy, Goldberger, & Tarule, 1986; Chodorow, 1978; Dinnerstein, 1976; Eisler, 1987; Ferguson, 1984; Gilligan, 1982; Glennon, 1979; Grace, 1995; Hartsock, 1983; Iannello, 1992; Klein, 1972; McMillan, 1982; Miller, 1976; Scott, 1992; Spender, 1984b; Tannen, 1990, 1994). (Fondas, 1997, p. 260)

By contrast, traits that have been culturally ascribed to men include the following:

an ability to be impersonal, self-interested, efficient, hierarchical, tough minded, and assertive; an interest in taking charge, control, and domination; a capacity to ignore personal, emotional considerations in order to succeed; a proclivity to rely on standardized or "objective" codes for judgment and evaluation of others; and a heroic orientation toward task accomplishment and a continual effort to act on the world and become something new or . . . [different] (cf. Brod & Kaufman, 1994; Gilligan, 1982; Glennon, 1979; Grace, 1995; Kanter, 1977a; Seidler, 1994). (Fondas, 1997, p. 260)

Studies focusing specifically on women managers—as opposed to women in general or senior-level women leaders—document their "orientation toward more participative, interactional, and relational styles of leading" (Fondas, 1997, p. 259, based on Helgesen, 1990; Lipman-Blumen, 1983; Marshall, 1984; Rosener, 1990). Frequently labeled as the feminine advantage (e.g., Chodorow, 1978; Helgesen, 1990; Rosener, 1990), a number of authors have suggested that all managers today need to incorporate a more feminine leadership style (Fondas, 1997, p. 259). As Fondas (1997) observes, these findings,

when juxtaposed against calls for companies to improve their competitiveness by transforming themselves into learning, self-managing, empowering, and continuously improving organizations—transformations that rely upon more interactional, relational, and participative management styles—led some writers to conclude that . . . [women] are well-suited for managerial roles in contemporary organizations and that male [managers] need to cultivate feminine leadership traits (Aburdene & Naisbitt, 1992; Godfrey, 1996; Grant, 1988; Peters, 1989). (p. 259)

The current implication is that both female and male leaders need to cultivate such feminine characteristics into their styles of leadership (see Klenke, 1996).

When considering the suggested differences in women's and men's approaches to leadership from a global perspective, caution is needed. Leadership approaches that have frequently been labeled as feminine in the North American management literature—including being more cooperative, participative, and interactional and using a more relational style—appear to reflect patterns of male-female differences specific to the American culture rather than broader, more universally valid patterns. For example, male managers in many other parts of the world, including in the fast-growing economies of Asia, exhibit a more supposedly feminine style that do American men. As Cambridge management scholar Charles Hampden-Turner (1994) notes,

> America's ultra-masculine corporate value system has been losing touch progressively with the wider world. It needs a change of values, desperately, or it will continue to under-perform, continue to lose touch with the value systems of foreigners, which ironically are much closer to the values in which American women are raised.
>
> American women, who are socialized to display values antithetical yet complementary to American men, have within their culture vitally important cures for [the] American econom[y]. (p. 3)

It appears that some of the male-female cultural distinctions documented in the United States among American women and men have been overgeneralized and, as such, offer poor guidance to those leading global organizations.

For example, as the economy shifts from the 20th century's emphasis on mass production capitalism to the 21st century's emphasis on mass customization—that is, from the 20th century's machine age emphasis on huge production runs of essentially undifferentiated products to the emerging era of products and services made in short runs and in great variety—the importance of interactional and relational styles increases. "The future for developed economies lies in products [and services] uniquely fashioned for special persons" (Hampden-Turner, 1994, p. 6). Whereas the more typically male (from a North American perspective) universalistic approach of treating everyone the same according to codified rules worked well for mass-producing products such as jeans, colas, and hamburgers sold to a mass domestic market, a more typically feminine (from a North American perspective) particularistic approach works best for developing products and services—such as software—that are tailored to the individual client's needs (Hampden-Turner, 1994, p. 6). To understand particular markets and clients well enough to fashion products and services to suit their needs requires deep relationships (Hampden-Turner, 1994, p. 6). Not surprisingly, relational skills (labeled by anthropologists as particularism and by North Americans as typically feminine) outperform the seemingly more objective approach of following the same rules with everyone (labeled as universalism by the anthropologists and as typically male by North Americans). The distinction does not appear to be strictly male/female but, rather, a difference between the approach of most American male managers and that of most other managers around the world. Results of research by Trompenaars (1993) and Hampden-Turner (1994) show that American male managers strongly prefer universalism (the less relational style), whereas executives from other economies, such as Hong Kong, Japan, and South Korea, emphasize more relational values that are opposite to those of their American male colleagues (Hampden-Turner, 1994). As Hampden-Turner (1994) summarizes, at the close of the 20th century:

> Most American male executives suddenly find themselves ill-suited to the wider world, trying to codify the uncodifiable, flanked by a huge surplus of lawyers using cumbersome rules where other nations enter trusting relationships with subtle communications. (p. 6)

According to the research, American women display a relational style of communicating that is closer to the style of most non-American managers around the world than it is to that of most American male managers. Given American women managers' concurrence with the relational styles of their non-American colleagues, it is not surprising that, on average, American women expatriate managers outperform their American male counterparts (Adler, 1994). It is not that the distinction between women and men identified in the American managerial literature is incorrect or inconsequential, but only that it is incomplete. Without appreciating American male managers as the outliers, it is difficult to appreciate what women's and men's approaches can bring to global leadership in the 21st century.

Global Women Leaders: An Emerging Portrait

Other than knowing that their numbers are increasing and their approaches to leadership appear to differ from those of men, what do we know about the women who are global leaders?[10]

Diversity defines pattern. The dominant pattern in women leaders' backgrounds as well as in the countries and companies that select them to lead is diversity. As highlighted in Tables 13.1 and 13.2, the 42 women political leaders and their business counterparts span the globe. They come from the world's largest and smallest, richest and poorest, and most socially and economically advantaged and disadvantaged countries, as well as from every geographical region. Countries led by women represent six of the major world religions, with four women prime ministers having led predominantly Muslim countries (see Adler, 1996, 1997a).

Many people believe that female-friendly countries and companies select more women leaders. They do not. Seemingly female-friendly countries (e.g., those that give women equal rights) do not elect a disproportionate number of women presidents and prime ministers. Similarly, companies that select women for their most senior leadership positions are not those that implement the most female-friendly policies, such as day care centers and flextime

(Wellington, 1996, as reported in Dobrzynski, 1996). For example, among the 61 *Fortune 500* companies employing women as chairmen, CEOs, board members, or one of the top five earners, only 3 were listed by *Working Woman* as among the most favorable companies for women employees (Dobrzynski, 1996).

The diversity among countries that elect women presidents and prime ministers and among major companies that select women CEOs suggests that the dominant pattern is simply that of selecting more women as senior leaders. The dominant pattern does not appear to be that a particular group of supposedly female-friendly countries and companies (such as the Scandinavian countries, companies such as Avon Products, or organizations such as Great Britain's National Health Service) are increasingly valuing women per se. The dominant pattern is one of women's leadership, not of companies and countries changed behavior toward women in general. The dominant pattern is that women are increasingly being selected to serve in senior leadership positions, not that a few countries, companies, or organizations with particularly feminine cultures are choosing to select women to lead them.

People's aspirations: Hope, change, and unity. Why are countries and companies, for the first time in modern history, increasingly choosing women for senior leadership positions? It appears that people worldwide want something that women leaders exhibit (e.g., feminine values and behavior) or something that they symbolize.

The most powerful and attractive symbolism of women leaders appears to be change. Women's assumption of the highest levels of leadership brings with it the symbolic possibility of fundamental societal and organizational change. The combination of a woman being an outsider at senior leadership levels previously controlled by men and of her beating the odds to become the first woman to lead her country or company provides powerful public imagery about the possibility of broadly based societal and organizational change.

Women assuming senior leadership positions literally bring change. When a woman is chosen to become president, prime minister, or CEO, when no other woman has ever held such an office and when few people thought that she would be selected, people begin to believe that other potential organizational and societal changes are possible. Mary Robinson's presidential acceptance speech captures the unique event of Ireland electing its first woman president coupled with the possibility of national change:

> I was elected by men and women of all parties and none, by many with great moral courage who stepped out from the faded flags of civil war and voted for a new Ireland. And above all by the women of Ireland . . . who instead

of rocking the cradle rocked the system, and who came out massively to make their mark on the ballot paper, and on a new Ireland. (RDS, Dublin, November 9, 1990, as reported in Finlay, 1990, p. 1)

In addition to symbolizing change, women leaders appear to symbolize unity. For example, Nicaragua's Violetta Chamorro and the Philippines' Corazon Aquino became symbols of national unity following their husbands' murders. Chamorro even claimed "to have no ideology beyond national 'reconciliation' " (Benn, 1995). Of Chamorro's four adult children, two are prominent Sandanistas and the other two equally prominently oppose the Sandanistas, not an unusual split in wartorn Nicaragua (Saint-Germain, 1993, p. 80). Chamorro's ability to bring all the members of her family together for Sunday dinner every week achieved near legendary status in Nicaragua (Saint-Germain, 1993, p. 80). As "the grieving matriarch who can still hold the family together" (Saint-Germain, 1993, p. 80), Chamorro gives symbolic hope to the nation that it too can find peace based on a unity that brings together all Nicaraguans. That a national symbol for a woman leader is family unity is neither surprising nor coincidental.

On the basis of similar dynamics in the Philippines, former president Corazon Aquino, as widow of the slain opposition leader, was seen as the only person who could credibly unify the people of the Philippines following Benigno Aquino's death. Although Aquino was widely condemned in the press for naiveté when she invited members of both her own and the opposition party into her cabinet, her choice was a conscious decision to attempt to reunify the deeply divided country.

Given that women leaders symbolize unity, it is perhaps not surprising that a woman business leader, Rebecca Mark, chief executive of Enron Development Corporation, was the first person to successfully negotiate a major commercial transaction following the Middle East peace accords. Mark brought the Israelis and Jordanians together to build a natural gas power generation station.

When, as Vaclav Havel (1994) has said, the world is "going through a transitional period, when it seems that something is on the way out and something else is painfully being born" (p. A27), it is not surprising that people worldwide are attracted to women leaders' symbolic message of bringing change, hope, and the possibility for unity.

Driven by vision, not by hierarchical status. What brings these women into senior leadership positions? Most women leaders are driven by a vision, mission, or cause. They are motivated by a compelling agenda that they want to achieve, not primarily by a desire for the hierarchical status of being president, prime minister, or CEO, or by a desire for power per se. Power and the presidency are means for achieving their mission, not the mission itself.

As children, none of the women political leaders dreamed about becoming president or prime minister, as have so many male politicians, including Bill Clinton and Bob Dole in the United States and Great Britain's Michael Hesseltine. For example, Golda Meir's mission was to create the State of Israel and to ensure its survival as a Jewish state. Not only did she not dream of becoming prime minister, she initially rejected the position when it was offered to her. Similarly, Anita Roddick (1991, p. 126), CEO of The Body Shop, describes her contemporary vision as "corporate idealism." Her vision transcends traditional, narrowly defined economic goals; she is neither motivated to be a traditional CEO nor to focus singularly on maximizing profits or shareholder wealth.

That women have not imagined or dreamed of leading a country or a major company is not surprising. The majority of the women are "firsts." For them, there have been no women predecessors or role models. The women political leaders, with only five exceptions, have been the first women to lead their countries.[11] Similarly, among the women corporate leaders, a disproportionate number are also firsts. The importance of this pattern for 21st-century leadership is that society, if it is to survive as a civilization, can no longer tolerate or support the leadership of self-aggrandizement at the expense of the greater, now highly interrelated whole—at the expense of the world's entire population and its physical, spiritual, and natural environment.

Sources of power: Broadly based. Who supports women in becoming senior leaders? Women leaders tend to develop and to use broadly based popular support, rather than relying primarily on traditional, hierarchical political party or corporate structural support. This is particularly apparent among the women political leaders who often are not seriously considered as potential candidates by their country's main political parties. They are consequently forced to gain support directly from the people, and thus foreshadow the dynamics of leadership in an organizationally flattened world of the 21st century.

Mary Robinson, for example, campaigned in more small communities in Ireland than any previous presidential candidate before either her party or the opposition took her seriously. The opposition later admitted that they did not seriously consider Robinson's candidacy until it was too late to stop her (Finlay, 1990).

Similarly, Corazon Aquino, whose campaign and victory were labeled the People's Revolution, held more than 1,000 rallies during her campaign, whereas incumbent Ferdinand Marcos held only 34 (Col, 1993, p. 25). Likewise, Benazir Bhutto, who succeeded in becoming Pakistan's first woman and youngest prime minister, campaigned in more communities than any politician before her. Her own party took her seriously only when more people showed up upon her return from exile to Pakistan than they, the opposition, or the international press had ever expected (Anderson, 1993; Weisman, 1986).

In business, the disproportionate number of women who choose to start their own companies echos the same pattern of broadly based support. Rather than attempting to climb the corporate ladder and to break through the glass ceiling into senior leadership positions in established corporations, these entrepreneurial women build their success directly on the marketplace. The types of broadly based support developed by women political leaders and entrepreneurs differ only in their source, with the former enjoying support directly from the electorate and the latter gaining support from the marketplace. In each case, the base of support is outside of the traditional power structure and therefore more representative of new and more diverse opinions and ideas. Their sources of support, and therefore of power, more closely reflect the flattened network of emerging 21st-century organizations and society than they do the more centralized and hierarchical power structures of most 20th-century organizations.

Path to power: Lateral transfer. How do women leaders gain power? Rather than following the traditional path up the hierarchy of an organization, profession, or political party, most women leaders laterally transfer into high office. For example, Gro Harlem Brundtland was a medical doctor; six years later she became Norway's first woman prime minister. Similarly, Charlotte Beers became both Ogilvy & Mather Worldwide's first woman chief executive as well as its first CEO brought in from outside the firm (Sackley & Ibarra, 1995). Marjorie Scardino, Pearson's first woman chief executive, is a triple outsider. As the first American CEO brought in to lead this traditional British firm, she is a cultural outsider. In addition, because Pearson owns only 50% of *The Economist,* where Scardino previously served as managing director, Scardino is an organizational outsider. The general public was so surprised when Pearson announced Scardino's selection that Pearson's stock initially dropped (Pogrebin, 1996).

Today's global organizations and society can only benefit from the dynamics of lateral transfers. The 21st century needs integration across geographies, sectors of society, and professions. Society can no longer tolerate leaders with "chimney stack" careers that, in the past, resulted in deep expertise in one area, organization, or country without any understanding of the context within which their particular organization or country operates. Transferring across organizations, sectors of society, and areas of the world allows leaders to develop alternative perspectives and an understanding of context that is almost impossible to acquire within a single setting. Due to the historic pattern of promoting men and failing to promote women to the most senior leadership positions from within organizations—most often referred to as the glass ceiling—women appear to have inadvertently become the prototypes of a career pattern that will be needed more broadly among all 21st-century leaders.

Global leadership: Global visibility. For the women who become global leaders, it is always salient that they are women. For example, the single most frequently asked question of former British prime minister Margaret Thatcher (1995) was, "What is it like being a woman prime minister?" (Thatcher generally responded that she could not answer because she had not tried the alternative.)

Women are new to most senior levels of both political and business leadership. As mentioned previously, only 5 of the 42 women presidents and prime ministers followed another woman into office. The remaining majority are firsts. Because women leaders are new, they benefit from enhanced visibility, including global visibility. Their unique status as their countries' first woman president or prime minister attracts worldwide media attention, thereby leveraging historically domestic leadership positions into ones with global visibility, and concomitantly, the potential for worldwide influence. For example, following the election of Mary Robinson as Ireland's first woman president,

> Newspapers and magazines in virtually every country in the world carried the story. . . . [T]he rest of the world understood Ireland to have made a huge leap forward . . . Mary Robinson had joined a very small number of women . . . who had been elected to their country's highest office. It was, quite properly, seen as historic. (Finlay, 1990, pp. 149-150)

President François Mitterrand purposely created a worldwide media event by appointing Edith Cresson as France's first woman prime minister. Similarly, Pakistan's former Prime Minister Benazir Bhutto's male predecessor not only complained about insufficient international press coverage while abroad, he also fired the Pakistani embassy's public relations officer when displeased with the small number of journalists who covered his arrival in London. Benazir Bhutto, however, always received extensive media coverage wherever she traveled.

Because of the worldwide media attention given women leaders, their leadership is becoming global even as they assume roles that were primarily domestic when previously held by men. Whether by intention or consequence, senior women leaders are at the forefront of moving from the domestic to the world stage.

Whereas many of the dynamics affecting senior women leaders are quite different from those affecting women managers (see Adler, 1997a), it should be noted that international business women also receive more visibility than do their male colleagues. Women expatriates as well as women on international business trips, for example, report being noticed and remembered more readily than are their male counterparts (Adler, 1994). Compared with businessmen, global business women gain easier access to new clients, suppliers, and government officials; receive more time when meeting with international contacts; and are more frequently remembered (Adler, 1994).

Global Women Leaders: What We Know, What We Need to Know

As we begin to focus on the women who are assuming the most senior levels of leadership, what do we know? We know that the number of women political leaders is rapidly increasing. We need to verify if the same is true for women business leaders. For both, we need to know why, at this particular point in history, there is such a marked increase in the number of senior women leaders.

For both political leaders and business leaders, we know that women's paths to power do not appear to replicate those of men. The initial women who are gaining political power are disproportionately relying on broadly based support rather than on party support. These women political leaders are more vision driven than office driven. Similarly, women business leaders are disproportionately relying on market-based support rather than on established corporate, hierarchical support. Their source of support is reflected in the domain of their leadership—disproportionately as entrepreneurs rather than as leaders of established corporations. What we need to know is why. Are women relying disproportionately on broadly based popular and market-based support because current political and business power structures refuse to accept and to support them? Is society as a whole moving from centralized and hierarchical power structures to more networked forms of organization, with women merely fitting into an overall societal trend? Or is the explanation that women are inherently attracted to less hierarchical sources and uses of influence?[12]

We know that these initial women leaders are not simply viewed as leaders but, rather, as women leaders. A woman leader is not viewed as androgynous or as undifferentiated from her male counterparts. She is viewed as a woman who is a leader. In recognizing women leaders as women, we know that they become more visible and enjoy a broader scope to their visibility than do their male counterparts. Is this visibility due strictly to women leaders' current novelty or to the unique confluence of women and power?

We know that women leaders today tend to symbolize unity, change, and modernity. We need to know if such symbolism is a result of the novelty of women in senior leadership positions or if it is based on some more enduring cultural symbolism attached to women.

Whereas research on women managers suggests that they lead in more inclusive and democratic ways than do men, we do not yet know if the same will be true of women leaders. Fundamentally, we need to know if women, on average, lead in ways similar to or different from men. Are women strictly moving into the roles and behaviors of male leaders, or are they bringing a more feminine approach to leadership? Only once we know if such differentiation exists can we ask one of the most fundamental questions: How can men's and women's styles of leadership complement each other to the benefit of organizations and society? Given the problems inherent in organizations and society today, we can hope for the potential benefit of a new, more feminine, style of senior leadership; however, as yet, no one can prove it.

Global Leaders: Women of Influence

The confluence of 21st-century business, political, and societal dynamics gives leaders a chance to create the type of world in which they, and we, would like to live. Such dynamics demand, as Havel (1994) reflected, that leaders find "the key to insure the survival of . . . [our] civilization . . . a civilization that is global and multicultural" (p. A27). The increasing number of women political and business leaders brings with it a set of experiences and perspectives that differs from that of the 20th century's primarily male leaders. The interplay of women's and men's styles of leadership will define the contours and potential success of 21st-century society. The risk is in encapsulating leaders, both women and men, in approaches that worked well in the 20th century but foretell disaster for the 21st century. Dr. Frene Ginwala, speaker of the South African National Assembly, has said that "the institutions that discriminate are man-shaped and must be made people-shaped. Only then will women be able to function as equals within those institutions. . . . [Ginwala's fundamental belief is that] women's struggle is not a struggle to transform the position of women in society but a struggle to transform society itself" (as reported in Iqtidar & Webster, 1996, p. 10). Recognizing the growing number of women leaders is the first step in creating and understanding the types of global leadership that will lead to success in the 21st century.

Notes

1. Quote is from U.S. Secretary of State Madeleine K. Albright's June 5, 1997 Harvard commencement address as reported in the *New York Times,* June 6, 1997, p. A8.

2. The opening section of this article is based on work originally presented in Adler's "Societal Leadership: The Wisdom of Peace" (1998).

3. For contemporary discussions of some of the widely read leadership theories and approaches, see Bennis (1989), Bennis and Nanus (1985), Conger (1989), Conger and Kanungo (1988), Gardner (1995), Kotter (1988), and Rosen (1996), among many others.

4. For descriptions of American societal and management culture contrasted with those of many other countries, see, among others, Hofstede (1980a), Kluckhohn and Strodbeck (1961), Laurent (1983), and Trompenaars (1993).

5. See Bernard Bass's (1991) extensive work on leadership in various countries around the world for an excellent example of worldwide comparative leadership

research. Note, however, that such comparisons are not the equivalent of global theory but, rather, exemplify the best of multidomestic theory building.

6. This is based on Fondas's (1997) observation "that the feminization of managers and managerial work is a significant development in management thinking" (p. 257). This section extends the focus from managers to leaders.

7. For further discussion on the divergent dynamics of the business and political spheres relative to overall societal well-being, see Adler and Bird (1988) and Adler (1998).

8. The Republic of San Marino, a city-state with a population of fewer than 25,000 people, has been led since 1243 by a consul, the co-captain regent, who acts as both head of government and head of state and is elected for a period of six months. In modern history, four women have held the position of co-captain regent: Maria Lea Pedini-Angelini (in 1981), Glorianna Ranocchini (in 1984 and 1989-1990), Edda Ceccoli (in 1991-1992), and Patricia Busignani (in 1993). Due to the small size of the country and the frequency of changing leaders, San Marino has not been included in the statistics on global women leaders.

9. Although the results are not yet available, the author is currently involved in a major worldwide survey identifying women who head global businesses with annual revenues in excess of U.S. $250 million.

10. For a more in-depth discussion of the issues raised in this section, see Adler (1997a, 1997b).

11. The exceptions are Sri Lanka's current executive president, Chandrika Kumaratunga, who followed her prime minister mother Sirimavo Bandaranaike into office; Bangladesh's Hasina Wajid, who followed Khaleda Zia into office, Ireland's Mary McAleese, who followed Mary Robinson into the presidency; and Bermuda's Jennifer Smith, who followed Pamela Gordon into office.

12. Whereas research on managers strongly suggests that women use more inclusive approaches than do men, no such research exists, as yet, on senior women leaders (Eagly & Johnson, 1990, as cited in Vinnicombe & Colwill, 1995, p. 32).

Chapter 14

A Multiperspective Framework of Sexual Harassment

Reviewing Two Decades of Research

Lynn Bowes-Sperry and Jasmine Tata

Sexual harassment is a pervasive and widespread problem in the workplace, with estimates of harassment ranging from 28% to 90% for female targets and 14% to 19% for male targets (Gelfand, Fitzgerald, & Drasgow, 1995; Gutek, 1985; Mazer & Percival, 1989; Schneider, Swan, & Fitzgerald, 1997; U.S. Merit Systems Protection Board, 1981, 1988, 1995). Recent watershed events in the United States, such as Paula Jones's sexual harassment lawsuit against President Bill Clinton, and Anita Hill's allegations of sexual harassment against Clarence Thomas during his Supreme Court confirmation hearings (Hill, 1997), have put this issue in the public eye. Public awareness has been accompanied by a growing interest in the topic by academicians and researchers, resulting in special issues of journals (e.g., *Basic and Applied Social Psychology,* Vol. 17, 1995 [see Fitzgerald, Gelfand, & Drasgow, 1995]; *Journal of Vocational Behavior,* Vol. 42, No. 1, 1993), a number of edited volumes (e.g., Stockdale, 1996), and over 500 citations in the literature. Recently, researchers have moved beyond documenting the mere existence of sexual harassment to examining its causes (e.g., Gutek, Cohen, & Konrad, 1990) and its consequences (e.g., Fitzgerald, 1993; Schneider et al., 1997), as well as the management of sexual harassment in organizations (e.g., Riger, 1991) and the legal aspects of harassment (e.g., Terpstra & Baker, 1988, 1992).

Sexual harassment is defined as both a subjective and an objective construct: subjective from an individual perspective, objective from a conceptual/behavioral perspective, and both subjective and objective from a legal perspective (because the plaintiff must prove that he or she was adversely affected and that a "reasonable person" would be similarly affected). The merits of these definitions have been debated in the literature. Some researchers believe that, because perceptions vary from person to person, using a subjective definition would classify an almost infinite number of behaviors as sexual harassment, increasing the difficulties involved in "trying to study a variable that means different things to different people . . . [and] result in the frustration expressed by some men that virtually anything they say or do may be construed by some women as sexual harassment" (Lengnick-Hall, 1995, p. 844). Others believe that targets may not perceive all objectively harassing behaviors as sexual harassment. Schneider et al. (1997) found that approximately 60% of women who stated that they had experienced at least one behavior listed on the Sexual Experiences Questionnaire (developed by Fitzgerald and her colleagues to *objectively* measure sexual harassment) failed to recognize or admit that they were sexually harassed.

To attain a fuller understanding of this phenomenon, organizational and legal scholars ultimately need to establish consensus on the objective behaviors and dimensions that constitute sexual harassment. This chapter examines the literature on sexual harassment, differentiating between subjective perceptions and objective occurrences, and presents a multiperspective framework that integrates two lines of research, one by legal scholars and one by psychological and organizational scholars. A framework is developed that answers five crucial questions:

1. What is sexual harassment?
2. What causes sexual harassment?
3. How do people and organizations respond to harassment?
4. What are the consequences of harassment?
5. What are the emerging issues and future directions in research on this topic?

What Is Sexual Harassment?

A review of the existing literature indicates that there are three fundamental responses to the question "What is sexual harassment?" This question can be answered from an individual/subjective perspective, a conceptual/behavioral perspective, or a legal perspective.

Individual/Subjective Perspective

From an individual perspective, sexual harassment is any behavior of a sexual nature that an individual subjectively perceives to be offensive and unwelcome (whether or not it is legally or conceptually defined as such). York (1989) emphasizes the importance of this concept when he states that "sexual harassment is not a purely objective phenomenon but one based on an individual's perception of another's behavior" (p. 831). Thus, sexual harassment is viewed as a subjective construct, with its definition differing from person to person.

Conceptual/Behavioral Perspective

The behavioral perspective seeks to objectively identify types of behavior that constitute sexual harassment (whether or not they are legally defined as harassment or are subjectively perceived by targets as such); thus, the definition of sexual harassment does not differ from person to person. Building on previous research by Till (1980), Gelfand et al. (1995, p. 164) propose that sexual harassment is a "stable behavioral construct distinct from but related to evolving legal formulations" consisting of three primary dimensions: *gender harassment* (i.e., behaviors that express hostile or insulting attitudes toward targets but are not initiated for the purpose of gaining sexual cooperation), *unwanted sexual attention* (i.e., behaviors that are initiated for the purpose of gaining sexual cooperation but are not welcomed by the target or tied to job-related outcomes), and *sexual coercion* (i.e., behaviors that explicitly or implicitly link sexual cooperation to job-related outcomes). Because research in this area generally examines the occurrence of objective behaviors, the definition of sexual harassment remains constant. In addition to direct exposure to sexually harassing behaviors, people can also be exposed to such behaviors indirectly. This phenomenon, known as *ambient sexual harassment,* has been defined as the general level of sexual harassment in a work group, that is, the frequency of sexually harassing behaviors experienced by others in a target's work group (Glomb et al., 1997).

Legal Perspective

From a legal perspective, sexual harassment is any behavior that violates the laws of the country in which it occurs. In the United States, the legal definition established by the U.S. Equal Employment Opportunity Commission (EEOC; 1981) states,

> Unwelcome sexual advances, requests for sexual favors, and other verbal or physical conduct of a sexual nature constitute sexual harassment when (1) submission to such conduct is made explicitly or implicitly a term or

condition of an individual's employment, (2) submission to or rejection of such conduct by an individual is used as a basis for employment decisions affecting such individual, or (3) such conduct has the purpose or effect of substantially interfering with an individual's work performance or creating an intimidating, hostile, or offensive working environment. (p. E-10)

This definition has been elevated to the status of law by a number of court decisions, including several by the U.S. Supreme Court (e.g., *Meritor Savings Bank, FSB v. Vinson,* 1986; *Oncale v. Sundowner Offshore Services, Inc.,* 1998). In *Meritor,* the Supreme Court first granted Title VII coverage to sexual harassment complaints by ruling that an intimidating, hostile, or offensive work environment and/or unwelcome sexual advances constitute sexual harassment and that sexual harassment could be established without the target suffering tangible economic loss. The *Oncale* decision broadened the definition to include same-sex sexual harassment.

Both the EEOC and case law recognize two types of harassment: quid pro quo, in which targets are threatened with punishment or promised rewards based on their response to initiators' sexual demands, and hostile environment, in which targets are made to feel uncomfortable in the workplace. Gender harassment and unwanted sexual attention constitute examples of a legal hostile work environment, whereas sexual coercion is similar to quid pro quo harassment (Gelfand et al., 1995).

Although the legal definition of sexual harassment has developed further in the Unites States than in most other countries, the European Union has established standards similar to those in the Unites States. The 1991 European Community Recommendations on Sexual Harassment define harassment as conduct (1) that is unwanted, unreasonable, and offensive to the target; (2) that creates a hostile and intimidating work environment; and (3) in which rejection or acceptance of such conduct is used as a basis for employment decisions (Collier, 1995). Although the recommendations are legally enforceable in the European Union, not all member states have passed national sexual harassment laws. Some countries (e.g., Spain and Denmark) merely have workers' charters and agreements that have no legal force, whereas others (e.g., Great Britain and France) have specific sexual harassment laws (Collier, 1995). Britain passed the Sex Discrimination Act in 1975, and a landmark case (*Porcelli v. Strathclyde Regional Council,* 1986, cited in Collier, 1995) recognized sexual harassment as sex discrimination. The legal definition of sexual harassment in Britain (based on the Sex Discrimination Act and case law) is similar to the one in the United States and includes both quid pro quo and hostile environment behaviors. In France, however, sexual harassment is defined as behaviors by supervisors intended to compel employees to provide sexual favors; this definition focuses solely on quid pro quo harassment and ignores harassment by peers (Collier, 1995). In general, most countries appear to be moving toward a legal definition of sexual harassment similar to that established by U.S. law.

What Causes Sexual Harassment?

Individual/Subjective Perspective

From the individual/subjective perspective, the question "What causes sexual harassment?" may be reframed as "What causes certain individuals to label certain behaviors as sexual harassment?" because sexual harassment exists only when a behavior is perceived and labeled as such. Although the difference is slight between men and women in recognizing the more extreme forms of harassment, women classify the more "ambiguous" incidents as sexual harassment more frequently than do men (Gutek, Morasch, & Cohen, 1983; Powell, 1986a; Roth & Fedor, 1993). Therefore, research in this area addresses factors such as gender that influence individuals to label behaviors as sexual harassment. Apart from gender, a number of other factors influence targets' perceptions of sexual harassment. Sociosexual behaviors are more likely to be labeled as harassment by people who have previously experienced sexual harassment (Blakely, Blakely, & Moorman, 1995; Roth & Fedor, 1993), have an internal locus of control (Booth-Butterfield, 1989), have feminist attitudes (Brooks & Perot, 1991), and perceive the initiator's intentions as hostile (Pryor & Day, 1988). In addition, third-party perceptions of sexual harassment can be influenced by perceptions of the target's complicity in the situation (Reilly, Carpenter, Dull, & Barlett, 1982; Workman & Johnson, 1991) and by the remedial accounts (explanations) provided by the initiator (Tata, 1998).

In addition to the individual-level factors described above, a number of organizational variables influence perceptions and labeling of sexual harassment. Pryor (1985) suggests that "the general unexpectedness or inappropriateness of a behavior for an actor's role and status contributes to the labeling of a behavior as sexual harassment" (p. 274). The status of the initiator, both in absolute terms and relative to the target, can influence such perceptions because people in supervisory roles are held to higher standards of behavior than coworkers (Pryor, 1985; Tata, 1993). Organizations with highly sexualized atmospheres or those that communicate a tolerance of harassment are more likely to have a greater number of occurrences of harassment (Fitzgerald, Drasgow, Hulin, Gelfand, & Magley, 1997; Pryor, LaVite, & Stoller, 1993). This finding is consistent with the power differences perspective to the extent that "there is power in numbers" because individuals who are contemplating sexual harassment are likely to believe that they will be supported (or at least not punished) by others. Another organizational factor to be considered is the physical setting (work vs. social) where the harassment occurs; sociosexual behaviors are more likely to be perceived as sexual harassment when occurring in work settings as opposed to social settings (Dougherty, Turban, Olson, Dwyer, & Lapreze, 1996; York, 1989).

Conceptual/Behavioral Perspective

Under the behavioral perspective, the very occurrence of certain behaviors (gender harassment, unwanted sexual attention, or sexual coercion) constitutes sexual harassment. To reduce the frequency of sexual harassment and deal effectively with it when it does occur, we must understand the factors contributing to its occurrence.

Sexual arousal as an explanation of sexual harassment. Tangri, Burt, and Johnson (1982) set forth three explanatory models of sexual harassment. Their natural/biological model suggests that sexual harassment results from biological sex drives or sexual arousal. Sexual arousal is central to Stockdale's (1993) misperception theory that suggests that some sexually harassing behaviors result from men's misperceptions of women's friendliness as the desire for a sexual relationship. In such instances, initiators may believe that their behavior is pleasing rather than harassing or harmful to their targets. Given that men are more likely than women to (mis)perceive friendly behavior as sexy (e.g., Abbey, 1982; Johnson, Stockdale, & Saal, 1991) and that men are more likely than women to initiate sexually harassing behaviors, the misperception explanation of sexual harassment is not without merit. However, based on his review of several studies designed to empirically assess this theory, Saal (1996) concluded that "considered all together, these studies failed to yield any notable support for this very plausible hypothesis" (p. 81).

Although the sexual arousal explanation may be tenable for sexual harassment between a heterosexual man and a heterosexual woman, two gay men, or two lesbians, it cannot account for same-sex sexual harassment among heterosexuals. Therefore, it is clear that other explanations for sexual harassment must exist.

Power differences as an explanation of sexual harassment. Differences in power are central to both the sociocultural and organizational models of sexual harassment proposed by Tangri et al. (1982). Although the sociocultural model suggests that sexual harassment is the result of gender-related power differences perpetuated by a patriarchal value system in society, the organizational model suggests that it results from the hierarchical structure of organizations. To the extent that societies with patriarchal value systems tend to have a disproportionate percentage of men in higher organizational positions, these models are consistent with one another.

The power differences explanation of sexual harassment was illustrated in the film *Disclosure* (Levinson, 1994) when Michael Douglas's character stated, "Sexual harassment is about power. When did I ever have the power?" In accordance with the organizational model, the answer to his question is that he *never* had the power because he is in a lower hierarchical position than the person who accused him of harassment. In accordance with the socio-cultural model, however, the answer to the question is that he *always* had the power because he is a man in a society that exhibits gender-related power differences that favor men.

A significant amount of empirical support exists for the power differences explanation of sexual harassment. Research indicates that sexual harassment occurs more often in firms that are not perceived as having equal employment opportunities for women (Lafontaine & Tredeau, 1986). By definition, such firms have more men in higher-level organizational positions. Because men tend to be the initiators of sexually harassing behaviors, this finding is consistent with a power differences perspective. Similarly, target charac-teristics associated with personal vulnerability (or reduced power) such as younger age and lower levels of education have been found to be correlates of sexual harassment (e.g., U.S. Merit Systems Protection Board, 1981, 1988, 1995).

Integrative explanations of sexual harassment. The sex-role spillover model (Gutek & Morasch, 1982) argues that when the sex ratio of employees at a particular location is skewed (i.e., when there are few members of one sex relative to the other) or when jobs/occupations are sex-typed, the characteristics of one gender become more salient and traditional sex roles spill over into the workplace. In partial support of this theory, Fitzgerald et al. (1997) found that workplaces with large numbers of men and traditionally male-oriented tasks exhibited higher levels of sexual harassment, although they did not find a similar effect for female-dominated workplaces. Gruber (1992) also found a higher occurrence of sexual harassment in male-dominated, blue-collar occupations.

Depending on which aspect of the female sex role we consider, the sex-role spillover model can be interpreted as either a sexual arousal or power differences explanation of sexual harassment. If "sexiness" is more salient as a result of skewed gender ratios, then this model is consistent with the sexual arousal explanation. Alternatively, if "weakness" is more salient as a result of skewed gender ratios, then this model is consistent with the power differences explanation.

In fact, Bargh, Raymond, Pryor, and Stack (1995) found that for some men, the notions of power and sexuality are inextricably intertwined. Specifi-cally, they found that men with propensities to sexually harass (e.g., those espousing adversarial sexual beliefs and traditional sex-role stereotypes) were more likely to associate power cues with sexual cues (i.e., were more sexually attracted to women when power themes had been primed) compared to other men. Other research by Pryor and his colleagues provides a framework that integrates the sexual arousal and power differences explanations of sexual harassment. Pryor et al. (1993) view sexual harassment as originating from the person/situation interaction, and they suggest that individual variables should be examined within their situational context because "neither qualities of the person nor qualities of the situation are typically sufficient to produce sexually harassing behavior" (p. 69). They found that men with proclivities to harass were more likely to initiate sexually harassing behaviors when the social norms of their department or organization allowed them to do so without penalty. In general, these theories suggest that both power differences and sexual arousal should be included in future theories on sexual harassment.

Legal Perspective

The courts have identified certain criteria that must exist for a target to establish a prima facie case and prove sexual harassment. Similar to the individual/subjective perspective, the legal perspective suggests that the target's complicity in the situation is an important factor in third-party perceptions of harassment. The courts may consider evidence regarding not only the target's response to the harassing conduct (e.g., *Cann v. Unilift Ltd.,* 1992, a British case cited in Collier, 1995) but also the target's appearance, manner of dress, or conduct (e.g., *Reed v. Shepard,* 1991). In addition, harassing conduct directed at other persons can strengthen the target's case (e.g., *Hall v. Gus Construction Company,* 1988).

The gender gap in perceptions of sexual harassment (discussed earlier) is reflected in legal discussions about the "reasonable woman" versus the "reasonable person" standard as the appropriate criterion for determining whether sexual harassment has occurred. For example, British law suggests that the legal test of a hostile work environment is whether a reasonable woman would be expected to find the workplace intimidating and humiliating (Collier, 1995). Similarly, the U.S. Ninth Circuit Court stated that "conduct that many men consider unobjectionable may offend many women. Because women are disproportionately victims of rape and assault, they have a stronger incentive to be concerned with sexual behavior" (*Ellison v. Brady,* 1991). This standard, however, does not have clear support at the U.S. Supreme Court level. *Harris v. Forklift Systems, Inc.* (1993) was expected to settle the issue of whose perspective should be considered, but the Supreme Court chose not to address this issue directly. Instead, the Court reemphasized the reasonable-person standard, thus hinting at rejecting the reasonable-woman perspective. Although courts tend to ignore organizational-level variables such as climate, gender of supervisor, and type of job, they do implicitly consider organizational climate when looking at the extent to which employers take prompt and appropriate remedial actions to end harassment.

How Do People and Organizations
Respond to Sexual Harassment?

The manner in which a target responds to sexual harassment can moderate the negative job-related, psychological, and health-related outcomes of harassment (Fitzgerald et al., 1997). Prompt and remedial actions by organizations may also reduce the negative impact of sexual harassment in terms of both individual consequences (e.g., retaliation from coworkers or supervisors) and organizational consequences (e.g., legal liability and reduced productivity).

Personal Responses to Sexual Harassment

Given the range of responses available to targets of sexual harassment and the increasing number of empirical studies (mainly from the individual/subjective perspective) investigating such responses, Knapp, Faley, Ekeberg, and Dubois (1997) developed a comprehensive typology of target responses to sexual harassment (see Figure 14.1). One response dimension classifies responses as self-focused versus initiator focused and the other as self-response versus supported response.

Research indicates that most women respond to sexual harassment by ignoring the situation and/or avoiding the initiator (a self-focused, self-response under Knapp et al.'s typology), even though this response is the least effective in terms of ending the harassment (Gutek & Koss, 1993; Loy & Stewart, 1984). Perhaps targets believe that ignoring, denying, or redefining the harassment can reduce the amount of stress they experience and allow them to maintain their "belief in a just world" (Lerner, 1980). Individuals who are younger, have previously experienced sexual harassment, or have low self-esteem are most likely to ignore the incident (Roth & Fedor, 1993).

Responses involving others (supported responses) such as filing a formal complaint, reporting to a boss or committee, and seeking legal assistance are among the least preferred actions by targets of sexual harassment (e.g., Gutek & Koss, 1993; Loy & Stewart, 1984; Roth & Fedor, 1993), despite the efficacy of such responses in ending harassment. Gutek (1985) estimates that for every woman who complains about or reports sexual harassment, there are up to eight more who do not report their experiences, perhaps because they do not define their experiences as harassment. Other targets define their experiences as sexual harassment but consciously decide not to report the incident. Their reasons for not reporting include the belief that they will not be taken seriously or should be able to handle the problem themselves; the emotional stress connected with reporting; fear of retaliation by the initiator, management, or coworkers; and/or a desire to avoid causing trouble for the initiator (Fitzgerald et al., 1988; Gutek, 1985; Knapp et al., 1997; Petersen & Massengill, 1992-1993; Riger, 1991).

MODE OF RESPONSE

	Self-Response	Supported Response
Self-Focus	*Avoidance/Denial* Most frequently used, yet least effective for ending harassment • avoiding the harasser • altering the job situation by transferring/quitting • ignoring the behavior • going along with the behavior • treating the behavior as a joke • self-blame	*Social Coping* Not effective for ending harassment, but may assist target in coping with negative consequences resulting from harassment • bringing along a friend when harasser will be present • discussing situation with sympathetic others • medical and/or emotional counseling
Initiator Focus	*Confrontation/Negotiation* Not frequently used, but very effective for ending harassment • asking or telling harasser to stop • threatening the harasser • disciplining the harasser (if in a position to do so)	*Advocacy Seeking* Not frequently used, but very effective for ending harassment • reporting the behavior to a supervisor, other internal official body, or outside agency • asking another person (e.g., a friend) to intervene • seeking legal remedies through the court system

(FOCUS OF RESPONSE — vertical label along left margin)

Figure 14.1. Typology of Target Responses to Sexual Harassment
SOURCE: From Knapp, Faley, Ekeberg, and Dubois (1997).

Research on those who do file complaints with the EEOC indicates that the majority are single women under the age of 40 with higher levels of education. These individuals are most likely to file complaints about repetitive incidents, incidents initiated by their supervisors, and incidents involving job discharge or involuntary quit (Terpstra & Cook, 1985). With regard to resolution of complaints, Terpstra and Baker (1988, 1992) found that severity of behavior, presence of witnesses, and notification of management before filing externally resulted in more favorable outcomes for the complainant.

Although a number of researchers have examined targets' responses to sexual harassment, there is very little research on the responses of third-party observers of sexual harassment (Kulik, Perry, & Schmidtke, 1997). Based on their review of the existing research, Kulik et al. concluded that observers of sexual harassment were likely to state that they would engage in direct responses (e.g., confronting or disciplining the harasser), especially in situations involving severe harassment or target noncompliance. Similarly, Bowes-Sperry and Powell (in press) found that observers responding to a hypothetical incident of harassment exhibited stronger intentions to intervene if they (1) identified the incident as an ethical issue, (2) believed that others would perceive the incident as harassment, and (3) were told that the target was upset by the incident. Possible responses of observers include testifying during investigations, reporting harassment to organizational officials, providing negative feedback to initiators regarding their behavior, and providing social support to targets of harassment (Bowes-Sperry & Powell, 1996). The fact that many targets do not report sexual harassment, even when the behavior is strongly offensive and harmful (Gutek, 1985; Ragins & Scandura, 1995), makes the role of observers especially important.

Kulik et al. (1997) argue that the responses of targets and observers to sexual harassment should vary in systematic ways because of differences in their access to information and in the consequences for each group. However, because different methodologies were used in the studies focusing on targets (several examined responses to actual incidents of harassment) than in the studies focusing on observers (all used hypothetical scenarios), it is not possible at this time to conclusively determine how these groups differ in terms of their responses.

Organizational Responses to Sexual Harassment

According to Gutek (1993), organizational policies and procedures may consider sexual harassment either as an issue between two individuals and direct solutions toward the individuals, or as an organizational issue and direct solutions toward the organization. The legal perspective emphasizes the first type of response. From a legal perspective, courts believe that employers should take appropriate actions to end harassment and deter the initiator from further harassment. An established sexual harassment policy or grievance procedure, however, does not prevent employer liability (e.g., *Meritor Savings Bank, FSB v. Vinson,* 1986); organizations can be held responsible even if the target does not use the internal formal grievance procedure (e.g., *EEOC v. Hacienda Hotel,* 1989) and even if the organization takes corrective action but does not prevent the harassment from occurring in the first place (e.g., *Carter v. Westcliff Hall Sidmouth Ltd.,* 1990, a British case cited in Collier, 1995). The continued presence of the harasser in the workplace even in the absence of future harassing behavior may also constitute a sexually hostile environment for the target (e.g., *Ellison v. Brady,* 1991).

In general, responses to sexual harassment should include (1) adopting, enforcing, and disseminating reasonable sexual harassment policies and grievance procedures; (2) appraising employees of charges against them immediately upon learning of the alleged misconduct; (3) conducting fair and full investigations of charges; and (4) ensuring that penalties are commensurate with the seriousness of the offense (Hames, 1994). In addition to responding to specific instances of harassment, organizations should try to prevent sexual harassment by disseminating information, changing employees' attitudes and behaviors, and transforming the organizational climate (Howard, 1991).

What Are the Consequences of Sexual Harassment?

Sexual harassment can result in a number of negative consequences for both individuals and organizations. Consequences of sexual harassment may be similar from the individual/subjective and the conceptual/behavioral perspectives, because even "relatively low-level but frequent types of sexual harassment" can result in negative outcomes for people exposed to such behavior whether or not they actually define their experiences as such (Schneider et al., 1997, p. 401).

Individual/Subjective and Conceptual/ Behavioral Perspectives

Consequences of sexual harassment can be categorized as job related, psychological/somatic, and organizational. Gutek and Koss (1993) note that negative job-related outcomes include voluntary quits, transfers and reassignments, terminations, deterioration of interpersonal relationships with coworkers, and decreases in job satisfaction and organizational commitment. Fitzgerald et al. (1997) found that women who were harassed reported lower levels of job satisfaction and higher levels of absenteeism and turnover intentions. Similarly, research on federal employees indicates that 10% of the women surveyed had quit a job because of sexual harassment (U.S. Merit Systems Protection Board, 1981, 1988, 1995). In addition, when people report sexual harassment, they are often retaliated against by coworkers and others in a manner similar to the well-documented "whistleblower" effect (Lewin, 1987).

Sexual harassment can also impair the target's health, resulting in headaches and sleep disturbances (Fitzgerald et al., 1997) as well as negative psychological outcomes. Psychological/somatic outcomes include reduced self-esteem and life satisfaction, as well as increased stress, anger, fear, depression, and anxiety. Loy and Stewart (1984) found that nervousness, irritability, uncontrolled anger, and loss of motivation were the most common personal effects of sexual harassment; 75% of those experiencing harassment had suffered at least one symptom of emotional or physical distress. In addition to the negative outcomes experienced by targets of sexual harassment, coworkers who witness, hear about, or are aware of the sexual harassment of others can also experience negative job-related, health-related, and psychological outcomes (Glomb et al., 1997).

Despite studies such as those described above, some people still refer to targets of sexual harassment who experience such consequences as hypersensitive or "whiners." The research of Schneider et al. (1997) and Glomb et al. (1997) addresses this "whiner" argument empirically. Their results indicate that the negative job-related and psychological effects associated with sexual harassment do not emanate from oversensitivity to harassment, high levels of general job stress, or negative dispositions of individuals experiencing those effects.

Legal Perspective

In addition to personal consequences for targets of sexual harassment, there are serious legal and financial consequences for organizations in which the harassment occurs. If sexual harassment is not dealt with effectively, organizations can incur huge legal costs along with unwanted publicity, preventing the organization from attracting and retaining valued employees (Bennett-Alexander & Pincus, 1995), although "legal damages associated with [sexual harassment] suits are minor when compared with the costs of reduced productivity, absenteeism, turnover, requests for transfer, and medical and emotional counseling" (Knapp et al., 1997, p. 688).

When a target files a sexual harassment case, liability can flow to both the organization and individuals who are considered its agents. An agent is a person who has supervisory authority (e.g., the authority to determine work assignments) and exercises control over the target's hiring, firing, or other conditions of employment (*Paroline v. Unisys Corp.*, 1989). Organizations are strictly liable for the conduct of their employees in quid pro quo cases of sexual harassment; they are liable in hostile environment cases if management had actual or constructive knowledge (i.e., knew or should have known) about the sexually hostile environment and failed to take action.

The Civil Rights Act of 1991 increased the severity of organizational consequences of sexual harassment, providing for both punitive and compensatory damages. It set maximum damages at $50,000 for companies with fewer than 100 workers and $300,000 for those with more than 500 workers. In addition, the act allows for jury trials of sexual harassment cases, which may increase organizational costs, because juries may be more sympathetic than judges in assessing damages arising from sexual harassment.

Given the potential for such financial losses, it is not surprising that some organizations are trying to circumnavigate the judicial system. Toward this end, one company argued that financial damages arising from sexual harassment should be covered by its insurance carrier (*State Farm Fire & Casualty Co. v. Compupay, Inc.*, 1995). Compupay asserted that State Farm's policy provided coverage for loss under the personal injury and bodily injury provisions. However, State Farm argued successfully during appeal that because the acts of sexual harassment were intentional, not accidental or "occurrences," the policy does not afford coverage. Other organizations have argued (with varying levels of success) that workers' compensation is the exclusive remedy for sexual harassment; Bowes-Sperry and Veglahn (1996) provide an analysis of legal cases regarding the interface between sexual harassment and workers' compensation. The increase in costly sexual harassment jury verdicts against organizations has also resulted in a new insurance product known as "employment practices liability insurance" that offers organizations protection against charges of workplace harassment and discrimination (Jidoun, 1998).

Emerging Issues and Future Directions in Sexual Harassment Research

Researchers need to broaden the context of their investigations by examining this phenomenon in a range of populations in various countries, cultures, and ethnic groups and by studying same-sex harassment. In addition, the gap between theory and application needs to be narrowed by connecting research on sexual harassment to practical issues such as organizational training programs.

Sexual Harassment in an International Context

Sexual harassment is prevalent in most, if not all, countries; studies suggest that harassment has been experienced by 30% to 34% of people in Belgium, 80% to 90% in Spain, 50% to 60% in Holland, 70% to 75% in Germany (Rubenstein, 1992), and 50% to 90% in Great Britain (Collier, 1995). Although sexual harassment is a concern in many countries and appears to be more prevalent in other parts of the world (Kanekar & Dhir, 1992), the literature consists almost entirely of research conducted in the United States. Few studies have examined this issue in other countries; these studies suggest that cultural norms can influence targets' perceptions of and responses to sexually harassing behaviors. For example, Matsui, Kakuyama, Onglatco, and Ogutu (1995) found that 53% of Japanese women were likely to ignore even physical instances of harassing behavior. In addition, over 90% of women surveyed stated that they would neither report the behavior nor protest verbally. Matsui et al. speculate that this lack of assertive responses could be due to two factors: (1) the prevalence of Confucian norms in Japanese society under which women are expected to be passive and subservient to men and/or (2) collective norms that emphasize acceptance of social values and discourage the assertion of individual rights.

Societal norms can also influence perceptions of sexual harassment. Tang, Yik, Cheung, Choi, and Au (1995) found that unwanted sexual advances from teachers in Hong Kong were perceived as sexually harassing by fewer than 20% of students, although most respondents (over 90%) labeled quid pro quo behaviors as harassing. In another investigation, male respondents claimed that sexual harassment did not exist in Chinese society, but that it was prevalent in Western countries with "lax sexual morality" (Choi, Au, Cheung, Tang, & Yik, 1993). Gruber, Smith, and Kauppinen-Toropainen (1995) compared the responses of Canadian, American, and former Soviet women and found that former Soviet women were less likely to label more ambiguous behaviors as sexual harassment. These studies suggest that cultural norms may decrease public sensitivity to sexually harassing behavior. In contrast, studies conducted in India found a high level of sensitivity to sexual harassment, along with gender differences in perceptions (Kanekar & Dhir, 1992; Menon & Kanekar, 1992); Indian men were more likely than Indian women to blame the target of harassment, and women were more likely than men to recommend severe penalties for harassment.

The high power differential between the sexes that exists in developing countries in Asia, Africa, Latin America, and the Middle East has the potential to result in rape and sexual harassment (Ruan & Matsumara, 1991; Vaz & Kanekar, 1990). In such cultures, unwanted sexual advances and sexist remarks may be part of the male sexual prerogative. A number of economic and societal factors increase this power differential between men and women and create a climate conducive to harassment: (1) unequal access to formal education and training, (2) new techniques and technologies that continually displace women into low-skill and part-time jobs, (3) the greater prevalence of women in temporary jobs without benefits such as health insurance or maternity leave, and (4) the large pay gap between men and women (Ramamurthy, 1985). Additional international research is necessary to examine the economic and cultural conditions that influence the incidence and perceptions of sexual harassment, as well as its antecedents and consequences. In addition, legal researchers need to provide comparative analyses of sexual harassment laws across countries.

Race, Ethnicity, and Sexual Harassment

We know almost nothing about minority women's perceptions of and responses to sexual harassment, despite the fact that a number of major sexual harassment cases have involved them (e.g., Michelle Vinson in *Meritor Savings Bank, FSB v. Vinson* [1986], and Anita Hill in the U.S. Supreme Court confirmation hearings for Clarence Thomas [Hill, 1997]). Researchers suggest that race and ethnicity influence vulnerability to sexual harassment for two reasons: (1) Minority status often denotes marginality, lack of power, and economic vulnerability (Fitzgerald & Shullman, 1993; MacKinnon, 1979); and (2) stereotypes of minority women as sexually driven (e.g., Black women) or submissive and easily dominated by men (e.g., Hispanic and Asian American women) may lead initiators to believe that they would be less upset about being harassed (Karsten, 1994). Some studies have found that Black women in low-status, blue-collar jobs report a greater severity and frequency of sexual harassment (Gruber & Bjorn, 1982, 1986; Mansfield et al., 1991).

Empirical research, however, shows equivocal support for this proposition. For example, Gowan and Zimmerman (1996) did not find differences in perceptions of sexual harassment between White and Hispanic respondents. Gutek (1985) found that minority respondents were no more vulnerable to harassment than White women, and Wyatt and Riederle (1995) determined that more White women than Black had experienced sexual harassment, although single Black women were at a greater risk of being harassed than single White women. These contradictory findings about the connection between race/ethnicity and vulnerability to sexual harassment may be due to varying perceptions and definitions of harassment among ethnic/racial groups. Also, Black women who have historically been stereotyped as highly sexual may feel that their community and society would not support them upon disclosure of harassment (Wyatt, 1992).

Ethnicity and race can also influence responses to sexual harassment. In contrast to the patterns found for White women, Yoder and Aniakudo (1995) found that all the Black women firefighters in their sample used initiator-focused responses such as confronting the harasser and filing complaints, which were effective at stopping ongoing harassment and deterring future incidents. They suggest that Black women may have already encountered an atmosphere of exclusion at the workplace and, thus, were less likely to perceive confrontation as a costly strategy. Gutek (1985) found that minority women who experienced sexual harassment were less likely to quit a job, perhaps because of economic vulnerability. The threat of sexual harassment can also lead to minority women limiting the nature of their interpersonal relationships at work, especially career-enhancing relationships with White male supervisors (Thomas, 1989), suggesting that they may perceive the adverse consequences of sexual harassment as more severe. Further research with multiethnic populations is necessary to determine how racial/ethnic differences and minority status influence the experience of, responses to, and consequences of sexual harassment.

Same-Sex Sexual Harassment

There has been a growing interest among legal researchers in same-sex sexual harassment, an interest that is expected to increase in light of a recent U.S. Supreme Court decision (*Oncale v. Sundowner Offshore Services, Inc.,* 1998). Previously, lower courts had been divided as to whether harassment in which the initiator and target were of the same sex constituted a cause of action under Title VII, with courts more likely to consider quid pro quo cases of same-sex harassment as actionable than hostile environment cases (Petersen & Massengill, 1997-1998). In *Oncale,* the Court unanimously ruled that the federal sex discrimination law applies to same-sex harassment cases and that factors such as sexual orientation (Oncale and his harassers are heterosexual) and whether the harassment is "motivated by sexual desire" should be irrelevant (Felsenthal, 1998).

This ruling puts pressure on researchers to examine the causes, antecedents, and consequences of same-sex sexual harassment, issues that have largely been ignored in the literature. A related area of research may be the harassment of homosexual individuals, a phenomenon that is often more prevalent than that of heterosexual individuals (D'Augelli, 1988).

Workplace Romances and Sexual Harassment

Workplace romances and sexual harassment have largely been treated as unrelated issues in the literature, although both entail a sexual component between two employees (Powell, 1993). Sexual harassment often occurs after a romance has gone sour (Galen, Schiller, Hamilton, & Hammonds, 1991). When this happens, "the negative affect experienced by the employees, combined with the inevitable repeated exposure to one another after the relationship has terminated, can increase the likelihood of one member of the dyad sexually harassing the other" (Pierce & Aguinis, 1997, p. 198). For example, one party may refuse to accept the termination of the romance and continue to make sexual advances, which could be interpreted as sexual harassment by the second party. An employee who is unwilling to end a romance may falsely accuse the other of sexual harassment out of revenge. Or a supervisor who has terminated a romance with a subordinate may transfer the subordinate; such conduct could result in a complaint of sexual harassment (Pierce & Aguinis, 1997).

The potential for a workplace romance to turn into sexual harassment increases with the imbalance of power in the romantic relationship (Mainiero, 1986); hence, romances between supervisors and subordinates are particularly susceptible. A prior romantic relationship with the initiator can also decrease the target's chances of redress. Summers and Myklebust (1992) found that a romantic history resulted in less sympathy for the target and greater leniency toward the initiator. Future research is needed to thoroughly understand the connections between workplace romances and sexual harassment.

Evaluation of Sexual Harassment Training

There is a plethora of books, videos, and consulting programs on sexual harassment awareness training, and most organizations use or are beginning to use training programs. At the same time, there are surprisingly few studies evaluating training programs. Researchers have largely focused on describing the content of training programs (e.g., Howard, 1991); very few studies (e.g., Barak, 1994; Gilbert, Heesacker, & Gannon, 1991; Licata & Popovich, 1987) have evaluated training outcomes such as increased sensitivity and skills for preventing sexual harassment. One reason for this scarcity of evaluation research could be an ambiguity concerning the training outcomes, especially if some organizations incorporate sexual harassment awareness training merely as insurance against legal liability.

Generally, these programs focus on disseminating information and attempting to change individual-level factors such as attitudes and behaviors. However, if harassment is the result of power differences embedded in organizational norms, then training should be directed toward changing organizational norms and recognizing the responsibility of the organization and management in eliminating undesirable and unacceptable behaviors. Future research comparing various training approaches can help identify the factors that contribute to training success; otherwise, there is little guidance for managers and organizations dealing with sexual harassment issues.

Conclusions

Sexual harassment is a pervasive phenomenon that has attracted the attention of both researchers and practitioners. Recent court cases and other newsworthy events have increased public awareness of the prevalence of this problem, resulting in a heightened sensitivity to harassment issues and a change in the way people perceive and define harassment. Public awareness, however, has not increased our understanding of how to resolve and deal with this problem in the workplace.

The literature on sexual harassment has often been criticized for consisting "mostly of anecdotal accounts . . . that mix personal opinion, legal issues, and a political or ideological agenda" (McDonald & Lees-Haley, 1995, p. 54) and for offering "little . . . in the way of guidance to managers and others in organizations who must deal with sexual harassment issues" (Lengnick-Hall, 1995, p. 860). This criticism is not without merit, because a large number of studies examine sexual harassment from a narrow perspective. Our integrative framework uses a multiperspective approach to examine the antecedents of, responses to, and consequences of sexual harassment and represents a first step toward a broad theory of sexual harassment that can help employees, managers, and organizations deal with this issue in the 21st century.

Chapter 15

Romantic Relationships in Organizational Settings

Something to Talk About

Gary N. Powell and Sharon Foley

In Bonnie Raitt's popular song "Something to Talk About" (1991), two people who are not at present romantic partners are being talked about as if they were. Romantic relationships in organizational settings are talked about at great length. They are frequently depicted in television shows, movies, and novels. When a public official is involved in a workplace romance, as was U.S. President Bill Clinton with White House intern Monica Lewinsky (Isikoff & Thomas, 1998), the relationship receives an enormous amount of public attention. However, such relationships are rarely talked about in the scholarly literature. The purpose of this chapter is to stimulate talk among scholars about romantic relationships in organizational settings by reviewing the meager scholarly literature on the subject and by suggesting directions for theory and future research.

AUTHORS' NOTE: An earlier version of this chapter appeared as "Something to Talk About: Romantic Relationships in Organizational Settings," in *Journal of Management, 24*(3), pp. 421-448, 1998. Used with permission of JAI Press.

It is of interest to consider why much more attention has been paid to workplace romances in the mass media as compared to scholarly journals. Why do people in work settings and the public at large talk about workplace romances so much? Why do researchers talk about workplace romances so little?

The answer to the first question seems straightforward. Workplace romances are likely to invoke issues of love, sex, family, power, justice, ethics, and norms regarding acceptable behavior in the workplace. When considered separately, each of these issues is a provocative topic of discussion; in combination, an irresistible topic of discussion. Workplace romances cause substantial gossip among organizational members, which may be positive or negative (Dillard & Miller, 1988; Quinn, 1977).

This suggests the answer to the second question: Workplace romances are likely to invoke issues of love, sex, family, power, justice, ethics, and norms regarding acceptable behavior in the workplace. Management and organizational behavior scholars do not appear to be comfortable talking about the issues at the beginning of this list. They certainly shy away from discussions of love. They also shy away from discussions of sex except when considering sexual harassment, or unwelcome expressions of sexuality in the workplace (see Chapter 14 by Bowes-Sperry and Tata for more on the topic of sexual harassment). Scholars in the area called "work and family" discuss how organizations may benefit from structuring work in ways that acknowledge employees' family needs (see Chapter 20 by Greenhaus and Parasuraman and Chapter 23 by Lobel for more on the topic of work and family). However, they do not discuss how romantic relationships in the workplace may disrupt family relationships and contribute to new family relationships, thereby influencing what family needs will be. Instead, scholars are more comfortable talking about power, justice, ethics, and workplace norms. Their discussions of these issues generally do not include the issues of love, sex, and family that may be a consequence of romantic relationships in organizational settings. Indeed, most scholars' views of the workplace, as conveyed through the topics that they deem most worthy of research, suggest a different question: "What's love got to do with it?" (Turner, 1983).

Some scholars may avoid the topic of romantic relationships in organizational settings precisely because such relationships receive extensive and sensationalist treatment in the mass media. They may feel that no self-respecting scholar should delve into such dubious subject matter. Other scholars may feel that little about such relationships warrants scholarly treatment. After all, when romantic relationships occur in organizational settings, they are supposed to be essentially extra-organizational. Such relationships may arise among people who happen to work together, but the relationships may have nothing to do with the conduct of work. If this is the case, why should scholars pay any attention to romantic relationships in organizational settings?

Why Scholars Should Talk About Romantic Relationships in Organizational Settings

We believe that romantic relationships in organizational settings are worth talking about by scholars. First, they may affect the conduct of work by individuals, groups, and organizations. Second, they differ from other kinds of relationships in organizational settings that receive scholarly attention.

Romantic Relationships May Affect the Conduct of Work

Many people believe that sexuality should be banned from the workplace altogether (Lobel, 1993). Margaret Mead (1980), a legendary anthropologist, argued that much like the taboos against sexual expression in the family that are necessary for children to grow up safely, taboos against sexual involvement at work are necessary for women and men to work together effectively. When expressions of sexuality appear in work settings, people who believe that such expressions should never appear at work inevitably get upset and expect management to do something.

Many people believe that certain kinds of romantic relationships are immoral in any setting. For example, relationships between two gay men or two lesbians are likely to provoke strongly negative reactions (Croteau, 1996). Extramarital relationships also provoke negative reactions (Mainiero, 1989). When individuals object to workplace romances that they observe, they are also likely to get upset and to expect management to do something.

Some organizations explicitly ban certain kinds of romantic relationships. For example, Wal-Mart, the discount retailer, fired two employees who were dating because one of them was married, although legally separated from her husband ("Can Smoking . . . ?" 1993); Wal-Mart later revised its policy to ban only dating between supervisors and individuals who report directly to them. In addition, the U.S. Armed Forces prohibit adultery by military personnel when it is seen as prejudicial to order and discipline or as bringing discredit on the military. The Armed Forces also prohibit same-sex relationships by military personnel (Herek, 1993). Both policies tend to be enforced in a "don't ask, don't tell" manner; the military does not investigate a case of alleged adultery or homosexuality unless someone calls attention to it. However, as demonstrated in a highly publicized case involving adultery by Kelly Flinn, the first female Air Force B-52 pilot (Gibbs, 1997), the consequences of investigation may be severe. Possible penalties for violating the ban on adultery include expulsion from the military and a prison sentence. When individuals violate official organizational policies by engaging in proscribed romantic relationships, they place their careers and livelihood at great risk. In addition, the organization may receive unwanted publicity by establishing and enforcing such policies, as did the Air Force in the Kelly Flinn case (Gibbs, 1997).

Involvement in a romantic relationship may affect how the partners conduct themselves in their formal work roles. Romantic relationships in organizational settings may result in conflicts of interest, flawed or biased decision making, and other workplace inequities that negatively affect performance and careers (Powell, 1993). On the other hand, workplace romances that lead to marriage may help individuals to work to their maximum potential because their personal needs are being satisfied (Mainiero, 1989).

Romantic relationships in organizational settings may also result in coworkers' perceptions of workplace inequities, accurate or not. Other group members may fear that their work-related interactions with the two partners will be altered because of the romantic relationship. In addition, they may fear that task or career rewards will be allocated for sexual favors, thereby creating an inequitable situation (Mainiero, 1986). Such fears may have direct negative impact on group morale and cohesiveness and indirect impact on organizational performance.

Romantic relationships in organizational settings are more prevalent in recent years due to changes in the workplace and in society. First, the gender composition of the workplace has changed considerably, with an increased proportion of women in the workforce and in managerial and professional positions in most countries. Thus, there is greater opportunity for the formation of heterosexual romantic relationships between people at the same organizational level than before. Second, organizational members are expected to work longer hours. They are spending more time with coworkers and less time with family members and individuals outside the organization, making the work environment increasingly conducive to the formation of romantic relationships with coworkers and increasingly threatening to family relationships. Third, the high divorce rate and relaxed sexual mores in recent years are likely to lead to a greater incidence of workplace romance (although divorce may also be a consequence of workplace romance).

As a result, romantic relationships in organizational settings have become quite common. Dillard and Miller (1988) reported that 71% of respondents in the combined samples of prior studies had observed at least one romantic relationship at work, and 31% of persons surveyed had themselves been involved in romantic relationships at work. Because romantic relationships in organizational settings are occurring at a high frequency, their potential impact on the conduct of work is considerable.

Romantic Relationships Differ
From Other Kinds of Relationships

Romantic relationships in organizational settings are unique relationships for scholars to consider. Much of organizational behavior occurs in relationships between two or more individuals. For example, interaction is a regular occurrence between leaders and subordinates, between mentors and protégés, and among work group members. Scholars regularly examine issues pertaining to the formation, dynamics, consequences, and effectiveness of each of these types of relationships. These relationships are organizationally sanctioned and have an explicit purpose related to organizational goals (e.g., to improve subordinate performance, to develop individuals for future organizational roles, and to stimulate creativity in group problem solving and decision making). In contrast, romantic relationships in work settings are not organizationally sanctioned and are unrelated to organizational goals; their "effectiveness" is not an issue from an organizational perspective. Instead, they satisfy individuals' personal needs outside of their work roles.

In addition, outsiders are likely to react to workplace romances differently than they react to other workplace relationships. As noted, people like to talk about workplace romances (Dillard & Miller, 1988; Quinn, 1977). People also like to talk about organizationally sanctioned relationships. The focus of such talk is typically on whether the relationship is carried out in an appropriate manner and on whether it benefits or hinders the individuals involved and the organization as a whole. However, no one questions whether organizationally sanctioned relationships should exist. This is not the case for workplace romances. As a result, workplace romances differ from non-work-related romances. When a romantic relationship is initiated and conducted at work, it is subject to the scrutiny of coworkers. When a work-related romance ends, the two ex-lovers may continue to see each other and interact on a regular basis at the workplace.

Thus, there is an additional evaluative component in coworkers' reactions to romantic relationships in work settings that is not present in their reactions to organizationally sanctioned relationships. When coworkers are upset about what is going on, or what they imagine is going on, in a workplace romance, they may experience lower morale and group cohesiveness that ultimately leads to lower organizational performance. Even if coworkers do not believe that there is anything improper in a workplace romance, they may object to the ensuing gossip as an unnecessary distraction.

Boundaries of the Review

We consider this relatively unexamined relationship between people in organizational settings and provide guidelines as to exactly what constitutes this kind of relationship.

First, the term *romantic relationship* suggests that we are examining relationships between two people in which there is some element of sexuality or physical intimacy. We note the difference between perceived romantic relationships (i.e., relationships that observers believe have a sexual component) and actual romantic relationships (i.e., relationships between participants that actually have a sexual component). One may lead to the other but not necessarily imply the other. Romantically involved coworkers may successfully keep that aspect of their relationship secret from others, and/or others may wrongly suspect that two people are romantically involved. For example, in "Something to Talk About" (Raitt, 1991), there is a perceived but not an actual romantic relationship. If the singer gets her way, however, there will be a romance.

Second, the term romantic relationship suggests that the relationship is wanted by both partners. If only one partner wants the relationship, even if it was once wanted by both, it is likely to constitute sexual harassment rather than what we would consider a romantic relationship. For examination of the interface between sexual harassment and workplace romance, including the effects of a dissolved workplace romance, see Witteman (1993), Pierce and Aguinis (1997), and Pierce, Aguinis, and Adams (1998).

Third, our reference to romantic relationships *in organizational settings* suggests that we are examining romantic relationships between two members of the same organization or between one person in a given organization and another person with a close work-related connection to that organization (e.g., customer, client, independent contractor, student in an academic program). Fourth, unlike in most prior discussions of romantic relationships in work settings (e.g., Lobel, 1993; Mainiero, 1986; Pierce, Byrne, & Aguinis, 1996; Quinn, 1977), we do not restrict our review to opposite-sex relationships. Fifth, we do not examine relationships that are psychologically but not physically intimate (Lobel, Quinn, St. Clair, & Warfield, 1994). Finally, we do not examine relationships between married couples who jointly own and manage businesses.

Review of the Literature

Quinn (1977) initiated the scholarly examination of romantic relationships in organizational settings. He asked workers to describe romantic relationships between pairs of their present or former coworkers. Content analysis of open-ended descriptions of workplace romances led to development of a survey that, after being pretested, was distributed to individuals in the waiting areas of New York's Albany and La Guardia airports. Individuals were asked to respond to questions about the workplace romance with which they were most familiar; 62% knew of at least one such relationship.

Quinn's (1977) survey yielded the first typology of romantic relationships in organizational settings. Specifically, Quinn identified different factors pertaining to the formation of workplace romances, the impact of workplace romances, and management actions (or lack of action) concerning workplace romances. He concluded that the model of organizational romance he had developed inductively was theoretically important because it examined a natural but deviant behavior pattern in organizations that in some cases has a significant negative consequence.

Since Quinn (1977), three major theoretical articles on organizational romances have been published. Mainiero (1986) offered a model of how issues of power, dependency, and social exchange influence the internal dynamics of romantic relationships in organizational settings, which in turn influence coworker reactions and management interventions. Pierce et al. (1996) offered a model that elaborated on the factors that influence the formation and impact of organizational romances. Foley and Powell (in press) offered a model that focused on coworkers' reactions to managerial interventions regarding workplace romances. Our review is structured according to the four principal research questions that were collectively suggested by Quinn (1977), Mainiero (1986), Pierce et al. (1996), and Foley and Powell (in press):

1. What are the *antecedents* of romantic relationships in organizational settings, or what factors contribute to or inhibit their formation?

2. What are the *dynamics* of romantic relationships in organizational settings, or what types of romances occur and how do they evolve over time?

3. What are the *consequences* of romantic relationships in organizational settings, and what factors influence their impact?

4. What are the *managerial actions* to be considered regarding romantic relationships in organizational settings? This question is divided into two parts:
    a. What kinds of *policies,* if any, do organizations establish about romantic relationships in general, and what factors influence whether a policy is established?
    b. What kinds of *responses,* if any, do managers make to specific romantic relationships that occur within organizational boundaries, and what factors influence the choice of response?

Table 15.1 summarizes the issues examined in the review.

Antecedents

Sternberg's (1986) triangular theory of love provides a perspective on loving relationships in general that may be applied to the formation of romantic relationships in organizational settings. Sternberg suggested that love is best understood in terms of three components that represent the vertices of a triangle. The three components are *intimacy,* or feelings of closeness and connectedness in a relationship; *passion,* or feelings of romance and sexual attraction and the desire for sexual consummation; and *decision/commitment,* or the decision that one loves someone else and the commitment to maintain that love. Intimacy is at the core of many kinds of

TABLE 15.1 Issues Regarding Romantic Relationships in Organizational Settings Examined in the Review

Antecedents	Dynamics	Consequences	Managerial Actions
Interpersonal attraction	Match between participants' motives	For participants	Policies
Physical proximity	Love	Positive vs. negative	Formal
Functional proximity	Fling	Attitudes	Informal
Attitude similarity	Utilitarian	Behavior	
	Mutual user		Interventions
Romantic attraction		For coworkers	No action vs. positive action vs.
Attractiveness	Dependencies	Approval vs. tolerance vs. objection	punitive action
	Task	Gossip	Treatment of higher-level vs.
Participation in a romance	Career	Coping strategies	lower-level participant
Attitudes toward workplace	Personal/sexual	Reactions to managerial action vs.	Treatment of women vs. men
romance in general		inaction	Prescriptions for interventions
Work group norms	Reporting relationship/organizational		
Job autonomy	level of participants	For organizations	
Culture		Positive vs. neutral vs. negative	
Motives of individual participants	Exploitation		
Benefits vs. risks			
	Attempts at secrecy		
	Evolution of dynamics over time		
	Termination of romance		

loving relationships, such as love of parent, sibling, child, or close friend. Passion is linked to certain kinds of loving relationships, especially romantic ones involving sexual activity. Decision/commitment is highly variable over different kinds of loving relationships. The importance of these components depends in part on whether the relationship is short term or long term, with passion playing a particularly important role in short-term romantic relationships.

Pierce et al. (1996) used Sternberg's (1986) theory to distinguish between factors that contribute to interpersonal attraction (i.e., feelings of intimacy) and factors that contribute to romantic attraction (i.e., feelings of passion and, in some cases, decision/commitment as well as feelings of intimacy). They depicted the formation of romantic relationships in organizational settings as occurring in three stages: First, feelings of interpersonal attraction arise toward another organizational member; second, feelings of romantic attraction arise toward the same person; and third, the decision is made to participate in a workplace romance.

Interpersonal attraction is influenced by proximity (Dillard & Miller, 1988; Mainiero, 1989; Quinn, 1977), which may be divided into physical and functional proximity (Pierce et al., 1996). Physical (or geographical) proximity refers to closeness that results from the location of employees' areas of work. Long work hours may lead to physical proximity over greater periods of time (Mainiero, 1989). Functional proximity refers to closeness that results from the actual conduct of work. Employees who interact with each other more frequently or more intensely because of ongoing work relationships are higher in functional proximity. Also, employees who are closer in rank and status are likely to be higher in functional proximity (Dillard & Witteman, 1985). In turn, employees with higher physical and functional proximity are more likely to be attracted to each other. Thus, business trips, which entail high levels of both physical and functional proximity away from the constraining influence of others, are particularly conducive to the formation of romantic relationships (Mainiero, 1989). Interpersonal attraction is also influenced by attitude similarity. According to the similarity-attraction paradigm (Byrne & Neuman, 1992), individuals who are more similar in attitudes to each other will like each other more.

Whether interpersonal attraction leads to romantic attraction may be influenced by two factors: the physical attractiveness of the other person and a generalized physiological arousal (Pierce et al., 1996). Whether romantic attraction in turn leads to participation in a workplace romance is influenced by several other factors. Pierce et al. (1996) proposed that individuals' attitudes toward workplace romance in general influence whether they act on feelings of romantic attraction. Powell (1986b) and Pierce (1998) found that women had more negative attitudes toward workplace romances in general than men; however, Pierce (1998) did not find a relationship between such attitudes and participation in a workplace romance. Work group norms regarding workplace romances may also influence whether group members get involved in such relationships, as will the presence of close supervision or close intragroup personal relationships (Quinn, 1977). However, individuals who hold more autonomous jobs are less subject to the influence of work group norms and thereby more likely to participate in workplace romances because they make more decisions about their own work and move more freely inside and outside the organization (Pierce et al., 1996).

In addition, the prevailing culture in a work setting may influence whether individuals participate in workplace romances. Mainiero (1989) distinguished between conservative cultures, which are characterized by an emphasis on traditional values and ways of doing things, and liberal cultures, which are characterized more by creativity and innovation. Conservative cultures are more steadfast in traditional beliefs regarding women's roles and less flexible in norms regarding appropriate employee behavior, making them less conducive to the formation of workplace romances, whereas liberal cultures are more supportive of the relaxed sexual mores associated with workplace romances. Individual departments within organizations may vary in whether their cultures are conservative or liberal. In addition, professions as a whole differ in whether they emphasize the creativity and innovation associated with liberal cultures (e.g., advertising) or the adherence to formal work styles and practices associated with conservative cultures (e.g., accounting). However, management actions to desexualize the organization may have the opposite effect if subordinates' resistance leads them to engage in behavior simply because it is forbidden (Burrell, 1984).

The culture of the organization, department, or profession regarding the acceptability of workplace romances may be influenced by the values of the organization's founders or current top management (Schneider, 1987). In addition, culture may be influenced by the ratio of one gender to the other in an organization, department, or group. Gutek (1985) suggested that sex-role spillover, or the carryover into the workplace of individuals' expectations based on gender roles, is more likely to occur when the sex ratio is skewed in favor of either men or women. Thus, individuals may be more inclined to become romantically involved when the work setting is numerically dominated by one sex because they are more inclined to see each other as sex objects. Mainiero (1989) suggested that younger and growing organizations are more likely to have a liberal culture regarding workplace romance. Dillard and Witteman (1985) found a curvilinear relationship between organizational size and the occurrence of workplace romances; fewer romances occurred in very large or very small organizations than in moderately large organizations.

Individuals may participate in romantic relationships in organizational settings for a variety of reasons. Quinn (1977) identified job motives (e.g., desire for advancement, job security, financial rewards), ego motives (e.g., desire for excitement, adventure, ego satisfaction), and love motives (e.g., desire for intimacy, passion, and decision/commitment; Sternberg, 1986) as reasons for individuals' participation in organizational romances. Mainiero (1986) identified the desire to increase power as an additional motive for involvement. Individuals may enter into romantic relationships with any or all of these motives. Also, coworkers and other observers attribute motives to participants. Anderson and Fisher (1991) and Powell (1998b) found that attributed motives for involvement in a workplace romance differed according to the gender of the participant, with love and job motives seen as more prevalent in women and ego motives in men.

However, Mainiero (1986) noted that individuals weigh the potential risks against the potential benefits when deciding whether to begin a workplace romance. These include risks to career (e.g., loss of coworkers' respect), risks to self-image and self-esteem (e.g., questioning of basis for work-related rewards from the higher-level participant), risks to home and family (e.g., marital strife and divorce), and risks due to violations of workplace norms (depending on the organizational, departmental, and/or professional culture).

Dynamics

Sternberg (1986) distinguished between different types of loving relationships in general according to the presence or absence of each of the three components of love: intimacy, passion, and decision/commitment. These types (with the components present in the relationship specified in parentheses) include liking (intimacy alone), infatuated love (passion alone), empty love (decision/commitment alone), romantic love (intimacy and passion), companionate love (intimacy and decision/commitment), fatuous love (passion and decision/commitment), and consummate love (all three components present). Nonloving relationships lack all three components.

Quinn (1977) distinguished between different types of workplace romances in particular according to the match between the motives (job, ego, or love) of the male and female participants. Nine different combinations of motives were possible. However, Quinn found significant correlations between the two partners' motives for only three combinations: ego for both male and female, a fling; love for both male and female, true love; and ego for the male and job for the female, utilitarian. Flings, similar to Sternberg's (1986) infatuated love relationships, were characterized by high excitement for both participants and were often expected to be temporary. True love relationships, similar to Sternberg's consummate love relationships, were characterized by the sincerity of both participants and the tendency to result in marriage. Utilitarian relationships involved a trade-off between different motives of the two participants, with the female seeking to further job-related goals through involvement with a male in pursuit of ego gratification.

Quinn's (1977) study inspired follow-up studies of motives in workplace romances. Dillard (1987) added two combinations of motives to the three combinations identified by Quinn (1977): job for both male and female, a mutual user relationship; and job for the male and ego for the female, with the male seeking to further job-related goals through involvement with a female in pursuit of ego gratification; the latter relationship complements what Quinn called simply a utilitarian relationship. The male ego-female job motive combination was more likely to occur when the male had greater organizational power, whereas the female ego-male job motive combination was more likely when the female had greater organizational power. In addition, Dillard, Hale, and Segrin (1994) suggested one more combination of motives: love and ego for both male and female, a passionate love relationship.

Power is a key variable in understanding the dynamics of organizational romances. Mainiero (1986) depicted these dynamics as a function of the relative dependency of each participant on the other for resources being exchanged in the relationship. The more powerful participant is the one who is giving more than he or she is getting, and therefore is less dependent on the relationship. Three types of dependency may be present in a work relationship. Task dependency occurs when a worker depends on another to perform his or her function effectively. Career dependency occurs when individuals desire advancement that is dependent on the consent of others; for example, in manager-subordinate relationships, subordinates exchange hard work (the manager is task dependent on the subordinate) for the reward of career advancement (the subordinate is dependent on the manager for advancement). In an organizational romance, a personal/sexual dependency is introduced. The addition of this third dependency to an otherwise work-oriented relationship threatens the balance between task and career dependencies.

When there is an imbalance of power in a romantic relationship, there is a high potential for exploitation of whoever is more dependent on the relationship. The higher-level participant can use the personal/sexual exchange to force the lower-level participant to increase task performance. In addition, the lower-level participant can use the personal/sexual exchange to argue for favorable task assignments or work conditions. When either of these instances occur, the relationship becomes utilitarian. The potential for exploitation is greater in hierarchical romances (i.e., in which participants are at different organizational levels with greater task and career dependency) than in lateral romances (i.e., in which participants are at the same organizational level with less task and career dependency). However, a power imbalance may occur simply because one participant is more dependent on the personal/sexual exchange than the other, even if task and career dependencies do not enter into the relationship. Mainiero's (1986) model suggested that organizational romances may be characterized according to the types of dependencies that are present, the balance of power in the relationship, the potential for exploitation of one participant by the other, and the extent to which exploitation actually occurs.

Workplace romances may also be characterized according to whether participants attempt to keep them secret from coworkers and whether such attempts are successful. Most couples try to keep their workplace romance hidden but fail in the attempt (Anderson & Hunsaker, 1985; Quinn, 1977). Mainiero (1989) argued that conservative cultures cause workplace romances to go underground, with participants making a greater effort to keep the relationship secret. Also, the work roles of the two participants influence whether they attempt to keep the relationship secret. For example, when teachers and students become romantically involved, discretion is important because of the likelihood of negative reactions (Quinn, 1977). Similarly, because coworkers disapprove of hierarchical romances more than lateral romances (Powell, 1986b), participants in hierarchical romances are more likely to attempt to hide the relationship. Also, workplace romances in which one or both participants are married cause dilemmas for coworkers who are aware of the romance and socialize with the other spouses involved, leading to greater attempts by participants to keep the relationship secret (Dillard et al., 1994; Mainiero, 1989).

Motives, dependencies, and components of love in workplace romances are not static and may evolve over time. Sternberg (1986) noted that levels of intimacy, passion, and decision/commitment felt by participants in a loving relationship seldom remain constant. Participants' motives in a workplace romance may also change; they may feel more or less satisfied with the relationship than originally and want to increase mutual commitment or to terminate the relationship. Even if one participant's feelings about the relationship are unchanged, he or she has to deal with the other's changes. Mainiero (1989) noted the difficulties associated with the return from being lovers to being only coworkers, including lower self-image and self-esteem for the participant who was dumped.

In addition, what was once workplace romance may become sexual harassment if one participant continues to pursue a romantic relationship that the other no longer desires. Pierce and Aguinis (1997) proposed that dissolved workplace romances between a supervisor and directly reporting subordinate are the relationships most likely to become sexual harassment.

Consequences

The consequences or outcomes of romantic relationships in organizational settings may be seen in the behavior and attitudes of individual participants, the reactions of coworkers and work group members, and the impact on the organization as a whole. We review the consequences of workplace romances in that order.

Quinn (1977) reported different kinds of behavioral changes in individual participants. In some instances, positive changes occurred as one or both participants became easier to get along with or more productive. In other instances, negative changes occurred as one or both participants became more preoccupied and less punctual, missed important meetings and commitments, made costly mistakes, or covered the mistakes of the other participant. Other changes involved alteration of power and occurred most often in hierarchical romances between a superior and subordinate. These changes included ignoring complaints about the subordinate's performance, increasing the subordinate's power, and showing favoritism toward the subordinate in task assignments, pay raises, and promotions.

Pierce et al.'s (1996) model of organizational romance proposed a variety of outcomes. Specifically, it proposed that participants experience decreases in productivity, work motivation, and job involvement during the early stages of the romance and increases in these three outcomes in the later stages; they argued that effects become more positive once the initial excitement of the relationship diminished. Their model suggested that hierarchical romances lead to lower productivity than do lateral romances. Participants who were more satisfied with the romance were also expected to have higher job satisfaction. Finally, participants who entered the romance with a love motive were expected to increase their productivity and job involvement, whereas those who entered the romance with a job or ego motive were not expected to exhibit a change in productivity or job involvement.

Clawson and Kram (1984) suggested that romance within mentoring relationships in particular leads to negative consequences for the protégé. They argued that successful mentoring relationships, judged by the development of the protégé, are characterized by a productive level of intimacy between the mentor and protégé that does not result in workplace romance. Less successful mentoring relationships are characterized by either unproductive intimacy, leading to a romantic relationship and poor development of the protégé, or unproductive distance, which also leads to insufficient development of the protégé.

In a partial test of Pierce et al.'s (1996) model, Pierce (1998) found that participation in a workplace romance had a marginally significant positive relationship with productivity but was unrelated to work motivation, job involvement, and job satisfaction. However, Dillard et al. (1994) found that women in female utilitarian relationships experienced declines in attendance and performance. Other data supported a positive impact of workplace romance on the performance, job involvement, and enthusiasm of participants who entered the romance with a love motive (Dillard, 1987; Dillard & Broetzmann, 1989). Dillard and Miller (1988) speculated that love-motivated individuals may attempt to impress their partners through higher productivity or to alleviate their supervisors' fears that the romance will have a negative impact on the conduct of work. On the other hand, love-motivated individuals may simply be happier people who have more time and energy available for task requirements because they have met their personal needs for companionship.

At a minimum, workplace romances stimulate gossip among coworkers (Dillard & Miller, 1988; Quinn, 1977). However, whether the inevitable gossip is positive or negative depends on the motives for the romance and type of romance. Romances between love-motivated participants are likely to stimulate more positive gossip, whereas romances between job-motivated participants are likely to stimulate more negative gossip, especially if the romance is between a superior and subordinate (Dillard, 1987; Pierce et al., 1996).

Otherwise, coworkers' reactions to workplace romances vary from approval to tolerance to outright objection expressed either to participants or to management (Quinn, 1977). In some cases, coworkers cope with romance by adopting extreme strategies such as blackmail (e.g., threatening to tell a spouse), ostracism of participants through informal interactions, or quitting the organization to remove themselves from an intolerable situation (Quinn, 1977). Devine and Markiewicz (1990) found that coworkers were expected to respond most positively when both participants had high-status positions and most negatively when the female participant had a higher-status position than the male participant. Powell (1998b) found that women who were romantically involved with a senior-level executive elicited more negative reactions from coworkers than men who were involved in such a relationship, primarily because they were seen as more motivated by job-related concerns; romances that negatively affected participants' productivity also elicited more negative reactions from coworkers. Hierarchical romances, more visible romances, job-motivated romances, and romances in which exploitation or disruption of productivity has occurred are likely to elicit the most negative reactions from coworkers and have the most negative effect on group morale (Devine & Markiewicz, 1990; Dillard et al., 1994; Mainiero, 1986; Pierce et al., 1996; Powell, 1998b).

Foley and Powell (in press) argued that coworkers' reactions to workplace romances are also based on the managerial intervention, if any, in response to the romance. They proposed that coworkers form perceptions of the justice of the managerial action directed toward romantic partners and the process by which this action is decided on. Coworkers' reactions to managerial action are influenced by such factors as the reporting relationship between participants (hierarchical or lateral), motives attributed to the participants (job-related or non-job-related), attitudes toward workplace romance in general, perceived disruption of the work group, and perceived conflict of interest. Coworkers' perceptions of justice in turn affect their other work-related attitudes and behaviors (Greenberg, 1996). Thus, coworkers are likely to be influenced by all of the ramifications of a workplace romance, not just the romance itself.

In summary, the possible effects of workplace romance on the organization or system range from positive (e.g., increased individual productivity, work motivation, and involvement; improved work climate) to neutral (e.g., increased levels of nondisruptive gossip with little other impact) to negative (e.g., decreased individual productivity, work motivation, and job involvement; lower group morale) (Quinn, 1977). The motives of participants, the stage and visibility of the romance, whether the romance is hierarchical or lateral, and management actions about the romance influence which of these overall effects occurs.

Managerial Actions

▨ Policies

There has been intense discussion among some scholars about whether sexuality can and should be banned from the workplace (Lobel, 1993). For example, MacKinnon (1979) argued that most of what passes for organizational romance is actually "coerced caring" or sexual harassment in disguise, that is, a result of a closed system of social depredation in which most women are powerless to avoid being exploited sexually or otherwise. Burrell (1984) argued that one of the basic goals of bureaucracies, which most organizations are assumed to be, is to suppress sexuality and other "irrational" behaviors and relegate them to the world of private interactions outside the workplace. Mainiero (1989) countered that the desire to suppress sexuality in the workplace is more associated with conservative than with liberal organizational cultures. As noted earlier, Mead (1980) argued in favor of a ban on sexual involvement in the workplace as a way of enabling women and men to work together effectively and to respect each other as individuals. In contrast, Lionel Tiger (1997), another well-known anthropologist, argued that the U.S. Armed Forces' ban on sexual involvement among soldiers was preposterous because sexuality is an important, pervasive, and healthy life force that cannot be as willingly and easily suppressed as the military would like.

Nonetheless, organizations have not been inclined to establish formal policies about workplace romances. *Business Week* ("Romance in the Workplace," 1984) reported that antinepotism policies that specified only that married couples must not work with or for each other were the most prevalent. Few organizations have written or unwritten policies about workplace romances (Society for Human Resource Management, 1998), and most chief executives regard workplace romance as none of the company's business (Fisher, 1994).

Mainiero (1989) suggested that companies with conservative cultures are more likely to develop informal policies that discourage close working relationships between married or unmarried romantic partners. In addition, direct-reporting hierarchical romances are more likely than lateral romances to be the subject of either formal or informal policies regardless of the firm's culture. Most organizations, however, are reluctant to develop strict policies regarding romantic relationships conducted within their boundaries. If companies have any policy at all, it is usually that workplace romances need to be treated on an individual basis (Mainiero, 1989).

▓ Responses

Quinn (1977) described three general kinds of responses that organizations make to specific organizational romances: no action, punitive action (e.g., reprimand, warning, transfer, termination), and positive action (e.g., open discussion, counseling). The most frequent response was no action (Anderson & Hunsaker, 1985; Quinn, 1977), involving either a decision to ignore the romance, a belief that whatever problem the romance presented would resolve itself, or an avoidance of the risk associated with taking action.

Pierce et al. (1996) proposed an effect of workplace romances on three types of managerial decisions: promotions, relocations, and terminations. They proposed that participants in workplace romances in more conservative cultures are less likely to be promoted than those in more liberal cultures. They also proposed that lower-level participants in hierarchical romances are more likely to be relocated or terminated than higher-level participants, especially if they are female, because they are seen as less valuable and more dispensable. Devine and Markiewicz (1990) found that participants in couples where both had high organizational status were seen as more likely to be promoted than participants in couples where both had low organizational status; also, female participants were seen as more at risk of losing their jobs than male participants. Similarly, Quinn (1977) found that female participants in workplace romances were twice as likely to be terminated as were male participants because they tended to be in lower-level positions. Summers and Myklebust (1992) found that managerial reactions to a complaint of sexual harassment by a female complainant against a male tended to be more lenient if the couple had previously been romantically involved.

Many prescriptions have been offered for managerial interventions in response to specific workplace romances. These prescriptions have varied in tone and complexity. For example, E. G. C. Collins (1983) recommended simply that the least essential person to the company, typically the lower-level participant, be terminated whenever an organizational romance occurred because such relationships represented an inevitable conflict of interest. Anderson and Hunsaker (1985), however, recommended a general strategy of noninterference, given the prevalence of workplace romance and the resistance to taboos on human behavior (Burrell, 1984). Mainiero (1986) recommended that managerial actions, ranging in severity from discussions and reprimands to transfers and terminations, be taken only when exploitation of one participant by the other had actually occurred in a romantic relationship.

Powell's (1993) recommendations were more complex. He recommended that the severity of a managerial intervention taken in response to a specific workplace romance be based on the potential for a work disruption, the certainty that a disruption occurred, and the severity of an alleged disruption. Unlike E. G. C. Collins (1983), he assumed that the mere existence of a workplace romance did not necessarily represent a work disruption. If there was no actual or potential disruption, Powell (1993) saw no need for any managerial intervention. Using Mainiero's (1986) terms, a romance that created the potential for task-related or career-related decisions to be influenced by personal/sexual considerations might interfere with work; even if important decisions had not been affected by the romance, coworkers might fear the worst and their morale and productivity could suffer. In such instances, Powell (1993) recommended either that the two participants be asked to "cool" the relationship or that one or both participants accept being transferred to an equivalent position elsewhere in the organization. However, when task-related or career-related decisions actually had been influenced by personal/sexual considerations, Powell (1993) recommended that strong punitive action be taken against both participants.

Implications for Future Research

For a small body of literature, the literature on romantic relationships in organizational settings has managed to shed some light on the phenomenon. Theory and empirical research provide a tentative understanding of issues pertaining to the antecedents, dynamics, consequences, and managerial actions related to organizational romances. We now discuss the implications of our review for future research on workplace romances.

Theory Testing Should Keep Pace With Theory Building

The primary attempts at theory building have been in articles by Quinn (1977), Mainiero (1986), Pierce et al. (1996), and Foley and Powell (in press). Their theories and models address most of the important issues pertaining to workplace romances. If all of the propositions based on these theories were supported empirically, there would not be gaping holes in our knowledge left to be filled (other than about same-sex workplace romances; see below). However, only a small portion of these theories has been tested. Empirical research has barely examined the dynamics of workplace romances (other than by identifying the combinations of participant motives that tend to occur), the consequences of workplace romances, or the managerial actions that workplace romances stimulate. We thus recommend an increased level of empirical research to support or disconfirm available theories of workplace romance.

Future Theory Building Should Make Greater Use of Existing Theoretical Frameworks

Limited use has been made of established theoretical frameworks in the few attempts at theory building regarding workplace romances. Pierce et al. (1996) based part of their model of the antecedents of workplace romance on the similarity-attraction paradigm (Byrne & Neuman, 1992). Foley and Powell (in press) used organizational justice theory (Greenberg, 1996) as the basis for a model of coworkers' reactions to managerial interventions in response to specific workplace romances. However, greater use may be made of existing theoretical frameworks in theorizing about workplace romances.

For example, it may be possible to explain coworkers' interventions in workplace romances using an ethical decision making framework. Jones's (1991) model of ethical decision making by individuals in organizations suggests that decisions about an issue that has a moral or ethical dimension occur in four stages: recognition of an ethical issue, making of a moral judgment, establishment of intentions to engage in ethical behavior, and actual ethical behavior. Jones further proposed that how far individuals proceed in the ethical decision making process is influenced by the moral intensity of the issue with which they are confronted. Moral intensity has six components: proximity, magnitude of consequences, social consensus, concentration of effect, probability of effect, and temporal immediacy. Bowes-Sperry and Powell (in press) found that coworkers' perceptions of moral intensity influenced their decisions about whether to intervene in incidents of sexual harassment that they witnessed. In the same vein, coworkers may decide what action to take (if any) in response to a workplace romance based on their perceptions of moral intensity. We recommend the use of theories beyond those already used to examine workplace romance to increase the theoretical base of our knowledge about the phenomenon.

Research Design Remains an Issue

Quinn (1977) observed, "The topic [of workplace romance] does not readily lend itself to rigorous research methods" (p. 31). Almost a decade later, Mainiero (1986) observed, "Researching the subject of organizational romances is somewhat problematic due to the sensitive nature of the phenomenon. As a result, much of the literature on the subject suffers from a lack of methodological rigor" (p. 750). One more decade later, Pierce et al. (1996) observed that "the existing literature on workplace romance demonstrates insufficient methodological rigor in addition to an equivocal theoretical and empirical bearing" (p. 6). Thus, it is not a particularly novel or bold stance for us to state that research on the phenomenon of romantic relationships in organizational settings lacks a certain amount of, shall we say, methodological rigor. We need to say more about this issue if we are to provide useful guidance for future research.

Quinn's (1977) methodology set the stage for the two decades of work that followed. Dillard (1987) argued that Quinn's (1977) findings were limited by his choice of population and research design. First, the nature of Quinn's subject population, travelers at two northeastern airports, was hardly representative of the workplace in its gender (71% were male) or professional status (at least 80% were in professional, technical, managerial, or sales occupations). Yet, in its predominantly white-collar nature, this population gave Quinn exactly the kind of middle-class sample that he said he was looking for. Since then, the term *office romance* (e.g., Anderson & Hunsaker, 1985; Mainiero, 1989; Horn & Horn, 1982) has often been used to label the phenomenon being examined. Although not everyone in the workplace has an office and not all workplace romances occur in offices, the linkage of workplace romance to the assumed offices of participants has influenced discussion of the topic. Anderson and Fisher (1991) observed, "The mere mention of office romance evokes guffaws and snickers. The term trivializes the extent and difficulties of the issue" (p. 165).

Second, the perspective of Quinn's (1977) survey respondents was that of observers of workplace romances, not that of participants. Jones and Nisbett (1972) observed that there are important differences between the perspectives of actors and observers in situations. Quinn believed that participants in organizational romances would be difficult to locate, difficult to approach if located, and difficult to persuade to talk about their romance if approached. He acknowledged that a third party may have limited information about the romance and may be influenced by romantic fantasies, feelings toward the participants, and other biases. However, he viewed collection of data from third-party observers as the best he could do to shed light on the phenomenon. Following in Quinn's footsteps, several studies of workplace romance have used observers rather than participants as subjects (e.g., Anderson & Fisher, 1991; Anderson & Hunsaker, 1985; Dillard et al., 1994). However, to their credit, other studies by Dillard and colleagues (Dillard, 1987; Dillard & Broetzmann, 1989; Dillard & Witteman, 1985) compared results obtained from samples of both observers and participants.

Quinn's (1977) findings, as well as those of many studies that followed, were also limited by their reliance on subjective data obtained in surveys. For example, Dillard and Miller (1988) observed that none of the research that has examined the effect of workplace romance on individual performance has used objective job performance data. Instead, observers have been asked their perceptions of changes in the performance of participants (e.g., Dillard et al., 1994) or participants have been asked their perceptions of changes in their own performance (e.g., Pierce, 1998). Findings based on these perceptions may not accurately reflect participants' actual performance or the actual effect of their romantic relationships on their performance.

We recognize the validity of Quinn's (1977) concerns about gaining access to data from actual participants in workplace romances. Conducting field studies of workplace romances that are based on something other than responses to surveys may seem an almost impossible task. However, there are other possible approaches to collecting data on actual workplace romances that do not rely on survey data. For example, in the classic qualitative study *Men and Women of the Corporation,* Kanter (1977a) reported and analyzed her observations of one corporation from the roles of consultant, participant-observer, and researcher over a five-year period. If a researcher had the time and access, he or she could conduct a qualitative study like Kanter's study to obtain firsthand observations of workplace romances, including their antecedents, dynamics, consequences, and resulting managerial actions.

Another approach to examining actual workplace romances would be to use process-tracing methods such as verbal protocol analysis (Ford, Schmitt, Schechtman, Hults, & Doherty, 1989) to generate data. Process-tracing methods may be used to gain a better understanding of individuals' decision processes. In this case, verbal protocols may be obtained on how decisions about workplace romances are made by participants in an actual romance, workers who have chosen not to get involved in a romance, coworkers, and management. When Quinn (1977) obtained open-ended descriptions of workplace romances, he could have analyzed their content as in verbal protocol analysis and reported conclusions based on this analysis. Instead, he used his coding of these descriptions as the basis of a subsequent survey and then reported only the survey results. Use of verbal protocol analysis could add to our knowledge about workplace romances in three ways: (1) by examining individual decision making about workplace romances using a different methodology than previous research; (2) by examining individual decisions that have not been examined before, for example, decisions by potential participants about whether to get involved in a workplace romance (discussed only in general terms in Mainiero, 1986) and decisions by coworkers about whether to intervene in workplace romances; and (3) by examining decisions made by couples about how to handle their romance as well as their work relationship.

Greater use may also be made of laboratory and experimental methods (Griffin & Kacmar, 1991) in examining romantic relationships in organizational settings. Griffin and Kacmar (1991) suggested that laboratory methods are particularly useful when a sensitive topic is being examined and when "real" subjects (i.e., in the field) are hard to identify or would be placing themselves at risk by participating in the research; these conditions apply to research on workplace romances. Some studies have already used paper-and-pencil designs in which subjects read vignettes that systematically vary in content and then provide their evaluations about the participants and/or decisions in the role of manager (e.g., Devine & Markiewicz, 1990; Summers & Myklebust, 1992); additional studies using such designs may be conducted. Policy capturing (Slovic & Lichtenstein, 1971), an experimental technique that systematically varies the content of a larger series of vignettes to obtain a separate decision policy for each individual, may be used to examine individual differences in managerial decisions about specific workplace romances. Studies based on experimental methods such as policy capturing, although lacking the realism of field studies, have the advantage of enabling stricter control by the researcher over the variables being considered as predictors.

We recognize that prior research on workplace romances has its methodological limitations. However, we do not believe that all future research must be handicapped by the same limitations. Although every methodology has its limitations, we recommend that research using a greater variety of methods than those exhibited in the literature to date be conducted so as to increase our knowledge about workplace romances substantially.

Gay and Lesbian Workplace Romances Should Not Be Ignored

Whether a romantic relationship in an organizational setting is between opposite-sex or same-sex participants seems a relevant distinction. The silence on this distinction in the literature has been deafening. Silence on same-sex romances is exhibited in the literature on workplace romances in general. All of the theoretical and empirical treatments of workplace romances in the scholarly literature that were identified for our review have been restricted to analysis of opposite-sex romances. For example, three theoretical articles (Mainiero, 1986; Pierce et al., 1996; Quinn, 1977) explicitly stated that they applied only to opposite-sex workplace romances. In Dillard (1987), the sole person interviewed who provided knowledge of a same-sex relationship was removed from the sample.

The literature on sexual orientation in the workplace is also silent on same-sex workplace romances. For example, Croteau's (1996) review of research on the work experiences of lesbians, gays, and bisexuals integrated findings within five areas of common content: pervasiveness of discrimination in the workplace, formal versus informal discrimination, fear of discrimination, variability in workplace openness about sexual orientation, and correlates of the degree of openness versus concealment of sexual orientation. However, Croteau did not discuss workplace romance as a possible component of these work experiences.

If the silence on the topic of same-sex workplace romances indicates anything, it is that either (1) such romances do not exist, which seems unlikely, or (2) scholars are even less inclined to talk about such romances than about opposite-sex workplace romances. We see no reason for this silence. Accordingly, we recommend empirical research to increase our understanding of the antecedents, dynamics, consequences, and managerial actions associated with same-sex versus opposite-sex workplace romances. In addition, we recommend studies that examine solely same-sex workplace romances to document the frequency of such relationships and to identify their unique characteristics.

What We Might Know About Romantic Relationships in Organizational Settings

Most of the propositions that have been offered in various theories about workplace romance seem plausible, even though few have been subjected to empirical scrutiny. Thus, we may know more about this unique kind of organizational relationship than prior reviews that have focused on the weaknesses of the literature have suggested. What might we know?

1. That workplace romances originate for different reasons pertaining to participants' motives, liking and attraction, attitudes toward workplace romance in general, and proximity in their work roles and physical environment. Thus, organizations stimulate expressions of sexuality among coworkers through the design of work environments and the structure of work as much as they suppress expressions of sexuality.

2. That the experiences of workplace romances range from positive to negative, temporary to permanent, exploitative to nonexploitative, and utilitarian to love motivated in nature.

3. That the effects of workplace romances at the group and organizational levels range from positive to neutral to negative, from mildly diverting to benign to damaging. Workplace romances sometimes present a threat to organizational effectiveness through their negative effects on participants and coworkers. At other times, workplace romances enhance organizational effectiveness through their positive effects on participants. Two kinds of romances have the most damaging effects on group morale and organizational effectiveness: (1) hierarchical romances in which one participant directly reports to the other and (2) utilitarian romances in which one participant satisfies personal/sexual needs in exchange for satisfying the other participant's task-related and/or career-related needs.

4. That policymakers in most organizations believe that workplace romances cannot be legislated away and should be ignored unless they present a threat to individual, group, or organizational effectiveness.

5. That decision makers in most organizations recognize that some form of managerial response is required when a workplace romance presents a

serious threat to the conduct of work or group morale. Hierarchical and utilitarian romances present the greatest threat.

6. That workplace romances are particularly hazardous for gay, lesbian, and bisexual employees due to negative reactions to homosexuality in general.

7. That the prevailing culture in a work setting influences the formation, dynamics, and consequences of workplace romances and management actions related to workplace romances.

In conclusion, whatever else they represent, workplace romances will always provide something for organizational members and people in general to talk about. Through this review, we hope we have demonstrated that workplace romances represent something for scholars to talk about more.

Part **IV**

Careers and the Quality of Life

Chapter 16

Gender and Careers

Present Experiences and Emerging Trends

Linda K. Stroh and Anne H. Reilly

Like so much else in our society, the concept of career has been changing. Career progression typically meant vertical advancement within one or more organizations, but today the term often describes lateral movements within an organization or from one company to another. In addition to these shifts in career progression, major changes have also occurred in how work gets done, a result of the dramatic advances in recent years in technology and information sharing and toward globalization. In combination with demographic and societal shifts, such as the rise in dual-career couples, these changes have led many scholars and practitioners to view careers from new perspectives (cf. Hall & Mirvis, 1996; Handy, 1989; Stroh, Brett, & Reilly, 1994).

This chapter explores one key dimension of today's changing careers: differences attributable to gender. We examine male and female differences in key career issues, including career choices, advancement, and attitudes. First, we review the literature on gender and careers, focusing primarily on managerial careers in the United States. Next, we compare many of these issues within the international context, and we conclude with a discussion of emerging trends that merit future study. Throughout the chapter, we strive to maintain a balanced perspective, to avoid viewing gender and careers as strictly a women's issue using men as the group for baseline comparison. Instead, we aim to point out areas in which there are gender differences and to explain these differences.

Our focus is on managerial and white-collar careers, primarily in the private sector, in the United States, Japan, Canada, and Germany. These countries share similar economic structures. The literature we discuss reflects a variety of theoretical and disciplinary perspectives used to explain differences in male and female career outcomes: human capital theory (economics), social roles and expectations (sociology), gender-related and individual personality characteristics and stereotypes (psychology), and organizational characteristics (management and organizational behavior) (Gerson, 1993; Melamed, 1995; Powell & Mainiero, 1992; Schneer & Reitman, 1995; Stroh, Brett, & Reilly, 1992). In examining this wide range of perspectives, we hope to convey the array of approaches that can be brought to bear on this topic.

Research on Gender and Careers in the United States

Education and Early Career Choices

Research suggests that gender-based expectations concerning career choices develop as early as elementary school. For example, a 1995 study by the American Association of University Women titled *How Schools Short-change Girls,* which compared the self-esteem, interest in math and science, and career aspirations of girls and boys 9 to 15 years of age, provides evidence of gender bias in schools. The study documents the subtle yet pervasive gender biases that encourage teachers to call on boys more frequently and to provide boys with more substantive feedback on written assignments. Furthermore, statistics compiled in 1994 by the U.S. National Center for Education Statistics (U.S. Department of Education, 1994) show that although computer use is roughly equal between boys and girls from prekindergarten through high school, women college students lag behind men college students in their use of computers at home (36.6% for males, 29.7% for females) and at home for schoolwork (26.3% for males, 20.5% for females).

Male and female differences also are evident in access to higher education and thus to career choices. McWhirter (1997) found significant gender differences in perceived barriers to education and careers among a large, ethnically diverse sample of male and female high school students. For example, female students were more likely than male students to anticipate sex discrimination and less likely to anticipate ethnic discrimination with respect to future jobs.

One of the major positive changes that has occurred during this century is that, overall, the average level of educational attainment among American women has increased dramatically, at the upper levels in particular. Nonetheless, although women received more than half (54.5%) of the bachelor's degrees earned in the United States in 1994, there were noticeable differences between men and women in their fields of study. In 1994, over 75% of the degrees in library science, home economics, health sciences, public affairs, and education were awarded to women. In comparison, over 70% of the degrees earned in engineering, military technologies, and computer and information sciences were awarded to men (U.S. Department of Education, 1996).

Gender differences are also evident in the percentage of men versus women who earn graduate degrees in business, a field generally associated with higher career achievement. In 1994, men earned 63.5% of the master's degrees in business management and administrative services fields awarded in the United States (U.S. Department of Education, 1996).

Clearly, education is only one of many variables that affect occupational choice, and many of these variables may be influenced by gender. For example, research has documented male and female differences in individual achievement orientation and vocational interests (Brown, Eisenberg, & Sawilowsky, 1997; Hansen, Collins, Swanson, & Fouad, 1993). Studies have also demonstrated that early socialization may determine the jobs women and men consider socially acceptable (Cohen & Swim, 1995; Melamed, 1995, 1996; Witkowski & Leicht, 1995). Finally, gender has been shown to influence job-search strategies (Leicht & Marx, 1997; Malen & Stroh, 1998).

Career Paths and Progression

The literature on career progression over time offers numerous models of career stages (e.g., Schein's nine stages, 1978; Levinson's four stages, 1978; Rosenbaum's tournament model, 1989; Hall & Mirvis's new career contract, 1995). According to Powell and Mainiero (1992), however, none of these models applies to women's careers, in part because women's career paths have always been more complex and ambiguous. Their approach depicts individual women *not* as placing themselves, at any point in time, in a specific career or life stage. Rather, women see themselves on a continuum between career and relationships, experiencing levels of success in both. Melamed (1995, 1996) also argued that the career paths of men and women differ significantly. Melamed developed and tested a gender-specific model of career success with three sets of predictors: human capital attributes (e.g., job experience, personality); career options (job type, relocation); and opportunity structure (organizational size, industry factors). The importance attached to specific predictors of career success varied between men and women.

One observed difference is that women's careers are more likely to follow a sequential, as opposed to a simultaneous, pattern (Powell & Mainiero, 1992; Sheehy, 1976)—that is, a period of employment, followed by a multiyear career interruption, then resumption of outside employment. Biological and social reasons—childbearing and child rearing, respectively—are the usual reasons for this pattern. Consequently, some high-profile, high-achieving women have been viewed as "tokens" who did not follow women's typical career paths. Another way to view the sequential career path is as the result of a proactive strategy balancing work and family responsibilities (Hall & Richter, 1990). In other words, this pattern may simply be an alternative to the simultaneous career pattern (concurrent employment and parenthood) typically adopted by men (Gerson, 1993).

In addition to observable gender differences in career paths, there are also measurable gender differences in career achievement outcomes, such as pay, promotion, and job opportunities. This disparity between men and women has most frequently been attributed to the *glass ceiling,* which restricts women from attaining the highest positions in corporations, compared to men with similar backgrounds and education (Brett & Stroh, 1997; Lyness & Thompson, 1997; Melamed, 1995, 1996; Schneer & Reitman, 1995; Stroh et al., 1992). Researchers have explained the glass ceiling barrier in a variety of ways. For example, gender differences have been observed in access to important career development opportunities, such as training, job challenges, mentoring, and job-relocation options, thus affecting human capital (Lyness & Thompson, 1997; Ohlott, Ruderman, & McCauley, 1994; Ragins, Townsend, & Mattis, 1998). Other explanations for the glass ceiling reference career interruptions (women have more than men), or industry differences (e.g., men are more likely than women to be promoted to executive positions in manufacturing companies).

Varma and Stroh (1998) provide yet another perspective on gender differences in career progression. Using leader-member exchange (whether one is in the "in-group" or "out-group" at work) as their theoretical basis (Dienesch & Liden, 1986), they found that men and women managers were more likely to have same-sex members in their in-groups. Their results further indicated that male managers rated their male subordinates higher than their female subordinates, whereas female managers rated their female subordinates higher. Consequently, because there are more men in managerial positions than women, especially at higher levels, male subordinates may be more likely to progress further in their careers than female subordinates.

Attitudes Toward Careers

Yet another intriguing explanation for the observed differences between men's and women's career progression patterns stems from differences in key career attitudes. The nature of these differences—and whether they really exist—highlights one of the most fundamental controversies in the gender and careers area: whether men and women bring similar or different personal qualities to the workplace. Powell (1993) discussed this controversy, identifying four basic positions about the presence of gender differences in managerial traits: no differences, stereotypical differences favoring men, stereotypical differences favoring women, and nonstereotypical differences.

Several observers have reported important differences between men and women in their attitudes about work (Cose, 1995; Gerson, 1993; "Giving Women," 1997; Horwitz, 1993; Morris, 1995). Grant (1988) suggested that women managers can offer organizations different yet valuable skills, compared to their male counterparts. According to one perspective, women are generally less involved in their careers because their family responsibilities are the primary focus of their attention (Schwartz, 1989). Another view focuses on male and female differences in perceptions of career success and advancement. In this view, men's self-concept is more strongly derived from career success as measured by traditional yardsticks such as pay and promotion, whereas women's self-concept is related more to factors such as balancing the various spheres of their lives (Gerson, 1993; Gordon & Whelan, 1998).

Morris (1995) noted an important distinction in men's and women's expectations: Because executive women often begin their careers with much lower expectations than do executive men, they are more willing than men to take career risks, and these risks often pay off. These women then may be more willing to take on additional career risks, such as leaving a corporate job to establish their own businesses. Moore's chapter in this book provides an in-depth look at gender and entrepreneurship.

Another reason why many women leave corporate America to strike out on their own may be a broader concept of personal fulfillment. According to some observers, women define career achievement less by their incomes and more by whether their careers allow them the autonomy to balance their personal and professional lives. Support for these observations comes from research that suggests that men and women seek different outcomes from their careers and define career achievement differently (see Gordon & Whelan, 1998; Karambayya, 1998; Lobel, 1991; Lobel & St. Clair, 1992).

In contrast, other research on gender and careers suggests that men and women in the workplace have similar career interests, skills, and attitudes. For example, Kanter (1977a) argued in *Men and Women of the Corporation* that career progress is determined more by the political and structural characteristics of the organization and the roles assigned to men and women than by the individual characteristics of male and female corporate employees. In his review of differences in managerial behavior between women and men managers, Powell (1990) found few significant differences. (See also Chapter 12 in this book by Butterfield and Grinnell about gender, leadership, and managerial behavior.)

Another debate in the career area is based on organizational commitment and its link to career outcomes. Articles in the popular press have suggested that currently neither men nor women are loyal to their organizations, and they are more committed to advancing their own careers (e.g., "Loyalty,"

1995). Women may be perceived as even less committed to their organizations than men because they do not advance as far in their careers (Davidson & Burke, 1994).

However, research by Stroh and Reilly (1997) showed that men and women differ very little in their organizational commitment. Rather, the major differences are between those managers who stay with their organizations and those who opt for what they perceive as "greener pastures" in other companies: Those employees who changed jobs were more committed to their new organizations than were their coworkers who stayed at their old organizations, and both the men and women who left their organizations fared better than those who stayed.

Gender Segregation and Discrimination in the Workforce

The Civil Rights Act of 1964 and its associated antidiscrimination laws were the impetus for reducing some of the gender discrimination existing in the U.S. workplace. Although the implementation of these laws did not change perceptions immediately, they have had some measurable positive effects on the hiring and promotion practices of American firms.

Between 1975 and 1995, the percentage of women in managerial and professional specialty occupations in the American workforce increased significantly. In 1995, women accounted for 43% of managerial and related employment, nearly double their share in 1975 (22%); women's share of employment in professional occupations also rose during this period, from 45% to 53% (Wootton, 1997). There were noticeable differences, however, in the functional areas women chose (or were channeled into) (Leicht & Marx, 1997; Witkowski & Leicht, 1995). Women were much more heavily represented in service occupations, as were men in precision production, craft, and repair occupations (Wootton, 1997). Employment in technician and sales occupations was evenly split.

Gender segregation exists throughout the management hierarchy, up to and including boards of directors and CEOs. Bilimoria and Piderit (1994) reported that boards assigned male and female directors to board committees based on stereotypical beliefs. For example, women board members were more likely to be placed on public affairs committees, and men on compensation, executive, and finance committees. Ragins, Townsend, and Mattis (1998) surveyed 325 *Fortune* 1000 CEOs and 461 of the highest-ranking women in their organizations and reported that the CEOs still held stereotypical beliefs about women. For example, 82% of the CEOs (compared to 47% of the highest-ranking women) responded that lack of significant general management or line experience prevents women from advancing to corporate leadership. Sixty-four percent (vs. 29% of women) stated that women have not been in the pipeline long enough. In contrast, 52% of the women perceived male stereotyping and preconceptions as a barrier to women's advancement (compared to 25% of the CEOs).

Whether the observed gender differences in functional areas reflect stereotypical role choices or are determined by entrenched organization and power structures (Kanter, 1977a; "Women in American Boardrooms," 1996), the outcome is unequivocal: Certain functional areas (e.g., finance, manufacturing, information systems) are associated with more career opportunities, greater compensation, higher levels of career achievement—and fewer women.

Work and Family Issues

No discussion of gender and career issues is complete without acknowledging the struggle employed women face in balancing work and family responsibilities, especially in light of studies that show that women are still responsible for most child-rearing and household chores, even when they work full-time (Hammonds, 1996; Hochschild, 1997; Stroh, Brett, & Reilly, 1996; Tenbrunsel, Brett, Stroh, & Reilly, 1995). Chapter 20 by Greenhaus and Parasuraman in this book reviews the extensive literature on work and family.

Passage of the Family and Medical Leave Act in 1993 appears to have prompted many American organizations to think more proactively about work and family issues (Hawthorne, 1993). The act entitles both men and women to receive up to 12 weeks of unpaid leave to care for new babies (natural birth or adopted), and it can also be taken to care for sick children, parents, or spouses. However, research shows that few men have taken advantage of the Family and Medical Leave Act (Hawthorne, 1993), and many of the women who have are concerned that doing so may have sidetracked their careers (Kantrowicz & Wingert, 1993; Morris, 1997). Companies that provide full menus of family-friendly benefits also report that more women than men take advantage of options such as parental leaves and flextime. Furthermore, research illustrates that although more organizations now offer some family-friendly benefits, they do so reluctantly and often on an ad hoc, one-by-one basis. For example, most employees have to request flexible work schedules individually (Kush & Stroh, 1994). (See also Chapter 23 in this volume by Lobel about work and family initiatives.)

The use of family-friendly benefits addresses a sensitive topic in the gender and career arena: the "mommy track." In 1989, Schwartz published an article in the *Harvard Business Review* in which she distinguished between "career-primary" and "career-family" women. Several studies followed on both "mommy" and "daddy" tracks (e.g., Schneer & Reitman, 1993; Stroh & Brett, 1996). These studies showed that there were disadvantages for *both* corporate men and women to being perceived as more committed to one's family than to the workplace. For example, in both studies, the fathers in the two-income households earned *less* on average than the traditional fathers (those whose spouses were at home caring for the children). Disagreement exists not only about whether there are indeed different career tracks for parents, and the degree of resentment felt by colleagues asked to cover for them, but also about whether men on the daddy track are seen as holding a 1990s cachet not extended to women on the mommy track (Lublin, 1995).

Career Interruptions and Breaks

Although many employees never leave the workforce from entry job until retirement, other employees experience one or more interruptions during the course of their careers. There are many types of career interruptions and breaks, with different implications for the men and women taking them. One of the most common reasons to take a leave is for pregnancy, maternity, or child rearing, and obviously, more women than men interrupt their careers for these reasons (Lyness & Thompson, 1997). Whether women take lengthy parental leaves is driven by the availability of leaves, such as through the Family and Medical Leave Act; the child care options available; financial considerations; the employee's role expectations concerning motherhood; and the corporate culture (Cose, 1995; Crompton, 1996; Morris, 1997). But regardless of the reasons underlying these leaves, the outcome for women employees is the same: lower pay than men in comparable positions who did not take leaves (Schneer & Reitman, 1990). It is worth noting, however, that several studies have shown that women executives who do not have children and therefore do not take parental leaves also earn less than men in comparable positions (Schneer & Reitman, 1995; Stroh et al., 1992).

Another type of career break may arise from career dislocation due to downsizing (Karambayya, 1998). Both in the United States and worldwide, in nearly two decades of corporate restructuring, hundreds of thousands of employees have lost their jobs. One question that has emerged is whether men and women react differently to being laid off. Some commentators (and a popular movie) have suggested that dislocated men who adopt the "Mr. Mom" role, either temporarily or long term, experience greater loss of self-esteem and more stress than dislocated women (Cose, 1995; Horwitz, 1993). However, empirical research does not support this claim. Leana and Feldman (1991) found no significant male and female differences in the behavior and distress associated with job loss: Job loss resulted in psychological stress in both men and women. Work by Malen and Stroh (1998) supported Leana and Feldman's findings. In both studies, the researchers found the only gender differences were in individuals' coping strategies. According to Leana and Feldman (1991), men tended to focus more on problem-solution behaviors to reduce their stress, whereas women focused more on support-seeking behaviors (i.e., social and financial support). In addition, Malen and Stroh (1998) found that women tended to be laid off longer than men.

Career Issues at Midcareer

The few studies that have investigated career progress at midcareer and beyond have found interesting gender differences. Midcareer has been found to be a time when men and women may undergo a type of role reversal (Stroh & Greller, 1995). For women, this is often a time when child care responsibilities diminish and they are freer to fulfill career-related goals.

Gordon and Whelan (1998) identified important differences in the needs of midcareer women, midcareer men, and younger women in areas ranging from child care and the use of personal time to achievement, advancement, and perceived value to organizations. Gordon and Whelan suggest, for example, that for younger women, logistical issues of child care dominate; for midlife women, these logistical issues are resolved; and for midlife men, they are typically not a concern. In contrast, when they were asked how to meet the challenges of the next decade, midlife men described their primary focus on their own mortality and, consequently, wanted to accomplish their goals immediately. Younger women appeared present oriented and not focused on the future. Midlife women reported they were beginning to acknowledge that they must prepare for different family, career, and personal challenges in the next decade (Gordon & Whelan, 1998, p. 11). Karambayya (1998) found a similar pattern of shifting priorities in her interviews with midcareer women managers who elected to leave a large utility in the midst of corporate restructuring.

At midcareer, the male-female earnings gap and access to promotion are as pervasive as ever. In their longitudinal study of the career paths of men and women who held MBAs, Schneer and Reitman (1995) found that the women who remained committed to their careers earned lower salaries and worked fewer hours than the men who remained committed to their careers, and they were less likely than men to rise to positions in top management.

One aspect of the challenges facing midcareer men and women that continues to receive attention is the midlife crisis. Midlife crises generally occur in the mid- to late 30s, and they supposedly reflect the point at which one stops growing up and starts growing old (Morris, 1995). The crisis may be precipitated by a significant reassessment of one's life, perhaps as a result of a friend's illness or death. It may be associated with reaching a career plateau; it may reflect an imbalance between work and nonwork interests and goals (Fierman, 1993). Anecdotal evidence suggests there are major differences in how men and women experience midlife crises (Morris, 1995). This topic merits further research, because there are important questions about not only the causes and consequences of midlife crises but also about their impact on men and women.

Career Challenges of Late Career

The literature offers some insights into the career outcomes and attitudes of late career (Levinson, 1978; Schein, 1978). For example, Greller and Stroh (1995) found that as employees approach midlife and beyond, social, cultural, and economic factors, including the possibility of fewer rewards, push them into retirement as their contribution in most organizations is undervalued. However, few studies explore how men and women compare in meeting the challenges of their later working lives, and the limited research suggests there may be important male and female differences.

Greller and Stroh (1995) found that older women whose children were grown and gone reported significantly higher levels of job/career satisfaction than older men. Assuming that women are socialized to be nurturing and relationship oriented, the focus on the development of others characteristic of the maintenance career stage (Levinson, 1978) may represent a comfortable role for women in their middle and older years. Another reason for the higher levels of career satisfaction reported among older women may be a shift in focus from family to self, and the resulting personal growth and renewal. However, this sense of renewal may lead some women to feel "out of sync" with their husbands, who are in the withdrawal stage of their careers (Levinson, 1978).

The challenges of late career are clearly an area that merits further study, including differences by gender. One important reason to extend this research is increased life expectancy and the opportunity and financial imperative to work into one's later years. Handy (1989) argues that the Third Age (from the French *Le Troisième Age,* originally meaning "retirement") should be viewed as an inherent part of one's career, lasting for 20 to 25 years beyond the final corporate job, and he emphasizes the importance of planning for two decades of another type of work.

Cross-Generational Career Issues

Important differences and corresponding conflicts have always existed between the generation in power and the next generation. In today's business world, members of three generations often work together: those in the over-50 generation (many at upper echelons of the firm); baby boomers (approximately 30 to 50 years of age, many in mid- and upper-level management); and members of Generation X (under 30, in entry-level and early-career positions). The dramatic differences in work attitudes and values among these employees have become important issues in human resource management (Caudron, 1997). For example, Conger (1998) suggests that what he labels the "Silent Generation" (those born between 1925 and 1942) was influenced by the Great Depression and World War II to treasure employment and be obedient employees respectful of hierarchy. In contrast, argues Conger, Gen X employees distrust hierarchy, prefer more informal arrangements, and are far less loyal to their companies. According to Hall and Richter's (1990) profile of baby boomers, boomers display both a strong concern for basic values as well as a focus on self and self-awareness, which some observers label "narcissism."

Because of the presence of women in the workforce throughout the age spectrum, an intriguing issue has evolved that only now is being explored: the interaction effect of gender and generation on career variables (Gordon & Whelan, 1998). The greater prevalence of dual-career families in today's corporate workforce has caused companies to make adjustments in job-transfer policies as well as to introduce family-friendly benefits. No longer do employees automatically accept geographic relocations, even for better jobs, if it means their spouses will suffer career setbacks (Brett, Stroh, & Reilly, 1992). In addition, anecdotal evidence suggests that younger women are insisting on career equality when making career-related decisions with their significant others. Women in the younger generation expect to work throughout their lifetimes, and, like their male counterparts, are so preparing themselves (Stern, 1991).

Other researchers have noted differences between men of prior generations and 1990s fathers. Gerson (1993) identified three categories of husbands/fathers based on her interviews with 138 men from diverse social backgrounds: primary breadwinners (men who defined family and work commitments according to the traditional breadwinner role, 36% of Gerson's sample); autonomous (men who had eschewed parenthood or significant parental involvement, 30% of the sample); and involved fathers (men whose outlook on parenthood included caretaking as well as economic support, 33%). Gerson's research suggests that American men's parental involvement has risen significantly since the 1950s, when traditional breadwinning fathers accounted for nearly two-thirds of American households.

Several other observers have noted that younger men appear to be more willing to make career sacrifices to spend more time with their families (Cose, 1995; Rubin, 1994). This shift may reflect one of the Gen X attitude changes reported by Caudron (1997). Caudron claims that unlike the baby boomers and members of older generations, who are willing to trade off short-term sacrifices for long-term gains, Gen Xers seek immediate gratification. Thus, they may value the present rewards of parental involvement more than the alleged long-term benefits of job involvement. Conger (1998) notes that most Gen Xers grew up in dual-earner families, and a high percentage are children of divorce. Therefore, he suggests that this generation is searching for a balance between work and personal life that was lacking in their parents' lives.

Perhaps these differences reflect a coming sea change in Americans' perceptions of the "traditional" family, toward what Schneer and Reitman

TABLE 16.1 Workforce Participation Rates

Country	1976 Male	1976 Female	1986 Male	1986 Female	1996 Male	1996 Female
United States	77.5	47.3	76.3	55.3	74.9	59.3
Canada	77.8	45.6	77.1	55.8	72.4	57.6
Japan	81.0	44.9	77.6	47.6	77.5	49.3
Germany	72.5	39.3	70.2	41.4	64.2[a]	44.1[a]

SOURCE: U.S. Department of Labor (1997c, p. 1).
a. 1994.

(1995) call a form of family that is "post-traditional." Or perhaps traditional roles have only gone underground (Stern, 1991). According to Cose (1995), "Many modern young professionals, despite their professed belief in sexual equality, cling to conventional roles reflexively" (p. 14). This issue, which will be played out in the years ahead, is another intriguing topic that merits further exploration.

Gender and Careers: An International Perspective

Our chapter so far has focused on gender and career issues within the United States. In this section, we examine key gender differences in other nations. The international perspective contributes to our understanding of careers in general, especially given the global nature of our economy. We have chosen to compare our findings for the United States with findings for Canada, Japan, and Germany, because their economies are similar to that of the United States.

Workforce Participation Rates

Workforce participation rates vary somewhat among these three countries, but in each, the percentage of men in the labor force outnumbers the percentage of women (see Table 16.1). The 1996 gap is greatest in Japan and smallest in Canada (U.S. Department of Labor, 1997c). Over time, these gaps have narrowed in all three countries, especially in Canada (from 32.2% in 1976 to 14.8% in 1996). In contrast, the gap narrowed the least in Japan (from 36.1% in 1976 to 28.2% in 1996), suggesting that Japan continues to be more male dominated, which has strong negative implications for working women in Japan, including American women working there.

Affirmative action policies and demographic changes in the workforce have had a great impact on the labor force participation rates worldwide (Mandelson, 1996). (See also Chapter 22 by Konrad and Linnehan in this book for more on affirmative action issues.) For example, according to a projection made by the Canadian government, by 2000 only 15% of new entrants into the Canadian workforce will be White males, and Canadian organizations have been forced to look to women and minorities to fill what had been considered stereotypical male jobs (Dingwall, 1992).

Work-Family Issues

Balancing work and family issues is of paramount concern to women in most Western countries and is becoming more important to Asian women as well.

Canada. In Canada, balancing a career track and maternity are problems left largely to individual women and their employers. In fact, many feminists believe that women who make it too far up the ladder have been co-opted by the "enemy" and thus are unlikely to sympathize with their entry-level sisters (Dingwall, 1992). The Canadian government has remained relatively uninvolved, although the government does provide an annual subsidy to all families with children, regardless of their income. One reason government-sponsored "free" national day care has been marginalized may be that day care issues in Canada largely concern entry-level workers and are often accompanied by the additional challenges of single parenthood (Dingwall, 1992).

Japan. Because children are seen as the major source of fulfillment in Japanese culture, Japanese women seek work that allows them to be good mothers in Japanese terms. Often, women say they prefer part-time work, as long as they can receive good benefits, so that they can be on call for "family duty" (White, 1991). Furthermore, many working women feel that men's work lives are too constrained to serve as good models, and thus they do not want to be male clones. They favor, instead, the introduction of flextime in the workplace, which would help them achieve balance in their triple roles of child rearer, household manager, and family representative in neighborhood and community activities (White, 1991).

In general, sex stereotyping is more pervasive in Japan than in the West. Although there is some evidence that views on women's roles are changing, both men and women tend to view working women with children primarily in their traditional role as mother (Davis, 1992). Hence, many women in Japan doubt that they will ever succeed professionally (Fisher, 1993) and break through the "bamboo barrier" (Bando, 1986; White, 1991) as it is called. Furthermore, few Japanese companies have formal systems for dealing with such predominantly female issues as sexual harassment, maternity leaves, and company-sponsored day care (Fisher, 1993). Although Japan enacted an Equal Employment Opportunity Act in 1986, it is viewed as having no teeth because there are no penalties for violators. The law is seen as a "failure for Japanese feminism" (White, 1991).

Germany. Research makes references to distinctions between the regions of the former Federal Republic of Germany (East Germany) and the former German Democratic Republic (West Germany). These differences can be attributed to the unique social, political, and economic conditions surrounding their historical development.

In West Germany, almost 60% of 25- to 35-year-old women with children leave the labor market at least temporarily. Only 40% of the women in middle management are mothers, and they typically have only one child; by contrast, almost all of their male colleagues have an average of two children. There is a general belief in West Germany that raising children represents one of the most significant barriers to equal opportunity in management careers (Antal & Krebsbach-Gnath, 1993; Einhorn, 1994).

The situation in East Germany has been markedly different, in part because of the broader availability of child care. Here, the vast majority (94%) of women with children remain in the labor force. In spite of their large representation in the labor force, women maintain primary responsibility for children, which creates a barrier to their professional advancement in organizations (Antal & Krebsbach-Gnath, 1993; Einhorn, 1994).

Several measures were introduced in East Germany in 1976 to help women combine their family and work responsibilities. As a result, the child care provisions for working mothers are more extensive than in any other country in the world. In large cities, almost 100% of child care needs for infants and preschool children and 82% of needs for after-school care are met at no cost (Antal & Krebsbach-Gnath, 1993; Einhorn, 1994).

In West Germany, the state's provision of child care is more extensive than in the United States but not considered sufficient. Ninety-seven percent of those eligible have taken parental leaves, but in 98.5% of those cases, it was taken by the mother; of the fathers who took leaves, 70% had been unemployed prior to doing so (Antal & Krebsbach-Gnath, 1993).

International comparative surveys indicate that men in Germany tend to maintain traditional conservative views on a woman's role in child rearing. Other surveys, however, show that a small but growing number of men are taking a more critical look at the traditional German work ethic and seeking more meaningful activities, both at work and in their leisure time (Antal & Krebsbach-Gnath, 1993).

Education

Education is a critical component and predictor of career success in all the countries we examined.

Canada. Canada has more women in postsecondary institutions than in any other Western country, including the United States. Women make up more than 50% of the graduates of Canada's universities, 50% of the graduates of MBA programs and law schools, 41% of the graduates of medical schools, and one-third of the graduates of advanced science programs (Dingwall, 1992).

Japan. At most levels, Japanese women are completing more years of education than are men: 95.3% of Japanese girls finish high school versus 93.0% of boys; 36.8% of Japanese girls go to college versus 34.8% of boys. As a result, female college graduates now outnumber men in the workplace; as of 1989, there were 243,000 female graduates versus 231,000 male graduates (White, 1991).

Germany. Women's education levels and vocational training in western Germany also have been rising significantly. But unlike the situation in Japan, female university graduates in western Germany have higher unemployment rates than do male graduates. Women represent 25% of the working population with university degrees but 45% of those with degrees who are unemployed (Antal & Krebsbach-Gnath, 1993; Einhorn, 1994).

In East Germany, the levels of education and vocational training of women also have been increasing steadily. The official statistics of the former East Germany show that by the 1980s men and women had attained equal levels of educational and vocational training. More women than men, however, work in jobs below their levels of qualification (Antal & Krebsbach-Gnath, 1993; Einhorn, 1994).

Representation in Professional Positions

Canada. Of the women who work for the federal government in Canada, three-quarters are employed in 4 of 72 subcategories as office workers, secretaries, administrators, and program managers; office workers alone account for 44% of these women ("The Case," 1996; Core, 1994; "Women Workers," 1997). Outside the government sector, most working women are found in service jobs, not in manufacturing or resource extraction, two sectors where there is a shortage of workers (Dingwall, 1992). As in the United States, women fill a small percentage (less than 2%) of Canada's top corporate positions.

Japan. In Japan, attracting female employees to mainstream companies is becoming an issue of survival, as the demand for skilled workers exceeds the supply. Although only a token number of female managers advance, their visibility as role models gives them the leverage, if they are persistent, to change the conditions of employment (Bando, 1986).

The picture may become brighter in the future, but currently women in Japan hold only 6.2% of administrative/managerial positions (not including the self-employed). According to a 1984 survey conducted by the Japanese Labor Ministry, 43.7% of Japanese companies fail to give women opportunities to gain promotion to managerial positions. And even in those companies that do give women the chance to advance, the majority do not promote them to positions above that of chief clerk (Bando, 1986; Creighton, 1996).

Because Japanese women generally work for only short periods of time, companies are reluctant to target even the highly educated for future management positions. Thus, women employees are excluded from in-company rotations and programs that develop talent over long periods of time. As male employees become older, they become specialists, but their female counterparts lag behind, remaining in low-level positions (Bando, 1986; Creighton, 1996). Compounding the problem, Japanese companies adhere closely to seniority policies. Thus, most male employees remain loyal to their companies, because they lose seniority if they change jobs. Not surprisingly, the rate of turnover is higher among women than among men (Bando, 1986; Creighton, 1996).

In a study that measured gender differences in a Japanese automobile assembly plant, it was found that women were often assigned to lower-level or "light duty" positions. Few women were in positions of leadership and upper management (Gottfried & Graham, 1993).

Germany. As in Canada and other parts of Europe, gender-specific labor segmentation is pervasive in both East and West Germany. Almost 70% of working women in West Germany are concentrated in the following occupational categories: health services (87.5%), social services (79%), retail (62.2%), and education (48.2%). In East Germany, these dominant categories are social services (91.8%), health services (83.1%), education (77%), retail (72%), and postal and phone services (68.9%).

Women in both East and West Germany generally have better chances of obtaining management positions in the government than in private industry (Frazee, 1997) and in the sectors of the economy where they are strongly represented. Thus, women are a rarity in management in heavy industry, construction, and science (Antal & Krebsbach-Gnath, 1993).

The glass ceiling is somewhat lower in Germany than in the United States and Canada and certainly higher than the bamboo barrier in Japan (Foreign Press Center, 1986). In West Germany, promotion decisions for higher management positions are based more on subjective criteria, such as professional competence and effectiveness, than on objective data, and promotions are often given to employees who have followed traditional male career patterns. Furthermore, women have to work harder than men to gain respect from their male peers (Frazee, 1997). The net effect is discrimination against women.

In summary, these data show a consistent pattern of gender differences in the career paths of men and women in Canada, Japan, and Germany. Important differences may also be observed in other nations. For example, the Scandinavian countries are known to have very progressive employment packages. Sweden pays maternity and paternity benefits up to nearly 75% of salaries for 12 months and allows an additional 3 months at a reduced pay (McShulskis, 1996). Examining the impact these employment packages may have on gender and careers would be important to this body of literature. Likewise, examining gender differences in emerging and transitioning markets (i.e., Vietnam, Poland) would be of interest.

Emerging Trends

Today's turbulent corporate environment has yielded some significant shifts in employees' career patterns, and numerous scholars have proposed new approaches to current models of careers. For example, Hall (1990; Hall & Mirvis, 1995) maintains that managers today follow a more "protean" pattern than in the past, evident in their taking more responsibility for their careers, their self-directedness, and their willingness to change jobs to meet personal career needs and goals. Handy (1989) suggests the notion of the portfolio career, in which one's current job is just one element in a lifetime portfolio of wages, contract fees, charity work, and study. Research by Stroh and Reilly (1997) and Karambayya (1998) indicates that employees may choose to switch organizations when downsizing and restructuring change the organizational culture so that it no longer fits the employees' career goals and opportunities. In fact, one major male-female distinction that emerged from the Stroh and Reilly (1997) research was that the women appeared more sensitive to highly politicized work environments where success was based more on *who* employees knew than on *what* they knew. Today's less linear career patterns may be easier for women than men to manage, as women's career paths have generally required greater flexibility and adaptability (Powell & Mainiero, 1992). Future research on gender and careers should track and take into account emerging notions of the very meaning of career.

Two decades of downsizing and restructuring have resulted in another shift, the shape of organizations themselves. Handy (1989) describes many firms as "shamrock organizations," which undertake only their core activities and outsource the rest through contract employees. Thus, the emergence of contract workers and temporary employees as important organizational resources is another area that merits study. Certainly, we can expect that the career outcomes and attitudes of contract workers and temporary workers will differ from those of permanent employees, and there may be gender differences as well. For example, many women's sequential career paths may include a period of self-selected contract employment, as they freelance in their specialty area while at home with children.

A related issue is the two-tier wage system that has emerged in organizations as diverse as airlines and academia. This arrangement is characterized by a set of senior employees, who receive higher pay (and usually better benefits) than a set of junior employees, even though both sets do similar work within the same organization. Because women are more likely to interrupt their careers for maternity and child rearing, they may sacrifice the seniority required to stay in the upper tier of higher-paid employment.

The continuing shifts in demographics and corresponding changes in family structure are other areas that offer promising possibilities for research. For example, the gender and career issues that emerge in the commuter couple are just beginning to be examined (Jehn, Stroh, & Von Glinow, 1997). Some of the research questions here are logistical: What distance is involved? Is commuting a temporary or permanent arrangement? But other questions are more fundamental: How far will men and women go to make compromises between work and family? Further study here is clearly in order.

Finally, as our review of the international careers and gender literature indicates, additional comparative international research is needed. In a 1996 study, Schein, Mueller, Lituchy, and Liu studied male and female managers in Japan and China, and then compared their results with previous studies done in the United States, Great Britain, and Germany. Their conclusion: "Think manager, think male" is a global phenomenon. New economies are emerging, providing different models of careers and new career patterns. Furthermore, the competitive nature of our global economy requires optimum use of all our human resources, regardless of gender.

As we enter the 21st century, other career issues and other areas for investigation are likely to emerge. We hope that the research described in this chapter provides some of the background for research to progress in the new directions that we can predict now and those that we can hardly yet imagine.

Reflections on the Glass Ceiling

Recent Trends and Future Prospects

Gary N. Powell

Numerous articles, books, and book chapters have reviewed the status of women in the workplace in general and in the managerial ranks of organizations in particular. Dipboye (1987) listed nine reviews that had appeared since 1974 (e.g., Bass, 1981; Kanter, 1977a; Larwood & Wood, 1977; Nieva & Gutek, 1981; O'Leary, 1974). Dipboye's list was not exhaustive; among others, it omitted reviews by Bartol (1978) and Riger and Galligan (1980). Since Dipboye's 1987 review, over a dozen reviews have appeared (e.g., Alvesson & Billing, 1997; Blau, Ferber, & Winkler, 1998; Burke & McKeen, 1992; Cahoon & Ramsey, 1993; Collinson, Knights, & Collinson, 1990; Davidson & Burke, 1994; Davidson & Cooper, 1992; Fagenson, 1993b; Kelley & Streeter, 1992; Morrison & Von Glinow, 1990; Powell, 1993; Stromberg & Harkess, 1988; Tanton, 1994; Wahl, 1995).

AUTHOR'S NOTE: I extend grateful appreciation to Laura Graves, Marcia Kropf, Mary Mattis, Patricia Ohlott, Marian Ruderman, and Mary Ann Von Glinow for discussions that contributed to the ideas in this chapter, and to Tony Butterfield, Belle Rose Ragins, Anne Reilly, and Linda Stroh for their reactions to an earlier draft. An abbreviated and earlier version of this chapter appeared in M. J. Davidson & R. J. Burke (Eds.), *Women in Management: Current Research Issues* (Vol. 2), London: Chapman, 1999.

Because of the many prior reviews, this review is necessarily selective and focuses on trends. The chapter begins by linking prior reviews to statistics about the status of women in management. The statistics provide insight into the change in emphasis of reviews over time. Questions about recent and future trends in such statistics are then addressed.

Prior Reviews and Related Statistics

In 1970, the proportion of women in the American labor force was 38% (U.S. Department of Labor, 1998a). However, the proportion of women in management positions in 1970 was only 16%, a proportion that had held constant for over a decade (U.S. Department of Labor, 1983). There were no systematic surveys of the proportion of women in top management positions at this time. However, there were so few female executives in the late 1960s that a study attempted by the Harvard Business School was abandoned due to lack of sufficient participants (Epstein, 1975).

In response to such statistics, the first generation of reviews of the status of women in management primarily asked the question "Why are there so few women in management?" For example, Riger and Galligan (1980) categorized causal explanations for the scarcity of women in management as focusing on either the person or the situation. Person-centered explanations suggested that socialization practices directed toward females encouraged the development of personality traits, skills, and behaviors that were contrary to the demands of the managerial role, including a fear of success (Horner, 1969) and an unwillingness to take risks (Hennig & Jardim, 1977). These explanations, which had received the greater attention in prior research, were seen as inadequate in accounting for women's low status in management. In contrast, situation-centered explanations suggested that the nature of the organizational work environment faced by women who aspired to management positions determined their fate more than their own traits, skills, and behaviors. The work environment included group dynamics directed toward "token" female members (Kanter, 1977a), attitudes toward female managers (O'Leary, 1974), differential attributions of causes of success for men and women (Garland & Price, 1977), and differential allocations of rewards (e.g., salary, promotion) to men and women. Riger and Galligan (1980) called for greater attention directed toward the influence of situation-centered variables and the interaction between person-centered and situation-centered variables on the status of women in management.[1]

Bartol (1978) also attempted to account for the relatively small number of women in managerial positions. After first reviewing research on sex differences in three leadership-related areas (leader behavior or style, job satisfaction of the leader and subordinates, and job performance), she rejected the person-centered explanation that women in leadership positions behave differently and generate different outcomes than men in such positions.

Instead, she suggested that filtering points at different career stages keep women from progressing up organizational hierarchies. For example, women may be filtered out of managerial careers at the pre-organizational-entry stage by socialization for traditional female roles, at the organizational-entry stage by selection discrimination, at the first-assignment stage by unchallenging work assignments, and at the promotion or leveling-off stage by promotion discrimination. Bartol recommended additional research on the internal (i.e., person-centered) and external (i.e., situation-centered and social-system-centered) factors that influence decisions by both individuals and organizations to learn more about the filtering out of women at different career stages. However, similar to Riger and Galligan (1980), as well as to other reviews not discussed here (e.g., Kanter, 1977a), Bartol stressed the utility of focusing on external phenomena over internal phenomena in explaining why so few women were in management positions.

The proportion of women in management positions in the United States dramatically increased during the 1970s and 1980s, from 16% in 1970 to 26% in 1980 and 39% in 1990 (U.S. Department of Labor, 1983, 1990). The proportion of women in the American labor force also grew during this period, from 38% in 1970 to 43% in 1980 and 45% in 1990, but at a slower rate (U.S. Department of Labor, 1998a). By the end of the 1980s, the gap between the proportions of women in the labor force and in management had narrowed considerably.

Government statistics are not kept regarding the proportion of women at various management levels, and surveys have differed in how *top management* has been defined. However, whatever definition was used, the proportion of women in top management positions was never reported as higher than 5% during the 1970s or 1980s. For example, the proportion of female executives in large American corporations was reported as 0.5% in 1979 and 2.9% in 1989 (Korn/Ferry International, 1990). The proportion of female corporate officers in *Fortune 500* corporations was 1.7% in 1986 (Morrison, White, Van Velsor, & the Center for Creative Leadership, 1987) and 2.6% in 1990 (Morrison, White, Van Velsor, & the Center for Creative Leadership, 1992). Finally, the proportion of female directors and executives listed in *Standard and Poor's Register of Corporations, Directors, and Executives* was 1.8% in 1982 and 2.7% in 1987 (J. B. Forbes, personal communication, 1988).

In response to these statistics, the second generation of reviews of the status of women in management primarily asked the question "Why are there so few women in top management?" For example, Dipboye (1987), in a book chapter titled "Problems and Progress of Women in Management," found both good news ("there are clearly more women in management today than there were 10 or 20 years ago," p. 118) and bad news ("women are still a distinct minority in management, particularly at the higher levels, and there are signs that this situation will continue for some time to come," p. 119). The balance of the chapter was devoted to possible person-centered (e.g., sex differences in managers' traits and behavior, women's biases against a managerial career), situation-centered (e.g., biases in the recruitment, selection, and treatment of women managers), and social-system-centered (e.g., sex stereotyping) explanations for the bad news. Applying the terms of his chapter title, Dipboye addressed the problems but not the progress of women in management.

Morrison and Von Glinow (1990) also found both good and bad news about the status of women in management. The good news, contained in one sentence and not discussed thereafter, was that "the number of women, Blacks, and Hispanics in management has quadrupled since 1970, and the number of Asians has increased eightfold" (p. 200). The remainder of the review focused on the bad news regarding the low rate of upward movement of women and minority managers within the managerial ranks. Morrison and Von Glinow (1990) suggested that White women and people of color encounter a *glass ceiling*, defined as "a barrier so subtle that it is transparent, yet so strong that it prevents women and minorities from moving up in the management hierarchy" (p. 200). Person-centered (e.g., sex- and race-related differences in traits, skills, and behaviors), situation-centered (e.g., women's and minorities' lack of opportunity for mentoring, inclusion in informal networks, and other developmental experiences), social-system-centered (e.g., structural discrimination, biases held by the dominant group), and interactional (e.g., interactions between opportunities for developmental experiences, internal self-evaluations, and subsequent self-limiting behavior) explanations for the existence of the glass ceiling were discussed. However, similar to Dipboye (1987), as well as to other reviews not discussed here (e.g., Burke & McKeen, 1992), Morrison and Von Glinow made little attempt to explain the recent increase in the proportion of women in management positions.

Turning to the most recent statistics available, the proportion of women in the American labor force was 46% in 1998, representing a 1% increase since 1990 (U.S. Department of Labor, 1998b). The proportion of women in management positions was 44% in 1998, representing a 5% increase since 1990. The proportion of female corporate officers in *Fortune* 500 corporations was 8.7% in 1995, 10.0% in 1996, 10.6% in 1997, and 11.2% in 1998 (Catalyst, 1998a); these statistics compare favorably with earlier statistics regarding the same proportion in 1986 (1.7%; Morrison et al., 1987) and 1990 (2.6%; Morrison et al., 1992). However, the statistics reported by Catalyst (1998a) and Morrison et al. (1987, 1992) were compiled by somewhat different methods. Also, definitions of *corporate officer* vary from company to company and may have expanded over time to include positions at lower levels where there tend to be more women. Supporting the latter notion, the proportion of women in "clout" officer positions that wield the most power and influence (chief executive officer, chairman, vice chairman, president, chief operating officer, senior executive vice president, and executive vice president) in *Fortune* 500 corporations was only 3.8% in 1998;

looking solely at the five highest titles of CEO, chairman, vice chairman, president, and COO, women represented less than 1% of office holders (Catalyst, 1998a).

We can see that the proportions of women in the American labor force, in management overall, and in top management have increased in recent years. Also, the gap between the proportions of women in the labor force and in management overall has virtually disappeared. However, the gap between the proportions of women in management overall and in top management remains large. In fact, the proportion of women in management overall in 1970 (16%; U.S. Department of Labor, 1983) was higher than the most recent estimate of the proportion of women in top management (11.2%; Catalyst, 1998a).

Similar trends have been exhibited in other countries. For example, as reported in the introduction in this book, the proportion of women in the labor force increased between 1985 and 1995 in a wide variety of countries around the globe (International Labour Office, 1986, 1996). Also, the proportion of women in management positions increased between 1985 and 1991 in 39 of 41 countries (International Labour Office, 1993). The proportion of women in management varies widely between countries due to differences in national culture and definitions of *manager*. However, within all countries, the proportion of women decreases at progressively higher levels in the managerial ranks (Burke & McKeen, 1992; Parker & Fagenson, 1994). Although the proportion of women in top management, however top management is defined, has increased over time within individual countries (Albertsen & Christensen, 1993; Hammond & Holton, 1994), this proportion is still typically reported as less than 5% (e.g., 1%-2% in Australia and the United Kingdom, Davidson & Cooper, 1992; 2%-4% in Denmark, Albertsen & Christensen, 1993; 3% in Italy, Olivares, 1993; 2% in Belgium, Woodward, 1993; 3% in Sweden, Wahl, 1995).

Thus, this chapter addresses the following questions:

1. Why has the proportion of women in management overall increased in recent years?

2. Why has the proportion of women in top management remained relatively small?

3. What forces will influence the proportion of women in management overall?

4. What forces will influence the proportion of women in top management?

The challenge for the next generation of reviews of the status of women in management is to explain both the good and bad news in recent trends as well as to offer predictions regarding the forces that will influence future trends. This chapter attempts to respond to this challenge.

Explaining Recent Trends

Why Has the Proportion of Women in Management Overall Increased in Recent Years?

Human capital theory (Becker, 1971) suggests that the quality of the labor supply is influenced by investments in human capital; resources that are invested in individuals today are likely to enhance their future productivity and career prospects. Higher education is an investment that enhances individuals' credentials by increasing their skills and knowledge, ranging from specific skills applicable only to certain jobs to general skills applicable to a wide variety of jobs (e.g., writing skills, reasoning ability, math proficiency). Educational institutions also teach behaviors that are valued in the workplace, such as punctuality, dependability, and the ability to follow instructions (Blau et al., 1998). Women have taken significant steps to increase their human capital through higher education in recent years. Between 1970 and 1995, the proportion of women earning college degrees in all disciplines in the United States increased from 43% to 55% at the bachelor's level and from 40% to 55% at the master's level. Moreover, during the same 25-year period, the proportion of women earning college degrees in business administration increased from 9% to 48% at the bachelor's level and from 4% to 37% at the master's level (U.S. Department of Education, 1997b). Increases in the proportion of women receiving college degrees at all levels in all disciplines and in business also have been exhibited in many other countries (United Nations Educational, Scientific, and Cultural Organization, 1998). These statistical trends depict a major societal shift toward the enhancement of women's academic credentials as well as an increased commitment of women to managerial and professional careers.

The size of the supply of available labor also influences women's employment in management. For example, the fertility rate of American women decreased by about half from 1957 (3.7 births/woman) to 1975 (1.8 births/woman) and remained at about the same level through 1990 (Schwartz, 1992a). Let's assume that the average entry-level manager is age 30. In 1987, 30-year-old managers were born in 1957, when the fertility rate was at its postwar peak. In 1997, 30-year-old managers were born in 1967, when the fertility rate was 2.6 births/woman. In 2005, 30-year-old managers will have been born in 1975, when the fertility rate fell to its low point. A reduced fertility rate contributes to a shortage of entrants to the workforce, including candidates for entry-level managerial positions. When there are fewer candidates for such positions, there are more opportunities for women (Schwartz, 1992a).

In addition, the gender composition of the labor supply, determined by women's and men's relative interest in belonging to the labor force, has influenced the status of women in management. As noted in the Introduction, the labor force participation rate, or the proportion of adult Americans who are engaged in or seeking paid employment, has declined somewhat in recent years for men (from 80% in 1970 to 74% in 1998) while it has substantially increased for women (from 43% in 1970 to 60% in 1998; U.S. Department of Labor, 1998a, 1998b). Increased labor force participation has been exhibited by women of all ages and mothers of children of all ages; for example, over half of mothers with children under 2 years old are now in the American labor force (U.S. Department of Labor, 1991b). Thus, the increased employment of women in traditionally male-dominated occupations such as management may be attributable to the reduced proportion of men in the labor force as well as to the increased proportion of women.

These changes in the labor supply, in quality, quantity, and gender composition, would not have occurred without changes in societal norms regarding women's roles in the home and the workplace. It has increasingly become the norm in most societies for women to be employed outside the home and to have more freedom to choose their own career interests. They are more likely to remain in the labor force after marriage and childbirth, and their roles are less likely to be defined solely as mother or wife; women's roles increasingly include manager, subordinate, and coworker. Increased control over reproduction has given couples more choice in when to start a family and women more freedom to plan their careers (Kelley & Streeter, 1992). Lower fertility rates suggest that women are experiencing less societal pressure to bear large numbers of children, which grants them freedom to pursue their careers with less interruption (Schwartz, 1992a). Also, an increase in single-parent households headed by women, fueled in part by high divorce rates, has meant that many women provide the sole economic support for their families; these women are likely to be drawn to higher-paying careers such as management.

An increased demand for labor also affects the status of women in management. When an economy is expanding, the increased demand for labor leads to an increased proportion of women in the labor force (Adler & Izraeli, 1988). In a growing economy, the rising demand for managers leads to a shortage of equally qualified men and thereby boosts the proportion of women in lower-level managerial jobs. In such cases, the women hired do not replace male managers as much as they fill newly created jobs.

Other economic developments such as the global shift from a manufacturing-based to an information- and service-based economy benefit women's employment in management positions. In an economy that increasingly values "brain power" over "muscle power," highly educated workers are increasingly in demand over less educated workers (Schwartz, 1992a). This advantage dovetails with women's increasing levels of educational attainment.

Societal policies as exhibited in laws promoting equal employment opportunity (EEO) and executive orders requiring affirmative action (AA) programs have contributed to substantial gains by women and people of color in the workplace in many countries (Hodges-Aeberhard & Raskin, 1997a; Lim, 1996). In Chapter 22, Konrad and Linnehan document improvements attributable to AA in women's access to education and employment in both the public and private sectors of the American economy. AA has also led to the development of formalized human resource management (HRM) structures that in turn have enhanced the status of women and people of color in management. Overall, EEO laws, AA programs, and resulting HRM practices have contributed to the enhancement of opportunities for women to enter the managerial ranks.

Organizational programs that influence the status of women in management may be initiated for reasons other than compliance with laws and executive orders. For example, organizations may seek to do a better job of anticipating and serving the needs of an increasingly diverse base of customers and coordinating the efforts of diverse employees. Many companies (e.g., Xerox, Gannett News Media, Merck, Grand Metropolitan) have thrived because of their clear and consistent commitment to valuing employee diversity in all jobs and at all levels (Powell, 1998c). Organizations may also seek to gain a competitive advantage by providing a work environment that attracts, retains, and takes advantage of the most talented women available in the labor market. To obtain such an advantage, an increasing number of successful companies (e.g., DuPont, GTE, Johnson & Johnson, Price Waterhouse, Motorola) have implemented work-family programs that help lowerlevel managers and other employees to meet their family-related needs while maintaining high levels of performance (Lewis & Lewis, 1996; Parasuraman & Greenhaus, 1997). In Chapter 23, Lobel offers many examples of corporate work-family initiatives and diversity initiatives and describes their impact on the attraction, retention, and performance of employees and the achievement of organizational objectives as well as the proportion of women in management.

Characteristics and practices of organizations other than AA programs, HRM practices, and work-family and diversity initiatives affect the proportion of women in management positions. Blum, Fields, and Goodman (1994) found that the proportion of women in management positions at all organizational levels was positively related to the proportion of women in nonmanagement positions, proportion of non-Whites in management positions, number of annual management vacancies, proportion of employees in professional and skilled positions, industry type (nonmanufacturing rather than manufacturing), and emphasis on training, development, and promotion from within the organization, and negatively related to the average management salary. Blum et al. (1994) concluded that the organizational context such as the existing social structure, HRM and compensation policies, and industry type may facilitate as well as restrict women's access to management positions.

Finally, the presence of women at higher managerial levels influences the entry, retention, and perceptions of women at lower managerial levels. In an analysis of hiring and promotion decisions, Cohen, Broschak, and Haveman (1998) found that women are more likely to be hired and promoted into a given managerial level when there is a substantial minority of women above that level, but not when women constitute the majority of managers in higher-level positions. Using an organizational-level analysis, Goodman, Fields, and Blum (1995) found that an organization's proportion of women in top management was positively related to its proportion of women in managerial jobs at all levels. Furthermore, in a study of law firms, Ely (1994, 1995) found that when the proportion of women partners (i.e., women at senior levels) is higher, women associates (i.e., women at junior levels) identify more with senior-level women, regard them as better role models, view their authority as more legitimate, perceive fewer psychological and behavioral differences between women and men at work, and evaluate women's attributes more favorably in relation to the firm's requirements for success.

The proportion of women in top management influences the proportion of women at lower managerial levels indirectly as well as directly. Foley (1998) found that female associates in law firms with a smaller proportion of women and minority partners were more likely to perceive the existence of a glass ceiling that would prevent them from attaining partner status themselves, which in turn led to greater intentions to quit the firm. Other studies have found that a smaller proportion of women at upper levels results in greater intentions to quit (Burke & McKeen, 1996) and actual turnover (Cohen & Elvira, 1997) for women at lower levels. These results suggest that a smaller proportion of women in top management may indirectly lead to a smaller proportion of women in lower-level managerial positions through its effect on women's voluntary departures from organizations.

In summary, social-system-centered, situation-centered, and person-centered explanations have been offered to account for the increased proportion of women in management in recent years. Social-system-centered explanations include a decreased supply of candidates for entry-level managerial jobs, an increased demand for managers due to a growing global economy, a global shift to an economy based less on manufacturing and more on information and services, a change in societal norms regarding women's roles, and societal policies that promote EEO. Situation-centered explanations include AA programs, work-family programs, organizational programs that promote and take advantage of diversity, and other organizational characteristics and practices. Person-centered explanations include women's increased educational attainment in all disciplines in general and in business in particular, which has accompanied as well as contributed to women's increased commitment to managerial and professional careers, and changes in the labor force participation rates of men (lower) and women (higher). In addition, within individual organizations, the presence of women in higher managerial levels may have both direct and indirect effects on the proportion of women in lower managerial levels.

Why Has the Proportion of Women in Top Management Remained Relatively Small?

The forces driving the increase in the proportion of women in management overall have had less effect on the proportion of women in top management. The higher the position within the managerial ranks, the less the importance of "objective" credentials that women may acquire, such as education (Antal & Krebsbach-Gnath, 1988). As a result, women's increased educational attainment, which represents a change in the quality of the labor supply, has had a greater effect on hiring and promotion into entry-level management positions than into those at the top. Discriminatory selection practices are more easily prevented and addressed when there is a greater reliance on objective credentials in selection; thus, the effects of EEO laws and AA programs are seen more in women's access to entry-level management positions than top management positions. Also, increases in the demand for labor due to a growing economy have relatively little effect on the proportion of women in top management because of the limited number of executive positions in any organization and the abundance of interested and qualified male candidates (Adler & Izraeli, 1994).

Furthermore, a change in societal norms to afford women more opportunities in the workplace does not necessarily imply that they have more opportunities to hold high-level positions with the greatest authority. Throughout recorded history, a patriarchal social system in which the male has power and authority over the female has prevailed (Marshall, 1984; Powell, 1993). Women's presence in top management positions violates the societal norm of men's higher status and superiority to a greater extent than women's presence in lower-level management positions. This norm may be perpetuated by direct discrimination on the part of the dominant group of males against women who violate the norm by seeking high-level positions (Morrison & Von Glinow, 1990). It may also be reinforced in indirect ways, such as in stereotypes of effective managers, the cognitive processes of decision makers, and the roles played by women and men in task-oriented groups.

In most societies, management has traditionally been regarded as a masculine domain, that is, one associated with men (Hearn & Parkin, 1988; Marshall, 1984). Schein (1973, 1975) compared middle managers' beliefs about the characteristics associated with women in general, men in general, and successful middle managers. She found that both female and male managers believed that successful middle managers possessed an abundance of characteristics that were more associated with men in general than with women in general. Similarly, Powell and Butterfield (1979) found that female and male business students at both the MBA and undergraduate levels described a good manager in predominantly masculine terms. Replications of both studies with different types of samples and in different countries have yielded essentially the same results: Women and men continue to describe good managers as higher in stereotypically masculine traits than stereotypically feminine traits (Powell, 1993). Thus, women who aspire to management positions in most societies contend with common stereotypes of their being unfit for the role. These stereotypes disadvantage women at all levels of management. However, such stereotypes are most invoked when women are being considered for top-level management positions because women's presence at such levels most violates the norm of male superiority.

The cognitive processes of decision makers about top management positions also reinforce the norm of male superiority. Perry, Davis-Blake, and Kulik (1994) noted that individual decision makers develop a schema or mental model about the attributes of job holders that influences their hiring and promotion decisions. A schema may be either gender based, incorporating the gender of jobholders in some way, or gender neutral, ignoring the gender of jobholders. According to Perry et al., gender is most likely to be incorporated into decision makers' jobholder schemas when persons primarily of one gender occupy the job under consideration and/or the applicant pool. A gender-based schema favoring men is more likely to arise in large than in small firms, because large firms have more formal job ladders from which women may have already been systematically excluded, leading to greater gender segregation of jobs (Baron, Davis-Blake, & Bielby, 1986) and triggering of gender-based schemas. Large firms also have more job titles, thus providing greater opportunity for the formation of gender-based schemas, and such firms fill more jobs and evaluate more job candidates, thus providing greater opportunity for the use of gender-based schemas.

According to the similarity-attraction paradigm (Byrne & Neuman, 1992), people tend to make the most positive evaluations of and decisions about people whom they see as similar to themselves. Kanter (1977a) characterized the results of such a preference in management ranks as homosocial reproduction. She argued that the primary motivation in bureaucracies in all decisions is to minimize uncertainty. Uncertainty is present whenever individuals are relied on, and the effects of such uncertainty are greatest when these individuals hold significant responsibility for the direction of the organization. One way to minimize uncertainty in the executive suite is to close top management positions to people who are regarded as "different." Thus, women have a difficult time in entering top management positions because they are seen as different by male incumbents (Kanter, 1977a).

Gender-based schemas and preferences for similar jobholders as a way to minimize uncertainty are cognitive processes that decision makers may use when filling any type of job. However, these processes are especially likely to be used when top management jobs are filled because the gender composition of the executive ranks most determines whether a societal norm of male superiority is upheld in the workplace. Cohen et al. (1998) found that women are more likely to be hired and promoted into a particular management level when women are already there. In turn, when women already hold some of the top management jobs in an organization, a gender-based schema favoring men is less likely to be used when top management jobs are filled (Perry et al., 1994) and the prospect of adding women to top management is less fraught with uncertainty (Kanter, 1977a). As Cohen et al. noted, the challenge then becomes getting women into top management jobs in the first place.

Men's higher status in society also influences the behavior of women and men in task-oriented groups in ways that are self-fulfilling. As Carli and Eagly suggest in Chapter 11 in this book, higher-status individuals are assumed by others to be more competent at tasks unless there is evidence to the contrary. As a result, men are assumed to be more competent than women in many work domains. This assumption affects the group behaviors that women and men exhibit, people's reactions to these behaviors, and the possibilities of exerting influence and emerging as the group leader. When women's task contributions are seen as less legitimate than those of men, women tend to participate less in mixed-sex groups and specialize less in strictly task-oriented behaviors, decreasing the likelihood that they will be viewed as future leaders of the organization and given the opportunity to move up management hierarchies.

The entry of women into top management is also influenced by the structure of the decision-making process and the accountability of the decision makers. Most organizations do not have a systematic procedure for making promotions to top management positions, handling each case on an ad hoc basis, and records of the promotional process are seldom kept. As a result, decisions about top management positions are relatively unstructured and unscrutinized, allowing decision makers' biases to influence decisions. In contrast, decisions for lower-level management positions that are based on more objective credentials may be scrutinized more readily, rendering decision makers more accountable.

Powell and Butterfield (1994) found that women's access to top management positions may be influenced by such practices. In their study of a cabinet-level department of the U.S. federal government, the sex of applicants for open top management positions that were not political appointments ("senior executive service" positions) influenced promotion decisions to the advantage of women. Powell and Butterfield (1994) suggested that women's advantage in such decisions may have been due to the federal government's special promotion procedures in addition to its strong commitment to EEO. First, all open senior executive service positions are made known through a public announcement. Second, all promotion decisions are made using the same basic procedure. Third, records must be kept of the entire decision-making process for at least two years. These practices provide structure to the decision-making process and enable identification of improperly made decisions, thereby making decision makers accountable for how promotion decisions are made. However, such practices are rare, especially in the private sector.

The proportion of women in top management is further influenced by the developmental experiences of lower-level managers. If lower-level female managers are not groomed for top management positions as often or as well as lower-level male managers, they will be at a disadvantage when competing for scarce top management positions. Ohlott, Ruderman, and McCauley (1994) found that male managers experienced greater task-related developmental challenges in their jobs, whereas female managers with equivalent backgrounds and jobs experienced greater developmental challenges stemming from obstacles encountered. Men had to learn how to handle a variety of types of responsibilities under fire; their jobs were higher in the need to handle high stakes (e.g., clear deadlines, pressure from senior management, high visibility, responsibility for key decisions), manage business diversity (e.g., handle multiple functions, groups, products, customers, or markets), and handle external pressure (e.g., work in a foreign culture, negotiate with unions or government agencies, cope with serious community problems). In contrast, women had to learn how to function on their own with little support due to their being excluded from key networks and receiving little encouragement from others. According to female executives, the developmental challenges faced more by male managers in Ohlott et al.'s study are ones that contribute to women's career advancement (Mainiero, 1994; Ragins, Townsend, & Mattis, 1998), whereas those faced more by female managers are ones that hinder women's career advancement (Morrison et al., 1987).

Another key developmental experience is having a mentor. As Ragins describes in Chapter 18, mentors significantly contribute to their protégés' career success and satisfaction. In addition, mentors buffer women from both overt and covert discrimination and help them to overcome obstacles to their attaining top management positions. However, male potential mentors are in greater abundance than female potential mentors. Male mentors may be reluctant to select female protégés because of concerns about possible sexual innuendoes and rumors or, as the similarity-attraction paradigm suggests (Byrne & Neuman, 1992), because they prefer to mentor people like themselves. If lower-level female managers have difficulty in obtaining mentors or have problematic mentoring relationships, they experience less career-enhancing benefits of being mentored and success in eventually attaining top management positions.

However, climbing to the top of management hierarchies is not necessarily good in itself, and not everyone wants to make such climbs. The typical executive job has enormous responsibilities, time demands, and pressures. It also calls for considerable sacrifices in personal life. According to prior theories of career development (Powell & Mainiero, 1992), such jobs hold greater interest for men than for women.

Powell and Mainiero (1992) differentiated between the "traditional" model of career success, based primarily on observations of men, and what may be called a "nontraditional" model of career success based primarily on observations of women. The traditional model emphasizes objective measures of career success such as salary, title, and number of levels from the top of the management hierarchy, whereas the nontraditional model places greater emphasis on subjective measures of career success such as satisfaction with the current job and prospects for future satisfaction. Also, the traditional model focuses primarily on work life, whereas the nontraditional model includes greater consideration of non-work as well as work life. Thus, people who follow the nontraditional model of career success attempt to strike a balance between their relationships with others and their personal achievements at work and seek some level of personal or subjective satisfaction in both realms (Powell & Mainiero, 1992). However, top management jobs do not encourage this kind of balancing act and tend to attract individuals who adhere to the traditional model of career success. If lower-level male managers adhere to the traditional model more than lower-level female managers, they will also be more interested in attaining top management positions.

Of course, not all women adhere to the nontraditional model of career success, nor do all men adhere to the traditional model. However, some women who might be interested in attaining top management jobs find that family responsibilities keep them from seriously entertaining the idea. Although the commonly held perception that successful career women have to forgo marriage and children to focus on work achievement is a myth (Catalyst, 1996), it is a fact that fewer female than male executives are married or have children (Korn/Ferry International, 1993). Lobel describes corporate work-family initiatives that make it easier for female lower-level managers to handle their family concerns and that serve to maintain their interest in eventually attaining top management jobs.

There are women interested in attaining top management jobs who find that a glass ceiling stops them. Such women experience frustration and consider other options. Stroh, Brett, and Reilly (1996) found that female managers who are frustrated at their lack of career opportunities are more likely to quit their organizations than male managers with a similar level of frustration. In other words, women managers have a lower tolerance for lack of career opportunities than men managers.

Where do these women go when they quit their organizations? Increasingly, into business for themselves. In Chapter 19, Moore reports that women have been starting businesses at a faster rate than men in recent years in many countries. There are five reasons female entrepreneurs tend to give for leaving their prior organizations to go into business for themselves: challenge (e.g., opportunity to be in charge), self-determination (e.g., to try to make it on one's own, freedom from bureaucracy), family concerns (e.g., balancing work and family, gaining control of time), blocks to advancement (e.g., discrimination, career barriers), and organizational dynamics (e.g., a demotivating organizational culture) (Moore & Buttner, 1997). Women who leave the corporate world to run their own businesses do not show up in published statistics about the proportion of women in top management, because such statistics typically focus on large publicly held firms such as *Fortune* 500 corporations (e.g., Catalyst, 1998a; Morrison et al., 1987, 1992). However, such women in effect become the top management of their own firms.

In summary, social-system-centered, situation-centered, and person-centered explanations have been offered to account for the relatively small proportion of women in top management, at least in the large firms for which such statistics are compiled. Social-system-centered explanations include patriarchal social systems, direct discrimination by the dominant group, and stereotypes of effective managers. Situation-centered explanations include decision makers' preferences to work with people like themselves and use of a gender-based schema when making hiring and promotion decisions for top management positions, organizational practices in making such decisions, and sex differences favoring men in developmental experiences at lower managerial levels such as challenging assignments, personal support, and access to mentoring. The social-system-centered and situation-centered explanations account for the glass ceiling as a barrier to the upward mobility of women in management hierarchies. In addition, person-centered explanations include sex differences in task-oriented behavior, influence, and emergent leadership in groups; interests in jobs at top management levels; the effect of family responsibilities and corporate work-family initiatives; and inclinations to quit organizations and the corporate world when faced with a lack of career opportunities.

Future Prospects

It is difficult to predict what the future holds for the glass ceiling and the status of women in management. The proportions of women in management overall and in top management are determined by definitions of *management* and *top management* in the compilation of statistics in particular countries. However, in many countries, these proportions are subject to a common set of interrelated forces. Based on this review, we may predict the forces that will influence the future status of women in management, both overall and in the executive ranks, with greater confidence.

*What Forces Will Influence the Proportion
of Women in Management Overall?*

The proportion of women in management overall is likely to be influenced by the following:

1. *Societal norms regarding women's roles.* Changes in societal norms have resulted in lessened expectations for women to devote their lives to bearing and raising children and more opportunities for women to participate in paid employment. As a result, women are freer to follow their career interests and pursue their careers with less fear of unwanted interruption. Increased societal recognition and reinforcement of the importance of women's role in the global economy will be likely to contribute to an increased proportion of women in higher-paying occupations such as management.

2. *Educational attainment.* Any change in the proportion of women earning college degrees, especially master's degrees in business, will be likely to affect the proportion of women in management.

3. *Size of the labor supply.* When the supply of individuals interested in managerial jobs is lessened, the proportion of women in such jobs is likely to increase. Thus, demographic trends that influence the size of the labor supply will in turn be likely to affect the proportion of women in management.

4. *Labor force participation rates of women relative to men.* When the proportion of women interested in paid employment increases relative to that of men, the proportion of women in fields such as management is likely to increase. The current trends in labor force participation rates for women (upward) and men (downward) are likely to contribute to increases in the proportion of women in management. However, a reversal of these trends would contribute to a reduction in the proportion of women in management.

5. *Demand for labor.* A growing economy will increase the demand for managers and in turn the opportunities for women to assume managerial positions. On the other hand, a shrinking economy will be likely to decrease the opportunities for women to retain managerial positions because female managers tend to have less seniority and status in their organizations than male managers.

6. *Structure of the economy.* A shift toward a global economy based less on the manufacture of products and more on the provision of information and services has contributed to an increase in the proportion of women in management. Trends in this direction will be likely to contribute to an increase in this proportion.

7. *Enactment, enforcement, and compliance with societal policies and legislation promoting equal employment opportunity and affirmative action.* EEO laws and AA programs have contributed to an increase in the proportion of women in management. Such laws and programs will be likely to increase or maintain the proportion of women in management in the future, as long as they are enforced by national and local governments and adhered to by organizations.

8. *Organizational attitudes toward cultural diversity and corporate diversity initiatives.* Cox (1991) distinguished between three types of organizations—monolithic, pluralistic (or plural), and multicultural—according to their attitudes toward diversity. Monolithic organizations have a large majority of one demographic group (typically White males), especially in top management positions. Women and minority group employees are expected to conform to the norms and values of the majority group. Pluralistic organizations have taken more steps to hire and promote women and minorities, but they still expect women and minorities to conform to majority group norms and values. A pluralistic organization is made up of many diverse groups of employees. Multicultural organizations value this diversity. They encourage the members of diverse groups to adopt some of the norms and values of the other groups. Organizations that adopt a multicultural approach to diversity and reinforce it with specific initiatives will be more likely to attract and retain female managers at all levels and thereby increase their proportion of women in management.

9. *Organizational work-family initiatives.* Organizations that implement work-family initiatives, such as flexible scheduling and assistance with child and elder care, become more attractive to women managers. Such programs help all employees meet their family needs without sacrificing work performance. Because wives usually bear greater family responsibilities within dual-earner households than their husbands, corporate work-family programs are particularly beneficial for women. Thus, an increase in organizational efforts to be family-friendly will be likely to lead to an increased proportion of women in management. However, some organizations are more abusive than family-friendly in their work practices, display a callous disregard for their employees' needs, and promote work-family programs solely for the public relations value (Powell, 1998a). Work-family initiatives in such organizations will have little actual impact on the proportion of women in management.

10. *Proportion of women in top management in the future.* Within a given organization, this proportion signals to lower-level female managers their prospects for career advancement, which may influence their decisions to remain with the organization. Thus, an increase (or decrease) in a firm's

proportion of women in top management will be likely to lead to an increase (or decrease) in the proportion of women in the firm's lower managerial levels.

What Forces Will Influence the Proportion of Women in Top Management?

The proportion of women in top management is likely to be influenced by the following:

1. *Societal norms regarding women's status.* A norm of male superiority resulting from patriarchal social systems is supported in practice when organizations are dominated by men at the top management levels. Any change in societal norms that grants women increased status relative to that of men will be likely to increase the proportion of women in top management.

2. *Masculine stereotypes of effective managers.* Stereotypes reinforce the norm of male superiority in the workplace because the preferred traits for managers have been traditionally associated with men more than women. Any change in managerial stereotypes that emphasizes traditionally feminine traits will increase the perceived fitness of women for top management jobs, regardless of whether female candidates actually differ in masculine or feminine traits from male candidates. The increased visibility of high-profile, successful female executives (e.g., Sellers, 1998) will counter these stereotypes.

3. *Use of gender-based schemas by decision makers.* Gender-based schemas favoring men are likely to be used by decision makers in filling top management jobs when most job incumbents or applicants are male. Any increase in the proportion of female candidates for such jobs will lead to more gender-neutral decisions. Such an increase will come about if the proportion of women in lower-level management positions, the most likely source of applicants for top management jobs, is greater. Thus, the proportion of women in top management will be likely both to influence and be influenced by the proportion of women at lower managerial levels.

4. *Uncertainties associated with having women in top management positions.* Women in top management positions pose the most uncertainty when there are no women in top management positions at present. Once women enter the top management levels in a given organization and become less of an uncertainty, the proportion of women in top management will be likely to rise further.

5. Task-oriented behavior, influence, and emergent leadership in groups. Any positive change in perceptions of women's competence to contribute to the accomplishment of tasks and serve as leaders of task-oriented groups will encourage them to exhibit more of the kinds of task-oriented behavior that are valued. In turn, such a change will be likely to influence perceptions of women's potential for top management positions and eventually the proportion of women in top management.

6. The decision-making process. A structured hiring and promotion process for top management positions that holds decision makers accountable reduces the likelihood of decisions' being based on personal biases. Organizational hiring and promotion processes modeled on those used by the U.S. government (Powell & Butterfield, 1994) will be likely to increase the proportion of women in top management.

7. Organizational attitudes toward cultural diversity and corporate diversity initiatives. Organizations that adopt a multicultural, rather than monolithic or pluralistic, approach to diversity (Cox, 1991) with specific initiatives will be more likely to attract and retain female executives and thereby increase their proportion of women in top management.

8. Developmental experiences of lower-level managers. Lower-level managers' experiences in their jobs, including opportunities for learning how to handle multiple and complex demands under pressure, personal support, obstacles faced, and mentoring, influence the extent to which they are prepared to assume top management responsibilities. Reduction in the favoring of men in developmental experiences will lessen the disadvantage of women in competing for top management positions and thereby will be likely to increase the proportion of women in top management.

9. Interest in holding a top management job. Top management jobs, especially those in large organizations, are generally unappealing to people who are interested in balancing their work and nonwork interests, despite the enhanced compensation and status. Any change in life interests such that either men become more interested or women become less interested in striking such a balance will be likely to contribute to an increase in the proportion of women in top management. Family supports provided by organizations, such as flexible scheduling and child and elder care assistance, that make it easier for women with family responsibilities to hold managerial positions will increase the proportion of women interested in holding top management positions.

10. *Inclinations to quit the corporate world when faced with limited career opportunities.* Some women quit their organizations and go into business for themselves when they perceive a lack of career opportunities due to a glass ceiling. Although women who leave organizations to go into business become the top management of their own firms, they take themselves out of the running for top management positions with their former employers and increase the likelihood that such positions will be filled by men. Thus, any reduction in women's inclinations to quit the corporate world when frustrated may increase the proportion of women in top management in the large publicly owned organizations for which such statistics are typically compiled.

Directions for Future Research

This chapter has suggested many different forces that may explain the existence of a glass ceiling in work settings and the relative status of women and men in the managerial ranks of organizations. However, there is not a well-defined body of glass ceiling research that has systematically examined the influence of such forces on the status of women in management. Some of the explanations for the status of women in management have been the subject of a considerable amount of research; for example, an entire chapter in this book by Ragins (Chapter 18) is devoted to mentoring relationships. Other explanations have not been researched sufficiently; for example, there has been little research of any type, not only gender related, on how promotion decisions are actually made for top management positions (Powell & Butterfield, 1994). Although this chapter offers a variety of explanations for the status of women in management, both overall and in the executive ranks, additional research is recommended in many of these areas.

Certain types of research would be most welcome. Most of the explanations that have been offered in this chapter have been stated as main effects, for example, the effect of societal norms regarding women's roles and status, organizational diversity and work-family initiatives, managers' developmental experiences at lower levels, and individuals' interest in holding top management positions. It is likely that many of these forces operate in tandem and interact with each other to influence the status of women in management. However, with few exceptions (e.g., Fagenson, 1990; Stroh et al., 1996), there is little research that may be considered interactional (Chatman, 1989). Interactional research is needed to examine the combined influence of various forces on the status of women in management.

In addition, virtually no cross-cultural research has been conducted on the forces that influence the status of women in management. Many reviews have examined the status of women in management in particular countries (e.g., individual chapters in Adler & Izraeli, 1988, 1994, and in Davidson & Cooper, 1993a). These reviews suggest that with some variation due to specific societal norms and laws, similar forces affect the status of women in management in many different countries. Little research has tested whether this is actually the case.

Finally, gender effects should not be considered in isolation from the effects of the wide range of personal characteristics that may influence people's sense of identity. In Chapter 2, Ferdman suggests that gender effects in the workplace may vary for individuals from different races, ethnic groups, and cultures; also, these variables may affect men and women differently. Thus, future research should simultaneously examine how sex and other personal characteristics influence the presence of women at all managerial levels.

Conclusions

An intricate web of forces has influenced the proportions of women in management overall and in top management. These interrelated forces seem likely to influence the status of women in management in the future as well. We must, however, be cautious in our predictions. The forces that will shape the future cannot be predicted with certainty. Also, individual women (and men) managers must decide how important moving up management hierarchies is in their own lives.

We have reason to be concerned whenever women who attempt to move up management hierarchies are unsuccessful because of external barriers exclusive only to them. Even though further glass ceiling research is needed, there can be no doubt that such barriers create a glass ceiling that restricts women's career advancement and satisfaction, especially in large organizations. Women deserve fair access to managerial positions at all levels. Without fair access, women will continue to see their reflections in the glass ceiling as they gaze up the management hierarchy.

Note

1. Many different schemes have been used to categorize explanations for gender-related phenomena in the workplace (e.g., Fagenson, 1990; Kanter, 1977a; Ragins & Sundstrom, 1989). This chapter adopts four categories of explanations: (1) person-centered; (2) situation-centered, originally suggested by Riger and Galligan (1980); (3) social-system-centered, suggested by Ragins and Sundstrom (1989); and (4) interactional, suggested for organizational research by Chatman (1989). These categories are defined as follows: *Person-centered explanations* focus on individual phenomena such as traits, skills, attitudes, and behaviors; *situation-centered explanations* focus on group and organizational phenomena such as group norms and organizational culture, policies, and programs; *social-system-centered explanations* focus on economic and societal phenomena such as trends in the global economy, societal norms and socialization practices, and legislation; and *interactional explanations* focus on interactions between the other three types of phenomena.

Chapter 18

Gender and Mentoring Relationships

A Review and Research Agenda for the Next Decade

Belle Rose Ragins

Research on mentoring relationships has evolved only over the past decade. The findings, however, are quite clear: Mentoring relationships are critical resources for employees in organizations. Protégés receive more promotions (Dreher & Ash, 1990), greater compensation (Chao, 1997; Dreher & Ash, 1990), and more career mobility (Scandura, 1992) than nonprotégés. Mentoring is related to greater career satisfaction (Fagenson, 1989), career commitment (Bachman & Gregory, 1993; Colarelli & Bishop, 1990), career planning (Chao, 1997), organizational socialization (Chao, 1997; Ostroff & Kozlowski, 1993), self-esteem at work (Koberg, Boss, & Goodman, 1998), job satisfaction (Bahniuk, Dobos, & Hill, 1990; Chao, 1997), job involvement (Koberg et al., 1998), and lower turnover intentions (Laband & Lentz, 1995; Viator & Scandura, 1991). Individuals with mentors receive more power in organizations (Fagenson, 1988) and advance at a faster rate than those without mentors (Dreher & Ash, 1990; Whitely, Dougherty, & Dreher, 1991). It is clear that individuals with mentoring relationships have a definite advantage over those lacking such relationships.

Mentorship theorists emphasize that although mentoring relationships are important for all organizational members, they are essential for women (Burke & McKeen, 1990; Noe, 1988b; Ragins, 1989, 1997a, 1997b). These researchers propose a number of gender-related benefits of mentoring relationships. A key benefit is that mentors can help women overcome barriers to advancement in organizations and break through the *glass ceiling,* an invisible barrier to advancement based on gender biases (Morrison, White, Van Velsor, & the Center for Creative Leadership, 1987). A recent study by Catalyst revealed that a full 91% of the female executives surveyed reported having a mentor, and the majority of respondents identified mentoring as a key strategy used to break through the glass ceiling (Ragins, Townsend, & Mattis, 1998).

According to theory, mentors can buffer women from both overt and covert forms of discrimination and help women navigate the obstacle course to the executive suite (Burke & McKeen, 1990; Ragins, 1989, 1997a, 1997b). By conferring legitimacy on their female protégés, mentors can alter stereotypic perceptions and send the message that the protégé has the mentor's powerful support and backing. Mentors provide "reflected power" (Kanter, 1977a) to their protégés, and they use their influence to build the protégé's base of power in the organization. Mentors train their female protégés in the "ins and outs" of corporate politics and provide valuable information on job openings and changes in the organization—information that is typically provided in the "old boy's network" (Ragins, 1989). These activities are particularly important, because women have been found to be less likely than men to receive personal support (Ohlott, Ruderman, & McCauley, 1994), job-related information, and developmental support from their supervisors (Cianni & Romberger, 1995). Finally, by building self-esteem and providing feedback, mentors help women develop the skills necessary to overcome the "male managerial model," which prescribes different behaviors for male and female managers (Schein, 1973).

Although existing theory suggests that mentoring relationships may be critical for women, research on gender and mentoring has evolved just over the past decade. What has this research told us about the effects of gender on mentoring relationships? What research questions need to be answered in the second decade of research on this topic? In this chapter, I attempt to answer these questions by providing a comprehensive review of the existing empirical research on gender and mentoring. I first define mentoring and then review the research findings on the effects of protégé gender, mentor gender, and the gender composition of the mentoring relationship on mentoring functions and outcomes. Important areas for future research are highlighted in the course of the review. I conclude with some caveats for conducting research on gender and mentorship and provide an agenda for the second decade of research on gender and mentoring.

Mentors are generally defined as individuals with advanced experience and knowledge who are committed to providing support and upward mobility to their protégés' careers (Hunt & Michael, 1983; Kram, 1985). According to Kram (1985), mentors provide two functions. First, they provide career development functions, which involve coaching, sponsoring advancement, protecting protégés from adverse forces, providing challenging assignments, and fostering positive visibility. Second, mentors provide psychosocial functions, which include personal support, friendship, acceptance, counseling, and role modeling. Mentors may provide some or all of these functions, which may vary not only from relationship to relationship but also over time in a given relationship. Research on mentorship behaviors reveals that the more functions the mentor provides, the greater the career and organizational benefits received by the protégé (Dreher & Ash, 1990; Orpen, 1995; Scandura, 1992).

Mentoring relationships may take a variety of forms, and three distinctions in particular are relevant when viewing the effects of gender on mentoring processes and outcomes. The first is that a mentor may or may not be a protégé's supervisor. Supervisory mentors have been found to provide functions different from mentors who are not protégés' supervisors (Burke & McKeen, 1997; Ragins & McFarlin, 1990). Women may be more likely than men to develop mentoring relationships with their supervisors because they have access to supervisory mentors but restricted access to higher-ranking mentors in other departments (Ragins, 1989; Ragins & Cotton, 1991). In spite of these issues, most mentoring studies have failed to distinguish between supervisory and nonsupervisory mentors.

The second distinction is that mentors may be "internal mentors," employed in the same organization as their protégé, or they may be "external mentors," employed outside the organization (Ragins, 1997b). Although there has been a lack of research on gender effects, research indicates that minority protégés may be more likely than their majority counterparts to seek external mentors (Thomas, 1990; Thomas & Higgins, 1996). Although it has been suggested that internal and external mentors have different access to resources and may therefore provide different functions for their protégés (Ragins, 1997b), few researchers have investigated or controlled for this type of relationship.

The final, and perhaps most important, distinction is that between formal and informal mentoring relationships. Informal mentoring relationships occur spontaneously and last between two and five years, whereas formal mentoring relationships last about one year and develop by the matching or assignment of protégés to mentors (Murray, 1991; Phillips-Jones, 1983). Only a few studies have compared formal and informal relationships, and these studies reveal that formal and informal mentoring relationships yield different mentoring functions and career outcomes (Chao, Walz, & Gardner, 1992; Fagenson-Eland, Marks, & Amendola, 1997; Ragins & Cotton, in press). Only one of these studies (Ragins & Cotton, in press) has focused on the effects of gender in formal and informal mentoring relationships.

Although most research to date has not distinguished between these types of mentoring relationships, research on gender and mentoring in the next decade should (1) examine the outcomes associated with these three types of mentoring relationships, (2) assess whether these relationships vary by gender, and (3) control for existing gender differences in these types of relationships when examining the effects of gender on outcomes of mentoring relationships.

A review of the effects of protégé gender, mentor gender, and the gender composition of the relationship on mentoring functions and outcomes is provided in the following sections.

Does Protégé Gender Affect Mentoring Relationships?

Most of the studies on gender and mentoring have been conducted from the protégé's perspective and have investigated whether protégé gender affects the presence of mentors, the reported functions of mentors, and the career outcomes associated with these relationships.

Presence of Mentors

Research on the relationship between protégé gender and the presence of a mentor has produced somewhat surprising results. Existing theory predicts that women encounter greater barriers to gaining mentors than men and would therefore be less likely to obtain mentors than men (Noe, 1988b; Ragins, 1989). Only partial support was obtained for this proposition. In a study of a matched sample of 510 male and female employees, Ragins and Cotton (1991) found that women reported greater barriers to getting mentors than men. Women were more likely than men to report that mentors were unwilling to mentor them, that supervisors and coworkers would disapprove of the relationship, that they had less access to mentors, and that they were hesitant to initiate the relationship for fear that their efforts would be misconstrued as being sexual by either the mentor or others in the organization. In spite of these reported barriers, women were as likely as men actually to have a mentor, suggesting that women overcame these barriers to develop these important relationships. In fact, most studies indicate that women are as likely as men to report having mentors (Corzine, Buntzman, & Busch, 1994; Dreher & Ash, 1990; Dreher & Cox, 1996; Fagenson, 1989; Ragins & Cotton, 1991; Scandura & Ragins, 1993; Swerdlik & Bardon, 1988) and to initiate mentoring relationships (Turban & Dougherty, 1994). As the exception, two studies found gender differences in the presence of mentors.

In a study of 224 professors, Hill, Bahniuk, and Dobos (1989) found that men were more likely than women to report that they had mentors and that they initiated the relationships. In contrast, in a study of employees in female-typed organizations, Bachman and Gregory (1993) found that women expressed greater motivation for getting mentors than men and were more likely to report having mentors, thereby suggesting that the gender typing of the organization may influence access to mentors. It is particularly perplexing that although barriers to obtaining mentors should be similar for women and people of color (e.g., Ragins, 1997a, 1997b; Thomas & Alderfer, 1989), research on the effects of race on the presence of mentors yields inconsistent results; some researchers found race differences in the presence of a mentor, whereas other researchers found no differences (for a complete review, see Ragins, 1995).

One question that arises when viewing the research on gender and reports of mentoring is whether these reports are influenced by social desirability or self-perceptions related to gender. Given sex-role stereotypes and prescriptions regarding nurturing (Eagly, 1987), men may feel less comfortable admitting the help of a mentor than women, and may therefore underreport these relationships. However, the reason may be more than just social desirability effects; at a deeper level, gender differences in sense of self may also affect reports of mentoring. According to self-construal theory (e.g., Cross & Madson, 1997), men maintain independent self-construals, whereas women maintain self-construals more interdependent in nature. Related theoretical perspectives hold that although a man's sense of self is based on defining himself as distinct and superior to others (e.g., Bakan, 1966; Gilligan, 1982; Jordan, Kaplan, Miller, Stiver, & Surrey, 1991), a woman's sense of self is based on developing interdependent relationships. These gender differences in sense of self may lead to gender differences in perceptions of work relationships and how these relationships are reported to others. Although it is difficult to disentangle some of these effects, one outcome may be that men underreport their mentoring relationships and the functions their mentors provide so that they can maintain the self-perception and social perception of career independence and status.

Asking mentors to identify their protégés does not provide an easy solution to this problem because gender may also affect reports of being a mentor. For example, male mentors may be more likely than female mentors to report mentoring relationships and to take credit for their protégés' accomplishments as a way of maintaining public status and superiority in relationships. Men may therefore overreport their experiences of being mentors and underreport their experiences of being protégés. Based on this theory, mentoring relationships may take different forms for female and male mentors; female mentors may seek mentoring relationships that are more interdependent and equal, whereas male mentors may seek more hierarchical relationships that provide greater public status and recognition to the mentor.

The gender composition of the relationship may also interact with reports of the presence of a mentor. Based on status differentials, men may be less likely to report having female than male mentors, and more likely to report having male protégés than female protégés. However, gender-role stereotypes may also have a countervailing effect that may lead to men overreporting mentoring women if they view their role in the relationship as "protector."

It is clear that research in the next decade should further examine these relationships. Future research should assess the impact of gender, self-construals, and reliance on gender-role stereotypes on the presence of mentors and reports of mentoring relationships.

Functions of Mentors

Even if gender does not affect the presence of a mentor, protégé gender may still affect the functions a mentor provides in the relationship. Before reviewing the results of these studies, it is important to highlight methodological and measurement issues that may contribute to the inconsistent findings in this area. As discussed previously, mentors may provide two sets of functions: career development and psychosocial (Kram, 1985). Currently, there are three established instruments that reliably assess these functions by asking protégés to report on the specific behaviors performed by their mentors (Noe, 1988a; Ragins & McFarlin, 1990; Scandura & Katerberg, 1988). Some studies on gender and mentoring functions use these measures, but far too many studies use newly developed measures, or even single-item measures that prevent reliability assessments. Given these psychometric limitations, the results of these studies must be interpreted with caution.

The research on the effects of protégé gender on mentoring functions yields mixed findings. In an early study, Noe (1988a) developed a 21-item mentor-roles instrument and used it to survey 74 female and 65 male educators enrolled in a formal mentoring program. After six months, female protégés reported receiving more psychosocial benefits from their mentors than male protégés. No gender differences were found for career development functions. In a study of 147 female and 173 male business school graduates, Dreher and Ash (1990) used 18 items selected from Noe's (1988a) and Whitely et al.'s (1991) instruments to measure career development and psychosocial functions. It is unfortunate that respondents were not asked to consider a specific mentor, but were asked to consider the degree to which influential *managers* served as their mentors over the course of their careers. The problem with this approach is that respondents were asked to report on the *specific* mentoring behaviors provided by *multiple* mentors, thus diluting the accuracy of the mentoring functions instrument and increasing the probability of central tendency biases in the ratings. In addition, separate analyses were not conducted for the psychosocial and career development functions. The men and women in the study reported experiencing the same frequency of mentoring activities from senior managers. The only gender difference that emerged was that women were more likely than men to report that their mentors conveyed empathy in the relationship. Using the same definition of mentoring and mentoring functions instrument, Turban and Dougherty (1994) surveyed 147 business school graduates and also found no gender differences in reports of mentoring functions. Koberg and her associates also used the same global definition of mentoring in their study of 635 hospital employees. The researchers first reported results using seven of the career development items from Noe's (1988a) instrument (Koberg, Boss, Chappell, & Ringer, 1994). In contrast to the studies reviewed previously, they found that men reported more career development functions than women, regardless of organizational rank. In another publication based on the same sample, the researchers presented results from the remaining 14 psychosocial items of Noe's (1988a) instrument and found no gender differences in reports of psychosocial functions (Koberg et al., 1998). It should be noted that these studies did not specify what proportion of the sample consisted of protégés; missing data were assumed to represent individuals who were not mentored by senior management.

Ragins and McFarlin (1990) used confirmatory factor analysis to develop a mentoring functions instrument, and then used the 33-item instrument to assess the impact of protégé gender, mentor gender, and gender composition of relationship on mentoring functions. The 181 male and female protégés in the sample were matched on rank, department, and specialization. In addition, five covariates that may have varied by gender were used in their analyses: number of previous mentoring relationships, the length of the current mentoring relationship, whether the mentor was the protégé's supervisor, and the protégé's age and rank. Reports of mentor functions did not vary by mentor gender or protégé gender, but gender composition did have a limited effect on the relationship, as discussed later in this chapter. The authors observed that the use of control variables are important when investigating gender differences, and to illustrate this point, they reran the analyses without control variables and found numerous gender main effects and interactions.

Ragins and Cotton (in press) used the Ragins and McFarlin (1990) mentor-roles instrument and controlled for occupation, position tenure, number of career interruptions, duration of prior mentoring relationships, and whether those relationships involved supervisory mentors in their national study of 614 protégés (352 female, 257 male, and 5 who did not report their gender). They found that although protégés with formal mentors reported fewer career development and psychosocial functions than protégés with informal mentors, this relationship was not equivalent for men and women. Although female protégés with formal mentors reported receiving less coaching, role modeling, and friendship and fewer social interactions than female protégés with informal mentors, these differences were not found for male protégés, who reported receiving equivalent functions from both formal and informal mentors. Moreover, male protégés actually reported receiving more counseling from formal than informal mentoring relationships. These findings suggest that formal mentors may be more beneficial for male than female protégés.

In an interview study of 27 male and 27 female faculty members, Stonewater, Eveslage, and Dingerson (1990) found that men and women differed when reporting the behaviors of their "career helpers." Although the study did not investigate the individual's current or prior mentor and was limited by the sample size, the researchers found that women reported receiving more personal and emotional support, whereas men reported receiving more work-related support from their mentors.

There is some evidence that gender-role orientation may be more important than gender in predicting the presence of a mentor and the functions of the relationship. In a study of 1,024 accounting professionals, Scandura and Ragins (1993) found that, although biological sex was unrelated to the presence of a mentor, both women and men with androgynous and masculine role orientations were more likely to have a mentor than individuals with feminine orientations. Moreover, gender-role orientation accounted for more of the variance in mentorship roles than biological sex; androgynous individuals reported more career development and psychosocial support from their mentors than individuals with either masculine or feminine role orientations.

In sum, research on the effects of protégé gender on mentoring functions has produced mixed results: Some studies found gender differences, and others found no differences. The inconsistency of these findings may be due to the instruments used, the definition of mentoring provided to the protégé, the type of mentor, and variations in the use of control variables. Perhaps the most important reason for these mixed results is that mentoring behaviors are not a function only of protégé gender, or mentor gender, but may be a function of the gender composition of the relationship. This point is discussed at length later in this chapter.

Outcomes of Mentoring Relationships

Most of the research indicates that male and female protégés receive equivalent benefits from mentoring relationships. In a survey of 246 health care employees, Fagenson (1989) found that protégé gender did not moderate the relationship between mentoring and career mobility, promotions, and job satisfaction. Similarly, in their study of 320 business school graduates, Dreher and Ash (1990) found that women were as likely as men to obtain outcomes associated with the relationship, such as promotions, compensation, and satisfaction with compensation. In a replication of these studies, Corzine et al. (1994) also found that the relationship between mentoring and job satisfaction and perceived likelihood of promotion was equivalent for male and female protégés. Other researchers have also concluded that male and female protégés receive equivalent organizational and career outcomes associated with having mentors (e.g., Baugh, Lankau, & Scandura, 1996; Johnson & Scandura, 1994; Mobley, Jaret, Marsh, & Lim, 1994). One exception is Bahniuk et al.'s (1990) study of 258 business professionals. They found that although having a mentor was associated with outcomes such as job satisfaction, positive self-perceptions, rank, and income, female protégés reported fewer of these outcomes than did male protégés and male nonprotégés. One limitation of this study was that the researchers did not control for gender differences in rank; rank has since been found to moderate the relationship between mentoring and job-related attitudes and outcomes (Gaskill & Sibley, 1990; Struthers, 1995). Because women generally hold lower ranks in organizations than men, and rank is related to mentoring outcomes, rank represents a potential confound in research on gender and mentoring outcomes.

Other Variables

A few studies have investigated the effects of protégé gender on other variables related to mentoring. Fagenson (1992) compared protégés and nonprotégés on the need for power, achievement, affiliation, and autonomy and found that men and women who became protégés had similar personality needs. Kalbfleisch (1997), in a survey of 50 students, found that male protégés perceived more events in mentoring relationships as conflict producing than did female protégés. Male protégés were more likely to report arguing with their mentors, but they were also more likely to report making sacrifices for their mentors and reported greater compliance with their mentor's wishes. Olian, Carroll, and Giannantonio (1993) conducted a field simulation in which 145 banking managers were placed in the role of mentors and were asked to select protégés represented by paper-and-pencil measures. They found no support for their hypothesis that mentors would expect greater rewards and be more willing to mentor single, as compared to married, protégés because of perceived work-family demands. They found an unexpected (and unexplained) gender by marital status interaction in which mentors reported greater willingness to help their protégés' careers and anticipated greater rewards to themselves if male protégés were married and female protégés were single.

Little research has been conducted on the relationship between protégé gender and stages in the mentoring relationship. According to Kram (1983, 1985), mentoring relationships evolve through four distinct phases: initiation, cultivation, separation, and redefinition. The relationship develops during the initiation phase and evolves into providing the full range of roles and functions during the cultivation phase. The separation phase occurs two to five years after initiation and involves the termination of the relationship because of physical separation or psychological reasons. The redefinition phase occurs several years after separation and, depending on the type of termination, may involve either the achievement of peer status or lack of interpersonal contact. Although there has been some research on the stages of mentoring relationships (e.g., Chao, 1997; Ragins & Scandura, 1997), there has been little on the effect of gender on the stages of mentoring relationships. One exception is a recent study on gender and the termination stage of mentoring relationships conducted by Ragins and Scandura (1997). Using a matched sample of 142 male and female ex-protégés, the researchers found that when controlling for gender differences in rank, salary, tenure, and other demographic and organizational variables, women did not differ from men in the number or duration of prior mentoring relationships or in their reasons for terminating the relationship. Their study revealed no support for the idea that women are more dependent on their mentors, are less likely to terminate the relationship once it has served its purpose, or use their mentors any less effectively than men. The lack of male protégés with female mentors in the study prevented an assessment of the impact of the gender composition of the relationship on the duration of the relationship and the reasons for termination.

Research in the next decade should explore whether protégé gender, mentor gender, and/or the gender composition of the relationship affect the stages of the relationship or the outcomes associated with various stages. For example, it is reasonable to expect that same-gender mentoring relationships may move from the initiation to the cultivation stage more quickly than cross-gender relationships because of perceived similarity and the degree of comfort in the relationship. Research indicates that the specific gender composition of the relationship affects mentoring functions and outcomes (Ragins & Cotton, in press), which highlights the importance of investigating the effects of gender composition on mentoring processes, stages, and outcomes. This is discussed at length later in the chapter.

Two studies examined the relationship between subordinate gender and subordinate reports of the degree to which a supervisor engaged in mentoring behaviors. In a study of 52 male and 24 female MBA students, Goh (1991) used a newly developed 11-item instrument on "supervisory mentoring behaviors" and found gender differences on only 2 of the items in the scale: Female subordinates were more likely than male subordinates to report that their supervisors excluded them from work-related discussions and, in seeming contrast, that their supervisors sought out their opinions on important company issues. In their study of 117 supervisors and their subordinates, Tepper, Brown, and Hunt (1993) concluded that men who employ stronger upward-influence tactics obtain more career-related mentoring functions and that women who employ weaker upward-influence tactics obtain more psychosocial mentoring functions. It should be emphasized that these two studies did not ask the respondents if they viewed their supervisors as mentors. Even if a supervisor engages in some mentoring functions (i.e., providing visible assignments, friendship, or counseling), that individual is not necessarily a mentor. Future research should avoid this confusion by providing respondents with the definition of a mentor and directly asking the respondent if the supervisor is a mentor.

Does Mentor Gender Affect Mentoring Relationships?

Relatively little research has been conducted on the mentoring relationship from the mentor's perspective. Three areas that have been investigated are (1) the relationship between mentor gender and the functions and outcomes of the relationship, (2) gender differences in the decision to mentor, and (3) gender differences in the costs and benefits associated with being a mentor.

Mentor Gender and Protégé Outcomes

Existing theory predicts that because men have more power than women in organizations (Ragins & Sundstrom, 1989), male mentors have greater ability to provide more career outcomes and career development functions (Ragins, 1995, 1997b). Moreover, as discussed earlier, self-construal and other feminist theories suggest that because many women define themselves in terms of interdependent relationships (Cross & Madson, 1997; Gilligan, 1982), women may provide more psychosocial or supportive mentoring functions than men when protégé gender is held constant (Ragins, 1995, 1997b).

Research provides some support for the idea that male mentors bring more power to the relationship than female mentors. Erkut and Mokros (1984) found that male students avoided selecting female faculty as mentors because they were seen as having less power and status than their male counterparts. Similarly, in a study of 89 female psychologists, Brefach (1986) found that protégés rated male mentors as having more power at work and more power in the relationship than female mentors.

Perceptions of greater power among male mentors may be well founded. In a study of 1,018 MBA graduates, Dreher and Cox (1996) found that protégés with nonsupervisory White male mentors earned significantly more than protégés with female mentors or mentors of color and that men were more likely than women to form mentoring relationships with White men. Bachman and Gregory (1993) found that in female-dominated organizations in which women had greater promotion rates than men, protégés with female mentors had equivalent promotion rates to protégés with male mentors. Along those same lines, Brefach (1986) found that women with male mentors rated themselves higher in professional success than women with female mentors. The female protégés in the study were also more likely to report that they sought approval for their actions from male mentors than female mentors and that male mentors encouraged less risk taking than female mentors. In a study of 352 female and 257 male protégés, Ragins and Cotton (in press) found that when controlling for occupation, position tenure, number of career interruptions, duration of prior mentoring relationships, and whether those relationships involved supervisory or formal mentors, protégés with a history of male mentors received significantly greater compensation than protégés with a history of female mentors. However, they found no support for the hypothesis that protégés with male mentors would report more career development functions than protégés with female mentors, thus suggesting that there may be some slippage between protégé reports of mentor behaviors and the outcomes associated with those behaviors.

There is mixed support for the proposition that female mentors provide more psychosocial functions than their male counterparts. In a study of 94 mentors, Burke, McKeen, and McKenna (1993) found that female mentors reported that they provided more psychosocial and career development functions than male mentors, and mentors of both genders reported that they provided more psychosocial functions to female than male protégés. In a study of 81 female protégés using a newly developed nine-item instrument of career development and psychosocial functions, Gaskill (1991) found significant differences for only two of the psychosocial items: Female protégés with female mentors were more likely than those with male mentors to report that their mentors were their role models and that female mentors were perceived as being better at helping female protégés explore personal concerns.

In contrast, Ensher and Murphy (1997) found no support for the hypothesis that female mentors would be perceived as providing more psychosocial functions than male mentors in their study of 104 protégés of color who were matched with same-gender mentors over an eight-week period. Similarly, in their study of 196 female protégés, Burke and McKeen (1997) also found that mentor gender did not affect protégé reports of mentor functions. In the Ragins and McFarlin (1990) study reviewed earlier in this chapter, the researchers found that protégés perceived male and female mentors as providing equivalent psychosocial and career development functions. Their study controlled for gender differences in rank, department, specialization, type of mentor, and mentoring history. When rerunning the analyses without the control variables, there were numerous significant main effects for mentor gender, thus suggesting that the inconsistent findings in this area may be due to variations in some of these control variables.

Other studies have examined the relationship between mentor gender and other protégé outcomes, such as job attitudes and descriptions of the mentoring relationship. Some studies have found gender effects, and others have not. For example, Mobley et al. (1994) surveyed 1,132 lawyers and found that although mentoring was positively related to job satisfaction, this relationship did not vary as a function of the gender of the mentor. Similarly, Gaskill (1991) found that mentor gender did not affect the duration of the relationship, the reasons for terminating the relationship, the problems in the relationship, or the reported value of the relationship. In the Burke and McKeen (1997) study of female protégés reviewed earlier, women with female mentors were more involved in their jobs but also reported greater intentions to quit their jobs than women with male mentors. However, in contrast to other studies (Dreher & Ash, 1990; Orpen, 1995; Scandura, 1992), a *negative* relationship was found between career development functions and job satisfaction and perceptions of future promotion prospects. Perhaps one reason for this puzzling finding is that the respondents were presented with a new mentoring functions instrument and were asked to consider a senior individual who provided those functions, but the word *mentor* was not used on the survey, so possibly the respondents believed the researchers were interested in information on a senior individual who was *not* their mentor. This illustrates the importance of providing a clear definition of mentoring for respondents.

Finally, a few studies investigated the effects of mentor gender on other protégé outcomes. These studies also reveal somewhat inconsistent findings. In a study of 89 female psychologists, Brefach (1986) found that female protégés with female mentors were more likely to report that their mentors helped them integrate personal and professional aspects of their lives than those with male mentors. In contrast, in a study of 20 female human services professionals, Quinn (1980) found that, counter to expectations, male mentors were perceived as providing more assistance in integrating feminine and professional self-concepts than female mentors. No gender differences were found in the mentors' influence on integrating family and career issues or in their assistance in the protégés' professional development.

As discussed earlier, the inconsistent research findings in this area may be due to variations in instrumentation, definitions of mentoring, use of control variables, and between-study differences in the gender composition of the mentoring relationship.

Gender Differences in the Decision to Mentor

Existing theory predicts that female managers face more obstacles to assuming a mentoring role than their male counterparts (e.g., Ragins, 1989, 1997a). Women's token status in male-dominated occupations increases their visibility and performance pressures (Kanter, 1977a). Due to their precarious position and limelight status, female mentors may be less willing and less able to withstand the risk of protégé failure, which is viewed as a direct reflection of the mentor's judgment and competency. The female mentor-female protégé relationship is the most visible of all gender combinations, and it faces the greatest risk, particularly if they are viewed as "plotting a revolution" (Ragins, 1989). Another barrier to becoming a mentor is the time involved with the relationship. Given the obstacles women face to advancement (Ragins & Sundstrom, 1989), they may need to spend their time advancing their own careers rather than helping others.

Research suggests that barriers to mentoring may be most salient at midlevel management positions. In an early study of midlevel managers, Ragins and Cotton (1993) investigated gender differences in willingness to mentor in a matched sample of 229 women and 281 men in three research and development organizations. Even though the respondents were matched on rank, department, and specialization, men were nearly twice as likely to be mentors as women. When controlling for gender differences in factors relating to decisions to mentor (age, rank, tenure, and mentorship experience), women expressed equivalent intentions to mentor as men, even though they anticipated more drawbacks to becoming a mentor. Drawbacks included such factors as being put in a bad light by their protégés' failures, lacking the time to be a mentor, and feeling unqualified in assuming a mentorship role. In an extension of this study to a national matched sample of 80 male and 80 female executives above the glass ceiling, Ragins and Scandura (1994) found that women were as likely to be mentors as men and expressed equivalent intentions to mentor others in the future, suggesting that women have greater freedom to mentor once they break through the glass ceiling. In a subsequent study using 607 first-line supervisors at a large government organization, Allen and her colleagues (Allen, Poteet, Russell, & Dobbins, 1997) found that although less than half of the sample actually were mentors, no significant gender differences were found in reported intentions to mentor, barriers to being a mentor, and actually being a mentor. In another study of 68 MBA students in a formal peer-mentoring program at a large university, Allen, Russell, and Maetzke (1997) found that full-time female graduate students reported greater intentions to mentor in the future than their male counterparts. Taken together, these studies suggest that gender differences in willingness to mentor may be directly affected by the organization's climate and by the potential mentor's rank in the organization. Given that women are more likely to be found in lower ranks, women holding entry-level positions are perhaps less visible than women at midlevel or upper-level positions. Women who have made it to executive positions are visible, but less vulnerable than women who are just beneath the glass ceiling. Midlevel female managers hold the most precarious positions, and therefore may be less willing to mentor than will women at other levels. These relationships highlight the importance of controlling for rank when investigating gender differences in mentoring relationships.

In general, we know little about the factors that contribute to an individual's decision to mentor (e.g., Allen, Russell, & Maetzke, 1997; Green & Bauer, 1995; Ragins & Cotton, 1993) and whether gender interacts with these variables. Some theoretical models have been developed (e.g., Ragins, 1997a), but more work is needed. Some initial research suggests gender differences in the processes underlying the decision to mentor. In a study of 53 male and 35 female managers, Horgan and Simeon (1990) found that although self-perceptions of competency predicted the decision to mentor for both men and women, greater pay was associated with being a mentor for men, whereas greater job dissatisfaction was associated with being a mentor for women. Future research could explore these relationships while controlling for potential confounds relating to job rank and tenure.

Gender Differences in Costs and Benefits

Mentors may receive both costs and benefits from assuming a mentorship role (e.g., Erickson, 1963; Kram, 1985; Levinson, Darrow, Klein, Levinson, & McKee, 1978; Ragins & Scandura, 1994). One primary benefit is the satisfaction and fulfillment received from nurturing the development of the protégé. Mentors may benefit from the creative and youthful energy of their protégés, which may rejuvenate the mentors' careers and improve their job performance. Finally, mentors benefit from the organization's recognition of the relationship, and the loyal base of support provided by their protégés. The costs associated with being a mentor include the time and energy in maintaining the relationship and the negative visibility from a poorly performing protégé (Halatin & Knotts, 1982; Myers & Humphreys, 1985). Mentors also run the risk of being displaced or "stabbed in the back" by ambitious or disloyal protégés, or being viewed as playing favorites with their protégés.

There has been little research assessing gender differences in the costs and benefits received by the mentor in the mentoring relationship. In a study of 80 matched male and female executives, Ragins and Scandura (1994) hypothesized that mentoring would represent more of a "high stakes" venture for women than for men. Specifically, the support and influence gained by being a mentor may be particularly advantageous for a female mentor facing the glass ceiling (e.g., Parker & Kram, 1993), but the mentor also stands to lose more in the relationship due to increased visibility and the potential risks involved with mentoring a poorly performing protégé. In contrast to these expectations, the female executives in the study reported equivalent costs and benefits to being a mentor as their male counterparts. As discussed earlier, the women were also as likely as the men to be mentors, and they expressed equivalent intentions to mentor in the future; however, rank may affect the barriers to becoming a mentor and the costs and benefits received from the relationship. Future research should expand on this study by using a matched sample of male and female employees from lower organizational ranks.

Gender Composition of the Relationship

Most research on gender and mentoring has tested for significant main effects for mentor gender or for protégé gender; very few studies have investigated the interaction of mentor and protégé gender. Yet theory suggests that the gender composition of the mentoring relationship may have the greatest impact on mentoring relationships (Ragins, 1997a, 1997b). Two research questions focus on the gender composition of mentoring relationships. The first is whether there are differences between same-gender and cross-gender relationships, and the second explores the effects of each of the four gender combinations on mentoring relationships.

Same-Gender Versus Cross-Gender Mentoring Relationships

Research indicates that women are more likely to be in cross-gender mentoring relationships than men (Burke, McKeen, & McKenna, 1990; Ragins & Cotton, 1991), a function of the lack of women at higher ranks in organizations. Many authors have observed that cross-gender relationships are more difficult to manage than same-gender relationships because of sexual issues, innuendoes, and negative reactions from others (Clawson & Kram, 1984; Hurley & Fagenson-Eland, 1996; Ragins, 1989). Research indicates support for this idea. In a study of 30 female managers, Fitt and Newton (1981) found that sexual tension was an issue in the mentoring relationships and that some of the relationships became romances. Bowen (1985), in a study of 32 cross-gender mentoring relationships, found that jealous spouses and resentful coworkers created problems for both mentors and protégés. Ragins and Cotton (1991) found that women were more likely than men to report that they hesitated to initiate a relationship with a potential mentor because they were afraid that the action would be misconstrued as a sexual advance by the mentor or others in the organization.

According to existing theory, cross-gender mentoring relationships are less likely to provide psychosocial and role-modeling functions than same-gender relationships (Ragins, 1989, 1997b) due to restrictions in perceived similarity and role modeling in the relationship. Only a few studies have examined this issue, and these findings provide mixed support for this theoretical prediction. In a study of 88 Black and 107 White male and female managers, Thomas (1990) found that, although there were no significant main effects for gender or race, protégés in same-gender relationships reported that their mentors provided more psychosocial and career development functions than protégés in cross-gender relationships and that protégés in same-race relationships reported more psychosocial functions than protégés in cross-race relationships. Thomas found that protégés in same-gender relationships reported more mutuality and trust than protégés in cross-gender relationships. He also found that same-gender relationships lasted a shorter period of time than cross-gender relationships and that there were less age differences between the mentor and protégé in same-gender than in cross-gender mentoring relationships.

Along similar lines, in a study of 92 male and 275 female hospital employees, Koberg et al. (1998) found that when controlling for rank, protégés in same-gender and same-race relationships reported that their mentors provided more psychosocial functions than protégés in cross-gender or cross-race relationships. Although the study was limited by the number of minority respondents ($n = 55$), majority protégés reported more psychosocial support from their mentors than minority protégés. However, male and female protégés did not significantly differ in reports of the psychosocial functions provided by their mentors.

In a study of 115 male and 66 female protégés, Ragins and McFarlin (1990) controlled for the number of previous mentoring relationships, the length of the current mentoring relationship, whether the mentor was the protégé's supervisor, and the protégé's age, rank, department, and specialization and found that cross-gender protégés were less likely than same-gender protégés to report engaging in after-work, social activities with their mentors. In addition, compared to other gender combinations, female protégés with female mentors were more likely to report that their mentor served a role-modeling function. However, cross- and same-gender mentoring relationships did not significantly differ in the other psychosocial roles or the career development functions.

Ragins and Cotton (in press) explored the effect of gender composition on the functions and outcomes of mentoring relationships in a study of 352 female and 257 male protégés. When controlling for occupation, type of mentoring relationship (formal or informal and supervisory or nonsupervisory), and duration of mentoring relationship, they found no support for the hypotheses that protégés in same-gender mentoring relationships would report more psychosocial functions than protégés in cross-gender relationships. However, they did find a significant three-way interaction between mentor gender, protégé gender, and type of relationship (formal vs. informal). Protégés in cross-gender relationships reported that their mentors provided less challenging assignments with formal, as compared to informal, relationships. Those in same-gender relationships, however, actually reported receiving more challenging assignments from their mentors when the mentor was formally assigned, and this was particularly true among female protégés with formally assigned female mentors.

One caveat that should remain in mind when viewing the results of these studies is that the male protégé/female mentor relationship is relatively infrequent. For example, 91% of the mentoring relationships in Thomas's (1990) study involved White male mentors. Similarly, there were only 11 male protégés with female mentors of the 510 respondents in Ragins and McFarlin's (1990) study. This situation creates unbalanced cells and decreases the statistical power necessary to find true effects. Comparisons of same- and cross-gender mentoring relationships in these studies may reflect the impact of cross- and same-gender mentors on relationships for female protégés, more than for male protégés.

In recognition of this issue, Ragins and Cotton (in press) designed their study to increase the number of female mentors in their sample. They started with a national survey of 3,000 men and women in male-typed, female-typed, and gender-integrated occupations. They received 1,162 responses, and the final sample (614 protégés) consisted of 352 female protégés, 257 male protégés, and 5 who did not report their gender. The gender composition of these relationships is telling: 233 male protégés with male mentors, 115 female protégés with female mentors, 237 female protégés with male mentors, and only 24 male protégés with female mentors. The authors noted that the relative rarity of the male protégé/female mentor relationship may be due not only to the scarcity of female mentors but also to the functions of the relationship, as discussed later in this chapter.

A few studies have examined whether protégés prefer same-gender or cross-gender mentoring relationships. In an early study, Olian, Carroll, Giannantonio, and Feren (1988) conducted a series of laboratory simulations using 675 undergraduate business students and found no consistent evidence of preference for same-gender mentors. In a recent study of 150 college students, Gumbiner (1998) found that both male and female students perceived male professors as more authoritative and female professors as more emotional, but still preferred mentors of their own gender. In a study of 280 female graduate business students, Burke and McKeen (1995) found that the women did not report a stronger preference for female than male mentors. The women in the study also, on a conceptual level, did not see cross-gender relationships as more difficult to manage than same-gender relationships and did not perceive that cross-gender relationships required special negotiations regarding managing the public image of the relationship. However, those respondents who *actually had* male mentors reported more concerns about managing the public image of the relationship and reported that same-gender mentorships were more desirable than cross-gender relationships. Although this study assessed only female protégés, it does illuminate the importance of using actual protégés and mentors rather than simulations or projected reports.

Other studies have investigated the impact of cross- and same-gender relationships on various outcomes of the relationship. Noe (1988a) surveyed 74 female and 65 male protégés assigned to formal mentors in an educational setting over a six-month period. Counter to expectations, he found that mentors in cross-gender relationships reported that their protégés used the relationship more effectively than mentors in same-gender relationships. In particular, male mentors with male protégés reported less effective use by their protégés than female mentors with female protégés or mentors in cross-gender relationships. In a laboratory study of 243 college students, Chao and O'Leary (1990) investigated how others respond to same- and cross-gender mentoring relationships and found that successful female protégés in same-gender mentoring relationships were viewed unfavorably by others. Participants perceived successful female protégés with female mentors to have a lower sense of identity resolution and less optimistic career future than female protégés with male mentors. However, plateaued female protégés were more likely to be viewed positively when mentored by a female than male mentor. Finally, in a study of cross- and same-sex role models, which relates peripherally to mentoring, Goldstein (1979) surveyed male and female scholars with male and female advisers and found that scholars with same-gender advisers published significantly more research than scholars with cross-gender advisers. These studies reveal some intriguing results that call for further exploration and investigation.

In sum, research that has investigated the effects of cross- and same-gender mentoring relationships indicates that female protégés are more likely than male protégés to be in cross-gender mentoring relationships, particularly in male-dominated organizations and occupations. Compared to cross-gender mentoring relationships, same-gender mentoring relationships between people who are assumed to be heterosexual by others are less susceptible to sexual innuendoes and rumors and have less potential to develop into romantic relationships. Some research indicates that formal mentors may provide more challenging assignments in same-gender than cross-gender relationships and that same-gender relationships may provide more role modeling than cross-gender relationships. However, the inconsistent findings on this topic suggest that although gender is a primary attribute associated with role modeling, other attributes (i.e., race, ethnicity, sexual orientation, age, profession) may also affect role modeling in mentoring relationships. Future research could tease out the specific demographic, social group, and personal characteristics of the mentor and protégé that best predict role-modeling and psychosocial functions. This research could also assess how gender interacts with other attributes to affect role-modeling and psychosocial functions, as well as career development functions and other career outcomes (e.g., Ragins, 1997b).

Specific Gender Composition of Relationship

Few studies have investigated the impact of the specific combination of mentor and protégé gender on mentoring functions and outcomes. Mobley et al. (1994) explored the relationship between mentoring and job satisfaction in a study of 248 female and 216 male attorneys. The authors stated that about 40% of the sample had mentors, but did not reveal the cell sizes of each of the four gender combinations of mentoring relationships. The researchers failed to find support for their hypothesis that mentor and protégé gender interact in predicting job satisfaction. In an exploratory study of 12 female and 8 male mentors in a university setting, Kalbfleisch (1997) reported that mentor gender interacted with protégé gender in the mentor's perception of the perceived effectiveness of the protégé's strategy for dealing with conflict in the relationship. Specifically, male mentors reported a higher level of esteem for female protégés who comply with their wishes than for male protégés who comply, and female mentors reported a higher level of esteem for male protégés who comply with their wishes than for female protégés who comply. Small samples and lack of information about cell sizes limit the findings of these studies. However, the Kalbfleisch (1997) study provides direction for future research that could investigate the effect of the gender composition of the relationship on interpersonal communication and influence processes.

In the Ragins and Cotton (in press) study of 352 female and 257 male protégés discussed earlier, the researchers tested diversified mentoring theory (Ragins, 1997b). Diversified mentoring theory predicts that male protégés with male mentors would receive greater compensation and promotion rates and report more career development and psychosocial functions than any other gender combination of mentoring relationship. This is because male protégés with male mentors benefit from their mentors' power and also from the gender similarity in the relationship. The researchers also tested the corollary hypothesis that male protégés with female mentors would receive less of these outcomes than any other gender combination. Although these hypotheses were only partially supported, the study revealed that the specific gender composition of the mentoring relationship affected mentoring functions and outcomes. As hypothesized, male protégés with a history of male mentors received more compensation than any other gender combination. In addition, male protégés with female mentors ($n = 24$) were less satisfied with their mentors and were less likely than all other gender combinations to report that their mentors provided acceptance in the relationship. Male protégés with female mentors were also less likely to report that their mentors provided challenging assignments and exposure in the organization than did female protégés with male mentors. Post hoc analyses revealed that female protégés with female mentors ($n = 115$) were more likely to report engaging in social activities with their mentors than female protégés with male mentors ($n = 237$). Future research needs to examine the effects of each of the four gender combinations of mentoring relationships, accepting the challenge of obtaining an adequate sample of male protégés with female mentors.

The relative scarcity of the male protégé/female mentor relationship may be due to a number of factors. First, the relative shortage of female mentors limits their availability as mentors. Some research indicates that male protégés may not select female mentors because they have or are perceived as having less power in organizations than their male counterparts (Ragins, 1997a). Psychosocial and role-modeling functions may also be limited in cross-gender relationships. Finally, female mentors may prefer female to male protégés. In a study of 649 female executives, Vincent and Seymour (1995) found that 41% of women reported that it was easier to mentor women and 8% found men easier to mentor. In addition, male protégés were viewed as having more confidence and a greater career orientation, whereas female protégés were perceived as having greater ability and as being more receptive to mentoring.

Caveats and Directions for Future Research on Gender and Mentoring

Research on gender and mentoring is only a decade old; we know substantially less than what we need to know. Areas for future research have been identified throughout this chapter. This section briefly highlights methodological issues inherent in research on gender and mentoring and points to new areas for research that have not been previously addressed.

Methodological Caveats

Mentoring research has suffered from problems relating to the definition of a mentor, the type of mentor (supervisory vs. nonsupervisory, formal vs. informal), the unit of analysis used (i.e., individual vs. dyad), the measurement of mentoring functions, and obtaining samples reflecting the full range of the gender composition of the relationship (for full description of these issues, see Ragins, 1999).

A number of control variables need to be employed when conducting research on gender and mentoring. Variables that affect mentoring functions and outcomes and also vary by gender represent a potential confound to the investigation. One such variable is organizational rank, which differs by gender and is related to barriers to gaining a mentor (Ragins & Cotton, 1991). The importance of controlling for rank is illustrated by Mobley et al. (1994); they found gender effects in mentoring, but this effect disappeared when the researchers controlled for rank and position. Struthers (1995) found that rank had a greater impact on mentoring outcomes than gender. Other potential control variables include organizational tenure, position tenure, education, age, and the size and type of the organization.

Mentoring-related variables that may differ according to gender should be used as control variables when assessing the relationship between gender and mentoring functions and outcomes. These variables include length of mentoring relationship, the number of prior relationships, and the type of mentoring relationship. Supervisory mentors provide different functions than nonsupervisory mentors (Burke, McKenna, & McKeen, 1991; Ragins & McFarlin, 1990; Tepper, 1995). Women may be more likely than men to have supervisory mentors because of the barriers to gaining mentors in other departments (Ragins, 1989). Similarly, formal and informal mentoring relationships yield different functions and outcomes (Ragins & Cotton, in press), and gender differences in this type of relationship should be controlled for when investigating the relationship between gender and mentoring functions and outcomes.

Directions for Future Research

In the course of this chapter, I have highlighted areas for future research that build on existing studies. However, the field of mentoring is moving into new areas, and there is a concomitant need to investigate the effects of gender within these new domains.

For example, mentoring relationships are evolving and are taking new forms, such as peer, group, and lateral mentoring (e.g., Eby, 1997) and formally assigned relationships (e.g., Chao et al., 1992; Ragins & Cotton, in press). What are the effects of gender and the gender composition of the mentoring relationship on these new forms of mentoring? Do these forms represent an advantage or a disadvantage for women when compared to more traditional forms of mentoring? What gender combination of the relationship best predicts effective functions and outcomes?

Mentoring researchers are beginning to move beyond the functions and outcomes of mentoring relationships and explore other processes in the relationship. For example, it would be instructive to understand how gender and the gender composition of the relationship affect communication processes using a dyadic framework (e.g., Mullen, 1994). Furthermore, it would be instructive to assess the communication processes over time and stages in the mentoring relationship (e.g., Kram, 1985; see also Chapter 11 by Carli and Eagly in this book). For example, cross-gender mentoring relationships may have more strained interpersonal communication in the initial stage of the relationship (Ragins, 1997a), but the members of the relationship may work through these issues over time. It would be interesting to assess the factors that facilitate the communication process in cross-gender mentoring relationships. In essence, what factors moderate the relationship between gender composition and communication in mentoring relationships?

Other perceptual processes in mentoring relationships should also be investigated. Processes that are particularly relevant to gender include perceptions of competence, performance attributions, stereotyping, attributions regarding power and influence, and the ability to influence (Ragins, 1997a, 1997b). These processes may affect the functions the mentor provides, the protégé's behaviors, and the outcomes associated with the relationship. For example, are female mentors perceived as having equivalent power as male mentors? Do these perceptions vary as a function of protégé gender and the gender composition of the relationship? These processes may also influence the mentor's and protégé's decision to enter and terminate the relationship, and the perception of the relationship by supervisors and coworkers. Do gender-based attributions affect the response of coworkers and supervisors to mentoring relationships? If mentoring is viewed as an important resource, does mentoring create jealousy or influence coworker perceptions of organizational equity and justice? How does the gender composition of the mentoring relationship affect these perceptions and reactions to the relationship? Research in the next decade should examine the effects of gender on these processes from the point of view of the mentor, the protégé, and others in the organization (supervisors, coworkers, and the work group).

A host of new dependent variables has been presented as fruitful areas for research, such as leader-member exchange, organizational citizenship, social support, and socialization (e.g., McManus & Russell, 1997). It would be fruitful to assess the effects of the gender composition of the relationship on these, as well as other, dependent variables. Does the gender composition of the mentoring relationship moderate the relationship between mentoring and these variables? Future research should provide us with insights into the effect of the gender composition of the mentoring relationship on these dependent variables. In addition, the form of the mentoring relationship (formal vs. informal, supervisory vs. nonsupervisory, group vs. dyad, peer vs. hierarchical) should be explored.

It is important to link gender research with the evolving area of diversity in organizational relationships. We need to understand the processes by which gender interacts with other dimensions of diversity to affect mentoring processes and outcomes (cf. Kram & Hall, 1996; Ragins, 1997a, 1997b; Thomas & Higgins, 1996), as well as the methodological issues involved with investigating diversified mentoring relationships (Ragins, 1999). There is some initial research that suggests that race may have more of an effect than gender on mentoring relationships (Cox & Nkomo, 1991; Kalbfleisch, & Davies, 1991), but more research is needed in this area. Theory holds that mentoring relationships vary along a dimension of diversity, which is defined as membership in power-related groups in organizations (Ragins, 1997b). This theory needs to be tested and refined.

Research on gender and mentoring assumes that members of mentoring relationships are heterosexual. For example, same-gender mentoring relation-ships are viewed as an inoculation against sexual innuendoes by coworkers and the potential for romantic involvement (Clawson & Kram, 1984; Hurley & Fagenson-Eland, 1996; Ragins, 1989). Like other areas of organizational research, these views assume heterosexuality among members of organiza-tions. There has been no research that investigates sexual orientation and mentoring. It would be particularly instructive to understand the interactions among sexual orientation, gender, race, and other dimensions of diversity as they affect mentoring relationships. Is sexual orientation more of an issue in same-gender relationships involving men than women? Is similarity in sexual orientation among members of the relationship more important than similar-ity in gender, race, or ethnicity? How are these relationships moderated by work group composition and organizational policies regarding gay and lesbian employees?

Finally, because most research on mentoring has been conducted on North American samples, there has been a lack of research and theory on the effects of national culture on mentoring relationships. Other cultures may produce mentoring relationships that provide different mentoring functions than the functions identified in North American samples; even the term *mentoring* may or may not translate to other cultures. Theory on cultural differences can be applied to the mentoring arena. For example, using Hofstede's theory of cultural differences (1993; Hofstede, Neuijen, Ohayv, & Sanders, 1990), individualistic cultures that emphasize status differentials and power distinctions may have entirely different forms of mentoring than cultures with collectivist orientations and low power distinctions. For example, psychosocial functions involving friendship, affirmation, and role modeling should be more likely to occur in collectivist than individualist cultures. Using Triandis's (1989) theoretical model, "tight" cultures, which have clear norms and little toleration for deviation, may develop mentoring relationships focused on socializing protégés to the norms of the organization, whereas "loose" cultures, which have greater tolerance for individual differences, may foster mentoring relationships that allow protégés to develop individualized career paths that extend beyond organizational boundaries. Similarly, cultures that value seniority and loyalty to the organization may produce very different types of mentoring relationships than cultures that value youth and entrepreneurial careers. Age may be a stronger prerequisite for being a mentor in cultures that value age, rather than in cultures that value youth. Cultures in which the individual's worth is judged by his or her contribution to the group or employer may produce mentoring relationships that focus less on the protégé's individual achievements or advancement and more on the protégé's contribution to the team and organization.

Embedded in these cultural differences is the subculture of gender. In some cultures, particularly those that restrict the civil rights and employment opportunities of women, the very idea of a senior woman mentoring a younger male protégé may be nearly incomprehensible. Although men and women have been found to be equally likely to have mentors in the United States, this finding may not generalize to other countries. It would be particularly interesting to discover the individual and interpersonal qualities that allow some women to be the exception to the rule in other cultures.

Little is known about how gender and culture interact to affect the development, processes, functions, and outcomes of mentoring relationships (e.g., Ragins, 1998). For example, the cultural construct of "masculinity" may interact with mentor or protégé gender to affect processes in mentoring relationships. According to Hofstede (1993; Hofstede et al., 1990), cultures that are masculine value aggressiveness, whereas cultures that are feminine value nurturing. How do these cultural values interact with gender expectations in mentoring relationships? How do "feminine" female mentors in a "masculine" culture fare? A related area of interest is cross-cultural mentoring relationships, which involve mentors and protégés from different cultures. Emerging theory suggest that these relationships may be particularly susceptible to conflicts in cultural values, work values, and gender expectations (Ragins, 1998).

In conclusion, although inroads have been made much work remains to be done in the study of gender and mentoring in organizations. This field provides an exciting opportunity for charting new terrain and making a real contribution to our understanding of this important and complex relationship.

Chapter 19

Women Entrepreneurs

Approaching a New Millennium

Dorothy Perrin Moore

The intense interest in entrepreneurship is unprecedented (U.S. Small Business Administration, 1995, 1997). A recent Gallup poll reported that over 90% of Americans would approve if either a daughter or son started a small business (Cooper, 1998; Dennis, 1997). The daughters have been especially active. The 78% increase in the number of women-owned firms between 1987 and 1996 nearly doubled the 47% increase for all U.S. firms (National Foundation for Women Business Owners [NFWBO], 1997e, p. 1; U.S. Small Business Administration, 1997, pp. 1-2). In 1996, there were approximately 8 million women-owned businesses in the United States. They were expected soon to employ approximately 26% of the U.S. workforce, a total of 18.5 million workers (NFWBO, 1996a, p. 1). In the United States, within the women's business segment, minority ownership now represents the sharpest increase (NFWBO, 1997b, 1998b). Worldwide, women-owned firms comprise between one-fourth and one-third of all businesses (NFWBO, 1997e). In Canada, women have been opening businesses at more than twice the rate of men (NFWBO, 1997e). In Australia, Canada, and Germany, the percentages of women-owned business are beginning to approach U.S. figures. Drawing on an array of research studies from the European Community, Turner (1993) notes that "women now account for about one in three enterprise creators in

Germany and Denmark; one in four in France, the UK, and the Netherlands; and one in five in Greece, Spain, Italy, and Ireland" (p. 134).

Overview of Research

Research on Women Entrepreneurs

Research on entrepreneurs has varied widely in topics, levels of sophistication in research designs and methodologies applied, types of data gathered, analytical tools, and research respondents. Early work predominantly focused on males, the most representative group by number (Moore, 1988, 1990; Stevenson, 1986). Women entrepreneurs were assumed to have the same value sets, characteristics, and drives as male entrepreneurs, and findings were all lumped together. This assumption is questioned today.

Research on women business owners as a separate group began to develop in the late 1970s. The early work was mainly comparative analyses of psychological and sociological characteristics (Schwartz, 1976) with some studies in male-dominated industries (Hisrich & O'Brien, 1981). Findings suggested the businesses could be divided by their location in fields that were traditional or nontraditional for women. In the 1980s, Moore (1987a, 1987b, 1988, 1990) regrouped female entrepreneurs into the classifications of *Traditional* and *Modern* based on their training, prior business experience, and orientation. But until the late 1980s, research on women entrepreneurs was a neglected area of academic study (Carter, 1993, pp. 148-149). Wortman and Kleis (1991) described research on women as "an entrepreneurship sub-field studied only by a small sub-set of researchers focused on behavioral characteristics."

Changes in the past few years have been dramatic. Brush (1992) applied Gartner's new venture creation framework to classify 57 empirical articles on women. Like Moore (1990) and Brush (1992), Beggs, Doolittle, and Garsombke (1994) and Baucus and Human (1994) called for new models and more comprehensive and rigorous research.

Women's Characteristics

For the most part, women entrepreneurs continued to be studied as part of the larger group of entrepreneurs as a whole. Because most female entrepreneurs operated service sector businesses (and still do), the dominant service sector characteristic often masked the nature and achievements of women in high-growth and nontraditional areas such as finance, insurance and real estate, wholesale trade, manufacturing, transportation, and communications (Allen & Carter, 1996; U.S. Department of Commerce, 1997a). Studies showed that women possessed all the inherent characteristics of a business culture (i.e., well educated, motivated by achievement, energetic;

Hisrich & Brush, 1987) and had higher self-confidence scores than those of their male counterparts (Stimpson, Narayanan, & Shanthakumar, 1993), but lagged in managerial and business start-up experience (Fischer, Reuber, & Dyke, 1993). This is perhaps reflected in parallel findings that many of the businesses owned by women are smaller in size, have fewer employees, and have slower income growth and lower sales volume than businesses owned by men (Chaganti & Parasuraman, 1996; Fischer et al., 1993).

The Emerging Classifications
of Female Entrepreneurs

Traditionals

Prior to the 1980s, the limited research on women entrepreneurs suggested a model of the traditional entrepreneur, that is, women who were associated with stereotypical female work roles. Schwartz (1976), Demarest (1977), and Diffley (1983) suggested that, when these women went into business, their motivations, psychology, and management styles reflected traditional values. Many of the businesses created during this period were sole proprietorships and low-income, low-equity, small, and slow-growing enterprises (U.S. Department of Commerce, 1986; Vesper, 1983). The business owners had limited access to capital (Hisrich & O'Brien, 1981; Pellegrino & Reese, 1982) and limited business and technical education and management experience (Moore, 1990; Scott, 1986; Stevenson, 1986).

Moderns

A new group, called Second Generation (Gregg, 1985), or Moderns (Moore, 1987a, 1987b, 1990), began appearing in larger numbers in the 1980s. These female entrepreneurs met Drucker's (1985) narrow definition of an entrepreneur as one who "drastically upgrades the yield from resources and creates a new market and a new customer" (pp. 21, 25, 33). Many were women who had left corporations to be their own bosses, to exercise their educational and technical skills, and not incidentally, to make money (Fried, 1989; Rosener, 1989; Scott, 1986). Differing from the Traditional in a number of important dimensions, they represented a revolution in the female entrepreneurial paradigm. Hisrich and O'Brien (1981) found that the Modern more commonly exhibited traits associated with male entrepreneurs and was engaged in business enterprises previously dominated by men, that is, finance, insurance, manufacturing, and construction. Moore (1987a, 1987b, 1990) found that a Modern's needs were also more in line with those identified for male entrepreneurs in the same fields. Moderns heading corporations, more than sole proprietors, prized assistance in the relatively sophisticated business areas of short- and long-term planning, cash flow analysis, networking, and identifying and expanding new markets (Moore, 1990). Demographically, a Modern was likely to be hardworking, white, older, and married and have some postsecondary education and administrative or management background (Devine, 1994).

Characteristics

The Incubator Transition

In the 1990s, it became clear that women entrepreneurs were not only opening business ventures in all kinds of markets and industry sectors but also bringing with them a great deal of skill and knowledge. Much of this knowledge came from previous organizational experience, most commonly 10 to 12 years in duration (Murphy, 1992). The fact that about three-fourths of all new business owners are employed elsewhere at the time of their business start-ups (U.S. Department of Commerce, 1997a) suggested that much of the expertise and motivation of female entrepreneurs came from experiences in previous organizational environments (Birley, 1989; Brush & Hisrich, 1988; Moore, 1990; Moore, Buttner, & Rosen, 1992; Murphy, 1992; Moore & Buttner, 1997). Entrepreneurs were establishing businesses in sectors or industries similar to the incubator experiences (Brush, 1992; Fischer et al., 1993) or dealing in familiar products and services (Cooper, Woo, & Dunkelberg, 1989). An entrepreneur's prior organization appeared to resemble an incubator (Cooper & Dunkelberg, 1987; Ireland & Van Auken, 1987), a valued training ground where financial, marketing, management, technical, and networking skills were refined (Moore & Buttner, 1997). Regarding the new ventures, Hisrich and Brush (1984) and Chaganti (1986) suggested that the survival of the women-headed businesses was not necessarily associated with high growth rates and profits but with the strong driving forces of personal accomplishment, freedom, and self-respect, attributes also associated with an incubator experience (Olson & Currie, 1992).

The Changing Profile

As noted by Moore (1990), Brush (1992), Carter (1993), and Beggs et al. (1994), the values, experiences, and thought processes that had been labeled typically entrepreneurial were based on conclusions drawn primarily from studying men. The American male norm formed the background against which female entrepreneurs were compared. As illustrated by the research chronicled by Adler and Izraeli (1994, pp. 182, 183, 211) in Sweden, the United Kingdom, Finland, and Germany; Davidson and Cooper (1992, 1993a) in the United Kingdom; and Symons (1993) in the United Kingdom, Ireland, Denmark, the Netherlands, Germany, France, Belgium, Greece, Italy,

Portugal, and Spain, the tendency to identify entrepreneurs with masculine characteristics has been worldwide.

In recent years, the NFWBO and Dun and Bradstreet have led the way in forming a national database on female entrepreneurs in the United States that includes corporate businesses owned by women, a segment of ownership not previously recorded in the census data. This collection of data has led to an interpretation of women entrepreneurs broader than the statistical data reports provided by the Small Business Administration and the Census Bureau. The NFWBO (1996a, 1996c) finds no differences in the United States in the level of education or the way men and women owners do their banking, nor do they find significant differences between women and men in the service sector in fiscal solidness. Differences exist in the increase in the number of businesses owned by women and the dramatic increases in the number of Black, Hispanic, Asian American, and Indian/Alaskan Native women-owned businesses, especially the increase among Hispanic women during the 1987 to 1996 comparative period. The greatest growth among minority women-owned firms has been in nontraditional sectors and especially in the fields of construction, wholesale trade, transportation/communications, and public utilities (NFWBO, 1997b).

Recent research by NFWBO (1996b, 1998c) has expanded our under-standing of women in international markets and across boundaries. A 1996 Canadian study in which NFWBO participated (commissioned by the Bank of Montreal's Institute for Small Business, Dun and Bradstreet Information Services, North America) provided a landmark comparison across borders of women-led firms in Canada and in the United States (NFWBO, 1996b, p. 1). The Women Entrepreneurs of Canada Foundation (WECF) developed a strategic alliance with NFWBO in 1997 to study the opportunities and challenges for women business owners in international trade (NFWBO, 1997c, p. 1). NFWBO has also continued with the challenge to develop an international profile of women entrepreneurs. In 1997, they surveyed 43 women from 14 countries (Australia, Canada, Cote d'Ivoire, Ethiopia, Ghana, Italy, Malta, Mexico, Nambia, Paraguay, Senegal, South Africa, Uganda, and the United States) at two international conferences for entrepreneurial leaders and reported on top business management issues (NFWBO, 1998c, p. 2). In a comparative analysis of entrepreneurial women in Africa, Russia, and the United States, the NFWBO (1997e) reported entrepreneurial demographics and shared business concerns (NFWBO, 1997e, see chart displays).

A considerable body of other work has recently been made available. In 1987, the European Community Commission, Women in Local Employment Initiatives, was launched to aid the development and professional opportunities for women entrepreneurs. The Department of Employment in the United Kingdom reported on the percentage increase in the number of self-employed women between 1981 and 1987 (Davidson & Cooper, 1993a, p. 25). Their 78% figure was an increase similar to that reported by the Small Business

Administration in the United States. The edited research reports of Davidson and Cooper (1993a) of entrepreneurs in the European Community profile a dramatic increase in women as a percentage of self-employed in Spain (37%), Ireland (31.5%), the United Kingdom and Italy (25% each), the Netherlands (24%), Germany (17%), France (16%), and Greece (pp. 13, 25, 84, 135, 156, 175, 196).

Status of Research Since 1991

Four extensive literature searches have examined the status of research on women entrepreneurs since 1991: Wortman and Kleis (1991), Brush (1992), Moore et al. (1992), and Beggs et al. (1994). The present study examines data from 70 journal articles plus proceedings papers and books that have appeared since Brush (1992) compiled her research. (Because her study was published early in 1992, of necessity, most of the references were made to studies prior to 1991.)

Brush (1992) identified 10 major resources for publications on women entrepreneurs. From the array of sources, she found 57 citable works on female entrepreneurs. Many were comparisons with businesses headed by males. She found published studies on women entrepreneurs in *Frontiers of Entrepreneurship Research* (the Babson Conference Proceedings) and *Journal of Small Business Management* (14 in each) and in two journals in the field, *Entrepreneurship Theory and Practice* and *Journal of Business Venturing* (5 articles each). The *United States Association of Small Business and Entrepreneurship Proceedings* had published three papers on women entrepreneurs. Some 16 other publications were scattered among *Entrepreneurship and Regional Development,* the *International Council of Small Business Proceedings, Academy of Management Journal, Wisconsin Small Business Forum,* and some book chapters. I have added to the Brush (1992) list the journals that did not overlap from J. A. Katz's (1997) list of the 26 academic journals that he described as "more or less totally dedicated to the field, with another half-dozen where entrepreneurship related papers or special issues regularly show up" (p. 2). In addition, I searched all Web sites and library servers to identify any academic studies that had been written about women entrepreneurs since 1991, the cutoff date for the Brush study. Depending on Brush's method of counting papers for the Babson Conference, there may be a decrease in papers published there. Her listing included 15 papers; I found 10 published papers and 11 summaries and posters. In all, I identified 70 journal articles (5 of these were actually from 1990 but not included in her list because they were published in *Journal of Business Ethics*) on female or female-male comparisons of entrepreneurs and three academic scholarly books.

From this array of sources, five definitive clusters of research on female entrepreneurs emerge:

1. Behaviors, stereotypes, and roles
2. Performance, transitions, ownership span, and loan status
3. Networks, the interactive approach, and affiliations
4. Global findings on gender differences
5. Career typing of entrepreneurs

Behaviors, Stereotypes, and Roles

Personal home life as well as the climate or culture of the workplace appear to have a great impact on whether an individual goes into business, stays in business, and thrives as an entrepreneur. A national study of the entrepreneurship knowledge and attitudes of female and male secondary school students suggests differences in approaches to entrepreneurship at a very young age. Kourlisky and Walstad (1998) find that although both female and male secondary school students exhibit a low level of entrepreneurial knowledge, high interest in learning about entrepreneurship and starting businesses, and giving back to their communities, females "are more aware of their deficiencies in this knowledge than are their male counterparts" (p. 77). Furthermore, although very interested in starting a business, "females still are significantly less likely than males (62% vs. 72%) to want to start a business of their own" (p. 78). The higher interest of males than of females in becoming entrepreneurs is also supported by the research findings of Matthews and Moser (1996). Because the results of Kourlisky and Walstad's (1998) research suggest less confidence among females in "their entrepreneurial abilities, less interest in starting a business, and more negatively predisposed toward market mechanisms" (p. 87), it appears that educational training and development is especially important to women.

Even though the pervasive dominate profile of entrepreneurs is associated with masculine characteristics, Fagenson and Marcus (1991) found that the climate or culture of business ownership or leadership has a strong effect on the rating. Women working in a company headed by women gave greater weight to feminine characteristics to describe entrepreneurs than women working in companies headed by men. Irrespective of perceptions, Brush (1992) points out that studies of psychological traits have found more similarities than differences between female and male entrepreneurs. Other works support this finding. As noted in Srinivasan, Woo, and Cooper (1994), researchers have found that women "scored equally well as men along scales of conformity, interpersonal effect, social adroitness, harm avoidance, and succorance" and that the score on succorance "is of particular significance in that it belies the commonly held notion that women are emotional and need constant external support" (p. 44). Fischer et al. (1993) found few differences in the education or motivation of women and men entrepreneurs. Fagenson (1993a) concluded that entrepreneurs, irrespective of gender, are more alike in their personal characteristics than they are similar to managers; in general, entrepreneurs more than managers gave high weights to the terminal values of self-respect, freedom, sense of accomplishment, and exciting life and to the instrumental values of being honest, ambitious, capable, independent, and imaginative.

Yet male and female entrepreneurs are not alike in a number of characteristics. Gatewood, Shaver, and Gartner (1995) found that potential female entrepreneurs value internal stable attributions ("I have always wanted to be my own boss") over the external stable attributions chosen by men about going into business ("I had identified a market need"). Fagenson (1993a) found that women value equality more than males do. Olson and Currie (1992) conclude that women in male-dominated fields may be forced into allowing external factors (customers, suppliers, environments, etc.) to dictate strategies rather than personal values.

Brush and Bird (1996) explained a high amount of gender variance in leadership. Women, they said, practiced *innovative realism,* defined as flexible, innovative, action oriented, integrated, changing, and inspirational rather than placing emphasis on long-range formalized and strategic planning. Luthans, Envick, and Anderson (1995) note that the need for achievement is significantly lower for women than for men, though their commitment to enterprise is similar. This suggests that, for women, the need for achievement may be satisfied in areas of their lives not related to the business. There is some support for this finding in the research of Parasuraman, Purohit, Godshalk, and Beutell (1996), who state that women business owners devote substantially more time to their families than do men business owners. However, their sample was small and there may be more explanations for this finding in their group. In a wider context, Winn and Stewart (1992) identify three distinct sets of female entrepreneurs. One set parallels the findings of Parasuraman et al. (1996) and fits the profile of the postulated *family woman group.* Among this group of entrepreneurs, it would be expected that individual career interest would be subordinated to the family.

Performance, Transitions, Ownership Span, and Loan Status

Career research on women entrepreneurs is in the initial stages of formulation. In developing a theoretical overview and extension of research on gender and entrepreneurship, Fischer et al. (1993) found that women who open their own businesses have less experience in similar industries and in management generally, as well as less experience in opening and managing the type of businesses they start. They attribute the absence of experience in these areas to the fact that women's firms are smaller and have less growth income and fewer sales per employee than do male-owned firms. The heart of the career development appears to lie in acquiring relevant management and industry related experience. Surveying 2,994 businesses (22.2% owned by women), Srinivasan et al. (1994) found differences in education and motivation between male and female entrepreneurs, with women tending to have less formal education. They also found that "most of the variables associated with entrepreneurial attributes, processes of starting, and firm characteristics differed for women-owned businesses as compared to those owned by men," and that, for women, a primary business initiation goal was "letting them do the work they wanted to do" and "less on making more money than they would otherwise" (p. 47). This conclusion is supported by the research of Gatewood et al. (1995), who found the internal stable attribution among potential women entrepreneurs to be based on the drive to be their own boss and by the research supporting the drive for credibility and independence (NFWBO, 1994a).

Although the desire to be in charge and to be one's own boss is strong and a most-cited reason for starting a business, it is important to note that, for women, launching a business is a gradual process. Srinivasan et al. (1994) and Gundry, Kowlake, and Robertson (1992) found that women were less likely to quit their current jobs because of plans for their ventures. Observers have noted the practice of layering of full-time with part-time work, often by moonlighting prior to starting a business. Although the pattern itself does not appear to be new, it has only recently been reported and may provide an important underlying key to the difference in performance among women- and men-owned businesses. But it is not the only difference in business start-ups by women. Although most women who start businesses now have had private sector work experience, Catalyst, the National Foundation for Women Business Owners, and the Committee of 200 Foundation (1998), in a joint study sponsored by Salomon Smith Barney, found that one-third (32%) of their respondents in a sample of 650 had "worked in small businesses (fewer than 100 employees), 9% for a medium-sized company (100 to 499 employees), and 17% have worked for a large corporation (500 or more employees)" (p. 2). Additional information about the respondent statistics also provides an interesting profile of the present entrepreneurial woman: 13% came from a public sector background, 11% had been out of the labor force before starting their businesses, 4% had worked for a nonprofit organization, and only 9% had been self-employed. One important finding is that, although 59% of men business owners are in a business closely related to previous careers, 56% of women are not; 42% are in a field unrelated to their previous careers and 14% turned a personal interest into a business pursuit (Catalyst et al., 1998, p. 3). This may have implications for success. Srinivasan et al. (1994) found that start-up variables for women play a crucial role in survival and success and that women who broke completely with an organization and launched a business in an industry sector very similar to the work environment where experience had been gained were the most successful.

There has been little research on the patterns of entry and exit in entrepreneurship. Dolinsky, Caputo, Pasumarty, and Quazi (1993) used data from the National Longitudinal Survey of Labor Market Experience that followed a national sample of women entrepreneurs from 1967 to 1984 to examine the variations in likelihood of entering, staying, and reentering self-employment by level of educational attainment. Their findings show that approximately two-thirds of women who enter self-employment leave after about three years but a substantial number later return to self-employment.

Goals appear to be directly related to business performance. Chaganti and Parasuraman (1996) found that, although women's businesses had significantly lower annual sales than men's firms, their employment growth and return on assets were similar. Women's achievement and financial goals were higher with a greater emphasis on product quality than that of men business owners. The NFWBO (1996a, 1996d) finds a "growing similarity between women and men business owners' sources of capital" with the primary difference in how credit is used. "Women use it primarily for growth and expansion; men are more likely to use it to smooth out cash flow and consolidate debt" (NFWBO, 1996d, p. 1). Although there is a pervasive impression that women have more difficulty acquiring credit from lending institutions than do men, recent studies do not support a contention that this is gender based. Fabowale, Orser, and Riding (1995) found, in a study of 2,763 entrepreneurs, of whom 759 were female, that, in general, women-owned businesses are smaller and have less capacity, less capital, a narrower range of collateral, and unproven track records relative to men-owned firms. With less managerial experience and overrepresentation in retail businesses, there is a greater perception of risk among banking institutions. When these structural differences are accounted for, the authors find no differences in the rate of loan rejections and terms of credit. At the same time, perception of differences may lead to an internal focus on equity among women entrepreneurs. Chaganti, DeCarolis, and Deeds (1995) found that women "tend to seek internal equity rather than external equity financing," which suggests "that difficulties that women entrepreneurs face in financial markets may extend into equity markets as well" (p. 16). Self-reliance appears to be a driving force for women.

Kalleberg and Leicht (1991), in a study of the relationship of survival and success of businesses headed by men and by women to industry type, found that women's businesses are not more likely to go out of business or to be less successful than those owned by men. Allen and Carter (1996) sought to move the research beyond examining all women entrepreneurs as a group to sort out the impact of new business openings in nontypical areas for women to determine if factors are in place when businesses are formed that predict performance and large-scale revenues in adolescent businesses (those in business from 2 to 8 years). The 1,400 female owner respondents were divided for analysis according to their sales revenues into the top 25% of their industry and the bottom 25%. The results clearly indicate that "having capital to grow and expand the business . . . , in addition to a personal banking relationship and a focus on profit and growth, contributes significantly to the high performance of women-owned businesses" (p. 2 of Summary). The authors did not find social or cultural barriers that inhibit or exclude women from growing companies nor did they find that situational variables, level of education, marital status, and having dependent children affect respondents toward either low- or high-performing businesses. The interesting analogy between this study and the one by Srinivasan et al. (1994) is that the research is based on data from the NFWBO, whereas the earlier study was based on responses from members of the National Federation of Independent Businesses where females represented 22% of the group.

Networks, the Interactive Approach, and Affiliations

Networks of trusted advisers serve women entrepreneurs as confidential sounding boards for voicing concerns and sharing solutions. Entrepreneurs consider personal and emotional support, which mostly comes from spouses or significant others, far more important than financial, operational, or other types of assistance in running their businesses. A spouse's business knowledge and experience, particularly if he is self-employed, can have a strong positive impact, however (Caputo & Dolinsky, 1998). There is compelling evidence of the importance of personal network strategies as an interrelated part of centrality, support, and in organizational transitions, an approach that has been labeled interactive (Brush, 1992; Rosener, 1989, 1990). This may carry over into the method of selection of advertising media by women during the first year of business operation and in successive years. Van Auken, Rittenburg, Doran, and Hsieh (1994) found that women entrepreneurs not only continued the same advertising media used during the first year but also reported greater usage of referrals, community events, telephone directories, and fliers than used by males, with referrals ranked the highest. Cromie and Birley (1992) found female networks very similar to those of men in terms of activity, contacts, and diversity and that women were no more likely to consult family and friends than were men (p. 238). However, little is known about women's patterns of interaction or how their networks are formed (Ibarra, 1993, 1995). Andre (1992) noted that power for the small business woman will come through more proactive participation in networks of small businesses. For example, he found women to be active in the economic development organizations (organizations composed of business leaders who organize to influence policies) "at the local rather than state levels and to achieve network membership in particular regions of the country" (p. 69). Tjosvold and Weicker (1993) found that cooperative goals and interaction contribute substantially to successful networking. For entrepreneurs, the absence of formal linkages across organizations can make networking even more compelling. Moore and Buttner (1997) found over 60% of their entrepreneurs to view their work and life as a central point connected to an overlapping series of network relation-

ships that included family, business, and society. The establishment of cooperative networks is clearly related as one of the most important factors in
gaining success. Women "derive satisfaction and success from building relationships with customers and employees, having control of their own destiny,
and doing something they consider worthwhile" (NFWBO, 1994b, p. 2).

Helgesen (1990, 1995) supports the contention that women leaders place
greater value on their relationships, with emphasis on cultivation and nurturance. Yammarino, Dubinsky, Comer, and Jolson (1997) found "that female
leaders form unique one-to-one interpersonal relationships with their male
and female subordinates" (p. 205) and that these relationships are independent of one another and group membership. Collectively, the findings
suggest that instead of the traditional top-down organizational chart, an image
of the businesses of these female entrepreneurs would be a wheel, with the
owner at the center, connected directly to each subordinate by a spoke, and
employees linked to each other along the rim (Moore & Buttner, 1997). The
image clearly conveys that a centrally located actor will not only have greater
control over relevant resources and enjoy benefits and opportunities not
always available to those on the periphery of the network but also will be
directly linked to individuals in her firm (Brass, 1992; Burt, 1982, cited in
Ibarra & Andrews, 1993, p. 279; Ibarra, 1995; Ibarra & Andrews, 1993).

Global Findings on Gender Differences

Research on gender in entrepreneurship differences suggests there is
much to be learned. Brush (1992) found distinctions between men and women
in education, occupational background, skills, approach to venture cre-
ation/acquisition, business goals, problems, and performance (pp. 6, 24). She
further postulated that women use an *integrative perspective,* rooted in
psychological and sociological theories that suggest that women's social
orientations are focused more on relationships and that this carries over to
the way they run businesses. Devine (1994), Moore and Buttner (1997),
Buttner and Moore (1997), and NFWBO (1994c, 1996e, 1997c, 1997d,
1998a) found some support for these propositions and also reported on other
variables that suggest how women set priorities, manage their businesses, and
network. According to NFWBO (1998a), women business owners not only
give priority to retirement plans but are "more likely to offer job sharing or
flex time and profit sharing than men-owned firms . . . and . . . a wider range
of investment options" (p. 1). Women business owners also take on more
volunteer activities in their communities (NFWBO, 1996e) and lead the way
in employee benefits overall (NFWBO, 1994b). As did Brandstatter (1997),
Moore and Buttner (1997) found differences between men and women
business owners in attributions of success and failure and further noted
patterns of perceptual difference in organizational training program availabil-

ity, how skills are used and transferred from the incubator organizations, and in loan and capital acquisition.

Studies of gender worldwide have yielded some provocative conclusions. Tilsson (1996) shows a sophisticated profile of Canadian women entrepreneurs similar to the description found in the United States by NFWBO (1996b; NFWBO & Dun and Bradstreet Information Services, 1995). The wide-ranging Hisrich, Koiranen, and Hyrsky (1996) study in northern Europe, the United Kingdom, Ireland, North America, and Australia found women owners to perceive entrepreneurship more positively than do men. Shane, Kolvereid, and Westhead (1991) examined start-ups in New Zealand, Norway, and Great Britain across gender and national boundaries and found that the driving force for starting a business, irrespective of gender or boundary, was the desire for independence. Their later research in 1993 noted that female entrepreneurs perceived higher political uncertainty than did males, a finding further supported by research in Pakistan by Shabbir and DiGregorio (1996), who found the desires for personal freedom, security, and satisfaction to be the driving forces for starting and persisting in business. Network affiliation (Cromie & Birley, 1992) in Northern Ireland, Staber (1997) in Canada, and Lerner, Brush, and Hisrich (1997), who also studied capital and motivation in Israel, show a highly significant effect on profitability. Studies of the relationship between gender and ownership in the United Kingdom (Rosa & Hamilton, 1994) and on the locus of control and entrepreneurship in the Russian Republic (Kaufman, Welsh, & Bushmarin, 1995) are equally enlightening. Findings in the Russian study indicate that, although entrepreneurs have a higher level of perceived internal control than either powerful others or chance, there is still a lag in the level of this control when compared to most other countries and cultures. That the transformation has a long way to go is further exemplified by the research of Mroczkowski (1997), who examined the widespread gender discrimination against women in the Polish job markets. For one Polish woman out of three, entrepreneurship is the way out of joblessness, and the decisive factor for Polish women in starting businesses is to become more independent (Rogut, 1994). Zapalska (1997) found that Polish women display traditionally masculine and feminine characteristics and that they, as do men, turned to self-employment to gain self-control, to alleviate dissatisfaction with previous employment, and for political and economic reasons.

Career Typing of Entrepreneurs

Entrepreneurs can be divided into groups in many different ways. Moore and Buttner (1997) found support for two career groupings of entrepreneurs that they labeled *corporate climbers* and *intentional entrepreneurs*. Of late, the first group, though smaller in number (Catalyst et al., 1998), has been attracting attention. Corporate climbers started out pursuing the American dream of advancing to the top of the organization. But restructuring, down-sizing (Uchitelle & Kleinfield, 1996), rightsizing, and other factors drove many to seek other options for application of their skills (Birley, 1989; Cooper, 1981; Rosener, 1989; Winn & Stewart, 1992). Systemic attitudinal and organizational barriers to women's career advancement (Adler, 1993; Belcourt, 1991; Fischer et al., 1993) and negative effects of the corporate culture (Hood & Koberg, 1994; Noble, 1993; Taylor, 1986) also provided incentives for business ownership (Knight, 1987; Scott, 1986; Shaver, Gate-wood, & Gartner, 1991). For many, it was combinations of organizational push and entrepreneurial pull that led to decisions to exit organizations (Birley & Westhead, 1993; Cooper & Dunkelberg, 1981; Denison & Alexander, 1986; Dubini, 1988; Scheinberg & MacMillan, 1988; Shane et al., 1991). Corporate climbers can be further subdivided for study on the basis of the three-cluster typology of psychological characteristics developed by Langan-Fox and Roth (1995): managerial entrepreneurs, pragmatists, and need achievers.

By contrast, the intentional entrepreneurs had never aspired to the organizational career ladder. With lifelong ambitions of creating businesses of their own (Schein, 1990, 1993), they entered corporate life to work for others to gain experience before starting businesses or because that was the best initial personal or financial choice. It is interesting that intentional entrepreneurs and corporate climbers both ultimately left organizations for many of the same reasons.

Intentional entrepreneurs may also be seen as sequential entrepreneurs or latent intentionals, according to Katz and Gartner (1988) and Katz (1994), who see intention as a label describing people who seek out information they may use to create a business. Under this definition, not only may en-trepreneurial intentions be short range, but also initially an entrepreneur may be unaware of her intention. Thus, the final move to opening a business, rather than being a complete break, occurs as a sequence of career strategy decisions (Naffziger, Hornsby, & Kuratko, 1994, p. 34). Another grouping of entrepre-neurs, which includes family concerns, is described by Winn and Stewart (1992). They suggested that the woman entrepreneur who has subordinated her career to family goals is not oriented to owning a business of her own or to developing an organizational career, and, although she may have held a number of organizational positions, they have been subordinate to family. Because this woman has left and reentered the workforce throughout her child-rearing years, taking positions to supplement family income, her skills may be outdated or obsolete. Her choice of a business thus will be conditioned by her family-employment "education" and closely linked to her family situation.

Yet another distinct grouping of entrepreneurs, little studied to date, consists of the rising number of "copreneurs." As with large numbers of women entrepreneurs, the increase in husband and wife entrepreneurs sharing business ownership equally is recent (69.3% of women-owned businesses were started after 1980, and 29% after 1990; 61.7% of copreneur businesses were started after 1980, 24% after 1990, and 21.8% were home based in 1994; Knutson, 1994). Marshack (1994) found that copreneurs were different from dual-career couples in sharing roles and responsibilities in that copreneur wives take on a traditional sex role (feminine or androgynous) and males a masculine role in the business. The role of the copreneur wife is disparate in the division of household responsibilities and child care. At work, she is primarily responsible for bookkeeping, accounting, secretarial, payroll, billing, and collections. The pattern is consistent with findings that masculine characteristics are dominant among entrepreneurs (Fagenson & Marcus, 1991) and that women entrepreneurs are the family caretakers (Parasuraman et al., 1996). Marshack (1998) notes that "copreneurs are different from other dual-career couples in that they work within the overlapping domains of love and work in a family firm" and that in general they share three basic qualities: "(1) they both work full-time in a joint venture, (2) they are predominantly all-rounders or organizers, and (3) they usually keep their businesses small enough to manage it themselves" (p. 24). Important gaps that occur in business and marriage partner relationships as they affect the success of the business have been addressed in a proposed model by Foley and Powell (1997).

Irrespective of the grouping variable, it appears that among women entrepreneurs, independence, personal development, job freedom, challenge, self-determination, family concerns, organizational dynamics, and blocks to advancement are important determinants of venture creation (Moore & Buttner, 1997; Scheinberg & MacMillan, 1988; Shane et al., 1991).

Although women-owned businesses represent the fastest growth segment of small businesses, the number of firms still lags behind that of men-owned businesses. Sales and incomes of women-owned firms are substantially lower (Carter, Williams, & Reynolds, 1997; Fischer et al., 1993), and there is a higher probability of discontinuance (Srinivasan et al., 1994). There are other differences. Women measure success differently, rating self-fulfillment and effectiveness highest, followed by profits, goal achievement, and employee satisfaction. Making a social contribution and business growth rank much lower (Moore & Buttner, 1997). Needs, attributions, and attitudes of women owners differ substantially from those of men. A lower need for achievement (Luthans et al., 1995) coupled with remaining in the corporate environment (the old job) while launching a new business (Gundry et al., 1992) also suggest a career strategy for women that differs from the previous male model of venture creation. Findings that women's leadership styles focus on innovative realism and vision formulation yielding a high capacity of flexibility, innovativeness, and action-oriented strategies (Brush & Bird, 1996) pose questions about the ability of the male model to explain women's entrepreneurial styles. Other findings show consistency between male and female entrepreneurs rather than differences. Women are more likely to survive if they establish a business in the same type of firm or industry that they left and if they make a complete break from the previous organization to become a full-time dedicated business operator (Srinivasan et al., 1994). This is also true for men (U.S. Department of Commerce, 1994).

In the conclusion of her survey of research on women business owners, Brush (1992, pp. 19-24) suggested that, in addition to the variables normally found in the (predominantly male) studies of entrepreneurship, future work on female entrepreneurs might focus on discrete dimensions: the individual (the motives of female entrepreneurs in starting a business, how they view their firms and their roles in them, and how they make decisions), the organization (firm goals, structure, and planning mechanisms), the business process (activities involved in business start-ups, obstacles to success, and management style), and the environment (business, work, family, and society). In 1994, Beggs et al. called for new models and research approaches to address the role of diversity in entrepreneurship, as did Baucus and Human (1994). These researchers were in step with the changing face of the workforce and the new impetus in the increase in minority-owned businesses.

Future Research Needs

As Wortman (1987) noted, "No theories have been developed in the entrepreneurship field" (p. 264). MacMillan and Katz (1992) call the absence of theory the "idiosyncratic milieus" of entrepreneurial research. With these milieus, a number of narrowly defined frameworks have emerged from the research, some more integrative than others (Bhave, 1994). One reason why more definitive typologies have not been developed is that the majority of the early field studies used questionnaire and interview formats relying on instruments developed in other disciplines, particularly psychology with its focus on personal characteristics. Other research lacked focus due to variations in sample sizes, frames of reference, and even definitions of entrepreneurship and the firm.

Disagreement on definitions of entrepreneurship and small business hampers the development of models and paradigms (Bowen & Hisrich, 1986; Gartner, 1985; Gartner, Shaver, Gatewood, & Katz, 1994; Sexton, 1987; U.S. Small Business Administration, 1985). Ambiguities in the study of women entrepreneurs begin with definitions. Lavoie (1984/1985) describes the woman entrepreneur "as the female head of a business who has taken the initiative of launching a new venture, who is accepting the associated risks and the financial, administrative, and social responsibilities, and who is effectively in charge of its day-to-day management" (p. 34). Moore and Buttner's (1997) definition is a woman who has initiated a business, is actively involved in managing it, owns at least 50% of the firm, and that the business has been in operation one year or longer. Starr and Yudkin (1997) define a woman entrepreneur as "a person who has played a significant management role in the start and building of the business and has held equity."

In the past decade, much progress has been made in entrepreneurial research on women business owners. Although a number of researchers have investigated many of the areas, and we have learned much, the work is still at an exploratory level. For a variety of reasons, we are a long way from developing a model of business ownership for women entrepreneurs. There are problems in current research on women entrepreneurs. Sample sizes vary; that is, females are a clear minority in many studies (Fischer et al., 1993), a majority in others (Fagenson, 1993a), or the complete sample (Gundry et al., 1992; Gundry & Welsch, 1993). Full descriptions of study respondents are not always included (Gatewood et al., 1995; Luthans et al., 1995). Statistical techniques vary in levels of sophistication, as do research design and selection of instruments. Although studies of women tended to concentrate on personal characteristics, as Caird (1993) notes, before such "psychological tests could be useful in correlating entrepreneurial traits with the characteristics of the small business enterprises, the instruments must be validated" (p. 11). In the near future, we can expect studies to continue to be focused over a number of areas with no generally agreed-on strategies guiding research.

There are additional developments. Researchers today have available the vast databases collected by the NFWBO, Dun and Bradstreet, and the Small Business Administration. The Small Business Administration has developed a "virtual women's center" that works concurrently with more than 60 women's business centers nationwide and more recently has reached out to establish international links (U.S. Small Business Association, 1997). In addition, there are the collaborative efforts in the United States of Catalyst, the NFWBO, and the Committee of 200 Foundation sponsored by Salomon Smith Barney (Catalyst et al., 1998) as well as the international collaborations of NFWBO in the collection of data, that is, Russia and Canada. The thrust for knowledge on women entrepreneurs worldwide is further illustrated by the NFWBO's (1997a) first selection of leading women entrepreneurs, which included women from Argentina, Australia, Brazil, Canada, France, Germany, Greece, Hong Kong, India, Ireland, Italy, Japan, Malaysia, Norway, the Philippines, Poland, Portugal, Scotland, Singapore, Sweden, South Africa, Taiwan, Thailand, the United Kingdom, and the United States. Mme. Yvonne Ed Foinant, who owned and managed a steelworks in France, founded the worldwide association Les Femmes Chefs d'Entreprises Mondiales (FCEM) in 1945 to help advance women business owners. In 1998, it celebrated its 46th world conference with 35 member countries and over 29,000 business owners and members. Other international associations of growing strength include the American Business Women International, founded in 1995 for the advancement of international trade, and the International Federation of Business and Professional Women. The availability of data from these sources, the more accurate reporting of business ownerships by the U.S. Census Bureau and

Departments of Labor and Commerce, and the increased support for women business ownerships by the Small Business Administration enable researchers to move beyond the initial stages of descriptive statistics to provide sharper profiles of the modern female entrepreneur. Needed particularly are more standard and scientific methods by which to collect data. These include clear definitions of entrepreneurs and small business owners by industry classification and type to provide a yardstick for the data collection.

It is time to stop clumping entrepreneurs together in one group. Much is to be learned by studying women entrepreneurs as members of various groups. Two divisions of women entrepreneurs, the Modern and the Traditional, appear clear-cut. Women who entered business during the past 10 years have a distinctly different operational style than those who became entrepreneurs in the previous decade. Within the two initial divisions there may be several subclassifications that lead to model building and hypotheses to be tested. It is also important to determine the impact of diversity on each of the subclassifications. In this chapter, a number of international studies were cited; however, many of these studies did not use a validated instrument. They varied in design, respondent selection, and overall instrumentation. Past patterns of instrumentation in the United States and reliance on the field of psychology also were reflected in many of the international studies.

Specifically, we need detailed studies on female entrepreneurs' use of incubators and other experiences in founding their businesses, needs according to industry classification and business type, networking to form business coalitions and constellations, leadership styles, and measures of success. In particular, we need to investigate the drive among women to open organizations in industry settings in which they do not have previous experience. We also need to conduct longitudinal studies to determine how initial start-up decisions of women with corporate experience in an industry sector differ from those of women who have opened businesses in areas new to them. A more careful examination is needed of women's transitions after they have decided to open their businesses. What impact does it have on their success when they do not quit their corporate position at the beginning phases of the new businesses? Could "hanging on" be related to the "hub effect" identified by Moore and Buttner (1997) or the "web effect" identified by Helgesen (1995) and as an interactive effect (Brush, 1992)? What differences evolve in the success and business strategies of the women entrepreneurs who left corporate environments because of the glass ceiling, as compared to those who left for greater flexibility? What long-range impact on strategy and success does the present profile of the modern entrepreneurial woman (in business for 10 years or less as defined by Catalyst et al., 1998) that depicts a workforce background where managerial, marketing, and sales experience are more prevalent than one in accounting and finance? Does this vary across industry? How?

The study of women entrepreneurs is no longer a subfield. Women now own more than 8 million businesses, generate nearly $2.3 trillion in revenues, and employ one in four company workers in the United States, more than 18.5 million people (NFWBO, 1998b, 1998c). They employ one-third more people than the *Fortune 500* companies worldwide.

Given the rapid growth of women-owned businesses one might reasonably expect an outpouring of new literature in the major research outlets. Not so. Journals published by the *Academy of Management* (inclusive of all publications at the national and regional levels) recognized by J. A. Katz (1997) and the USASBE Web listing had a grand total of three articles dealing with either women entrepreneurs or comparisons of male and female entrepreneurs. Only one of these articles was published in *Academy of Management Journal.* No papers on women entrepreneurs have been included in the *Academy of Management Best Papers Proceedings* during the seven years since the Brush study, and only nine abstracts have been published in only three Divisions, Careers (1), Women in Management (2), and Entrepreneurship (6). If the field of women's entrepreneurial studies is to move forward, more scholars in this field must submit research to the major journals, become part of the conference program planning teams, and gain access to the editorial boards. It is hoped that this chapter will inspire such developments.

Chapter 20

Research on Work, Family, and Gender

Current Status and Future Directions

Jeffrey H. Greenhaus and Saroj Parasuraman

Research on the work-family interface has proliferated in the past 25 years, and an extensive body of literature has accumulated on the nature of the interdependencies between the worlds of work and family (Barling & Sorensen, 1997; Greenhaus, 1989; Greenhaus & Parasuraman, 1994; Zedeck, 1992). The sustained research in this area has been fueled by dramatic changes in the demographic composition of the workforce, most notably the growing proportion of employees who are dual-earner partners or single parents. These changes have focused sharp attention on the salience of work-family concerns to an increasingly large segment of employed men and women. Therefore, the scholarly interest in work-family issues has been accompanied by legislative and employer initiatives aimed at helping working parents and those with responsibility for the care of elders to manage the increasingly complex responsibilities and pressures of work and family.

As we approach the new millennium, changes in the workplace accompanying the ongoing downsizing and restructuring of organizations are anticipated to radically transform work and careers (Arthur & Rousseau, 1996). Therefore, it is an appropriate time to take stock of the current status of the research on work-family connections, and to draw up a new work-family research agenda to address salient but underresearched issues as well as those with inconclusive findings. In addition, despite the growing influx of women into nontraditional occupations and jobs, there appears to be little erosion in the strength of gender-based role expectations held by society regarding men and women in work and family roles. Thus, the links between work and family need to be examined with attention given to similarities and differences in the work and family experiences of men and women in the context of a gendered society and gendered work organizations.

Work-family researchers have identified several types of linkages to explain the nature of the interdependence between work and family roles, including compensation, conflict, spillover, accommodation, and segmentation (Lambert, 1990; Repetti, 1987; Staines, 1980). However, the overwhelming majority of the studies on work-family linkages are based implicitly or explicitly on a conflict perspective that has provided an incomplete view of the relationships between work and family.

The aim of this chapter is to identify the pattern of linkages observed between individuals' work and family lives. In doing so, we do not attempt an exhaustive review of the literature, but rather focus primarily on recent research and theory. It should be noted that the majority of the studies we examined were conducted on American samples. We return to this issue later in the chapter when we identify areas for future research.

In this chapter, we first distinguish the dominant work-family conflict perspective from a more positive, integrative approach. We then review the theory and research on work-family linkages, focusing specifically on the role played by gender in shaping these connections. We conclude with an agenda identifying areas for future research.

Work-Family Conflict

Much of the early research on work-family conflict stems from the pioneering study of organizational stress by Kahn, Wolfe, Quinn, Snoek, and Rosenthal (1964), who identified interrole conflict as a significant source of work stress. Applying Kahn et al.'s role conflict perspective, Greenhaus and Beutell (1985) defined work-family conflict as arising from the "simultaneous pressures from both work and family which are mutually incompatible in some respect" (p. 77). Because of this incompatibility, participation in one role is made more difficult by virtue of participation in the other role.

The popularity of the work-family conflict perspective stems from a scarcity hypothesis, which assumes that time and energy are fixed and that individuals who participate in multiple roles inevitably experience conflict that impairs their well-being (Marks, 1977; Sieber, 1974). Some of the initial research in this area questioned whether women's multiple roles (family *and* work) were detrimental to the welfare of the women and their families.

Although research generally does not support the major tenets of the scarcity hypothesis (Baruch & Barnett, 1986; Greenberger & O'Neil, 1993), studies of work-family conflict appear unabatedly in the literature.

The research on work-family conflict has produced valuable insights into the connections between work and family life. It is clear, for example, that extensive conflict can produce dissatisfaction and distress within the work and family domains (Frone, Yardley, & Markel, 1997; Netemeyer, Boles, & McMurrian, 1996; Parasuraman, Purohit, Godshalk, & Beutell, 1996), and can adversely affect one's quality of life (Higgins, Duxbury, & Irving, 1992; Rice, Frone, & McFarlin, 1992). Moreover, excessive work-family conflict can produce dysfunctional social behaviors as disparate as destructive parenting (Stewart & Barling, 1996), alcohol consumption (Frone, Russell, & Cooper, 1993), and withdrawal from work or family responsibilities (MacEwen & Barling, 1994).

It is also clear that a variety of pressures arising from work and family can trigger conflict between the two domains. These forces can take the form of time pressures to participate in work or family activities, stressors in the work or family domains, or high levels of psychological involvement in work or family life (Adams, King, & King, 1996; Aryee, 1992; Frone et al., 1997; Hammer, Allen, & Grigsby, 1997; Higgins et al., 1992; Judge, Boudreau, & Bretz, 1994; O'Driscoll, Ilgen, & Hildreth, 1992; Parasuraman et al., 1996). In fact, many recent studies have viewed work-family conflict as a mediator of relationships between work and family role pressures and employee well-being (Frone et al., 1997; Judge et al., 1994; Parasuraman et al., 1996).

Because work-family conflict represents interference between the two roles, the specific nature of the interference has often been examined. For example, some studies have distinguished the specific subroles within the family domain (spouse and parent) that are in conflict with the work role (Aryee, 1992; Blanchard-Fields, Chen, & Hebert, 1997). Additionally, Greenhaus and Beutell (1985) suggested that there are three types of work-family conflict: (1) time-based conflict, (2) strain-based conflict, and (3) behavior-based conflict. Subsequent research indicates that different work and family factors may be responsible for the three types of work-family conflict (Greenhaus, Parasuraman, Granrose, Rabinowitz, & Beutell, 1989; Loerch, Russell, & Rush, 1989).

Recent research has also explored the direction of the interference between work and family roles. Because work-family conflict is produced by *simultaneous* pressures from the two roles, there are times when work demands interfere with the quality of family life (WF conflict), and other times when family pressures interfere with responsibilities at work (FW conflict). It has consistently been found that WF conflict is more likely to occur than FW conflict (Eagle, Miles, & Icenogle, 1997; Frone, Russell, & Cooper, 1992b; Gutek, Searle, & Klepa, 1991; Matsui, Ohsawa, & Onglotco, 1995; Netemeyer et al., 1996; Williams & Alliger, 1994). This is attributed to the organization's demands on the time and energy of an employee being more compelling than those of the family because of the economic contribution of work to the well-being of the family. Individuals are also likely to have somewhat more latitude in adjusting family schedules than work schedules (Gutek et al., 1991). Generally speaking, work pressures are the most powerful predictors of WF conflict and family pressures are most strongly related to FW conflict (Frone, Russell, & Cooper, 1992a; Frone et al., 1997; Judge et al., 1994). Moreover, a recent meta-analysis (Kossek & Ozeki, 1998) revealed that WF conflict bears stronger negative relationships with job satisfaction and life satisfaction than does FW conflict.

Pleck (1977) proposed that the direction of role interference is different for men and women. Given men's socially defined role as "providers," their work is more likely to intrude into family life than is the case with women. For women, however, who still shoulder the primary responsibility for home life, family demands are expected to intrude into the work domain. According to this view, men should experience more WF conflict than women, and women should experience more FW conflict than men. However, empirical research has not supported Pleck's assertion. None of the three direct tests of the hypothesis detected the necessary interaction between gender and the direction of the conflict (Eagle et al., 1997; Frone et al., 1992b; Gutek et al., 1991).

Instead, the literature reveals two patterns of findings. Most of the studies indicate that men and women experience a similar level of work-family conflict (Bedeian, Burke, & Moffett, 1988; Blanchard-Fields et al., 1997; Duxbury & Higgins, 1991; Frone & Rice, 1987; Loerch et al., 1989; Voydanoff, 1988). The vast majority of the studies that did observe a gender difference reported that women experience more conflict than men (Frone et al., 1992b; Hammer et al., 1997; Wiersma, 1990; Williams & Alliger, 1994). Because women typically spend more combined time on work and family activities than men (Hochschild, 1989), the results of these latter studies are not surprising.

The studies that find no gender difference in conflict are more difficult to explain. First, it is possible that women self-select into occupations and jobs that are less demanding and less likely to generate work-family conflict. It is also possible that women have already responded to the conflicting demands of work and family by reducing their involvement in work or by deciding not to get married or have children (Parasuraman & Greenhaus, 1993; Powell, 1988). These actions might lower women's work-family conflict to a level experienced by men. Alternatively, women may be better than men at "multitasking" or at adopting other coping strategies that reduce work-family conflict to a more manageable level.

These post hoc speculations rest on an assumption that people respond to anticipated or actual conflict in ways that reduce the conflict. Unfortunately, a snapshot view of work-family conflict at one particular point in time cannot identify the adjustments that are made at the time that work-family conflict is initially assessed. As we discuss in a later section, additional research is needed to understand the process by which work-family conflict unfolds over time.

In summary, extensive research has examined the antecedents and consequences of work-family conflict and the paths that link pressures and demands in the work and family domains to well-being. This research, however, explains only the negative linkages between work and family life. Only a relatively few studies have acknowledged the possibility that work and family roles can have positive or enriching effects on one another. A different concept—work-family integration—is necessary to explore this issue (Friedman & Greenhaus, in press).

Work-Family Integration

Several researchers have recognized opportunities for enhancement or integration between work and family roles. Marks (1977) proposed that participation in multiple roles can expand (rather than deplete) resources and create energy, thereby enhancing overall well-being. Sieber (1974) identified several mechanisms by which role participation can promote psychological health. Two of these mechanisms—status enhancement and personality enrichment— are particularly relevant to our examination of work-family linkages.

Status enhancement refers to the application of resources derived from one role to another role. Thus, money, status, connections, and other resources from work or family can promote well-being in the other domain (Kanter, 1977c; Piotrkowski, Rapoport, & Rapoport, 1987). Personality enrichment is the transfer of skills, attitudes, or perspectives developed within one role to solve problems in the other role. Other researchers have discussed this concept under a variety of names: educational spillover (Crouter, 1984); socialization transfer (Repetti, 1987); work as a socializer (Kanter, 1977c); and occupational conditions, values, and socialization (Piotrkowski et al., 1987).

In a series of studies that explored spillover from family to work, Kirchmeyer (1992a, 1992b, 1993) developed measures to assess positive (enhancement) and negative (conflict) connections from family to work. She found that positive spillover from family to work was more prevalent than negative spillover. Moreover, conflict and enhancement may be independent dimensions of the work-family interface (Kirchmeyer, 1992b; Tiedje et al., 1990), suggesting that, for a given individual, work and family roles can conflict with one another in some respects and enrich each other in other ways.

In summary, work-family linkages can produce conflict or integration. In the next section, we discuss three mechanisms that can be used to explain both the positive and negative linkages between work and family roles. In addition, we present research findings that bear on these mechanisms, discussing the role of gender whenever applicable.

Work-Family Linkages: Role Experiences, Involvement, And Attitudes

Three critical dimensions of role membership are the experiences encountered in a role, the level of involvement invested in a role, and the attitudinal reactions to participation in a role. Experiences, involvement, and attitudes within a role have the capacity to influence opportunities, competence, involvement, and attitudes in another role, and thereby affect outcomes in that role (Friedman & Greenhaus, in press).

We use the term *role experiences* broadly to include structural characteristics of a role and an individual's experiences that result from participating in the role. In the work domain, structural role characteristics include task characteristics, work stressors, social support received from supervisors and coworkers, compensation, job level, socialization practices, and career development opportunities. Individual work experiences can include knowledge, skills, or perspectives developed at work, perceptions of control over the work environment, status and work-related contacts, and self-esteem derived from work.

In the family domain, structural role characteristics include marital status; employment and income of spouse; presence, number, and ages of children; responsibility for the care of elders; and social support received from the spouse or other family members. Individual family experiences can include knowledge, skills, or perspectives developed within the family; status and family contacts; and the level of proficiency achieved within the family domain.

Role involvement has two components. Behavioral involvement refers to the amount of time devoted to in-role activities. Many studies have examined such indicators of behavioral involvement as hours worked, time spent on parenting, and time devoted to home maintenance. Psychological involvement refers to the level of ego involvement attached to a particular role or the salience of the role in an individual's life. Job involvement, career involvement, work role salience, work commitment, and family involvement are frequently studied indicators of psychological involvement.

Role attitudes refer to affective reactions to role membership and experiences therein. Job satisfaction, career satisfaction, quality of work life, work tension, and work distress illustrate specific work attitudes examined in the work-family literature. Family-related attitudes include family satisfaction, marital satisfaction, parenting satisfaction, quality of family life, family tension, and family distress.

Although the aim of this chapter is to illustrate the linkages between work and family roles, it should be noted that experiences, involvement, and attitudes within a given role may be interrelated, thereby having indirect effects on outcomes in the other role. For example, job scope, social support, and socialization practices might heighten work involvement and contribute to positive work attitudes (Brown, 1996; Chao, O'Leary-Kelly, Wolf, Klein, & Gardner, 1994; Schaubroeck & Fink, 1998). Similar observations may be made about relationships among experiences, involvement, and attitudes within the family domain. Family conflict and stress have shown consistent negative relationships with family satisfaction (Frone et al., 1992b; Higgins et al., 1992), and family support can promote marital and family satisfaction (Beatty, 1996; Frone et al., 1997; Leiter & Durup, 1996; Parasuraman et al., 1996).

In short, experiences, involvement, and attitudes are interrelated dimensions of membership in a particular role. We now discuss how these variables, in conjunction with gender, explain the work-family linkages proposed or observed in the literature. Because role experiences can operate through attitudes and involvement in the same role to have indirect effects on life in another role, we first discuss work-family linkages based on role attitudes and role involvement and then consider the impact of role experiences.

Attitude Spillover

Many scholars have proposed that attitudes or moods that arise within one role produce similar affect in another role. Some concepts focus on the transfer of negative emotions from one role to another, such as Evans and Bartolome's (1980) negative emotional spillover, Greenhaus and Beutell's (1985) strain-based conflict, and Small and Riley's (1990) energy interference. Other researchers have recognized that attitudinal or mood spillover can be positive as well as negative (Kanter, 1977c; Repetti, 1987).

On the negative side, individuals who are dissatisfied or anxious at work may bring these emotions home and become dissatisfied, preoccupied, or anxious within the family. Similarly, difficulties and frustrations at home can be so distracting that they prevent employees from enjoying and concentrating on work. Positive attitude spillover occurs when feelings of satisfaction or fulfillment that arise within one role are transferred into the other role, permitting fuller and more enjoyable participation in that role.

Staines (1980) interpreted positive correlations between satisfaction in one role and equivalent variables in another role as support for the spillover hypothesis. Many other researchers have reported positive relationships between satisfaction at work and satisfaction at home (Duxbury & Higgins, 1991; Friedman & Greenhaus, in press; Frone et al., 1992a; Frone et al., 1997; Parasuraman et al., 1996; Rice et al., 1992; Tiedje et al., 1990; Williams & Alliger, 1994). However, because most of the studies are based on cross-sectional data, it is impossible to determine whether a positive correlation reflects spillover from work to family or from family to work, or whether the spillover is positive or negative. In fact, these correlations may simply reflect dispositional tendencies to be happy or unhappy with work as well as other life roles (Judge, Locke, Durham, & Kluger, 1998). Kirchmeyer's (1992a, 1992b, 1993) research on spillover is unique in assessing positive and negative spillover with independent self-report scales. She found evidence of both types of spillover, with positive spillover being more prominent than negative spillover.

Several studies have examined relationships between attitudes at work and behaviors or outcomes within the family domain. For example, the relationship between job satisfaction and positive (or "authoritative") parenting (Stewart & Barling, 1996) might explain why fathers who are satisfied with their jobs have children with relatively few conduct problems (Barling, 1986) and why satisfied employees believe they are performing well as parents (Friedman & Greenhaus, in press). Moreover, stress at work has been associated with a tendency to withdraw emotionally from parent-child interactions (Repetti & Wood, 1997) and to use punitive parenting behavior (Stewart & Barling, 1996), and parents' feelings of job insecurity have been related to children's negative work beliefs and work attitudes (Barling, Dupre, & Hepburn, 1998). These findings suggest that the impact of work attitudes may go beyond the transfer of mood to influence specific behaviors and outcomes at home.

There are no consistent gender differences in attitude spillover. Staines (1980) observed that positive relationships between attitudes in the work and family domains were more likely to be observed for men than for women. In addition, home-to-work stress spillover has been found to be more pronounced for men than for women (Bolger, DeLongis, Kessler, & Wethington, 1989; Forthofer, Markman, Cox, Stanley, & Kessler, 1996). On the other hand, Williams and Alliger (1994) found stronger relationships between work and family attitudes for women than men. None of the studies we reviewed formally examined sex as a moderator of the relationship between work satisfaction and family satisfaction. We believe that a different methodology is necessary to determine whether there is a gender difference in attitude spillover, a point to which we will return in a later section of the chapter.

In summary, attitudes or mood that arise within one role can affect attitudes, mood, and behavior in another role. When negative attitudes spill over from one role to another, the first role conflicts with—or interferes with—participation in the second role. When positive attitudes spill over, then the originating role enriches the quality of life in the other role, fostering work-family integration.

Involvement in Work and Family Roles

Does a deep involvement in one role diminish, enhance, or bear no relationship to involvement in another role? Because it is often considered a fixed resource, time spent in one role cannot be devoted to another role (Greenhaus & Beutell, 1985; Kanter, 1977c; Small & Riley, 1990). In addition, psychological absorption with a role (Kanter, 1977c; Small & Riley, 1990) may produce a preoccupation with that role that interferes with full participation in another role.

The literature suggests that involvement in one role can inhibit involvement in another role. For example, the number of hours an employee works is inversely related to the time spent on nonwork activities in general (O'Driscoll et al., 1992) and on family activities in particular (Frone et al., 1997; Parasuraman et al., 1996; Staines & Pleck, 1984). Because the magnitude of these relationships is often small and occasionally nonsignificant (Gutek et al., 1991), there are likely to be exceptions to the time scarcity hypothesis. Research has also revealed a negative relationship between psychological involvement in work and psychological involvement in family (Friedman & Greenhaus, in press; Hammer et al., 1997; Howard, 1992; Parasuraman et al., 1996), although there have been exceptions to this relationship as well (Adams et al., 1996; Frone et al., 1992a; Williams & Alliger, 1994).

In a direct test of the relationship between work involvement and family involvement, Friedman and Greenhaus (in press) classified managers on the basis of the priority they attach to different roles. Their analyses revealed four life role priority groups: career focused, family focused, career *and* family focused, and self- or society focused. As might be expected, the career-focused managers spent less time with their families and were less psychologically involved in family life than the family-focused group. On the other hand, the family-focused managers were less involved in their work—behaviorally and psychologically—than the career-focused group.

These analyses indicate that many people focus their time and emotion on either work *or* family and suggest that an intense involvement in one role may interfere with full participation in the other role. It is not surprising, then, that a high level of work involvement reduces satisfaction and performance within the family domain, and an intense involvement in family life encourages individuals to restructure their work to meet family needs and reduce their career aspirations (Friedman & Greenhaus, in press; Karambayya & Reilly, 1992).

Many of the findings on work and family involvement suggest a process of accommodation (Lambert, 1990) in which an individual reduces involvement in the less salient role to participate actively in the more prominent role. Taken to the extreme, accommodation can produce a "spiraling imbalance" between work and family (Kofodimos, 1990). In her study of male executives, Kofodimos observed that work-family imbalance originates during the early career years, when long work hours and full commitment to the job can strain relationships within the family. As family life further deteriorates, the executives invest even more of themselves in work, which provides more rewards and more satisfaction than their families do. These men avoid the uncomfortable intimacy of family life in favor of satisfying their well-developed mastery needs at work. Work, then, becomes an "alibi" (Bartolome, 1983) for not investing themselves more fully in the lives of their family, a situation that is perpetuated by the organization's reward system. Hochschild's (1997a) recent analysis suggests that many women may also use work as an escape from increasingly demanding family responsibilities.

Although some degree of accommodation seems to be a prevalent strategy, it is possible to be moderately or highly involved in both work and family. As noted earlier, Friedman and Greenhaus (in press) found that a segment of their sample was career *and* family focused. These managers, who constituted nearly 30% of the sample, worked long hours, were psychologically involved in their careers, and aspired to senior management positions. However, they also were likely to be married with children, psychologically involved in their family lives, adjust their work schedules for family and personal reasons, and spend significant time with their children and on home chores. Thus, an extreme accommodation of one role for another is not inevitable.

In sum, it is our belief that a high level of involvement in one role is usually associated with a lower level of involvement in another role. In this respect, the linkages between work involvement and family involvement offer stronger support for a conflict perspective than for an integration perspective. However, most of the existing research cannot determine whether work-involved individuals reduce their participation in family life, or whether family-involved individuals reduce their involvement in work. We return to this issue when we discuss areas for future research.

Gender is a key factor that is associated with involvement in work and family roles. Women generally devote fewer hours than men to paid work (Greenberger & O'Neil, 1993; Parasuraman et al., 1996; Singh, Greenhaus, Parasuraman, & Collins, 1998), especially when there are children in the family (Friedman & Greenhaus, in press). On the one hand, women continue to spend more time than men on home and family activities (Burley, 1991; Greenberger & O'Neil, 1993; Greenhaus et al., 1989; Parasuraman et al., 1996; Wiersma & van den Berg, 1991), even when the women are employed outside the home (Hochschild, 1989). On the other hand, the research on gender differences in *psychological* involvement in work and family roles is inconclusive (Friedman & Greenhaus, in press; Greenberger & O'Neil, 1993; Greenhaus et al., 1989; Parasuraman et al., 1996; Singh et al., 1998).

It might be expected that the negative relationship between work involvement and family involvement would be stronger for women than men. Women experience more substantial trade-offs between their work and family lives than men (Friedman & Greenhaus, in press), and, as we see in the next section, mothers are more likely than fathers to reduce their work involvement in response to the demands of parenthood.

Yet we found no evidence that behavioral or psychological involvement in one role affects involvement in the other role differently for men and women. Indeed, virtually no studies have examined the relationship between work involvement and family involvement separately for men and women. However, there are likely to be gender differences in the extent to which specific experiences (e.g., parenthood) trigger involvement in a role. We elaborate this point in the next section.

Role Experiences

Experiences within a role can directly and indirectly affect the quality of life in another role. When the effects are positive, role experiences act as resources that provide opportunities for work-family integration. When the effects are negative, interference or conflict arises at the work-family interface (Friedman & Greenhaus, in press). Next, we discuss the impact of work experiences on family life and then examine the effects of family experiences on work.

▨ The Impact of Work Experiences on Family Life

Perhaps the most basic dimension of work experience is whether an individual is employed. Based on the scarcity hypothesis and normative beliefs concerning the appropriate roles for women and men, it was widely assumed that a woman's employment would be detrimental to her family's well-being. The literature in this area has provided more support for the enhancement hypothesis than for the scarcity hypothesis. A woman's employment has been shown to enhance her emotional well-being (Baruch & Barnett, 1986), particularly if she wishes to work (Ross, Mirowsky, & Huber, 1983) and her job is interesting and challenging (Valdez & Gutek, 1987).

Research has also indicated that a woman's employment need not have deleterious effects on her children (Piotrkowski et al., 1987). The impact of a mother's work on her children also seems to depend on the quality of the woman's work experiences (Baruch & Barnett, 1986) and the congruence of her employment status with her commitment to work (Barling, Fullager, & Marchl-Dingle, 1988).

The effect of a woman's employment on her husband's well-being is inconclusive. Most of the studies show either no effect or a negative effect. Husbands of employed women who report decreased well-being may feel inadequate as income providers (Rosenfield, 1992; Staines, Pottick, & Fudge, 1986), or may devote more time to the home (Rosenfield, 1992) and less time to work (Parasuraman, Greenhaus, Rabinowitz, Bedeian, & Mossholder, 1989) than they would like, thereby experiencing decreased job satisfaction.

Turning to the conditions of employment, one of the most significant rewards provided by a job is income. Although money does not guarantee personal fulfillment or marital well-being, it does establish a family's standard of living. Moreover, a high income can provide a positive home environment for children (Menaghan & Parcel, 1995), promote children's health (Friedman & Greenhaus, in press), and enable parents to hire outside help to handle certain household responsibilities, permitting them to spend more time with their children (Miller, 1997). Money can serve as a resource that enriches the quality of family life.

The literature also suggests that the content of a job, in particular, its level of autonomy, can affect one's family. Autonomy enhances feelings of work satisfaction (Parasuraman et al., 1996), which can spill over and affect attitudes within the family, eventually enhancing the quality of a marriage (Hughes, Galinsky, & Morris, 1992) and the way a parent interacts with children (Stewart & Barling, 1996). Moreover, autonomy often enables employees to determine the timing and location of their work, which may explain why individuals with extensive autonomy experience relatively little work-family conflict (Aryee, 1992; Greenhaus et al., 1989; Parasuraman et al., 1996). These findings illustrate the indirect effects of job autonomy on family life through positive work-related attitudes and control over the time spent at work.

Work schedule flexibility, which often accompanies highly autonomous jobs, has also been linked to low levels of work-family conflict (Hammer et al., 1997). Because flexibility enables an individual to fulfill home responsibilities more effectively, it is not surprising that the flexibility of an employee's work schedule is associated with increased satisfaction with family life (Parasuraman et al., 1996).

Flexibility can also be derived from broader organizational work-family practices that provide more personal control over work life. Perhaps because employees working in family-supportive organizations tend to spend more time with their children, they see themselves as effective parents, experience little work-family conflict, and feel the need to make relatively few work-family trade-offs (Friedman & Greenhaus, in press; Judge et al., 1994).

Social support from the workplace need not involve formal, organizational work-family initiatives. Employees who receive extensive support from their supervisors or coworkers experience little work-family conflict (Goff, Mount, & Jamison, 1990; Warren & Johnson, 1995), in part because of the greater control over work gained by having supportive colleagues (Thomas & Ganster, 1995). In short, social support from work is a resource that can enhance performance and well-being in the family domain (Frone et al., 1997). It is reasonable to expect that a supportive work environment not only provides flexibility, information, and direct help to employees but also enhances their feelings of acceptance and self-esteem.

Gender and work experiences. There is some evidence that work role experiences may have different effects on the family lives of men and of women. For example, Friedman and Greenhaus (in press) found that women (but not men) who engage in extensive networking have healthy children who do well in school and have satisfactory child care arrangements. They also observed that a woman's job autonomy has a positive effect on the well-being of her children. It was concluded that women, more so than men, use their work experiences to benefit their families. For example, women may be more likely than men to use the freedom provided by autonomous jobs to make themselves available to their children. They may also use the relationships established through networking to seek information and advice, share family concerns, and provide and receive emotional support regarding work-family problems.

In addition, women have been found to respond more positively than men to the presence of a flexible work schedule (Scandura & Lankau, 1997), and to place more importance than men on receiving parenting support in the form of child care, alternative work hours, and flexible work schedules (Wiersma, 1990). Consistent with these studies, Friedman and Greenhaus (in press) found that an organization's family supportiveness expands women's expenditure of time on home and family more than it affects men's time allocations, although in most respects, supportiveness had similar benefits for men and women.

The picture is less clear when it comes to informal support from the work domain. Although women receive more social support from coworkers than do men, women and men receive similar levels of support from their supervisors (Parasuraman & Greenhaus, 1993). Moreover, there is no consistent evidence that women benefit more or less than men from support provided by their supervisors or coworkers (Greenberger, Goldberg, Hamill, O'Neil, & Payne, 1989; Parasuraman, Greenhaus, & Granrose, 1992).

Summary. Work experiences can affect involvement, behavior, attitudes, and outcomes in the family domain. Positive work experiences—high autonomy and control, work schedule flexibility, and social support—can enrich family life, promoting work-family integration. The absence of these resources, and the presence of extensive stress within the work environment, may produce work-family conflict that has harmful effects on the family.

The Impact of Family Experiences on Work Life

In the previous section, we noted that employment often enhances the well-being of the employee's family. Does having a spouse and children enhance the quality of one's work life? In this section, we examine the effects of marriage and children on individuals' work lives and discuss the impact of support from family members on the work domain.

Marriage and children. Research partially supports the belief that marriage hinders a woman's career. Married women are more likely than unmarried women to hold low-status and part-time jobs (Rosin & Korabik, 1990; Valdez & Gutek, 1987), and women in upper-management positions are less likely to be married than men in similar positions (Parasuraman & Greenhaus, 1993). Nevertheless, marriage does not seem to affect the career success of women once they have entered managerial and professional positions (Friedman & Greenhaus, in press). It is likely that the presence of children (see below) has a more substantial effect on women's work lives than their marital status.

Married men, on the other hand, may experience a "family bonus" that has a positive effect on work-related achievements. Pfeffer and Ross (1982) noted that marriage had a positive impact on men's financial rewards from work. More recently, Friedman and Greenhaus (in press) found that married men occupied higher-level positions, earned more money, and were more satisfied with their careers than unmarried men, even after controlling for the men's age. The family bonus was attributed to the high level of job autonomy experienced by married men. It is not clear, however, whether married men seek out additional autonomy—perhaps because their marital status increases their ambition—or whether they are provided more freedom by organizations that view married men as particularly mature and responsible.

The presence of children does appear to inhibit the careers of many women. Although several studies found that parental responsibilities have no effect on women's work outcomes (Lobel & St. Clair, 1992; Schneer & Reitman, 1993), other studies suggest that a "family penalty" may accompany motherhood. Tharenou, Latimer, and Conroy (1994) observed that married women with children experienced less rapid advancement in their managerial careers than did women without children. In addition, Friedman and Greenhaus (in press) found that mothers made less money and were less satisfied with their careers than women without children. The impact of children—especially preschool children—on income and career satisfaction was attributed to several factors. Mothers of young children spent less time at work, were less psychologically involved in work, and received less coaching and fewer developmental assignments than women without children. Singh et al. (1998) also observed that women with young children spent less time working and were less involved in their work than women with lesser parental demands.

Taken together, these findings indicate that many women with substantial family responsibilities reduce their behavioral and psychological involvement in work, in response to actual or anticipated work-family conflict (Parasuraman & Greenhaus, 1993). Why these women have fewer opportunities for coaching and career development is not clear. Although some mothers of young children turn down special assignments and other developmental opportunities (Friedman & Greenhaus, in press), it is also likely that some organizations are less willing to invest in the career development of these women (Lewis & Cooper, 1988). The importance of organizational support is reinforced by the finding that mothers' family penalty is substantially reduced in family-responsive organizations (Friedman & Greenhaus, in press).

Do family responsibilities also influence women's decisions to change employers? Although work-family initiatives in many organizations are intended to curb voluntary turnover (Connor, Hooks, & McGuire, 1997; Riley & McCloskey, 1997), the role of family responsibilities in women's turnover decisions is unclear. Rosin and Korabik (1991) found that women's turnover intentions were unrelated to the inflexibility of their work schedules, their desire to spend more time with their children, their difficulty arranging for quality child care, and their level of work-family conflict. Similarly, marital status, number of children, and other family variables failed to predict the turnover intentions of men or women (Rosin & Korabik, 1995; Stroh, Brett, & Reilly, 1996).

It appears that women consider leaving organizations for the same reasons that men do: dissatisfying jobs and limited career advancement opportunities (Rosin & Korabik, 1995; Stroh et al., 1996). Work-related factors also seem to be primarily responsible for women's decision to leave their career field (Greenhaus, Collins, Singh, & Parasuraman, 1997). Therefore, despite many assertions to the contrary, family responsibilities are generally not a substantial factor in a woman's decision to leave her employer. We return to this point in a later section of the chapter.

Research examining the effects of children on men's work lives has produced inconsistent results. Lobel and St. Clair (1992) found no effect of the number or age of children on men's level of effort at work or their financial rewards. Also, Singh et al. (1998) observed that parental demands did not influence men's behavioral and psychological involvement in work.

On the other hand, Friedman and Greenhaus (in press) found that fathers experience a family bonus: They occupy higher-level jobs, earn more money, and are more satisfied with their careers than men without children. The enhanced career success of fathers was also observed by Tharenou et al. (1994), who found that fathers participated in more extensive training and development activities than men without children. These findings are consistent with Gould and Werbel's (1983) observation that fathers are more highly involved in their jobs than men without children.

Yet the financial bonus enjoyed by fathers applies primarily to single-earner fathers (Friedman & Greenhaus, in press), who tend to earn higher salaries than dual-earner fathers (Brett, 1997; Schneer & Reitman, 1993). Because the dual-earner father penalty is not fully explained by differences in education, tenure, or work hours, Brett (1997) concluded that wives who are not in the workforce might provide more indirect career support to their husbands than employed wives. It is also possible that organizations tend to reward single-earner fathers because they are thought to have more substantial financial needs than men whose wives are in the workforce.

Social support from the family. Although extensive family responsibilities can be a drain on an individual's career—especially a woman's—families can also provide social support that enriches work life. For example, there is consistent evidence that support from a spouse or other family member has a positive effect on an individual's work attitudes (Adams et al., 1996; Friedman & Greenhaus, in press; Frone et al., 1997). There are several plausible reasons for this effect.

First, it is likely that supportive family members participate more actively in family life, permitting an individual to work longer hours and avail themselves of more career development opportunities (Parasuraman, Singh, & Greenhaus, 1997). This would explain why support from the family enables individuals to make fewer adjustments of their work schedules for family reasons (Friedman & Greenhaus, in press). Family support also reduces individuals' work-family conflict (Aryee, 1992; Greenberger & O'Neil, 1993), particularly the interference of family with work (Adams et al., 1996; Parasuraman et al., 1996), and promotes high levels of job performance (Friedman & Greenhaus, in press; Frone et al., 1997).

Moreover, individuals who receive extensive emotional support from their spouses have more opportunities for coaching and developmental assignments, participate more extensively in networking activities, feel more accepted by their coworkers, and have more autonomy on the job than those who receive little emotional support (Friedman & Greenhaus, in press). The researchers speculated that the self-acceptance and self-esteem derived from emotional support (Cohen & Wills, 1985) and the different perspectives provided by an empathic and insightful spouse can help employees pursue their careers more assertively.

It is not clear whether family support differentially affects the work experiences of men and women, because the research on sex differences in social support has yielded inconsistent findings. The studies we reviewed clearly indicate that husbands receive more instrumental support from their wives than they provide, specifically in terms of home maintenance and child care. Men and women seem to provide each other with a similar level of emotional support (Parasuraman & Greenhaus, 1994) and appear to benefit equally from the support (Cutrona & Suhr, 1992).

Summary. Experiences in the family domain can affect work life positively or negatively. The presence of young children is more likely to interfere with work for women than for men, and many women have undoubtedly reduced their work involvement to alleviate the daily conflicts between family and work. Social support from family members, on the other hand, can enhance work life for women and men by reducing work-family conflict and by providing information, advice, and encouragement that can be applied to the work domain.

Integration and Agenda for Future Research

The literature clearly indicates that work and family lives are interconnected in many ways. The three-dimensional framework (Friedman & Greenhaus, in press) we adopted for reviewing the literature was useful in identifying specific features of the role experiences, involvements, and attitudes of women and men that shape the nature of the linkages between work and family. Work-family integration occurs when positive attitudes in one role spill over into the other role, or when experiences in one role serve as resources that enrich life in the other role. Work-family conflict, on the other hand, arises when negative attitudes intrude into the other role, or when experiences and intense involvement in a role interfere with active participation in the other role. In this section, we reexamine the effect of gender on the linkages between work and family roles and identify several areas in which additional inquiry would be particularly fruitful.

The influence of gender on work-family linkages rests on the disparities between men's and women's involvement in work and family roles, especially when there are children in the family. From a behavioral perspective, a gendered division of labor seems to have withstood dramatic changes in family structure and the world of work. Mothers in dual-earner families continue to spend considerably more time on home and children than their husbands, whereas the fathers devote more time to their jobs than do their wives. If actions speak louder than words, then there are clear differences in the involvement that women and men invest in the worlds of family and work.

Yet the fact that the empirical research has not revealed consistent gender differences in the psychological involvement attached to work and family roles suggests that involvement may mean something different for men and women. In particular, we suspect that men who report a high level of family involvement may be referring primarily to their role as economic provider, whereas women who report high involvement may be referring to their role as nurturer. Therefore, the family involvement of men and women may have different behavioral implications. This may explain why men who work long hours are highly satisfied with their family lives, whereas women who work long hours tend to be dissatisfied with their family roles (Friedman & Greenhaus, in press).

Future research should investigate whether men and women attribute different meanings to involvement in family life. One strategy would be to determine the relationship between family involvement and behavioral indicators of family participation separately for men and women. Such studies should use new measures that capture the multidimensionality of family involvement.

An understanding of gender differences in role involvement is necessary to discern how involvement in one role affects involvement in another role. Although the negative relationship between work involvement and family involvement seems to exist for both men and women, the empirical research does not distinguish the causality of the relationship. This relationship could indicate that individuals who are highly involved in their family roles reduce their career involvement, or that those who are highly involved in their careers restrict their involvement in family life. Of course, both scenarios are plausible and may, in fact, be different for men and women.

A variety of methodologies will be required to detect the causal directionality of the relationship between work involvement and family involvement. Cross-sectional, correlational studies will continue to contribute to the literature by documenting relationships among variables. They should be supplemented, however, by additional methodologies that are more capable of revealing different causal relationships. The ongoing assessment of work and family variables on a daily basis (Williams & Alliger, 1994) and other short-term longitudinal approaches (Leiter & Durup, 1996; MacEwen & Barling, 1994) should be employed in a greater variety of situations. A combination of quantitative and qualitative analyses within the same study (Crouter, 1984) can provide particularly rich data. Moreover, vignette studies—used so frequently in other areas of organizational behavior—can strengthen causal inferences through the manipulation of independent variables and the random assignment of respondents to the different treatment conditions.

The literature also suggests that attitudes or emotions may spill over from one role to another. Yet the usefulness of much of the research is limited by its reliance on correlations between work attitudes and family attitudes to provide evidence for the spillover process. As noted earlier, the presence of positive correlations cannot distinguish the roles that are the origin and the recipient of the spillover, and cannot determine whether the attitude spillover is positive or negative in its consequence.

New measures should be developed that distinguish the causal direction (WF or FW) and the sign (positive or negative) of attitude spillover, perhaps using additional sources of data (e.g., spouse, coworkers) that supplement self-reports. This would enable researchers to study the conditions under which individuals carry attitudes or moods from one role to another, the relative likelihood of work attitudes and family attitudes crossing role boundaries, and the actions that individuals or organizations can take to reduce negative attitude spillover.

Research should also examine the conditions under which there are gender differences in attitude spillover. Sex-role stereotypes might suggest that men are more likely than women to bring home their job-induced emotions (positive or negative), whereas women are more likely to carry their family satisfactions or frustrations to the workplace. This proposition is based on the assumption that attitudes or moods are more likely to spill over when they originate in roles that are central to an individual's self-concept. Yet the limited research suggests the opposite; men may have more difficulty than women preventing home-related stress from extending into the workplace (Bolger et al., 1989). New theories and new measures will be needed to examine this phenomenon further.

Our review also reveals how experiences in one role can have a positive or negative effect on the other role. Stressful, rigid work environments that demand extended time commitments can interfere with family life, whereas supportive, flexible work environments that provide opportunities for self-control can enrich family life.

Although positive work experiences can serve as resources for parents, women may be more likely than men to use these resources—job autonomy, social relationships, supportive work-family initiatives—for the welfare of their children (Friedman & Greenhaus, in press). Are women more motivated than men to use the work environment for the benefit of their children? Are they more comfortable sharing their work-family problems with others at work? Does a woman's relationship orientation provide more opportunities to receive advice or support from work colleagues? Research is needed to understand gender differences in the application of work-related resources to family life. We also need to understand the impact of parents' work experiences on children's well-being. Although research on this topic has been expanding in recent years (Barling et al., 1998; Friedman & Greenhaus, in press; Repetti & Wood, 1997; Stewart & Barling, 1996), a great deal of work remains to be done.

As work experiences affect family life, so too can family experiences influence the work role. Support from a spouse or other family member can promote involvement, success, and satisfaction in the work domain for men and women. Yet family experiences can also constrain opportunities and involvement at work, and it is in this regard that gender differences are most pronounced. Women's family responsibilities can severely limit their careers in ways that do not generally affect men. Women tend to choose occupations that are compatible with their family's needs. They also limit their aspirations for career advancement, reduce their behavioral and psychological involvement in work, adjust their work schedules for family reasons, and turn down opportunities for career development and growth that would interfere with their family responsibilities.

Although family interferes with work more extensively for women than men, this difference is not consistently reflected in the empirical research on work-family conflict. Of the nine studies we located that explicitly examined FW conflict, five revealed no gender difference, three observed greater interference for women than men, and one found greater interference for men than women. We believe that the method employed to study work-family conflict is responsible for this apparent contradiction.

Elsewhere (Greenhaus & Parasuraman, 1994), we suggested that work-family conflict should be studied as a stress episode—much like Kahn et al.'s (1964) original conceptualization—rather than as a chronic or ongoing state.

This perspective would enable researchers to trace a work-family conflict incident from its beginning—a preliminary appraisal of conflict in the environment—and study an individual's reactions to the incipient conflict, including the search for social support and the activation of different coping behaviors. We believe a focus on work-family conflict episodes can promote a better understanding of the conditions under which environmental factors arouse psychological conflict and the usefulness of different coping and support mechanisms in resolving work-family conflict.

An examination of work-family conflict episodes can also help us understand the reasons behind the absence of gender differences reported in many studies of work-family conflict. Women may respond to an initial appraisal of conflict by reducing their behavioral and psychological involvement in work. Although objectively their family responsibilities interfere with work, they may not experience psychological conflict because the simultaneous pressures (family *and* work) required to arouse conflict are no longer as intense. Moreover, women's initial conflict may subside because of the extensive coping strategies they adopt in response to work-family difficulties (Kirchmeyer, 1993). In addition, because women are more likely than men to acknowledge the need to prioritize roles and to make trade-offs (Friedman & Greenhaus, in press), they may perceive family-work interference as inevitable rather than as a source of intense conflict.

We believe that research that views work-family conflict as an episode can reveal the similarities and differences in the ways that men and women respond to pressures in the work and family domains. This research will require a methodology that focuses on a specific instance of potential conflict and follows the episode through a series of cognitive and behavioral responses. A qualitative approach that concentrates on a current or very recent conflict episode and a vignette methodology that requires individuals to respond to hypothetical pressures from work and family seem particularly promising.

We also believe that the role of gender in work and family life should be studied in the context of development across the life course. Prior research has revealed changes in the work involvement of married women when they become parents (Friedman & Greenhaus, in press). Moreover, parents' feelings of work-family conflict are likely to be heightened during major child-rearing periods (Blanchard-Fields et al., 1997).

The adoption of a life stage perspective could reveal many subtle gender differences in work-family linkages that might otherwise go undetected, especially because the careers of women and men may evolve in different sequences or patterns (Gallos, 1989; Sekaran & Hall, 1989). For example, does the impact of the family vary for men and women making turnover decisions at different stages of their lives? Does the usefulness of different types of social support from work and family depend on family stage? And do work (family) role experiences enrich or conflict with family (work) life in different ways for men and women at varying stages of family development? We believe that analyses that incorporate family or life stage may reveal when work-family linkages are similar for men and women and when they are different.

We would add that most of the research on work and family treats the role involvements and experiences of dual-earner partners as the product of individual decision making aimed at maximizing each partner's outcomes. We recommend that more research be conducted at the dual-earner couple or the family level of analysis. We need to understand how dual-earner partners make decisions regarding the role of each partner in career and family, the consequences of these decisions for individual and family well-being, and the crossover of stress and strain from one partner to another (Westman & Etzion, 1995). An examination of the family as the unit of analysis can also reveal a great deal about power dynamics between partners, communication and conflict resolution styles, and changes in partners' work and family involvements over time.

We noted earlier that most of the research we reviewed was conducted on American samples. Of the 59 empirical studies of work-family conflict reviewed in this chapter, 14 (nearly 25%) were based on non-U.S. samples, with the majority of these coming from Canada. However, because our chapter focused primarily on relatively recent studies, the representation of non-U.S. samples in work-family research as a whole is likely to be larger than 25%. Indeed, some of the pioneering research on work-family dynamics was conducted with data gathered from participants in Canada (Burke, Weir, & DuWors, 1979) and Europe (Evans & Bartolome, 1984). Moreover, international researchers have contributed to the growing literature on work-family issues in such countries and regions as Australia (Tharenou et al., 1994), India (Komarraju, 1997; Sekaran, 1992; Shukla & Kapoor, 1990), Israel (Izraeli, 1992; Richter, 1992), Japan (Ishii-Kuntz, 1993; Watanabe, Takahashi, & Minami, 1998), and Singapore (Aryee, 1992; Yuen & Lim, 1992).

It is important to note that work and family systems operate within, influence, and are influenced by the wider social, economic, and political context (Lewis, 1992, 1997b), which includes cultural norms and values, gender-role ideology, and public policy. Although the likelihood and prevalence of differences in culture and values have been recognized, few studies on the work-family interface have assessed specific cultural dimensions of the countries in which the studies were conducted. There is also little comparative research examining cross-country differences in the pattern of linkages between work and family. Thus, we recommend that investigations of cross-cultural and cross-national influences play a prominent role in the future research agenda on the work-family interface.

Finally, we propose that researchers go beyond the study of work-family conflict to identify mechanisms that integrate work and family lives. The process by which work and family experiences are used as resources requires greater scrutiny. The research by Kirchmeyer is especially instructive in this regard because she developed a measure of several mechanisms by which one role (the family) can have positive effects on another role. Moreover, it is plausible that personal characteristics—such as life values or positive/negative affectivity—moderate the cross-role relationship between experiences and well-being.

In sum, it is time to supplement our study of work-family conflict with an equally vigorous effort to understand work-family integration. Such an approach will provide a more balanced view of the linkages between the worlds of work and family for both women and men.

Stress and the Working Woman

Marilyn J. Davidson and Sandra Fielden

The costs of occupational stress for organizations are substantial. According to Discoll and Cooper (1996), 360 million working days are lost annually in the United Kingdom through sickness at a cost to organizations of £ 8 billion. Moreover, the United Kingdom Health and Safety Executive estimates that approximately half of these lost days are stress related (Discoll & Cooper, 1996). Similarly, Elkin and Rosch (1990) estimate that of the 550 million working days lost per year due in America to absenteeism, around 54% are stress related in some way. Due to the rapid demographic, social, and economic changes over the past few decades, there has been a large increase in the number of women entering paid employment throughout Western Europe, North America, and Australia (Davidson, 1996). For example, in 1997 women accounted for just over 49.5% of the United Kingdom's workforce (Employment Service, 1998); this figure will continue to rise until the year 2006, according to recent government projections ("British Labour Force Projections," 1995). Although paid employment provides many positive benefits for women, for some (especially the working wife and mother), the excessive pressure and scarcity of free time can adversely affect their ability to cope, sometimes resulting in physical and mental illnesses such as depression, anxiety, high blood pressure, and headaches. This, in turn, may lead to alcohol and drug abuse, absenteeism, poor personal relationships with colleagues, changed sleeping habits, and decreased work performance (Davidson & Cooper, 1992; Devanna, 1987). This chapter examines the current literature pertaining to gender and occupational stress with special emphasis on the effects of stress on the working woman.

The Nature of Stress

The term *stress* has been used to signify environmental agents that disturb structure and functions, as well as responses to such agents by psychological, physiological, and sociological systems.

Hans Selye (1976) was one of the first to try to explain the process of stress-related illness with his "general adaptation syndrome" theory, which describes three stages an individual encounters in stressful situations:

1. *The alarm reaction,* in which an initial shock phase of lowered resistance is followed by countershock during which the individual's defense mechanisms become active.

2. *Resistance,* the stage of maximum adaptation and, it is hoped, a successful return to equilibrium for the individual. If, however, the stressor continues or the defense does not work, the individual will move on to the third stage.

3. *Exhaustion,* when adaptive mechanisms collapse.

This theory reflected the prevalent feeling of the 1930s and 1940s that stress could be understood exclusively by a simple stimulus-response model. Although many of the current definitions of stress still stick fairly close to the stimulus-response or energy-exchange model, there is a movement toward viewing it more as an *interactive process.* This more sophisticated viewpoint is particularly well articulated by Lazarus (1971) and is the beginning of interactionist thinking. Although both the environmental stimulus and the reacting individual are vital elements, it is the nature of the relationship between the two that is crucial: "Stress refers, then, to a very broad class of problems differentiated from other problem areas because it deals with *any demands which tax the system,* whatever it is, a physiological system, a social system, or a psychological system, and the response of that system"; "reaction depends on how the person interprets or appraises (consciously or unconsciously) the significance of a harmful, threatening or challenging event" (Lazarus, 1971, p. 196).

Cognitive appraisal is an essentially individual-based affair: "The appraisal of threat is not a simple perception of the elements of the situation, but a judgment, an inference in which the data are assembled to a constellation of ideas and expectations" (Lazarus, 1966, p. 27). Change in any one element (e.g., the background situation against which the stimulus is perceived) can radically alter the perceiver's interpretation. Appley (1962) agrees that this cognitive element (he calls it "threat perception") is the vital link between the individual's environment and his or her experience of stress. Arnold (1960), who prefers the term "sense judgment," emphasizes that elaborate levels of awareness are not necessarily involved.

Once this perceptual viewpoint becomes theoretically acceptable, stress researchers ascribe some of the (indisputable) individual variations in nature and levels of stress to individual characteristics, rather than to environmental ones. Appley and Turnbull (1967) talk of a person's "vulnerability profile" (i.e., personality, demographic factors, physical makeup, past experience, and motivation) and provide substantiating research that finds that well-adjusted, integrated, mature individuals are best able to cope in stressful situations. They add that the more the stimulus relies on prior conditioning, the more individual differences are likely to play a part.

Turning our attention to occupational stress, it is now generally accepted that sources of work stress can be adequately investigated only by taking a multidisciplinary approach (Cooper, Cooper, & Eaker, 1988; Davidson & Cooper, 1992), that is, investigating psychological, sociological, and physiological problems that tax individuals by the demands made on them. Figure 21.1 presents a multifaceted approach to occupational stress in females. In particular, it includes organizational and extra-organizational stressors on the individual at work, which have been isolated as being particularly pertinent to women (i.e., "work stressors" and "home-work conflicts"). The first includes problems associated with discrimination and prejudice (e.g., career blocks, sexual harassment) and being a token woman (e.g., performance pressure, sex stereotyping, isolation, lack of role models), as well as specific stressors associated with Black and ethnic minority women (e.g., racism, sexism, bicultural role stressors). The second focuses on the interface between home and work and such conflicts as lack of social and domestic support, dilemmas about starting a family, and so on (Davidson, 1997; Davidson & Cooper, 1992).

This model demonstrates that work stressors can also affect an individual in the home and social environment, and vice versa. Thus, when isolating the sources of stress in working women, one also has to be aware of the importance of extra-organizational sources of stress that can affect the behavior, performance, and mental and physical health of an individual at work. Figure 21.1 shows that the major settings for behavior (work and home) form an integrated whole of forces that impinge on and interact with the individual. Therefore, the stressor(s) from one area that affect the individual may change the amount of stressor(s) in relationships in other areas.

When an individual is stressed to a sufficient extent in one or more areas, then stress will materialize. Exactly how depends on a number of individual coping factors (determined by variables such as personality, behavior, demographics), but clearly it is an "individual within context" situation. Thus, when exposed to the same apparent stressor, one individual may engage in escapist drinking, whereas another may develop hypertension (Cartwright & Cooper, 1997; Davidson & Cooper, 1992; Davidson, Cooper, & Baldini, 1995).

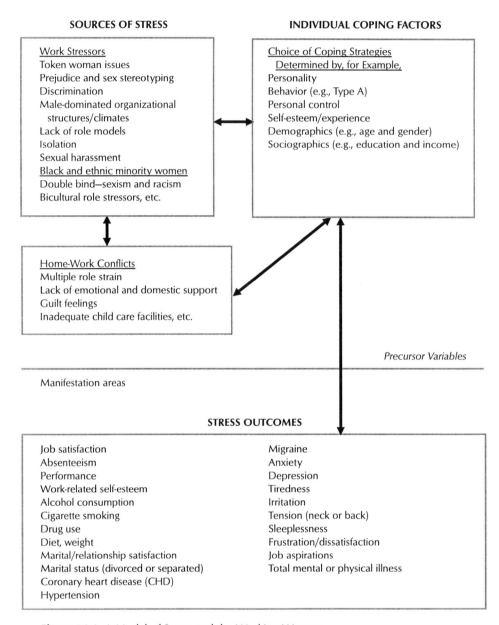

Figure 21.1. A Model of Stress and the Working Woman

Sources of Stress and the Working Woman

The majority of research into occupational stress has been predominantly North American and European and has focused primarily on White, professional men; many gaps and biases still exist in the current approach to stress and working women (Clark, Chandler, & Barry, 1996; Rydstedt, Johansson,

& Evans, 1998; Trocki & Orioli, 1994). The gender segregation prevalent in the examination of how work affects people has led to the conclusion that "the widely held belief that there are sex differences in occupational stress is not supported" (Martocchio & O'Leary, 1989, p. 498). Studies that have attempted to compare men's and women's work experiences have failed to accurately represent the current picture of women and work stress because occupational roles, in general, are associated with good psychological health (Dunahoo, Geller, & Hobfoll, 1996). However, studies controlling for marital status and children have shown that women with multiple roles (e.g., work and motherhood) experience poorer mental health than their nonworking counterparts (Arber, Gilbert, & Dale, 1985). This has frequently led to the assumption that women should experience increased mental well-being during unemployment due to role reduction, a fact not supported by studies into managerial and nonmanagerial female unemployment (Fielden & Davidson, 1996; Waldron & Herold, 1986).

In the past, studies of gender differences in the workplace have often suffered from the fact that, in many organizations, women are employed in substantially different roles than men (Guppy & Rick, 1996). Potential gender-based differences in stress appear to have been masked by role differentiation in much of the research. Stress experienced by women working in male-dominated industries or male-dominated professions is frequently exacerbated by gender-based barriers. "Token women" working in nontraditional jobs, whether blue or white collar, suffer most from stress related to discrimination and prejudice at work (Davidson & Cooper, 1984; Rosin & Korabik, 1991). However, recent research (Terborg, 1995) has shown that a number of female-dominated jobs, such as clinical technician, secretary, and waitress, although also stressful, can provide high levels of job satisfaction that can offset the negative effect of stress on health and well-being (Guppy & Rick, 1996; Sevastos, Smith, & Cordery, 1992).

Recent studies have also concluded that managerial and professional women experience unique sources of stress related to their minority status and gender and that these stressors result in higher levels of overall occupational stress compared with their male counterparts. Devanna (1987) and Greenglass (1993a) found that high role conflict in family and work areas correlated with high Type A coronary-prone behavior scores for professional women. Type A behavior, characterized by extremes of competitiveness, striving for achievement, aggressiveness, and haste, has been found to be a significant source of stress-related illness. Individuals' ability to cope with stress may be adversely affected by their tendency toward Type A behavior patterns (Greenglass, 1993b), which are often elicited by environmental stressors or challenges. Type A individuals are particularly challenged by situations in which their control is threatened; their primary response in such situations is to act aggressively to maintain control over their environment (Caplan, 1983).

Stress-related illness tends to manifest itself more as physical ill health for men and mental ill health for women (Walters, 1993). However, although coronary heart disease (CHD) is generally more prevalent in men than in women, it is now widely recognized that the link between stress and CHD is a major concern for both sexes (Elliott, 1995; Kirtz-Silverstein, Wingard, & Barrett-Connor, 1992). For example, Haynes and Feinleib (1980) reanalyzed prospective data drawn from the Framingham Heart Study and discovered that working women did not have a significantly higher incidence of CHD than homemakers and that their rates were lower than for working men. However, analyzing the data in terms of married (including divorced, widowed, and separated) versus single working women yielded a substantial increase in heart disease among married women. Comparing married working women with children to those without revealed that among working women, the incidence of CHD rose as the number of children increased (Haynes & Feinleib, 1980). Homemakers, however, showed a slight decrease in heart disease as the number of children increased. Couple these findings with the strong association between Type A behavior and CHD (along with hypertension) and one could hypothesize that those female managers most at risk are high Type A married women with children. Cooper et al. (1988) refer to a review of the research literature on marital adjustment in dual-career marriages, in which a University of Michigan team found that of the 13 important studies using a U.S. national or regional sample, at least 11 indicated that marital adjustment was worse for working wives (Staines, Pleck, Shepard, & O'Connor, 1979).

To date, one of the largest U.K. studies investigating the occupational stressors and stress outcomes for female managers is that of Davidson and Cooper (1983). Qualitative data were obtained from in-depth interviews with a stratified, random sample of 60 female managers, with larger-scale questionnaire survey data collected on 696 female and 185 male managers. The results indicated that women managers experienced more external, discriminatory-based pressures at work compared to male managers. Specific stressors that were isolated as being unique to female managers included strains of coping with prejudice and sex stereotyping; overt and indirect discrimination from fellow employees, employers, and the organizational structure and climate; lack of role models and feelings of isolation; and burdens of coping with the role of the token woman. Women managers had significantly higher Type A coronary-prone behavior scores compared to their male counterparts. As for stress manifestations, female managers reported experiencing a far greater number of psychosomatic symptoms compared to men; their total mean psychosomatic ill-health score was significantly higher.

Cooper and Melhuish (1984) supplemented and reinforced some of the original findings of Davidson and Cooper (1983) by carrying out a longitudinal health and stress study on 311 senior male managers and 171 senior female managers. Several interesting findings emerged, which help to further explain previous work. First, when male executives experience stress-related illness, it tends to emerge as physical ill health, whereas female managers are more likely to suffer mental ill health. Second, Type A behavior is predictive of cardiovascular risk and poor physical and mental health for both male and female managers, but particularly so for women. Third, a significant predictor of adverse health manifestations for women managers is having responsibility for large numbers of people, perhaps because female executives seem to face difficulty in delegating responsibility, as Davidson and Cooper (1983) found. Fourth, male executives have higher stressor scores for the following work factors: responsibility for people, frequent promotions, frequent relocations, more nights away from home on business, and overall stress at work. Although not particularly strong predictors of ill health (i.e., cardiovascular risk, physical or mental health) among men, they are significant factors for female managers. It could be that although men find these job factors stressful, they have lived with them long enough to adapt, whereas women, having only comparatively recently entered the management field, have less tolerance to these work stressors, even at low levels. Because frequently only physical sickness is considered "genuine," male managers may consider physical illness more compatible with their self-concept and more acceptable in others' appraisals of them than they would mental illness (Miles, 1988). Often, findings suggest that women who experience higher levels of psychological distress tend to normalize their mental health problems (Walters, 1993).

Scase and Goffee (1989) also confirmed Davidson and Cooper's (1983) findings that junior and middle managers are far more vulnerable to occupational stress compared to senior executives. They reported that 84% of the male managers and 88% of the female managers claimed to work an average week in excess of 50 hours, due mainly to work overload and time pressures exacerbated by resource cutbacks. An increase in the length of the working week was especially true for younger managers (particularly women), and almost 40% of men and women reported frequent feelings of frustration.

More recently, Davidson et al. (1995) studied occupational stress in 126 female and 220 male graduate managers (i.e., those who had gained university undergraduate management degrees) occupying a range of managerial jobs throughout the United Kingdom and found substantial adverse consequences of stress for management graduates, particularly in terms of mental and physical ill health and job dissatisfaction. Male management graduates, especially middle managers, had a more competitive and thrusting attitude to living, a high Type A behavior. This trend becomes even worse when the sample of female management graduates is analyzed. Very little has changed in the past decade to help eliminate the extra sources of pressure suffered by female managers; many of these results mirror those found by Davidson and Cooper in 1983. Female middle and junior graduate managers were under much higher pressure than their male counterparts. In addition, female senior managers also reported higher pressure scores relating to gender issues such as discrimination and prejudice, home-work conflicts, and so on. They had high Type A scores, exhibited rushed behavior, tended to be more abrupt in speech and manner, and were more hard driving and time oriented in their jobs. Gender differences were also found on reported levels of mental and physical ill-health symptoms. The reported higher ill-health scores by female management graduates and female middle managers is consistent with the literature on occupational stress (e.g., Davidson & Cooper, 1983). No significant differences were found on measures of job satisfaction in managerial levels; however, when the total sample was taken into account, management graduate women were less satisfied with their jobs than male management graduates (Davidson et al., 1995).

Despite the fact that the proportion of minority group members in the total workforce in the United Kingdom and the United States is increasing (and projected to do so further), little research has examined work stress among minority employees (James, 1994; James, Lovato, & Khoo, 1994). Although numerous cross-cultural studies conclude that White managerial women experience unique sources of stress compared with their White male counterparts, research confirms that Black and ethnic minority managers (particularly women) are doubly disadvantaged in terms of upward mobility by high levels of work stress and pressure (Greenhaus, Parasuraman, & Wormley, 1990; Hite, 1996). Bell's (1990) studies of Black women managers and professionals in America reveals that these women perceive themselves as living in a bicultural world (one Black, the other White). Consequently, they feel a constant "push and pull" between the different cultural contexts in their lives, which results in high stress levels particularly linked to role conflict stressors. Denton (1990) also emphasizes the importance of these bicultural role stressors and the combined effects of racism and sexism, which enhance the stresses endemic to today's cadre of Black professional women. Furthermore, compared with their White female counterparts, Black women managers are more likely to be in token and test-case positions (Bell, 1990; Davidson, 1997).

In Davidson's (1997) study of 30 Black and ethnic minority female managers in the United Kingdom, similar work stressors were isolated and compared to White women managers. The most commonly cited stressor was performance pressure, followed by work overload/deadlines/time pressures; feeling undervalued/underutilized; feeling powerless; needing to gain more qualifications; and problems with delegating. However, what made these stressors different from those experienced by White females was that they were often linked to the double bind (i.e., sexism and racism). American researchers such as Frone, Russell, and Cooper (1990) and James et al. (1994) have found that perceived prejudice and discrimination in European American organizations are unique sources of stress for minority workers above and beyond other work stressors. James (1994) and James et al. (1994) strongly emphasize the importance of social identities and minority workers' health and view the former as important in terms of sources of stress-coping ability. Variables involved in social identity processes in organizations that have been previously correlated with minority workers' health include individual expressiveness; levels of perceived prejudice and discrimination experienced in the job; perceived differences in values between minority and majority organization members (addressed separately for supervisors and for peers); and levels of self-esteem and collective (ethnic-group-based) esteem (James et al., 1994).

Another potential source of stress for working women is sexual harassment (unwanted conduct of a sexual nature, or other conduct based on sex affecting the dignity of women and men at work) (Rubenstein, 1991). Victims of sexual harassment often experience negative behavioral, physical, psychological, and health-related outcomes such as depression, anger, fear, irritability, anxiety, nausea, headaches, insomnia, tiredness, and increased alcohol drinking and smoking, as well as dependence on drugs (Terpstra & Baker, 1991; Wright & Bean, 1993). Earnshaw and Davidson's (1994) study of British women who had taken sexual harassment claims to industrial tribunals indicated that over half of those interviewed had to seek medical help and were prescribed drugs such as sleeping tablets, antidepressants, and so on. Not surprisingly, the victims' relationships with others (particularly men) can be adversely affected, as can their general attitude toward work in terms of lowered motivation, job satisfaction, confidence, and organizational commitment (Gutek, 1985). One of the most serious negative work-related outcomes as a result of sexual harassment is loss of one's job. Female victims of sexual harassment are much more likely than the (male) harasser to be relocated within the company, quit, or lose their job. Although research shows that all women are at risk regardless of their appearance or age, certain groups of women appear to be more vulnerable to sexual harassment (e.g., those working in masculine sex-typed jobs, women in nonsenior positions, younger women, and divorced and separated women) (Earnshaw & Davidson, 1994; Terpstra & Baker, 1991).

Home-Work Conflicts

Besides being subjected to additional pressures at work, the majority of working women, especially those with children, are far more affected by the burdens and pressures of their home and child care duties than are most employed men. Indeed, women in paid employment who appear most vulnerable to stress-related maladies are those who combine paid work with unpaid domestic work (Pugliesi, 1988). Multiple-role strain is a major source of overload for employed women, especially in a society that prescribes certain expectations and behaviors to women's roles that are often contradictory. The resulting conflicts and frustration increase the demands on women, potentially leading to fatigue and poorer mental health (Repetti, Matthews, &

Waldron, 1989). The main forms of multiple-role conflict for many working women revolve around guilt feelings, lack of emotional and domestic social support from partners, and inadequate child care facilities. Thus, in families where both partners have full-time jobs, a major source of stress is that the number of demands on a partner (particularly a female) often exceeds the time and energy to deal with them (Lewis & Cooper, 1996). In addition, increasing numbers of working women and men are caring for elderly or disabled relatives (Brannen, Meszaros, Moss, & Poland, 1994).

The once traditional family of male breadwinner and female homemaker is now a memory in much of the industrialized world (Lewis, Izraeli, & Hootsmans, 1992). In the United Kingdom, when both partners work, women spend over two hours a day on housework and cooking compared to 45 minutes spent by their spouses (Jamieson, 1998). These findings are also paralleled by American studies, which have shown that in partnerships where both individuals are employed, women spend at least 15 hours per week on domestic labor (Swiss & Squires, 1993). Although British research indicates that, compared to a decade ago, fathers are spending more time with their children, job segregation at home based on gender still persists (Jamieson, 1998). For example, a U.K. report noted that although 69% of the males and females sampled maintained that men ought to share household jobs, in reality 85% of the women did the laundry, 77% the cooking, 75% the cleaning, and 66% the shopping (Ferri, 1993).

Some evidence suggests that both men and women are placing greater value on shorter working hours, to achieve a more balanced life (Schor, 1991). Unfortunately, this is viewed by many as reduced job commitment, rather than a reaction to changing family roles. This resistance to change may arise in some part from the fact that such changes are most likely to benefit women rather than men. Parasuraman, Greenhaus, and Granrose (1992) found that in dual-career couples, men were reluctant to increase their participation at home, even though their wives experienced high levels of work and family role stressors. Although this inequality is perpetuated by men, it has adverse effects for both men and women, with women reporting higher levels of distress and men experiencing greater levels of stress through increased work-family conflict (Barnett & Brennan, 1997; Parasuraman et al., 1992).

Stress Outcomes and Gender Differences

One of the most consistent results in mental health surveys is that women report significantly more symptoms than men (Tousignant, Brosseau, & Tremblay, 1987), perhaps for one or more of the following reasons: (1) Women are more willing to tell their symptoms to others, either because of greater social acceptance of sickness among women or greater concern for health among women; (2) the "vocabulary of illness" differs for men and women (women often discuss both psychological effects and physical outcomes); and (3) women genuinely experience poorer mental health than men (Tousignant et al., 1987; Verbrugge, 1985). Deaux (1984) suggests that inherent gender differences in mental health are a reflection of the gender socialization process and its role in influencing attitudes and behaviors. These differences will probably continue as long as researchers continue to assume that "normality = White, middle-class male," a model in comparison to which all other groups are still being judged (Frosh, 1987).

Nelson and Quick (1985) maintain that women suffer from poorer mental health not because they are inherently less stable than men, but because they experience greater sources of both psychological and physiological stress. Women are also more likely to experience psychosocial sources of stress than men; a significant relationship between psychosocial stressors and susceptibility to infectious disease has been found (Arnetz et al., 1987). The deleterious behavioral consequences of stress, in terms of smoking and drinking, also differ between men and women. In general, women are more likely to smoke than men regardless of employment status. Although unemployment is associated with an overall increase in smoking, unemployed women smoke more than unemployed men (Hammarstrom & Janlert, 1994). In contrast, health problems due to drinking are more frequently reported among men in general, whereas unemployed women report fewer drinking problems than their employed counterparts (Lahelma, Kangas, & Manderbacka, 1995).

The evidence clearly indicates that there are differences between the psychological, physiological, and behavioral reactions of men and women to stressors, although the reasons for those differences continue to elicit conflicting conclusions. The mediators of those reactions (e.g., coping strategies) are also influenced by gender and may explain the difference in reported stress outcomes.

Individual Coping Factors

Coping is generally defined as constantly changing one's mental and physical behavior to manage the internal and external demands of transactions that tax or exceed a person's resources (Latack, Kinicki, & Prussia, 1995). Coping with stressful events is complex and highly dynamic and is directed toward moderating the impact of such events on an individual's physical, social, and emotional functioning. The choice of coping strategies is determined by a number of factors: personality and behavioral variables (e.g., personal control, self-esteem, experience, and Type A behavior patterns), demographic factors (e.g., age and gender), and sociodemographic factors (e.g., education and income) (Gist & Mitchell, 1992; Holahan & Moos, 1987). On the other hand, the effect of Type A behavior patterns on psychological and psychosomatic symptoms is strongly influenced by the type of coping strategy employed (Edwards, Baglioni, & Cooper, 1990). Problem-focused coping in conjunction with Type A behavior results in a decrease in symptoms, whereas emotional-focused coping in conjunction with Type A behavior results in an increase in symptoms.

It is common to distinguish between two major dimensions of coping: *problem-focused coping,* which addresses the stressful situation, and *emotional-focused coping,* which deals with the feelings and reactions to the stressful event (Latack et al., 1995). Problem-focused coping decreases emotional distress and is negatively related to depression, whereas emotional-focused coping causes an increase in distress and is positively related to depression (Mitchell, Cronkite, & Moos, 1983; Vitaliano, Maiuro, Russo, & Becker, 1987); this is also true when viewed in conjunction with Type A behavior patterns. It is important to further distinguish between four main types of emotional-focused coping to understand its impact: wishful thinking, self-blame, avoidance, and positive appraisal (i.e., efforts to regulate one's own feelings and to create positive meaning or a positive outline). Wishful thinking and self-blame are significant predictors of overall psychological and psychosomatic symptoms, whereas avoidance and positive appraisal both serve as stress moderators (Nakano, 1991). Vingerhoets and Van Heck (1990) found that men are more inclined to use active, problem-focused coping strategies (they plan and rationalize their actions; they engage in positive thinking, perseverance, self-adaptation, and personal growth). In contrast, women prefer emotional-focused solutions (they engage in self-blame and wishful thinking; they seek social support and a forum to express their emotions). Ptacek, Smith, and Dodge (1994) propose that gender differences in coping arise from early socialization that promotes stereotypes of men as independent, instrumental, and rational, compared to women, who are portrayed as emotional, supportive, and dependent. However, although men theoretically have a more effective approach to coping, women are more likely to actively engage in behavioral coping than men (i.e., they attempt to deal directly with the problem and its effects by taking positive action) (Astor-Dubin & Hammen, 1984; Fielden & Davidson, 1996).

Coping is often protracted and unpredictable, especially when other people are involved. In such circumstances, the "coper" has to take into account the goals and expectations of others as well as his or her own (Oakland & Ostell, 1996). Initial strategies may have to be revised radically depending on how others respond to the copers' behavior; sometimes wide varieties of strategies employed over long periods of time prove ineffectual, leaving the problem unchanged or worse. This lack of coping efficacy can have profound effects on psychological stress reactions, subsequent coping behaviors, and ultimately on personal and situational outcomes (Oakland & Ostell, 1996). Women are more likely to engage in behaviors that involve external recognition, allowing others to label and offer help, whereas men tend to deal with their problems internally (Astor-Dubin & Hammen, 1984).

This external focus is also reflected in women's perception of their control over their situation. In general, women tend to believe that they have less control over interpersonal relationships and uncontrollable life events than men (Sherman, Higgs, & Williams, 1997). Although women undoubtedly gain a positive health advantage from their pursuit of social relationships, they may also be a source of stress because of their perceived uncontrollability. In addition, women tend to feel they have less control over their achievements than their male counterparts, a situation that may arise because women have fewer opportunities for real achievement or independence within organizations (Riipinen, 1994). This can lead to decreased self-esteem and job satisfaction, further reducing the effective coping strategies available to women and hence their ability to cope with occupational stress.

Summary and Future Research

As the number of employed women rises, so too does the cost to organizations of occupational stress. Stress affects women both psychologically and physically, yet only relatively recently have the effects of stress on working women received any real attention. Studies have found that women encounter greater sources of stress than their male counterparts, especially those working in male-dominated professions, such as managers. Women managers experience high levels of gender stereotyping, prejudice, and discrimination and report greater pressure at all management levels than their male counterparts. In addition to work stressors, women have to deal with substantially more domestic pressures than the majority of men. For Black and ethnic minority women, this is further compounded by bicultural demands and increased feelings of isolation (see Figure 21.1).

Women, faced with different stressors than men, tend to employ different coping strategies. Emotional support is a key factor in women's ability to cope with work stress; however, it is frequently counteracted by the negative effects of the socialization process, which undermine the importance of women's work and frequently result in a lack of perceived personal control. This may also be responsible for the reported difference in the response of women and men to the stress process, with researchers continuing to use a health model based on the assumption that "normality = White, middle-class male." In comparison to men, women tend to report significantly poorer mental well-being, characterized by low self-esteem, increased self-doubt, and self-blame. Often, this is viewed as an example of the instability of women rather than a legitimate outcome of the stress process, whereas the physical outcomes of stress generally suffered by men are viewed with much more gravity. Thus, not only do working women experience more sources of stress than men, but those stressors are often viewed as having less impact on women's health, a situation that is clearly inaccurate and one that could prove extremely costly to organizations if it continues to be ignored.

Clearly, there is a need for additional comparative high-quality quantitative and qualitative research, to further investigate and compare the stress factors experienced by working women from different ethnic, cultural, occupational, and socioeconomic groups. To date, published research has been predominantly European and North American, with a tendency to concentrate on White, professional, full-time working women. Frequently, research has taken a retrospective approach to the study of stress, yet increasingly it is recognized that a longitudinal, prospective approach is the most valid. According to Link and Shrout (1992), it is the main panacea for problems of casual inference raised by traditional stress research methodology. Consequently, if we are truly to advance our understanding of stress and the working woman, future work needs to take a far more generic approach that accurately identifies the ongoing sources of stress encountered by women at work, their changing reactions to those stressors, and the impact that continued exposure to such stressors has on their physical and mental well-being.

Part **V**

Organizational Initiatives

Chapter 22

Affirmative Action

History, Effects, and Attitudes

Alison M. Konrad and Frank Linnehan

Affirmative action (AA) programs consist of organizational goals for increasing the representation of historically excluded groups, timetables for achieving those goals, and organizational practices designed to achieve the goals within the stated time frames. In the United States, AA programs usually target African Americans, Hispanic Americans, Asian Americans, Native Americans, and White women. AA is clearly under attack, particularly in the popular business press (e.g., D'Souza, 1997; Munk, 1994). Many in both academia and business continue to defend it (e.g., Reed, 1995; Steinberg, 1995). The conclusions we draw from a review of the research place us squarely in favor of AA policy. Because much of the research does not distinguish among women by race/ethnicity or among people of color by sex, we review the literature on both the sex and race effects of AA.

Research shows that AA has been an important policy for improving the economic status of people of color and White women in the United States. Because AA has been important in improving the economic status of historically excluded groups, weakening it will hurt progress toward equality. AA programs have greatly increased diversity among professionals, managers,

AUTHORS' NOTE: The authors' names are listed in alphabetical order. Both contributed equally to the chapter.

students of higher education, civil servants, and federal contractors. The gains made from AA programs are tenuous, however, and the effects of AA's recent dismantling in California and Texas demonstrate how devastating it would be to end AA at this time. In the following sections, we discuss the legislative history of AA, its economic effects, its social and psychological effects, and determinants of attitudes toward AA.

The History of Affirmative Action

In the United States, AA was created from a series of executive orders (Anderson, 1996), but AA today is not the result of the actions of only the executive branch. In fact, AA evolved from the interplay between the executive, legislative, and judicial branches of the federal government. We begin by examining some of the significant events in each branch of government that have converged to create AA. We first discuss the history of AA in the United States in detail because it is illustrative and serves to accentuate the differences between the U.S. approach and the approaches used in other countries to achieve equality in the workforce.

The Executive Branch

AA originated in a succession of executive orders (EOs), beginning with EOs 8587 (1940) and 8802 (1941) signed by President Roosevelt (Clayton & Crosby, 1992). A. Philip Randolph's threat to stage a mass march on Washington protesting race discrimination by defense contractors was the impetus for Roosevelt's action (Kellough, 1992). EO 8587 prohibited discrimination in the federal service, but it had no provisions for enforcement. Similarly, EO 8802 banned discrimination in employment by the federal government, but it also established the Fair Employment Practice Committee to hear discrimination complaints. This committee, however, lacked power to enforce the order (Herring & Collins, 1995).

Subsequent executive orders strengthened the government's position against discrimination and its enforcement. President Truman's EO 9980 (1948) established another agency, the Fair Employment Board in the Civil Service Commission, that, as Kellough (1992) points out, was also charged with initiating "constructive action" to increase the employment and advancement of minorities in the federal government. Other executive orders relevant to the evolution of AA were signed throughout the Eisenhower and Kennedy administrations. President Kennedy signed EO 10925 (1961), which established the President's Committee on Employment Opportunity and reaffirmed the concept of constructive action. In fact, it was in EO 10925 that the term *affirmative action* was first used in an executive order (Graham, 1992).

Most consider President Johnson's EO 11246 (1965) a milestone in the history of AA (Anderson, 1996). Although previous executive orders had prohibited employment discrimination and called for AA, the real effect of this order was its impact on enforcement. Prior to EO 11246, these policies were enforced by two agencies, both of which were headed by the vice president. In effect, 11246 abolished these agencies and transferred the responsibility of enforcement from the White House to the Labor Department, which subsequently created the Office of Federal Contract Compliance Programs to meet this obligation (Graham, 1992).

Two conclusions emerge in tracing AA's roots in the executive branch. First, it is clear that the objective was to reduce racial discrimination both in the federal government and by federal contractors. Neither sex nor age discrimination was addressed by any of the executive orders through EO 11246. In fact, sex discrimination was added by EO 11375 (1967), which was signed two years after EO 11246.

The second conclusion is that the executive orders were very specific; not only did they prohibit discrimination, but also they made it incumbent on the federal government and its contractors to be proactive in their employment practices (Clayton & Crosby, 1992; Steinberg, 1995). That language makes it clear that in the early 1960s, race was an issue that not only must be taken into consideration in employment decisions of the federal government and its contractors but also that required positive action. It is this "active" orientation (Steinberg, 1995) that differentiates the policies enacted by the executive branch from the laws eventually passed by Congress. This difference in orientation is the crux of the AA debate. We now discuss the federal civil rights laws, their perspectives and their differences with the executive orders.

The Legislative Branch

> It is claimed that the bill would require racial quotas for all hiring, when in fact it provides that race shall not be a basis for making personnel decisions. (U.S. Congressional Record, 1964, p. 6553)

On March 30, 1964, Hubert Humphrey opened the debate on the Senate floor on H.R. 7152, the Civil Rights Act of 1964. Humphrey's words depict the clear distinction between the legislative and executive orientation to employment discrimination. In general, federal civil rights laws are what Steinberg (1995, p. 165) has termed "passive injunctions" against discrimination, whereas the executive orders are based on the obligation to "go a step beyond non-discrimination and to *actively* seek out targeted groups in employment." In addition to prohibiting discrimination in the private sector, the Civil Rights Act of 1964 also created an enforcement agency, the Equal Employment Opportunity Commission.

Title VII of the Civil Rights Act of 1964 banned discrimination in employment on grounds of race, color, religion, sex, or national origin; however, it is the only provision of the act that includes sex as a criterion for discrimination. In fact, similar to the executive branch actions, which initially omitted sex as a basis for discrimination, sex was not included in the original bill, but was added to Title VII during the House debates (U.S. Congressional Record, 1964, p. 6548). Sex was also omitted from Title VI of the act, which prohibits discrimination on the basis of race, color, or national origin "under any program or activity receiving Federal financial assistance" (U.S. Congressional Record, 1964, p. 6544).

Arguments in the AA debate focus on inherent contradictions in the orientations of the civil rights laws and the executive orders of AA. Federal civil rights legislation has at its foundation standards of equality, meritocracy, and even individualism. These values assume individuals can and should be judged on their merit alone. From this perspective, what has happened in the past is irrelevant, and only the present matters. Alternatively, the proactive orientation found in the more recent executive orders is rooted in the past. Equity is a critical consideration of the orders that were signed by Presidents Kennedy and Johnson (Kellough, 1992). As such, these directives take into consideration a past that AA proponents believe can be remedied only by taking race into consideration and giving preferences to those groups that experienced past discrimination. Thus, the arguments of both proponents and opponents of AA are rooted in different fundamental values.

Is past injustice relevant or does only the present matter? These are the opposite poles of the civil rights-AA continuum that have been established by the legislative and executive branches of government. The judicial branch has bounced between these extremes in exerting its influence over AA.

The Judicial Branch

The Supreme Court decisions that have affected civil rights and AA have reflected the diversity of these policies. In a decision known as the Civil Rights Case of 1883, which overturned the Civil Rights Act of 1875, Justice Joseph Bradley wrote it was time that the Black American "take the rank of a mere citizen and ceases to be the special favorite of the laws" (Reed, 1995, p. 19). Bradley's opinion is certainly an early outcry against proactive remedies based on past injustice and one that advocates a passive approach to racial inequality. Justice John Harlan extended this interpretation in his 1896 dissent to *Plessy v. Ferguson* (1894), which established the legality of separate but equal facilities for people of different races by upholding a Louisiana law that allowed separate railroad accommodations for Blacks and Whites (Simmons, 1982).

However, this separate-but-equal doctrine came under fire in later Court decisions, many of which involved cases in educational settings (Simmons,

1982). The separate-but-equal doctrine established by *Plessy* was reversed by the Court in *Brown v. Board of Education of Topeka* (1954). In this decision, all local, state, and federal ordinances that enforced segregation were declared unconstitutional (Mosely & Capaldi, 1996; Simmons, 1982). Not only was this a landmark case against segregation, but it also became a springboard for a much stronger position taken by the Court in later race-related decisions. For example, in *Green v. County School Board* (1968), the Court ruled that desegregating school systems should "take race into account" and that school boards had an "affirmative duty" to produce racial integration (Graham, 1992, p. 59). This was a clear indication that the Court had swung toward the proactive orientation of the executive orders.

Other pro-AA decisions that allowed public and private entities to use race to remedy past discrimination include *United Steelworkers of America v. Weber* (1979), *Fullilove v. Klutznick* (1980), and *Metro Broadcasting, Inc. v. FCC* (1990). In *Fullilove,* the Court upheld a minority business enterprise (MBE) set-aside provision of the Public Works Employment Act of 1977. Although falling under greater scrutiny since *City of Richmond v. Croson* (1989), these set-asides continue and were expanded to women by the Women's Business Ownership Act of 1988.

Legal cases involving AA have usually been argued on the basis of the Fourteenth Amendment, which provides all individuals equal protection under the law (Mosely & Capaldi, 1996). Opponents argue that AA denies this right. As such, they contend race should not be a consideration in such activities as granting contracts or making staffing decisions in an organization. In Supreme Court decisions of the early 1970s, which are considered to be favorable toward AA, the Court used a standard of "intermediate scrutiny" when determining the legality of using race in employment and contractor decisions (Johnson-Jackson, 1995). This implies that race classifications can be used if they serve "important government interests" and they are "rationally related" to the achievement of those interests (Mosely & Capaldi, 1996).

The Court's rulings began to swing slowly away from the proactive side of the continuum in the late 1970s. This can be seen in *University of California Regents v. Bakke* (1978). In *Bakke,* the Court ruled that the special admissions program of the Medical School at the University of California at Davis was unconstitutional. It concluded that race could, however, be considered in admission decisions as long as it was not the sole criterion.

In its more recent decisions, the Court has turned away from racial preferences by employing a narrower, "strict scrutiny" standard (Johnson-Jackson, 1995). In *City of Richmond v. Croson* (1989), the Court ruled that minority-owned enterprise set-asides were illegal unless there was a "significant statistical disparity between the number of qualified minority contractors willing and able to do the work and the number of minority firms that received contracts" (Munk, 1994, p. 50). The Court concluded that "if racial classifications are necessary in extreme cases, they should be narrowly tailored"

(LaNoue, 1992, p. 114). In set-aside programs, then, strict scrutiny allows for race to be used in contractor decisions only if it can be shown that minority contractors experienced discrimination. In another case, *Adarand v. Pena* (1995), the Court ruled that "strict scrutiny applies to *all* government classifications based on race" (Johnson-Jackson, 1995, p. 33). *Pena* shows that some justices are now willing to "ban racial preferences in all circumstances" (Rosen, 1995, p. 22).

The Supreme Court's positions on the civil rights-AA continuum fall between those of the executive and legislative branches and have moved away from proactive to more passive enforcement of nondiscrimination. Similar to the actions of the other branches, these Supreme Court decisions have focused the AA debate on race rather than sex.

Affirmative Action Outside the United States

With the exception of Canada, it may be somewhat misleading to label the antidiscrimination policies that have been enacted by countries outside the United States as AA programs. Many countries, however, have made significant commitments to the goal of equal employment opportunity. In this section, we examine the policies and practices of countries that have adopted a proactive equal employment approach. Whereas AA in the United States has evolved through the interaction of internal forces created by its three branches of government, in many other countries external forces have shaped equal employment opportunity practices. These external forces have included the laws that exist in countries such as Canada and the United States, the pressure imposed by multinational associations such as the European Community (EC), and the influence of the United Nations (UN) (Davidson & Cooper, 1993b).

For example, Japan's 1994 Equal Employment Opportunity Act is based on a UN resolution calling for all signatory countries to prohibit discrimination against women (Bergeson & Oba, 1994). The Russian Federation's stance against discrimination has its roots in the UN's Universal Declaration of Human Rights, which prohibits discrimination on the basis of national characteristics or ethnic origin, as well as the provisions adopted by the International Labour Organization's Discrimination Convention of 1958 (Tkachencko, Koryukhina, & Matveeva, 1997). Within the EC, there is a growing interest in Greece, Belgium, Italy, and Germany in establishing quotas for hiring women in entry and senior management positions (Davidson & Cooper, 1993b). Commenting on this trend, Davidson and Cooper (1993b) conclude, "It is obvious that exposure to the United States' experience in this field has led many EC countries to consider this approach" (pp. 11-12).

Some countries have developed relatively weak antidiscrimination policies. For example, Belgium's antidiscrimination policy is voluntary, and this may be why very few private firms in Belgium have implemented programs

(Woodward, 1993b). Japan's 1985 Equal Employment Law bans sex discrimination in employment, but includes no penalties for noncompliance (Brinton, 1994). In Italy, antidiscrimination efforts are weakened by the codification of an unequal division of labor within the family in the Constitution, which states, "The working woman has the same rights and the same remuneration for equal work as a man. Working conditions should permit the fulfillment of her essential family function and ensure to the mother and her child a special adequate protection" (Olivares, 1993, p. 163).

In some countries, internal forces have resulted in preferential policies designed to benefit the majority. In India, for example, governmental policy reserves a certain percentage of public sector jobs for the Special Castes and Special Tribes, as well as for those considered to be part of the backward classes (Kaur, 1997). In some areas, however, these governmental reservationist policies have been extended to protect the rights of the majority who are indigenous to the area, against minority populations who have migrated to these areas (Joseph, 1991). These minority groups are usually more economically successful and better educated than the so-called sons of the soil or indigenous populations. Malaysia has also instituted a set of reservationist policies protecting the majority indigenous population. Here, governmental policies mandate quotas in employment, admission to universities, equity ownership, and public sector employment for the *bumiputras,* the indigenous majority. These quotas were filled often at the expense of the ethnic Chinese, who make up 32% of the Malaysian population (Hodges-Aeberhard & Raskin, 1997b).

Member of nonprotected groups in the United States and Canada who feel that AA is unfair may advocate the adoption of similar governmental policies to protect the rights of the majority. There are, however, two very important distinctions that would argue against importing these types of practices. First, in both India and Malaysia, the majority groups that are given these reservations by the government are less educated and less successful economically than the minority, immigrant groups. This clearly is not the case in the United States and Canada, where White males have historically achieved more economic success than women and people of color. Also, the minority groups in India and Malaysia have migrated to those countries voluntarily; this is not the case for many African Americans, whose ancestors were brought to the United States against their will as slaves.

Examining the effects of proactive antidiscrimination programs outside the United States is an area in need of more extensive research. Some significant results have emerged, however. In Canada, Leck and Saunders (1992) found that fewer than 50% of the Canadian employers they studied had formalized their AA plans and only 18% had plans in place, despite the fact they are required to do so. Yet Leck and Saunders (1996) reported the Employment Equity Act has had a positive effect on the number of organizations employing a representative number of visible minorities. Additionally,

Leck, St. Onge, and LaLancette (1995) found evidence that this act also contributed to lowering the wage gap between men and women. Finally, Leck and Saunders (1992) reported those organizations that adopted Employment Equity Programs were more likely to hire a representative number of women than companies that did not adopt these programs.

In Great Britain, Zabalza and Tzannatos (1994) attributed the 1975-1981 rise in the relative earnings and employment of women to the implementation of the Equal Pay Act and the Sex Discrimination Act. In Japan, Cannings and Lazonick (1994) found that the enactment of the 1985 Equal Employment Law had a significant, positive effect on employment opportunities for university-educated women. However, Brinton (1994) found that men were more likely than women to be offered career-track positions in large Japanese firms. She attributed this finding to the fact that Japan's Equal Employment Law contains no penalties for violations.

Empirical studies that examine the effects of antidiscrimination laws are much more prevalent in the United States. The evidence presented in the next section indicates that AA has been an important factor in the progress made toward greater equality in the United States.

Economic Effects of Affirmative Action

White women and people of color have made substantial economic gains since the inception of AA policy. Although it is difficult to identify exactly what portion of these gains are attributable to AA alone, many indicators demonstrate that AA has been an important factor in reducing inequality. In this section, we review the gains made in higher education, general employment, and federal contracting receipts.

Affirmative Action and Access to Education

AA policy has allowed women to increase greatly their representation in higher education. Sex discrimination in college and university admissions was substantially reduced by a combination of EOs, Title IX of the Civil Rights Act of 1972, and legal actions on the part of the Women's Equity Action League against over 250 institutions. From 1958 to 1995, the proportion of M.D.s awarded to women rose from 5% to 39%, the proportion of law degrees from 3% to 43%, and the proportion of Ph.D.s from 10% to 39%. The representation of people of color among students has risen as well, for all groups except African American men (U.S. Department of Education, 1997a; Orlans, 1992).

Targeted groups have also increased their presence among college and university faculty. In 1979, 68% of faculty were White men. In 1993, 57% of faculty were White men, 28% were White women, 2.5% were African American men, 2.2% were African American women, 1.4% were Hispanic

American men, 0.8% were Hispanic American women, 3.5% were Asian American men, 1.2% were Asian American women, 0.2% were Native American men, and 0.1% were Native American women (U.S. Department of Education, 1997a; Orlans, 1992). The change in the distribution of African Americans among institutions has been significant also. By 1982-1983, only 16% of African American students (but 44% of full-time faculty) were located at historically African American institutions (Orlans, 1992).

Although it is difficult to determine exactly what percentage of these gains are directly attributable to AA, other statistics underscore its importance. Bowen and Bok (1998) provide the most comprehensive data available to date on the effects of AA in undergraduate admissions. They start from the premise that only about 20%-30% of all four-year colleges and universities have enough applicants to be selective, on the basis of race or any other criterion. For this reason, they focused their research on selective institutions. They found that Black applicants were considerably more likely than White applicants with the same SAT scores to be admitted. Because there were relatively few African American applicants at these institutions, however, the potential number of White students displaced by race-based admissions was small. Bowen and Bok (1998) estimated that eliminating race-based admissions would have increased the percentage of White applicants admitted to these selective institutions from 25% to only 26.5%. But eliminating race-based admissions would have cut African American admissions by almost half.

Additionally, African American students who entered selective institutions were far more likely to graduate (75%) than their counterparts who attended unselective institutions (40%). Importantly, the improvement in probability of graduation was largest for those with the lowest SAT scores, refuting the argument that African American students admitted with SAT scores that are low relative to the institutional average suffer negative academic consequences. African American students who attended selective institutions were considerably more likely to obtain graduate degrees, and they earned higher salaries than their counterparts attending unselective institutions. Hence, entering high-quality institutions helped African American students even though they entered with lower SAT scores on average. The implication of Bowen and Bok's (1998) findings is that disallowing the use of race as an admissions criterion would cut the number of African American students at selective institutions by half, with devastating consequences for the numbers of African American doctors, lawyers, executives, and community leaders.

In her nationwide study of African American women lawyers, Simpson (1996) found that AA played a substantial role in many of the women's entry into law school. She reported that 24% of her respondents had participated in a prelaw summer preparatory program for minorities as a precursor to law school admission. Thirty-one percent received minority scholarships from their colleges, 45% from their law schools. AA admissions programs were important to most of the women who had attended highly prestigious law schools. Wightman's (1997) research examining the qualifications of all applicants at 173 U.S. law schools in 1990-1991 corroborated the importance of AA. She estimated that eliminating AA in law school admissions would have cut the number of African American law students in half.

The dismantling of AA admissions programs in California and Texas in 1996 has had debilitating effects on African Americans' access to legal and medical education. The number of African Americans admitted to U.C. Berkeley's prestigious law school dropped from 75 in 1996 to 14 in 1997, when the AA admissions program was eliminated (Bunzel, 1997). In the same year, the dismantling of the AA admissions program at the University of Texas Southwestern Medical Center in Dallas resulted in only 1 African American entering the school in a class of about 200 (Suhler, 1997). The loss of African American medical students is particularly distressing because African American physicians are far more likely than their White counterparts to provide health care for underserved populations (Komaromy et al., 1996).

Affirmative Action and Government Employment

AA policy has resulted in substantial gains in public sector employment for women and African Americans. Steinberg (1995) argued that during the 1970s, African Americans increased their numbers in public employment at double the rate of Whites. By 1982, almost one-quarter of all African American workers were government employees (S. M. Collins, 1983). Government has been a particularly important source of employment for African American managers and professionals. Between 1960 and 1970, the number of African American managers in government increased almost 275% compared to an 82% increase in the number of White managers. The increase for African Americans between 1970 and 1980 was a little over 200% compared to a 29% increase among Whites (S. M. Collins, 1983).

Kellough (1989) found that African American employment in the federal civil service as a whole grew steadily from the early 1960s to 1984 at about 0.5% per year. Although the federal government's 1971 adoption of goals and timetables had little effect on African American employment in the federal civil service as a whole, it was effective in opening opportunities for African Americans in agencies other than those serving a disproportionately high number of African American citizens (S. M. Collins, 1983). For example, goals and timetables had no effect on African American employment in Housing and Urban Development, but a positive effect in the Federal Trade Commission, National Aeronautics and Space Administration, the National Labor Relations Board, the Federal Deposit Insurance Corporation, and the Securities and Exchange Commission (Kellough, 1989). Examining specific agencies in depth, Kellough (1989) found that AA had greater impact when agencies devoted a relatively high level of resources to it, when agency leaders showed a high level of commitment to it, and when goals and timetables were in effect for a longer period of time.

For women, Kellough (1989) found that AA goals and timetables had positive effects on federal civil service employment across the board. In the lower grades, female employment grew at an average rate of 0.5% per year from 1968 to 1971 but at 1.25% per year from 1972 to 1984. In the higher grades, female employment increased by 0.1% per year before and 0.6% per year after the authorization of goals and timetables. Powell and Butterfield (1994) found that between 1987 and 1992, White women had better promotion opportunities than did White men at the highest ranks of the federal civil service. Men of color, however, fared poorly relative to White men in top-level promotion decisions (Powell & Butterfield, 1997).

Court-ordered AA programs have been effective in opening public sector employment opportunities to targeted groups. For example, about 40% of police departments had court-ordered AA programs during the 1970s and 1980s because they had systematically discriminated against women and people of color in hiring. Another 42% of departments adopted voluntary AA plans during the same period. As a result, the percentage of police officers who were people of color increased from 7% to 23%, and the percentage who were women increased from 2% to 9% (Martin, 1991). Hacker (1992) documented that between 1970 and 1990 the number of African American police officers rose from 24,000 to 64,000. African Americans accounted for 41% of all new hires during that period.

Affirmative Action and Employment in the Private Sector

AA policy has also had substantial effects on employment in the private sector. Studies examining the effects of EOs 11246 and 11375 compare federal contractors covered by the executive orders with other employers having at least 100 employees. Findings show that when a variety of firm characteristics are controlled, the employment of African American men and women increased more rapidly among federal contractors than among employers not covered by the executive orders.

Leonard (1994) reports figures comparing the growth of employment shares in contracting and noncontracting establishments. He found that between 1974 and 1980, the employment of targeted groups grew significantly faster in contracting than in noncontracting establishments. Specifically, the employment share held by African American men increased from 5.8% to 6.7% of the total workforce among contractors. The comparison statistics for noncontractors are 5.3% in 1974 and 5.9% in 1980. Rodgers and Spriggs (1996) report similar effects. Between 1982 and 1992, the employment share held by African Americans was about 1% higher in contracting than in noncontracting establishments. Given that federal contractors include many of the largest U.S. employers, these apparently small percentages represent tens of thousands of jobs.

In the private sector, African Americans have benefited more from AA than either Asian or Hispanic Americans. People categorized as "other minorities" in Leonard's analysis did not gain significantly more employment among contractors than among noncontractors. Rodgers and Spriggs (1996) found that in 1992, the employment share held by Asian Americans was about 0.25% higher among contractors than among noncontractors, but the employment share held by Hispanic Americans was 0.45% *lower*.

White women benefited from private sector AA programs. Leonard (1994) found that the employment share held by White women among federal contractors increased from 27.6% in 1974 to 28.8% in 1980. The percentages for noncontractors were 39.4 in 1974 and 40 in 1980. White women were less likely to be employed by contractors than noncontractors overall because contractors tend to be in industries, such as defense and construction, that traditionally employed relatively few women. Hence, the faster gains made by women among contractors indicate improvement in the sectors where women have historically encountered the greatest barriers.

Herring and Collins (1995) used survey data to compare the employment outcomes of respondents who reported that they worked for an AA employer with those who did not. They found that people who worked for an AA employer reported that higher percentages of African Americans and women were employed in their organizations. Also, when White women and people of color worked for an AA employer, they had higher annual earnings by thousands of dollars. In large firms, their earnings approached parity with those of White men.

It is possible that the findings reported by Herring and Collins overstate the earnings impact of AA because other factors affecting earnings, such as education and work experience, were not controlled in the analysis. It is possible that AA firms attracted the most productive White women and people of color. This reasoning implies, however, that AA programs attract highly qualified applicants, refuting arguments that AA results in hiring the unqualified.

Among contractors, undergoing a compliance review has a significant effect on employment statistics. Leonard (1994) argued that during the 1970s, African American men's employment shares increased twice as quickly among reviewed than among nonreviewed contractors. Reviews had a similar positive effect for African American women.

Other evidence suggests that the gains achieved among federal contractors are relatively tenuous. Leonard (1994) argued that the contract compliance review program "virtually ceased to exist in all but name after 1980" (p. 29). With a reduction in staff and budget, the Office of Federal Contract Compliance Programs doubled the number of compliance reviews conducted annually. The reason for this increase was a vast reduction in the number of in-depth audits and an increase in the number of desk reviews. Back-pay awards were phased out and debarments almost extinguished. The lack of substantive enforcement reversed the gains made by African Americans. Between 1980 and 1984, both male and female African American employment grew more slowly among contractors than among noncontractors (Leonard, 1994).

Affirmative Action and Human Resource Management Practices

One of the most significant economic effects of the executive orders has been the elaboration of the Human Resource Management (HRM) function. AA requires contractors to conduct utilization analyses to determine whether women and people of color are employed in numbers reflecting their availability in the local population. In areas where underutilization is found, employers must establish goals and timetables for increasing the employment shares of the relevant group. Additionally, employers are to develop means by which to achieve their goals within a reasonable time period. Examples of suggested means include (1) ensuring that hiring and promotion decisions are based on valid criteria, (2) developing relationships with recruiting sources likely to refer large numbers of women or people of color, (3) posting promotion opportunities internally, (4) evaluating supervisors on the basis of their equal employment opportunity efforts, and (5) encouraging child care and transportation programs designed to improve access for women and people of color (see Revised Order 4, 1974). Many of these practices, such as job posting and requiring the use of valid selection criteria, equalize opportunities for all applicants, not just targeted groups.

As a result of AA, employers have developed extensive HRM structures designed to ensure that equal employment opportunity occurs. Konrad and Linnehan (1995a) identified 117 discrete HRM activities undertaken by firms in response to equal employment and AA pressures. They divided these activities into two types. Identity-blind activities do not consider demographic characteristics, whereas identity-conscious activities do. On average, the 138 firms in their sample had implemented 58% of the identity-blind and 37% of the identity-conscious activities. Being a federal contractor increased the presence of identity-conscious structures by 7%, being the subject of an equal employment lawsuit increased it by 6% more, and being subjected to a compliance review increased it by an additional 8%. None of these factors affected the presence of identity-blind structures. Identity-blind structures also had no impact on the employment shares of women or people of color. Identity-conscious structures increased the presence of people of color in management as well as the rank of the highest-status woman.

The elaboration of HRM structures resulting from AA has been important in enhancing management opportunities for African Americans. Collins

(1997) found that upward mobility among African American managers has often been due to their promotion to head of the firm's AA program. Konrad and Pfeffer (1991) report similarly that African Americans in higher education administration are concentrated in the position of director of AA. White women also often head college and university AA programs.

Although the development of AA programs opened management opportunities to African Americans, these opportunities have not led to the highest corporate echelons. Rather, channeling the careers of African American managers into racialized roles such as head of AA has limited their opportunities to acquire the skills and accomplishments needed to qualify for top executive jobs. Jobs in AA programs are also vulnerable to changes in public policy. If the federal government disbands its AA program, the positions of directors of corporate AA programs may be eliminated (Collins, 1997).

Affirmative Action and Small Business Opportunities

Contract set-aside programs have been important in providing opportunities for entrepreneurs to found and grow their own businesses. Between 1969 and 1980, the percentage of federal government purchasing dollars going to MBEs increased 100-fold from 0.03% to 3.2%. In 1980, the federal government did business worth over $3 billion with MBEs (S. M. Collins, 1983). The Small Business Administration's set-aside program, better known as the 8(a) Program (named after section 8(a) of the Small Business Act), secured $4.5 billion in federal contracts for MBEs in 1995 (Brown & Shakespeare, 1996).

In 1988, the year that federal contract set-asides were extended to women, women-owned business enterprises received $1.75 billion in contracts (LaNoue, 1992). In 1993, due to the Department of Transportation set-asides for the federal highway program, women-owned business contracts with the department rose from $307 million to $879 million (Munk, 1994).

The long-term value of these preferential procurement programs, however, has been called into question recently, as evidence from one study indicated that MBEs that rely on government contracts might be more prone to failure than those that do not (Bates & Williams, 1996). The findings of this study are limited to MBEs doing business with state and local governments. Bates and Williams did not study MBEs contracting with the federal government. Another problem with this study was that the authors did not make a comparison with similar non-minority-owned businesses. If non-minority-owned businesses also fail more often when they rely on government contracts, then the minority set-asides cannot be said to be damaging MBEs. Finally, reliance on government contracts was confounded with the age of the business. In the first year of the study, 39% of the MBEs that relied heavily on the government for business had been in existence for two years or less.

New businesses are more likely to fail than established ones for a variety of reasons.

Summary

Many different statistics show that greater equality has been attained by White women and people of color since the implementation of the federal government AA programs. AA has increased access to higher education for women and people of color. AA programs have increased the employment of targeted groups in the public sector and have been particularly important in providing professional and managerial opportunities to women and people of color. Federal contractors covered by AA policy have increased the diversity of their workforces considerably more rapidly than similar noncontractors. Private sector employers have changed their HRM systems in response to AA, and these changes have increased employment opportunities for people of color and White women. Some of the changes have increased the fairness of employment decisions for everyone. Finally, minority set-asides in government procurement have increased the percentage of federal dollars going to businesses owned by women and people of color.

Other data suggest that these gains may be so tenuous that dismantling AA policy will cause their reversal. Many African American women lawyers relied on AA for access to their legal education. When AA was rescinded in California and Texas, the admission of African Americans to prestigious law schools there plummeted. These findings imply that ending AA will hurt the opportunities African Americans have to obtain the qualifications needed for middle-class jobs. During Ronald Reagan's presidency, the lack of substantive enforcement of AA among federal contractors led to reduced hiring of African Americans in those firms. This shows that ending AA will result in lost employment opportunities for African Americans. Identity-conscious HRM structures are adopted by firms in response to AA pressures. These structures enhance management opportunities for people of color and White women. Identity-blind structures do not. It is unclear whether companies will dismantle their identity-conscious HRM structures if AA is abolished; however, it seems clear that companies with few such structures will not adopt them voluntarily.

Finally, many African Americans and White women are employed in positions overseeing AA programs in colleges, universities, companies, and civil service administrations. The dismantling of AA would put all of their jobs in jeopardy. As S. M. Collins (1983) argues, public policy and not the market has driven the demand for African American labor, especially among professional and managerial positions. The fact that African Americans are primarily sought for racialized positions implies that if AA is dismantled, they will have relatively poor prospects in the labor market.

Social and Psychological Effects of Affirmative Action

In this section, we outline the major trends in the research on the psychology of AA. We have divided the studies into two categories, which we have termed *outcome focused* and *process focused*. Outcome-focused studies examine the social and psychological effects of AA on individuals. Process-focused studies attempt to explain how these outcomes are reached. We review some key studies and findings in each of these categories.

Outcome-Focused Studies

Outcome-focused studies have shown that preferential selection may have adverse effects on the self-perceptions of beneficiaries. Furthermore, these adverse effects seem to be felt significantly more by women than by men. For example, Heilman, Simon, and Repper (1987) reported that preferential selection had a negative effect on the self-assessment of leadership competence and the desire to remain a leader for the female students in their experiment, but not for their male student counterparts. Similarly, women who were selected on a preferential basis were found to choose a less complex task over a more demanding one, but method of selection (preferential or merit) had no impact on the task choice of men in this same study (Heilman, Rivero, & Brett, 1991). Apparently, women, but not men, assume they are less competent when they are told they were selected on the basis of sex rather than merit.

Although this research documents the potential of AA programs to have unintended negative consequences, it is limited in several ways. First, most of these studies have defined AA as basing selection decisions solely on demographics. This definition of AA restricts the generalizability of this research because AA programs rarely comprise selection based exclusively on sex or race (Crosby & Cordova, 1996). Another limitation is that this research has focused primarily on White women (Turner & Pratkanis, 1994). White women's reactions to preferential selection may differ from those of other targeted groups (Eberhardt & Fiske, 1994). Finally, most of the studies have used high school and college student participants who may be less certain than adult workers of their competencies and hence more susceptible to experimenters' statements about their skills and abilities.

Due to these limitations, it is important to examine whether the adverse effects of preferential selection demonstrated in the laboratory generalize to the field. Findings have seldom replicated negative effects of AA outside the laboratory. In a study of 188 graduates of an MBA program, Graves and Powell (1994) found that both women and men had more positive job attitudes when their own sex was given preferential treatment than when decisions were sex neutral. In a study of over 7,000 employees at a large, federal government agency, Parker, Baltes, and Christiansen (1997) found positive attitudinal reactions to AA for all employees, including White men. Finally, Taylor's (1994) analysis of General Social Survey data showed no differences in job satisfaction, intrinsic interest in work, and ambition between White women employed in AA companies and those employed in firms that did not practice AA. Additionally, African Americans in AA firms had higher levels of ambition than their counterparts employed in non-AA firms.

Outcome-focused research has also examined how others perceive the beneficiaries of AA. Some are thought to evaluate AA beneficiaries negatively due to a stigma created by the perception of preferential treatment. Kelley's (1972) discounting principle is a theoretical foundation often used to explain the phenomenon of stigmatization. Kelley believed that when multiple explanations of behavior exist, any one cause of that behavior can be discounted. Garcia, Erskine, Hawn, and Casmay (1981) use this idea to explain how individuals underestimate the qualifications of those perceived to benefit from AA. They found that when study participants were told that a school had an AA policy, their estimates of minority applicants' grade point averages and qualifications were lower than when AA was not mentioned. The existence of an AA policy provided an alternative explanation, allowing the participants to discount the role qualifications played in the admission decision. Summers (1991) and Heilman, Block, and Lucas (1992) conducted laboratory studies demonstrating the discounting effect when women were the beneficiaries of AA programs.

Heilman, Block, and Stathatos (1997) tried to generalize the discounting effect to the field by demonstrating that managers discounted White women's qualifications under an AA program. This study was limited in two ways, however. First, the managers judged a hypothetical person on the basis of an employment application alone. In a real hiring situation, applicants for employment are usually interviewed. The richer information provided in an interview may reduce the effects of the presence of an AA program. Second, the managers knew they were participating in a research study. Hence, they knew that their decisions did not have any real consequences and they may have acted differently than they would in an actual hiring situation.

Other research shows that the discounting effect may not generalize to the field. Using General Social Survey data, Herring and Collins (1995) found that White men employed by firms with AA programs evaluated the work habits of African Americans more favorably than those from firms without AA programs. Women in firms with AA programs, however, had slightly less favorable perceptions of the work habits of African Americans than those in firms without AA programs, a finding that is consistent with the discounting principle.

In summary, there is considerable evidence from the laboratory that AA may have negative social and psychological effects. There is little evidence, however, that these effects generalize to the field.

Process-Focused Studies

Process-focused studies examine the effects of manipulating the process through which AA selection decisions are made. Results demonstrate that changing the decision-making process significantly affects the outcomes of AA programs.

Nacoste (1985, 1987) has examined effects of perceived process fairness on the outcomes of AA. For example, he found that the perceived fairness of selection criteria was a significant predictor of the attractiveness of the organization (Nacoste, 1987). When an organization's selection criteria for a research grant included both gender and the qualifications of the applicant, respondents were more willing to work for the organization than when the decision was made on the sex of the applicant alone (Nacoste, 1985).

Major, Feinstein, and Crocker (1994) argued that selection based on group membership creates attributional ambiguity for AA beneficiaries. In their view, an AA program makes the cause of positive career outcomes less clear for beneficiaries because success might be due to group membership rather than personal merit. As a result, success in an AA context has a weaker positive impact on self-confidence and self-esteem. They and others have shown, however, that this potential adverse effect can be eliminated by knowledge that decisions were based on merit in addition to group membership (Heilman, Lucas, & Kaplow, 1990; Heilman et al., 1991). White men also respond more positively to AA when told that decisions are based on merit as well as group membership (Heilman, McCullough, & Gilbert, 1996).

The AA as help model provides more detailed insight into AA processes likely to produce positive outcomes (Turner & Pratkanis, 1994). In this model, AA procedures are dichotomized into the categories of self-threatening and self-supportive actions. These categories are determined by three factors: (a) what is implied by the procedures, (b) how they conform to social norms, and (c) the instrumental benefits of the procedures. Self-threatening AA procedures include actions that imply failure and inferiority, are perceived as unfair, and fail to give indications of future success. Self-supportive AA procedures are those that do not imply that assistance is needed in obtaining a job, emphasize independence, and give indications of future success. It is thought that these procedures lead to a number of positive short- and long-term consequences, such as positive affect, positive evaluations (of self and by others), and nondefensive behaviors. Research is needed to examine these propositions.

In summary, laboratory evidence indicates that the specific AA procedures used have significant effects on people's reactions to AA. Procedures that include consideration of qualifications in addition to demographics are perceived to be more fair and are less likely to have negative social and psychological consequences. They also more closely conform to the way AA is practiced in organizations. Hence, they provide further evidence that the unintended negative effects of AA demonstrated in the laboratory are unlikely to generalize to the field.

Determinants of Attitudes Toward Affirmative Action

Attitudes toward AA have been studied a great deal. Generally speaking, White Americans have negative responses to the term *affirmative action,* but positive responses to many of the activities that it entails. Consistent predictors of positive AA attitudes include (1) being a member of a targeted group, (2) holding antiracist attitudes, (3) espousing liberal views, (4) believing that race and sex discrimination occurs, and (5) believing that AA has desirable effects. Among these, the strongest predictors are racism, beliefs about discrimination, and beliefs about AA programs.

Demographics as Predictors of AA Attitudes

Research shows that race/ethnicity and sex are fairly consistent predictors of attitudes toward AA (Steeh & Krysan, 1996). Demographics are not the strongest predictors of AA attitudes, however, and generally show weak to moderate effect sizes. In general, White men are less supportive of AA programs than other demographic groups (Bobo & Kluegel, 1993; Kluegel & Smith, 1983). White women are less supportive of AA programs designed to eliminate race discrimination than are African Americans. Studies examining the attitudes of Asian or Hispanic Americans are relatively rare and have shown that these groups fall between African Americans and White Americans in their level of support for AA (Bell, McLaughlin, & Harrison, 1996; Kravitz & Platania, 1993).

Most of this research has examined attitudes toward AA programs targeting people of color, and relatively few studies have examined attitudes toward AA programs targeting women. The studies examining AA programs targeting women have found that women support these programs more than men do (Tougas & Beaton, 1993) and White women support programs targeting women more strongly than programs targeting people of color (Smith & Witt, 1990).

The reasons for these demographic group differences are not self-evident. Although attributing racial, ethnic, and sex differences in AA attitudes to self-interest may appeal to common sense, in general, measures of self-interest are only weakly associated with policy attitudes (Sears & Funk, 1990). The following sections explore other determinants of AA attitudes to try to identify the underlying causes of these demographic group differences.

Racism

Many authors argue that negative attitudes toward AA stem from racism. Research results support this contention, and the correlations between measures of racism and AA attitudes are moderate to strong (Bobo & Kluegel, 1993; Kluegel & Smith, 1983). Findings that people are less likely to endorse AA programs targeting African Americans than AA programs targeting other groups, such as the poor or the disabled, also imply that racism may be a factor affecting attitudes (Bobo & Kluegel, 1993; Kravitz & Platania, 1993; Steeh & Krysan, 1996).

Theorists argue that contemporary racism is expressed more subtly than blatant statements about the inferiority of African Americans. The concept of symbolic racism (Sears, 1988) argues that the two roots of anti-AA attitudes are negative affect and attachment to traditional values such as individualism. Symbolic racists believe that African Americans violate cherished values such as individual responsibility and social mobility through individual merit. These feelings are not expressed directly. Instead, racists express their feelings indirectly and symbolically in opposition to public policies such as busing and AA. The reason for this is because it is easier in contemporary society to develop socially acceptable arguments for opposition to a specific government policy than to justify racist sentiments.

Critics of symbolic racism research argue that this approach does not measure racism independently of policy attitudes and is therefore tautological (Sniderman & Tetlock, 1986). To counter that argument, Little, Murry, and Wimbush (1998) developed a measure of symbolic racism that did not include items about attitudes toward AA. Their symbolic racism measure was a strong predictor of anti-AA attitudes.

Other theorists have applied the concept of aversive racism to explain AA attitudes. Aversive racists endorse an egalitarian value system while holding racist beliefs (Dovidio, Mann, & Gaertner, 1989). They desire to be racially tolerant but hold negative feelings toward other racial or ethnic groups. The result of aversive racism is that when norms prescribing appropriate behavior are clear, people will not discriminate on the basis of race. However, when the normative structure of the situation is weak, ambiguous, or conflicting, or if a racist can justify or rationalize a negative action, he or she will discriminate. In this way, aversive racists can engage in racial discrimination without challenging their egalitarian self-images.

Examining the link between aversive racism and AA attitudes, Murrell, Dietz-Uhler, Dovidio, Gaertner, and Drout (1994) found that undergraduates had more negative attitudes toward AA for African Americans than for the disabled or elderly persons. Attitudes were more positive when the policy was justified as compensating for past discrimination or providing diversity for the organization than when the policy was not justified. The justification effect was stronger for policies targeted at African Americans than for policies targeted at disabled or elderly persons, suggesting the operation of aversive racism. In the absence of macrolevel justifications, participants could more easily rationalize their negative attitudes on the basis of factors other than race. More research of this type needs to be done to demonstrate the association between AA attitudes and aversive racism.

Political Ideology and Beliefs About the Merit System

Liberalism-conservatism is a consistent predictor of AA attitudes (Feldman, 1988; Kinder & Sanders, 1990). Another consistent predictor is the respondent's beliefs about the merit system in the United States. Liberalism-conservatism and beliefs about the merit system are linked. Conservatives are more likely to endorse statements supporting the efficacy of the merit system, such as "Any person who is willing to work hard has a good chance of succeeding." Conservatives are less likely to endorse statements calling for greater equality in society, such as "If people were treated more equally in this country, we would have many fewer problems" (Feldman, 1988). People who support the need for greater equality in society are more likely to support AA programs (Feldman, 1988; Kluegel & Smith, 1983). Also, people who believe that structural barriers to opportunity exist are more likely to support AA programs (Bobo & Kluegel, 1993; Jacobson, 1983; Kluegel & Smith, 1983).

One of the strongest predictors of AA attitudes is the extent to which respondents believe that race discrimination exists in society. Correlations between belief in race discrimination and AA attitudes are moderate to strong in magnitude (Bobo & Kluegel, 1993; Kluegel & Smith, 1983). Belief in the existence of sex discrimination is also strongly associated with positive attitudes toward AA programs targeting women (Tougas & Beaton, 1993; Tougas, Beaton, & Veilleux, 1991; Tougas & Veilleux, 1990).

Whites are less likely than African Americans to believe that race discrimination exists (Bobo & Kluegel, 1993), and men are less likely than women to believe that sex discrimination exists (Kern, 1994; Tougas & Beaton, 1993). Unfortunately, no studies have examined whether beliefs in the merit system mediate the relationship between demographic characteristics and AA attitudes. Research examining these mediating effects would be useful for determining whether demographic group differences are due to self-interest or political beliefs.

Beliefs About the Effects of Affirmative Action

Research has shown that people who believe that AA programs lead to positive outcomes have more favorable attitudes toward AA. The effect sizes are moderate to strong (Jacobson, 1983; Tougas & Beaton, 1993). Other research has shown that people's beliefs about AA programs are often incorrect (Kravitz & Platania, 1993). For example, people believed that AA programs do not compare the proportion hired to the proportion of qualified people in the area population, when, in fact, this is how AA programs operate. Respondents approved of AA programs functioning in the actual way that they do. The authors concluded that educating the public about how AA programs actually work would help to increase support for AA.

Supporting Kravitz and Platania's (1993) contention, research has shown that when people are given specific information about the content of AA programs, their support increases dramatically. For example, when asked "All in all, do you favor or oppose AA programs in industry for Blacks provided there are no rigid quotas?" about 70% of Whites agreed in both 1978 and 1988 Harris polls (Steeh & Krysan, 1996). Konrad and Linnehan (1995b) found that although managers had negative attitudes toward "female or minority hiring quotas," they had neutral to favorable attitudes toward many specific activities involved in AA programs.

Large demographic group differences exist in beliefs about AA's effects. Men have more negative beliefs about AA programs targeting women (Tougas & Beaton, 1993), and Whites have more negative beliefs about AA than African, Hispanic, or Asian Americans (Bell, Harrison, & McLaughlin, 1997). For example, 74% of African Americans and 26% of Whites agree that without AA, African Americans would not get a "fair shake," and fewer than 20% of African Americans but 40% of Whites agree that AA will lead to reverse discrimination (Sigelman & Welch, 1991).

To determine whether differences in beliefs about AA mediate the relationship between demographic characteristics and AA attitudes, further research is needed that links specific beliefs about AA to global measures of AA attitudes. Other important outcome variables to examine include behavioral intentions regarding AA programs. Beliefs about AA programs may predict the behavioral intentions of decision makers who have the power to take proactive action to reduce race and sex inequality.

Directions for Future Research on Affirmative Action Attitudes

Most of the research examining determinants of AA attitudes has focused on Whites. More research should examine AA attitudes among other groups. Research should disaggregate demographic groups as much as possible by analyzing data for African Americans, Asian Americans, and Hispanic Americans separately and by comparing women and men within race and ethnic categories. Also, research is needed to examine whether determinants such as racism, beliefs about the existence of discrimination, or beliefs about AA's effects mediate the association between demographic characteristics and AA attitudes. Such research would help us to understand why demographic groups differ in their attitudes toward AA.

Research should measure attitudes toward AA programs targeting women and people of color separately because reactions to AA depend on the beneficiary group. The question of why people respond differently to AA programs targeting different groups also needs to be examined. In particular, research should document the reasons why people have more negative attitudes toward AA programs for African Americans than for other groups. Racism undoubtedly plays a part, and beliefs about AA's effects and about the existence of discrimination in society may also be important. Also, though racism has been shown to be a strong predictor of anti-AA attitudes, no research has examined whether there is a significant association between sexism and attitudes toward AA for women.

Finally, more research needs to be conducted to improve our understanding of media effects on AA attitudes (Kinder & Sanders, 1990). Research could examine media effects by manipulating the determinants of AA attitudes identified above. For example, certain issue frames may make AA more appealing to aversive racists. Others may influence beliefs about the existence of discrimination and about AA's effects. By identifying AA portrayals that increase the accuracy of beliefs about AA and reduce the ability of aversive racists to rationalize anti-AA attitudes, research could help AA proponents garner greater support among the public.

Discussion

AA programs are under attack. The executive orders on which AA is based conflict with the position taken by the federal antidiscrimination laws. Although the executive orders require remedial steps because of the historical context, federal laws deny the necessity of such action. In a series of decisions, the judiciary has moved away from the doctrine of proactive action in recent years. This is troubling. As Crosby and Cordova (1996) point out, AA is "the *only* legal remedy in the United States for discrimination that does not require the victims to notice their condition and come forward in grievance on their own behalf" (p. 44). Proactive action to promote equal opportunity is important because discrimination is difficult to detect on a case-by-case basis. Only when aggregate data are presented can people detect a systematic pattern of discrimination (Cordova, 1992). As such, without AA, systematic patterns of discrimination will go unnoticed and unremedied more often than they do now.

It is also troubling that attacks on AA programs have targeted institutions of higher education. Opponents argue that AA is ineffective because there is a lack of qualified candidates from targeted classes. The disparity in the quality of public education between the urban, rural, and suburban areas should be reduced to provide institutions of higher education with a more diverse group of qualified applicants for admission. But college and university AA programs must·be kept in place to ensure that institutions produce a diverse pool of qualified job applicants. Without diversity in degree-granting programs, it will be difficult for employers to increase employee diversity at all levels and in all job categories.

Research has demonstrated positive economic effects for AA beneficiaries. But the argument that AA has unintended negative social and psychological effects has been used to justify its dismantling (e.g., Steele, 1990). Research with student participants has documented such negative effects on beneficiaries of AA, yet other research has shown that these effects often do not generalize to adult workers. For targeted groups, the documented material benefits of AA probably outweigh the costs of potential social and psychological problems, especially because these problems seem to be rather easily remedied by procedural initiatives that emphasize the beneficiaries' qualifications.

Public support could pressure lawmakers to strengthen AA. Support for AA appears weak because the term *affirmative action* has pejorative implications for many. However, these negative connotations disappear when people rate the specific activities that are at the heart of an AA program. Eberhardt and Fiske (1994) argue that research should examine ways to effectively communicate AA procedures to the public. Anti-AA attitudes are linked to racist sentiments that contemporary Americans hesitate to express to others or even admit to themselves (Dovidio et al., 1989; Sears, 1988). As such, it is not surprising that opponents have attacked AA on the basis of race rather than sex, both in the media and in the courts. Ambiguous cases where Whites lose out to African Americans because of AA provide modern racists with rationalizations that allow them to express anti-AA attitudes without explicitly acknowledging racist feelings. Providing people with information on the prevalence of discrimination and the ways AA programs work renders such rationalizations less plausible. Research should examine ways to counter the processes through which unacknowledged racist feelings influence AA attitudes.

Although research has shown that AA has generally had a positive impact on the economic status of White women and people of color, attacks on AA mean that its effectiveness must continue to be demonstrated. To do this, more research should be conducted on the economic, psychological, and social effects of AA. This will require closer collaboration between governmental enforcement agencies, academia, and organizations. Government data should be made available to researchers in greater detail, organizations can sponsor and participate in this research, and researchers must use women and men who are members of all racial and ethnic groups in their studies. Longitudinal data collection designs will help to establish causality and determine whether effects are short-term or long-lasting.

Chapter 23

Impacts of Diversity and Work-Life Initiatives in Organizations

Sharon A. Lobel

As of 1997, about one-third of the 500 largest companies in the United States had workplace diversity programs and another one-third had programs in planning stages (Blackmon, 1997). Despite evidence of growth in the number and range of diversity initiatives in organizations, the political, economic, and social climate is not altogether favorable for diversity management (Lobel, 1996). Continued support and investment in diversity cannot be taken for granted.

In the 1980s and 1990s, the political climate moved away from government intervention to create diversity and achieve equal opportunity in organizations (see Chapter 22 by Konrad and Linnehan in this volume for more on affirmative action issues). During the Reagan and Bush eras, enforcement of Title VII was relaxed (Yakura, 1996) and, most recently, affirmative action has become a visible target. In a recent survey, 39% of Americans said affirmative action programs have gone "too far," up from 24% less than four years ago. Seventy-five percent of Whites and 58% of Blacks believe that racial preferences should be outlawed (Decker, 1995). Although advocates of diversity management have argued that it is distinct from affirmative action

AUTHOR'S NOTE: The author wishes to acknowledge Marilyn Gist and Gary Powell for their seminal contributions to the development and express of these ideas.

(Yakura, 1996), negative attitudes expressed about affirmative action may also be directed at diversity practices in general.

The future of diversity initiatives is especially uncertain when their links to business objectives are not firmly established in the minds of decision makers (Kossek & Lobel, 1996; Robinson & Dechant, 1997). Unfortunately, as reported in a Center for the American Workforce (1994) survey, many companies engage in diversity practices only because of government mandates, not for their value to organizational effectiveness. The Glass Ceiling Commission study (U.S. Department of Labor, 1991a) found that a majority of CEOs report commitment to a diverse workforce because of federal directives; only 30% to 40% are committed for business reasons. Therefore, if federal mandates continue to weaken, commitment to diversity may also decline.

Although diversity initiatives may lose momentum due to the political climate, initiatives to help employees manage work and personal life demands face other challenges. Like diversity initiatives (see Table 23.1), work-life initiatives (see Table 23.2) have developed in response to changing demographics. The increasing complexity of family life and employee needs for flexibility have also fueled the work-life movement (Lobel, Googins, & Bankert, 1999). At the same time, single adults with no dependent children resent working overtime and weekends, and traveling more frequently than coworkers with families (Lafayette, 1994). Furthermore, work-life management tends to be perceived as costly, a deterrent to support in economic downturns. Heightened pressures to cost justify work-life initiatives and sentiments of resentment signal that these programs are being carefully scrutinized.

Other prevalent challenges to managing diversity and work-life within organizations are competition with other issues, belief that demographics will not affect a company's ability to attract employees, and lack of middle- and senior management support (Winterle, 1992). In this political, economic, and social climate, the major challenge is to link initiatives to organizational effectiveness.

Toward this end, this chapter reviews the research on impacts of diversity and work-life management in organizations. The most frequently cited diversity and work-life objectives are discussed, and their associated measures of effectiveness are examined. Then, the existing empirical research on diversity and work-life impacts are reviewed, noting trends and gaps. Research needs for the future are then described.

Objectives of Diversity and Work-Life Practices

Tables 23.1 and 23.2 reveal a substantial variety and number of programs and policies. The objectives of these programs and policies are directed toward

TABLE 23.1　Diversity Initiatives in Organizations

Career development and planning initiatives
　Database tracking of workforce demographics
　Informal mentoring
　Formal mentoring programs
　Identification process for "high potential"
　　employees
　Expanded job posting up to vice president levels
　Individual development plans
　Executive MBA programs
　Targeted recruitment
　Cross-training to learn nontraditional, technical
　　objectives
　Developmental assignments: lateral, rotational,
　　special short term, task forces
　Partnerships with educational institutions
　Internships
　Recruitment incentives
　Exit interviews

Employee involvement initiatives
　Network and support groups
　Issue study groups
　Focus groups
　Advisory task force

Legal
　Internal grievance procedures
　Monitor frequency of complaints by locations
　EEO statistics and profiles
　Affirmative action/EEO office

Culture change initiatives
　Internal diagnostic studies
　　Glass ceiling audit
　　Equity studies
　　Culture audits
　　Employee needs assessment

Monitoring of compensation systems for equity
Incorporate diversity issue items into employee
　attitude surveys
Benchmark other companies
Revise policies/benefits to support diverse needs
Amend performance appraisal systems, for
　example, use multiple sources of feedback
Hold managers accountable for results in
　performance appraisal and compensation

Communication initiatives
　Speeches by CEO/senior executives; top
　　management support
　Special newsletters/status reports
　Articulated diversity philosophy or mission
　　statement
　Recognition events, awards
　Public relations to highlight diversity

Education and training initiatives
　Sexual harassment training
　Awareness training for managers
　Classes/lectures/seminars
　Cross-cultural skill building
　Reference library
　Training for recruiters

Outreach
　Start-up loans
　Technical assistance

Other
　Board of director activities
　Selection of nontraditional vendors
　Customer satisfaction audits
　Community involvement
　Diversity coordinator position in company

individual change and development, work group performance, and overall organizational effectiveness.

Table 23.3 summarizes the major objectives outlined in the diversity and work-life literature. For each objective, I have developed a list of desired, measurable indicators of impact. In the context of the review of research on impacts that follows, we will evaluate those objectives in Table 23.3 that have been most frequently highlighted by researchers and practitioners.

Some of the objectives listed in Table 23.3, such as attracting a wider pool of talent or reducing legal costs, are more closely associated with affirmative action. Others such as effecting culture change are more directly linked with managing diversity. Affirmative action *creates* diversity within organizations.

TABLE 23.2   Work-Life Initiatives in Organizations

Flexibility initiatives
   Part-time
   Job share
   Work-at-home
   Short increments of time off
   Phased retirement
   Phased-in work schedule following leave
   Compressed work week
   Flexible benefits

Dependent care
   Information and referral
   On-site, near-site child care
   Child care consortium
   Sponsors community-based child care
   Dependent care leave
   Sick/emergency child or elder care services
   Summer/holiday care program
   Before/after school program
   Caregiver fairs

Paid leaves of absence
   Maternity
   Parental
   Adoption
   Family personal
   Sabbatical
   Job guarantee

Financial benefits
   Flexible spending accounts
   Reimbursement of dependent care costs
      (i.e., with travel overnight)
   Tuition or subsidy programs

Culture change initiatives
   Needs assessment

Incorporate work-life items into employee
   attitude surveys
Benchmark other companies
Hold managers accountable for support for
   flexibility

Other employee involvement initiatives
   Network and support groups
   Issue study groups
   Focus groups
   Advisory task force

Communication initiatives
   Speeches by CEO/senior executives
   Articulated work-life philosophy or mission
      statement
   Public relations to highlight flexibility
   Participation in regional or national award
      ceremonies
   Guides (internal or external) on implementation

Other
   Work-life coordinator position in company
   Handbook of work-life benefits and policies
   Work-life seminars or workshops

Unpaid leaves
   Leaves beyond those mandated by state or
      federal legislation

Partnerships with communities
   Corporate gifts to community organizations
      dealing in dependent care
   Partnerships with schools to enhance skills and
      interest of applicant pool

Managing diversity differs from affirmative action in that the presence of diversity can be assumed. The focus of managing diversity initiatives is to *develop* the talents within the workforce. Organizations, such as Xerox Corporation, that have proven to be benchmarks for managing diversity have built their success on strong affirmative action programs (Sessa, 1992). Recruitment of women and minorities goes hand-in-hand with changes that decrease their turnover in organizations. Therefore, although affirmative action and managing diversity can be distinguished, I do not do so in this chapter.

TABLE 23.3   Objectives and Indicators of Effective Diversity and Work-Life Management

Objectives	Indicators of Achievement of Objectives
Enhanced organizational effectiveness	
Meet a moral imperative; do the "right thing"	Assessment of corporate citizenship
	Assess impacts on multiple stakeholders (shareholders, employees, communities)
	Outside recognition, reputation
Reduce labor costs	Absenteeism
	Turnover
	Productivity
Reduce legal costs associated with lawsuits and grievances	Number of EEO complaints and grievances; associated costs
	Distribution of economic and social benefits, for example, rates of advancement, access to training and development opportunities across levels, functions, titles
Have policies and programs that are responsive to the changing demographic profile of employees and that support work and personal life effectiveness	Number of relevant programs and policies (e.g., training)
	Program utilization rates
	Employee satisfaction with programs and policies (measurement not limited to beneficiaries)
	Management accountability
Enhance the organization's reputation	Public knowledge and assessment
	Awards
Attract a wider pool of talent	Demographic characteristics of candidates
	Demographic characteristics of hires
Retain a wider pool of talent	Demographic characteristics for voluntary and involuntary turnover populations
	Retention rate of high-potential employees
	Retention rate by function, level
Effect culture change consistent with program and policy changes	Cultural audit
	Integration of diversity and work-life with other programs, for example, orientation
	Top management support
	Number and level of managers involved in diversity and work-life initiatives
	Frequency of communication about importance of diversity and work-life in organization
Offer better service and marketing for a diverse customer base	Customer satisfaction with quality of products and services
	Market share for target population or region
Enhance ability to innovate because of use of diverse perspectives	Quality and profitability of new products and services

(continued)

TABLE 23.3 Continued

Objectives	Indicators of Achievement of Objectives
Reinforce business strategies	Profitability
	Progress toward globalization
	Quality
	Customer service and marketing
Enhanced individual and work group effectiveness	
Improved job satisfaction and performance of individuals	Individual job satisfaction and performance
	Existence of support networks; frequency of meetings; impact
	Promotion rates of trainees
Increased awareness and understanding of issues	Changes in perception, for example, stereotypes
Improved quality of team problem solving	Team commitment and performance
Improved abilities to work with and manage people of diverse backgrounds	Satisfaction with coworkers
	Managerial skill development (e.g., flexibility, interpersonal and communication skills)
	Individual accountability for climate, hiring records
Improved ability to manage work and personal life commitments across a wide spectrum of career and life patterns/stages	Reduced work-life conflict
	Satisfaction with work and personal life

Existing Research on Impacts

Tables 23.4 and 23.5 summarize the existing research on impacts of diversity and work-life, respectively, for organizations and individuals. Because of the difficulties inherent in evaluating impacts, Cox (1994) proposed that researchers begin with variables that are more easily studied and progress to more difficult indicators. Therefore, I organized the tables into four categories, roughly reflecting the ease with which data can be collected. The categories show effects of initiatives on (1) attitudes, (2) individual and team performance, (3) organizational human resource management indicators, and (4) organizational strategic goals. In the next section, I will summarize the research results associated with each category.

Tables 23.4 and 23.5 do not include the numerous sources that rely on testimonials about effects of work-life and diversity. Testimonials are claims that are unsubstantiated by empirical research. In most cases, the claims are made by company spokespersons to journalists and reported in the popular press. For example, a wide range of diversity and work-life initiatives brought

(text continues on page 464)

TABLE 23.4   Review of Research on Impacts of Diversity Initiatives

Initiative	Impact	Author
Effects on attitudes		
Diversity training	More positive attitudes toward diversity	Rynes and Rosen (1995)
Active top management support for diversity	Managers' judge organization as effective in managing diversity	Morrison, White, Van Velsor, and the Center for Creative Leadership (1987); Rynes and Rosen (1995); Hitt and Keats (1984)
Management accountability for development of diversity	HR professionals rate organization as effective in managing diversity	Schreiber, Price, and Morrison (1993)
Increasing number of women on boards of directors	Women board members perceive lack of influence on management succession	Briggins (1998)
Higher proportion of women in upper management	Reduction in stereotyping	Ely (1995)
AA hiring status	Lower ratings of competence, lower recommended salary increase	Heilman, Block, and Stathatos (1997)
Diversity training	Positive attitudes toward diversity	Alderfer (1992); Adler (1983)
Increased gender diversity	Positive attitudes toward diversity initiatives	Kossek and Zonia (1993)
Superior-subordinate gender difference	Superior rates subordinate as performing more poorly; less liking for subordinate	Tsui and O'Reilly (1989)
Increasing proportion of women in work unit	Men report less job satisfaction and organizational attachment	Tsui, Egan, and O'Reilly (1992); Wharton and Baron (1987)
Increased team diversity	Reduced organizational and team attachment	Tsui et al. (1992); Watson, Kumar, and Michaelson (1993); Riordan and Shore (1997); Alagna, Reddy, and Collins (1982)
Top team gender diversity	Women report less intention to quit, more job satisfaction	Burke and McKeen (1996)
Effects on individual and team performance		
Increased diversity of social networks	More promotion potential	Ibarra (1995)
Increased team diversity	Better quality of team solutions	McLeod, Lobel, and Cox (1996); Jackson, May, and Whitney (1995)
Increased team diversity	Increased team turnover	Jackson (1991); Tolbert, Simons, Andrews, and Rhee (1995); O'Reilly, Caldwell, and Barnett (1989)
Increased team diversity	More creativity and innovation	Bantel and Jackson (1989); Jackson (1991)
Increased team diversity	Less technical and interpersonal communication	Hoffman (1985); Zenger and Lawrence (1989)
Increasing difference from others in work unit	Increased absence for men and Whites; No effect for women and non-Whites	Tsui et al. (1992)
Superior-subordinate gender difference	Subordinates report more role ambiguity	Tsui and O'Reilly (1989)
Superior-subordinate gender difference (Mexico)	Increased absence	Pelled and Xin (1997)

(continued)

TABLE 23.4 Continued

Initiative	Impact	Author
Effects on organizational human resource management indicators		
AA, balanced workforce goals and caucus groups (Xerox)	Upward mobility for all groups	Sessa (1992)
Active commitment of senior management to diversity	Upward mobility for women and minorities	Morrison et al. (1987)
Valuing differences discussion groups (Digital)	Positive company reputation	Walker and Hanson (1992)
Recruitment of minorities for management (Pacific Bell)	More minorities in management	Roberson and Gutierrez (1992)
Presence of EEO/AA offices and rules	*More EEO-/AA-related lawsuits*	Edelman (1992)
Diversity training	*Training-related lawsuit*	Caudron (1993)
Glass ceiling interventions	More Black managers	Alderfer (1992)
Increased number of HR structures to manage diversity	More managerial level of women and people of color	Konrad and Linnehan (1995a)
Equal opportunity office and program (IBM–Germany)	Increased percentage of women in management	Antal and Krebsbach-Gnath (1988)
Both man and woman must be nominated for board and public council appointments (Denmark)	Increased representation of women on Boards and councils	Albertsen and Christensen (1993)
Increased proportion of women in job class	*Decline in salary level for job class*	Pfeffer and Davis-Blake (1987)
Higher pay for AA officer compared to other employees in same organization	Increased percentage of women and minorities	Pfeffer, Davis-Blake, and Julius (1995)
Personal development program for women (Bank of Ireland)	Increased representation of women in management	Murphy (1993)
Effects on organizational strategic goals		
Progressive HR practices	Profitability	Kanter (1983)
Top management team diversity	More organizational innovation	Eisenhardt and Schoonhoven (1990)
More women in management	Return on assets, return on investments, return on equity	Shrader, Blackburn, and Iles (1997)

NOTE: Italicized entries under "Impact" represent undesirable or neutral impacts. HR = human resource; AA = affirmative action; EEO = equal employment opportunity.

TABLE 23.5   Review of Research on Impacts of Work-Life Initiatives

Initiative	Impact	Author
Effects on attitudes		
Availability of family responsive practices	Organizational attachment	Grover and Crooker (1995)
Work-family supports	Job satisfaction	National Council of Jewish Women (1987)
Work-family workshops	Lower stress	Kline and Snow (1994)
On-site child care	Organizational commitment and job satisfaction	Greenberger, Goldberg, Hamill, O'Neil, and Payne (1989); Youngblood and Chambers-Cook (1984)
On-site child care	Perceived positive impact on recruitment, absenteeism, employee attitudes, and public relations	Perry (1982)
On-site child care	Would recommend employer	Dawson, Mikel, Lorenz, and King (1984); Marquart (1988)
On-site child care	Beliefs about positive impacts on productivity, recruitment, and absenteeism	Burge and Stewart (1988)
On-site child care	Improved morale	Ransom, Aschbacher, and Burud (1989)
On-site child care	Manager perceptions of positive impacts	Perry (1982)
Use of on-site child care	*Not related to managers' assessments of users' performance or absenteeism*	Kossek and Nichol (1992)
Flexible work schedules	Organizational commitment	Pierce and Newstrom (1982, 1983); Rothausen (1994)
Flexible schedules and supportive supervisors	Reduced job dissatisfaction; lower levels of depression and somatic complaints	Thomas and Ganster (1995)
Flextime	Perceptions of improved work group and superior-subordinate relations	Narayanan and Nath (1982)
Flextime	Perceptions of improved productivity	Golembiewski, Yeager, and Hilles (1976); Golembiewski, Hilles, and Kagno (1974)
Flextime	Improved job satisfaction and morale of users; *supervisor ambivalence*	Ronen (1984)
Flextime	Reduced work-family conflict	Winett, Neale, and Williams (1982); Lee (1983)
Flextime	*No impact on work-family conflict or satisfaction with family life*	Shinn, Wong, Simko, and Ortiz-Torres (1989); Bohen and Viveros-Long (1981)
Flextime	Increase in satisfaction with work environment	Evans (1973); McGuire and Liro (1986)
Flexible work arrangements, child care subsidies, part-time benefits (American Express)	Positive assessments by employees	Morrison and Herlihy (1992)
Parental leave	Perceived positive impact on company's business	Staines and Galinsky (1992)

(continued)

TABLE 23.5 Continued

Initiative	Impact	Author
Effects on individual and team performance		
Use of flexible work arrangements and other work-life programs	Improved individual performance	Catalyst (1998b); Dawson, Mikel, Lorenz, and King (1984); Lambert (1993); Rowe (1973)
Flexible work arrangements	Better team performance measures	Rayman (1998)
Flextime	No change in productivity	Narayanan and Nath (1982); Schein, Maurer, and Novak (1977); Milkovich and Gomez (1976)
Flextime	Improvement in productivity and performance	Ronen (1984); Pierce and Newstrom (1983); Kim and Campagna (1981)
Flextime	Mixed effects on productivity	Harrick, Vanek, and Michlitsch (1986)
Use of on-site child care	Ability to work overtime	Dawson et al. (1984)
On-site day care	No change in productivity	Miller (1984)
Use of work-family benefits	Participation in quality improvement circles	Lambert (1993)
Effects on organizational human resource management indicators		
Flexible work arrangements	Reduced absenteeism	Kim and Campagna (1981); Narayanan and Nath (1982); Pierce and Newstrom (1982, 1983); Golembiewski et al. (1976)
Flextime	Reduced use of sick days; reduced tardiness	Ronen (1984); Harrick et al. (1986)
Flextime	Reduced turnover	Ronen (1984); Nollen and Martin (1978)
On-site day care	No effect on absenteeism	Goff, Mount, and Jamison (1990); Miller (1984); Krug, Palmour, and Ballassai (1972)
Child care programs	Reduced absenteeism	Petersen and Massengill (1988); Kwasha Lipton (1995); Milkovich and Gomez (1976); Marquart (1988); Burud, Aschbacher, and McCroskey (1984); Rowe (1973); Ransom et al. (1989)
On-site child care	Positive impact on recruitment	Dawson et al. (1984); Marquart (1988); Ransom et al. (1989)

	Impact	References
On-site day care	Reduced turnover	Kossek and Nichol (1992); Marquart (1988); Milkovich and Gomez (1976); Youngblood and Chambers-Cook (1984); Dawson et al. (1984); Solomon (1985); Rowe (1973); Ransom et al. (1989); Burud et al. (1984)
Liberal leave policies	Reduced turnover	Marra and Lindner (1992)
Job protected maternity leave (U.S., Japan, Britain)	Higher pay than mothers without leave coverage	Waldfogel (1995, 1998); Higuchi, Waldfogel, and Abe (1998)
Work/life supports	Reduced turnover	National Council of Jewish Women (1987)
Work-life supports	Fewer sick days taken	National Council of Jewish Women (1987)
Effects on organizational strategic goals		
Working Mother list award	Positive impact on stock price	Chauvin and Guthrie (1994)
Flextime	Reduction in overtime expenditures; *no impact on suppliers or customers*	Ronen (1984)

NOTE: Italicized entries under "Impact" represent undesirable or neutral impacts.

about an increase in the number of women in management at Avon Corporation according to Caudron (1993). Although these claims may be legitimate, access to sources and information about research methods can be limited and the implications for researchers and practitioners unknown. Unfortunately, given the small amount of empirical research, especially for diversity impacts, advocates often have to rely on testimonials to promote their agenda.

Most of the existing research has been done in the United States. Although other countries have introduced initiatives, commonly designed to further the progress of women in organizations, there is only sparse mention of their known impacts in the literature. For example, Hammond (1988) describes several initiatives for equal opportunity in Great Britain. At National Westminster Bank, female managers are allowed a "career break" to care for children under age 5. They are guaranteed a return to management, provided that they work at least two weeks a year at the bank and participate in training activities. Although Hammond mentions the bank's need to recruit and retain a dwindling supply of high-potential employees, she does not report whether the career break has helped in these efforts. According to Erwee (1994), U.S. multinational signatories to the Sullivan Code, which offered Black South Africans equal opportunities in education, union organization, and employment, had a "direct, positive influence on the upward mobility of black women" (p. 337). No supporting data are presented, however. The Sullivan Code was discontinued in 1991 due to changes in South African policy supporting Black advancement. Davidson and Cooper's (1993a) book on European women in business and management and Adler and Izraeli's (1994) book on women in management contain descriptions of public and private efforts in 11 and 21 countries, respectively. Despite detailed descriptions of a wide array of initiatives that address work-life and women's career issues in each country, the contributors do not apparently have access to information about impacts. One exception involves a course titled "Do I Want to Be a Manager?" that was designed to help women in three Danish companies discover their aptitudes for management (Albertsen & Christensen, 1993). A total of 150 women participated in the course, and within a two-year period, 20% of them had assumed management positions.

The reasons for lack of data on impacts of initiatives in other countries vary. Researchers may not be able to gain access to company data or companies may not keep reliable records. For example, some multinational companies may routinely measure employee satisfaction with diversity or work-life initiatives as part of a global survey process, but this information is not typically shared with outsiders. In Mexico, a human resource management consultant observed that companies are not strict about record-keeping for employee behaviors, such as tardiness. Therefore, reliable measures may be difficult to obtain even if the company were willing to share them (Lobel, 1999). In many countries, mandatory diversity or work-life initiatives may be ineffective because of lack of compliance. For example, in Germany, the federal government passed guidelines on recruitment, promotion, and training of women as well as measures designed to help women balance work with family responsibilities (Antal & Krebsbach-Gnath, 1994). Although the guidelines are mandatory, there are no sanctions for lack of compliance. Antal and Krebsbach-Gnath suggest that the weak incentive system may be behind the limited effects of these guidelines. Similarly in Israel, the Equal Opportunity Law has no provision for affirmative action or enforcement of regulations (Izraeli, 1994). In France, an equal opportunity law passed in 1983 requires that employers with more than 50 employees present an annual report to their work council and union representatives, detailing what was done during the previous year to improve the situation for women. The government offers financial support to prepare a "positive action plan." Serdjenian (1994) reports that most eligible French companies prefer not to receive financial support rather than undertake the recommended planning. French unions are responsible for negotiating equal opportunity on behalf of women, but the unions appear to lack motivation to do so. In Hong Kong, sex discrimination in employment is still legal (deLeon & Ho, 1994).

Impacts of Diversity and Work-Life Initiatives on Attitudes

Measures of attitude changes before and after implementation of an initiative can reflect either *directional* changes (e.g., more positive attitudes toward diversity management practices) or changes in *strength* of attitudes (e.g., respondents think about diversity more frequently or hold specific attitudes more strongly) (Abelson, 1988). Researchers have measured the actual effects or the perceived effectiveness of initiatives on attitudes such as employee perceptions of how much the organization values diversity, commitment to the organization, and attachment to the work group.

Some research has focused on impacts of heightened diversity on attitudes of respondents in natural and experimental settings. Although these studies do not reflect evaluation of an actual diversity initiative, they do contribute to our understanding of the impact of one of the desirable outcomes of diversity management, namely, heightened diversity in work groups and organizations. On the positive side, Ely (1995) reported that an increase in the proportion of women in upper management is associated with a reduction in gender stereotyping. On the negative side, heightened diversity within work groups appears to have a negative impact on members' attachment to the group (Tsui, Egan, & O'Reilly, 1992; Watson, Kumar, & Michaelson, 1993). In other words, as heterogeneity within a group increases, group members report less group cohesiveness. Recent work suggests, however, that effects of demographic heterogeneity on attachment may diminish over time, as group members engage in meaningful interactions (Harrison, Price, & Bell, 1998; Watson et al., 1993).

Other research has measured perceived impacts of actual initiatives. For example, Rynes and Rosen (1995) surveyed human resource managers about changes in attitude toward diversity before and after diversity training. According to the managers' estimates, whereas only 9% of "typical employees" hold positive attitudes toward diversity prior to training, that number increases to 73% after training. Nonetheless, only one-third of respondents rated their diversity training programs as quite successful. We can infer, therefore, that the respondents hope for broader impacts as determinants of success.

When comparing the perceived impacts of a variety of diversity and work-life initiatives, human resource managers gave high ratings to formal and informal grievance procedures, communication of commitment from top managers, managers' accountability for increasing diversity, special training programs, mandatory attendance for all managers at training, and reduction of pressure to relocate as a prerequisite for career advancement (Hitt & Keats, 1984; Rosen, Miguel, & Peirce, 1989; Rynes & Rosen, 1995). These initiatives were perceived as highly effective for reducing discrimination and stemming the exodus of women and minority managers.

As mentioned earlier, a growing number of Americans have expressed negative attitudes toward affirmative action. One study investigated the stigma of being identified as an affirmative action hire. Heilman, Block, and Stathatos (1997) gave hypothetical information about job performance to male and female managers. If the employee was portrayed as an affirmative action hire, study participants rated her as less competent and recommended smaller salary increases than they did when the individual was not associated with affirmative action—even if disconfirming evidence was presented.

Not surprisingly, researchers have reported that attitudes about the value of different diversity initiatives vary with the demographic characteristics of respondents. For example, Tickamyer, Scollay, Bokemeier, and Wood (1989) surveyed affirmative action officers and university administrators about their perceptions of the impact of affirmative action programs on campuses. Women were less likely than men to feel that the programs had had an impact. Affirmative action officers were more likely than college administrators to feel that programs had an impact. Alderfer (1992) reports that Black employees at XYZ Corporation were more likely to report having benefited from the race relations competence workshops and more likely to recommend strengthening this and other diversity interventions, relative to White employees. Similarly, Kossek and Zonia (1993) found that women and minorities were more likely than White men to value employer efforts to promote diversity. These results indicate that personal characteristics of respondents will affect their attitudes about impact and that actual evaluations of impact are all the more necessary.

Results reported in Table 23.5 indicate largely positive effects of work-life practices on employee attitudes—such as organizational commitment, job satisfaction, and morale—and subjective assessments of performance. For example, Burge and Stewart (1988) reported that employees believed that their performances had improved as a result of access to on-site child care, although actual performance was not measured. As with diversity, assessments of effectiveness vary according to the characteristics of the respondent. For example, men and managers evaluate a leave of absence program for elder care as more effective than do women and nonmanagers (Kossek, DeMarr, Backman, & Kollar, 1993).

Despite the ease with which researchers can collect data on attitudes, the research is slim, especially for diversity. There are a number of anecdotal press accounts of impacts on attitudes, such as the report that "training and relentless communication seem to have softened opposition" to work-life policies at Corning, Inc. (Hammonds, 1997). More published research is needed. In addition, we need to look to broader populations to measure impacts on attitudes. Program users or targets are the obvious beneficiaries of specific initiatives, but programs and policies can have impacts on attitudes of other stakeholders. For example, Grover and Crooker (1995) reported that family-responsive policies affect work attitudes of those who directly benefit from the policies, as well as those who do not. Aside from employees and shareholders, customers, suppliers, communities, and families are also important stakeholders and potential beneficiaries. Just as organizational decision makers have designed outreach diversity and work-life initiatives, researchers also need to design outreach studies that measure impacts on a wider range of stakeholders. For example, in addition to measuring employee perceptions of equitable treatment in the workplace, researchers can measure customer and supplier perceptions as well.

Beyond the few published studies listed in Tables 23.4 and 23.5, there are undoubtedly in-house surveys of employee reactions to diversity training, one of the more common types of diversity initiatives. A major objective of training is to facilitate changed behavior in the workplace. Because reactions are not indicators of the learning that occurs, practitioners and researchers need to articulate how they expect the training to affect employee behaviors and skills. Then we can use surveys to measure perceptions of managerial and coworker skill enhancement following training. Companies should also include questions about employee morale in relation to climate for women and people of color in employee surveys and as part of the performance appraisal process. Ultimately, training-related behavior change needs to be anticipated and assessed in performance appraisals. For example, how might training affect the way that the trainee mentors coworkers or responds to customers from other cultures? This kind of research has not been widely done.

*Impacts of Diversity and Work-Life Initiatives
on Individual and Team Performance*

In describing some of the competitive advantages of diversity, Cox and Blake (1991) suggested that workforce diversity should generate diversity of perspectives, which in turn should improve creative output. They also proposed that encouragement of diverse perspectives can potentially contribute to better problem solving at the team level, and more system flexibility at the organizational level. There have been several reviews, mostly based on laboratory study research, of effects of team diversity on team performance (e.g., Thompson & Gooler, 1996) that support these arguments. In one such study, McLeod, Lobel, and Cox (1996) found that heterogeneous teams produced more feasible and effective solutions on a brainstorming task, relative to homogeneous teams.

Research in organizations is more limited, but consistent, with laboratory findings. As with the laboratory work, this research examines factors associated with one of the desired outcomes of diversity management, namely, heightened workforce diversity, although it does not directly assess the impact of a specific diversity initiative. In her review of the literature on effects of team diversity in work settings, Jackson (1991) concluded that heterogeneous teams are generally more creative and innovative. For example, in a study of 199 top management teams in the banking industry, Bantel and Jackson (1989) reported that teams diverse in functional background and education were more innovative in decision making.

Research on behavior changes in individuals as a result of diversity management activities is unfortunately absent. In the cross-cultural management literature, there has been a body of research on how cross-cultural training affects skill development, adaptation, and performance of expatriate employees (see review in Black & Mendenhall, 1990). Rigorous research with control groups and longitudinal designs has shown that cross-cultural training is effective (e.g., Earley, 1987). This stream of research, clearly related to diversity management, could serve as a resource for diversity researchers more often than it has in the past.

By and large, the results of research examining impacts of work-life initiatives on individual and team performance have been encouraging. For example, in a major study conducted by Catalyst (1998b), researchers surveyed and interviewed more than 2,000 people from four organizations over a two-year period to investigate impacts of flexible work arrangements on the performance of participants, as well as on their colleagues and supervisors. The researchers found that in many cases, impacts for these multiple stakeholders were positive or neutral. Negative assessments of user performance were most often reported by full-time colleagues and least often by users of flexible work arrangements and their managers. Actual performance of participants in flexible work arrangements apparently did not decrease;

however, some of their colleagues perceived that it did. The researchers concluded that the perceptions of negative impacts could be avoided by better communication and management of the expectations and processes associated with implementation of workplace flexibility.

One of the most interesting studies of work-life management on *team* performance was done by Lotte Bailyn, Leslie Perlow, and colleagues at Xerox Corporation (Perlow, 1997). The researchers worked with a small group of engineers who responded to a survey about work processes that interfered with their ability to integrate work and personal life. The respondents expressed a need for more quiet time. A work log revealed that 52% of engineers' work time was being spent meeting with others, formally or informally. Therefore, the group instituted a formal morning quiet time of two hours free of interruptions. As a result, they were able to achieve the first on-time launch of a new product in the business's history and also reduced absenteeism by 30%. The importance of this example is that the effort was driven by work-life concerns. This perspective mobilized people with a zest that a campaign for excellence in customer service might not have been able to match.

Another recent study (Rayman, 1998) measured the impact of flextime, telecommuting, and work redesign on team performance at two worksites of the Fleet Financial Group, the 11th largest bank holding company in the United States. The new work processes had positive impacts on team productivity, measured as completion times for loan turnarounds and time spent on administrative tasks. In addition, the initiatives improved retention rates, employee morale, and employee ability to integrate work and personal life. The researchers plan to monitor impacts over the long term and to expand their research to four additional Fleet worksites.

Impacts on Human Resource Management Indicators

In a survey of over 100 organizations, Konrad and Linnehan (1995a) examined the impact of a wide range of diversity programs on advancement of women and minorities. They wanted to investigate whether organizations with a greater number of programs specifically targeted for women and minorities (identity-conscious structures) have a better record of upward mobility for women and people of color, relative to organizations that have standardized, development programs to benefit all employees (identity-blind structures). They found that identity-blind structures, such as formal mentoring programs for all managers, employee assistance programs, and internal reviews to determine pay equity, have no noticeable impact on the progress of women and minorities. By contrast, identity-conscious programs were strongly associated with higher levels of employment status for women and minorities. This study provides strong evidence that despite resistance, expressed by both beneficiaries and members of the majority culture, to "special treatment" for women and minorities, these programs work; that is, they have their intended effect.

Elmes and Connelley (1997) have argued that diversity interventions might exacerbate existing problems by focusing awareness on group differences and threatening established status and power relationships. There is no reliable research on this topic. One of the few negative outcomes associated with diversity management is misperceived discrimination. For example, at a training session at Lucky Stores, participants listed commonly held stereotypes of minority groups. The list was found by an employee who had not attended the session. Thinking that the list was used for selection and promotion decisions, the employee sued successfully for intentional discrimination (Joplin & Daus, 1997). Because increased awareness and understanding is one of the goals of diversity management, this case challenges the development of training curriculum to identify the negative attitudes that might hinder change.

Although work-life and diversity may seem to be candidates for a natural alliance of goals and objectives, these two initiatives may have opposite impacts on organizational patterns of mobility. For example, a *Wall Street Journal* survey of 38,000 companies found that those known for being "family friendly" often have poor records for promoting women (Sharpe, 1994). Many work-life initiatives are designed to help individuals deal with immediate conflicts and do not necessarily consider the impact on careers (Lobel & Kossek, 1996). Because many women are leaving corporations, not for family reasons but because of advancement barriers (Tashjian, 1990), family-friendly programs that do not attend to women's advancement will be unsuccessful in retaining valued employees. Successful recruitment and retention of female professionals require comprehensive policies for removing barriers to advancement and allowing employees to balance work with other aspects of life (Rosen et al., 1989).

When diversity and work-life practices are designed together, their effects may be more consistent. For example, Corning, Inc. pinpointed a need to reduce their $5 million yearly cost for hiring and training replacements associated with the attrition of women and minorities. With a range of diversity and work-life programs, they were able to significantly reduce the attrition of women from 16.2% to 7.6% and of Blacks from 15.3% to 11.3% in three years (Morrison, 1992). Anecdotal evidence suggests that a wide range of diversity initiatives has stemmed turnover and improved representation of women and people of color in levels of management at Ortho Pharmaceuticals, Hewlett-Packard, Avon, and Prudential (Caudron, 1993).

In relation to the objectives of diversity and work-life management, the research on turnover and absenteeism provides convincing evidence of effectiveness in reducing labor costs. Organizations should maintain internal databases on the distribution of economic and social benefits, including rates of advancement and compensation, access to training and development opportunities, and representation across levels and functions.

Research findings about reduced turnover and absenteeism should be translated into dollar amounts where appropriate (Phillips & Reisman, 1992). Calculations to describe the costs associated with absenteeism or attrition are not complicated (e.g., Kwasha Lipton, 1995; Lobel & Faught, 1996). Assessments of labor costs associated with lawsuits and grievances would be more difficult to compute but could provide powerful evidence for the value of managing diversity effectively. Returns on investments in relation to important business strategies need to be demonstrated.

Impacts on Organizational Strategic Goals

As is evident in Tables 23.4 and 23.5, there is scant research to measure the degree to which diversity or work-life initiatives reinforce business strategies. For example, using event study methodology, some researchers have argued that announcements of company awards for progressive diversity practices, such as *Working Mother* magazine's annual list of best companies for working mothers, have a positive impact on stock price valuation (Chauvin & Guthrie, 1994; Wright, Ferris, Hiller, & Kroll, 1995). Others have argued that management researchers who experiment with these research methodologies have failed to conform to standard procedures, such as controlling for confounding events (McWilliams & Siegel, 1997). The encouraging results may be invalid.

To build a solid body of research, policymakers need to determine how specific initiatives are linked to important strategies. For example, flexible scheduling can support strategies of globalization or superior customer service. By having employees work nontraditional hours, the organization can be responsive to customers outside of typical business hours and in various time zones. Members of the workforce who are culturally sensitive to target markets can enhance the organization's ability to develop products and provide customer service to these markets. Once linkages to strategy are identified and communicated, it will be easier for researchers to design studies that collect data on these specific issues.

One promising area for research is what Cox and Blake (1991) refer to as system flexibility. Modern organizations require flexibility to survive in the global economy. Researchers need to explore how effective work-life and diversity management contributes to this flexibility. Perhaps as managers learn to support a diverse workforce with a broad array of work and personal lifestyles, their adaptability will translate into better management in general. *Integrating Work and Life: The Wharton Resource Guide* (Friedman, DeGroot, & Christensen, 1998) identifies managerial competencies for work-life balance. Some of these competencies, such as "rewarding performance and productivity, not just time spent working" and "questioning assumptions and encouraging creative experimentation in the way work is done," are skills that will serve broader organizational effectiveness goals. As work-life training for these competencies begins, how management development benefits the organization at large should be monitored.

Next Steps for Research

Research on impacts leaves much room for improvement in terms of quantity and quality. More research in all areas is needed to determine what degree of effectiveness can be expected within a given time frame, to give guidance in the development of initiatives, and to provide concrete evidence of success for cost-conscious critics.

Although there has been more work-life research than diversity research, there are several critiques of the quality of the existing research on impacts of work-life initiatives. For example, Grover and Crooker (1995) question the reliability of single-company studies and the usefulness of studies that investigate only direct beneficiaries. Miller (1984) notes that well-planned evaluations with proper controls have been absent. Friedman (1988) indicates that the research has not been "pure in its methods or realistic in its conclusions" (p. 40). Christensen and Staines (1990) suggest that the modest benefits of flextime in reducing work-family conflict may be attributed to problems in research design. There are no similar critiques of diversity research, with one exception (McWilliams & Siegel, 1997); perhaps this is so because there have been fewer studies on diversity impacts published in refereed journals.

The benefits of diversity and work-life management, namely, improved abilities to work with and manage people of diverse backgrounds and lifestyles, deserve more attention. To the extent that researchers focus on measuring more easily quantified costs and benefits, they may fail to assess valuable impacts such as improvements in managerial flexibility. Therefore, when facing scrutiny of program costs, diversity and work-life advocates should translate results into bottom-line metrics while persuading decision makers that other types of results are equally significant (Lobel & Faught, 1996).

In the human resource field in the 1990s, a movement to measure the impact of progressive human resource practices on firm financial performance has developed. For example, a major Society for Human Resource Management study found that higher-quality human resource practices are significantly linked to market/book value, productivity, market value, and sales (Ulrich, 1997). There are a number of methods for measuring human resource effectiveness, many of which attempt to quantify impacts in financial terms or in terms of effects on important stakeholders (Yeung & Berman, 1997).

Nonetheless, as Pfeffer (1997) notes, what is most easily measured is not necessarily what is most important to measure:

> The question is not how many people were hired at what cost, but rather whether the right people were hired who will remain in the organization and do effective work over a long period of time. The question is not how many people were trained, but whether the training was retained and accomplished anything that enhanced the organization's operations. (p. 361)

He broadly challenges widely accepted objectives of human resource activities, namely, that their purpose is to contribute to organizational efficiency, productivity, and profit and that the human resource function ought to be held accountable for the same organizational outcomes as are other staff groups. He suggests that the human resource function may play a unique role in preserving intangible organizational culture and values in the face of contrary pressures. Human resource practitioners and researchers fulfill critical "soft" objectives that no other organizational discipline will entertain; this role needs to be preserved (Lobel, 1997). The challenge, then, is how to measure impacts in such a way as to identify and support these intangible objectives.

One specific area that has been touted as being central to effective diversity and work-life management, but that has received almost no attention in research, is organizational culture (Trice & Beyer, 1993). Organizational culture encompasses informal practices, such as the quality of relationships between superiors and subordinates, and symbolic events, such as giving an individual an undeserved promotion or failing to dismiss an individual known to have sexually harassed someone. Formal policies and programs may exist, but if the organizational culture does not mirror the formal practices, beneficiaries of programs may be stigmatized and employees may become increasingly frustrated with managers' failure to "walk the talk." Measuring impacts of specific programs is easier than measuring impacts of changes in culture or measuring organizational culture itself. We need to develop widely accepted tools for monitoring organizational progress in terms of culture change, one of the key objectives mentioned in Table 23.3.

In both the work-life and diversity fields, researchers have developed models to describe the relative position of an organization along a continuum of progressively more broad-ranging and effective culture change efforts (Cox, 1991; Friedman & Galinksy, 1992). These models may serve as a foundation for the development of measurement tools.

For example, in Cox's description of culture change, organizations evolve from monolithic to plural and, finally, to multicultural organizations. In multicultural organizations (Cox, 1991) there is a two-way process of adaptation, understanding and appreciation of members of the organization. At the same time that organizational members note and accept differences, perhaps as a consequence of diversity training, they also identify similarities and superordinate goals. In this stage of cultural development, diversity management includes a focus on appropriate interpersonal and communication skills for a wide range of organizational interactions such as coaching, providing performance feedback, and conflict resolution. As mentioned previously, *Integrating Work and Life: The Wharton Resource Guide* (Friedman et al., 1998) has identified managerial skills that comprise the ability to support the balance of work and personal life for all employees. If managers throughout an organization were able to develop and to improve these skills, clearly organizational change toward multiculturalism would ensue.

Gentile (1996) and Arredondo (1996) have prepared guidelines for measuring impacts of diversity initiatives. Ideally, we need random samples of organizations that cross industry, geography, and economic and cultural development. In future research, I hope that researchers and practitioners will be able to generalize from findings to a broad range of situations.

A research project of the desired scope must have practical value, as well as make a contribution to the academic literature. Therefore, for all phases of the research, from deciding on the principal research questions to considerations of length of questionnaire, researchers need to evaluate whether the projected value to practitioners justifies the investment of their time. Practitioners and researchers seek a high ratio of value to time.

One project is under way that may address a number of the concerns mentioned in this chapter. The Boston College Center for Work & Family has created the National Work/Life Measurement Project, which will include cost-benefit analyses, assessment of attitudes toward benefits, and aspects of workplace culture that affect utilization rates and attitudes. In the first two years, the project will focus on the key work-life area of information and education, for example, resource and referral, seminars, and training. Assessment tools will be designed to gather a wide range of information on impact. Although it is too early to say, perhaps this study will serve as a model for the kind of comprehensive research we hope to see more of in the future.

Part **VI**

Conducting
Future Research

Chapter 24

Methodological Issues in Conducting Research on Gender in Organizations

Elizabeth A. Cooper and Susan M. Bosco

This chapter reviews the methodology that has been used to study the field previously known as women in management, commonly now referred to as gender in organizations (GIO). More than just the actual statistical technique involved in a study, research methodology encompasses the interwoven issues of research ideology, political and practical constraints, research design, topic of investigation, and the choice of participants. Over the past 30 years, much has changed in both general research methodology and GIO research. All of these issues are discussed from the viewpoint of GIO. In addition, a review of recent GIO research is conducted to follow the actual path of this field. From this, directions for the future are suggested.

Research methodology is a broad area; different topics are more relevant to some fields of study than others. Research methods in GIO are distinct because information is drawn from the fields of sociology, anthropology, economics, psychology, and of course, management. This leads to a field rich in diversity; however, different factions work without knowledge, or without understanding, of others. The need to work in organizations can be problematic. Companies may not allow access to people and/or information without acquiring some advantage. Pressure for research results to lead to practical consequences for the organization may make fieldwork difficult and constrict the research questions. Most important is the focus on women and gender, which brings a different viewpoint to organizational research that had been missing prior to this work.

Research Ideology

With the varied theoretical background of GIO come the many paradigms of research. Paradigms can be defined as a general perspective or way of thinking that reflects one's fundamental beliefs and assumptions (Gioia & Pitre, 1990; Guba & Lincoln, 1994), thus affecting all aspects of the way one does research. Burrell and Morgan (1979) break down these key assumptions into two dimensions. The first, *subjective versus objective,* asks, Do we create reality or just discover it? whereas the second, *radical change versus regulation,* asks, Should science serve to change society or maintain the existing structure? The intersection of these two dimensions results in four research paradigms: radical humanism, radical structuralism, interpretivism, and functionalism. The first three are combinations of the two dimensions, and the last, functionalism, is the objective, regulatory model common in much of the research with which we are familiar. Authors have at times referred to the qualitative difference between functionalism and the other paradigms as positivism and phenomenology (Easterby-Smith, Thorpe, & Lowe, 1991).

The positivist tradition espouses that the truth is out there and through objective data collection and analysis the truth will be realized (Cook & Campbell, 1979; Easterby-Smith et al., 1991; Gioia & Pitre, 1990). Although not all positivists may agree, the following generalities can be made:

1. The observer is independent of what is being observed.
2. The choice of what is to be studied can be determined by objective criteria.
3. The purpose of the research is to determine causality.
4. Science works best in the hypothetico-deductive process.
5. Problems are best understood when broken down to the smallest components.
6. Because generalizability is critical, large samples are required.

This "normal" science can only subsume what is learned into what is already known (Kuhn, 1962). Therefore, research moves in tiny steps. Theory development requires the nomological net (Cronbach & Meehl, 1955), which is a web of information that connects new discoveries to old. Articles based on previous work, or "coupling," are the most common. In fact, having one's work cited by someone else is considered a major form of recognition. The citation is the link between what was, what is, and what will be. In a study of academic recognition, Newman and Cooper (1993) classified 257 articles from the *Journal of Applied Psychology* by "research plot," ranging from replication to new theory. In this sample only two articles are clearly new theory.

Positivism has been the traditional method of research in many fields, particularly psychology, and is used in many texts and reports on research (Cook & Campbell, 1979; Kerlinger, 1986; Rosenthal & Rosnow, 1991; Sackett & Larson, 1990; Schmitt & Klimoski, 1991). It places the researcher in a higher position where he or she observes, records, and often deceives the participant. Rarely, though, is the issue addressed of whether the approach to research is appropriate; usually, there is just a reiteration on what should be done and how to do it better. There is, however, a realization that research is not always as rational a process as it appears to be in written articles, as indicated by the phrase "Think Yiddish, write British" (Rosenthal & Rosnow, 1991).

The other category of thought, phenomenology, encompasses many different views and beliefs (Denzin & Lincoln, 1994). However, they have enough in common as a group to be discussed as a single view. More common in the fields of sociology and anthropology, phenomenology is characterized by the view that "reality" is not objective and external to the being, but is socially constructed and given meaning by people (Burrell & Morgan, 1979; Easterby-Smith et al., 1991; Gioia & Pitre, 1990; Guba & Lincoln, 1994; Patton, 1990). Rather than gathering facts to construct the truth, researchers study how people construct a situation rather than how they react to it. Morgan and Smircich (1980) classified this difference as a continuum on the nature of reality—from the subjectivist to the objectivist, reality moves from the projection of human imagination to a concrete structure.

Unlike positivists, who believe that we are not to affect what we study but to only observe, phenomenologists believe that the mere process of observing changes the situation (Gioia & Pitre, 1990; Patton, 1990). Others believe that the purpose of the research is to create change (Burrell & Morgan, 1979; Chio, 1993; Hyde, 1995). Although positivists see research as being objective and value free, phenomenologists strongly state that what we value determines what we study and how we research it (Guba & Lincoln, 1994; Patton, 1990; Peplau & Conrad, 1989).

One particular method within phenomenology, with direct bearing on GIO, is feminist research. Feminism is an ideology and a sociopolitical movement (Hyde, 1995). Any research that grows out of this movement shares its values (Peplau & Conrad, 1989). Feminists criticize positivist researchers for treating women as absent and invisible (Olesen, 1994), ignoring context, creating artificial situations, and using experimental methodology, which, with its strong hierarchy of power, creates inequity in the research setting. Feminist researchers believe that qualitative methodology is the only appropriate method. Some claim that only women can be feminists, a radical view that rejects all previous scientific methods and desires to replace them with a "successor science" (Peplau & Conrad, 1989).

The above discussion presents extreme views of positivism and feminism. Many researchers try to reconcile the differences between the two and take the best from each. There is an awareness in feminist thought of a need for more empirical work (Hyde, 1995). Peplau and Conrad (1989) claim that how a method is used determines whether or not it is feminist. Similarly, positivist researchers recognize the reality of value-laden research and the inevitability of subjectivity in research (McCall & Bobko, 1990; Rosenthal & Rosnow, 1991).

At the heart of the issue between positivists and phenomenological research is where to set priorities. What we know is strongly influenced by how we discovered it. If how we do research is affected by our views and values, so are the results of the work. We cannot separate the results of the data from the method of the data. There are no right answers, simply a set of choices that researchers make that meets with their interests, abilities, and beliefs. The field of GIO is slowly changing as researchers broaden their beliefs in how research should be conducted and their knowledge of qualitative research methods. As GIO matures as a field, components from both views are being incorporated into a more comprehensive science. This ability to cross paradigmatic lines is an important step in theory building (Gioia & Pitre, 1990; Guba & Lincoln, 1994).

This issue of paradigm, however, does not end with one's own beliefs on how research should be conducted. We do not do research in a vacuum. We work within specific organizations and publish and present our work at specific outlets. Positivists and phenomenologists are often at odds, each claiming their own method as superior. However, one may change or present research in such a way as to be more acceptable to those who would evaluate it (Kulka, 1982).

Research Methodology: Issues and Choices

Research involves choices. Some are clearly conscious choices, some are clearly political, and some occur randomly. Some of these choices are aligned with different philosophical research ideologies. In research design, the paradigmatic debate continues as positivists lean heavily toward quantitative methods (Sackett & Larson, 1990, Schmitt & Klimoski, 1991) and feminists lean toward qualitative ones (Peplau & Conrad, 1989). This difference, however, is more theoretical than actual, as there is discussion of meta-analysis in feminist research (Hyde, 1995), and qualitative methods are found in traditional research tomes (Rosenthal & Rosnow, 1991).

What follows is an attempt to highlight those decisions critical to GIO research, each aspect of which is closely intertwined with the others.

Research Question

The research question affects the choice of setting, participants, variables of interest, and data collection and analysis. Typically, this choice comes from a combination of internal and external factors ranging from curiosity and conformity to resource allocation and reward systems (Sackett & Larson, 1990). Or, as Rosabeth Kanter stated,

> I did not enter this field the way some researchers do, which is to see a new field like the study of women as a chance for me to carve out a niche. I did it out of annoyance. I felt that research that was narrowly psychological, that looked at people outside of any context whatsoever, and then made generalizations [without] taking into account the setting which was pushing them to do those things was very misleading to say the least. (quoted in Kulka, 1982, p. 49)

An important component in the choice of the question is the way the question is asked. The framing of the question and the role of context are a marker of differences between positivists and feminists. Will this be a description of variables or the study of the interrelationships among variables? The description of variables by asking Can X occur? or Can X affect Y? omits the setting. Asking *Does* X occur? or *Does* X affect Y? includes context in the question.

Research Design

In designing a GIO study, the researcher often has lofty goals in obtaining a relevant sample from one or more organizations. As we all know, however, this can be difficult. Organizations may decline to cooperate, relevant participants may be inaccessible, or, even if they are, money may be an issue. The choice of where the research occurs and who will participate is as much a function of reality as ideology.

A point of difference between positivists and feminists is the choice of research setting. Positivists tend toward studies that allow for control rather than context (i.e., lab studies, surveys, simulations). In experimentation, the researcher is actively involved in controlling the context, which allows for better determination of causation (Cook & Campbell, 1979; Sackett & Larson, 1990). The amount of control can vary by setting (lab vs. field) or by the availability of randomization (i.e., quasi-experimentation). Even in a quasi-experiment, where there is a lack of randomization, there is an opportunity for more control and causal interpretation than in a nonexperimental setting (Cook & Campbell, 1979).

Feminists focusing on the importance of context prefer field studies and field experiments as well as nonexperimental designs such as studies that correlate various beliefs, attitudes, and/or behaviors. In these situations, nothing is manipulated, only observed; social context becomes a variable of study, not a variable to be controlled. For example, research on the impact of gender on employment gap issues found that an employment gap results in less satisfaction for men than for women (Schneer & Reitman, 1993). It would be easy to conclude that women don't mind being out of work or, as these authors surmised, that the lost income effect was worse for men than women. However, if a contextual approach were taken, one would consider the reasons and how they usually differ for men and women. That is, women often experience employment gaps to be home with their children, whereas men may have been fired or laid off from their jobs. Certainly, looking at the problem this way raises the possibility that women's employment gaps are often filled with some rewarding activity, whereas men's are more likely to be filled with anxiety. Ignoring context to focus on gender causes the omission of issues that may be pertinent to finding the answer to a research question.

According to McGrath (1982), three issues are important in choosing setting and participants: (1) *generalizability* with respect to populations, (2) *precision* in control and measurement of variables, and (3) existential *realism* for the participants. Yet the maximization of one of these necessarily minimizes the others. At the most, the researcher may be able to focus on two of the three requirements, but never all three at the same time. Only with additional research, which focuses on different components, will enough information be amassed for conclusions to be drawn. No one approach to research is better than another because all are necessary for understanding. Too much of one type of research will not give us an entire picture.

Closely tied to the question of setting is that of sample. A major question in GIO research is whom to study. The first answer may appear obvious: women in management. But as we all know, getting a "real" sample is not always possible. When is it appropriate to rely on a "convenience" sample of college students or MBAs? In the organization, what level do we study: first-line supervisors? midlevel managers? top-level executives?

The issues of who and how many are addressed differently by positivists and feminists. Positivists prefer large samples (Easterby-Smith et al., 1991) and are most likely to obtain them by using college students (who are readily available) and surveys (which are easy to mail to large groups). Because small samples do not provide stable estimates (Tversky & Kahneman, 1971), large samples are needed for quantitative analysis.

Feminists, on the other hand, prefer small samples, which provide a depth of information and make it easier to obtain samples in context. It is easier to obtain information from 20 individuals than 200. Williams and Alliger (1994) studied shift work and its impact on work and family with only 41 participants. These individuals completed diaries for seven days, eight times each day, which yielded a rich pool of information on task perceptions as well as work influence on family and vice versa. This would not have been possible by surveying 1,000 respondents. Last, feminists are more interested in women and may be less likely to include men in their research.

Data Collection

The method of data collection is intimately tied to the research setting and choice of participants. Experimentation involves first manipulating a stimulus, then recording the reaction of the participants, each of which can be done in a number of ways.

One of the most popular methods of evoking a stimulus is by analogue (Worrell & Robinson, 1994). Analogue methods, which create a situation that is analogous to a naturally occurring event, may include (a) using volunteers as confederates to enact live situations, (b) using video- or audiotaped volunteers to serve as a stimulus, and (c) using vignettes or stories to describe various situations. Although these methods are very common and allow a great deal of control over the stimulus, they necessarily reduce context and often elicit stereotypical responses.

Closer to reality are simulations. Simulations have ranged from a short period of group work to complex workplaces, which have been created solely for the purpose of collecting data. In these latter cases, individuals may be "hired" to work for a number of weeks without realizing they are really working at being participants in a study.

Regardless of the stimulus, there are a number of choices in how to collect the data. A common choice is a survey or questionnaire filled out by the participants that assesses attitudes, values, beliefs, and so on as well as participants' perceptions of events, which can be compared to some objective measure such as Likert-type scales, semantic differentials, or forced-choice items. The questionnaire may also include open-ended questions, which allow participants to respond in their own words. Data may also be recorded via an interview, which allows for more tailoring of questions as well as follow-up questions.

Both the questionnaire and the survey serve as substitutes for direct observations. Although participants can be observers, nonparticipant observation is the most common. In direct observation, which requires training and extensive time and energy, the researcher observes and records participants' activities. This can involve both participant and nonparticipant observation with the latter being more common. However, it can also be obtrusive and affect the situation enough for participants to change their behavior (Sackett & Larson, 1990).

The most common unobtrusive observation is the use of archival data, where information is obtained from previous studies, performance appraisals, or other organizational materials. This method of data collection may be the least invasive, but the original data were not collected for the purpose of research and may not be complete enough to answer the research question.

Often, researchers choose more than one method by which to collect data to capture the most information and to counteract any impact of one method. This methodology pluralism (Rosenthal & Rosnow, 1991) reduces the possibility of subject-experimenter artifacts as well as single-method variance.

Data Analysis

How the data are collected affects how they are analyzed. The more quantitative the data, the more likely a statistical measure will be used. Similarly, observational data may be interpreted qualitatively rather than analyzed (Denzin & Lincoln, 1994). However, these methods are not mutually exclusive. A typical example is using content analysis to categorize open-ended responses on questionnaires or using computers to analyze qualitative data. Yet, even with the acceptance of qualitative data collection, the emphasis in GIO is still on quantitative data analysis.

Quantitative data analysis suffers from a number of weaknesses, including the use of too many small (low power) studies, the overreliance on dichotomous hypotheses testing paired with the overimportance of significance level, and relying too heavily on what is easy to do rather than on what should be done (Cohen, 1994; Cortina & Dunlup, 1997; Rosenthal & Rosnow, 1991). The debate over hypotheses testing versus meta-analysis goes beyond the scope of this chapter (Cortina & Dunlup, 1997; Schmidt, 1996) but does affect GIO research in that it calls for more meta-analysis, something demanded by GIO authors themselves (Eagly, 1995; Hyde, 1995).

Research results vary by paradigm as well. The positivist writes a scientific report, which is objective, logical, and factual. The feminist researcher is more likely to engage in experimental writing wherein he or she describes and details the data and the impact that the observer has made (Denzin & Lincoln, 1994).

Politics and Research Methodology

In a time of political correctness some have argued that there are some questions that should not be asked, research that should not be conducted. In GIO such a topic is differences between men and women. This issue was brought to the fore in a series of articles and rejoinders in a special issue of *The American Psychologist* (1995). Eagly (1995) reviewed research on differences following the publication of Maccoby and Jacklin's *Psychology of Sex Differences* (1974), a book that set the stage by questioning if not the existence, then the practicality of previously discovered sex differences. According to Eagly, feminist researchers strove to show that differences occurred due to stereotypes and negative attitudes toward women. Findings of no differences between men and women lead to gender-neutral opportunities and gender equality, whereas research that indicated sex differences was seen as limiting women's opportunities and justifying unequal treatment. Eagly points out, however, that the development of meta-analyses (which became feasible after the publication of Maccoby and Jacklin's book) indicated that there are indeed stable, consequential sex differences. Because the prevailing political view was that there were no differences, these meta-analysis results were treated with suspicion and distrust. Attempts were made to dismiss these differences as being too small, inconsistent, artifactual, and inconsistent with stereotypes; however, research does not show this to be the case.

In response to Eagly (1995), Hyde and Plant (1995) argue that not all feminists take a "null" standpoint on sex differences; some feminist works describe large difference effects. They do point out, however, that compared to other effects in psychology, sex differences fall in the small range. Maracek (1995) believes it is not the fear of finding gender differences but the way in which the question is asked that fuels debate. She argues that the question of gender needs to shift the focus from the individual to the interpersonal and institutional arenas, as did Perry, Davis-Blake, and Kulik (1994), who studied gender-based selection using a contextual explanation that included organizational structure. This echoes the view of Gilbert (1994), who warns against the use of the "gender as difference" view rather than the "gender in context" view. The former method (popular with both feminist and nonfeminist researchers) removes the person from the social context. In phenomenological research, context is critical. Without a framework for the initial research question or the interpretation of the results, the researcher may be led away from explanations that include the person's history or social circumstances. (The reader should note that such a concern would not occur to a positivist, because by definition, science occurs independent of context.)

We are left with an unsatisfactory resolution to the issue of gender differences and political correctness. Of interest, however, is that this is not new. In the creation of the Stanford-Binet Intelligence Test, many months were spent developing questions that would result in equal scores for males and females on the spatial and verbal tests. Not surprisingly, males scored higher on the spatial components, females on the verbal. The developers of the test believed, however, that it should not have sex differences (Moir, 1991).

A Review of Recent Gender in Organizations Research

Considering all of these issues in evaluating the research trends in GIO necessarily raises some important questions. What is the prevailing paradigm in GIO research? What questions are being asked and how are they being analyzed? Is GIO keeping up with research trends in other fields? How is GIO developing as a research field? To determine the answers to these and other questions, we conducted a review of articles published from 1985 to 1997. During this time period, women made sufficient inroads into the workplace,

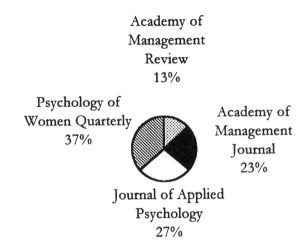

Figure 24.1. Gender in Organizations Articles, by Journal

allowing for a variety of GIO topics to be researched. Because of the exploratory nature of this research, no propositions or hypotheses are made as to the results of our analysis.

We wanted to follow research in GIO over a period of time to evaluate the research methods used and whether these methods have changed over time. Because there is no specific GIO journal, four journals were chosen to represent the GIO field: *Journal of Applied Psychology (JAP), Academy of Management Review (AMR), Academy of Management Journal (AMJ),* and *Psychology of Women Quarterly (PWQ).* They are considered top journals in the fields of psychology and management and publish GIO-type articles.

Every article from 1985 to 1997 that dealt with an issue relevant to GIO was included. To be chosen, the article had to deal with gender and an aspect of the work environment. The following information was obtained: purpose of study, participant information (i.e., gender, numbers, student vs. working), method of data collection, time frame of study, and statistical technique used. If there was more than one study in an article, this information was obtained for each study. We purposely did not include articles on sex difference that were not directly work related (i.e., children as subjects) or that did not include gender as a variable of study.

This resulted in 175 articles with a total of 186 individual studies. Figure 24.1 indicates the breakdown of the articles by journal. The two psychology journals, *JAP* and *PWQ,* account for most (71%) of the articles. Only 29% were published in the management journals. *AMR,* which has the smallest number of GIO articles, publishes mainly conceptual, theory-building pieces; GIO has not been one of those areas chosen to be developed. Clearly, this affects the choice of research question for those interested in publishing in the top-tier management journals. If publication is a priority, GIO will not be the topic of study.

TABLE 24.1 Popular Topics in Gender in Organizations Research

Topic	Number of Articles
General workplace issues	37
Work and family	30
Performance and compensation	19
Attitudes toward female managers	17
Women and promotion	13
Gender and leadership	11
Stress	11
Recruitment	11

Coding of Research Topics

The next step in the analysis was a review of the major topics of research in GIO represented in Table 24.1. After coding each article's main theme, we grouped topics into meaningful categories. Two important research themes are not included in the table because they are cross-topic themes: gender discrimination and gender differences. Of the 175 articles reviewed, 33 are on some form of gender discrimination. These articles cross nine different topic areas; the top four are affirmative action (7 articles), promotion (6 articles), recruitment (6 articles), and compensation (5 articles).

The second cross-topic theme is gender differences. Of the reviewed articles, 70% (123) include sex/gender differences in their analysis. This is surprising given the controversy of gender difference research discussed previously. In *PWQ*, 58% of articles examine sex/gender differences (42 of 72 articles). It appears the rhetoric concerning gender differences has not affected their actual investigation. There is, however, a particular reason why so many articles include this analysis. It is easy. Once gender information is recorded, it is easy to test for differences, even if there is no theoretical basis for believing a difference will exist. In only one article did the authors specifically state they did not analyze the data by gender, as it was not central to the research question (Malovich & Stake, 1990).

Summaries of top research topics. Accounting for more than 50% of topics in the articles reviewed are general workplace issues (37 articles, 21%), work and family (30 articles, 17%), performance and compensation (19 articles, 11%), and attitudes toward female managers (17 articles, 10%). Each is composed of subtopics, which are grouped together for better understanding. General workplace issues includes job satisfaction, sexual harassment, arbitration, union activities, shift work, and organizational dress. Work and family includes role conflict, effects of maternal employment on children, and organizational structure effects. Performance and compensation includes evaluation, merit increases, family structure and performance, and job evaluation. Attitudes toward

TABLE 24.2   Frequency of Topics, by Journal

Journal	Work and Family	Attitudes Toward Female Managers	Performance and Compensation	General Workplace Issues
Academy of Management Journal	3	9	2	6
Academy of Management Review	2	1	1	2
Journal of Applied Psychology	6	4	10	10
Psychology of Women Quarterly	19	3	6	7

female managers includes management traits, subordinate attitudes, and female representation in management positions.

Other areas of research in GIO are gender and leadership, mentoring, recruitment of women, sexual harassment, stress, promotion of women, career choice, motivational differences between genders, women in nontraditional jobs, and occupational segregation; however, none of these are represented to a significant degree as far as numbers of articles.

One area that is researched rarely is international issues in GIO. Of all the studies reviewed, only seven were conducted in countries other than the United States. Three additional studies used American participants with foreign cultural backgrounds. This weakness may be due to the ethnocentric nature of these journals. Considering the frequent comparisons with particularly European organizations in the area of work and family, it is surprising that not more actual research is done to substantiate claims that European organizations are more family-friendly. Topics were disbursed throughout many of the areas of interest noted above. Methods of data collection and analysis varied as well, including both functionalist and feminist types. This research area seems ripe for expansion in the future, especially as the global economy moves from dream to reality.

Coverage of topics across journals and across time. Table 24.2 represents the publication trends of the most frequently researched areas in GIO in the four journals reviewed. In *AMJ*, the topics of attitude toward female managers and general workplace issues receive the most attention. This journal is developing and testing theory that investigates whether women are truly progressing in their quest to occupy more positions of authority in the workplace. *AMR* has published articles in the areas of workplace and role stress. This may reflect a focus on the negative aspects of workplace participation on women.

The topics are evenly researched in *JAP*. The most frequent topics researched are performance and compensation, and general workplace issues, which include work groups, job satisfaction, union membership, and attitudes toward work. Sexual harassment, a cross-topic area, and stress are also researched, which, considering their psychological nature, is to be expected.

TABLE 24.3 Sample Type, by Year of Publication

Year	Studies With Working People	Studies With Students
1985	16	6
1986	8	4
1987	9	3
1988	7	6
1989	9	4
1990	8	2
1991	13	5
1992	8	3
1993	5	4
1994	12	5
1995	14	1
1996	0	2
1997	3	1
Total	112	46

Here, GIO includes a wide range of topics important to both the organization and the individual.

PWQ also provides coverage of a wider range of topics in GIO than does either of the management journals, although its emphasis is clearly on work and family. Similar to *JAP*, it frequently publishes topics in the areas of sexual harassment and stress.

We also examined coverage of research topics by year of publication and found no clear pattern. Coverage of topics is uneven, driven by popular interests rather than the progression of the field of study itself. Therefore, topics may be abandoned for several years, making development beyond basic investigation very difficult, if it happens at all.

Characteristics of Samples

The samples found in GIO vary in gender composition, type (student vs. workplace participants), and size, with sample sizes ranging from 3 to over 54,000 (a survey of military personnel). Excluding the 10 studies that included over 2,000 participants, the average number of participants per study was 400, which still included 11 studies with between 1,000 and 2,000 participants. The large sample studies were mostly composed of nonexperimental survey data. The majority of studies included both women and men (only 25 studies did not include men). Participants of color were not as well represented: Only 19 studies included non-Whites. Some of these studies were composed of specific non-White groups such as Hispanic (Romero, Castro, & Cervantes, 1988) or Asian (Chow, 1987).

Table 24.3 makes it clear that GIO research has consistently favored the use of participants who are currently in the workplace. Slightly more than two-thirds of the participants are working individuals, including managers

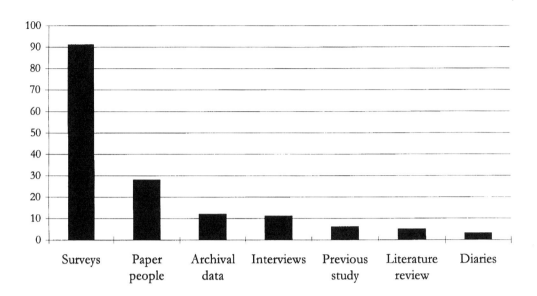

Figure 24.2. Types of Data Collection

(63 studies), clerical personnel (23 studies) and laborers (25 studies). Many studies (23) included individuals from more than one level (some were large-scale mail surveys). Seven studies included non-working women and/or men as well.

In the study of gender in *organizations,* it is imperative that study participants who have work experience are used, to obtain more accurate and generalizable results. Student workplace experiences are usually brief and are certainly different in nature from those of the employee who makes his or her living from the workplace. The use of primarily nonstudent participants is one of the strengths of this field and also allows for a greater range of data when open-ended instruments and methods are used because of the variation in types of positions and responsibilities.

Data Collection Methods

The major data collection methods used in GIO research are illustrated in Figure 24.2, with the primary method being the self-administered question-naire or survey. Although it is certainly permissible to use this type of method in this research area, using it to the exclusion of other methods may lead to monomethod bias in the results. Surveys and questionnaires are usually the easiest way to obtain data, particularly when a large sample size is needed; however, because they are primarily closed-ended, they do not allow for a great amount of detail to be provided by the respondent. It is also relatively easy for a respondent to answer in a socially desirable manner, especially when surveys address personal lives as they do in the work and family literature.

Asking participants to perform tasks such as reviewing résumés of potential employees for positions ("paper people" tasks) is the next most widely used method of data collection. As discussed earlier, this analogue method does not always provide a true representation of situations where actual people's lives are on the line and politics becomes a consideration in decision making.

Other methods provide different perspectives on data. For example, diaries and interviews are excellent ways of following a respondent's thought process or of obtaining a better understanding of responses provided through another method. It is important to note, however, that several of these methods (archival data review, interviews, and literature reviews) are susceptible to researcher biases in the manner in which data are selected for review and are ultimately analyzed. Despite this shortcoming, however, using a variety of methods of data collection is necessary to provide a fuller understanding of many GIO issues.

Trends in Analysis

Throughout the years covered in this review, the primary methods of data analysis continue to be univariate methods, such as analysis of variance (ANOVA), regression, and correlation. Because 70% of GIO research includes the comparison of females to males, differences between these two groups are usually analyzed by ANOVAs. Multivariate analysis is also often used, the most frequent types being multiple regression and MANOVAs. In recent years, computer applications have made it easier to perform the necessary calculations for these analyses. Multivariate methods are used to develop and test theories that encompass elements other than gender alone. Since 1990, path analysis and structural equation modeling, more complex multivariate analyses, are used to test models that contain many variables, not only independent and dependent, but moderating and mediating ones as well.

Qualitative methods, so few they did not appear on the "most popular" lists, are summarized in Table 24.4 (data collection and analysis) by journal. As might be expected, the feminist journal *PWQ* has the greatest number of articles (19) that use qualitative methods, although they account for only 26% of its 73 GIO articles (the remainder use quantitative methods). Surprisingly, *AMJ* is second for percentage of qualitative methods with 18% (7 of 39). *JAP*, a strong methodological journal, favors quantitative methods; only 10% (5 of 50) of its GIO articles use qualitative methods. *AMR* included 1 qualitative article, or 8% (1 of 13).

TABLE 24.4   Qualitative Methods, by Journal

Method Type	Academy of Management Journal	Academy of Management Review	Journal of Applied Psychology	Psychology of Women Quarterly
Diary	1		3	
Open-ended survey			1	3
Open-ended interview	3		1	7
Content analysis	1			1
Descriptive analysis	1			7
Textual analysis		1		
Theme analysis	1			1

Discussion and Conclusions

This review of four journals allows several conclusions to be drawn. One is that most of the research on GIO is published in psychology journals. The feminist journal *Psychology of Women Quarterly* published the most articles in this field during the review period. However, feminist research has yet to make a strong impact in GIO research. There is little qualitative work in any of the journals. The most common data collection method is the survey with the data then analyzed by ANOVAs.

The strongest impact of feminism is in the area of research questions. There is a difference in the types of questions found in *PWQ* than in the other journals. These questions look more at women in context, family as well as organization. However, one is almost as likely to find research on sex/gender difference in *PWQ* as in any journal.

Over the years, the number of articles per year did not change much, perhaps indicating that either interest in GIO remains steady or has not increased over the years. In addition, certain issues keep arising over and over. In a casual Internet survey, when searching for "women in management" articles, the majority are still classified as "differences in gender" articles. They appear to be updates of gender differences aimed at new settings or occupations (journalists, accountants, advertising, etc.).

To move this field of study beyond basic gender differences research, it may be helpful to observe the progression of the work and family topics in recent years that have moved into the area of context. Including antecedent and consequential variables when considering larger models allows researchers to better understand the *environment* in which gender operates. This change in orientation will make research in the field of GIO more cohesive and focused so that it can progress.

This inclusion of context is mirrored in this book, specifically in the chapters on the changing nature of work (Chapter 3 by C. Cooper and Lewis) and the gendered nature of organizations (Chapter 5 by Maier) and service work (Chapter 4 by Gutek, Cherry, and Groth). The scope of topics is broadened with the inclusion of non-White women and the issues of diversity. Gender in context is also recognized.

As we speak of diversity, however, the majority of the participants in these studies were White, middle-class professionals. Although the inclusion of other than white-collar participants was more common in *PWQ*, the lack of minorities and cross-cultural work crosses all four journals. As a field of study, women in management focused heavily on White, middle-class managers. As we move to GIO, we are including all individuals; our samples are slowly reflecting this change with the inclusion of nonmanagerial women (in both traditional and nontraditional fields) and women of different cultures and colors in research studies.

Feminist research has made little impact on the data collection or analysis aspect of research methodology. Most articles rely on survey instruments analyzed by ANOVAs, MANOVAs, and/or multiple regression. The vast majority of studies are cross-sectional, with only a handful involving longitudinal work. In many of the quantitative studies the samples are small, often too few for the analysis chosen. In survey-based studies, researchers commonly analyze and reanalyze the data looking for relationships among the variables. There is very little theory development; most articles take a small component from previous work and either expand on it or modify it in some way (i.e., coupling).

There is a strong monomethod bias both across and within this research, due as much to the politics of "publish or perish" as to personal predilection or ease of analysis. Working toward promotion and tenure does not always allow for qualitative work, which can be time-consuming and cost-intensive. Although few studies used qualitative methods, there does appear to be a growing acceptance within certain journals.

There is a heavy reliance on null hypotheses testing in GIO. This is a part of the sex/gender difference debate: If we reject H_0, there are differences; if we fail to reject, there are no differences! Yet we all know this decision is a function of sample size and power as well as the size of any real difference. Asking Yes or No questions does not provide the theoretical information in which we are really interested. Data analysis needs to include information on effect size and confidence intervals, as appropriate. In addition, meta-analyses need to be conducted in those areas in which multiple studies exist.

Research methodology in GIO is varied and encompasses many different themes. However, researchers need to look beyond gender differences and use participants who reflect the reality of the workforce. A variety of data collection and analysis methods should also be used to expand knowledge.

References

Abbey, A. (1982). Sex differences in attributions for friendly behavior: Do males misperceive females' friendliness? *Journal of Personality and Social Psychology, 32,* 830-838.

Abelson, R. P. (1988). Conviction. *American Psychologist, 43,* 267-275.

Aburdene, P., & Naisbitt, J. (1992). *Megatrends for women.* New York: Villard.

Acker, J. (1990). Women and stratification: A review of recent literature. *Contemporary Sociology, 9,* 25-34.

Acker, J. (1992). Gendering organizational theory. In A. J. Mills & P. Tancred (Eds.), *Gendering organizational analysis* (pp. 248-260). Newbury Park, CA: Sage.

Acker, J., & Van Houten, D. (1974). Differential recruitment and control: The sex structuring of organizations. *Administrative Science Quarterly, 19,* 152-163.

Adams, G. A., King, L. A., & King, D. W. (1996). Relationships of job and family involvement, family social support, and work-family conflict with job and life satisfaction. *Journal of Applied Psychology, 81,* 411-420.

Adams, J., Rice, R. W., & Instone, D. (1984). Follower attitudes toward women and judgments concerning performance by female and male leaders. *Academy of Management Journal, 27,* 636-643.

Adarand v. Pena (No. 93-1841). (1995, June 13). *The United States Law Week* (63 U.S.L.W. 4523).

Adkins, L. (1995). *Gendered work: Sexuality, family and the labour market.* Buckingham, UK: Open University Press.

Adler, N. J. (1983). Organizational development in a multicultural environment. *Journal of Applied Behavioral Science, 19*(3), 349-365.

Adler, N. J. (1987). Pacific Basin managers: A *gaijin,* not a woman. *Human Resource Management, 26,* 169-192.

Adler, N. J. (1993). Competitive frontiers: Women managers in the triad. *International Studies of Management and Organization, 23*(2), 3-23.

Adler, N. J. (1994). Competitive frontiers: Women managing across borders. In N. J. Adler & D. N. Izraeli (Eds.), *Competitive frontiers: Women managers in a global economy* (pp. 22-40). Cambridge, MA: Blackwell.

Adler, N. J. (1996). Global women political leaders: An invisible history, an increasingly important future. *Leadership Quarterly, 7*(1), 133-161.

Adler, N. J. (1997a). Global leaders: A dialogue with future history. *International Management, 1*(2), 1997, 21-33.

Adler, N. J. (1997b). Global leadership: Women leaders. *Management International Review, 37*(1) [Special issue], 135-143.

Adler, N. J. (1998). Societal leadership: The wisdom of peace. In S. Srivastva (Ed.), *Executive wisdom and organizational change* (pp. 205-221). San Francisco: Jossey-Bass.

Adler, N. J., & Bird, F. B. (1988). International dimensions of executive integrity: Who is responsible for the world? In S. Srivastva (Ed.), *The functioning of executive integrity* (pp. 243-337). San Francisco: Jossey-Bass.

Adler, N. J., & Izraeli, D. N. (Eds.). (1988). *Women in management worldwide*. Armonk, NY: M. E. Sharpe.

Adler, N. J., & Izraeli, D. N. (Eds.). (1994). *Competitive frontiers: Women managers in a global economy*. Cambridge, MA: Blackwell.

Alagna, S., Reddy, D., & Collins, D. (1982). Perceptions of functioning in mixed-sex and male medical training groups. *Journal of Medical Education, 57*, 801-803.

Albert, A. A., & Porter, J. R. (1988). Children's gender-role stereotypes: A sociological investigation of psychological models. *Sociological Forum, 3*, 184-210.

Albertsen, J., & Christensen, B. (1993). Women in business and management—Denmark. In M. J. Davidson & C. L. Cooper (Eds.), *European women in business and management* (pp. 58-78). London: Paul Chapman.

Albrecht, K., & Zemke, R. (1985). *Service America! Doing business in the new economy*. Homewood, IL: Dow Jones-Irwin.

Alderfer, C. (1972). *Existence, relatedness and growth: Human needs in organizational settings*. New York: Free Press.

Alderfer, C. (1991, August). *The new corporate language for race relations*. Paper presented at the annual meeting of the Academy of Management, Miami Beach, FL.

Alderfer, C. (1992). Changing race relations embedded in corporations: Report on a long-term project with the XYZ Corporation. In S. E. Jackson (Ed.), *Diversity in the workplace: Human resource initiatives* (pp. 138-166). New York: Guilford.

Alexander, V. D., & Thoits, P. A. (1985). Token achievement: An examination of proportional representation and performance outcomes. *Social Forces, 64*(3), 332-340.

Allen, J. G., & Haccoun, D. M. (1976). Sex differences in emotionality: A multidimensional approach. *Human Relations, 29*, 711-722.

Allen, K. R., & Carter, N. M. (1996). Women entrepreneurs: Profile differences across high and low performing adolescent firms. In W. D. Bygrave, B. J. Bird, S. Birley, N. C. Churchill, M. G. Hay, R. H. Kelley, & W. E. Wetzel, Jr. (Eds.), *Frontiers of entrepreneurship research* (Summary). Babson Park, MA: Center for Entrepreneurial Studies, Babson College. [On-line]. Available: www.babson.edu/entrep/fer/papers96/summ96/allen.html

Allen, T. D., Poteet, M. L., Russell, J. E. A., & Dobbins, G. H. (1997). A field study of factors related to supervisors' willingness to mentor others. *Journal of Vocational Behavior, 50,* 1-22.

Allen, T. D., Russell, J. E., & Maetzke, S. B. (1997). Formal peer mentoring: Factors related to protégés' satisfaction and willingness to mentor others. *Group & Organization Management, 22,* 488-507.

Allmendinger, J., & Hackman, R. R. (1995). The more, the better? A four-nation study of the inclusion of women in symphony orchestras. *Social Forces, 74*(3), 423-460.

Allport, G. (1954). *The nature of prejudice.* Cambridge, MA: Addison-Wesley.

Altemeyer, R. A., & Jones, K. (1974). Sexual identity, physical attractiveness and seating position as determinants of influence in discussion groups. *Canadian Journal of Behavioral Science, 6,* 357-375.

Althauser, R. P., & Kalleberg, A. L. (1981). Firms, occupations, and the structure of labor markets: A conceptual analysis. In I. Berg (Ed.), *Sociological perspectives on labor markets* (pp. 119-149). New York: Academic Press.

Alvesson, M., & Billing, Y. D. (1997). *Understanding gender and organizations.* London: Sage.

American Association of University Women. (1995). *How schools shortchange girls.* Washington, DC: Author.

Anat, A. B., & Izraeli, D. N. (1993). A global comparison of women in management: Women managers in their homelands as expatriates. In E. A. Fagenson (Ed.), *Women in management: Trends, issues, and challenges in managerial diversity* (pp. 52-96). Newbury Park, CA: Sage.

Anderson, B. E. (1996). The ebb and flow of enforcing Executive Order 11246. *American Economic Review, 86,* 298-301.

Anderson, C. I., & Hunsaker, P. L. (1985). Why there's romancing at the office and why it's everyone's problem. *Personnel, 62*(2), 57-63.

Anderson, C. J., & Fisher, C. (1991). Male-female relationships in the workplace: Perceived motivations in office romance. *Sex Roles, 25,* 163-180.

Anderson, L. R., & Blanchard, P. N. (1982). Sex differences in task and social-emotional behavior. *Basic and Applied Social Psychology, 3,* 109-139.

Anderson, N. F. (1993). Benazir Bhutto and dynastic politics: Her father's daughter, her people's sister. In M. A. Genovese (Ed.), *Women as national leaders* (pp. 41-69). Newbury Park, CA: Sage.

Andre, R. (1992). A national profile of women's participation in networks of small business leaders. *Journal of Small Business Management, 30*(1), 66-73.

Antal, A. B., & Krebsbach-Gnath, C. (1988). Women in management: Unused resources in the Federal Republic of Germany. In N. J. Adler & D. N. Izraeli (Eds.), *Women in management worldwide* (pp. 141-156). Armonk, NY: M. E. Sharpe.

Antal, A. B., & Krebsbach-Gnath, C. (1993). Women in management in Germany: East, West, and reunited. *International Studies of Management and Organizations, 23,* 49-69.

Antal, A. B., & Krebsbach-Gnath, C. (1994). Women in management in Germany: East, West, and reunited. In N. J. Adler & D. N. Izraeli (Eds.), *Competitive frontiers: Women managers in a global economy* (pp. 206-223). Cambridge, MA: Blackwell.

Apfelbaum, E. (1993). Norwegian and French women in high leadership positions: The importance of cultural contexts upon gendered relations. *Psychology of Women Quarterly, 17,* 409-429.

Appelbaum, E., & Batt, R. (1994). *The new American workplace: Transforming work systems in the United States.* Ithaca, NY: ILR.

Appiah, K. A. (1996). Race, culture, identity: Misunderstood connections. In K. A. Appiah & A. Gutmann, *Color conscious: The political morality of race* (pp. 30-105). Princeton, NJ: Princeton University Press.

Appley, M. H. (1962). Motivation, threat perception and the introduction of psychological stress. *Proceedings of the Sixteenth International Congress of Psychology* (pp. 880-881). Bonn and Amsterdam: North-Holland.

Appley, M. H., & Turnbull, R. (1967). *Psychological stress.* Englewood Cliffs, NJ: Prentice Hall.

Arber, S., Gilbert, N., & Dale, A. (1985). Paid employment and women's health: A benefit or a source of strain? *Sociology of Health and Illness, 7(3),* 375-399.

Argyris, C. (1993). *Knowledge for action: A guide to overcoming barriers to organizational change.* San Francisco: Jossey-Bass.

Argyris, C., & Schön, D. (1992). *Theory in practice.* San Francisco: Jossey-Bass.

Aries, E. (1976). Interaction patterns and themes of male, female, and mixed groups. *Small Group Behavior, 7,* 7-18.

Aries, E. (1996). *Men and women in interaction: Reconsidering the differences.* New York: Oxford University Press.

Aries, E., Olver, R. R., Blount, K., Christaldi, K., Fredman, S., & Lee, T. (1998). Race and gender as components of the working self-concept. *Journal of Social Psychology, 138,* 277-290.

Arkkelin, D., & O'Connor, R., Jr. (1992). The "good" professional: Effects of trait-profile gender type, androgyny, and likableness on impressions of incumbents of sex-typed organizations. *Sex Roles, 27,* 517-532.

Arkkelin, D., & Simmons, S. (1985). The "good manager": Sex-typed, androgynous, or likable? *Sex Roles, 12,* 1187-1198.

Arnetz, B. B., Wasserman, J., Petrinin, B., Brenner, S. O., Levi, L., Eneroth, P., Salovaara, H., Hielm, R., Salovaara, L., Theorell, T., & Petterson, L. L. (1987). Immune function in unemployed women. *Psychosomatic Medicine, 49(1),* 3-12.

Arnold, M. (1960). *Emotions and personality* (Vols. 1-2). New York: Columbia University Press.

Arredondo, P. (1996). *Successful diversity management initiatives: A blueprint for planning and implementation.* Thousand Oaks, CA: Sage.

Arthur, M. B., & Rousseau, D. M. (1996). A career lexicon for the 21st century. *Academy of Management Executive, 10(4),* 28-39.

Arvey, R. D. (1979). Unfair discrimination in the employment interview: Legal and psychological perspectives. *Psychological Bulletin, 86,* 736-765.

Arvey, R. D., & Campion, J. E. (1982). The employment interview: A summary and review of recent research. *Personnel Psychology, 35,* 281-322.

Arvey, R. D., & Faley, R. H. (1988). *Fairness in selecting employees.* Reading, MA: Addison-Wesley.

Aryee, S. (1992). Antecedents and outcomes of work-family conflict among married professional women: Evidence from Singapore. *Human Relations, 45,* 813-837.

Ashforth, B. E., & Mael, F. (1989). Social identity theory and the organization. *Academy of Management Review, 14(1),* 20-39.

Ashmore, R. D. (1993). Sex, gender, and the individual. In L. A. Pervin (Ed.), *Handbook of personality theory and research* (pp. 486-526). New York: Guilford.

Astin, H. S., & Leland, C. (1991). *Women of influence, women of vision.* San Francisco: Jossey-Bass.

Astor-Dubin, L., & Hammen, C. (1984). Cognitive versus behavioral coping responses of men and women: A brief report. *Cognitive Therapy and Research, 8,* 85-90.

Atkins, L., & Dunning, J. (1998). Female and male R and D team leaders: Differences and similarities in leadership profile. *Proceedings of the International Work Psychology Conference.* Sheffield, UK: University of Sheffield.

Atwater, L. E. (1998). The advantages and pitfalls of self-assessment in organizations. In J. W. Smither (Ed.), *Performance appraisal: State of the art in practice* (pp. 331-369). San Francisco: Jossey-Bass.

Atwater, L. E., & Van Fleet, D. D. (1997). Another ceiling? Can males compete for traditionally female jobs? *Journal of Management, 23,* 603-626.

Atwater, L., & Waldman, D. (1998, May). Accountability in 360-degree feedback: Is it time to take the 360-degree feedback method to its next step? *HRMagazine, 43,* 96-102.

Bachman, S. I., & Gregory, K. (1993, April). *Mentor and protégé gender: Effects on mentoring roles and outcomes.* Paper presented at the Society for Industrial and Organizational Psychology Conference, San Francisco.

Baderschneider, J. (1989, August 12). *The impact of family issues on career development at Mobil Oil Corporation.* Study results presented at the 49th annual meetings of the Academy of Management, Washington, DC.

Bahniuk, M. H., Dobos, J., & Hill, S. E. K. (1990). The impact of mentoring, collegial support, and information adequacy on career success: A replication. *Journal of Social Behavior and Personality, 5,* 431-451.

Bakan, D. (1966). *The duality of human existence: An essay on psychology and religion.* Chicago: Rand McNally.

Baker, J. (1987). The role of the environment in marketing services: The consumer perspective. In J. Czepiel, C. Congram, & J. Shanahan (Eds.), *The services challenge: Integrating for competitive advantage.* Chicago: American Marketing Association.

Bales, R. F. (1950). *Interaction process analysis: A method for the study of small groups.* Cambridge, MA: Addison-Wesley.

Bandura, A. (1997). *Self-efficacy: The exercise of control.* New York: Freeman.

Bando, M. S. (1986). When women change jobs. *Japan Quarterly, 33,* 177-182.

Bantel, K. A., & Jackson, S. E. (1989). Top management and innovations in banking: Does the composition of the top team make a difference? *Strategic Management Journal, 10,* 108-124.

Banton, M. (1988). *Racial consciousness.* London: Longman.

Barak, A. (1994). A cognitive-behavioral educational workshop to combat sexual harassment in the workplace. *Journal of Counseling and Development, 72,* 595-602.

Bargh, J. A., Raymond, P., Pryor, J. B., & Strack, F. (1995). Attractiveness of the underling: An automatic power → sex association and its consequences for sexual harassment and aggression. *Journal of Personality and Social Psychology, 68,* 768-781.

Baril, G. L., Elbert, N., Mahar-Potter, S., & Reavy, G. C. (1989). Are androgynous managers really more effective? *Group and Organization Studies, 14,* 234-249.

Barling, J. (1986). Interrole conflict and marital functioning amongst employed fathers. *Journal of Occupational Behaviour, 7*, 1-8.

Barling, J., Dupre, K. E., & Hepburn, C. G. (1998). Effect of parents' job insecurity on children's work beliefs and attitudes. *Journal of Applied Psychology, 83*, 112-118.

Barling, J., Fullager, C., & Marchl-Dingle, J. (1988). Employment commitment as a moderator of the maternal employment status/child behavior relationship. *Journal of Organizational Behavior, 9*, 113-122.

Barling, J., & Sorensen, D. (1997). Work and family: In search of a relevant research agenda. In C. L. Cooper & S. E. Jackson (Eds.), *Creating tomorrow's organizations* (pp. 157-169). New York: John Wiley.

Barnes-Farrell, J. L., L'Heureux-Barrett, T. J., & Conway, J. M. (1991). Impact of gender-related job features on the accurate evaluation of performance information. *Organizational Behavior and Human Decision Processes, 48*, 23-35.

Barnett, R. C., & Brennan, R. T. (1997). Changes in job conditions, changes in psychological distress, and gender: A longitudinal study of dual-earner couples. *Journal of Organizational Behavior, 18*, 253-274.

Barnum, P., Liden, R. C., & DiTomaso, N. (1995). Double jeopardy for women and minorities: Pay differences with age. *Academy of Management Journal, 38*, 863-880.

Baron, J. N., & Bielby, W. T. (1984). The organization of work in a segmented economy. *American Sociological Review, 49*, 454-473.

Baron, J. N., Davis-Blake, A., & Bielby, W. T. (1986). The structure of opportunity: How promotion ladders vary within and among organizations. *Administrative Science Quarterly, 31*, 248-273.

Baron, J. N., Mittman, B. S., & Newman, A. E. (1991). Targets of opportunity: Organizational and environmental determinants of gender integration within the California civil service, 1979-1985. *American Journal of Sociology, 96*(6), 1362-1401.

Baron, J. N., & Newman, A. E. (1989). Pay the man: Effects of demographic composition on prescribed wage rates in the California civil service. In R. T. Michael, H. I. Hartmann, & B. O'Farrell (Eds.), *Pay equity: Empirical inquiries* (pp. 107-130). Washington, DC: National Academy Press.

Barrentine, P. (Ed.). (1993). *When the canary stops singing: Women's perspectives on transforming business.* San Francisco: Berrett-Koehler.

Barron, J. M., Black, D. A., & Loewenstein, M. A. (1993). Gender differences in training, capital and wages. *Journal of Human Resources, 28*, 343-364.

Bartol, K. M. (1974). Male versus female leaders: The effects of leader needs for dominance and follower satisfaction. *Academy of Management Journal, 17*, 225-233.

Bartol, K. M. (1978). The sex structuring of organizations: A search for possible causes. *Academy of Management Review, 3*, 805-815.

Bartol, K. M., & Butterfield, D. A. (1976). Sex effects in evaluating leaders. *Journal of Applied Psychology, 67*, 446-454.

Bartol, K. M., & Martin, D. C. (1986). Women and men in task groups. In R. D. Ashmore & F. K. Del Boca (Eds.), *The social psychology of female-male relations: A critical analysis of central concepts* (pp. 259-310). Orlando, FL: Academic Press.

Bartol, K. M., & Martin, D. C. (1988). Influences on managerial pay allocations: A dependency perspective. *Personnel Psychology, 41*, 361-378.

Bartol, K. M., & Martin, D. C. (1989). Effects of dependence, dependency threats, and pay secrecy on managerial pay allocations. *Journal of Applied Psychology, 74,* 105-113.

Bartol, K. M., & Martin, D. C. (1990). When politics pays: Factors influencing managerial compensation decisions. *Personnel Psychology, 43,* 599-614.

Bartolome, F. (1983). The work alibi: When it's harder to go home. *Harvard Business Review, 61*(2), 67-74.

Baruch, G. K., & Barnett, R. (1986). Role quality, multiple role involvement, and psychological well-being in midlife women. *Journal of Personality and Social Psychology, 51,* 578-585.

Bass, B. M. (1981). Women and leadership. In *Stogdill's handbook of leadership: A survey of theory and research* (Rev. and expanded ed., pp. 491-507). New York: Free Press.

Bass, B. M., Avolio, B. J., & Atwater, L. E. (1996). The transformational and transactional leadership on men and women. *Applied Psychology: An International Review, 45,* 5-34.

Bass, B. M. (1991). *Bass & Stogdill's handbook of leadership* (3rd ed.). New York: Free Press.

Bates, T., & Williams, D. (1996). Do preferential procurement programs benefit minority business? *American Economic Review, 86,* 294-298.

Baucus, D. A., & Human, S. E. (1994). Second-career entrepreneurs: A multiple case study analysis of entrepreneurial processes and antecedent variables. *Entrepreneurship Theory and Practice, 19*(2), 41-71.

Baugh, S. G., Lankau, M. J., & Scandura, T. A. (1996). An investigation of the effects of protégé gender on responses to mentoring. *Journal of Vocational Behavior, 49,* 309-323.

Beatty, C. A. (1996). The stress of managerial and professional women: Is the price too high? *Journal of Organizational Behavior, 17,* 233-251.

Beck, E. M., Horan, P. M., & Tolbert, C. M., II. (1978). Stratification in a dual economy: A sectoral model of earnings determination. *American Sociological Review, 43,* 704-720.

Beck, E. M., & Tolnay, S. (1990). The killing fields of the Deep South: The market for cotton and the lynching of Blacks, 1882-1930. *American Sociological Review, 55*(4), 526-539.

Becker, G. (1985). Human capital, effort, and the sexual division of labor. *Journal of Labor Economics, 17,* S33-S58.

Becker, G. S. (1971). *The economics of discrimination* (2nd ed.). Chicago: University of Chicago Press.

Bedeian, A. G., Burke, B. G., & Moffett, R. G. (1988). Outcomes of work-family conflict among married male and female professionals. *Journal of Management, 14,* 475-491.

Beggs, J. M., Doolittle, D., & Garsombke, D. (1994, August). Diversity in entrepreneurship: Integrating issues of sex, race, and class. In D. P. Moore (Ed.), *Academy of Management best papers proceedings* (Abstract, p. 482). Madison, WI: Omnipress.

Belcourt, M. (1991). From the frying pan into the fire: Exploring entrepreneurship as a solution to the glass ceiling. *Journal of Small Business and Entrepreneurship, 8*(3), 49-55.

Belenky, M. F., Clinchy, B. M., Goldberger, N. R., & Tarule, J. M. (1986). *Women's ways of knowing: The development of self, voice, and mind.* New York: Basic Books.

Bell, D. (1976). *The coming post-industrial society: A venture in social forecasting.* New York: Basic Books.

Bell, E. L. (1990). The bicultural life experience of career-oriented Black women. *Journal of Organizational Behavior, 11*(6), 459-478.

Bell, E. L., Denton, T. C., & Nkomo, S. (1993). Women of color in management: Toward an inclusive analysis. In E. A. Fagenson (Ed.), *Women in management: Trends, issues, and challenges in managerial diversity* (pp. 105-130). Newbury Park, CA: Sage.

Bell, M. P., Harrison, D. A., & McLaughlin, M. E. (1997). Asian American attitudes toward affirmative action in employment: Implications for the model minority myth. *Journal of Applied Behavioral Science, 33,* 356-377.

Bell, M. P., McLaughlin, M. E., & Harrison, D. A. (1996, August). *The belief structure of attitudes toward affirmative action: Sex, race and population differences.* Paper presented at the annual meeting of the Academy of Management, Cincinnati, OH.

Bem, S. L. (1974). The measurement of psychological androgyny. *Journal of Consulting and Clinical Psychology, 42,* 155-162.

Bem, S. L. (1981a). *Bem Sex Role Inventory: Professional manual.* Palo Alto, CA: Consulting Psychologists Press.

Bem, S. L. (1981b). Gender schema theory: A cognitive account of sex-typing. *Psychological Review, 88,* 354-364.

Bem, S. L. (1986). Masculinity and femininity exist only in the mind of the perceiver. In J. M. Reinisch, L. A. Rosenblum, & S. A. Sanders (Eds.), *Masculinity/femininity: Basic perspectives* (pp. 304-311). New York: Oxford University Press.

Bem, S. L. (1993). *The lenses of gender.* New Haven, CT: Yale University Press.

Benedict, M. E., & Levine, E. L. (1988). Delay and distortion: Tacit influences on performance appraisal effectiveness. *Journal of Applied Psychology, 73,* 507-514.

Benhabib, S. (1987). The generalized other and the concrete other: The Kohlberg-Gilligan controversy and feminist theory. In S. Benhabib & D. Cornell (Eds.), *Feminism as critique* (pp. 77-95). Minneapolis: University of Minnesota Press.

Benhabib, S., & Cornell, D. (Eds.). (1987). *Feminism as critique.* Minneapolis: University of Minnesota Press.

Benn, M. (1995, February). Women who rule the world. *Cosmopolitan.*

Bennett-Alexander, D. D., & Pincus, L. B. (1995). *Employment law for business.* Chicago: Irwin.

Bennis, W. (1989). *Why leaders can't lead: The unconscious conspiracy continues.* San Francisco: Jossey-Bass.

Bennis, W., & Nanus, B. (1985). *Leaders: Strategies of taking charge.* New York: Harper & Row.

Bento, R. F. (1997). When good intentions are not enough: Unintentional subtle discrimination against Latinas in the workplace. In N. V. Benokraitis (Ed.), *Subtle sexism: Current practice and prospects for change* (pp. 91-116). Thousand Oaks, CA: Sage.

Berger, J., Fisek, M. H., Norman, R. Z., & Zelditch, M., Jr. (1977). *Status characteristics and social interactions: An expectation states approach.* New York: Elsevier Science.

Berger, J., Wagner, D. G., & Zelditch, M., Jr. (1985). Introduction: Expectations states theory: Review and assessment. In J. Berger & M. Zelditch, Jr. (Eds.), *Status, rewards, and influence: How expectations organize behavior* (pp. 1-72). San Francisco: Jossey-Bass.

Berger, J., Webster, M., Jr., Ridgeway, C. L., & Rosenholtz, S. J. (1986). Status cues, expectations, and behaviors. In E. Lawler (Ed.), *Advances in group processes* (Vol. 3, pp. 1-22). Greenwich, CT: JAI.

Bergeson, J. M., & Oba, K. Y. (1994). Japan's new equal opportunity employment law: Real weapon or heirloom sword? In P. Burstein (Ed.), *Equal employment opportunity, labor market discrimination and public policy* (pp. 357-365). New York: Walter de Gruyter.

Bergmann, B. (1986). *The economic emergence of women.* New York: Basic Books.

Bernhardt, A., Morris, M., & Handcock, M. S. (1995). Women's gains or men's losses? A closer look at the shrinking gender gap in earnings. *American Journal of Sociology, 101*(2), 302-328.

Bernhardt, A., Morris, M., & Handcock, M. S. (1997). Percentages, odds, and the meaning of inequality: Reply to Cotter et al. *American Journal of Sociology, 102*(4), 1154-1162.

Berry, J. W. (1983). Acculturation: A comparative analysis of alternative forms. In R. J. Samuda & A. L. Woods (Eds.), *Perspectives in immigrant and minority education* (pp. 66-77). Lanham, MD: University Press of America.

Berry, L. L. (1983). Relationship marketing. In L. L. Berry, G. L. Shostack, & G. D. Upah (Eds.), *Emerging perspectives on services marketing* (pp. 25-28). Chicago: American Marketing Association.

Betz, N. E., & Fitzgerald, L. F. (1987). *The career psychology of women.* New York: Academic Press.

Bhatnagar, D., & Swamy, R. (1995). Attitudes toward women as managers: Does interaction make a difference? *Human Relations, 48*(11), 1285-1307.

Bhave, M. P. (1994). A process model of entrepreneurial venture creation. *Journal of Business Venturing, 9,* 223-242.

Bianchi, S. M. (1995). The changing economic roles of women and men. In R. Farley (Ed.), *State of the union: America in the 1990s* (Vol. 1, pp. 107-154). New York: Russell Sage.

Bielby, D. D., & Bielby, W. T. (1988). She works hard for the money: Household responsibilities and the allocation of work effort. *American Journal of Sociology, 93*(5), 1031-1059.

Bielby, W. T., & Baron, J. N. (1984). A woman's place is with other women: Sex segregation within organizations. In B. F. Reskin (Ed.), *Sex segregation in the workplace: Trends, explanations, remedies* (pp. 27-55). Washington, DC: National Academy Press.

Bielby, W. T., & Baron, J. N. (1986). Men and women at work: Sex segregation and statistical discrimination. *American Journal of Sociology, 91*(4), 759-799.

Biernat, M., & Kobrynowicz, D. (1997). Gender- and race-based standards of competence: Lower minimum standards but higher ability standards for devalued groups. *Journal of Personality and Social Psychology, 72,* 544-557.

Bigoness, W. J. (1976). Effect of applicant's sex, race, and performance on employers' performance ratings: Some additional findings. *Journal of Applied Psychology, 61,* 80-84.

Bilimoria, D., & Piderit, S. K. (1994). Board committee membership: Effects of sex-based bias. *Academy of Management Journal, 37,* 1453-1477.

Binning, J. F., Goldstein, M. A., Garcia, M. F., & Scattaregia, J. H. (1988). Effects of preinterview impressions on questioning strategies in same- and opposite-sex interviews. *Journal of Applied Psychology, 73,* 30-37.

Birley, S. (1989). Female entrepreneurs: Are they really any different? *Journal of Small Business Management, 27*(1), 32-37.

Birley, S., & Westhead, P. (1993). A taxonomy of business start-up reasons and their impact on firm growth and size. *Journal of Business Venturing, 9,* 7-31.

Bitner, M. J. (1992). Servicescapes: The impact of surroundings on customers and employees. *Journal of Marketing, 56,* 57-71.

Black, J. S., & Mendenhall, M. (1990). Cross-cultural training effectiveness: A review and a theoretical framework for future research. *Academy of Management Review, 15,* 113-136.

Black, J. S., Stephens, G. K., & Rosener, J. B. (1992). Women in management around the world: Some glimpses. In U. Sekaran & F. T. Leong (Eds.), *Womanpower: Managing in times of demographic turbulence* (pp. 223-251). Newbury Park, CA: Sage.

Blackmon, D. (1997, March 11). Consultant's advice on diversity was anything but diverse. *New York Times,* pp. 1, 4.

Blake, R., & Mouton, J. (1978). *The new managerial grid.* Houston, TX: Gulf.

Blake, S. (1999). At the crossroads of race and gender: Lessons from the mentoring experiences of professional Black women. In A. J. Murrell, F. Crosby, & R. Ely (Eds.), *Mentoring dilemmas: Developmental relationships in multicultural organizations.* Mahwah, NJ: Lawrence Erlbaum.

Blakely, G. L., Blakely, E. H., & Moorman, R. H. (1995). The relationship between gender, personal work experience, and perceptions of sexual harassment in the workplace. *Employee Responsibilities and Rights Journal, 8,* 263-274.

Blalock, H. (1967). *Toward a theory of minority group relations.* New York: Capricorn.

Blanchard-Fields, F., Chen, Y., & Hebert, C. E. (1997). Interrole conflict as a function of life stage, gender, and gender-related personality attributes. *Sex Roles, 37,* 155-174.

Blau, F. D. (1996). *Where are we in the economics of gender? The gender pay gap* (NBER Working Paper No. 5664). Cambridge, MA: National Bureau of Economic Research.

Blau, F. D., & Ferber, M. A. (1986). *The economics of women, men, and work.* Englewood Cliffs, NJ: Prentice Hall.

Blau, F. D., & Ferber, M. A. (1992). *The economics of women, men and work* (2nd ed.). Englewood Cliffs, NJ: Prentice Hall.

Blau, F. D., Ferber, M. A., & Winkler, A. E. (1998). *The economics of women, men, and work* (3rd ed.). Upper Saddle River, NJ: Prentice Hall.

Blau, F. D., & Hendricks, W. E. (1979). Occupational segregation by sex: Trends and prospects. *Journal of Human Resources, 14*(2), 197-210.

Blau, F. D., & Kahn, L. M. (1992). The gender earnings gap: Learning from international comparisons. *American Economic Review (Papers and Proceedings), 82*(2), 533-538.

Blau, F. D., & Kahn, L. M. (1994). Rising wage inequality and the U.S. gender gap. *American Economic Review (Papers and Proceedings), 84*(2), 23-28.

Blau, F. D., & Kahn, L. M. (1996). International differences in male wage inequality: Institutions versus market forces. *Journal of Political Economy, 104*(4), 791-837.

Blau, F. D., & Kahn, L. M. (1997). Swimming upstream: Trends in the gender wage differential in the 1980s. *Journal of Labor Economics, 15*(1), 1-42.

Blau, P. (1977a). *Inequality and heterogeneity.* New York: Free Press.

Blau, P. (1977b). A macrosociological theory of social structure. *American Journal of Sociology, 83*, 26-54.

Block, J. H. (1973). Conceptions of sex role: Some cross-cultural and longitudinal perspectives. *American Psychologist, 28*, 512-526.

Block, P. (1991). *The empowered manager.* San Francisco: Jossey-Bass.

Block, P. (1993). *Stewardship: Choosing service over self-interest.* San Francisco: Berrett-Koehler.

Blossfeld, H.-P. (1987). Labour market entry and the sexual segregation of careers in the Federal Republic of Germany. *American Journal of Sociology, 93*(1), 89-118.

Bluestone, B. (1994, Winter). The inequality express. *The American Prospect, 20*, 81-93.

Blum, T. C., Fields, D. L., & Goodman, J. S. (1994). Organization-level determinants of women in management. *Academy of Management Journal, 37*, 241-268.

Bobko, P., & Colella, A. (1994). Employee reactions to performance standards: A review and research propositions. *Personnel Psychology, 47*, 1-29.

Bobo, L., & Kluegel, J. R. (1993). Opposition to race-targeting: Self-interest, stratification ideology, or racial attitudes? *American Sociological Review, 58*, 443-464.

Bohen, H. H., & Viveros-Long, A. (1981). *Balancing jobs and family life: Do flexible work schedules help?* Philadelphia: Temple University Press.

Bolger, N., DeLongis, A., Kessler, R. C., & Wethington, E. (1989). The contagion of stress across multiple roles. *Journal of Marriage and the Family, 51*, 175-183.

Bolman, L., & Deal, T. (1995). *Leading with soul.* San Francisco: Jossey-Bass.

Bolman, L., & Deal, T. (1997). *Reframing organizations* (2nd ed.). San Francisco: Jossey-Bass.

Bonacich, E. (1972). A theory of ethnic antagonism: The split labor market. *American Sociological Review, 37*(5), 547-559.

Booth-Butterfield, M. (1989). Perception of harassing communication as a function of locus of control, work force participation, and gender. *Communication Quarterly, 37*, 262-275.

Bowen, D. D. (1985). Were men meant to mentor women? *Training and Development Journal, 39*(2), 31-34.

Bowen, D. D., & Hisrich, R. D. (1986). The female entrepreneur: A career development perspective. *Academy of Management Review, 11*(2), 393-407.

Bowen, D. E., & Jones, G. R. (1986). Transaction cost analysis of organization-customer exchange. *Academy of Management Review, 11*(2), 428-441.

Bowen, W. G., & Bok, D. (1998). *The shape of the river: Long-term consequences of considering race in college and university admissions.* Princeton, NJ: Princeton University Press.

Bowen-Willer, K., & Korabik, K. (1997, June). *Desirable and undesirable gender-role attributes and conflict resolution among supervisors and subordinates.* Paper presented at the annual meeting of the Canadian Psychological Association, Toronto, Ontario, Canada.

Bowes-Sperry, L., & Powell, G. N. (1996). Sexual harassment as a moral issue: An ethical decision making perspective. In M. S. Stockdale (Ed.), *Sexual harassment: Perspectives, frontiers, and response strategies* (Vol. 5, pp. 105-124). Thousand Oaks, CA: Sage.

Bowes-Sperry, L., & Powell, G. N. (in press). Observers' reactions to social-sexual behavior at work: An ethical decision making perspective. *Journal of Management.*

Bowes-Sperry, L., & Veglahn, P. A. (1996). Sexual harassment and workers' compensation. *Labor Law Journal, 47*(9), 597-601.

Boyacigiller, N., & Adler, N. J. (1991). The parochial dinosaur: The organizational sciences in a global context. *Academy of Management Review, 16*(2), 262-290.

Boyacigiller, N., & Adler, N. J. (1996). Insiders and outsiders: Bridging the worlds of organizational behavior and international management. In B. Toyne & D. Nigh (Eds.), *International business inquiry: An emerging vision* (pp. 22-1020. Columbia: University of South Carolina Press.

Brandstatter, H. (1997). Becoming an entrepreneur: A question of personality structure? *Journal of Economic Psychology, 18*(2-3), 157-177.

Brannen, J. P., Meszaros, P., Moss, H., & Poland, G. (1994). *Employment and family life: A review of research in the UK (1980-1994)*. London: Department of Employment.

Brass, D. P. (1992). Power in organizations: A social network perspective. In G. Moore & J. Whitt (Eds.), *Research in politics and society* (pp. 295-323). Greenwich, CT: JAI.

Brefach, S. M. (1986). *The mentor experience: The influences of female/male mentors on the personal and professional growth of female psychologists.* Unpublished doctoral dissertation, Boston University.

Brenner, O. C., Tomkiewicz, J., & Schein, V. E. (1989). The relationship between sex role stereotypes and requisite management characteristics revisited. *Academy of Management Journal, 32*, 662-669.

Brett, J. M. (1997). Family, sex, and career advancement. In S. Parasuraman & J. H. Greenhaus (Eds.), *Integrating work and family: Challenges and choices for a changing world* (pp. 143-153). Westport, CT: Quorum Books.

Brett, J. M., & Stroh, L. K. (1997). Jumping ship: Who does better on the external labor market? *Journal of Applied Psychology, 82*, 331-341.

Brett, J. M., Stroh, L. K., & Reilly, A. H. (1992). What is it like being a dual-career manager in the 1990s? In S. Zedeck (Ed.), *Work and family* (pp. 138-167). San Francisco: Jossey-Bass.

Brewer, M. B., & Miller, N. (1996). *Intergroup relations.* Pacific Grove, CA: Brooks/Cole.

Brewer, N., Socha, L., & Potter, R. (1996). Gender differences in supervisors' use of performance feedback. *Journal of Applied Social Psychology, 26*, 786-803.

Bridges, W. P., & Nelson, R. L. (1989). Markets in hierarchies: Organizational and market influences on gender inequality in a state pay system. *American Journal of Sociology, 95*(3), 616-658.

Briggins, A. (1998). Equity lacking in the boardroom. *Management Review, 87*(6).

Brinton, M. (1994). Gender stratification in contemporary urban Japan. In P. Burstein (Ed.), *Equal employment opportunity, labor market discrimination and public policy* (pp. 343-356). New York: Walter de Gruyter.

Brinton, M. C. (1993). *Women and the economic miracle: Gender and work in postwar Japan.* Berkeley: University of California Press.

Brinton, M. C., & Ngo, H.-Y. (1993). Age and sex in the occupational structure: A United States-Japan comparison. *Sociological Forum, 8*(1), 93-111.

Briskin, A. (1998). *The stirring of soul in the workplace.* San Francisco: Berrett-Koehler.

British labour force projections: 1995-2006. (1995, April). *Employment Gazette,* pp. 153-158.

Brod, H. (Ed.). (1987). *The making of masculinities: The new men's studies*. New York: Routledge.

Brod, H., & Kaufman, M. (Eds.). (1994). *Theorizing masculinities*. Thousand Oaks, CA: Sage.

Brooks, L., & Perot, A. R. (1991). Reporting sexual harassment: Exploring a predictive model. *Psychology of Women Quarterly, 15,* 31-47.

Broverman, I. K., Vogel, S. R., Broverman, D. M., Clarkson, F. E., & Rosenkrantz, P. S. (1972). Sex-role stereotypes: A current appraisal. *Journal of Social Issues, 28*(2), 59-78.

Brown v. Board of Education of Topeka, 347 U.S. 483 (1954).

Brown, C. M., & Shakespeare, T. L. (1996). A call to arms for Black business. *Black Enterprise, 27*(4), 79-86.

Brown, D., & Fuguitt, G. (1972). Percent nonwhite and racial disparity in non-metropolitan cities in the South. *Social Science Quarterly, 53*(4), 573-582.

Brown, M. T., Eisenberg, A. I., & Sawilowsky, S. S. (1997). Traditionality and the discriminating effect of expectations of occupational success and occupational values for women within math-oriented fields. *Journal of Vocational Behavior, 50,* 418-431.

Brown, S. P. (1996). A meta-analysis and review of organizational research on job involvement. *Psychological Bulletin, 120,* 235-255.

Brush, C. (1992). Research on women business owners: Past trends, a new perspective and future directions. *Entrepreneurship Theory and Practice, 16*(4), 5-30.

Brush, C. G., & Bird, B. J. (1996). Leadership vision of successful women entrepreneurs: Dimensions and characteristics. In W. D. Bygrave, B. J. Bird, S. Birley, N. C. Churchill, M. G. Hay, R. H. Kelley, & W. E. Wetzel, Jr. (Eds.), *Frontiers of entrepreneurship research* (Summary). Babson Park, MA: Center for Entrepreneurial Studies, Babson College. [On-line]. Available: www.babson.edu/entrep/fer/papers96/summ96/brush.html

Brush, C. G., & Hisrich, R. D. (1988). Women entrepreneurs: Strategic origins impact on growth. In B. A. Kirchoff, W. A. Long, W. E. McMillan, K. H. Vesper, & W. E. Wetzel, Jr. (Eds.), *Frontiers of entrepreneurship research* (pp. 612-625). Wellesley, MA: Babson College.

Bulan, H. F., Erickson, R. J., & Wharton, A. S. (1997). Doing for others on the job: The affective requirements of service work, gender, and emotional well-being. *Social Problems, 44*(2), 235-256.

Bunch, C. (1991). Foreword. In H. S. Astin & C. Leland, *Women of influence, women of vision* (pp. xi-xiv). San Francisco: Jossey-Bass.

Bunzel, J. H. (1997, October 12). Hard facts about falling minority admissions. *Washington Post*, p. C3.

Bureau of Economic Analysis. (1998a, September 24). [On-line]. Available: http://www.bea.doc.gov/bea/dn/niptbl-d.htm

Bureau of Economic Analysis. (1998b, September 25). [On-line]. Available: http://www.bea.doc.gov/bea/dn/pitbl.htm

Burge, D. L., & Stewart, D. L. (1988). *The Dominion Bank story*. Roanoke: Virginia Tech University Press.

Burke, R. J., & McKeen, C. A. (1990). Mentoring in organizations: Implications for women. *Journal of Business Ethics, 9,* 317-332.

Burke, R. J., & McKeen, C. A. (1992). Women in management. In C. L. Cooper & I. T. Robertson (Eds.), *International review of industrial and organizational psychology* (Vol. 7, pp. 245-283). Chichester, UK: Wiley.

Burke, R. J., & McKeen, C. A. (1995). Do managerial women prefer mentors? *Psychological Reports, 76,* 688-690.

Burke, R. J., & McKeen, C. A. (1996). Do women at the top make a difference? Gender proportions and the experiences of managerial and professional women. *Human Relations, 49,* 1093-1104.

Burke, R. J., & McKeen, C. A. (1997). Benefits of mentoring relationships among managerial and professional women: A cautionary tale. *Journal of Vocational Behavior, 51,* 43-57.

Burke, R. J., McKeen, C. A., & McKenna, C. (1990). Sex differences and cross-sex effects on mentoring: Some preliminary data. *Psychological Reports, 67,* 1011-1023.

Burke, R. J., McKeen, C. A., & McKenna, C. (1993). Correlates of mentoring in organizations: The mentor's perspective. *Psychological Reports, 72,* 883-896.

Burke, R. J., McKenna, C. S., & McKeen, C. A. (1991). How do mentorships differ from typical supervisory relationships? *Psychological Reports, 68,* 459-466.

Burke, R. J., Weir, T., & DuWors, R. E. (1979). Type A behavior of administrators and wives' reports of marital satisfaction and well-being. *Journal of Applied Psychology, 64,* 57-65.

Burley, K. A. (1991). Family-work spillover in dual-career couples: A comparison of two time perspectives. *Psychological Reports, 68,* 471-480.

Burrell, G. (1984). Sex and organizational analysis. *Organization Studies, 5*(2), 97-118.

Burrell, G. (1988). Modernism, postmodernism, and organizational analysis 2: The contributions of Michel Foucault. *Organization Studies, 9,* 221-235.

Burrell, G. (1992). Sex and organizational analysis. In A. J. Mills & P. Tancred (Eds.), *Gendering organizational analysis* (pp. 71-92). Newbury Park, CA: Sage.

Burrell, G., & Morgan, G. (1979). *Sociological paradigms and organisational analysis.* London: Heinemann.

Burt, R. S. (1982). *Toward a structural theory of action.* New York: Academic Press.

Burud, S. L., Aschbacher, P. R., & McCroskey, J. (1984). *Employer-supported child care: Investing in human resources.* Boston: Auburn House.

Busch, P., & Bush, R. F. (1978). Women contrasted to men in the industrial salesforce: Job satisfaction, values, role clarity, performance, and propensity to leave. *Journal of Marketing Research, 25,* 438-448.

Buss, D. M. (1995). Psychological sex differences: Origins through sexual selection. *American Psychologist, 50,* 164-168.

Butler, D., & Geis, F. L. (1990). Nonverbal affect responses to male and female leaders: Implications for leadership evaluations. *Journal of Personality and Social Psychology, 58,* 48-59.

Butterfield, D. A., & Bartol, K. M. (1977). Evaluators of leader behavior: A missing element on leadership theory. In J. G. Hunt & L. L. Larson (Eds.), *Leadership: The cutting edge* (pp. 67-188). Carbondale: Southern Illinois University Press.

Butterfield, D. A., & Powell, G. N. (1981). Effects of groups performance, leader sex, and rater sex on ratings of leader behavior. *Organizational Behavior and Human Performance, 28,* 129-141.

Buttner, E. H., & McEnally, M. (1996). The interactive effect of influence tactic, applicant gender, and type of job on hiring recommendations. *Sex Roles, 34,* 581-591.

Buttner, E. H., & Moore, D. P. (1997). Women's organizational exodus to entrepreneurship: Self-reported motivations and correlates with success. *Journal of Small Business Management, 35*(1), 34-46.

Byrne, D. E. (1971). *The attraction paradigm.* New York: Academic Press.

Byrne, D., & Neuman, J. H. (1992). The implications of attraction research for organizational issues. In K. Kelley (Ed.), *Issues, theory, and research in industrial/organizational psychology* (pp. 29-70). Amsterdam: Elsevier Science.

Cable, D. M., & Judge, T. A. (1997). Interviewers' perceptions of person-organization fit and organizational selection decisions. *Journal of Applied Psychology, 82,* 546-561.

Cahoon, A. R., & Ramsey, J. (1993). Valuing differences: Organization and gender. In R. T. Golembiewski (Ed.), *Handbook of organizational behavior* (pp. 339-354). New York: Marcel Dekker.

Caird, S. P. (1993). What do psychological tests suggest about entrepreneurs? *Journal of Managerial Psychology, 8*(6), 11-21.

Calás, M., & Smircich, L. (1992). Using the "F" word: Feminist theories and the social consequences of organizational research. In A. J. Mills & P. Tancred (Eds.), *Gendering organizational theory* (pp. 222-234). Newbury Park, CA: Sage.

Calás, M., & Smircich, L. (1996). From "the woman's" point of view: Feminist approaches to organization studies. In S. Clegg, C. Hardy, & W. Nord (Eds.), *Handbook of organization studies* (pp. 218-257). London: Sage.

Calás, M. B. (1993). Deconstructing charismatic leadership: Re-reading Weber from the darker side. *Leadership Quarterly, 4*(3/4), 305-328.

Calás, M. B., & Smircich, L. (1991a). Re-writing gender into organizational theorizing: Directions from feminist perspectives. In M. I. Reed & M. D. Hughes (Eds.), *Rethinking organization: New directions in organizational research and analysis.* Newbury Park, CA: Sage.

Calás, M. B., & Smircich, L. (1991b). Voicing seduction to silence leadership. *Organization Studies, 12,* 567-601.

Calás, M. B., & Smircich, L. (1993). Dangerous liaisons: The "feminine-in-management" meets "globalization." *Business Horizons, 36*(2), 71-81.

Caligiuri, P. M., & Cascio, W. F. (in press). Can we send her there? Maximizing the success of Western women on global assignments. *Journal of World Business.*

Campion, J. E., & Arvey, R. D. (1989). Unfair discrimination in the interview. In R. W. Eder & G. R. Ferris (Eds.), *The employment interview: Theory, practice, and research* (pp. 61-73). Newbury Park, CA: Sage.

Campion, M. A., Palmer, D. K., & Campion, J. E. (1997). A review of structure in the selection interview. *Personnel Psychology, 50,* 655-702.

Can smoking or bungee jumping get you canned? (1993, August 9). *Fortune,* p. 92.

Canary, D. J., & Dindia, K. (Eds.). (1998). *Sex differences and similarities in communication: Critical essays and empirical investigations of sex and gender in interaction.* Mahwah, NJ: Lawrence Erlbaum.

Canary, D. J., & Hause, K. S. (1993). Is there any reason to research sex differences in communications? *Communications Quarterly, 41,* 129-144.

Cann, A., & Siegfried, W. (1990). Gender stereotypes and dimensions of effective leader behavior. *Sex Roles, 23*(7/8), 413-419.

Cann, A., & Siegfried, W. D., Jr. (1987). Sex stereotypes and the leadership role. *Sex Roles, 17,* 401-408.

Cannings, K., & Lazonick, W. (1994). Equal employment opportunity and the "managerial woman" in Japan. *Industrial Relations, 33,* 44-69.

Cantor, D., & Bernay, T. (1992). *Women in power.* New York: Houghton Mifflin.

Caplan, R. D. (1983). Person-environment fit: Past, present and future. In C. L. Cooper (Ed.), *Stress research* (pp. 35-52). Chichester, UK: Wiley.

Caputo, R. K., & Dolinsky, A. (1998). Women's choice to pursue self-employment: The role of financial and human capital of household members. *Journal of Small Business Management, 36*(3), 8-17.

Carbonell, J. L. (1984). Sex roles and leadership revisited. *Journal of Applied Psychology, 69,* 44-49.

Carli, L. L. (1981, August). *Sex differences in small group interaction.* Paper presented at the 89th annual meeting of the American Psychological Association, Los Angeles.

Carli, L. L. (1989). Gender differences in interaction style and influence. *Journal of Personality and Social Psychology, 56,* 565-576.

Carli, L. L. (1990). Gender, language, and influence. *Journal of Personality and Social Psychology, 59,* 941-951.

Carli, L. L. (1991). Gender, status, and influence. In E. J. Lawler, B. Markovsky, C. Ridgeway, & H. A. Walker (Eds.), *Advances in group processes* (Vol. 8, pp. 89-113). Greenwich, CT: JAI.

Carli, L. L. (1997, October). *Effect of gender composition on self-evaluation.* Paper presented at the meeting of the New England Social Psychological Association, Williams College, Williamstown, MA.

Carli, L. L. (1998, June). *Gender effects in social influence.* Paper presented at the meeting of the Society for the Psychological Study of Social Issues, Ann Arbor, MI.

Carli, L. L., LaFleur, S. J., & Loeber, C. C. (1995). Nonverbal behavior, gender, and influence. *Journal of Personality and Social Psychology, 68,* 1030-1041.

Carter, N. M., Williams, M., & Reynolds, P. D. (1997). Discontinuance among new firms in retail: The influence of initial resources, strategy, and gender. *Journal of Business Venturing, 12,* 126-145.

Carter, S. (1993). Female business ownership: Current research and possibilities for the future. In S. Allen & C. Truman (Eds.), *Women in business—Perspectives on women entrepreneurs* (pp. 148-160). New York: Routledge.

Cartwright, S., & Cooper, C. L. (1997). *Managing workplace stress.* London: Sage.

The case for pay equity. (1996). *Worklife Report, 10,* 14-15.

Cash, T. E., Gillen, B., & Burns, D. S. (1977). Sexism and "beautyism" in personnel consultants' decision making. *Journal of Applied Psychology, 62,* 301-307.

Cashman, K. (1998). *Leadership from the inside out.* Provo, UT: Executive Excellence.

Cassirer, N. (1997). *The restructuring of work and workers' lives: Determinants and consequences of externalized employment.* Unpublished doctoral dissertation, Ohio State University, Columbus.

Catalyst. (1996). *Women in corporate leadership: Progress and prospects.* New York: Author.

Catalyst. (1998a). *Census of women corporate officers and top earners.* New York: Author.

Catalyst. (1998b). *A new approach to flexibility.* New York: Author.

Catalyst, the National Foundation for Women Business Owners (NFWBO), & the Committee of 200 Foundation. (1998, February). *Paths to entrepreneurship: New directions for women in business* (Sponsored by Salomon Smith Barney). New York: Catalyst.

Caudron, S. (1993, April). Training can damage diversity efforts. *Personnel Journal,* pp. 51-62.

Caudron, S. (1997). Can Generation Xers be trained? *Training and Development, 51,* 20-24.

Cejka, M. A., & Eagly, A. H. (1999). Gender-stereotypic images of occupations correspond to the sex segregation of employment. *Personality and Social Psychology Bulletin, 25,* 413-423.

Center for the New American Workforce. (1994). *Corporate responses to diversity: A benchmark study.* New York: Queens College, City University of New York.

Chaganti, R. (1986, October). Management in women-owned enterprises. *Journal of Small Business Management, 24,* 18-29.

Chaganti, R., DeCarolis, D., & Deeds, D. (1995). Predictors of capital structure in small ventures. *Entrepreneurship Theory and Practice, 20*(2), 7-18.

Chaganti, R., & Parasuraman, S. (1996). A study of the impacts of gender on business performance and management patterns in small business. *Entrepreneurship Theory and Practice, 21*(2), 73-75.

Chao, G. T. (1997). Mentoring phases and outcomes. *Journal of Vocational Behavior, 51,* 15-28.

Chao, G. T., & O'Leary, A. M. (1990). How others see same- and cross-gender mentoring. *Mentoring International, 6*(3), 3-12.

Chao, G. T., O'Leary-Kelly, A. M., Wolf, S., Klein, H. J., & Gardner, P. D. (1994). Organizational socialization: Its content and consequences. *Journal of Applied Psychology, 79,* 730-743.

Chao, G. T., Walz, P. M., & Gardner, P. D. (1992). Formal and informal mentorships: A comparison on mentoring functions and contrast with nonmentored counterparts. *Personnel Psychology, 45,* 619-636.

Chapman, J. B. (1975). Comparison of male and female leadership styles. *Academy of Management Journal, 18,* 645-650.

Charles, M. (1992). Accounting for cross-national variation in occupational sex segregation. *American Sociological Review, 57*(4), 483-502.

Chatman, J. A. (1989). Improving interactional organizational research: A model of person-organization fit. *Academy of Management Research, 14,* 333-349.

Chauvin, K. W., & Guthrie, J. P. (1994). Labor market reputation and the value of the firm. *Managerial and Decision Economics, 15,* 543-552.

Cheng, C. (Ed.). (1996a). *Masculinities in organizations.* Thousand Oaks, CA: Sage.

Cheng, C. (1996b). "We choose not to compete": The "merit" discourse in the selection process, and Asian and Asian American men and their masculinity. In C. Cheng (Ed.), *Masculinities in organizations* (pp. 177-200). Thousand Oaks, CA: Sage.

Chio, V. (1993). Feminist theories and feminists' conceptualizations of work: Research agendas and questions for WIM researchers. In S. M. Schor (Ed.), *Proceedings of the 30th meeting of the Eastern Academy of Management* (pp. 282-285). Minneapolis, MN: Omnipress.

Chodorow, N. (1978). *The reproduction of mothering*. Berkeley: University of California Press.

Chodorow, N. (1993). What is the relation between psychoanalytic feminism and the psychoanalytic psychology of women? In D. Rhode (Ed.), *Theoretical perspectives on sexual difference* (pp. 114-130). New Haven, CT: Yale University Press.

Choi, P. K., Au, K. C., Cheung, F. M., Tang, S. K., & Yik, S. M. (1993). *Power and dignity: Sexual harassment on campus in Hong Kong*. Hong Kong: Hong Kong Institute of Asia-Pacific Studies.

Chow, E., & Berheide, C. (1988). The interdependence of family and work: A framework for family life education, policy and practice. *Family Relations, 37*(1), 23-28.

Chow, E. N. (1987). The influence of sex-role identity and occupational attainment on the psychological well-being of Asian American women. *Psychology of Women Quarterly, 11,* 69-82.

Christensen, K. E., & Staines, G. L. (1990). Flextime: A viable solution to work/family conflict? *Journal of Family Issues, 4,* 455-477.

Cialdini, R. B., & Trost, M. R. (1998). Social influence: Social norms, conformity, and compliance. In D. T. Gilbert, S. T. Fiske, & G. Lindzey (Eds.), *The handbook of social psychology* (4th ed., Vol. 2, pp. 151-192). Boston: McGraw-Hill.

Cianni, M., & Romberger, B. (1995). Perceived racial, ethnic, and gender differences in access to developmental experiences. *Group & Organization Management, 20,* 440-459.

City of Richmond v. Croson, 488 U.S. 469 (1989).

Civil Rights Act, 3(1), 101 (1991).

Clark, H., Chandler, J., & Barry, J. (1996). Work psychology, women and stress: Silence, identity and the boundaries of conventional wisdom. *Gender, Work and Organization, 3*(2), 65-77.

Clawson, J. G., & Kram, K. E. (1984). Managing cross-gender mentoring. *Business Horizons, 27*(3), 22-32.

Clayton, S. D., & Crosby, F. J. (1992). *Justice, gender, and affirmative action*. Ann Arbor: University of Michigan Press.

Cleveland, J. N., Murphy, K. R., & Williams, R. E. (1989). Multiple uses of performance appraisal: Prevalence and correlates. *Journal of Applied Psychology, 74,* 130-135.

Cockburn, C. (1991). *In the way of women: Men's resistance to sex equality in organizations*. Ithaca, NY: ILR.

Cohen, J. (1994). The earth is round (*p* < .05). *American Psychologist, 45,* 997-1003.

Cohen, L. E., Broschak, J. P., & Haveman, H. A. (1998). And then there were more? The effect of organizational sex composition on the hiring and promotion of managers. *American Sociological Review, 63,* 711-727.

Cohen, L. E., & Elvira, M. M. (1997, August). *The effects of organizational sex composition on the turnover of men and women: Is leaving just the same?* Paper presented at the annual meeting of the Academy of Management, Boston.

Cohen, L. L., & Swim, J. K. (1995). The differential impact of gender ratios on women and men: Tokenism, self-confidence, and expectations. *Personality and Social Psychology Bulletin, 21*(9), 876-884.

Cohen, S. (1989). *Tender power*. Reading, MA: Addison-Wesley.

Cohen, S., & Wills, T. A. (1985). Stress, social support, and the buffering hypothesis. *Psychological Bulletin, 98,* 310-357.

Cohn, S. (1985). *The process of occupational sex-typing: The feminization of clerical labor in Great Britain.* Philadelphia: Temple University Press.

Col, J.-M. (1993). Managing softly in turbulent times: Corazon C. Aquino, president of the Philippines. In M. A. Genovese (Ed.), *Women as national leaders* (pp. 13-40). Newbury Park, CA: Sage.

Colarelli, S. M., & Bishop, R. C. (1990). Career commitment: Functions, correlates, and management. *Group and Organization Studies, 15,* 158-176.

Collier, R. (1995). *Combating sexual harassment in the workplace.* Buckingham, UK: Open University Press.

Collins, E. G. C. (1983). Managers and lovers. *Harvard Business Review, 61*(5), 142-153.

Collins, P. H. (1998). Toward a new vision: Race, class, and gender as categories of analysis and connection. In J. Ferrante & P. Brown, Jr. (Eds.), *The social construction of race and ethnicity in the United States* (pp. 478-495). New York: Longman.

Collins, S. M. (1983). The making of the Black middle class. *Social Problems, 30,* 369-382.

Collins, S. M. (1997). Black mobility in White corporations: Up the corporate ladder but out on a limb. *Social Problems, 44,* 55-67.

Collinson, D. L., & Hearn, J. (1994). Naming men as men: Implications for work, organization and management. *Gender, Work and Organization, 1*(1), 2-22.

Collinson, D. L., & Hearn, J. (1996). Breaking the silence: On men, masculinities, and managements. In D. L. Collinson & J. Hearn (Eds.), *Men as managers, managers as men: Critical perspectives on men, masculinities, and managements* (pp. 1-24). Thousand Oaks, CA: Sage.

Collinson, D. L., Knights, D., & Collinson, M. (1990). *Managing to discriminate.* London: Routledge.

Conger, J. A. (1989). *The charismatic leader: Behind the mystique of exceptional leadership.* San Francisco: Jossey-Bass.

Conger, J. A. (1994). *Spirit at work.* San Francisco: Jossey-Bass.

Conger, J. A. (1998). How "Gen X" managers manage. *Strategy & Business, 10,* 21-31.

Conger, J. A., & Kanungo, R. (1988). *Charismatic leadership.* San Francisco: Jossey-Bass.

Connell, R. W. (1987). *Gender and power: Society, the person and sexual politics.* Stanford, CA: Stanford University Press.

Connell, R. W. (1995). *Masculinities.* Berkeley: University of California Press.

Connor, M., Hooks, K., & McGuire, T. (1997). Gaining legitimacy for flexible work arrangements and career paths: The business case for public accounting and professional services firms. In S. Parasuraman & J. H. Greenhaus (Eds.), *Integrating work and family: Challenges and choices for a changing world* (pp. 154-166). Westport, CT: Quorum Books.

Constantinople, A. (1973). Masculinity-femininity: An exception to a famous dictum? *Psychological Bulletin, 80,* 389-407.

Cook, A. (1992). Can work requirements accommodate to the needs of dual-earner families? In S. Lewis, D. N. Izraeli, & H. Hootsmans (Eds.), *Dual-earner families: International perspectives* (pp. 201-220). London: Sage.

Cook, E. P. (1985). *Psychological androgyny.* New York: Pergamon.

Cook, T. D., & Campbell, S. T. (1979). *Quasi-experimentation: Design and analysis issues for field settings.* Boston: Houghton Mifflin.

Cooper, A. C. (1981). Strategic management: New ventures and small business. *Long Range Planning, 14*(5), 39-45.

Cooper, A. C. (1998, January). *Entrepreneurship: The past, the present, the future.* Paper presented at the annual meeting of the United States Association of Small Business and Entrepreneurship, Clearwater, FL.

Cooper, A. C., & Dunkelberg, W. C. (1981). A new look at business entry: Experiences of 1805 entrepreneurs. In K. Vesper, (Ed.), *Frontiers of entrepreneurship research* (pp. 1-20). Wellesley, MA: Center for Entrepreneurial Studies, Babson College.

Cooper, A. C., & Dunkelberg, W. C. (1987). Entrepreneurial research: Old questions, new answers and methodological issues. *American Journal of Small Business, 11*(3), 11-23.

Cooper, A. C., Woo, C., & Dunkelberg, W. (1989). Entrepreneurship and the initial size of firms. *Journal of Business Venturing, 4,* 317-332.

Cooper, C. L. (1996). Corporate relocation policies. In S. Lewis & J. Lewis (Eds.), *The work-family challenge: Rethinking employment* (pp. 93-102). London: Sage.

Cooper, C. L. (1998). The psychological implications of the changing patterns of work. *RSA Journal, 1*(4), 74-81.

Cooper, C. L., Cooper, C. R., & Eaker, L. H. (1988). *Living with stress.* London: Penguin.

Cooper, C. L., & Jackson, S. (1997). *Creating tomorrow's organizations: A handbook for future research in organizational behaviour.* Chichester, UK: Wiley.

Cooper, C. L., & Melhuish, A. (1984). Executive stress and health: Differences between men and women. *Journal of Occupational Medicine, 26*(2), 99-103.

Cooper, R. (1989). Modernism, postmodernism, and organizational analysis 3: The contributions of Jacques Derrida. *Organization Studies, 10,* 479-502.

Cooper, V. W. (1997). Homophily or the queen bee syndrome: Female evaluation of female leadership. *Small Group Research, 28,* 483-499.

Copeland, C. L., Driskell, J. E., & Salas, E. (1995). Gender and reactions to dominance. *Journal of Social Behavior and Personality, 10* [Special issue], 53-68.

Corcoran, M., & Duncan, G. J. (1979, Winter). Work history, labor force attachment, and earnings differences between the races and sexes. *Journal of Human Resources, 14,* 3-20.

Cordova, D. I. (1992). Cognitive limitations and affirmative action: The effects of aggregate versus sequential data in the perception of discrimination. *Social Justice Research, 5,* 319-333.

Core, F. (1994). Women and the restructuring of employment. *OECD Observer, 186,* 5-12.

Cortina, J. M., & Dunlup, W. P. (1997). On the logic and purpose of significant testing. *Psychological Methods, 2,* 161-172.

Corzine, J. B., Buntzman, G. F., & Busch, E. T. (1994). Mentoring, downsizing, gender and career outcomes. *Journal of Social Behavior and Personality, 9,* 517-528.

Cose, E. (1995, June 18). The daddy trap. *Chicago Tribune Magazine,* pp. 14-18.

Coser, L. (1974). *Greedy institutions.* New York: Free Press.

Cotter, D. A., DeFiore, J., Hermsen, J. M., Kowalewski, B. M., & Vanneman, R. (1995). Occupational gender segregation and the earnings gap: Changes in the 1980s. *Social Science Research, 24,* 439-454.

Cotter, D. A., DeFiore, J. M., Hermsen, J. M., Kowalewski, B. M., & Vanneman, R. (1997a). All women benefit: The macro-level effect of occupational integration on gender earnings inequality. *American Sociological Review, 62,* 714-734.

Cotter, D. A., DeFiore, J. M., Hermsen, J. M., Kowalewski, B. M., & Vanneman, R. (1997b). Same data, different conclusions: Comment on Bernhardt et al. *American Journal of Sociology, 102*(4), 1143-1154.

Coverman, S. (1986). Occupational segmentation and sex differences in earnings. In R. V. Robinson (Ed.), *Research in social stratification and mobility: A research annual* (Vol. 5, pp. 139-172). Greenwich, CT: JAI.

Coverman, S. (1988). Sociological explanations of the male-female wage gap: Individualist and structuralist theories. In A. H. Stromberg & S. Harkess (Eds.), *Women working: Theories and facts in perspective* (pp. 101-115). Mountain View, CA: Mayfield.

Cox, T., Jr. (1991). The multicultural organization. *Academy of Management Executive, 5*(2), 34-47.

Cox, T., Jr. (1993). *Cultural diversity in organizations: Theory, research & practice.* San Francisco: Berrett-Koehler.

Cox, T., Jr., & Nkomo, S. (1993). Race and ethnicity. In R. J. Golembiewski (Ed.), *Handbook of organizational behavior* (pp. 205-229). New York: Marcel Dekker.

Cox, T., Jr., & Nkomo, S. M. (1990). Invisible men and women: An overview of research on minorities in organizations. *Journal of Organizational Behavior, 11,* 419-431.

Cox, T. H., & Blake, S. (1991). Managing cultural diversity: Implications for organizational competitiveness. *The Executive, 5*(3), 45-56.

Cox, T. H., & Nkomo, S. M. (1991). A race and gender-group analysis of the early career experience of MBAs. *Work and Occupations, 18,* 431-446.

Craig, J. M., & Sherif, C. W. (1986). The effectiveness of men and women in problem-solving groups as a function of group gender composition. *Sex Roles, 14,* 453-466.

Crawford, M. (1995). *Talking difference: On gender and language.* Thousand Oaks, CA: Sage.

Creighton, M. R. (1996). Marriage, motherhood, and career management in a Japanese "counter culture." In A. E. Imamura (Ed.), *Re-imaging Japanese women* (pp. 192-220). Berkeley: University of California Press.

Cromie, S., & Birley, S. (1992). Networking by female business owners in Northern Ireland. *Journal of Business Venturing, 7*(3), 237-251.

Crompton, R. (1996). Paid employment and the changing system of gender relations: A cross-national comparison. *Sociology: The Journal of the British Sociological Association, 30,* 427-445.

Cronbach, L., & Meehl, P. E. (1955). Construct validity in psychological tests. *Psychological Bulletin, 52,* 281-302.

Crosby, F. (1982). *Relative deprivation and working women.* New York: Oxford University Press.

Crosby, F., & Nyquist, L. (1977). The female register: An empirical study of Lakoff's hypothesis. *Language in Society, 6,* 313-322.

Crosby, F. J., & Cordova, D. I. (1996). Words worth of wisdom: Toward an understanding of affirmative action. *Journal of Social Issues, 52*(4), 33-49.

Cross, S. E., & Madson, L. (1997). Models of the self: Self-construals and gender. *Psychological Bulletin, 122,* 5-37.

Croteau, J. M. (1996). Research on the work experiences of lesbian, gay, and bisexual people: An integrative review of methodology and findings. *Journal of Vocational Behavior, 48,* 195-209.

Crouter, A. C. (1984). Spillover from family to work: The neglected side of the work-family interface. *Human Relations, 37,* 425-442.

Crow, S. M., Fok, L. Y., & Hartman, S. J. (1995). Priorities of hiring discrimination: Who is at the greatest risk—Women, Blacks, or homosexuals? In *Academy of Management best papers proceedings* (pp. 443-447).

Cullen, J. B., & Perrewe, P. L. (1981). Superiors' and subordinates' gender: Does it really matter? *Psychological Reports, 48,* 435-438.

Culler, J. (1982). *On deconstruction.* Ithaca, NY: Cornell University Press.

Cutrona, C. E., & Suhr, J. A. (1992). Controllability of stressful events and satisfaction with spouse support behaviors. *Communication Research, 19,* 154-176.

Daly, K. J. (1996). *Families and time: Keeping pace in a hurried culture.* Thousand Oaks, CA: Sage.

Das Gupta, M. (1997). "What is Indian about you?" A gendered, transnational approach to ethnicity. *Gender & Society, 11,* 572-596.

Daubman, J., Heatherington, I., & Ahn, A. (1992). Gender and self-presentation of academic achievement. *Sex Roles, 27,* 187-204.

D'Augelli, A. R. (1988). Sexual harassment and affectional status: The hidden discrimination. *The Community Psychologist, 21,* 11-12.

Davidson, M. J. (1996). Women and employment. In P. Warr (Ed.), *Psychology at work* (pp. 279-307). London: Penguin.

Davidson, M. J. (1997). *The Black and ethnic minority woman manager: Cracking the concrete ceiling.* London: Paul Chapman.

Davidson, M. J., & Burke, R. J. (Eds.). (1994). *Women in management: Current research issues.* London: Paul Chapman.

Davidson, M. J., & Cooper, C. L. (1983). *Stress and the woman manager.* London: Martin Roberston.

Davidson, M. J., & Cooper, C. L. (1984). Occupational stress in female managers: A comparative study. *Journal of Management Studies, 21,* 185-205.

Davidson, M. J., & Cooper, C. L. (1992). *Shattering the glass ceiling: The woman manager.* London: Paul Chapman.

Davidson, M. J., & Cooper, C. L. (Eds.). (1993a). *European women in business and management.* London: Paul Chapman.

Davidson, M. J., & Cooper, C. L. (1993b). European women in business and management—An overview. In M. J. Davidson & C. L. Cooper (Eds.), *European women in business and management* (pp. 1-16). London: Paul Chapman.

Davidson, M. J., Cooper, C. L., & Baldini, V. (1995). Occupational stress in female and male graduate managers. *Stress Medicine, 11,* 157-175.

Davis, D. D. (1998). International performance measurement and management. In J. W. Smither (Ed.), *Performance appraisal: State of the art in practice* (pp. 95-131). San Francisco: Jossey-Bass.

Davis, S. T. W. (1992). Japan's working women are a "new breed" of consumer. *Marketing News, 26*(17), 12.

Dawson, A. G., Mikel, C. S., Lorenz, C. S., & King, J. (1984). *An experimental study of effects of employer-sponsored child care services on selected employee behaviors.* Chicago: Foundation for Human Services.

Day, D. R., & Stogdill, R. M. (1972). Leader behavior of male and female supervisors: A comparative study. *Personnel Psychology, 25,* 353-360.

Deal, J. J., & Stevenson, M. A. (1998). Perceptions of female and male managers in the 1990s: Plus ça change. . . . *Sex Roles, 38,* 287-300.

Deaux, K. (1976). *The behavior of women and men.* Belmont, CA: Wadsworth.

Deaux, K. (1979). Self-evaluations of male and female managers. *Sex Roles, 5,* 571-580.

Deaux, K. (1984). From individual differences to social categories: Analysis of a decade's research on gender. *American Psychologist, 39,* 105-116.

Deaux, K. (1993). Commentary: Sorry, wrong number—A reply to Gentile's call. *Psychological Science, 4,* 125-126.

Deaux, K. (1996). Social identification. In E. T. Higgins & A. Kruglanski (Eds.), *Social psychology: Handbook of basic principles* (pp. 777-798). New York: Guilford.

Deaux, K., & Kite, M. (1993). Gender stereotypes. In F. L. Denmark & M. A. Paludi (Eds.), *Psychology of women: A handbook of issues and theories* (pp. 107-139). Westport, CT: Greenwood.

Deaux, K., & LaFrance, M. (1998). Gender. In D. T. Gilbert, S. T. Fiske, & G. Lindzey (Eds.), *The handbook of social psychology* (Vol. 1, 4th ed., pp. 788-827). Boston: McGraw-Hill.

Deaux, K., & Major, B. (1987). Putting gender into context: An interactive model of gender-related behavior. *Psychological Review, 94,* 369-389.

Decker, C. (1995, February 19). California test for affirmative action. *Seattle Times,* p. A20.

Deldycke, T. (1968). *The working population and its structure.* Brussels, Belgium: Free University of Brussels.

deLeon, C. T., & Ho, S. (1994). The third identity of modern Chinese women: Women managers in Hong Kong. In N. J. Adler & D. N. Izraeli (Eds.), *Competitive frontiers: Women managers in a global economy* (pp. 43-56). Cambridge, MA: Blackwell.

Demarest, J. L. (1977). *Women minding their own businesses: A pilot study of independent business and professional women and their enterprises.* Unpublished doctoral dissertation, University of Colorado, Boulder.

Demos. (1995). *The time squeeze.* London: Author.

Denison, D., & Alexander, J. (1986). Patterns and profiles of entrepreneurs: Data from entrepreneurship forums. In R. Ronstadt, R. J. Hornaday, R. Peterson, & K. Vesper (Eds.), *Frontiers of entrepreneurship research* (pp. 578-593). Wellesley, MA: Center for Entrepreneurial Studies, Babson College.

Denmark, F. L., & Diggory, J. C. (1966). Sex differences in attitudes toward leader's display of authoritarian behavior. *Psychological Reports, 18,* 863-872.

Dennis, W. J., Jr. (1997). *The public reviews small business.* Washington, DC: NFIB Education Foundation.

Denton, T. (1990). Bonding and supportive relationships among Black professional women: Rituals of restoration. *Journal of Organizational Behavior, 11,* 447-457.

Denzin, N. K., & Lincoln, Y. S. (1994). Introduction: Entering the field of qualitative research. In N. K. Denzin & Y. S. Lincoln (Eds.), *Handbook of qualitative research* (pp. 1-18). Newbury Park, CA: Sage.

Devanna, M. A. (1987). Women in management: Progress and promise. *Human Resource Management, 26,* 409-481.

Devine, I., & Markiewicz, D. (1990). Cross-sex relationships at work and the impact of gender stereotypes. *Journal of Business Ethics, 9,* 333-338.

Devine, T. J. (1994). Characteristics of self-employed women in the United States. *Monthly Labor Review,* 117(3), 20-34.

Dienesch, R. M., & Liden, R. C. (1986). Leader-member exchange model of leadership: A critique and further development. *Academy of Management Review, 11,* 618-634.

Diffley, J. H. (1983). Important business competencies for the woman entrepreneur. *Business Education Forum, 37*(3), 31-33.

Dillard, J. P. (1987). Close relationships at work: Perceptions of the motives and performance of relational participants. *Journal of Social and Personal Relationships, 4,* 179-193.

Dillard, J. P., & Broetzmann, S. M. (1989). Romantic relationships at work: Perceived changes in job-related behaviors as a function of participant's motive, partner's motive, and gender. *Journal of Applied Social Psychology, 19*(2), 93-110.

Dillard, J. P., Hale, J. L., & Segrin, C. (1994). Close relationships in task environments: Perceptions of relational types, illicitness, and power. *Management Communication Quarterly, 7*(3), 227-255.

Dillard, J. P., & Miller, K. I. (1988). Intimate relationships in task environments. In S. W. Duck (Ed.), *Handbook of personal relationships* (pp. 449-465). New York: John Wiley.

Dillard, J. P., & Witteman, H. (1985). Romantic relationships at work: Organizational and personal influences. *Human Communication Research, 12*(1), 99-116.

Dingwall, J. (1992). The woman weapon. *D&B Reports, 40,* 60-61.

Dinnerstein, D. (1976). *The mermaid and the minotaur.* New York: Harper & Row.

Dipboye, R. L. (1985). Some neglected variables in research on discrimination in appraisals. *Academy of Management Review, 10,* 116-127.

Dipboye, R. L. (1987). Problems and progress of women in management. In K. S. Koziara, M. H. Moskow, & L. D. Tanner (Eds.), *Working women: Past, present, future* (pp. 118-153). Washington, DC: Bureau of National Affairs.

Dipboye, R. L. (1992). *Selection interviews: Process perspectives.* Cincinnati, OH: South-Western.

Discoll, M. P., & Cooper, C. L. (1996). Sources and management of executive job stress and burnout. In P. Warr (Ed.), *Psychology at work* (pp. 188-223). London: Penguin.

DiTomaso, N. (1989). Sexuality in the workplace: Discrimination and harassment. In J. Hearn, D. L. Sheppard, P. Tancred-Sheriff, & G. Burrell (Eds.), *The sexuality of organizations* (pp. 71-90). Newbury Park, CA: Sage.

Dobbins, G. H. (1986). Equity vs. equality: Sex differences in leadership. *Sex Roles, 15,* 513-525.

Dobbins, G. H., Cardy, R. L., & Truxillo, D. M. (1986). Effect of ratee sex and purpose of appraisal on the accuracy of performance evaluations. *Basic and Applied Social Psychology, 7,* 225-241.

Dobbins, G. H., Pence, E. C., Orban, J. A., & Sgro, J. A. (1983). The effects of sex of the leader and sex of the subordinate on the use of organizational control policy. *Organizational Behavior and Human Performance, 32,* 325-343.

Dobbins, G. H., & Platz, S. J. (1986). Sex differences in leadership: How real are they? *Academy of Management Review, 11,* 118-127.

Dobrzynski, J. H. (1996, November 6). Somber news for women on corporate ladder. *New York Times*, p. D1.

Dodge, K. A., Gilroy, F. D., & Fenzel, L. M. (1995). Requisite management characteristics revisited: Two decades later. *Journal of Social Behavior and Personality, 10,* 253-264.

Doeringer, P. G., & Piore, M. J. (1971). *Internal labor markets and manpower analysis.* Lexington, MA: D. C. Heath.

Dolinsky, A. L., Caputo, R. K., Pasumarty, K., & Quazi, H. (1993). The effects of education on business ownership: A longitudinal study of women. *Entrepreneurship Theory and Practice, 18*(1), 43-54.

Donnell, S., & Hall, J. (1980). Men and women as managers: A significant case of no significant difference. *Organizational Dynamics,* No. 8, pp. 60-77.

Dooley, B. (1996). At work away from home. *The Psychologist, 9*(4), 155-158.

Dorfman, P. W. (1996). International and cross-cultural leadership. In B. J. Punnett & O. Shenkar (Eds.), *Handbook for international management research* (pp. 267-349). Cambridge, MA: Blackwell.

Dorfman, P. W., & Howell, J. P. (1988). Dimensions of national culture and effective leadership patterns: Hofstede revisited. In S. B. Prasad (Ed.), *Advances in international comparative management* (Vol. 3, pp. 127-150). Greenwich, CT: JAI.

Dorfman, P. W., & Ronen, S. (1991). *The universality of leadership theories: Challenges and paradoxes.* Paper presented at the annual meeting of the National Academy of Management, Miami, FL.

Doss, B. D., & Hopkins, J. R. (1998). The Multicultural Masculinity Ideology Scale: Validation from three cultural perspectives. *Sex Roles, 38,* 719-741.

Dougherty, T. W., Turban, D. B., Olson, D. E., Dwyer, P. D., & Lapreze, M. W. (1996). Factors affecting perceptions of workplace sexual harassment. *Journal of Organizational Behavior, 17,* 489-501.

Douglas, A. (1977). *The feminization of American culture.* New York: Avon.

Dovidio, J. F., Brown, C. E., Heltman, S. L., Ellyson, K., & Keating, C. F. (1988). Power displays between men and women in discussions of gender-linked tasks: A multichannel study. *Journal of Personality and Social Psychology, 55,* 580-587.

Dovidio, J. F., Ellyson, S. L., Keating, C. F., Heltman, K., & Brown, C. E. (1988). The relationship of social power to visual displays of dominance between men and women. *Journal of Personality and Social Psychology, 54,* 233-242.

Dovidio, J. F., Mann, J., & Gaertner, S. L. (1989). Resistance to affirmative action: The implications of aversive racism. In F. A. Blanchard & F. J. Crosby (Eds.), *Affirmative action in perspective* (pp. 85-102). New York: Springer-Verlag.

Dreher, G. F., & Ash, R. A. (1990). A comparative study of mentoring among men and women in managerial, professional, and technical positions. *Journal of Applied Psychology, 75,* 539-546.

Dreher, G. F., & Cox, T. H. (1996). Race, gender, and opportunity: A study of compensation attainment and the establishment of mentoring relationships. *Journal of Applied Psychology, 81,* 297-308.

Dreher, G. F., Dougherty, T. W., & Whitely, W. (1989). Influence tactics and salary attainment: A gender-specific analysis. *Sex Roles, 20,* 535-550.

Drucker, P. F. (1985). *Innovation and entrepreneurship.* New York: Harper & Row.

Druskat, V. (1994). Gender and leadership style: Transformational and transactional leadership in the Roman Catholic Church. *Leadership Quarterly, 5,* 99-119.

D'Souza, D. (1997). The education of Ward Connerly. *Forbes, 159*(9), 90.

Dubini, P. (1988). The influence of motivations and environment in business startups: Some hints for public policies. *Journal of Business Venturing, 4*, 11-26.

duCille, A. (1994). The occult of true Black womanhood: Critical demeanor and Black feminist studies. *Signs: Journal of Women in Culture and Society, 19*, 591-629.

Dugger, K. (1996). Social location and gender-role attitudes: A comparison of Black and White women. In E. N. Chow, D. Wilkinson, & M. B. Zinn (Eds.), *Race, class, & gender: Common bonds, different voices* (pp. 32-51). Thousand Oaks, CA: Sage.

Dumas, R. G. (1979). Dilemmas of Black females in leadership. *Journal of Personality and Social Systems, 2*, 3-26.

Dunahoo, C. L., Geller, P. A., & Hobfoll, S. E. (1996). Women's coping: Communal versus individualistic orientation. In M. J. Schabracq, J. A. M. Winnubst, & C. L. Cooper (Eds.), *Handbook of work and health psychology* (pp. 183-204). London: Wiley.

Dunn, D. (1996). Gender-segregated occupations. In P. J. Dubeck & K. Borman (Eds.), *Women and work: A handbook* (pp. 91-94). New York: Garland.

Durden, G. C., & Gaynor, P. E. (1998). More on the cost of being other than White and male: Measurement of race, ethnic, and gender effects on yearly earnings. *American Journal of Economics and Sociology, 57*, 95-103.

Duxbury, L. E., & Higgins, C. A. (1991). Gender differences in work-family conflict. *Journal of Applied Psychology, 76*, 60-74.

Eagle, B. W., Miles, E. W., & Icenogle, M. L. (1997). Interrole conflicts and the permeability of work and family domains: Are there gender differences? *Journal of Vocational Behavior, 50*, 168-184.

Eagly, A. H. (1987). *Sex differences in social behavior: A social-role interpretation.* Hillsdale, NJ: Lawrence Erlbaum.

Eagly, A. H. (1995). The science and politics of comparing women and men. *American Psychologist, 50*, 145-158.

Eagly, A. H. (1997). Sex differences in social behavior: Comparing social role theory and evolutionary psychology. *American Psychologist, 52*, 1380-1383.

Eagly, A. H., & Johnson, B. T. (1990). Gender and leadership style: A meta-analysis. *Psychological Bulletin, 108*(2), 233-256.

Eagly, A. H., & Karau, S. J. (1991). Gender and the emergence of leaders: A meta-analysis. *Journal of Personality and Social Psychology, 60*, 685-710.

Eagly, A. H., Karau, S. J., & Makhijani, M. G. (1995). Gender and the effectiveness of leaders: A meta-analysis. *Psychological Bulletin, 117*, 125-145.

Eagly, A. H., Makhijani, M. G., & Klonsky, B. G. (1992). Gender and the evaluation of leaders: A meta-analysis. *Psychological Bulletin, 111*, 3-22.

Eagly, A. H., & Mladinic, A. (1989). Gender stereotypes and attitudes toward women and men. *Personality and Social Psychology Bulletin, 15*, 543-558.

Eagly, A. H., & Mladinic, A. (1994). Are people prejudiced against women? Some answers from research on attitudes, gender stereotypes, and judgments of competence. In W. Stroebe & M. Hewstone (Eds.), *European review of social psychology* (Vol. 5, pp. 1-35). New York: John Wiley.

Eagly, A. H., Mladinic, A., & Otto, S. (1991). Are women evaluated more favorably than men? An analysis of attitudes, beliefs, and emotions. *Psychology of Women Quarterly, 15*, 203-216.

Eagly, A. H., & Steffen, V. J. (1984). Gender stereotypes stem from the distribution of women and men into social roles. *Journal of Personality and Social Psychology, 46,* 735-754.

Earley, P. C. (1987). Intercultural training for managers: A comparison of documentary and interpersonal methods. *Academy of Management Journal, 30,* 685-698.

Earnshaw, J., & Davidson, M. J. (1994). Remedying sexual harassment via industrial tribunal claims: An investigation of the legal and psychological process. *Personnel Review, 23*(8), 3-16.

Easterby-Smith, M., Thorpe, R., & Lowe, A. (1991). *Management research: An introduction.* London: Sage.

Eberhardt, J. L., & Fiske, S. T. (1994). Affirmative action in theory and practice: Issues of power, ambiguity, and gender versus race. *Basic and Applied Social Psychology, 15,* 201-220.

Eby, L. T. (1997). Alternative forms of mentoring in changing organizational environments: A conceptual extension of the mentoring literature. *Journal of Vocational Behavior, 51,* 125-144.

Edelman, L. B. (1992). Legal ambiguity and symbolic structures: Organizational mediation of civil rights law. *American Journal of Sociology, 97,* 1531-1576.

Eder, R. W., & Buckley, M. R. (1988). The employment interview: An interactionist perspective. In G. R. Ferris & K. W. Rowland (Eds.), *Research in personnel and human resources management* (pp. 75-107). Greenwich, CT: JAI.

Edgeworth, F. Y. (1922). Equal pay to men and women. *Economics Journal, 32,* 431-457.

Edwards, J. R. (1994). The study of congruence in organizational behavior research: Critique and a proposed alternative. *Organizational Behavior and Human Decision Processes, 58*(1), 51-100.

Edwards, J. R., Baglioni, A. J., & Cooper, C. L. (1990). Stress, type-A coping and psychological and physical symptoms: A multi-sample test of alternative methods. *Human Relations, 43*(10), 919-956.

EEOC v. Hacienda Hotel, 881 F.2d 1504 (9th Cir. 1989).

Einhorn, B. (1994). Women in the new federal states after the Wende: The impact of unification on women's employment opportunities. In E. Boa & J. Wharton (Eds.), *Women and the Wende* (pp. 18-37). Atlanta, GA: Rodopi.

Eisenhardt, K. M., & Schoonhoven, C. B. (1990). Organizational growth: Linking founding team, strategy, environment, and growth among U.S. semiconductor ventures, 1978-1988. *Administrative Science Quarterly, 35,* 504-529.

Eisler, R. (1987). *The chalice and the blade.* San Francisco: HarperCollins.

Eisler, R. (1993). Women, men and management: Redesigning our future. In P. Barrentine (Ed.), *When the canary stops singing: Women's perspectives on transforming business* (pp. 27-40). San Francisco: Berrett-Koehler.

Elkin, A., & Rosch, P. (1990). Promoting mental health at the workplace: The prevention side of stress management. *Occupational Medicine: State of the Art Review, 5,* 739-754.

Elliott, S. J. (1995). Psychological stress, women and heart health: A critical review. *Social Science Medicine, 40*(1), 105-115.

Ellison v. Brady, CA 9, 54 FEP Cases 1346 (1991).

Ellyson, S. L., Dovidio, J. F., & Brown, C. E. (1992). The look of power: Gender differences in visual dominance behavior. In C. L. Ridgeway (Ed.), *Gender, interaction, and inequality* (pp. 50-80). New York: Springer-Verlag.

Elmes, M., & Connelley, D. L. (1997). Dreams of diversity and the realities of intergroup relations in organizations. In P. Prasad, A. J. Mills, M. Elmes, & A. Prasad (Eds.), *Managing the organizational melting pot: Dilemmas of workplace diversity* (pp. 148-167). Thousand Oaks, CA: Sage.

Elsass, P. M., & Graves, L. M. (1997). Demographic diversity in decision-making groups: The experiences of women and people of color. *Academy of Management Review, 22,* 946-973.

Ely, R. (1991, August). *Gender difference: What difference does it make?* Paper presented at the annual meeting of the Academy of Management, Miami, FL.

Ely, R. J. (1994). The effects of organizational demographics and social identity on relationships among professional women. *Administrative Science Quarterly, 39*(2), 203-238.

Ely, R. J. (1995). The power in demography: Women's social constructions of gender identity at work. *Academy of Management Journal, 38*(3), 589-634.

Employment Service. (1998). *British labour force statistics 1997.* London: HMSO.

England, P. (1982). The failure of human capital theory to explain occupational sex segregation. *Journal of Human Resources, 18,* 358-370.

England, P. (1984). Wage appreciation and depreciation: A test of neoclassical economic explanations of occupational sex segregation. *Social Forces, 62*(3), 726-749.

England, P. (1997). The sex gap in pay. In D. Dunn (Ed.), *Workplace/women's place: An anthology* (pp. 74-87). Los Angeles: Roxbury.

England, P., Farkas, G., Kilbourne, B. S., & Dou, T. (1988). Explaining occupational sex segregation and wages: Findings from a model with fixed effects. *American Sociological Review, 53*(4), 544-558.

England, P., Herbert, M. S., Kilbourne, B. S., Reid, L. L., & Medgal, L. M. (1994). The gendered valuation of occupations and skills: Earnings in 1980 census occupations. *Social Forces, 73*(1), 65-99.

Ensher, E. A., & Murphy, S. E. (1997). Effects of race, gender, perceived similarity, and contact on mentor relationships. *Journal of Vocational Behavior, 50,* 460-481.

Epstein, C. F. (1975). Institutional barriers: What keeps women out of the executive suite? In F. E. Gordon & M. H. Strober (Eds.), *Bringing women into management* (pp. 7-21). New York: McGraw-Hill.

Erickson, E. (1963). *Childhood and society.* New York: Norton.

Eriksen, T. H. (1996). Ethnicity, race, class and nation. In J. Hutchinson & A. D. Smith (Eds.), *Ethnicity* (pp. 28-31). Oxford, UK: Oxford University Press.

Erkut, S., & Mokros, J. R. (1984). Professors as models and mentors for college students. *American Educational Research Journal, 21*(2), 399-417.

Erwee, R. (1994). South African women: Changing career patterns. In N. J. Adler & D. N. Izraeli (Eds.), *Competitive frontiers: Women managers in a global economy* (pp. 325-342). Cambridge, MA: Blackwell.

Eskilson, A., & Wiley, M. G. (1976). Sex composition and leadership in small groups. *Sociometry, 39*(3), 183-194.

Essed, P. (1991). *Understanding everyday racism: An interdisciplinary theory.* Newbury Park, CA: Sage.

European Commission. (1997). *Youth in the European Union: From education to working life.* Luxembourg: Office for Publications of the European Communities.

Eurostat. (1997). *Demographic statistics.* Luxembourg: European Commission.

Evans, M. G. (1973). Notes on the impact of flexitime in a large insurance company. *Occupational Psychology, 47,* 237-401.

Evans, P. A. L., & Bartolome, F. (1980). *Must success cost so much?* New York: Basic Books.

Evans, P. A. L., & Bartolome, F. (1984). The changing pictures of the relationship between career and family. *Journal of Occupational Behaviour, 5,* 9-21.

Executive Order No. 8587, U.S., *Federal Register,* 13 Nov. 1940, pp. 4445-4448.

Executive Order No. 8802, U.S., *Federal Register,* 27 June 1941, p. 3109.

Executive Order No. 9980, U.S., *Federal Register,* 28 July 1948, pp. 4311-4313.

Executive Order No. 10925, U.S., *Federal Register,* 8 March 1961, pp. 1977-1979.

Executive Order No. 11246, U.S., *Federal Register,* 28 September 1965, pp. 12319-12325.

Executive Order No. 11375, U.S., *Federal Register,* 17 October 1967, pp. 14303-14304.

Fabowale, L., Orser, B., & Riding, A. (1995). Gender, structural factors, and credit terms between Canadian small businesses and financial institutions. *Entrepreneurship Theory and Practice, 19*(4), 41-65.

Fagenson, E. A. (1988). The power of a mentor: Protégés' and nonprotégés' perceptions of their own power in organizations. *Group and Organization Studies, 13,* 182-192.

Fagenson, E. A. (1989). The mentor advantage: Perceived career/job experiences of protégés vs. non-protégés. *Journal of Organizational Behavior, 10,* 309-320.

Fagenson, E. A. (1990). Perceived masculine and feminine attributes examined as a function of individuals' sex and level in the organizational power hierarchy: A test of four theoretical perspectives. *Journal of Applied Psychology, 75,* 204-211.

Fagenson, E. A. (1992). Mentoring—Who needs it? A comparison of protégés' and nonprotégés' needs for power, achievement, affiliation, and autonomy. *Journal of Vocational Behavior, 41,* 48-60.

Fagenson, E. A. (1993a). Personal value systems of men and women entrepreneurs versus managers. *Journal of Business Venturing, 8*(5), 409-430.

Fagenson, E. A. (Ed.). (1993b). *Women in management: Trends, issues, and challenges in managerial diversity.* Newbury Park, CA: Sage.

Fagenson, E. A., & Marcus, E. (1991). Perceptions of the sex role characteristics of entrepreneurs. *Entrepreneurship Theory and Practice, 15*(4), 33-47.

Fagenson-Eland, E. A., Marks, M. A., & Amendola, K. L. (1997). Perceptions of mentoring relationships. *Journal of Vocational Behavior, 51,* 29-42.

Fagnani, J. (1998). Helping mothers to combine paid and unpaid work–or fighting unemployment? The ambiguities of French family policy. *Community, Work and Family, 1*(3), 297-312.

Farley, R., & Allen, W. R. (1989). *The color line and the quality of life in America.* New York: Russell Sage.

Fassel, D. (1990). *Working ourselves to death: The high costs of workaholism and the rewards of recovery.* San Francisco: HarperCollins.

Federal Glass Ceiling Commission. (1995). *A solid investment: Making full use of the nation's human capital: Recommendations of the Federal Glass Ceiling Commission.* Washington, DC: U.S. Department of Labor, Glass Ceiling Commission.

Feild, H. S., & Holley, W. H. (1977). Subordinates' characteristics, supervisors' ratings, and decisions to discuss appraisal results. *Academy of Management Journal, 20,* 315-321.

Feingold, A. (1994). Gender differences in personality: A meta-analysis. *Psychological Bulletin, 116,* 429-456.

Feldman, S. (1988). Structure and consistency in public opinion: The role of core beliefs and values. *American Journal of Political Science, 32,* 416-440.

Felsenthal, E. (1998, March 5). Justices' ruling further defines sexual harassment. *Wall Street Journal,* pp. B1-B2.

Ferdman, B. M. (1990). Literacy and cultural identity. *Harvard Educational Review, 60,* 181-204.

Ferdman, B. M. (1992). The dynamics of ethnic diversity in organizations. In K. Kelley (Ed.), *Issues, theory and research in industrial/organizational psychology* (pp. 339-384). Amsterdam: North Holland.

Ferdman, B. M. (1995). Cultural identity and diversity in organizations: Bridging the gap between group differences and individual uniqueness. In M. Chemers, S. Oskamp, & M. A. Costanzo (Eds.), *Diversity in organizations: New perspectives for a changing workplace* (pp. 37-61). Thousand Oaks, CA: Sage.

Ferdman, B. M. (1997). Values about fairness in the ethnically diverse workplace. *Business and the Contemporary World, 9*(1), 191-208.

Ferdman, B. M., & Brody, S. E. (1996). Models of diversity training. In D. Landis & R. S. Bhagat (Eds.), *Handbook of intercultural training* (2nd ed., pp. 282-303). Thousand Oaks, CA: Sage.

Ferdman, B. M., & Horenczyk, G. (in press). Cultural identity and immigration: Reconstructing the group during cultural transitions. In E. Olshtain & G. Horenczyk (Eds.), *Language, identity, and immigration.* Jerusalem: Magnes.

Ferguson, K. (1991, April 19). *Lessons from* Challenger (Symposium). GTE lectureship in technology and ethics, Binghamton, NY.

Ferguson, K. E. (1984). *The feminist case against bureaucracy.* Philadelphia: Temple University Press.

Ferrante, J., & Brown, P., Jr. (Eds.). (1998). *The social construction of race and ethnicity in the United States.* New York: Longman.

Ferree, M. M., & Hall, E. J. (1996). Rethinking stratification from a feminist perspective: Gender, race, and class in mainstream textbooks. *American Sociological Review, 61,* 929-950.

Ferree, M. M., & McQuillan, J. (1998). Gender-based pay gaps: Methodological and policy issues in university salary studies. *Gender & Society, 12*(1), 7-39.

Ferri, E. (Ed.). (1993). *Life at 33.* London: National Children's Bureau/ESRC & City University.

Fiedler, F. E. (1967). *A theory of leadership effectiveness.* New York: McGraw-Hill.

Fielden, S. L., & Davidson, M. J. (1996). Sources of stress in unemployed female managers—An exploratory study. *International Review of Women and Leadership, 2*(2), 73-97.

Fields, D. L., & Blum, T. C. (1997). Employee satisfaction in work groups with different gender composition. *Journal of Organizational Behavior, 18*(2), 181-196.

Fierman, J. (1993, September 6). Beating the midlife career crisis. *Fortune,* pp. 52-62.

Filardo, E. K. (1996). Gender patterns in African American and White adolescents' social interactions in same-race, mixed-gender groups. *Journal of Personality and Social Psychology, 71*, 71-82.

Filer, R. K. (1989). Occupational segregation, compensating differentials, and comparable worth. In R. T. Michael, H. I. Hartmann, & B. O'Farrell (Eds.), *Pay equity: Empirical inquiries* (pp. 153-170). Washington, DC: National Academy Press.

Fine, M. (1997). Witnessing whiteness. In M. Fine, L. Weis, L. C. Powell, & L. Mun Wong (Eds.), *Off White: Readings on race, power, and society* (pp. 57-65). New York: Routledge.

Fine, M., Weis, L., Addelston, J., & Marusza, J. (1997). (In)secure times: Constructing White working-class masculinities in the late 20th century. *Gender & Society, 11*, 52-68.

Fine, M., Weis, L., Powell, L. C., & Mun Wong, L. (Eds.). (1997). *Off White: Readings on race, power, and society.* New York: Routledge.

Finlay, F. (1990). *Mary Robinson: A president with a purpose.* Dublin, Ireland: O'Brien.

Fischer, E., Gainer, B., & Bristor, J. (1997). The sex of the service provider: Does it influence perceptions of service quality? *Journal of Retailing, 73*(3), 361-382.

Fischer, E., Gainer, B., & Bristor, J. (1998). Beauty salon and barbershop: Gendered servicescapes. In J. F. Sherry (Ed.), *Servicescapes* (pp. 565-590). Chicago: American Marketing Association.

Fischer, E. M., Reuber, A. R., & Dyke, L. S. (1993). A theoretical overview and extension of research on sex, gender, and entrepreneurship. *Journal of Business Venturing, 8*(2), 151-168.

Fisher, A. B. (1993, December 7). Japanese working women strike back. *Fortune*, p. 22.

Fisher, A. B. (1994, October 3). Getting comfortable with couples in the workplace. *Fortune*, pp. 138-144.

Fishman, J. A. (1989). *Language and ethnicity in minority sociolinguistic perspective.* Philadelphia: Multilingual Matters.

Fiske, S. T., & Neuberg, S. L. (1990). A continuum of impression formation from category-based to individuating processes: Influences of information and motivation on attention and interpretation. In M. P. Zanna (Ed.), *Advances in experimental social psychology* (Vol. 23, pp. 1-74). New York: Academic Press.

Fitt, L. W., & Newton, D. A. (1981). When the mentor is a man and the protégée is a woman. *Harvard Business Review, 59*, 56-60.

Fitzgerald, L. F. (1993). Sexual harassment: Violence against women in the workplace. *American Psychologist, 48*, 1070-1076.

Fitzgerald, L. F., Drasgow, F., Hulin, C. L., Gelfand, M. J., & Magley, V. J. (1997). Antecedents and consequences of sexual harassment in organizations: A test of an integrated model. *Journal of Applied Psychology, 82*(4), 578-589.

Fitzgerald, L. F., Gelfand, M. J., & Drasgow, F. (1995). Measuring sexual harassment: Theoretical and psychometric advances. *Basic and Applied Social Psychology, 17* [Special issue], 425-445.

Fitzgerald, L. F., & Shullman, S. L. (1993). Sexual harassment: A research analysis and agenda for the 1990s. *Journal of Vocational Behavior, 42*, 5-27.

Fitzgerald, L. F., Shullman, S. L., Bailey, N., Richards, M., Swecker, J., Gold, Y., Ormerod, M., & Weitzman, L. (1988). The incidence and dimensions of sexual harassment in academia and the workplace. *Journal of Vocational Behavior, 32*, 152-175.

Flax, J. (1987). Postmodernism and gender relations in feminist theory. *Signs: Journal of Women in Culture and Society, 12,* 621-643.

Foley, S. (1998). *The effects of the actual and perceived glass ceiling on perceptions of promotion fairness.* Unpublished doctoral dissertation, University of Connecticut.

Foley, S., & Powell, G. N. (1997). Reconceptualizing work-family conflict for business/marriage partners: A theoretical model. *Journal of Small Business Management, 35*(4), 36-47.

Foley, S., & Powell, G. N. (in press). Not all is fair in love and work: Coworkers' preferences for and responses to managerial interventions regarding workplace romances. *Journal of Organizational Behavior.*

Fondas, N. (1993). *The feminization of American management* (Working Paper No. 93-05). Riverside: University of California, Graduate School of Management.

Fondas, N. (1997). The origins of feminization. *Academy of Management Review, 22*(1), 257-282.

Ford Foundation. (1989). *Work and family responsibilities: Achieving a balance.* New York: Author.

Ford, J. K., Schmitt, N., Schechtman, S. L., Hults, B. M., & Doherty, M. L. (1989). Process tracing methods: Contributions, problems, and neglected research questions. *Organizational Behavior and Human Decision Processes, 43,* 75-117.

Foreign Press Center. (1986). *Japanese women yesterday and today.* Tokyo: Author.

Forsythe, S. M. (1990). Effect of applicant's clothing on interviewers' decision to hire. *Journal of Applied Social Psychology, 20,* 1579-1595.

Forthofer, M. S., Markman, H. J., Cox, M., Stanley, S., & Kessler, R. C. (1996). Associations between marital distress and work loss in a national sample. *Journal of Marriage and the Family, 58,* 597-605.

Foschi, M. (1992). Gender and double standards for competence. In C. L. Ridgeway (Ed.), *Gender, interaction, and inequality* (pp. 181-207). New York: Springer-Verlag.

Foschi, M. (1996). Double standards in the evaluation of men and women. *Social Psychology Quarterly, 59,* 237-254.

Foschi, M., Lai, L., & Sigerson, K. (1994). Gender and double standards in the assessment of job applicants. *Social Psychology Quarterly, 57,* 326-339.

Frank, E. J. (1988). Business students' perceptions of women in management. *Sex Roles, 19,* 107-118.

Frank, F. D., & Drucker, J. (1977). The influence of evaluatee's sex on evaluations of a response on a managerial selection instrument. *Sex Roles, 3,* 59-64.

Franklin, C. (1984). *The changing definition of masculinity.* New York: Plenum.

Frazee, V. (1997). Establishing relations in Germany. *Workforce—Global Workforce Supplement,* pp. 16-17.

Freedman, S. M., & Phillips, J. S. (1988). The changing nature of research on women at work. *Journal of Management, 14,* 231-251.

Freeman, J. (1979). *Women: A feminist perspective* (2nd ed.). Palo Alto, CA: Mayfield.

Fried, L. I. (1989). A new breed of entrepreneur—Women. *Management Review, 78*(12), 18-25.

Friedan, B. (1963). *The feminine mystique.* New York: Norton.

Friedman, D. (1988). *Linking work-family issues to the bottom line* (Report No. 962). New York: Conference Board.

Friedman, D. E., & Galinsky, E. (1992). Work and family issues: A legitimate business concern. In S. Zedeck (Ed.), *Work, families, and organizations* (pp. 168-207). San Francisco: Jossey-Bass.

Friedman, S. D., DeGroot, J., & Christensen, P. (Eds.). (1998). *Integrating work and life: The Wharton resource guide.* San Francisco: Jossey-Bass/Pfeiffer.

Friedman, S. D., & Greenhaus, J. H. (in press). *Allies or enemies? How choices about work and family affect the quality of men's and women's lives.* New York: Oxford University Press.

Frieze, I. H., & McHugh, M. C. (Eds.). (1997). Measuring beliefs about appropriate roles for men and women [Special issue]. *Psychology of Women Quarterly, 21*(1).

Frone, M. R., & Rice, R. W. (1987). Work-family conflict: The effect of job and family involvement. *Journal of Occupational Behaviour, 8,* 45-53.

Frone, M. R., Russell, M., & Cooper, M. L. (1990). *Occupational stressors, psychological resources and psychological distress: A comparison of Black and White workers.* Paper presented at the annual meeting of the Academy of Management, San Francisco.

Frone, M. R., Russell, M., & Cooper, M. L. (1992a). Antecedents and outcomes of work-family conflict: Testing a model of the work-family interface. *Journal of Applied Psychology, 77,* 65-78.

Frone, M. R., Russell, M., & Cooper, M. L. (1992b). Prevalence of work-family conflict: Are work and family boundaries asymmetrically permeable? *Journal of Organizational Behavior, 13,* 723-729.

Frone, M. R., Russell, M., & Cooper, M. L. (1993). Relationship of work-family conflict, gender, and alcohol expectancies to alcohol use/abuse. *Journal of Organizational Behavior, 14,* 545-558.

Frone, M. R., Yardley, J. K., & Markel, K. S. (1997). Developing and testing an integrative model of the work-family interface. *Journal of Vocational Behavior, 50,* 145-167.

Frosh, S. (1987). *The politics of psychoanalysis: An introduction to Freudian and post-Freudian theory.* London: Macmillan Educational.

Frost, P., Mitchell, V., & Nord, W. (1997). *Organizational reality: Reports from the firing line* (4th ed., rev.). Reading, MA: Addison-Wesley.

Frye, M. (1983). *The politics of reality: Essays in feminist theory.* Freedom, CA: Crossing.

Fuller, F. F. (1964). Preferences for male and female counselors. *Personnel and Guidance Journal, 42,* 463-467.

Fullilove v. Klutznick, 448 U.S. 448 (1980).

Gaines, S. O., Jr., Barájas, L., Hicks, D., Lyde, M., Takahashi, Y., Yum, N., García, B. F., Marelich, W. D., Bledsoe, K. L., Steers, W. N., Henderson, M. C., Granrose, C. S., Ríos, D. I., Farris, K. R., & Page, M. S. (1997). Links between race/ethnicity and cultural values as mediated by racial/ethnic identity and moderated by gender. *Journal of Personality and Social Psychology, 72,* 1460-1476.

Galen, M., Schiller, Z., Hamilton, J., & Hammonds, K. H. (1991, March). Ending sexual harassment: Business is getting the message. *Business Week,* pp. 98-100.

Gallois, C., Callan, V. J., & Palmer, J. (1992). The influence of applicant communication style and interviewer characteristics on hiring decisions. *Journal of Applied Social Psychology, 22,* 1041-1060.

Gallos, J. V. (1989). Exploring women's development: Implications for career theory, practice, and research. In M. B. Arthur, D. T. Hall, & B. S. Lawrence (Eds.),

Handbook of career theory (pp. 110-132). Cambridge, UK: Cambridge University Press.

Garcia, J. L. A. (1997). Racism as a model for understanding sexism. In N. Zack (Ed.), *Race/sex: Their sameness, difference, and interplay* (pp. 45-59). New York: Routledge.

Garcia, L. T., Erskine, N., Hawn, K., & Casmay, S. R. (1981). The effect of affirmative action on attributions about minority group members. *Journal of Personality, 49,* 427-437.

Gardner, H. (1995). *Leading minds: An anatomy of leadership.* New York: Basic Books.

Garland, H., & Price, K. H. (1977). Attitudes toward women in management and attributions for their success or failure in a managerial position. *Journal of Applied Psychology, 62,* 29-33.

Gartner, W. B. (1985). A conceptual framework for describing the phenomenon of new venture creation. *Academy of Management Review, 10*(4), 696-706.

Gartner, W. B., Shaver, K. G., Gatewood, E., & Katz, J. A. (1994). Finding the entrepreneur in entrepreneurship. *Entrepreneurship Theory and Practice, 18*(3), 5-9.

Gaskill, L. R. (1991). Same-sex and cross-sex mentoring of female protégés: A comparative analysis. *Career Development Quarterly, 40,* 48-63.

Gaskill, L. R., & Sibley, L. R. (1990). Mentoring relationships for women in retailing: Prevalence, perceived importance, and characteristics. *Clothing and Textile Research Journal, 9,* 1-10.

Gatewood, E. J., Shaver, K. G., & Gartner, W. B. (1995). A longitudinal study of cognitive factors influencing start-up behaviors and success at venture creation. *Journal of Business Venturing, 10*(5), 371-391.

Gay, C., & Tate, K. (1998). Doubly bound: The impact of gender and race on the politics of Black women. *Political Psychology, 19,* 169-184.

Geis, F. L. (1993). Self-fulfilling prophecies: A social psychological view of gender. In A. E. Beall & R. J. Sternberg (Eds.), *The psychology of gender* (pp. 9-54). New York: Guilford.

Gelfand, M. J., Fitzgerald, L. F., & Drasgow, F. (1995). The structure of sexual harassment: A confirmatory analysis across cultures and settings. *Journal of Vocational Behavior, 47,* 164-177.

Gender and management. (1996). *Monthly Labor Review, 119*(12), 84.

Gentile, D. A. (1993). Just what are sex and gender anyway? A call for a new terminological standard. *Psychological Science, 4,* 120-122.

Gentile, M. C. (1996). Managerial effectiveness and diversity: Organizational choices. In M. C. Gentile, *Managerial excellence through diversity* (pp. 225-255). Chicago: Irwin.

Gerson, K. (1993). *No man's land: Men's changing commitments to family and work.* New York: Basic Books.

Giaciolone, R. A., & Riordan, C. A. (1990). Effect of self-presentation on perceptions and recognition in an organization. *Journal of Psychology, 124,* 25-38.

Giannantonio, C. M., Olian, J. D., & Carroll, S. J. (1995). An experimental study of gender and situational effects in a performance evaluation of a manager. *Psychological Reports, 76,* 1004-1006.

Gibbs, N. (1997, June 2). Wings of desire. *Time,* pp. 28-34.

Gibson, C. B. (1995). An investigation of leadership across four countries. *Journal of International Business Studies, 26,* 255-276.

Gibson, C. K., & Swan, J. E. (1981). Sex roles and the desirability of job rewards, expectations, and aspirations of male versus female salespeople. *Journal of Personal Selling & Sales Management, 2,* 39-45.

Gilbert, B. J., Heesacker, M., & Gannon, L. J. (1991). Changing the sexual aggression-supportive attitudes of men: A psycho-educational intervention. *Journal of Counseling Psychology, 38,* 197-203.

Gilbert, L. A. (1994). Reclaiming and returning gender to context. *Psychology of Women Quarterly, 18,* 539-558.

Gilligan, C. (1982). *In a different voice: Psychological theory and women's development.* Cambridge, MA: Harvard University Press.

Gioia, D. A., & Pitre, E. (1990). Multiparadigm perspectives on theory building. *Academy of Management Review, 15,* 584-602.

Gist, M., & Mitchell, T. (1992). Self-efficacy: A theoretical analysis of its dimensions and malleability. *Academy of Management Review, 17,* 183-211.

Giving women the business: On winning, losing, and leaving the corporate game. (1997). *Harper's Magazine, 294, 1771,* 47-58.

Glazer, J. (1997). Beyond male theory: A feminist perspective on teaching motivation. In J. L. Bess (Ed.), *Teaching well and liking it: Motivating faculty to teach effectively* (pp. 37-54). Baltimore: Johns Hopkins University Press.

Glennon, L. M. (1979). *Women and dualism.* New York: Longman.

Glick, P. (1991). Trait-based and sex-based discrimination in occupational prestige, occupational salary, and hiring. *Sex Roles, 25,* 351-378.

Glick, P., & Fiske, S. (1996). The Ambivalent Sexism Inventory: Differentiating hostile and benevolent sexism. *Journal of Personality and Social Psychology, 70,* 491-512.

Glick, P., Zion, C., & Nelson, C. (1988). What mediates sex discrimination in hiring decisions? *Journal of Personality and Social Psychology, 55,* 178-186.

Glomb, T. M., Richman, W. L., Hulin, C. L., Drasgow, F., Schneider, K. T., & Fitzgerald, L. F. (1997). Ambient sexual harassment: An integrated model of antecedents and consequences. *Organizational Behavior and Human Decision Processes, 71,* 309-328.

Godfrey, J. (1996). Mind of the manager. *Inc., 18*(3), 21.

Goff, S. J., Mount, M. K., & Jamison, R. L. (1990). Employer supported child care, work/family conflict, and absenteeism: A field study. *Personnel Psychology, 43*(4), 793-809.

Goh, S. C. (1991). Sex differences in perceptions of interpersonal work style, career emphasis, supervisory mentoring behavior, and job satisfaction. *Sex Roles, 24,* 701-710.

Goktepe, J. R., & Schneier, C. E. (1988). Sex and gender effects in evaluating emergent leaders in small groups. *Sex Roles, 19,* 29-36.

Goldberg, P. (1968). Are women prejudiced against women? *Transaction, 5,* 316-322.

Goldberg, S. (1993). *Why men rule: A theory of male dominance.* Chicago: Open Court.

Goldin, C. (1990). *Understanding the gender gap: An economic history of American women.* New York: Oxford University Press.

Goldstein, E. (1979). Effects of same-sex and cross-sex role models on the subsequent academic activity of scholars. *American Psychologist, 34*(5), 407-410.

Golembiewski, R. T., Hilles, R., & Kagno, M. S. (1974). A longitudinal study of flexitime effects: Some consequences of an OD structural intervention. *Journal of Applied Behavioral Science, 10*, 503-532.

Golembiewski, R. T., Yeager, S., & Hilles, R. (1976). Some attitudinal consequences of a flexitime installation. In R. H. Kilmann, L. R. Pondy, & D. P. Slevin (Eds.), *Management of organization design* (Vol. 2). New York: North-Holland.

Gonyea, J., & Googins, B. (1996). The restructuring of work and family in the United States: A new challenge for American corporations. In S. Lewis & J. Lewis (Eds.), *The work-family challenge: Rethinking employment* (pp. 63-78). London: Sage.

Goodman, J. S., Fields, D. L., & Blum, T. C. (1995, August). *An organizational level study of the glass ceiling.* Paper presented at the annual meeting of the Academy of Management, Vancouver, BC, Canada.

Goodwin, D. K. (1995). *No ordinary time: Franklin & Eleanor Roosevelt: The home front in World War II.* New York: Simon & Schuster.

Gordon, J. R., & Whelan, K. S. (1998). Successful professional women in midlife: How organizations can more effectively understand and respond to the challenges. *Academy of Management Executive, 12*(1), 8-27.

Gordon, S. (1990). *Prisoners of men's dreams: Striking out for a new feminine future.* Boston: Little, Brown.

Gornick, J. C., & Jacobs, J. A. (1998). Gender, the welfare state, and public employment: A comparative study of seven industrialized countries. *American Sociological Review, 63*(5), 688-710.

Gottfried, H., & Graham, L. (1993). Constructing difference: The making of gendered subcultures in a Japanese automobile assembly plant. *Sociology: The Journal of the British Sociological Association, 27*, 611-628.

Gould, S., & Werbel, J. D. (1983). Work involvement: A comparison of dual wage earner and single wage earner families. *Journal of Applied Psychology, 68*, 313-319.

Gowan, M. A., & Zimmerman, R. A. (1996). Impact of ethnicity, gender, and previous experience on juror judgments in sexual harassment cases. *Journal of Applied Social Psychology, 26*, 596-617.

Grace, N. M. (1995). *The feminized male character in twentieth-century literature.* Lewiston, NY: Edwin Mellen.

Grady, K. E. (1981). Sex bias in research design. *Psychology of Women Quarterly, 5*, 628-636.

Graham, H. D. (1992). The origins of affirmative action: Civil rights and the regulatory state. *Annals of the American Academy of Political and Social Science, 523*, 50-62.

Graham, M. E., & Welbourne, T. M. (in press). Gainsharing and the relative pay satisfaction of women and men. *Journal of Organizational Behavior.*

Grant, J. (1988). Women as managers: What can they offer organizations? *Organizational Dynamics, 16*, 56-63.

Graves, L. M. (1993). Sources of individual differences in interviewer effectiveness: A model and implications for future research. *Journal of Organizational Behavior, 14*, 349-370.

Graves, L. M., & Powell, G. N. (1988). An investigation of sex discrimination in recruiters' evaluations of actual applicants. *Journal of Applied Psychology, 73*, 20-29.

Graves, L. M., & Powell, G. N. (1994). Effects of sex-based preferential selection and discrimination on job attitudes. *Human Relations, 47*, 133-156.

Graves, L. M., & Powell, G. N. (1995). The effect of sex similarity on recruiters' evaluations of actual applicants: A test of the similarity-attraction paradigm. *Personnel Psychology, 48*(1), 85-98.

Graves, L. M., & Powell, G. N. (1996). Sex similarity, quality of the employment interview and recruiters' evaluations of actual applicants. *Journal of Occupational and Organizational Psychology, 69,* 243-261.

Green v. County School Board, 391 U.S. 430, 441 (1968).

Green, S. G., & Bauer, T. N. (1995). Supervisory mentoring by advisers: Relationships with doctoral student potential, productivity, and commitment. *Personnel Psychology, 48,* 537-561.

Greenberg, J. (1996). *The quest for justice on the job: Essays and experiments.* Thousand Oaks, CA: Sage.

Greenberger, E., Goldberg, W. A., Hamill, S., O'Neil, R., & Payne, C. K. (1989). Contributions of a supportive work environment to parents' well-being and orientation to work. *American Journal of Community Psychology, 17,* 755-783.

Greenberger, E., & O'Neil, R. (1993). Spouse, parent, worker: Role commitments and role-related experiences in the construction of adults' well-being. *Developmental Psychology, 29,* 181-197.

Greenglass, E. R. (1993a). The contribution of social support to coping strategies. *Applied Psychology: An International Review, 42*(4), 323-340.

Greenglass, E. R. (1993b). Structural and social-psychological factors associated with job functioning by women managers. *Psychological Reports, 73*(3), 979-986.

Greenhaus, J. H. (1989). The intersection of work and family roles: Individual, interpersonal, and organizational issues. In E. Goldsmith (Ed.), *Work and family: Theory, research, and applications* (pp. 23-44). Newbury Park, CA: Sage.

Greenhaus, J. H., & Beutell, N. J. (1985). Sources of conflict between work and family roles. *Academy of Management Review, 10,* 76-88.

Greenhaus, J. H., Collins, K. M., Singh, R., & Parasuraman, S. (1997). Work and family influences on departure from public accounting. *Journal of Vocational Behavior, 50,* 249-270.

Greenhaus, J. H., & Parasuraman, S. (1994). Work-family conflict, social support, and well-being. In M. J. Davidson & R. J. Burke (Eds.), *Women in management: Current research issues* (pp. 213-229). London: Paul Chapman.

Greenhaus, J. H., Parasuraman, S., Granrose, C. S., Rabinowitz, S., & Beutell, N. J. (1989). Sources of work-family conflict among two-career couples. *Journal of Vocational Behavior, 34,* 133-153.

Greenhaus, J. H., Parasuraman, S., & Wormley, W. M. (1990). Effects of race on organizational experiences, job performance, evaluation and career outcomes. *Academy of Management Review, 33*(1), 66-86.

Greenleaf, R. K. (1998). *The power of servant leadership.* San Francisco: Berrett-Koehler.

Gregg, G. (1985). Woman entrepreneurs: The second generation. *Across the Board,* pp. 10-18.

Gregory, R. G., Anstie, R., Daly, A., & Ho, V. (1989). Women's pay in Australia, Great Britain, and the United States: The role of laws, regulations, and human capital. In R. T. Michael, H. I. Hartmann, & B. O'Farrell (Eds.), *Pay equity: Empirical inquiries* (pp. 222-242). Washington, DC: National Academy Press.

Greller, M., & Stroh, L. K. (1995). A fallow field in need of sustenance. *Journal of Vocational Behavior, 47,* 232-247.

Griffeth, R. W., & Bedeian, A. G. (1989). Employee performance evaluations: Effects of ratee age, rater age, and ratee gender. *Journal of Organizational Behavior, 10,* 83-90.

Griffin, R., & Kacmar, K. M. (1991). Laboratory research in management: Misconceptions and missed opportunities. *Journal of Organizational Behavior, 12,* 301-311.

Grönroos, C. (1983). *A service quality model and its management implications.* Helsinki, Finland: Swedish School of Economics.

Grönroos, C. (1990). *Service marketing and management.* Toronto, ON: Lexington Books.

Grover, S. L., & Crooker, K. J. (1995). Who appreciates family-responsive human resource policies? The impact of family-friendly policies on the organizational attachment of parents and non-parents. *Personnel Psychology, 48,* 271-288.

Gruber, J. E. (1992). A typology of personal and environmental sexual harassment: Research and policy implications for the 1990s. *Sex Roles, 26,* 447-464.

Gruber, J. E., & Bjorn, L. (1982). Blue-collar blues: The sexual harassment of women autoworkers. *Work and Occupations, 9,* 271-298.

Gruber, J. E., & Bjorn, L. (1986). Women's responses to sexual harassment: An analysis of sociocultural, organizational, and personal resource models. *Social Science Quarterly, 67,* pp. 814-826.

Gruber, J. E., Smith, M., & Kauppinen-Toropainen, K. (1995). Sexual harassment types and severity: Linking research and policy. In M. S. Stockdale (Ed.), *Sexual harassment: Perspectives, frontiers, and response strategies* (Vol. 5, pp. 151-173). Thousand Oaks, CA: Sage.

Guba, E. G., & Lincoln, Y. S. (1994). Competing paradigms in qualitative research. In N. K. Denzin & Y. S. Lincoln (Eds.), *Handbook of qualitative research* (pp. 105-117). Newbury Park, CA: Sage.

Guest, D., & Mackenzie-Davies, K. (1996). Don't write off the traditional career. *People Management, 2*(4), 22-25.

Gumbiner, J. (1998). Professors as models and mentors: Does gender matter? *Psychological Reports, 82,* 94.

Gundry, L. K., Kowlake, C., & Robertson, B. L. (1992). Women-owned businesses in start-up and growth stages: A comparison of information needs and performance. In D. Naffziger & J. Hornsby, *United States Association of Small Business and Entrepreneurship proceedings: Emerging entrepreneurial strategies in the 1990s* (pp. 184-191). Muncie, IN: Ball State University.

Gundry, L. K., & Welsch, H. P. (1993). Differences in familial influence among women-owned businesses. In R. G. Russell (Ed.), *United States Association of Small Business and Entrepreneurship proceedings: Preparing the entrepreneur for 2000 and beyond* (pp. 103-110). Harrisburg, PA: Penn State University.

Guppy, A., & Rick, J. (1996). The influence of gender and grade on perceived work stress and job satisfaction in white collar employees. *Work & Stress, 10*(2), 154-164.

Gurman, E. B., & Long, K. (1992). Emergent leadership and female sex role identity. *Journal of Psychology, 126,* 309-316.

Gurr, T. R. (1970). *Why men rebel.* Princeton, NJ: Princeton University Press.

Gutek, B. A. (1985). *Sex and the workplace: The impact of sexual behavior and harassment on women, men, and organizations.* San Francisco: Jossey-Bass.

Gutek, B. A. (1993). Sexual harassment: Rights and responsibilities. *Employee Responsibilities and Rights Journal, 6,* 325-340.

Gutek, B. A. (1995). *The dynamics of service: Reflections on the changing nature of customer/provider interactions.* San Francisco: Jossey-Bass.

Gutek, B. A., Bhappu, A. D., Liao-Troth, M. A., & Cherry, B. (1999). Distinguishing between service relationships and encounters. *Journal of Applied Psychology, 84*(2).

Gutek, B. A., Cohen, A. G., & Konrad, A. M. (1990). Predicting social-sexual behavior at work: A contact hypothesis. *Academy of Management Journal, 33*(3), 560-577.

Gutek, B. A., & Koss, M. P. (1993). Changed women and changed organizations: Consequences of and coping with sexual harassment. *Journal of Vocational Behavior, 42,* 28-48.

Gutek, B. A., & Morasch, B. (1982). Sex-ratios, sex-role spillover, and sexual harassment at work. *Journal of Social Issues, 38,* 55-74.

Gutek, B. A., Morasch, B., & Cohen, A. G. (1983). Interpreting social-sexual behavior in a work setting. *Journal of Vocational Behavior, 22,* 30-48.

Gutek, B. A., Searle, S., & Klepa, L. (1991). Rational versus gender role explanations for work-family conflict. *Journal of Applied Psychology, 76,* 560-568.

Haccoun, D. M., Haccoun, R. R., & Sallay, G. (1978). Sex differences in the appropriateness of supervisory styles: A nonmanagement view. *Journal of Applied Psychology, 63,* 124-127.

Hacker, A. (1992). *Two nations.* New York: Macmillan.

Haddon, L., & Silverstone, R. (1993). *Teleworking in the 1990s: A view from the home.* (SPRU CICT Report No. 10). Sussex, UK: SPRU University of Sussex, CICT.

Halatin, T. J., & Knotts, R. E. (1982). Becoming a mentor: Are the risks worth the rewards? *Supervisory Management, 27*(2), 27-29.

Hall v. Gus Construction Company, 842 F.2d 1010 (8th Cir. 1988).

Hall, D. T. (1990). Promoting work/family balance: An organization change approach. *Organizational Dynamics, 18*(3), 5-18.

Hall, D. T., & Mirvis, P. H. (1995). The new career contract: Development of the whole person at midlife and beyond. *Journal of Vocational Behavior, 47,* 269-289.

Hall, D. T., & Richter, J. (1990). Career gridlock: Baby boomers hit the wall. *Academy of Management Executive, 4*(3), 7-22.

Hall, E. J. (1993). Smiling, deferring, and flirting. *Work and Occupations, 20*(4), 452-471.

Hall, F. S., & Hall, D. T. (1976). Effects of job incumbents' race and sex on evaluations of managerial performance. *Academy of Management Journal, 19,* 476-481.

Hall, J. (1984). *Nonverbal sex differences: Communication accuracy and expressive style.* Baltimore: Johns Hopkins University Press.

Hames, D. S. (1994). Disciplining sexual harassers: What's fair? *Employee Responsibilities and Rights Journal, 7,* 207-217.

Hammarstrom, A., & Janlert, U. (1994). Unemployment and change of tobacco habits: A study of young people from 16 to 21 years of age. *Addiction, 89,* 1691-1696.

Hammer, L. B., Allen, E., & Grigsby, T. D. (1997). Work-family conflict in dual-earner couples: Within-individual and crossover effects of work and family. *Journal of Vocational Behavior, 50,* 185-203.

Hammond, V. (1988). Women in management in Great Britain. In N. J. Adler & D. N. Izraeli (Eds.), *Women in management worldwide* (pp. 168-185). Armonk, NY: M. E. Sharpe.

Hammond, V., & Holton, V. (1994). The scenario for women managers in Britain in the 1990s. In N. J. Adler & D. N. Izraeli (Eds.), *Competitive frontiers: Women managers in a global economy* (pp. 224-242). Cambridge, MA: Blackwell.

Hammonds, K. (1996). Balancing work and family. *Business Week, 3493,* 74-80.

Hammonds, K. (1997, July 21). A close-up at Corning: It's the home-wrecking company in a new book, but improving. *Business Week,* pp. 93, 96.

Hamner, W. C., Kim, J. S., Baird, L., & Bigoness, W. J. (1974). Race and sex as determinants of ratings by potential employers in a simulated work-sampling task. *Journal of Applied Psychology, 59,* 705-711.

Hampden-Turner, C. (1994). The structure of entrapment: Dilemmas standing in the way of women managers and strategies to resolve these. *The Deeper News: Global Business Network Publication, 5*(1), 3-42.

Handy, C. (1989). *The age of unreason.* Boston: Harvard Business School Press.

Hansen, J. C., Collins, R. C., Swanson, J. C., & Fouad, N. A. (1993). Gender differences in the structure of interests. *Journal of Vocational Behavior, 42,* 200-211.

Harding, S. (1986). *The science question in feminism.* Ithaca, NY: Cornell University Press.

Hare-Mustin, R., & Marecek, J. (1986). Autonomy and gender: Some questions for therapists. *Psychotherapy, 23,* 205-212.

Harley, S. (1997). Speaking up: The politics of Black women's labor history. In E. Higginbotham & M. Romero (Eds.), *Women and work: Exploring race, ethnicity, and class* (pp. 28-51). Thousand Oaks, CA: Sage.

Harman, S. J., Griffeth, R. W., Crino, M. D., & Harris, O. J. (1991). Gender-based influences: The promotion recommendation. *Sex Roles, 25,* 285-300.

Harrick, E. J., Vanek, G. R., & Michlitsch, J. F. (1986, Summer). Alternate work schedules, productivity, leave usage, and employee attitudes: A field study. *Public Personnel Management, 15*(2), 159-169.

Harriman, A. (1985). *Women/men, management.* New York: Praeger.

Harris v. Forklift Systems Inc., U.S. Sup. Ct., 63 FEP Cases 225 (1993).

Harris, L. (1995). *Women: The new providers.* (Whirlpool Foundation study). New York: Families and Work Institute.

Harris, M. M. (1989). Reconsidering the employment interview: A review of recent literature and suggestions for future research. *Personnel Psychology, 42,* 691-726.

Harrison, D. A., Price, K. H., & Bell, M. P. (1998). Beyond relational demography: Time and the effects of surface- and deep-level diversity on work group cohesion. *Academy of Management Journal, 41,* 96-107.

Hartsock, N. C. (1983). *Money, sex, and power: Toward a feminist historical materialism.* New York: Longman.

Hassard, J. (1993). Postmodernism and organizational analysis: An overview. In J. Hassard & M. Parker (Eds.), *Postmodernism and organizations.* London: Sage.

Havel, V. (1994, July 8). The new measure of man. *New York Times,* p. A27.

Hawkins, K. W. (1995). Effects of gender and communication content of leadership emergence in small task-oriented groups. *Small Group Research, 26,* 234-249.

Hawthorne, F. (1993). Why family leave shouldn't scare employers. *Institutional Investor, 27,* 31-34.

Haynes, S. G., & Feinleib, M. (1980). Women, work and coronary heart disease: Heart study. *American Journal of Public Health, 70,* 133-141.

Hearn, J., & Parkin, P. W. (1988). Women, men, and leadership: A critical review of assumptions, practices, and change in the industrialized nations. In N. J. Adler & D. N. Izraeli (Eds.), *Women in management worldwide* (pp. 17-40). Armonk, NY: M. E. Sharpe.

Hearn, J., Sheppard, D., Tancred-Sheriff, P., & Burrell, G. (Eds.). (1989). *The sexuality of organization.* Newbury Park, CA: Sage.

Heatherington, L., Daubman, K. A., Bates, C., Ahn, A., Brown, H., & Preston, C. (1993). Tow investigations of "female modesty" in achievement situations. *Sex Roles, 29,* 739-754.

Heilman, M. E. (1980). The impact of situational factors on personnel decisions concerning women: Varying the sex composition of the applicant pool. *Organizational Behavior and Human Performance, 26,* 386-395.

Heilman, M. E. (1995). Sex stereotypes and their effects in the workplace: What we know and what we don't know. *Journal of Social Behavior and Personality, 10,* 3-26. [Special issue: Gender in the workplace]

Heilman, M. E., Block, C. J., & Lucas, J. A. (1992). Presumed incompetent? Stigmatization and affirmative action efforts. *Journal of Applied Psychology, 77,* 536-544.

Heilman, M. E., Block, C. J., & Martell, R. F. (1995). Sex stereotypes: Do they influence perceptions of managers? *Journal of Social Behavior and Personality, 10,* 237-252.

Heilman, M. E., Block, C. J., Martell, R. F., & Simon, M. C. (1989). Has anything changed? Current characterizations of men, women, and managers. *Journal of Applied Psychology, 74,* 935-942.

Heilman, M. E., Block, C. J., & Stathatos, P. (1997). The affirmative action stigma of incompetence: Effects of performance information ambiguity. *Academy of Management Journal, 40,* 603-625.

Heilman, M. E., Lucas, J. A., & Kaplow, S. R. (1990). Self-derogating consequences of sex-based preferential selection: The moderating role of initial self-confidence. *Organizational Behavior and Human Decision Processes, 46,* 202-216.

Heilman, M. E., McCullough, W. F., & Gilbert, D. (1996). The other side of affirmative action: Reactions of nonbeneficiaries to sex-based preferential selection. *Journal of Applied Psychology, 81,* 346-357.

Heilman, M. E., Rivero, J. C., & Brett, J. F. (1991). Skirting the competence issue: Effects of sex-based preferential selection on task choices of women and men. *Journal of Applied Psychology, 76,* 99-103.

Heilman, M. E., & Saruwatari, L. R. (1979). When beauty is beastly: The effects of appearance and sex on evaluations of job applicants for managerial and nonmanagerial jobs. *Organizational Behavior and Human Performance, 23,* 360-372.

Heilman, M. E., Simon, M. C., & Repper, D. P. (1987). Intentionally favored, unintentionally harmed? Impact of sex-based preferential selection on self-perceptions and self-evaluations. *Journal of Applied Psychology, 72,* 62-68.

Helgesen, S. (1990). *The female advantage: Women's ways of leadership.* New York: Doubleday Currency.

Helgesen, S. (1995). *The web of inclusion.* New York: Doubleday.

Helms, J. E. (1995). An update of Helms's White and people of color racial identity models. In J. Ponterotto, J. M. Casas, L. A. Suzuki, & C. M. Alexander (Eds.), *Handbook of multicultural counseling* (pp. 181-198). Thousand Oaks, CA: Sage.

Helms, J. E. (1996). Toward a methodology for measuring and assessing racial as distinguished from ethnic identity. In G. Sodowsky & J. Impara (Eds.), *Multi-*

cultural assessment in counseling and clinical psychology (pp. 143-192). Lincoln, NE: Buros Institute.

Hennig, M., & Jardim, A. (1977). *The managerial woman.* Garden City, NY: Anchor.

Herek, G. M. (1993). Sexual orientation and military service: A social science perspective. *American Psychologist, 48,* 538-549.

Herring, C., & Collins, S. M. (1995). Retreat from equal opportunity? The case of affirmative action. In M. P. Smith & J. R. Feagin (Eds.), *The bubbling cauldron: Race, ethnicity and the urban crisis* (pp. 163-181). Minneapolis: University of Minnesota Press.

Hersey, P., & Blanchard, K. (1988). *The management of organizational behavior* (5th ed.). Englewood Cliffs, NJ: Prentice Hall.

Hesselbein, F., Goldsmith, M., & Beckhard, R. (Eds.). (1996). *The leader of the future.* San Francisco: Jossey-Bass.

Hewitt, P. (1991). The place of part time employment. In P. Meadows (Ed.), *Work out or work in? Contributions to the debate on the future of work* (pp. 39-58). York, UK: Joseph Rowntree Foundation.

Hewlett, S., & West, C. (1998). *The war against parents: What we can do for America's beleaguered moms and dads.* New York: Houghton Mifflin.

Hewstone, M., & Brown, R. (1986). *Contact and conflict in intergroup relations.* New York: Blackwell.

Higginbotham, E. (1997). Introduction. In E. Higginbotham & M. Romero (Eds.), *Women and work: Exploring race, ethnicity, and class* (pp. xv-xxxii). Thousand Oaks, CA: Sage.

Higginbotham, E., & Romero, M. (Eds.). (1997). *Women and work: Exploring race, ethnicity, and class.* Thousand Oaks, CA: Sage.

Higgins, C. A., Duxbury, L. E., & Irving, R. H. (1992). Work-family conflict in the dual-career family. *Organizational Behavior and Human Decision Processes, 51,* 51-75.

Higuchi, Y., Waldfogel, J., & Abe, M. (1998, January). *Family leave and women's earnings in the United States, Britain, and Japan.* Paper presented at the meeting of the American Economic Association, Chicago.

Hill, A. (1997). *Speaking truth to power.* New York: Doubleday.

Hill, E. J., Hawkins, A. J., & Miller, B. C. (1996). Work and family in the virtual office: Perceived influences of mobile telework. *Family Relations, 45*(3), 293-301.

Hill, M. S. (1979). The wage effects of marital status and children. *Journal of Human Resources, 14,* 579-593.

Hill, S. E. K., Bahniuk, M. H., & Dobos, J. (1989). The impact of mentoring and collegial support on faculty success: An analysis of support behavior, information adequacy, and communication apprehension. *Communication Education, 38,* 15-33.

Himelstein, L. (1996, October 28). Shatterproof glass ceiling. *Business Week,* p. 55.

Hines, M. (1993). Hormonal and neural correlates of sex-typed behavioral development in human beings. In M. Haug, R. E. Whalen, C. Aron, & K. L. Olsen (Eds.), *The development of sex differences and similarities in behavior* (pp. 131-149). Dordrecht, the Netherlands: Kluwer Academic.

Hisrich, R. D., & Brush, C. G. (1984). The woman entrepreneur: Management skills and business problems. *Journal of Small Business Management, 22*(1), 30-37.

Hisrich, R. D., & Brush, C. G. (1987). Women entrepreneurs: A longitudinal study. In N. C. Churchill, J. A. Hornaday, B. A. Kirchoff, O. J. Krasner, & K. H. Vesper (Eds.), *Frontiers of entrepreneurship research* (pp. 187-189). Wellesley, MA: Center for Entrepreneurial Studies, Babson College.

Hisrich, R. D., Koiranen, M., & Hyrsky, K. (1996). A comparison of men and women entrepreneurs: A cross-national exploratory study. In W. D. Bygrave, B. J. Bird, S. Birley, N. C. Churchill, M. G. Hay, R. H. Kelley, & W. E. Wetzel, Jr. (Eds.), *Frontiers of entrepreneurship research* (Summary). Babson Park, MA: Center for Entrepreneurial Studies, Babson College. [On-line]. Available: www.babson.edu/entrep/fer/summ96/hisrich.html

Hisrich, R. D., & O'Brien, M. (1981). The woman entrepreneur from a business and sociological perspective. In K. Vesper (Ed.), *Frontiers of entrepreneurship research* (pp. 21-29). Wellesley, MA: Center for Entrepreneurial Studies, Babson College.

Hite, L. M. (1996). Black women managers and administrators: Experiences and implications. *Women in Management Review, 11*(6), 11-17.

Hitt, M. A., & Barr, S. H. (1989). Managerial selection decision models: Examination of configural cue processing. *Journal of Applied Psychology, 74,* 53-61.

Hitt, M. A., & Keats, B. W. (1984). Empirical identification of the criteria for effective affirmative action programs. *Journal of Applied Behavioral Science, 20*(3), 203-222.

Hochschild, A. (1989). *The second shift.* New York: Avon.

Hochschild, A. R. (1983). *The managed heart.* Berkeley: University of California Press.

Hochschild, A. R. (1997a). *The time bind: When work becomes home and home becomes work.* New York: Metropolitan.

Hochschild, A. R. (1997b). When work becomes home and home becomes work. *California Management Review, 39*(4), 79-97.

Hodges-Aeberhard, J., & Raskin, C. (Eds.). (1997a). *Affirmative action in the employment of ethnic minorities and persons with disabilities.* Geneva: International Labour Office.

Hodges-Aeberhard, J., & Raskin, C. (1997b). Malaysia. In J. Hodges-Aeberhard & C. Raskin (Eds.), *Affirmative action in the employment of ethnic minorities and persons with disabilities* (pp. 55-64). Geneva: International Labour Office.

Hodson, R., & England, P. (1986). Industrial structure and sex differences in earnings. *Industrial Relations, 25*(1), 16-32.

Hoffman, E. (1985). The effect of race-ratio composition on the frequency of organizational communication. *Social Psychology Quarterly, 48,* 17-26.

Hofstede, G. (1980a). *Culture's consequences: International differences in work-related values.* Beverly Hills, CA: Sage.

Hofstede, G. (1980b). Motivation, leadership, and organization: Do American theories apply abroad? *Organizational Dynamics, 9*(1), 4-21.

Hofstede, G. (1991). *Cultures and organizations: Software of the mind.* London: McGraw-Hill.

Hofstede, G. (1993). Cultural constraints in management theories. *Academy of Management Executive, 7,* 81-94.

Hofstede, G. (1998). *Masculinity and femininity: The taboo dimension of national attitudes.* Thousand Oaks, CA: Sage.

Hofstede, G., Neuijen, B., Ohayv, D. D., & Sanders, G. (1990). Measuring organizational cultures: A qualitative and quantitative study across twenty cases. *Administrative Science Quarterly, 35,* 286-316.

Holahan, C. J., & Moos, R. H. (1987). Personal and contextual determinants of coping strategies. *Journal of Personality and Social Psychology, 52,* 946-955.

Hollander, E. P. (1985). Leadership and power. In G. Lindzey & E. Aronson (Eds.), *Handbook of social psychology* New York: Random House.

Holvino, E. (1994). Women of color in organizations: Revising our models of gender at work. In E. Y. Cross, J. H. Katz, F. A. Miller, & E. W. Seashore (Eds.), *The promise of diversity: Over 40 voices discuss strategies for eliminating discrimination in organizations* (pp. 52-59). Burr Ridge, IL: Irwin.

Hood, J. N., & Koberg, C. S. (1994). Patterns of differential assimilation and acculturation for women in business organizations. *Human Relations, 47*(2), 159-181.

Horgan, D. D., & Simeon, R. J. (1990). Gender, mentoring, and tacit knowledge. *Journal of Social Behavior and Personality, 5,* 453-471.

Horn, P. D., & Horn, J. C. (1982). *Sex in the office.* Reading, MA: Addison-Wesley.

Horner, M. (1969, November). Fail: Bright women. *Psychology Today,* pp. 36-38, 62.

Horwitz, S. (1993, September 20). Jobless male managers proliferate in suburbs, causing subtle malaise. *Wall Street Journal,* pp. A1, A5.

Howard, A. (1992). Work and family crossroads spanning the career. In S. Zedeck (Ed.), *Work, families, and organizations* (pp. 70-137). San Francisco: Jossey-Bass.

Howard, J. A., Blumstein, P., & Schwartz, P. (1986). Sex, power, and influence tactics in intimate relationships. *Journal of Personality and Social Psychology, 51,* 102-109.

Howard, S. (1991). Organizational resources for addressing sexual harassment. *Journal of Counseling and Development, 69,* 507-511.

Howard, S. (1998, July 5). Men behaving badly at school put girls on top. *Sunday Times* (London).

Howell, J. P., Dorfman, P. W., Hibino, S., Lee, J. K., & Tate, U. (1994). *Leadership in Western and Asian countries: Commonalties and differences in effective leadership processes and substitutes across cultures.* New Mexico State University, Center for Business Research.

Huffman, M. L., & Velasco, S. C. (1997). When more is less: Sex composition, organizations, and earnings in U.S. firms. *Work and Occupations, 24*(2), 214-244.

Hughes, D. L., Galinsky, E., & Morris, A. (1992). The effects of job characteristics on marital quality: Specifying linking mechanisms. *Journal of Marriage and the Family, 54,* 31-42.

Hunt, D. M., & Michael, C. (1983). Mentorship: A career training and development tool. *Academy of Management Review, 8,* 475-485.

Hunter College Women's Studies Collective. (1983). *Women's realities, women's choices.* New York: Oxford University Press.

Hurley, A. E., & Fagenson-Eland, E. A. (1996). Challenges in cross-gender mentoring relationships: Psychological intimacy, myths, rumours, innuendoes and sexual harassment. *Leadership & Organization Development Journal, 17,* 42-49.

Hurtado, A. (1996). *The color of privilege: Three blasphemies on race and feminism.* Ann Arbor: University of Michigan Press.

Hurtado, A. (1997). Understanding multiple group identities: Inserting women into cultural transformations. *Journal of Social Issues, 53,* 299-328.

Hurtado, A., & Stewart, A. J. (1997). Through the looking glass: Implications of studying whiteness for feminist methods. In M. Fine, L. Weis, L. C. Powell, & L. Mun Wong (Eds.), *Off White: Readings on race, power, and society* (pp. 297-311). New York: Routledge.

Hutchinson, J., & Smith, A. D. (1996). Introduction. In J. Hutchinson & A. D. Smith (Eds.), *Ethnicity* (pp. 3-14). Oxford, UK: Oxford University Press.

Hutson-Comeaux, S. L., & Kelly, J. R. (1996). Sex differences in interaction style and group task performance: The process-performance relationship. *Journal of Social Behavior and Personality, 11* [Special issue], 255-275.

Huws, U., Podro, S., Gunnarsson, E., Weijers, T., Arvanitaki, K., & Trova, V. (1996). *Teleworking and gender.* Brighton, UK: Institute of Employment Studies.

Hyde, J. S. (1995). Women and maternity leave: Empirical data and public policy. *Psychology of Women Quarterly, 19,* 299-313.

Hyde, J. S., & Plant, E. A. (1995). Magnitude of psychological gender differences: Another side to the story. *American Psychologist, 50,* 159-161.

Iacobucci, D., Grayson, K., & Ostrom, A. (1994). Opinion: Customer satisfaction fables. *Sloan Management Review, 35*(4), 93-96.

Iacobucci, D., & Ostrom, A. (1993). Gender differences in the impact of core and relational aspects of services on the evaluation of service encounters. *Journal of Consumer Psychology, 2,* 257-286.

Iannello, K. P. (1992). *Decisions without hierarchy: Feminist interventions in organization theory and practice.* New York: Routledge.

Ibarra, H. (1993). Personal networks of women and minorities in management: A conceptual framework. *Academy of Management Review, 18*(1), 56-87.

Ibarra, H. (1995). Race, opportunity, and diversity of social circles in managerial networks. *Academy of Management Journal, 38*(3), 673-703.

Ibarra, H., & Andrews, S. B. (1993). Power, social influence, and sense making: Effects of network centrality and proximity on employee perceptions. *Administrative Science Quarterly, 38,* 277-303.

Inderlied, S. D., & Powell, G. (1979). Sex-role identity and leadership style: Different labels for the same concept? *Sex Roles, 5,* 613-623.

Institute for Women's Policy Research. (1996). *The wage gap: Women's and men's earnings.* Washington, DC: Author.

International Labour Office. (1985). *Yearbook of labour statistics.* Geneva: Author.

International Labour Office. (1986). *Yearbook of labour statistics* (46th ed., pp. 295-306, Table 3A). Geneva: Author.

International Labour Office. (1993). Unequal race to the top. *World of Work: The Magazine of the International Labour Office* (U.S. ed.), No. 2, pp. 6-7.

International Labour Office. (1995). *Yearbook of labour statistics.* Geneva: Author.

International Labour Office. (1996). *Yearbook of labour statistics* (55th ed., pp. 73-84, Table 2A). Geneva: Author.

International Survey Research. (1995). *Employee satisfaction: Tracking European trends.* London: Author.

Iqtidar, H., & Webster, L. J. (1996). *Frene Ginwala: Speaker of the South African National Assembly.* Unpublished manuscript, McGill University, Faculty of Management, Montreal.

Ireland, R. D., & Van Auken, P. M. (1987). Entrepreneurship and small business research: An historical typology and directions for future research. *American Journal of Small Business, 11*(4), 9-20.

Ishii-Kuntz, M. (1993). Japanese fathers: Work demands and family roles. In J. C. Hood (Ed.), *Men, work, and family* (pp. 45-67). Newbury Park, CA: Sage.

Isikoff, M., & Thomas, E. (1998, February 2). Clinton and the intern. *Newsweek,* pp. 30-46.

Izraeli, D. N. (1983). Sex effects of structural effects? An empirical test of Kanter's theory of proportions. *Social Forces, 62*(2), 153-165.

Izraeli, D. N. (1992). Culture, policy, and women in dual-earner families in Israel. In S. Lewis, D. N. Izraeli, & H. Hootsmans (Eds.), *Dual-earner families: International perspectives* (pp. 19-45). London: Sage.

Izraeli, D. N. (1994). Outsiders in the promised land: Women managers in Israel. In N. J. Adler & D. N. Izraeli (Eds.), *Competitive frontiers: Women managers in a global economy* (pp. 301-324). Cambridge, MA: Blackwell.

Jacklin, C. N., & Reynolds, C. (1993). Gender and childhood socialization. In A. E. Beall & R. J. Sternberg (Eds.), *The psychology of gender* (pp. 197-214). New York: Guilford.

Jackman, M. R. (1994). *The velvet glove: Paternalism and conflict in gender, class, and race relations.* Berkeley: University of California Press.

Jackson, S. E. (1991). Team composition in organizational settings: Issues in managing an increasingly diverse work force. In S. Worchel, W. Wood, & J. A. Simpson (Eds.), *Group process and productivity* (pp. 138-173). Newbury Park, CA: Sage.

Jackson, S. E., May, K. E., & Whitney, K. (1995). Understanding the dynamics of diversity in decision-making teams. In R. Guzzo, E. Salas, & Associates (Eds.), *Team effectiveness and decision making in organizations.* San Francisco: Jossey-Bass.

Jacobs, J. A. (1989a). Long term trends in occupational segregation by sex. *American Journal of Sociology, 95*(1), 160-173.

Jacobs, J. A. (1989b). *Revolving doors: Sex segregation and women's careers.* Stanford, CA: Stanford University Press.

Jacobs, J. A. (1992). Women's entry into management: Trends in earnings, authority, and values among salaried women. *Administrative Science Quarterly, 37,* 282-301.

Jacobs, J. A. (1993). Theoretical and measurement issues in the study of sex segregation in the workplace. *European Sociological Review, 9*(3), 325-330.

Jacobs, J. A. (1995). Gender and academic specialties: Trends among recipients of college degrees during the 1980s. *Sociology of Education, 68*(2), 81-98.

Jacobs, J. A., & Lim, S. T. (1992). Trends in occupational and industrial segregation by sex in 56 countries, 1960-1980. *Work and Occupations, 19*(4), 450-486.

Jacobs, J. A., & Steinberg, R. (1990). Compensating differentials and the male-female wage gap: Evidence from the New York State Comparable Worth Study. *Social Forces, 69*(2), 439-468.

Jacobs, J. A., & Steinberg, R. J. (1995). Further evidence on compensating differentials and the gender gap in wages. In J. A. Jacobs (Ed.), *Gender inequality at work* (pp. 93-124). Thousand Oaks, CA: Sage.

Jacobs, S. C. (1995). Changing patterns of sex segregation occupations throughout the life-course. *European Sociological Review, 11*(2), 157-171.

Jacobson, C. K. (1983). Black support for affirmative action programs. *Phylon, 44,* 299-311.

Jacobson, M. B., & Effertz, J. (1974). Sex roles and leadership: Perceptions of the leader and the led. *Organizational Behavior and Human Performance, 12,* 383-396.

Jacques, R. (1996). *Manufacturing the employee: Management knowledge from the 20th to 21st centuries.* Thousand Oaks, CA: Sage.

Jacques, R. (1997). The unbearable whiteness of being: Reflections of a pale, stale male. In P. Prasad, A. J. Mills, M. Elmes, & A. Prasad (Eds.), *Managing the organizational melting pot: Dilemmas of workplace diversity* (pp. 80-106). Thousand Oaks, CA: Sage.

Jago, A. G., & Vroom, V. H. (1982). Sex differences in the incidence and evaluation of participative leader behavior. *Journal of Applied Psychology, 67,* 776-783.

James, D., & Drakitch, J. (1993). Understanding gender differences in amount of talk: A critical review of research. In D. Tannen (Ed.), *Gender and conversational interaction* (pp. 281-312). New York: Oxford University Press.

James, K. (1994). Social identity, work stress and minority workers' health. In G. P. Keita & J. J. Hurrell (Eds.), *Job stress in a changing workforce* (pp. 127-146). Washington, DC: American Psychological Association.

James, K., Lovato, C., & Khoo, G. (1994). Social identity correlates of minority workers' health. *Academy of Management Journal, 37*(2), 383-391.

James, N. (1989). Emotional labor: Skill and work in the social regulation of feelings. *Sociological Focus, 37*(1), 15-42.

Jamieson, L. (1998). *Intimacy: Personal relationships in modern societies.* Malden, MA: Polity.

Jaworski, J. (1996). *Synchronicity: The inner path of leadership.* San Francisco: Berrett-Koehler.

Jehn, K. A., Stroh, L. K., & Von Glinow, M. A. (1997). The commuting couple: Oxymoron or career freedom? In Y. Altunex (Ed.), *Careers in the new millennium* (pp. 163-178). Brussels, Belgium: Academic Cooperative.

Jennings, E. (1960). *The anatomy of leadership.* New York: Harper & Row.

Jidoun, G. (1998, October). Covering up. *Working Woman,* p. 12.

Johnson, A., & Jackson, P. (1998, July). A longitudinal investigation into the experience of male managers who have re-entered the workforce after a redundancy, and their families. In *Proceedings of the International Work Psychology Conference.* Sheffield, UK: University of Sheffield.

Johnson, C., Clay-Warner, J., & Funk, S. J. (1996). Effects of authority structures and gender on interaction in same-sex groups. *Social Psychology Quarterly, 59,* 221-236.

Johnson, C. B., Stockdale, M. S., & Saal, F. E. (1991). Persistence of men's misperceptions of friendly cues across a variety of interpersonal encounters. *Psychology of Women Quarterly, 15,* 463-475.

Johnson, N. B., & Scandura, T. A. (1994). The effect of mentorship and sex-role style on male-female earnings. *Industrial Relations, 33,* 263-274.

Johnson-Jackson, J. (1995). Race-based affirmative action: Mend it or end it? *The Black Scholar, 25,* 30-42.

Jones, E. E., & Nisbett, R. E. (1972). The actor and the observer: Divergent perception of the causes of behavior. In E. E. Jones, D. E. Kanouse, H. H. Kelley, R. E. Nisbett, S. Valins, & B. Weiner (Eds.), *Attribution: Perceiving the causes of behavior* (pp. 79-94). Morristown, NJ: General Learning.

Jones, E. E., & Pittman, T. S. (1982). Toward a general theory of strategic self-presentation. In J. Suls (Ed.), *Psychological perspectives on the self* (Vol. 1, pp. 231-262). Hillsdale, NJ: Lawrence Erlbaum.

Jones, F., & Fletcher, B. (1993). An empirical study of occupational stress transmission in working couples. *Human Relations, 46*(7), 881-903.

Jones, J. M. (1997). *Prejudice and racism* (2nd ed.). New York: McGraw-Hill.

Jones, T. M. (1991). Ethical decision making by individuals in organizations: An issue-contingent model. *Academy of Management Review, 16*, 366-395.

Joplin, J. R. W., & Daus, C. S. (1997). Challenges of leading a diverse workforce. *Academy of Management Executive, 11*(3), 32-47.

Jordan, J. V. (1991). The meaning of mutuality. In J. V. Jordan, A. G. Kaplan, J. B. Miller, I. P. Stiver, & J. L. Surrey (Eds.), *Women's growth in connection: Writings from the Stone Center* (pp. 81-96). New York: Guilford.

Jordan, J. V., Kaplan, A. G., Miller, J. B., Stiver, I. P., & Surrey, J. L. (Eds.) (1991). *Women's growth in connection: Writings from the Stone Center.* New York: Guilford.

Josefowitz, N. (1983). *Is this where I was going?* New York: Warner.

Joseph, M. (1991). Reservations for "Sons of the Soil." *The Eastern Anthropologist, 44,* 189-192.

Judge, T. A., Boudreau, J. W., & Bretz, R. D. (1994). Job and life attitudes of male executives. *Journal of Applied Psychology, 79,* 767-782.

Judge, T. A., Locke, E. A., Durham, C. C., & Kluger, A. N. (1998). Dispositional effects on job and life satisfaction: The role of core evaluations. *Journal of Applied Psychology, 83,* 17-34.

Kacmar, K. M., & Carlson, D. S. (1994). Using impression management in women's job search processes. *American Behavioral Scientist, 37,* 682-696.

Kacmar, K. M., & Hochwarter, W. A. (1995). The interview as a communication event: An examination of demographic effects on interview outcomes. *Journal of Business Communication, 32,* 207-232.

Kahn, R. L., Wolfe, D. M., Quinn, R., Snoek, J. D., & Rosenthal, R. A. (1964). *Organizational stress.* New York: John Wiley.

Kakar, S. (1971). Authority patterns and subordinate behavior in Indian organizations. *Administrative Science Quarterly, 16*(3), 298-308.

Kalbfleisch, P. J. (1997). Appeasing the mentor. *Aggressive Behavior, 23,* 389-403.

Kalbfleisch, P. J., & Davies, A. B. (1991). Minorities and mentoring: Managing the multicultural institution. *Communication Education, 40,* 266-271.

Kalleberg, A. L., & Leicht, K. T. (1991). Gender and organizational performance: Determinants of small business survival and success. *Academy of Management Journal, 34*(1), 131-161.

Kalleberg, A. L., Reskin, B. F., & Hudson, K. (in press). Bad jobs in America: Nonstandard, contingent and secondary employment relations in the United States. *American Sociological Review.*

Kane, E. W. (1992). Race, gender, and attitudes toward gender stratification. *Social Psychology Quarterly, 55,* 311-320.

Kanekar, S., & Dhir, V. L. (1992). Sex-related differences in perceptions of sexual harassment of women in India. *Journal of Social Psychology, 133,* 119-120.

Kanter, R. M. (1977a). *Men and women of the corporation.* New York: Basic Books.

Kanter, R. M. (1977b). Some effects of proportions on group life: Skewed sex ratios and responses to token women. *American Journal of Sociology, 82,* 965-990.

Kanter, R. M. (1977c). *Work and family in the United States: A critical review and agenda for research and policy* (Social Science Frontiers No. 9). New York: Russell Sage.

Kanter, R. M. (1983). *The change masters.* New York: Simon & Schuster.

Kantrowicz, B., & Wingert, P. (1993). Being smart about the mommy track. *Working Woman, 18,* 48-51.

Kapalka, G. M., & Lachenmeyer, J. R. (1988). Sex-role flexibility, locus of control, and occupational status. *Sex Roles, 19,* 417-427.

Karambayya, R. (1997). In shouts and whispers: Paradoxes facing women of colour in organizations. *Journal of Business Ethics, 16,* 891-897.

Karambayya, R. (1998, May). *Moving on: Women, careers and corporate restructuring.* Paper presented at the Administrative Sciences Association of Canada annual conference, Saskatoon, Saskatchewan.

Karambayya, R., & Reilly, A. H. (1992). Dual earner couples: Attitudes and actions in restructuring work for family. *Journal of Organizational Behavior, 13,* 585-601.

Karsten, M. F. (1994). *Management and gender: Issues and attitudes.* Westport, CT: Praeger.

Kasarda, J. D. (1995). Industrial restructuring and the changing location of jobs. In R. Farley (Ed.), *State of the union: America in the 1990s: Vol. 1. Economic trends* (pp. 215-267). New York: Russell Sage.

Katz, D. (1987). Sex discrimination in hiring: The influence of organizational climate and need for approval on decision making behavior. *Psychology of Women Quarterly, 11,* 11-20.

Katz, I., & Hass, R. G. (1988). Racial ambivalence and value conflict: Correlational and priming studies of dual cognitive structures. *Journal of Personality and Social Psychology, 55,* 893-905.

Katz, J., & Gartner, W. B. (1988). Properties of emerging organizations. *Academy of Management Review, 13*(3), 429-441.

Katz, J. A. (1994). Modeling entrepreneurial career progressions: Concepts and considerations. *Entrepreneurship Theory and Practice, 19*(2), 23-39.

Katz, J. A. (1997, November). *Core publications in entrepreneurship and related fields: A guide to getting published* [On-line]. United States Association of Small Business and Entrepreneurship (USASBE) Web listing. Available: www.usasbe.org/search/search.htm; www.slu.edu/eweb/booklist.htm

Katz, L. F., & Murphy, K. M. (1992). Changes in relative wages, 1963-87: Supply and demand factors. *Quarterly Journal of Economics, 107*(1), 35-78.

Katz, P., & Katz, M. (1997). *The feminist dollar.* New York: Plenum.

Katz, R. (1997). *The can-do girls.* Oxford, UK: Oxford University Press.

Kaufman, P. J., Welsh, D. H. B., & Bushmarin, N. V. (1995). Locus of control and entrepreneurship in the Russian Republic. *Entrepreneurship Theory and Practice, 20*(1), 43-57.

Kaur, A. (1997). India. In J. Hodges-Aeberhard & C. Raskin (Eds.), *Affirmative action in the employment of ethnic minorities and persons with disabilities* (pp. 29-44). Geneva: International Labour Office.

Keating, K. (1993). Organizational gardening: A metaphor for the new business paradigm. In P. Barrentine (Ed.), *When the canary stops singing: Women's perspectives on transforming business* (pp. 55-68). San Francisco: Berrett-Koehler.

Kelley, H. H. (1972). Attribution in social interactions. In E. E. Jones, D. E. Kanouse, H. H. Kelley, R. E. Nisbett, S. Valins & B. Weiner (Eds.), *Attribution: Perceiving the causes of behavior* (pp. 1-26). Morristown, NJ: General Learning Press.

Kelley, K., & Streeter, D. (1992). The roles of gender in organizations. In K. Kelley (Ed.), *Issues, theory and research in industrial/organizational psychology* (pp. 285-337). Amsterdam: Elsevier Science.

Kellough, J. E. (1989). *Federal equal employment opportunity policy and numerical goals and timetables: An impact assessment.* New York: Praeger.

Kellough, J. E. (1992). Affirmative action in government employment. *Annals of the American Academy of Political and Social Science, 523,* 117-130.

Kelly, C. (1996). 50 world-class executives. *Worldbusiness, 2*(2), 20-31.

Kerfoot, D., & Knights, D. (1993). Management, masculinity and manipulation: From paternalism to corporate strategy in financial services in Britain. *Journal of Management Studies, 30*(4), 659-677.

Kerlinger, F. N. (1986). *Foundations of behavioral research.* Fort Worth, TX: Harcourt Brace Jovanovich.

Kern, J. A. (1994, August). *Making sense of gender inequality: An investigation of ideology in organizations.* Paper presented at the meeting of the Academy of Management, Dallas, TX.

Kerwin, C., & Ponterotto, J. G. (1995). Biracial identity development: Theory and research. In J. G. Ponterotto, J. M. Casas, L. A. Suzuki, & C. M. Alexander (Eds.), *Handbook of multicultural counseling* (pp. 199-217). Thousand Oaks, CA: Sage.

Kilbourne, B. S., England, P., Farkas, G., Beron, K., & Weir, D. (1994). Returns to skill, compensating differentials, and gender bias: Effects of occupational characteristics on the wages of White women and men. *American Journal of Sociology, 100*(3), 689-719.

Kilduff, M., & Mehra, A. (1996). Hegemonic masculinity among the elite: Power, identity and homophiliy in social networks. In C. Cheng (Ed.), *Masculinities in organizations* (pp. 115-129). Thousand Oaks, CA: Sage.

Kim, J. S., & Campagna, A. F. (1981). Effects of flextime on employee attendance and performance: A field experiment. *Academy of Management Journal, 24,* 729-741.

Kimmel, M. (1993). What do men want? *Harvard Business Review, 71*(6), 4-12.

Kimmel, M., & Messner, M. (1989). *Men's lives.* New York: Macmillan.

Kinder, D. R., & Sanders, L. M. (1990). Mimicking political debate with survey questions: The case of White opinion on affirmative action for Blacks. *Social Cognition, 8,* 73-103.

King, M. C. (1975). Oppression and power: The unique status of the Black woman in the American political system. *Social Science Quarterly, 56,* 116-128.

Kipnis, D., & Schmidt, S. M. (1988). Upward-influence styles: Relationship with performance evaluations, salary, and stress. *Administrative Science Quarterly, 33,* 528-542.

Kirchmeyer, C. (1992a). Nonwork participation and work attitudes: A test of scarcity vs. expansion models of personal resources. *Human Relations, 45,* 775-795.

Kirchmeyer, C. (1992b). Perceptions of nonwork-to-work spillover: Challenging the common view of conflict-ridden domain relationships. *Basic and Applied Social Psychology, 13,* 231-249.

Kirchmeyer, C. (1993). Nonwork-to-work spillover: A more balanced view of the experiences and coping of professional women and men. *Sex Roles, 28,* 531-552.

Kirchmeyer, C. (1995). Demographic similarity to the work group: A longitudinal study of managers at the early career stages. *Journal of Organizational Behavior, 16,* 67-83.

Kirso, K., & Korabik, K. (1996, August). *The relationship of undesirable gender-role characteristics to leadership and conflict management styles.* Paper presented at the International Congress of Psychology, Montreal, Quebec.

Kirtz-Silverstein, D., Wingard, D. L., & Barrett-Connor, E. (1992). Employment status and heart disease risk factors in middle-aged women: The Rancho Bernardo study. *American Journal of Public Health, 82*(2), 215-219.

Klein, V. (1972). *The feminine character: History of an ideology.* Urbana: University of Illinois Press.

Kleinke, C. L., & Nicholson, T. A. (1979). Black and White children's awareness of de facto race and sex differences. *Developmental Psychology, 15,* 84-86.

Klenke, K. (1996). *Women and leadership: A contextual perspective.* New York: Springer-Verlag.

Kline, M. L., & Snow, D. L. (1994). Effects of a worksite coping skills intervention on the stress, social support, and health outcomes of working mothers. *Journal of Primary Prevention, 15*(2), 105-121.

Klonoff, E. A., & Landrine, H. (1995). The Schedule of Sexist Events: A measure of lifetime and recent sexist discrimination in women's lives. *Psychology of Women Quarterly, 19,* 439-472.

Klose, A., & Finkle, T. (1995). Service quality and the congruency of employee perceptions and customer expectations: The case of an electric utility. *Psychology & Marketing, 12*(7), 637-646.

Kluckhohn, F. R., & Strodbeck, F. L. (1961). *Variations in value orientations.* Evanston, IL: Row, Peterson.

Kluegel, J. R., & Smith, E. R. (1983). Affirmative action attitudes: Effects of self-interest, racial affect, and stratification beliefs on Whites' views. *Social Forces, 61,* 797-824.

Knapp, D. E., Faley, R. H., Ekeberg, W. C., & Dubois, C. L. Z. (1997). Determinants of target responses to sexual harassment: A conceptual framework. *Academy of Management Review, 22*(3), 687-729.

Knight, P. A., & Saal, F. E. (1984). Effects of gender differences and selection agent expertise on leader influence and performance evaluations. *Organizational Behavior and Human Performance, 34,* 225-243.

Knight, R. M. (1987). Can business schools produce entrepreneurs? In N. C. Churchill, J. A. Hornaday, B. A. Kirchoff, O. J. Krasner, & K. H. Vesper (Eds.), *Frontiers of entrepreneurship research* (pp. 603-604). Wellesley, MA: Center for Entrepreneurial Studies, Babson College.

Knutson, D. (1994). *Characteristics of business by gender* [On-line]. Available: http://www.census.gov/agfs/gender/gend_res.htm [U.S. Census Bureau, Office of Statistics, revised April 24, 1997].

Koberg, C. S., Boss, R. W., Chappell, D., & Ringer, R. C. (1994). Correlates and consequences of protégé mentoring in a large hospital. *Group & Organization Management, 19,* 219-239.

Koberg, C. S., Boss, R. W., & Goodman, E. (1998). Factors and outcomes associated with mentoring among health-care professionals. *Journal of Vocational Behavior, 53,* 58-72.

Koen, S. (1984). *Feminist workplaces: Alternative models for the organization of work.* Unpublished doctoral dissertation, Union for Experimenting Colleges, University of Michigan Dissertation Information Service.

Kofodimos, J. R. (1990). Why executives lose their balance. *Organizational Dynamics, 19*(1), 58-73.

Kohlberg, L. (1981). *The philosophy of moral development.* New York: Harper & Row.

Kohlberg, L. (1984). *The psychology of moral development.* New York: Harper & Row.

Kolb, J. A. (1997). Are we still stereotyping leadership? A look at gender and other predictors of leader emergence. *Small Group Research, 28,* 370-393.

Komaromy, M., Grumbach, K., Drake, M., Vranizan, K., Lurie, N., Keane, D., & Bindman, A. B. (1996). The role of Black and Hispanic physicians in providing health care for underserved populations. *New England Journal of Medicine, 334,* 1305-1310.

Komarraju, M. (1997). The work-family interface in India. In S. Parasuraman & J. H. Greenhaus (Eds.), *Integrating work and family: Challenges and choices for a changing world* (pp. 104-114). Westport, CT: Quorum Books.

Komives, S. R. (1991). Gender differences in the relationship of hall directors' transformational and transactional leadership and achieving styles. *Journal of College Student Development, 32,* 155-165.

Konrad, A. M., & Linnehan, F. (1995a). Formalized HRM structures: Coordinating equal employment opportunity or concealing organizational practices? *Academy of Management Journal, 38,* 787-820.

Konrad, A. M., & Linnehan, F. (1995b). Race and sex differences in line managers' reactions to equal employment opportunity and affirmative action interventions. *Group & Organization Management, 20,* 409-439.

Konrad, A. M., & Pfeffer, J. (1991). Understanding the hiring of women and minorities in educational institutions. *Sociology of Education, 64,* 141-157.

Konrad, A. M., & Cummings, K. (1997). The effects of gender role congruence and statistical discrimination on managerial advancement. *Human Relations, 50*(10), 1305-1328.

Konrad, A. M., Winter, S., & Gutek, B. (1992). Diversity in work group sex composition: Implications for majority and minority members. *Research in the Sociology of Organizations, 10,* 115-140.

Korabik, K. (1990). Androgyny and leadership style. *Journal of Business Ethics, 9,* 9-18.

Korabik, K. (1993, May). Strangers in a strange land: Women managers and the legitimization of authority. *SWAP Newsletter, 17,* 26-34.

Korabik, K. (1996). *Gender, leadership style, and managerial effectiveness. Proceedings of the International Association of Management.* Toronto, Ontario: Association of Management.

Korabik, K. (1997). Applied gender issues. In S. W. Sadava & D. R. McCreary (Eds.), *Applied social psychology* (pp. 292-302). Upper Saddle River, NJ: Prentice Hall.

Korabik, K., & Ayman, R. (1989). Should women managers have to act like men? *Journal of Management Development, 8*(6), 23-32.

Korabik, K., Baril, G. L., & Watson, C. (1993). Managers' conflict management style and leadership effectiveness: The moderating effects of gender. *Sex Roles, 29,* 405-420.

Korabik, K., & McCreary, D. R. (1995, July). *Gender roles and interpersonal problems.* Paper presented at a meeting of the European Congress of Psychology, Athens, Greece.

Korabik, K., & Whiltshire, T. (1993, June). *Sex and gender: Terms frequently confused in the psychological literature.* Poster presented at the annual meeting of the American Psychological Society, Chicago.

Korn/Ferry International. (1990). *A decade of change in corporate leadership.* New York: Author.

Korn/Ferry International. (1993). *Decade of the executive woman.* New York: Author.

Kossek, E. E., DeMarr, B. J., Backman, K., & Kollar, M. (1993). Assessing employees' emerging elder care needs and reactions to dependent care benefits. *Public Personnel Management, 22*(4), 617-638.

Kossek, E. E., & Lobel, S. A. (1996). Transforming human resource systems to manage diversity—An introduction and orienting framework. In E. E. Kossek & S. A. Lobel (Eds.), *Managing diversity: Human resource strategies for transforming the workplace* (pp. 1-20). Cambridge, MA: Blackwell.

Kossek, E. E., & Nichol, V. (1992). The effects of on-site child care on employee attitudes and performance. *Personnel Psychology, 45,* 485-509.

Kossek, E. E., & Ozeki, C. (1998). Work-family conflict, policies, and the job-life satisfaction relationship: A review and directions for organizational behavior-human resources research. *Journal of Applied Psychology, 83,* 139-149.

Kossek, E. E., & Zonia, S. C. (1993). Assessing diversity climate: A field study of reactions to employer efforts to promote diversity. *Journal of Organizational Behavior, 14*(1), 61-81.

Kotter, J. (1988). *The leadership factor.* New York: Free Press.

Kourlisky, M. L., & Walstad, W. B. (1998). Entrepreneurship and female youth: Knowledge, attitudes, gender differences, and educational practices. *Journal of Business Venturing, 13*(1), 77-88.

Kram, K. E. (1983). Phases of the mentor relationship. *Academy of Management Journal, 26,* 608-625.

Kram, K. E. (1985). *Mentoring at work.* Glenview, IL: Scott, Foresman.

Kram, K. E., & Hall, D. T. (1996). Mentoring in a context of diversity and turbulence. In E. E. Kossek & S. A. Lobel (Eds.), *Managing diversity: Human resource strategy for transforming the workplace* (pp. 108-136). Cambridge, MA: Blackwell.

Kravitz, D. A., & Platania, J. (1993). Attitudes and beliefs about affirmative action: Effects of target and of respondent sex and ethnicity. *Journal of Applied Psychology, 78,* 928-938.

Krug, D. N., Palmour, V. E., & Ballassai, M. C. (1972). *Evaluation of the Office of Economic Opportunity Child Development Center.* Rockville, MD: Westat.

Kruse, L., & Wintermantel, M. (1986). Leadership ms.-qualified: The gender bias in everyday and scientific thinking. In C. F. Graumann & S. Moscovici (Eds.), *Changing conceptions of leadership* (pp. 171-197). New York: Springer-Verlag.

Kuchler, C. (1997). Integrating the feminine into organizational change work. *Journal of the Organization Development Practitioner, 29*(3), 17-25.

Kuhn, T. S. (1962). *The structure of the scientific revolution.* Chicago: University of Chicago Press.

Kulik, C. T., & Holbrook, R. L., Jr. (1998). *Demographics in service encounters: Effects of racial and gender congruence on perceived fairness.* Paper presented at the annual meeting of the Academy of Management, San Diego, CA.

Kulik, C. T., Perry, E. L., & Schmidtke, J. M. (1997). Responses to sexual harassment: The effect of perspective. *Journal of Managerial Issues, 9,* 37-53.

Kulka, R. A. (1982). Idiosyncrasy and circumstance: Choices and constraints in the research process. In J. E. McGrath, J. Martin, & R. Kulka (Eds.), *Judgement calls in research* (pp. 41-68). Beverly Hills, CA: Sage.

Kush, K. A., & Stroh, L. K. (1994). Flextime: Myth or reality? *Business Horizons, 37,* 51-55.

Kushell, E., & Newton, R. (1986). Gender, leadership style, and subordinate satisfaction: An experiment. *Sex Roles, 14,* 203-209.

Laband, D. N., & Lentz, B. F. (1995). Workplace mentoring in the legal profession. *Southern Economic Journal, 61,* 783-802.

Lafayette, L. (1994, October 16). Fair play for the childless worker. *New York Times,* p. F11.

Lafontaine, E., & Tredeau, L. (1986). The frequency, sources, and correlates of sexual harassment among women in traditional male occupations. *Sex Roles, 15,* 433-442.

Lahelma, E., Kangas, R., & Manderbacka, K. (1995). Drinking and unemployment: Contrasting patterns among men and women. *Drug and Alcohol Dependency, 37,* 71-82.

Lambert, S. (1993). *Added benefits: The link between family-responsive policies and work performance at Fel-Pro Incorporated.* Chicago: University of Chicago.

Lambert, S. J. (1990). Processes linking work and family: A critical review and research agenda. *Human Relations, 43,* 239-257.

Landrine, H., & Klonoff, E. A. (1996). *African American acculturation: Deconstructing race and reviving culture.* Thousand Oaks, CA: Sage.

Landrine, H., Klonoff, E. A., Alcaraz, R., Scott, J., & Wilkins, P. (1995). Multiple variables in discrimination. In B. Lott & D. Maluso (Eds.), *The social psychology of interpersonal discrimination* (pp. 183-224). New York: Guilford.

Landy, R. J., & Farr, J. L. (1980). Performance rating. *Psychological Bulletin, 87,* 72-107.

Langan-Fox, J., & Roth, S. (1995). Achievement motivation and female entrepreneurs. *Journal of Occupational and Organizational Psychology, 68*(3), 209-229.

LaNoue, G. R. (1992). Split visions: Minority business set-asides. *Annals of the American Academy of Political and Social Science, 523,* 104-116.

Larwood, L., & Wood, M. M. (1977). *Women in management.* Lexington, MA: Lexington Books.

Latack, J. C., Kinicki, A. J., & Prussia, G. E. (1995). An integrated process model of coping with job loss. *Academy of Management Review, 20*(2), 311-342.

Laurent, A. (1983). The cultural diversity of Western conceptions of management. *International Studies of Management and Organization, 13*(1-2), 75-96.

Lauterbach, K. E., & Weiner, B. J. (1996). Dynamics of upward influence: How male and female managers get their way. *Leadership Quarterly, 7,* 87-107.

Lavoie, D. (1984/1985, Winter). A new era for female entrepreneurship in the 80s. *Journal of Small Business,* pp. 34-43. (Canada)

Lawler, E. (1977). Reward systems. In J. Hackman & J. Suttle (Eds.), *Improving life at work: Behavioral science approaches to organizational change* (pp. 163-226). Santa Monica, CA: Goodyear.

Laws, J. L. (1979). *The second X: Sex role and social role.* New York: Elsevier.

Lazarus, R. S. (1966). *Psychological stress and the coping process.* New York: McGraw-Hill.

Lazarus, R. S. (1971). The concept of stress and disease. In L. Levi (Ed.), *Society, stress and disease* (Vol. 1, pp. 177-214). London: Oxford University Press.

Leana, C. R., & Feldman, D. C. (1991). Individual responses to job loss: Empirical findings from two field studies. *Human Relations, 43,* 1155-1181.

Leck, J. D., & Saunders, D. M. (1992). Hiring women: The effects of Canada's Employment Equity Act. *Canadian Public Policy, 18,* 203-220.

Leck, J. D., & Saunders, D. M. (1996). Achieving diversity in the workplace: Canada's Employment Equity Act and members of visible minorities. *International Journal of Public Administration, 19,* 299-221.

Leck, J. D., St. Onge, S., & LaLancette, I. (1995). Wage gap changes among organizations subject to the Employment Equity Act. *Canadian Public Policy, 21,* 387-400.

Lee, D. M., & Alvares, K. M. (1977). Effects of sex on descriptions and evaluations of supervisory behavior in a simulated industrial setting. *Journal of Applied Psychology, 62,* 405-410.

Lee, M. (1991). Gender, group composition, and peer interaction in computer-based cooperative learning. *Journal of Educational Computing Research, 9,* 549-577.

Lee, R. A. (1983). Flextime and conjugal roles. *Journal of Occupational Behaviour, 4,* 297-315.

Lee, S. M. (1993). Racial classifications in the U.S. census: 1890-1990. *Ethnic and Racial Studies, 16,* 75-94.

Lefkowitz, J. (1994). Sex-related differences in job attitudes and dispositional variables: Now you see them, . . . *Academy of Management Journal, 37,* 323-349.

Leicht, K. T., & Marx, J. (1997). The consequences of informal job finding for men and women. *Academy of Management Journal, 40,* 967-987.

Leidner, R. (1991). Serving hamburgers and selling insurance: Gender, work, and identity in interactive service jobs. *Gender & Society, 5*(2), 154-177.

Leidner, R. (1993). *Fast food, fast talk: Service work and the routinization of everyday life.* Berkeley: University of California Press.

Leiter, M. P., & Durup, M. J. (1996). Work, home, and in-between: A longitudinal study of spillover. *Journal of Applied Behavioral Science, 32,* 29-47.

Lengnick-Hall, M. L. (1995). Sexual harassment research: A methodology critique. *Personnel Psychology, 48,* 841-864.

Lenney, E. (1977). Women's self-confidence in achievement settings. *Psychological Bulletin, 84,* 1-13.

Lenney, E., Browning, C., & Mitchell, L. (1980). What you don't know can hurt you: The effects of performance criteria ambiguity on sex differences in self-confidence. *Journal of Personality, 48,* 306-322.

Leonard, J. S. (1994). Affirmative action: Symbolic accommodation and conflict. *New Approaches to Employee Management, 2,* 13-33.

Lerner, M., Brush, C., & Hisrich, R. (1997). Israeli women entrepreneurs: An examination of factors affecting performance. *Journal of Business Venturing, 12*(4), 315-339.

Lerner, M. J. (1980). *The belief in a just world.* New York: Plenum.

Levant, R. F., Majors, R. G., & Kelley, M. L. (1998). Masculinity ideology among young African American and European American women and men in different regions of the United States. *Cultural Diversity and Mental Health, 4,* 227-236.

Levin, S., Sinclair, S., Veniegas, R. C., & Taylor, P. L. (1998, May). *Gender, ethnicity, and perceived discrimination: Is double jeopardy in jeopardy?* Poster presented at the 10th annual convention of the American Psychological Society, Washington, DC.

Levine, P. B., & Zimmerman, D. J. (1995). A comparison of the sex-type of occupational aspirations and subsequent achievement. *Work and Occupations, 22*(1), 73-84.

Levinson, B. (Director). (1994). *Disclosure* [Film]. Burbank, CA: Warner Bros.

Levinson, D. J., Darrow, C. N., Klein, E. B., Levinson, M. H., & McKee, B. (1978). *The seasons of a man's life.* New York: Knopf.

Levy, F., & Murnane, R. J. (1992, September). U.S. earnings levels and earnings inequality: A review of recent trends and proposed explanations. *Journal of Economic Literature, 30,* 1333-1381.

Lewin, D. (1987). Dispute resolution in the nonunion firm. *Journal of Conflict Resolution, 31,* 465-502.

Lewin, T. (1997, September 15). Women losing ground to men in widening income difference. *New York Times,* pp. A1, A12.

Lewis, S. (1992). Work and families in the United Kingdom. In S. Zedeck (Ed.), *Work, families, and organizations* (pp. 395-431). San Francisco: Jossey-Bass.

Lewis, S. (1996). Rethinking employment: An organizational culture change framework. In S. Lewis & J. Lewis (Eds.), *The work-family challenge* (pp. 1-19). Thousand Oaks, CA: Sage.

Lewis, S. (1997a). Family friendly organizational policies: A route to organizational change or playing about at the margins. *Gender, Work and Organization, 4,* 13-23.

Lewis, S. (1997b). An international perspective on work-family issues. In S. Parasuraman & J. H. Greenhaus (Eds.), *Integrating work and family: Challenges and choices for a changing world* (pp. 91-103). Westport, CT: Quorum Books.

Lewis, S., & Cooper, C. L. (1988). Stress in dual-career families. In B. A. Gutek, A. H. Stromberg, & L. Larwood (Eds.), *Women and work: An annual review* (Vol. 3, pp. 139-168). Newbury Park, CA: Sage.

Lewis, S., & Cooper, C. L. (1996). Balancing the work-family interface. A European perspective. *Human Resource Management Review, 5,* 289-305.

Lewis, S., Izraeli, D. N., & Hootsmans, H. (Eds.). (1992). *Dual-earner families: International perspectives.* London: Sage.

Lewis, S., & Lewis, J. (Eds.). (1996). *The work-family challenge: Rethinking employment.* London: Sage.

Lewis, S., Smithson, J., Brannen, J., Das Dores Guerreiro, M., Kugelberg, C., Nilsen, A., & O'Connor, P. (1998). *Futures on hold. Young Europeans talk about combining work and family.* London: Midland Bank and Work-Family Research Centre.

Licata, B. J., & Popovich, P. M. (1987). Preventing sexual harassment: A proactive approach. *Training and Development, 69,* 512-517.

Liden, R. C., Wayne, S. J., & Stilwell, D. (1993). A longitudinal study on the early development of leader member exchange. *Journal of Applied Psychology, 78,* 662-674.

Lieberson, S. (1980). *A piece of the pie.* Berkeley: University of California Press.

Likert, R. (1967). *The human organization.* New York: McGraw-Hill.

Lim, L. L. (1996). *More and better jobs for women: An action guide.* Geneva: International Labour Office.

Link, B., & Shrout, P. (1992). Spurious association in longitudinal research. In J. Greenley & P. Leaf (Eds.), *Research in community and mental health* (pp. 301-321). Greenwich, CT: JAI.

Lipman-Blumen, J. (1983). Emerging patterns of female leadership in formal organizations. In M. Horner, C. C. Nadelson, & M. T. Notman (Eds.), *The challenge of change* (pp. 61-91). New York: Plenum.

Lipton, K. (1995). Back-up child care. *Kaleidoscope, 3*(4), 6.

Little, B. L., Murry, W. D., & Wimbush, J. C. (1998). Perceptions of workplace affirmative action plans: A psychological perspective. *Group & Organization Management, 23,* 27-47.

Lobel, S. A. (1991). Allocation of investment in work and family roles: Alternative theories and implications for research. *Academy of Management Review, 16*(3), 507-521.

Lobel, S. A. (1993). Sexuality at work: Where do we go from here? *Journal of Vocational Behavior, 42,* 136-152.

Lobel, S. A. (1996). *Work/life and diversity: Perspectives of workplace responses.* (Work-Family Policy Paper Series). Boston: Boston College.

Lobel, S. A. (1997). In praise of the soft stuff: A vision for human resource leadership. *Human Resource Management, 36*(1), 135-140.

Lobel, S. A. (1999). *Work/life issues in Brazil and Mexico: Expanding our understanding of work and family experiences in Latin America.* (Work-Family Policy Paper Series). Boston: Boston College.

Lobel, S. A., & Faught, L. (1996, November/December). Four methods for proving the value of work/life interventions. *Compensation and Benefits Review,* pp. 50-57.

Lobel, S. A., Googins, B., & Bankert, E. (in press). The future of work and family: Critical trends for policy, practice, and research. *Human Resource Management, 38*(3).

Lobel, S. A., & Kossek, E. E. (1996). Human resource strategies to support diversity in work and personal lifestyles: Beyond the "family friendly organization." In E. E. Kossek & S. A. Lobel (Eds.), *Managing diversity: Human resource strategies for transforming the workplace* (pp. 221-244). Cambridge, MA: Blackwell.

Lobel, S. A., Quinn, R. E., St. Clair, L., & Warfield, A. (1994). Love without sex: The impact of psychological intimacy between men and women at work. *Organizational Dynamics, 23*(1), 4-16.

Lobel, S. A., & St. Clair, L. (1992). Effects of family responsibilities, gender, and career identity salience on performance outcomes. *Academy of Management Journal, 35*(5), 1057-1069.

Lockheed, M. E. (1985). Sex and social influence: A meta-analysis guided by theory. In J. Berger & M. Zelditch, Jr. (Eds.), *Status, rewards, and influence: How expectations organize behavior* (pp. 406-429). San Francisco: Jossey-Bass.

Lockheed, M. E., & Hall, K. P. (1976). Conceptualizing sex as a status characteristic: Application to leadership training strategies. *Journal of Social Issues, 32*(3), 111-124.

Loden, M. (1985). *Feminine leadership: How to succeed in business without being one of the boys.* New York: New York Times Books.

Loerch, K. J., Russell, J. E. A., & Rush, M. C. (1989). The relationships among family domain variables and work-family conflict for men and women. *Journal of Vocational Behavior, 35,* 288-308.

London, M., & Poplawski, J. R. (1976). Effects of information on stereotype development in performance appraisal and interview context. *Journal of Applied Psychology, 61,* 199-205.

London, M., & Stumpf, S. A. (1983). Effects of candidate characteristics on management promotion decisions: An experimental study. *Personnel Psychology, 36,* 241-259.

London, M., & Wohlers, A. J. (1991). Agreement between subordinate and self-ratings in upward feedback. *Personnel Psychology, 44,* 375-390.

Longenecker, C. O., Gioia, D. A., & Sims, H. P. (1987). Behind the mask: The politics of employee appraisal. *Academy of Management Executive, 1,* 183-193.

Lord, R. G., Phillips, J. S., & Rush, M. C. (1980). Effects of sex and personality on perceptions of emergent leadership, influence, and social power. *Journal of Applied Psychology, 65,* 176-182.

Loscocco, K., & Spitze, G. (1991). The organizational context of women's and men's pay satisfaction. *Social Science Quarterly, 72*(1), 3-19.

Loy, P. H., & Stewart, L. P. (1984). The extent and effects of the sexual harassment of working women. *Sociological Focus, 17*(1), 31-43.

Loyalty no longer a model for corporate life. (1995, February 12). *New York Times.*

Lublin, J. S. (1995, June 13). Yea to that 90's dad, devoted to the kids . . . but he's out again? *Wall Street Journal,* pp. A1, A11.

Luthans, F. (1988). Successful vs. effective real managers. *Academy of Management Executive, 2*(2), 127-132.

Luthans, F., Envick, B. R., & Anderson, R. D. (1995). The need for achievement and organizational commitment of entrepreneurs: A gender comparison. In W. D. Bygrave, B. J. Bird, S. Birley, N. C. Churchill, M. Hay, R. H. Keeley, & W. E. Wetzel, Jr. (Eds.), *Frontiers of entrepreneurship research* (pp. 379-380). Babson Park, MA: Center for Entrepreneurial Studies, Babson College.

Luthar, H. K. (1996). Gender differences in evaluation of performance and leadership ability: Autocratic vs. democratic managers. *Sex Roles, 5/6,* 337-161.

Lyness, K. S., & Thompson, D. E. (1997). Above the glass ceiling? A comparison of matched samples of female and male executives. *Journal of Applied Psychology, 82,* 359-375.

Mabry, E. (1985). The effects of gender composition and task structure on small group interaction. *Small Group Behavior, 16,* 75-96.

Maccoby, E. E., & Jacklin, C. N. (1974). *The psychology of sex differences.* Stanford, CA: Stanford University Press.

MacDonald, C. L., & Sirianni, C. (1996). *Working in the service society.* Philadelphia: Temple University Press.

MacEwen, K. E., & Barling, J. (1994). Daily consequences of work interference with family and family interference with work. *Work & Stress, 8,* 244-254.

MacKinnon, C. A. (1979). *Sexual harassment of working women.* New Haven, CT: Yale University Press.

MacMillan, I. C., & Katz, J. A. (1992). Idiosyncratic milieus of entrepreneurial research: The need for comprehensive theories. *Journal of Business Venturing, 7*(1), 1-10.

Macpherson, D. A., & Hirsch, B. T. (1995). Wages and gender composition: Why do women's jobs pay less? *Journal of Labor Economics, 13*(3), 426-471.

Madden, J. F. (1985). The persistence of pay differentials: The economics of sex discrimination. In L. Larwood, A. H. Stromberg, & B. A. Gutek (Eds.), *Women and work: An annual review* (Vol. 1, pp. 76-114). Beverly Hills, CA: Sage.

Maher, K. J. (1997). Gender-related stereotypes of transformational and transactional leadership. *Sex Roles, 3*, 209-225.

Maier, M. (1992). Evolving paradigms of management in organizations: A gendered analysis. *Journal of Management Systems, 4*(1), 29-45.

Maier, M. (1994). Glass ceilings, glass prisons: Reflections on the gender barrier. *The Diversity Factor, 2*(3), 32-37.

Maier, M. (1997a). Confronting the (f)laws of the pyramid: Challenger's legacy for leadership and organizational development. *Public Administration Quarterly, 21*(3), 258-293.

Maier, M. (1997b, Summer). Invisible privilege: What White men don't see. *The Diversity Factor, 5*(4), 28-33.

Maier, M. (1997c). "We have to make a MANagement decision": *Challenger* and the dysfunctions of corporate masculinity. In P. Prasad, A. J. Mills, M. Elmes, & A. Prasad (Eds.), *Managing the organizational melting pot: Dilemmas of workplace diversity* (pp. 226-254). Thousand Oaks, CA: Sage.

Maier, M. (1998). Preparing managers for the 21st century: Perspectives on contemporary leadership education. *Journal of Management Systems, 10*(2), 1-12.

Mainiero, L. A. (1986). A review and analysis of power dynamics in organizational romances. *Academy of Management Review, 11*, 750-762.

Mainiero, L. A. (1989). *Office romance: Love, power, and sex in the workplace.* New York: Rawson Associates.

Mainiero, L. A. (1994). Getting anointed for advancement: The case of executive women. *Academy of Management Executive, 8*(2), 53-67.

Major, B. (1993). Gender, entitlement and the distribution of family labour. *Journal of Social Issues, 3*, 141-159.

Major, B. (1994). From social inequality to personal entitlement: The role of social comparisons, legitimacy appraisals, and group membership. *Advances in Experimental Social Psychology, 26*, 293-355.

Major, B., Feinstein, J., & Crocker, J. (1994). Attributional ambiguity of affirmative action. *Basic and Applied Social Psychology, 15*, 113-141.

Malen, E. A., & Stroh, L. K. (1998). The influence of gender on job loss coping behavior & career search efficacy among unemployed managers. *Journal of Employment Counseling, 35*, 26-39.

Malovich, N. J., & Stake, J. E. (1990). Sexual harassment on campus: Individual differences in attitudes and beliefs. *Psychology of Women Quarterly, 14*, 63-81.

Mandelson, D. A. (1996). Women's changing labor force participation in the United States. In P. J. Dubeck & K. Borman (Eds.), *Women and work* (pp. 3-6). New York: Garland.

Mansfield, P. K., Koch, P. B., Henderson, J., Vicary, J. R., Cohn, M., & Young, E. W. (1991). The job climate for women in traditionally male blue-collar occupations. *Sex Roles, 25*, 63-79.

Manz, C. C. (1998). *The leadership wisdom of Jesus: Practical lessons for today.* San Francisco: Berrett-Koehler.

Maracek, J. (1995). Gender, politics and psychology's ways of knowing. *American Psychologist, 50,* 162-163.

Marcic, D. (1997). *Managing with the wisdom of love.* San Francisco: Jossey-Bass.

Marini, M. M. (1989). Sex differences in earnings in the United States. *Annual Review of Sociology, 15,* 343-380.

Marini, M. M., & Brinton, M. C. (1984). Sex typing in occupational socialization. In B. Reskin (Ed.), *Sex segregation in the workplace: Trends, explanations, remedies* (pp. 192-232). Washington, DC: National Academy Press.

Marini, M. M., & Fan, P. L. (1997, August). The gender gap in earnings at career entry. *American Sociological Review, 62,* 588-604.

Marks, S. R. (1977). Multiple roles and role strain: Some notes on human energy, time and commitment. *American Sociological Review, 42,* 921-936.

Markus, H., Crane, M., Bernstein, S., & Siladi, M. (1982). Self-schemas and gender. *Journal of Personality and Social Psychology, 42,* 38-50.

Markus, M. (1987). Women, success and civil society: Submission to, or subversion of, the achievement principle. In S. Benhabib & D. Cornell (Eds.), *Feminism as critique: Essays on the politics of gender in late-capitalist societies* (pp. 96-109). Minneapolis: University of Minnesota Press.

Marlowe, C. M., Schneider, S. L., & Nelson, C. E. (1996). Gender and attractiveness bias in hiring decisions: Are more experienced managers less biased? *Journal of Applied Psychology, 81,* 11-21.

Marquart, J. M. (1988). *A pattern matching approach to link program theory and evaluation data: The case of employer-sponsored child care.* Unpublished doctoral dissertation, Cornell University, Ithaca, NY.

Marra, R., & Lindner, J. (1992). The true cost of parental leave: The parental leave cost model. In E. Friedman, E. Galinsky, & V. Plowden (Eds.), *Parental leave and productivity: Current research* (pp. 55-78). New York: Families and Work Institute.

Marsh, H. W. (1987). Masculinity, femininity, and androgyny: Their relations to multiple dimensions of self-concept. *Multivariate Behavioral Research, 22,* 427-449.

Marsh, H. W., & Byrne, B. M. (1991). Differentiated additive androgyny model: Relations between masculinity, femininity and multiple dimensions of self-concept. *Journal of Personality and Social Psychology, 61,* 811-828.

Marshack, K. J. (1994). Copreneurs and dual-career couples: Are they different? *Entrepreneurship Theory and Practice, 19*(1), 49-70.

Marshack, K. J. (1998). *Entrepreneurial couples—Making it work at work and at home.* Palo Alto, CA: Davies-Black.

Marshall, J. (1984). *Women managers: Travellers in a male world.* Chichester, UK and New York: Wiley.

Marshall, J. (1995). *Women managers moving on: Exploring career and life choices.* London: Routledge.

Martin, J. (1990a). Deconstructing organizational taboos: The suppression of gender conflict in organizations. *Organizational Science, 1*(4), 339-359.

Martin, J. (1990b). *Re-reading Weber: Searching for feminist alternatives to bureaucracy.* Paper presented at the annual meeting of the Academy of Management, San Francisco.

Martin, P. Y. (1985). Group sex composition in work organizations: A structural-normative model. *Research in the Sociology of Organizations, 4,* 311-349.

Martin, P. Y. (1993). Feminist practice in organizations: Implications for management. In E. Fagenson (Ed.), *Women in management: Trends, perspectives and challenges* (pp. 274-296). Newbury Park, CA: Sage.

Martin, P. Y. (1996). Gendering and evaluating dynamics: Men, masculinities, and managements. In D. L. Collinson & J. Hearn (Eds.), *Men as managers, managers as men: Critical perspectives on men, masculinities, and managements* (pp. 186-209). Thousand Oaks, CA: Sage.

Martin, P. Y., & Harkreader, S. (1993). Multiple gender contexts and employee rewards. *Work and Occupations, 20*(3), 296-336.

Martin, S. E. (1991). The effectiveness of affirmative action: The case of women in policing. *Justice Quarterly, 8*, 489-504.

Martocchio, J. J., & O'Leary, A. M. (1989). Sex differences in occupational stress: A meta-analytic review. *Journal of Applied Psychology, 74*, 495-501.

Maslow, A. (1943). A theory of human motivation. *Psychological Review, 50*, 370-396.

Maslow, A. (1954). *Motivation and personality.* New York: Harper.

Massey, D. S., & Denton, N. A. (1989). The dimensions of residential segregation. *Social Forces, 67*(2), 281-315.

Matsui, T., Kakuyama, T., Onglatco, M., & Ogutu, M. (1995). Women's perceptions of socio-sexual behavior: A cross-cultural replication. *Journal of Vocational Behavior, 46*, 203-215.

Matsui, T., Ohsawa, T., & Onglotco, M. (1995). Work-family conflict and the stress-buffering effects of husband support and coping behavior among Japanese married working women. *Journal of Vocational Behavior, 47*, 178-192.

Matthews, C. H., & Moser, S. B. (1996). A longitudinal investigation of the impact of family background and gender on interest in small firm ownership. *Journal of Small Business Management, 34*(2), 29-43.

Maurer, T. J., & Taylor, M. A. (1994). Is sex by itself enough? An explanation of gender bias issues in performance appraisal. *Organizational Behavior and Human Decision Processes, 60*, 231-251.

Mazer, D. B., & Percival, E. F. (1989). Ideology or experience? The relationships among perceptions, attitudes, and experiences of sexual harassment in university students. *Sex Roles, 20*, 135-147.

McCall, L. (1998a). *Spatial configurations of inequality: Restructuring gender, class, and race.* Unpublished manuscript, Rutgers University, New Brunswick, NJ.

McCall, L. (1998b). Spatial routes to gender wage (in)equality: Regional restructuring and wage differentials by gender and education. *Economic Geography, 74*, 379-404.

McCall, M. W., Jr., & Bobko, P. (1990). Research methods in service of discovery. In M. D. Dunnette & L. Hough (Eds.), *Handbook of industrial and organizational psychology* (2nd ed., Vol. 1). Palo Alto, CA: Consulting Psychologists Press.

McClelland, D. (1984). How motives, skills, and values determine what people do. In D. McClelland (Ed.), *Motives, personality and society: Selected papers* (pp. 213-236). New York: Praeger.

McClelland, D., Atkinson, J., Clark, R., & Lowell, E. (1953). *The achievement motive.* New York: Appleton-Century-Crofts.

McCreary, D. R., & Korabik, K. (1994). Examining the relationships between socially desirable and undesirable aspects of agency and communion. *Sex Roles, 31*, 637-651.

McDonald, J. J., & Lees-Haley, P. R. (1995). Avoiding "junk science" in sexual harassment litigation. *Employee Relations, 21,* 51-71.

McGrath, J. E. (1982). Dilemmatics: The study of research choices and dilemmas. In J. E. McGrath, J. Martin, & R. Kulka (Eds.), *Judgement calls in research* (pp. 69-102). Beverly Hills, CA: Sage.

McGregor, D. (1960). *The human side of enterprise.* New York: McGraw-Hill.

McGuire, J. B., & Liro, J. R. (1986). Flexible work schedules, work attitudes, and perceptions of productivity. *Public Personnel Management, 15,* 65-73.

McIntosh, P. (1988). *White privilege and male privilege: A personal account of coming to see correspondences through work in women's studies* (Working Paper No. 189). Wellesley, MA Center for Research on Women, Wellesley College.

McKenna, E. (1997). *When work doesn't work anymore: Women, work and identity.* New York: Delacorte.

McLeod, P. L., Lobel, S. A., & Cox, T. H. (1996). Ethnic diversity and creativity in small groups. *Small Group Research, 27*(2), 248-264.

McManus, S. E., & Russell, J. E. A. (1997). New directions for mentoring research: An examination of related constructs. *Journal of Vocational Behavior, 51,* 145-161.

McMillan, C. (1982). *Reason, women and nature: Some philosophical problems with nature.* Princeton, NJ: Princeton University Press.

McPherson, M., & Smith-Lovin, L. (1986). Sex segregation in voluntary associations. *American Sociological Review, 51*(1), 61-79.

McRae, M. B. (1994). Influence of sex role stereotypes on personnel decisions of Black managers. *Journal of Applied Psychology, 79,* 306-309.

McShulskis, E. (1996). Bringing up baby. *HRMagazine, 41*(12), 24.

McWhirter, E. H. (1997). Perceived barriers to education and career: Ethnic and gender differences. *Journal of Vocational Behavior, 50,* 124-140.

McWilliams, A., & Siegel, D. (1997). Event studies in management research: Theoretical and empirical issues. *Academy of Management Journal, 40*(3), 626-657.

Mead, M. (1980). A proposal: We need taboos on sex at work. In D. A. Neugarten & J. M. Shafritz (Eds.), *Sexuality in organizations: Romantic and coercive behaviors at work* (pp. 53-56). Oak Park, IL: Moore.

Meeker, B. F., & Weitzel-O'Neill, P. A. (1985). Sex roles and interpersonal behavior in task-oriented groups. In J. Berger & M. Zelditch, Jr. (Eds.), *Status, rewards, and influence: How expectations organize behavior* (pp. 379-405). San Francisco: Jossey-Bass.

Megargee, E. I. (1969). Influence of sex roles on the manifestation of leadership. *Journal of Applied Psychology, 53,* 377-382.

Melamed, T. (1995). Career success: The moderating effect of gender. *Journal of Vocational Behavior, 47,* 35-60.

Melamed, T. (1996). An assessment of a gender-specific model. *Journal of Occupational and Organizational Psychology, 69,* 217-242.

Mellor, S. (1995). Gender composition and gender representation in local unions: Relationships between women's participation in local office and women's participation in local activities. *Journal of Applied Psychology, 80*(6), 706-720.

Menaghan, E. G., & Parcel, T. L. (1995). Social sources of change in children's home environments: The effects of parental occupational experiences and family conditions. *Journal of Marriage and the Family, 57,* 69-84.

Menon, S. A., & Kanekar, S. (1992). Attitudes toward sexual harassment of women in India. *Journal of Applied Social Psychology, 22,* 1940-1952.

Meritor Savings Bank, FSB v. Vinson, 477 U.S. 57, 40 FEP Cases 1822 (1986).

Messerschmidt, J. W. (1995). Managing to kill: Masculinities and the Space Shuttle *Challenger* explosion. *Masculinities, 3*(4), 1-22.

Metro Broadcasting, Inc. v. FCC, 110 S. Ct. 2997 (1990).

Michael, R. T., Hartmann, H. I., & O'Farrell, B. (Eds.). (1989). *Pay equity: Empirical inquiries.* Washington, DC: National Academy Press.

Mighty, E. J. (1997). Triple jeopardy: Immigrant women of color in the labor force. In P. Prasad, A. J. Mills, M. Elmes, & A. Prasad (Eds.), *Managing the organizational melting pot: Dilemmas of workplace diversity* (pp. 312-339). Thousand Oaks, CA: Sage.

Miles, A. (1988). *Women and mental illness.* Brighton, UK: Wheatsheaf.

Milkovich, G., & Gomez, L. R. (1976). Child care and selected work behaviors. *Academy of Management Journal, 19,* 111-115.

Miller, J. B. (1976). *Toward a new psychology of women.* Boston: Beacon.

Miller, S. (1997). The role of a juggler. In S. Parasuraman & J. H. Greenhaus (Eds.), *Integrating work and family: Challenges and choices for a changing world* (pp. 48-56). Westport, CT: Quorum Books.

Miller, T. I. (1984). The effects of employer-sponsored child care on employee absenteeism, turnover, productivity, recruitment or job satisfaction: What is claimed and what is known. *Personnel Psychology, 37*(2), 277-289.

Mills, A. (1989). Gender, sexuality, and organization theory. In J. Hearn, D. Sheppard, P. Tancred-Sheriff, & G. Burrell (Eds.), *The sexuality of organization* (pp. 29-44). Newbury Park, CA: Sage.

Mills, A. (1997). Gender, bureaucracy, and the business curriculum. *Journal of Management Education, 21*(3), 325-342.

Mills, P. K., Chase, R. B., & Margulies, N. (1983). Motivating the client/employee system as a service production strategy. *Academy of Management Review, 8*(2), 301-310.

Mincer, J., & Polachek, S. (1974). Family investments in human capital: Earnings of women. *Journal of Political Economy, 82,* S76-S108.

Mitchell, R. E., Cronkite, R. C., & Moos, R. H. (1983). Stress, coping and depression among married couples. *Journal of Abnormal Psychology, 92,* 433-448.

Mobley, G. M., Jaret, C., Marsh, K., & Lim, Y. Y. (1994). Mentoring, job satisfaction, gender, and the legal profession. *Sex Roles, 31,* 79-98.

Mobley, W. H. (1982). Supervisor and employee race and sex effects on performance appraisals: A field study of adverse impact and generalizability. *Academy of Management Journal, 25,* 598-606.

Mohr, L. A., & Henson, S. W. (1996). Impact of employee gender and job congruency on customer satisfaction. *Journal of Consumer Psychology, 5*(2), 161-187.

Moir, A. (1991). *Brain sex: The real difference between men and women.* Secaucus, NJ: Carol Publishing Group.

The mommy track vs. the fast track. (1989, May 21). *New York Times,* p. D2.

Moore, D. P. (1984). Evaluating in-role and out-of-role performers. *Academy of Management Journal, 27,* 603-618.

Moore, D. P. (1987a). First- and second-generation female entrepreneurs—Identifying the needs and differences. In D. F. Ray (Ed.), *Southern Management Association proceedings* (pp. 175-177). Mississippi State: Mississippi State University.

Moore, D. P. (1987b). *Identifying the needs of women entrepreneurs in South Carolina* (Tech. Rep. No. 2). (For distribution to South Carolina Development Board, Small Business Administration, and other government bodies.) Charleston, SC: The Citadel Development Foundation.

Moore, D. P. (1988). Female entrepreneurs: New methodologies and research directions in the 1990s. In *Research Methodology Conference proceedings* (Vol. 38, pp. 1-44). Halifax, Nova Scotia: Mount Saint Vincent University.

Moore, D. P. (1990). An examination of present research on the female entrepreneur— Suggested research strategies for the 1990s. *Journal of Business Ethics, 9*(4/5), 275-281.

Moore, D. P., & Buttner, E. H. (1997). *Women entrepreneurs: Moving beyond the glass ceiling.* Thousand Oaks, CA: Sage.

Moore, D. P., Buttner, E. H., & Rosen, B. (1992). Stepping off the corporate track: The entrepreneurial alternative. In U. Sekaran & F. Leong (Eds.), *Womanpower: Managing in times of demographic turbulence* (pp. 85-110). Newbury Park, CA: Sage.

Moreno, J. L. (1943). *Sociometry and the cultural order.* New York: Beacon.

Morgan, D. H. J. (1992). *Discovering men.* New York: Routledge.

Morgan, D. H. J. (1996). The gender of bureaucracy. In D. L. Collinson & J. Hearn (Eds.), *Men as managers, managers as men: Critical perspectives on men, masculinities, and managements* (pp. 43-60). Thousand Oaks, CA: Sage.

Morgan, G. (1986). *Images of organization.* Beverly Hills, CA: Sage.

Morgan, G., & Smircich, L. (1980). The case for qualitative research. *Academy of Management Review, 5,* 491-500.

Morris, B. (1995, September 18). Executive women confront midlife crisis. *Fortune,* pp. 60-68.

Morris, B. (1997, March 17). Is your family wrecking your career? *Fortune,* pp. 70-90.

Morris, B. (1998, February 2). What's a corporate wife worth? (It's her job too). *Fortune,* pp. 65-78.

Morris, C. G., & Hackman, J. R. (1969). Behavioral correlates of perceived leadership. *Journal of Personality and Social Psychology, 13,* 350-361.

Morrison, A. M. (1992). *The new leaders: Guidelines on leadership diversity in America.* San Francisco: Jossey-Bass.

Morrison, A. M., & Von Glinow, M. A. (1990). Women and minorities in management. *American Psychologist, 45,* 200-208.

Morrison, A. M., White, R. P., Van Velsor, E., & the Center for Creative Leadership. (1987). *Breaking the glass ceiling: Can women reach the top of America's largest corporations?* Reading, MA: Addison-Wesley.

Morrison, A. M., White, R. P., Van Velsor, E., & the Center for Creative Leadership. (1992). *Breaking the glass ceiling: Can women reach the top of America's largest corporations?* (Updated ed.). Reading, MA: Addison-Wesley.

Morrison, E. W., & Herlihy, J. M. (1992). Becoming the best place to work: Managing diversity at American Express Travel Related Services. In S. E. Jackson (Ed.), *Diversity in the workplace: Human resource initiatives* (pp. 203-226). New York: Guilford.

Mosely, A. G., & Capaldi, N. (1996). *Affirmative action: Social injustice or unfair precedent?* Lanham, MD: Rowman & Littlefield.

Moses, J. L. (1973). The development of an assessment center for the early identification of supervisory potential. *Personnel Psychology, 26,* 569-580.

Moses, J. L., & Boehm, V. R. (1975). Relationship of assessment-center performance to management progress of women. *Journal of Applied Psychology, 60,* 527-529.

Moskowitz, D. W., Suh, E. J., & Desaulniers, J. (1994). Situational influences on gender differences in agency and communion. *Journal of Personality and Social Psychology, 66,* 753-761.

Moss, S. E., & Kent, R. L. (1994). Effects of sex and gender role on leader emergence. *Academy of Management Journal, 37,* 1335-1346.

Moss, S. E., & Kent, R. L. (1996). Gender and gender-role categorization of emergent leaders: A critical review and comprehensive analysis. *Sex Roles, 35,* 79-96.

Motherhood: At what cost to career and family? (1998). *Women in Management, 8*(7), 1-5.

Mroczkowski, T. (1997). Women as employees and entrepreneurs in the Polish transformation. *Industrial Relations Journal, 28*(2), 83-92.

Mulac, A. (1998). The gender-linked language effect: Do language differences really make a difference? In D. J. Canary & K. Dindia (Eds.), *Sex differences and similarities in communication: Critical essays and empirical investigations of sex and gender in interaction* (pp. 127-153). Mahwah, NJ: Lawrence Erlbaum.

Mulac, A., Lundell, T. L., & Bradac, J. J. (1986). Male/female language differences and attributional consequences in a public speaking situation: Toward an explanation of the gender-linked language effect. *Communication Monographs, 53,* 115-129.

Mullen, B., Salas, E., & Driskell, J. E. (1989). Salience, motivation, and artifact as contributions to the relation between participation rate and leadership. *Journal of Experimental Social Psychology, 25,* 545-559.

Mullen, E. J. (1994). Framing the mentoring relationship as an information exchange. *Human Resource Management Review, 4,* 257-281.

Muller, H. J. (1998). American Indian women managers: Living in two worlds. *Journal of Management Inquiry, 7,* 4-28.

Munk, N. (1994, August 15). Fighting over the spoils. *Forbes,* pp. 50-51.

Murphy, A. (1992). The start-up of the '90s. *Inc., 14*(3), 32-40.

Murphy, K. R., & Cleveland, J. N. (1991). *Performance appraisal: An organizational perspective.* Boston: Allyn & Bacon.

Murphy, Y. (1993). Women in business and management—Ireland. In M. J. Davidson & C. L. Cooper (Eds.), *European women in business and management* (pp. 43-57). London: Paul Chapman.

Murray, M. (1991). *Beyond the myths and magic of mentoring: How to facilitate an effective mentoring program.* San Francisco: Jossey-Bass.

Murrell, A. J., Dietz-Uhler, B. L., Dovidio, J. F., Gaertner, S. L., & Drout, C. (1994). Aversive racism and resistance to affirmative action: Perceptions of justice are not necessarily color blind. *Basic and Applied Social Psychology, 15,* 71-86.

Myers, D. W., & Humphreys, N. J. (1985). The caveats in mentorship. *Business Horizons, 28*(4), 9-14.

Nacoste, R. W. (1985). Selection procedure and responses to affirmative action. *Law and Human Behavior, 9,* 225-242.

Nacoste, R. W. (1987). But do they care about fairness? The dynamics of preferential treatment and minority interest. *Basic and Applied Social Psychology, 8,* 177-191.

Naffziger, D. W., Hornsby, J. S., & Kuratko, D. F. (1994). A proposed research model of entrepreneurial motivation. *Entrepreneurship Theory and Practice, 18*(3), 29-42.

Nagel, J. (1994). Constructing ethnicity: Creating and recreating ethnic identity and culture. *Social Problems, 41,* 152-176.

Nakano, K. (1991). The role of coping strategies on psychological and physical well-being. *Journal of Psychological Research, 33*(4), 160-167.

Narayanan, V. K., & Nath, R. (1982). A field test of some attitudinal and behavioral consequences of flexitime. *Journal of Applied Psychology, 67*(2), 214-218.

Nash, M. (1996). The core elements of ethnicity. In J. Hutchinson & A. D. Smith (Eds.), *Ethnicity* (pp. 24-28). Oxford, UK: Oxford University Press.

National Council of Jewish Women. (1987, November). *Accommodating pregnancy in the workplace* (NCJW Center for the Child report). New York: Author.

National Foundation for Women Business Owners & Dun and Bradstreet Information Services. (1995, April). *Women-owned businesses: Breaking the boundaries—The progress and achievement of women-owned enterprises.* Silver Spring, MD: Author.

National Foundation for Women Business Owners. (1994a, September 30). *Credibility and independence: Women business owners voice greatest challenges and biggest rewards of entrepreneurship* [On-line]. Available: http://www.NFWBO.org/ rm012. htm (Press release).

National Foundation for Women Business Owners. (1994b, July 19). *New study quantifies thinking and management style differences between women and men business owners* [On-line]. Available: http://www.NFWBO.org/rr003.htm (Press release).

National Foundation for Women Business Owners. (1994c, May 17). *Women-owned businesses lead the way in providing employee benefits* [On-line]. Available: http://www.NFWBO.org/rm011.htm (Press release).

National Foundation for Women Business Owners. (1996a). *Capital, credit and financing: Comparing women and men business owners' sources and uses of capital.* Silver Spring, MD: Author.

National Foundation for Women Business Owners. (1996b). *Growth of women-led businesses in Canada echoes increases in the U.S.* [On-line]. Available: http://www. NFWBO.org/rr009.htm.

National Foundation for Women Business Owners. (1996c). *Women business owners' economic impact re-affirmed* [On-line]. Available: http://www.NFWBO.org.

National Foundation for Women Business Owners. (1996d, October). *Women business owners make progress in access to capital; still lag men-owned businesses in credit levels* [On-line]. Available: http://www.NFWBO.org/rr010.htm (Press release).

National Foundation for Women Business Owners. (1996e, May 24). *Women business owners: Leaders in volunteerism* [On-line]. Available: http://www.NFWBO.org/ ao19710.htm (Press release).

National Foundation for Women Business Owners. (1997a, April 14). *First selection of leading women entrepreneurs worldwide* [On-line]. Available: http://www. NFWBO.org/rr013.htm (Press release).

National Foundation for Women Business Owners. (1997b, June 25). *Minority women-owned firms thriving—Growth is triple the rate of overall business growth* [On-line]. Available: http://www.NFWBO.org//rr014.htm (Press release).

National Foundation for Women Business Owners. (1997c, November 13). *Organizations to research global trade by women entrepreneurs—Alliance to benefit women business owners in U.S., Canada* [On-line]. Available: http://www.NFWBO.org/a049701.htm (Press release).

National Foundation for Women Business Owners. (1997d, November 13). *Women business owners give priority to retirement plans—They also offer more plan options; seek to minimize risks* [On-line]. Available: http://www.NFWBO.org/rr016.htm (Press release).

National Foundation for Women Business Owners. (1997e, February 29). *Women entrepreneurs are a growing international trend* [On-line]. Available: http://www.NFWBO.org/na001.htm (Press release).

National Foundation for Women Business Owners. (1998a, March). *NFWBO news, 1998, No. 1—Women business owners give priority to retirement plans* [On-line]. Available: http://www.NFWBO.org/News9801.htm#980101 (Press release).

National Foundation for Women Business Owners. (1998b, April 28). *Women of all races share entrepreneurial spirit—Women of color start businesses in record numbers* [On-line]. Available: http://www.NFWBO.org/rr020.htm (Press release).

National Foundation for Women Business Owners. (1998c, March 3). *Women entrepreneurs worldwide voice optimism—Also embrace technology and international trade* [On-line]. Available: http://www.NFWBO.org/rr019.htm (Press release).

Nelson, D. L., & Quick, J. C. (1985). Professional women: Are distress and disease inevitable? *Academy of Management Review, 10,* 206-218.

Nelton, S. (1991, May). Men, women, and leadership. *Nation's Business,* pp. 16-22.

Netemeyer, R. G., Boles, J. S., & McMurrian, R. (1996). Development and validation of work-family conflict and family-work conflict scales. *Journal of Applied Psychology, 81,* 400-410.

Newcomb, T. (1943). *Personality and social change: Attitude formation in a student community.* New York: Dryden.

Newman, J. M., & Cooper, E. (1993). Determinants of academic recognition: The case of the *Journal of Applied Psychology. Journal of Applied Psychology, 78,* 518-526.

Nieva, V. F., & Gutek, B. A. (1980). Sex effects on evaluation. *Academy of Management Review, 5,* 267-276.

Nieva, V. F., & Gutek, B. A. (1981). *Women and work: A psychological perspective.* New York: Praeger.

Nkomo, S. M. (1992). The emperor has no clothes: Rewriting "race in organizations." *Academy of Management Review, 17,* 487-513.

Nkomo, S. M., & Cox, T., Jr. (1996). Diverse identities in organizations. In S. R. Clegg, C. Hardy, & W. Nord (Eds.), *Handbook of organization studies* (pp. 338-356). London: Sage.

Noble, B. P. (1993, October 17). Reforming the talk on labor reform. *New York Times,* p. F25.

Noe, R. A. (1988a). An investigation of the determinants of successful assigned mentoring relationships. *Personnel Psychology, 41,* 457-479.

Noe, R. A. (1988b). Women and mentoring: A review and research agenda. *Academy of Management Review, 13,* 65-78.

Nollen, S. D., & Martin, V. H. (1978). *Alternative work schedules* (Pts. 1, 2, 3). New York: AMACOM, American Management Association.

Nyquist, L. V., & Spence, J. T. (1986). Effects of dispositional dominance and sex-role expectations on leadership behaviors. *Journal of Personality and Social Psychology, 50,* 87-93.

Oakland, S., & Ostell, A. (1996). Measuring coping: A review and critique. *Human Relations, 49*(2), 133-155.

O'Driscoll, M. P., Ilgen, D. R., & Hildreth, K. (1992). Time devoted to job and off-job activities, interrole conflict, and affective experiences. *Journal of Applied Psychology, 77,* 272-279.

Offerman L. R., & Kearney, C. T. (1988). Supervisor and subordinate influence strategies. *Personality and Social Psychology Bulletin, 14,* 360-367.

Ohlott, P. J., Ruderman, M. N., & McCauley, C. D. (1994). Gender differences in managers' developmental job experiences. *Academy of Management Journal, 37,* 46-67.

O'Leary, V. E. (1974). Some attitudinal barriers to occupational aspirations in women. *Psychological Bulletin, 81,* 809-826.

Olesen, V. (1994). Feminisms and models of qualitative research. In N. K. Denzin & Y. S. Lincoln (Eds.), *Handbook of qualitative research* (pp. 158-175). Newbury Park, CA: Sage.

Olian, J. D., Carroll, S. J., & Giannantonio, C. M. (1993). Mentor reactions to protégés: An experiment with managers. *Journal of Vocational Behavior, 43,* 266-278.

Olian, J. D., Carroll, S. J., Giannantonio, C. M., & Feren, D. B. (1988). What do protégés look for in a mentor? Results of three experimental studies. *Journal of Vocational Behavior, 33,* 15-37.

Olian, J. D., Schwab, D. P., & Haberfeld, Y. (1988). The impact of applicant gender compared to qualifications on hiring recommendations. *Organizational Behavior and Human Decision Processes, 41,* 180-195.

Olivares, F. (1993). Women in business and management—Italy. In M. J. Davidson & C. L. Cooper (Eds.), *European women in business and management* (pp. 161-173). London: Paul Chapman.

Olson, J. M., Roese, N. J., & Zanna, M. P. (1996). Expectancies. In E. T. Higgins & A. W. Kruglanski (Eds.), *Social psychology: Handbook of basic principles* (pp. 211-238). New York: Guilford.

Olson, S. F., & Currie, H. M. (1992). Female entrepreneurs: Personal value systems and business strategies in a male-dominated industry. *Journal of Small Business Management, 30*(1), 49-56.

Oncale v. Sundowner Offshore Services, Inc. 118 S. Ct. 998 (1998).

O'Neill, J. (1985). Role differentiation and the gender gap. In L. Larwood, A. H. Stromberg, & B. A. Gutek (Eds.), *Women and work: An annual review* (Vol. 1, pp. 50-75). Beverly Hills, CA: Sage.

O'Neill, J., & Polachek, S. (1993). Why the gender gap in wages narrowed in the 1980s. *Journal of Labor Economics, 11*(No. 1, Pt. 1), 205-228.

Ontiveros, M. L. (1998). Three perspectives on workplace harassment of women of color. In R. Delgado & J. Stefancic (Eds.), *The Latino/a condition: A critical reader* (pp. 531-535). New York: New York University Press.

Oquendo, A. R. (1998). Re-imagining the Latino/a race. In R. Delgado & J. Stefancic (Eds.), *The Latino/a condition: A critical reader* (pp. 60-71). New York: New York University Press.

O'Reilly, C. A., Caldwell, D. F., & Barnett, W. P. (1989). Work group demography, social integration, and turnover. *Administrative Science Quarterly, 34,* 21-37.

Orlans, H. (1992). Affirmative action in higher education. *Annals of the American Academy of Political and Social Science, 523*, 144-158.

Orpen, C. (1995). The effects of mentoring on employees' career success. *Journal of Social Psychology, 135*, 667-668.

Osborn, R. N., & Vicars, W. M. (1976). Sex stereotypes: An artifact in leader behavior and subordinate satisfaction analysis? *Academy of Management Journal, 19*, 439-449.

Ostroff, C., & Kozlowski, S. W. J. (1993). The role of mentoring in the information gathering processes of newcomers during early organizational socialization. *Journal of Vocational Behavior, 42*, 170-183.

O'Toole, J. (1995). *Leading change: Overcoming the ideology of comfort and the tyranny of custom.* San Francisco: Jossey-Bass.

Papanek, H. (1973). Men, women and work: Reflections on the two-person career. In J. Huber (Ed.), *Changing women in a changing society* (pp. 90-110). Chicago: University of Chicago Press.

Parasuraman, S., & Greenhaus, J. H. (1993). Personal portrait: The life-style of the woman manager. In E. A. Fagenson (Ed.), *Women in management: Trends, issues, and challenges in managerial diversity* (Vol. 4, pp. 186-211). Newbury Park, CA: Sage.

Parasuraman, S., & Greenhaus, J. H. (1994). Determinants of support provided and received by partners in two-career relationships. In L. A. Heslop (Ed.), *The ties that bind* (pp. 121-145). Calgary, Alberta: Canadian Consortium of Management Schools.

Parasuraman, S., & Greenhaus, J. H. (Eds.). (1997). *Integrating work and family: Challenges and choices for a changing world.* Westport, CT: Quorum.

Parasuraman, S., Greenhaus, J. H., & Granrose, C. S. (1992). Role stressors, social support, and well-being among two-career couples. *Journal of Organizational Behavior, 13*, 339-356.

Parasuraman, S., Greenhaus, J. H., Rabinowitz, S., Bedeian, A. G., & Mossholder, K. W. (1989). Work and family variables as mediators of the relationship between wives' employment and husbands' well-being. *Academy of Management Journal, 32*, 185-201.

Parasuraman, S., Purohit, Y. S., Godshalk, V. M., & Beutell, N. J. (1996). Work and family variables, entrepreneurial career success, and psychological well-being. *Journal of Vocational Behavior, 48*, 275-300.

Parasuraman, S., Singh, R., & Greenhaus, J. H. (1997). The influence of self and partner family variables on career development opportunities of professional women and men. In P. Tharenou (Ed.), *Best paper and abstract proceedings of the Australian Industrial and Organizational Psychology Conference* (pp. 125-129). Melbourne: Australian Psychological Society.

Parcel, T. L. (1989). Comparable worth, occupational labor markets, and occupational earnings: Results from the 1980 census. In R. T. Michael, H. I. Hartmann, & B. O'Farrell (Eds.), *Pay equity: Empirical inquiries* (pp. 134-152). Washington, DC: National Academy Press.

Parker, B., & Fagenson, E. A. (1994). An introductory overview of women in corporate management. In M. J. Davidson & R. J. Burke (Eds.), *Women in management: Current research issues* (pp. 11-28). London: Paul Chapman.

Parker, C. P., Baltes, B. B., & Christiansen, N. D. (1997). Support for affirmative action, justice perceptions, and work attitudes: A study of gender and racial-ethnic group differences. *Journal of Applied Psychology, 82,* 376-389.

Parker, I. (1989). Discourse and power. In J. Shotter & J. Gergen (Eds.), *Texts of identity* (pp. 56-69). London: Sage.

Parker, P. S., & ogilvie, dt. (1996). Gender, culture, and leadership: Toward a culturally distinct model of African-American women executives' leadership strategies. *Leadership Quarterly, 7,* 189-214.

Parker, V. A., & Kram, K. E. (1993). Women mentoring women: Creating conditions for connection. *Business Horizons, 36,* 42-51.

Paroline v. Unisys Corporation, 879 F.2d 100 (4th Cir. 1989).

Parsons, T., & Bales, R. F. (1955). *Family, socialization and interaction process.* New York: Free Press.

Parsons, T., Bales, R. F., & Shils, E. A. (1953). *Working papers in the theory of action.* Glencoe, IL: Free Press.

Patton, M. Q. (1990). *Qualitative evaluation and research methods* (2nd ed.). Newbury Park, CA: Sage.

Pazy, A. (1986). The persistence of pro-male bias despite identical information regarding causes of success. *Organizational Behavior and Human Decision Processes, 38,* 366-377.

Pearson, J. (1985). *Gender and communication.* Dubuque, IA: William C. Brown.

Pelled, L., & Xin, K. (1997). Birds of a feather: Leader-member demographic similarity and organizational attachment in Mexico. *Leadership Quarterly, 8*(4), 433-450.

Pelled, L. H. (1996). Relational demography and perceptions of group conflict and performance: A field investigation. *International Journal of Conflict Management, 7*(3), 230-246.

Pellegrino, E., & Reese, B. (1982). Perceived formative and operational problems encountered by female entrepreneurs in retail and service firms. *Journal of Small Business Management, 20*(2), 15-24.

Peplau, L. A., & Conrad, E. (1989). Beyond non-sexist research: The perils of feminist methods in psychology. *Psychology of Women Quarterly, 13,* 379-400.

Perlow, L. A. (1997). *Finding time: How corporations, individuals, and families can benefit from new work practices.* Ithaca, NY: ILR.

Perry, E. (1994). A prototype matching approach to understanding the role of applicant gender and age in the evaluation of job applicants. *Journal of Applied Social Psychology, 24,* 1433-1473.

Perry, E. L., Davis-Blake, A., & Kulik, C. T. (1994). Explaining gender-based selection decisions: A synthesis of contextual and cognitive approaches. *Academy of Management Review, 19,* 786-820.

Perry, K. (1982). *Employers and child care: Establishing services through the workplace.* Washington, DC: U.S. Department of Labor, Women's Bureau.

Pessar, P. R. (1987). The Dominicans: Women in the household and the garment industry. In N. Foner (Ed.), *New immigrants in New York* (pp. 103-129). New York: Columbia University Press.

Peters, T. (1989, April 11). Listen up, guys: Women fit profile of execs of future. *Seattle Post-Intelligencer,* p. B6.

Petersen, D. J., & Massengill, D. (1988, May). Childcare programs benefit employers too. *Personnel, 65,* 58-62.

Petersen, D. J., & Massengill, D. P. (1992-1993). Sexual harassment cases five years after *Meritor Savings Bank v. Vinson. Employee Relations, 18,* 489-515.

Petersen, D. J., & Massengill, D. (1997-1998). Same-sex sexual harassment—Is it actionable under the Civil Rights Act? *Journal of Individual Employment Rights,* 6, 119-126.

Petersen, T., & Morgan, L. A. (1995). Separate and unequal: Occupation establishment sex segregation and the gender wage gap. *American Journal of Sociology, 101*(2), 329-365.

Petty, M. M., & Lee, G. K., Jr. (1975). Moderating effects of sex of supervisor and subordinate on relationships between supervisory behavior and subordinate satisfaction. *Journal of Applied Psychology, 60,* 624-628.

Pfeffer, J. (1997). Pitfalls on the road to measurement: The dangerous liaison of human resources with the ideas of accounting and finance. *Human Resource Management,* 36(3), 357-366.

Pfeffer, J., & Davis-Blake, A. (1987). The effect of the proportion of women on salaries: The case of college administrators. *Administrative Science Quarterly, 32*(1), 1-24.

Pfeffer, J., Davis-Blake, A., & Julius, D. (1995). AA officer salaries and managerial diversity: Efficiency wages or status? *Industrial Relations, 34*(1), 73-94.

Pfeffer, J., & Ross, J. (1982). The effects of marriage and a working wife on occupational and wage attainment. *Administrative Science Quarterly, 27,* 66-80.

Pheterson, G. I., Kiesler, S. B., & Goldberg, P. A. (1971). Evaluation of performance of women as a function of their sex, achievement, and personal history. *Journal of Personality and Social Psychology, 19,* 114-118.

Phillips, J. D., & Reisman, B. (1992). Turnover and return on investment models for family leave. In D. E. Friedman, E. Galinsky, & V. Plowden (Eds.), *Parental leave and productivity: Current research* (pp. 33-45). New York: Families and Work Institute.

Phillips-Jones, L. L. (1983). Establishing a formalized mentoring program. *Training and Development Journal, 37*(2), 38-42.

Phinney, J. S. (1996). When we talk about American ethnic groups, what do we mean? *American Psychologist, 51,* 918-927.

Pierce, C. A. (1998). Factors associated with participating in a romantic relationship in a work environment. *Journal of Applied Social Psychology, 28,* 1712-1730.

Pierce, C. A., & Aguinis, H. (1997). Bridging the gap between romantic relationships and sexual harassment in organizations. *Journal of Organizational Behavior, 18,* 197-200.

Pierce, C. A., Aguinis, H., & Adams, S. K. R. (1998). *Effects of a dissolved workplace romance and rater characteristics on judgments and responses to a sexual harassment accusation.* Paper presented at the annual meeting of the Academy of Management, San Diego, CA.

Pierce, C. A., Byrne, D., & Aguinis, H. (1996). Attraction in organizations: A model of workplace romance. *Journal of Organizational Behavior, 17,* 5-32.

Pierce, J. (1995). *Gender trials: Emotional lives in contemporary law firms.* Berkeley: University of California Press.

Pierce, J. L., & Newstrom, J. W. (1982). Employee responses to flexible work schedules: An inter-organization, inter-system comparison. *Journal of Management, 8*(1), 9-25.

Pierce, J. L., & Newstrom, J. W. (1983). The design of flexible work schedules and employee responses: Relationships and process. *Journal of Occupational Behaviour, 4*, 247-262.

Piliavin, J. A., & Martin, R. R. (1978). The effects of sex composition of groups on style of social interaction. *Sex Roles, 4*, 281-296.

Pingitore, R., Dugoni, B. L., Tindale, R. S., & Spring, B. (1994). Bias against overweight job applicants in a simulated employment interview. *Journal of Applied Psychology, 79*, 909-917.

Piore, M. J. (1971). The dual labor market: Theory and implications. In D. M. Gordon (Ed.), *Problems in political economy: An urban perspective* (pp. 90-94). Lexington, MA: D. C. Heath.

Piore, M. J. (1975). Notes for a theory of labor market stratification. In R. C. Edwards, M. Reich, & D. M. Gordon (Eds.), *Labor market segmentation* (pp. 125-150). Lexington, MA: D. C. Heath.

Piotrkowski, C. S., Rapoport, R. N., & Rapoport, R. (1987). Families and work. In M. B. Sussman & S. K. Steinmetz (Eds.), *Handbook of marriage and the family* (pp. 251-283). New York: Plenum.

Pleck, J. H. (1985). *Working wives, working husbands.* Beverly Hills, CA: Sage.

Pleck, J. H. (1977). The work-family role system. *Social Problems, 24*(4), 417-427.

Plessy v. Ferguson, 163 U.S. 537 (1894).

Pogrebin, R. (1996, October 18). Pearson picks an American as executive. *New York Times*, p. D7.

Polachek, S. (1979). Occupational segregation among women: Theory, evidence, and a prognosis. In C. B. Lloyd, E. S. Andrews, & C. L. Gilroy (Eds.), *Women in the labor market* (pp. 137-157). New York: Columbia University Press.

Polachek, S. W. (1987). Occupational segregation and the gender wage gap. *Population Research and Policy Review, 6*, 47-67.

Pond, E. (1996). Women in leadership: A letter from Stockholm. *Washington Quarterly, 19*(4), 59.

Popielarz, P., & McPherson, M. (1995). On the edge or in between: Niche position, niche overlap, and the duration of voluntary association memberships. *American Journal of Sociology, 101*(3), 698-720.

Porter, N., Geis, F. L., & Walstedt, J. J. (1983). Are women invisible as leaders? *Sex Roles, 9*, 1035-1049.

Potuchek, J. L. (1992). Employed wives' orientation to breadwinning: A gender theory analysis. *Journal of Marriage and the Family, 55*, 133-145.

Powell, G. N. (1986a). Effects of sex role identity and sex on definitions of sexual harassment. *Sex Roles, 14*, 919.

Powell, G. N. (1986b). What do tomorrow's managers think about sexual intimacy in the workplace? *Business Horizons, 29*(4), 30-35.

Powell, G. N. (1987). The effects of sex and gender on recruitment. *Academy of Management Review, 12*, 731-743.

Powell, G. N. (1988). *Women and men in management.* Newbury Park, CA: Sage.

Powell, G. N. (1990). One more time: Do male and female managers differ? *Academy of Management Executive, 4*(4), 68-75.

Powell, G. N. (1993). *Women and men in management* (2nd ed.). Newbury Park, CA: Sage.

Powell, G. N. (1998a). The abusive organization. *Academy of Management Executive,* 12(2), 95-96.

Powell, G. N. (1998b). *Coworkers' reactions to cross-level organizational romances.* Paper presented at the meeting of the Southern Management Association, New Orleans, LA.

Powell, G. N. (1998c). Reinforcing and extending today's organizations: The simultaneous pursuit of person-organization fit and diversity. *Organizational Dynamics,* 26(3), 50-61.

Powell, G. N., & Butterfield, D. A. (1979). The "good manager": Masculine or androgynous? *Academy of Management Journal, 22,* 395-403.

Powell, G. N., & Butterfield, D. A. (1982). Sex, attributions, and leadership: A brief review. *Psychological Reports, 51,* 1171-1174.

Powell, G. N., & Butterfield, D. A. (1984). If "good managers" are masculine, what are "bad managers"? *Sex Roles, 10,* 477-484.

Powell, G. N., & Butterfield, D. A. (1989). The "good manager": Did androgyny fare better in the 1980s? *Group and Organization Studies, 14,* 216-233.

Powell, G. N., & Butterfield, D. A. (1994). Investigating the "glass ceiling" phenomenon: An empirical study of actual promotions to top management. *Academy of Management Journal, 37,* 68-86.

Powell, G. N., & Butterfield, D. A. (1997). Effect of race on promotions to top management in a federal department. *Academy of Management Journal, 40,* 112-128.

Powell, G. N., & Kido, Y. (1994). Managerial stereotypes in a global economy: A comparative study of Japanese and American business students' perspectives. *Psychological Reports, 74,* 219-226.

Powell, G. N., & Mainiero, L. A. (1992). Cross-currents in the river of time: Conceptualizing the complexities of women's careers. *Journal of Management, 18,* 215-237.

Prasad, P. (1997). The Protestant ethic and the myths of the frontier: Cultural imprints, organizational structuring, and workplace diversity. In P. Prasad, A. J. Mills, M. Elmes, & A. Prasad (Eds.), *Managing the organizational melting pot: Dilemmas of workplace diversity* (pp. 129-147). Thousand Oaks, CA: Sage.

Prasad, P., & Caproni, P. (1997). Critical theory in the management classroom: Engaging power, ideology and praxis. *Journal of Management Education, 21*(3), 284-291.

Propp, K. M. (1995). An experimental examination of biological sex as a status cue in decision-making groups and its influence on information use. *Small Group Research, 26,* 451-474.

Pryor, J. B. (1985). The lay person's understanding of sexual harassment. *Sex Roles, 13,* 273-286.

Pryor, J. B., & Day, J. D. (1988). Interpretations of sexual harassment: An attributional analysis. *Sex Roles, 18,* 405-417.

Pryor, J. B., LaVite, C. M., & Stoller, L. M. (1993). A social psychological analysis of sexual harassment: The person/situation interaction. *Journal of Vocational Behavior, 42,* 68-83.

Ptacek, J. T., Smith, R. E., & Dodge, K. L. (1994). Gender differences in coping with stress: When stressor and appraisals do not differ. *Personality and Social Psychology Bulletin, 20*(4), 421-430.

Pugh, M. D., & Wahrman, R. (1983). Neutralizing sexism in mixed-sex groups: Do women have to be better than men? *American Journal of Sociology, 88,* 746-762.

Pugliesi, K. (1988). Employment characteristics, social support and the well-being of women. *Women and Health, 14*(1), 35-58.

Pugliesi, K., & Shook, S. L. (1998). Gender, ethnicity, and network characteristics: Variation in social support resources. *Sex Roles, 38,* 215-238.

Pulakos, E. D., & Wexley, K. N. (1983). The relationship among perceptual similarity, sex and performance ratings in manager-subordinate dyads. *Academy of Management Journal, 26,* 129-139.

Pulakos, E. D., White, L. A., Oppler, S. H., & Borman, W. C. (1989). Examination of race and sex effects on performance ratings. *Journal of Applied Psychology, 74,* 770-780.

Quinn, B. S. C. (1980). *The influence of same-sex and cross-sex mentors on the professional development and personality characteristics of women in human services.* Unpublished doctoral dissertation, Western Michigan University.

Quinn, R. (1977). Coping with Cupid: The formation, impact, and management of romantic relationships in organizations. *Administrative Science Quarterly, 22,* 30-45.

Raabe, P. (1996). Constructing pluralistic work and career arrangements. In S. Lewis & J. Lewis (Eds.), *The work-family challenge: Rethinking employment* (pp. 128-141). London: Sage.

Rafaeli, A. (1989a). When cashiers meet customers: An analysis of the role of supermarket cashiers. *Academy of Management Journal, 32*(2), 245-273.

Rafaeli, A. (1989b). When clerks and customers meet: A test of variables related to emotional expressions on the job. *Journal of Applied Psychology, 74*(3), 385-393.

Ragins, B. R. (1989). Barriers to mentoring: The female manager's dilemma. *Human Relations, 42,* 1-22.

Ragins, B. R. (1991). Gender effects in subordinate evaluations of leaders: Real or artifact? *Journal of Organizational Behavior, 12,* 259-268.

Ragins, B. R. (1995). Diversity, power and mentoring in organizations: A cultural, structural and behavioral perspective. In M. Chemers, M. Costanzo, & S. Oskamp (Eds.), *Diversity in organizations* (pp. 91-132). Thousand Oaks, CA: Sage.

Ragins, B. R. (1997a). Antecedents of diversified mentoring relationships. *Journal of Vocational Behavior, 51,* 90-109.

Ragins, B. R. (1997b). Diversified mentoring relationships in organizations: A power perspective. *Academy of Management Review, 22,* 482-521.

Ragins, B. R. (1998). Work values in cross-cultural mentoring relationships. In International Society for the Study of Work and Organizational Values (ISSWOV) (Ed.), *Proceedings for the 6th Annual Conference on Work Values and Behavior* (pp. 224-228). Istanbul, Turkey: ISSWOV.

Ragins, B. R. (1999). Where do we go from here and how do we get there? Methodological issues in conducting research on diversity and mentoring relationships. In A. J. Murrell, F. J. Crosby, & R. J. Ely (Eds.), *Mentoring dilemmas: Developmental relationships within multicultural organizations* (pp. 227-246). Mahwah, NJ: Lawrence Erlbaum.

Ragins, B. R., & Cotton, J. (1991). Easier said than done: Gender differences in perceived barriers to gaining a mentor. *Academy of Management Journal, 34,* 939-951.

Ragins, B. R., & Cotton, J. (1993). Gender and willingness to mentor in organizations. *Journal of Management, 19,* 97-111.

Ragins, B. R., & Cotton, J. (in press). Mentor functions and outcomes: A comparison of men and women in formal and informal mentoring relationships. *Journal of Applied Psychology.*

Ragins, B. R., & McFarlin, D. (1990). Perception of mentor roles in cross-gender mentoring relationships. *Journal of Vocational Behavior, 37,* 321-339.

Ragins, B. R., & Scandura, T. (1994). Gender differences in expected outcomes of mentoring relationships. *Academy of Management Journal, 37,* 957-971.

Ragins, B. R., & Scandura, T. A. (1995). Antecedents and work-related correlates of reported sexual harassment: An empirical investigation of competing hypotheses. *Sex Roles, 32*(7/8), 429-455.

Ragins, B. R., & Scandura, T. A. (1997). The way we were: Gender and the termination of mentoring relationships. *Journal of Applied Psychology, 82,* 945-953.

Ragins, B. R., & Sundstrom, E. (1989). Gender and power in organizations: A longitudinal perspective. *Psychological Bulletin, 105,* 51-88.

Ragins, B. R., Townsend, B., & Mattis, M. (1998). Gender gap in the executive suite: CEOs and female executives report on breaking the glass ceiling. *Academy of Management Executive, 12*(1), 28-42.

Raitt, B. (1991). Something to talk about. On *Luck of the draw* [Compact disc]. Hollywood: Capitol Records.

Rakow, L. (1986). Rethinking gender research in communication. *Journal of Communication, 36,* 11-24.

Ramamurthy, L. (1985). Women in the developing countries. In L. D. Knezek, M. C. Barrett, & S. K. Collins (Eds.), *Women and work* (pp. 117-124). Arlington, TX: Women and Work Research and Resource Center.

Random House. (1987). *The Random House dictionary of the English language* (2nd ed., unabridged). New York: Author.

Ransford, H. E. (1980). The prediction of social behavior and attitudes. In V. Jeffries & H. Ransford (Eds.), *Social stratification: A multiple hierarchy approach* (pp. 265-295). Boston: Allyn & Bacon.

Ransom, C., Aschbacher, P. R., & Burud, S. (1989). The return in the child-care investment. *Personnel Administrator, 34*(10), 54-58.

Rayman, P. (1998). *The Radcliffe Fleet work/life integration project.* Cambridge, UK: Radcliffe Public Policy Institute.

Rechtschaffen, S. (1996). *Timeshifting.* New York: Bantam Doubleday Dell Audio.

Reed v. Shepard, 939 F.2d 484 (7th Cir. 1991).

Reed, A. (1995, June 3). Assault on affirmative action. *The Progressive, 59,* 18-20.

Reed, I. (Ed.). (1997). *Multiamerica: Essays on cultural wars and cultural peace.* New York: Viking.

Reid, P. T. (1988). Racism and sexism: Comparisons and conflicts. In P. A. Katz & D. A. Taylor (Eds.), *Eliminating racism: Profiles in controversy* (pp. 203-221). New York: Plenum.

Reilly, T., Carpenter, S., Dull, V., & Barlett, K. (1982). The factorial survey technique: An approach to defining sexual harassment on campus. *Journal of Social Issues, 38,* 99-110.

Repetti, R. L. (1987). Linkages between work and family roles. In S. Oskamp (Ed.), *Family processes and problems: Social psychological aspects* (pp. 98-127). Newbury Park, CA: Sage.

Repetti, R. L., Matthews, K. A., & Waldron, I. (1989). Employment and women's health: Effects of paid employment on women's mental and physical health. *American Psychologist, 44*(11), 1394-1401.

Repetti, R. L., & Wood, J. (1997). Effects of daily stress at work on mothers' interactions with preschoolers. *Journal of Family Psychology, 11,* 90-108.

Reskin, B. F. (1993). Sex segregation in the workplace. *Annual Review of Sociology, 19,* 241-270.

Reskin, B. F., & Hartmann, H. I. (1986). *Women's work, men's work: Sex segregation on the job.* Washington, DC: National Academy Press.

Reskin, B. F., & Padavic, I. (1994). *Women and men at work.* Newbury Park, CA: Pine Forge.

Reskin, B. F., & Roos, P. A. (1990). *Job queues, gender queues: Explaining women's inroads into male occupations.* Philadelphia: Temple University Press.

Revised Order 4, 41 C. F. R. § 60-2 (1974).

Rhey, W. L., Rustogi, H., & Watson, M. A. (1992). Buyer's perceptions of automobile saleswomen: A field study. In *Proceedings of the Southwestern Marketing Association* (pp. 41-46). Baton Rouge: Louisiana State University & Southwestern Marketing Association.

Rice, R. W., Frone, M. R., & McFarlin, D. B. (1992). Work-nonwork conflict and the perceived quality of life. *Journal of Organizational Behavior, 13,* 155-168.

Richmond, S. (1997). *The demands-control model in a fast-food organization: Effects of emotional labor, customer behavior, demands, controls, and support.* Unpublished doctoral dissertation, Department of Management and Policy, University of Arizona.

Richter, J. (1992). Balancing work and family in Israel. In S. Zedeck (Ed.), *Work, families, and organizations* (pp. 362-394). San Francisco: Jossey-Bass.

Ridgeway, C. (1997). Interaction and the conservation of gender inequality: Considering employment. *American Sociological Review, 62*(2), 218-235.

Ridgeway, C. L. (1978). Conformity, group-oriented motivation, and status attainment in small groups. *Social Psychology, 41,* 175-188.

Ridgeway, C. L. (1982). Status in groups: The importance of motivation. *American Sociological Review, 47,* 76-88.

Ridgeway, C. L. (Ed.). (1992). *Gender, interaction, and inequality.* New York: Springer-Verlag.

Ridgeway, C. L., & Berger, J. (1986). Expectations, legitimation, and dominance behavior in task groups. *American Sociological Review, 51,* 603-617.

Ridgeway, C. L., & Diekema, D. (1992). Are gender differences status differences? In C. L. Ridgeway (Ed.), *Gender, interaction, and inequality* (pp. 157-180). New York: Springer-Verlag.

Rifkin, J. (1987). *Time wars: The primary conflict in human history.* New York: Touchstone.

Riger, S. (1991). Gender dilemmas in sexual harassment policies and procedures. *American Psychologist, 46,* 497-507.

Riger, S., & Galligan, P. (1980). Women in management: An exploration of competing paradigms. *American Psychologist, 35,* 902-910.

Riipinen, M. (1994). Occupational needs as moderators between locus of control and job involvement. *Psychological Reports, 74*(2), 371-379.

Riley, F., & McCloskey, D. W. (1997). Telecommuting as a response to helping people balance work and family. In S. Parasuraman & J. H. Greenhaus (Eds.), *Integrating work and family: Challenges and choices for a changing world* (pp. 133-142). Westport, CT: Quorum Books.

Rind, B., & Bordia, P. (1995). Effect of server's "thank you" and personalization on restaurant tipping. *Journal of Applied Social Psychology, 25,* 745-751.

Rind, B., & Bordia, P. (1996). Effect of restaurant tipping on male and female servers drawing a happy, smiling face on the backs of customers' checks. *Journal of Applied Social Psychology, 26*(3), 218-225.

Riordan, C., & Shore, L. (1997). Demographic diversity and employee attitudes: Examination of relational demography within work units. *Journal of Applied Psychology, 82,* 342-358.

Ritchie, R. J., & Moses, J. L. (1983). Assessment center correlates of women's advancement into middle management: A 7-year longitudinal analysis. *Journal of Applied Psychology, 68,* 227-231.

Robbins, T. L., & DeNisi, A. S. (1993). Moderators of sex bias in the performance appraisal process: A cognitive analysis. *Journal of Management, 19,* 113-126.

Roberson, L., & Gutierrez, N. C. (1992). Beyond good faith: Commitment to recruiting management diversity at Pacific Bell. In S. E. Jackson (Ed.), *Diversity in the workplace: Human resource initiatives* (pp. 65-88). New York: Guilford.

Roberts, T., & Nolen-Hoeksema, S. (1989). Sex differences in reactions to evaluative feedback. *Sex Roles, 21,* 725-747.

Roberts, T., & Nolen-Hoeksema, S. (1994). Gender comparisons in responsiveness to others' evaluations in achievement settings. *Psychology of Women Quarterly, 18,* 221-240.

Roberts, T. A. (1991). Gender and the influence of evaluations on self-assessments in achievement settings. *Psychological Bulletin, 109,* 297-308.

Robinson, G., & Dechant, K. (1997). Building a business case for diversity. *Academy of Management Executive, 43*(5), 455-472.

Robinson, M. (1996, May). [Speech to International Women's Leadership Forum]. Stockholm, Sweden.

Robles, B. J. (1997). An economic profile of women in the United States. In E. Higginbotham & M. Romero (Eds.), *Women and work: Exploring race, ethnicity, and class* (pp. 5-27). Thousand Oaks, CA: Sage.

Roddick, A. (1991). *Body and soul.* New York: Crown.

Rodgers, W. M., III, & Spriggs, W. E. (1996). The effect of federal contractor status on racial differences in establishment-level employment shares: 1979-1992. *American Economic Review, 86,* 290-295.

Rogers, J. (1988). New paradigm leadership: Integrating the female ethos. *Journal of the National Association of Women Deans, Administrators and Counselors, 5*(9), 1-8.

Rogut, A. (1994). *Polish women in private business.* Warsaw, Poland: Institute for Private Enterprise and Democracy.

Rojahn, K., & Willemsen, T. M. (1994). The evaluation of effectiveness and likability of gender-role congruent and gender-role incongruent leaders. *Sex Roles, 30,* 109-119.

Romance in the workplace: Corporate rules for the game of love. (1984, June 18). *Business Week,* pp. 70-71.

Romero, G. J., Castro, F. G., & Cervantes, R. C. (1988). Latinas without work: Family, occupational and economic stress following unemployment. *Psychology of Women Quarterly, 12,* 281-297.

Romero, M. (1997). Epilogue. In E. Higginbotham & M. Romero (Eds.), *Women and work: Exploring race, ethnicity, and class* (pp. 235-248). Thousand Oaks, CA: Sage.

Ronen, S. (1984). *Alternative work schedules: Selecting, implementing and evaluating.* Homewood, IL: Dow Jones-Irwin.

Roos, P. A. (1981). Sex stratification in the workplace: Male-female differences in economic returns to occupation. *Social Science Research, 10,* 195-224.

Roos, P. A. (1983, December). Marriage and women's occupational attainment in cross-cultural perspective. *American Sociological Review, 48,* 852-864.

Roos, P. A. (1985). *Gender and work: A comparative analysis of industrial societies.* Albany: State University of New York Press.

Roos, P. A., & Reskin, B. F. (1984). Institutional factors contributing to sex segregation in the workplace. In B. F. Reskin (Ed.), *Sex segregation in the workplace: Trends, explanations, remedies* (pp. 235-260). Washington, DC: National Academy Press.

Roos, P. A., & Reskin, B. F. (1996). *Trends in occupational sex and race composition, 1970-1990: Codebooks and technical documentation.* Unpublished codebook, Rutgers University, Department of Sociology, New Brunswick, NJ.

Rosa, P., & Hamilton, D. (1994). Gender and ownership in UK small firms. *Entrepreneurship Theory and Practice, 18*(3), 11-17.

Rose, G. L., & Andiappan, P. (1978). Sex effects on managerial hiring decisions. *Academy of Management Journal, 21,* 104-112.

Rosen, A. C., & Rekers, G. A. (1980). Toward a taxonomic framework for variables of sex and gender. *Genetic Psychology Monographs, 102,* 191-218.

Rosen, B., & Jerdee, T. H. (1973). The influence of sex-role stereotypes on the evaluations of male and female supervisory behavior. *Journal of Applied Psychology, 57,* 44-48.

Rosen, B., & Mericle, M. F. (1979). Influence of strong versus weak fair employment policies and applicants' sex on selection decisions and salary recommendations in a management simulation. *Journal of Applied Psychology, 64,* 435-439.

Rosen, B., Miguel, M., & Peirce, E. (1989). Stemming the exodus of women managers. *Human Resource Management, 28*(4), 475-491.

Rosen, J. (1995, July 31). The color-blind court. *The New Republic, 213,* 19-24.

Rosen, R. H. (1996). *Leading people.* New York: Viking.

Rosenbaum, J. (1984). *Career mobility in a corporate hierarchy.* Orlando, FL: Academic Press.

Rosener, J. B. (1989, August). *"Corporate flight" and female entrepreneurs: Is there a connection?* Paper presented at the annual meeting of the Academy of Management, Washington, DC.

Rosener, J. B. (1990). Ways women lead. *Harvard Business Review, 68*(6), 119-225.

Rosener, J. B. (1995). *America's competitive secret: Utilizing women as a management strategy.* New York: Oxford University Press.

Rosenfeld, R. A., & Kalleberg, A. L. (1990). A cross-national comparison of the gender gap in income. *American Journal of Sociology, 96*(1), 69-106.

Rosenfeld, R. A., & Spenner, K. I. (1995). Occupational sex segregation and women's early career job shifts. In J. A. Jacobs (Ed.), *Gender inequality at work* (pp. 231-258). Thousand Oaks, CA: Sage.

Rosenfield, S. (1992). The costs of sharing: Wives' employment and husbands' mental health. *Journal of Health and Social Behavior, 33,* 213-225.

Rosenkrantz, P., Vogel, S., Bee, H., Broverman, I., & Broverman, D. M. (1968). Sex-role stereotypes and the self-concepts in college students. *Journal of Consulting and Clinical Psychology, 32,* 287-295.

Rosenthal, R., & Rosnow, R. L. (1991). *Essentials of behavioral research: Methods and data analysis.* New York: McGraw-Hill.

Rosin, H. M., & Korabik, K. (1990). Marital and family correlates of women managers' attrition from organizations. *Journal of Vocational Behavior, 37,* 104-120.

Rosin, H. M., & Korabik, K. (1991). Workplace variables, affective responses, and intention to leave among women managers. *Journal of Occupational Psychology, 64,* 317-330.

Rosin, H. M., & Korabik, K. (1995). Organizational experiences and propensity to leave: A multivariate investigation of men and women managers. *Journal of Vocational Behavior, 46,* 1-16.

Ross, C. E., & Mirowsky, J. (1996). Economic and interpersonal work rewards: Subjective utilities of men's and women's compensation. *Social Forces, 75*(1), 223-246.

Ross, C. E., Mirowsky, J., & Huber, J. (1983). Dividing work, sharing work, and in-between: Marriage patterns and depression. *American Sociological Review, 48,* 809-823.

Rost, J. (1991). *Leadership for the 21st century.* New York: Praeger.

Roth, J., & Fedor, D. B. (1993). *In the eye of the beholder: Naming, blaming, and claiming in the sexual harassment process.* Paper presented at the annual meeting of the Academy of Management, Atlanta, GA.

Rothausen, T. J. (1994). Job satisfaction and the parent worker: The role of flexibility and rewards. *Journal of Vocational Behavior, 44*(3), 317-336.

Rothschild, J. (1992). *Principles of feminist trade union organizations.* Paper presented at the Workshop on Feminist Organizations, Washington, DC.

Rothstein, B. (1984, August). *Corporate culture—Sex/war/games: Where do managerial women fit in?* Paper presented at the third annual Women and Organizations Conference, Boston.

Rothwell, S. (1985). Is management a masculine role? *Management Education and Development, 16*(2), 79-98.

Rowe, M. P. (1973, Spring). When the employer faces day care decisions: Cost-benefit analysis and other decision-making tools. *Sloan Management Review, 14,* 1-11.

Royce, A. P. (1982). *Ethnic identity: Strategies of diversity.* Bloomington: Indiana University Press.

Ruan, F. F., & Matsumara, M. (1991). *Sex in China: Studies in sexology in Chinese culture.* New York: Plenum.

Rubenstein, M. (1991, February). Devising a sexual harassment policy. *Personnel Management,* pp. 8-10.

Rubenstein, M. (1992). *Preventing and remedying sexual harassment at work: A resource manual.* London: Eclipse.

Rubin, B. M. (1994, March 23). Dads find their place is in the home also. *Chicago Tribune*, sec. 1, pp. 1, 15.

Ruble, T. L. (1983). Sex stereotypes: Issues of change in the 1970s. *Sex Roles, 9,* 397-402.

Ruddick, S. (1989). *Maternal thinking.* Boston: Beacon.

Rudman, L. A. (1998). Self-promotion as a risk factor for women: The costs and benefits of counterstereotypical impression management. *Journal of Personality and Social Psychology, 74,* 629-645.

Runciman, W. G. (1966). *Relative deprivation and social justice.* Berkeley: University of California Press.

Russell, J. E., Rush, M. C., & Herd, A. M. (1988). An exploration of women's expectations of effective male and female leadership. *Sex Roles, 18,* 279-287.

Rydstedt, L. W., Johansson, G., & Evans, C. W. (1998). A longitudinal study of workload, health and well-being among male and female women bus drivers. *Journal of Occupational and Organizational Psychology, 71*(1), 35-45.

Rynes, S., & Rosen, B. (1995). A field survey of factors affecting the adoption and perceived success of diversity training. *Personnel Psychology, 48,* 247-270.

Ryujin, D. H., & Herrold, A. J. (1989). Cross-sex comparisons: A word of caution. *Sex Roles, 20,* 713-719.

Saal, F. E. (1996). Men's misperceptions of women's interpersonal behaviors and sexual harassment. In M. S. Stockdale (Ed.), *Sexual harassment: Perspectives, frontiers, and response strategies* (Vol. 5, pp. 67-84). Thousand Oaks, CA: Sage.

Sackett, P. R., DuBois, C. L., & Noe, A. W. (1991). Tokenism in performance evaluation: The effects of work group representation on male-female and White-Black differences in performance ratings. *Journal of Applied Psychology, 76,* 263-267.

Sackett, P. R., & Larson, J. R., Jr. (1990). Research strategies and tactics in industrial and organizational psychology. In M. D. Dunnette & L. Hough (Eds.), *Handbook of industrial and organizational psychology* (2nd ed., Vol. 1). Palo Alto, CA: Consulting Psychologists Press.

Sackley, N., & Ibarra, H. (1995). *Charlotte Beers at Ogilvy & Mather worldwide.* Harvard Business School, Case 9-495-031.

Saint-Germain, M. A. (1993). Women in power in Nicaragua: Myth and reality. In M. A. Genovese (Ed.), *Women as national leaders* (pp. 70-102). Newbury Park, CA: Sage.

Sánchez, J. I., & Brock, P. (1996). Outcomes of perceived discrimination among Hispanic employees: Is diversity management a luxury or a necessity? *Academy of Management Journal, 39,* 704-719.

Sapp, S. G., Harrod, W. J., & Zhao, L. (1996). Leadership emergence in task groups with egalitarian gender-role expectations. *Sex Roles, 34,* 65-80.

Sargent, A. (1981). *The androgynous manager.* New York: American Management Association Communications (AMACOM).

Sargent, A. (1983, April). Women and men working together: Toward androgyny. *Training and Development Journal,* pp. 72-76.

Scandura, T. A. (1992). Mentorship and career mobility: An empirical investigation. *Journal of Organizational Behavior, 13,* 169-174.

Scandura, T. A., & Katerberg, R. J. (1988, August). *Much ado about mentors and little about measurement: Development of an instrument.* Paper presented at the annual meeting of the National Academy of Management, Anaheim, CA.

Scandura, T. A., & Lankau, M. J. (1997). Relationships of gender, family responsibility and flexible work hours to organizational commitment and job satisfaction. *Journal of Organizational Behavior, 18,* 377-391.

Scandura, T. A., & Ragins, B. R. (1993). The effects of sex and gender role orientation on mentorship in male-dominated occupations. *Journal of Vocational Behavior, 43,* 251-265.

Scase, R., & Goffee, R. (1989). *Reluctant managers: Their work and life style.* London: Unwin Hyman.

Schaef, A. (1981). *Women's reality.* New York: HarperCollins.

Schaef, A., & Fassel, D. (1988). *The addictive organization: Why we overwork, cover up, pick up the pieces, please the boss and perpetuate sick organizations.* New York: Harper & Row.

Schaubroeck, J., & Fink, L. S. (1998). Facilitating and inhibiting effects of job control and social support on stress outcomes and role behavior: A contingency model. *Journal of Organizational Behavior, 19,* 167-195.

Schein, E. H. (1978). *Career dynamics: Matching individual and organizational needs.* Reading, MA: Addison-Wesley.

Schein, E. H. (1990). *Career anchors: Discovering your real values.* San Diego, CA: Pfeiffer.

Schein, E. H. (1993). *Career anchors: Discovering your real values* (Rev. ed.). San Diego, CA: Pfeiffer.

Schein, V. E. (1973). The relationship between sex-role stereotypes and requisite management characteristics, *Journal of Applied Psychology, 57*(2), 95-100.

Schein, V. E. (1975). Relationships between sex role stereotypes and requisite management characteristics among female managers. *Journal of Applied Psychology, 60,* 340-344.

Schein, V. E. (1994). Managerial sex typing: A persistent and pervasive barriers to women's opportunities. In M. J. Davidson & R. J. Burke (Eds.), *Women in management: Current research issues* (pp. 41-52). London: Paul Chapman.

Schein, V. E., Maurer, V. H., & Novak, J. F. (1977). Impact of flexible working hours on productivity. *Journal of Applied Psychology, 62,* 463-465.

Schein, V. E., & Mueller, R. (1992). Sex role stereotyping and requisite management characteristics: A cross cultural look. *Journal of Organizational Behavior, 13,* 439-447.

Schein, V. E., Mueller, R., & Jacobson, C. (1989). The relationship between sex role stereotypes and requisite management characteristics among college students. *Sex Roles, 20*(1/2), 103-127.

Schein, V. E., Mueller, R., Lituchy, T., & Liu, J. (1996). Think manager—think male: A global phenomenon? *Journal of Organizational Behavior, 17,* 33-41.

Scheinberg, S., & MacMillan, I. C. (1988). An 11 county study of motivations to start a business. In B. A. Kirchoff, W. A. Long, W. E. McMillan, K. H. Vesper, & W. E. Wetzel, Jr. (Eds.), *Frontiers of entrepreneurship research* (pp. 669-687). Wellesley, MA: Center for Entrepreneurial Studies, Babson College.

Schermerhorn, R. (1996). Ethnicity and minority groups. In J. Hutchinson & A. D. Smith (Eds.), *Ethnicity* (pp. 17-18). Oxford, UK: Oxford University Press.

Schmidt, F. L. (1996). Statistical significance testing and cumulative knowledge in psychology: Implications for training of researchers. *Psychological Methods, 1,* 115-129.

Schmidt, R. A., & Sapsford, R. (1995). Issues of gender and servicescape: Marketing UK public houses to women. *International Journal of Retail & Distribution Management, 23,* 34-40.

Schmitt, N., & Hill, T. E. (1977). Sex and race composition of assessment center groups as a determinant of peer and assessor ratings. *Journal of Applied Psychology, 62*(3), 261-264.

Schmitt, N., & Klimoski, R. J. (1991). *Research methods in human resource management.* Cincinnati, OH: South-Western.

Schneer, J. A., & Reitman, F. (1990). Effects of employment gaps on the careers of MBA's: More damaging for men than for women? *Academy of Management Journal, 33,* 391-406.

Schneer, J. A., & Reitman, F. (1993). Effects of alternative family structures on managerial career paths. *Academy of Management Journal, 36,* 830-843.

Schneer, J. A., & Reitman, F. (1995). The impact of gender as managerial careers unfold. *Journal of Vocational Behavior, 47,* 290-315.

Schneider, B. (1987). The people make the place. *Personnel Psychology, 40,* 437-453.

Schneider, B., & Bowen, D. E. (1985). Employee and customer perceptions of service in banks: Replication and extension. *Journal of Applied Psychology, 70,* 423-433.

Schneider, K. T., Swan, S., & Fitzgerald, L. F. (1997). Job-related and psychological effects of sexual harassment in the workplace: Empirical evidence from two organizations. *Journal of Applied Psychology, 82*(3), 401-415.

Schoeni, R. F. (1998). Labor market assimilation of immigrant women. *Industrial and Labor Relations Review, 51,* 483-504.

Schön, D. (1983). *The reflective practitioner: How professionals think in action.* New York: Basic Books/HarperCollins.

Schor, J. (1991). *The overworked American.* New York: Basic Books.

Schreiber, C. T., Price, K. F., & Morrison, A. (1993). Workforce diversity and the glass ceiling: Practice, barriers, possibilities. *Human Resource Planning, 16*(2), 51-69.

Schwartz, E. B. (1976). Entrepreneurship: A new female frontier. *Journal of Contemporary Business, 5*(1), 47-76.

Schwartz, F. (1989). Management women and the new facts of life. *Harvard Business Review, 67,* 65-76.

Schwartz, F. (1992a). *Breaking with tradition: Women and work, the new facts of life.* New York: Times Warner.

Schwartz, F. (1992b). Women as a business imperative. *Harvard Business Review, 70*(2), 103-113.

Scott, A. F. (1992). *Natural allies: Women's associations in American history.* Urbana: University of Illinois Press.

Scott, C. (1986). Why more women are becoming entrepreneurs. *Journal of Small Business Management, 24*(4), 37-44.

Sears, D. O. (1988). Symbolic racism. In P. A. Katz & D. A. Taylor (Eds.), *Eliminating racism: Profiles in controversy* (pp. 53-84). New York: Plenum.

Sears, D. O., & Funk, C. L. (1990). Self-interest in American's political opinions. In J. J. Mansbridge (Ed.), *Beyond self-interest* (pp. 147-170). Chicago: University of Chicago Press.

Seidler, V. J. (1994). *Unreasonable men: Masculinity and social theory.* London: Routledge.

Sekaran, U. (1992). Middle-class dual-earner families and their support systems in India. In S. Lewis, D. N. Izraeli, & H. Hootsmans (Eds.), *Dual-earner families: International perspectives* (pp. 46-61). London: Sage.

Sekaran, U., & Hall, D. T. (1989). Asynchronism in dual-career couples. In M. B. Arthur, D. T. Hall, & B. S. Lawrence (Eds.), *Handbook of career theory* (pp. 159-180). Cambridge, UK: Cambridge University Press.

Sellers, P. (1998, October 12). The 50 most powerful women in American business. *Fortune*, pp. 76-96.

Selye, H. (1976). The general adaptation syndrome and the diseases of adaptation. *Journal of Clinical Endocrinology, 6*, 117.

Serdjenian, E. (1994). Women managers in France. In N. J. Adler & D. N. Izraeli (Eds.), *Competitive frontiers: Women managers in a global economy* (pp. 175-189). Cambridge, MA: Blackwell.

Sessa, V. I. (1992). Managing diversity at the Xerox Corporation: Balanced workforce goals and caucus groups. In S. E. Jackson (Ed.), *Diversity in the workplace: Human resource initiatives* (pp. 37-64). New York: Guilford.

Sevastos, P., Smith, L., & Cordery, J. L. (1992). Evidence on the reliability and construct validity of Warr's (1990) well-being and mental health measure. *Journal of Occupational Psychology, 65*, 185-205.

Sexton, D. L. (1987). Advancing small business research: Utilizing research from other areas. *American Journal of Small Business, 11*(3), 25-31.

Shabbir, A., & DiGregorio, S. D. (1996). An examination of the relationship between women's personal goals and structural factors influencing their decision to start a business: The case of Pakistan. *Journal of Business Venturing, 11*(6), 507-530.

Shackelford, S., Wood, W., & Worchel, S. (1996). Behavioral styles and the influence of women in mixed-sex groups. *Social Psychology Quarterly, 59*, 284-293.

Shane, S., Kolvereid, L., & Westhead, P. (1991). An exploratory examination of the reasons leading to new firms' formation across country and gender (Part 1). *Journal of Business Venturing, 6*(6), 431-446.

Sharp, C., & Post, R. (1980). Evaluations of male and female applicants for sex-congruent and sex-incongruent jobs. *Sex Roles, 6*, 391-401.

Sharpe, R. (1994, March 29). Family friendly firms don't always promote females. *Wall Street Journal*, pp. B1, B12.

Shaver, K. G., Gatewood, E. J., & Gartner, W. B. (1991). Attributions for new venture creation: An experimental comparison. In N. C. Churchill, W. D. Bygrave, J. G. Covin, D. L. Sexton, D. P. Slevin, K. H. Vesper, & W. E. Wetzel, Jr. (Eds.), *Frontiers of entrepreneurship research* (pp. 32-49). Babson Park, MA: Center for Entrepreneurial Studies, Babson College.

Sheehy, G. (1976). *Passages: Predictable crises of adult life.* New York: Dutton.

Sheets, T. L., & Bushardt, S. C. (1994). Effect of the applicant's gender appropriateness and qualifications and rater self-monitoring propensities on hiring decisions. *Public Personnel Management, 23*, 373-382.

Sheffey, S., & Tindale, R. S. (1992). Perceptions of sexual harassment in the workplace. *Journal of Applied Social Psychology, 22*, 1502-1520.

Shellenbarger, S. (1998a, April 15). Work & family: Good news at last in battle of the sexes—Men are helping more. *Wall Street Journal*, p. B1.

Shellenbarger, S. (1998b, March 11). Work & family: More executives cite need for family time as reason for quitting. *Wall Street Journal*, p. B1.

Shelton, B. A. (1992). *Women, men, and time: Gender differences in paid work, housework, and leisure.* New York: Greenwood.

Sherif, C. W. (1982). Needed concepts in the study of gender identity. *Psychology of Women Quarterly, 6,* 375-398.

Sherman, A. C., Higgs, G. E., & Williams, R. L. (1997). Gender differences in the locus of control construct. *Psychology and Health, 12,* 239-248.

Shimanoff, S. B., & Jenkins, M. M. (1991). Leadership and gender: Challenging assumptions and recognizing resources. In R. S. Cathcart & L. A. Samovar (Eds.), *Small group communication: A reader.* Dubuque, IA: William C. Brown.

Shinn, M., Wong, N. W., Simko, P. A., & Ortiz-Torres, B. (1989). Promoting the well-being of working parents: Coping, social support, and flexible job schedules. *American Journal of Community Psychology, 17,* 31-55.

Shore, L. M., & Thornton, G. C., III. (1986). Effects of gender on self- and supervisory ratings. *Academy of Management Journal, 29,* 115-129.

Shore, T. H. (1992). Subtle gender bias in the assessment of managerial potential. *Sex Roles, 27,* 499-515.

Shrader, C. B., Blackburn, V. B., & Iles, P. (1997). Women in management and firm financial performance: An exploratory study. *Journal of Managerial Issues, 9*(3), 355-372.

Shukla, A., & Kapoor, M. (1990). Sex role identity, marital power, and marital satisfaction among middle-class couples in India. *Sex Roles, 22,* 693-706.

Sidanius, J., & Crane, M. (1989). Job evaluation and gender: The case of university faculty. *Journal of Applied Social Psychology, 19,* 174-197.

Sidanius, J., & Pratto, F. (in press). *Social dominance: An intergroup theory of social hierarchy and oppression.* Cambridge, UK: Cambridge University Press.

Sieber, S. D. (1974). Toward a theory of role accumulation. *American Sociological Review, 39,* 567-578.

Sigelman, L., & Welch, S. (1991). *Black Americans' views of racial inequality: The dream deferred.* New York: Cambridge University Press.

Siguaw, J. A., & Honeycutt, E. D. (1995). An examination of gender differences in selling behaviors and job attitudes. *Industrial Marketing Management, 24,* 45-52.

Silver, H. (1993). Homework and domestic work. *Sociological Forum, 8*(2), 181-204.

Simas, K., & McCarrey, M. (1979). Impact of recruiter authoritarianism and applicant sex on evaluation and selection decisions in a recruitment interview analogue study. *Journal of Applied Psychology, 64,* 483-491.

Simmel, G. (1908). *Soziologie* [Sociology]. Berlin: Leipzig, Duncker and Humbolt.

Simmons, R. (1982). *Affirmative action: Conflict and change in higher education after Bakke.* Cambridge, MA: Schenkman.

Simpson, G. (1996). The plexiglass ceiling: The careers of Black women lawyers. *Career Development Quarterly, 45,* 173-188.

Singh, R., Greenhaus, J. H., Parasuraman, S., & Collins, K. M. (1998, May). *The influence of family responsibilities, gender, and social support on the career involvement of professionals.* Paper presented at the annual meeting of the Eastern Academy of Management, Springfield, MA.

Sitt, C., Schmidt, S., Price, K., & Kipnis, D. (1983). Sex of leader, leader behavior, and subordinate satisfaction. *Sex Roles, 9,* 31-42.

Skrypnek, B. J., & Snyder, M. (1982). On the self-perpetuating nature of stereotypes about women and men. *Journal of Experimental Social Psychology, 18,* 277-291.

Slovic, P., & Lichtenstein, S. (1971). Comparison of Bayesian and regression approaches to the study of information processing in judgment. *Organizational Behavior and Human Performance, 6,* 649-744.

Small, S. A., & Riley, D. (1990). Toward a multidimensional assessment of work spillover into family life. *Journal of Marriage and the Family, 52,* 51-61.

Smith, E., & Witt, S. (1990). Black faculty and affirmative action at predominantly White institutions. *Western Journal of Black Studies, 14*(1), 9-16.

Smith, J. P. (1989). Commentary. In R. T. Michael, H. I. Hartmann, & B. O'Farrell (Eds.), *Pay equity: Empirical inquiries* (pp. 171-175). Washington, DC: National Academy Press.

Smith, J. P., & Ward, M. P. (1984). *Women's wages and work in the twentieth century.* Santa Monica, CA: RAND.

Smith, P., & Smits, S. (1994). The feminization of leadership? *Training and Development Journal, 48*(2), 43-46.

Smith-Lovin, L., & Brody, C. (1989). Interruptions in group discussions: The effects of gender and group composition. *American Sociological Review, 54*(3), 424-435.

Smith-Lovin, L., Skvoretz, J. V., & Hudson, C. G. (1986). Status and participation in six-person groups: A test of Skvoretz's comparative status model. *Social Forces, 64,* 992-1005.

Sniderman, P. M., & Tetlock, P. E. (1986). Symbolic racism: Problems of motive attribution in political analysis. *Journal of Social Issues, 42,* 129-150.

Society for Human Resource Management. (1998). *Workplace romance survey.* Alexandria, VA: Author.

Solomon, B. A. (1985, February). A company that benefits from child-care benefits. *Personnel, 62,* 4-6.

Sorensen, E. (1989). Measuring the effect of occupational sex and race composition on earnings. In R. T. Michael, H. I. Hartmann, & B. O'Farrell (Eds.), *Pay equity: Empirical inquiries* (pp. 49-69). Washington, DC: National Academy Press.

Sorensen, E. (1990). The crowding hypothesis and comparable worth. *Journal of Human Resources, 25*(1), 55-89.

South, S. J., Bonjean, C. M., Markham, W. T., & Corder, J. (1982). Social structure and intergroup interaction: Men and women of the federal bureaucracy. *American Sociological Review, 47*(5), 587-599.

South, S. J., Markham, W. T., Bonjean, C. M., & Corder, J. (1987). Sex differences in support for organizational advancement. *Work and Occupations, 14*(2), 261-285.

Spain, D., & Bianchi, S. M. (1996). *Balancing act: Motherhood, marriage, and employment among American women.* New York: Russell Sage.

Spalter-Roth, R., & Hartmann, H. (1992). Raising women's earnings: The family issue of the 1990s. In J. Greenberg & W. Kistler (Eds.), *Buying America back: Economic choices for the 1990s* (pp. 384-395). Tulsa, OK: Council Oak.

Spangler, E., Gordon, M. A., & Pipkin, R. M. (1978). Token women: An empirical test of Kanter's hypothesis. *American Journal of Sociology,* No. 2, pp. 160-170.

Spears, L. (1998). *Robert K. Greenleaf: The power of servant leadership.* San Francisco: Berrett-Koehler.

Spence, J. T. (1985). Gender identity and its implications for the concepts of masculinity and femininity. In T. B. Sondergger (Ed.), *Nebraska Symposium on Motivation: Psychology and gender* (Vol. 32, pp. 59-95). Lincoln: University of Nebraska Press.

Spence, J. T., Helmreich, R. L., & Holahan, C. K. (1979). Negative and positive components of psychological masculinity and femininity and their relationships to self-reports of neurotic and acting out behaviors. *Journal of Personal and Social Psychology, 37,* 1673-1682.

Spence, J. T., Helmreich, R., & Stapp, J. (1975). Ratings of self and peers on sex role attributes and their relation to self-esteem and the conceptions of masculinity and femininity. *Journal of Personality and Social Psychology, 32,* 29-39.

Spender, D. (1984a). Defining reality: A powerful tool. In C. Kramarae, M. Schulz, & W. O'Barr (Eds.), *Language and power* (pp. 194-205). Beverly Hills, CA: Sage.

Spender, D. (1984b). *Women of ideas and what men have done to them from Alpra Behn to Adrienne Rich.* Boston: Routledge & Kegan Paul.

Srinivasan, R., Woo, C. Y., & Cooper, A. C. (1994). Performance determinants for male and female entrepreneurs. In W. D. Bygrave, S. Birley, N. C. Churchill, E. Gatewood, F. Hoy, R. Keeley, & W. E. Wetzel, Jr. (Eds.), *Frontiers of entrepreneurship research* (pp. 43-56). Babson Park, MA: Center for Entrepreneurial Studies, Babson College.

St. Jean, Y., & Feagin, J. R. (1997). Racial masques: Black women and subtle gendered racism. In N. V. Benokraitis (Ed.), *Subtle sexism: Current practice and prospects for change* (pp. 179-200). Thousand Oaks, CA: Sage.

Staber, U. (1997). Entrepreneurial network structures: Gender differences and performance outcomes. In L. N. Dosier & J. B. Keys (Eds.), *Academy of Management best papers proceedings* (Abstract, p. 524). Statesboro: Georgia Southern University, Faculty Research Services, College of Business.

Stack, S. (1997). Women's opposition to race-targeted interventions. *Sex Roles, 36,* 543-558.

Staines, G., & Galinsky, E. (1992). Parental leave and productivity: The supervisor's view. In D. E. Friedman, E. Galinsky, & V. Plowden (Eds.), *Parental leave and productivity* (pp. 21-32). New York: Families and Work Institute.

Staines, G. L. (1980). Spillover versus compensation: A review of the literature on the relationships between work and nonwork. *Human Relations, 33,* 111-129.

Staines, G. L., & Pleck, J. H. (1984). Nonstandard work schedules and family life. *Journal of Applied Psychology, 69,* 515-523.

Staines, G. L., Pleck, J. H., Shepard, L., & O'Connor, P. (1979). *Wives' employment status and marital adjustment.* Ann Arbor: University of Michigan, Institute of Social Research.

Staines, G. L., Pottick, K. J., & Fudge, D. A. (1986). Wives' employment and husbands' attitudes toward work and life. *Journal of Applied Psychology, 71,* 118-128.

Stamler, V. L., Christiansen, M. D., Staley, K. H., & Macagno-Shang, L. (1991). Client preference for counselor gender. *Psychology of Women Quarterly, 15,* 317-321.

Starr, J., & Yudkin, M. (1997). What is an entrepreneur? *Executive Female, 20*(2), 35.

State Farm Fire & Casualty Co. v. Compupay, Inc., 654 So.2d 944 (Fla. Ct. App. 1995).

Stead, B. A., & Zinkhan, G. M. (1986). Service priority in department stores: The effects of customer gender and dress. *Sex Roles, 15,* 601-611.

Steeh, C., & Krysan, M. (1996). Affirmative action and the public, 1970-1995. *Public Opinion Quarterly, 60,* 128-158.

Steele, S. (1990). *The content of our character: A new vision of race in America*. New York: St. Martin's.

Steil, J. M., & Weltman, K. (1992). Influence strategies at home and work: A study of sixty dual career couples. *Journal of Social and Personal Relationships, 9*, 65-88.

Stein, R. T., & Heller, T. (1979). An empirical analysis between leadership status and participation rates reported in the literature. *Journal of Personality and Social Psychology, 37*, 1993-2002.

Steinberg, R. J. (1990). The social construction of skill: Gender, power and comparable worth. *Work and Occupations, 17*(4), 449-482.

Steinberg, S. (1995). *Turning back: The retreat from racial justice in American thought and policy*. Boston: Beacon.

Sterba, J. P. (1997). Racism and sexism: The common ground. In N. Zack (Ed.), *Race/sex: Their sameness, difference, and interplay* (pp. 61-71). New York: Routledge.

Stern, B. B., Gould, S. J., & Tewari, S. (1993). Sex-typed service images: An empirical investigation of self-service variables. *The Service Industries Journal, 13*, 74-96.

Stern, G. (1991, September 16). Young women insist on career equality, forcing the men in their lives to adjust. *Wall Street Journal*, p. B1.

Sternberg, R. J. (1986). A triangular theory of love. *Psychological Review, 93*, 119-135.

Stevens, C. K., & Kristof, A. L. (1995). Making the right impression: A field study of applicant impression management during job interviews. *Journal of Applied Psychology, 80*, 587-606.

Stevenson, L. (1986). Against all odds: The entrepreneurship of women. *Journal of Small Business Management, 24*(3), 30-36.

Stevenson, M. H. (1988). Some economic approaches to the persistence of wage differences between men and women. In A. H. Stromberg & S. Harkess (Eds.), *Women working: Theories and facts in perspective* (pp. 87-100). Mountain View, CA: Mayfield.

Stewart, W., & Barling, J. (1996). Fathers' work experiences effect children's behaviors via job-related affect and parenting behaviors. *Journal of Organizational Behavior, 17*, 221-232.

The stigma facing mommies. (1989, March 27). *Newsday*, Sec. 3, pp. 1, 8-9.

Stimpson, D. V., Narayanan, S., & Shanthakumar, D. K. (1993). Attitudinal characteristics of male and female entrepreneurs in the United States and India. *Psychological Studies, 38*(2), 64-68.

Stockdale, M. S. (1993). The role of sexual misperceptions of women's friendliness in an emerging theory of sexual harassment. *Journal of Vocational Behavior, 42*, 83-100.

Stockdale, M. S. (Ed.). (1996). *Sexual harassment in the workplace: Perspectives, frontiers, and response strategies*. Thousand Oaks, CA: Sage.

Stogdill, R. M. (1974). *Handbook of leadership*. New York: Free Press.

Stolzenberg, R. M. (1975). Occupations, labor markets, and the process of wage attainment. *American Sociological Review, 40*(5), 645-665.

Stonewater, B. B., Eveslage, S. A., & Dingerson, M. R. (1990). Gender differences in career helping relationships. *Career Development Quarterly, 39*, 72-85.

Stouffer, S. A., Suchman, E., DeVinney, L., Starr, S., & Williams, R. (1949). The American soldier: Adjustment during Army life. In *Studies in social psychology in World War II* (Vol. 1). Princeton, NJ: Princeton University Press.

Stover, D. L. (1994). The horizontal distribution of female managers within organizations. *Work and Occupations, 21*(4), 385-402.

Stroh, L. K., & Brett, J. M. (1996). The dual-earner daddy penalty in salary progression. *Human Resource Management Journal, 35,* 1-21.

Stroh, L. K., Brett, J. M., & Reilly, A. H. (1992). All the right stuff: A comparison of female and male career patterns. *Journal of Applied Psychology, 77,* 251-260.

Stroh, L. K., Brett, J. M., & Reilly, A. H. (1994). A decade of change: Mobile managers' attachment to their organizations and their jobs. *Human Resource Management Journal, 33,* 531-548.

Stroh, L. K., Brett, J. M., & Reilly, A. H. (1996). Family structure, glass ceiling, and traditional explanations for the differential rate of turnover of female and male managers. *Journal of Vocational Behavior, 49,* 99-118.

Stroh, L. K., & Greller, M. M. (1995). Introduction to special issues on careers from midlife. *Journal of Vocational Behavior, 47,* 229-231.

Stroh, L. K., & Reilly, A. H. (1997). Rekindling organization loyalty: The impact of career mobility. *Journal of Career Development, 24*(1), 39-54.

Stromberg, A. H., & Harkess, S. (Eds.). (1988). *Women working: Theories and facts in perspective* (2nd ed.). Mountain View, CA: Mayfield.

Struthers, N. J. (1995). Differences in mentoring: A function of gender or organizational rank? *Journal of Social Behavior and Personality, 10,* 265-272.

Stumpf, S. A., & London, M. (1981a). Capturing rater policies in evaluating candidates for promotion. *Academy of Management Journal, 24,* 752-766.

Stumpf, S. A., & London, M. (1981b). Management promotions: Individual and organizational factors influencing the promotion decision process. *Academy of Management Review, 6,* 539-549.

Suhler, J. N. (1997, October 21). Affirmative action case has ripple effect; UT Southwestern, SMU say Black enrollment down. *Dallas Morning News,* p. 19A.

Sullivan, C., & Lewis, S. (1998). *Home based telework, gender and the synchronisation of work and family.* Proceedings of the Gender, Work and Organization Conference, Manchester, UK.

Summers, R. J. (1991). The influence of affirmative action on perceptions of a beneficiary's qualifications. *Journal of Applied Social Psychology, 21,* 1265-1276.

Summers, R. J., & Myklebust, K. (1992). The influence of a history of romance on judgments and responses to a complaint of sexual harassment. *Sex Roles, 27,* 345-357.

Surrey, J. L. (1991). The "self-in-relation": A theory of women's development. In J. V. Jordan, A. G. Kaplan, J. B. Miller, I. P. Stiver, & J. L. Surrey (Eds.), *Women's growth in connection: Writings from the Stone Center* (pp. 51-66). New York: Guilford.

Sutton, R. I., & Rafaeli, A. (1988). Untangling the relationship between displayed emotions and organizational sales: The case of convenience stores. *Academy of Management Journal, 31*(3), 461-487.

Swerdlik, M. E., & Bardon, J. I. (1988). A survey of mentoring experiences in school psychology. *Journal of School Psychology, 26,* 213-224.

Swim, J., Borgida, E., Maruyama, G., & Myers, D. G. (1989). Joan McKay versus John McKay: Do gender stereotypes bias evaluations? *Psychological Bulletin, 105,* 409-429.

Swiss, D., & Squires, J. (1993). *Women and the work/family dilemma.* Chichester, UK: Wiley.

Symons, G. L. (1993). Women's occupational careers in business: Managers and entrepreneurs in France and in Canada. In N. J. Adler & D. N. Izraeli (Eds.), *Women in management worldwide* (pp. 41-52). New York: M. E. Sharpe.

Tajfel, H. (1978). *Differentiation between social groups.* New York: Academic Press.

Tajfel, H. (1982). *Social identity and intergroup relations.* Cambridge, UK: Cambridge University Press.

Tajfel, H., & Turner, J. (1985). The social identity theory of intergroup behavior. In S. Worchel & W. G. Austin (Eds.), *Psychology of intergroup relations* (pp. 7-24). Chicago: Nelson-Hall.

Tam, T. (1997). Sex segregation and occupational gender inequality in the United States: Devaluation or specialized training? *American Journal of Sociology, 102*(6), 1652-1692.

Tang, C. S., Yik, M. S., Cheung, F. M. C., Choi, P., & Au, K. (1995). How do Chinese college students define sexual harassment? *Journal of Interpersonal Violence, 10,* 503-515.

Tangri, S., Burt, M., & Johnson, L. (1982). Sexual harassment at work: Three explanatory models. *Journal of Social Issues, 38,* 33-54.

Tannen, D. (1990). *You just don't understand: Women and men in conversation.* New York: Ballantine.

Tannen, D. (Ed.). (1993). *Gender and conversational interaction.* New York: Oxford University Press.

Tannen, D. (1994). *Talking from 9 to 5: How women's and men's conversational styles affect who gets heard, who gets credit, and what gets done at work.* New York: William Morrow.

Tanton, M. (Ed.). (1994). *Women in management: A developing presence.* London: Routledge.

Tashjian, V. W. (1990). *Don't blame the baby: Why women leave corporations.* Wilmington, DE: Wick & Company.

Tata, J. (1993). The structure and phenomenon of sexual harassment: Impact of category of sexually harassing behavior, gender, and hierarchical level. *Journal of Applied Social Psychology, 23,* 199-211.

Tata, J. (1998). He said, she said: Remedial accounts and judgments of coworker sexual harassment. In S. J. Havlovic (Ed.), *Best paper proceedings of the 58th annual meeting of the Academy of Management* [CD-ROM]. Briarcliff Manor, NY: Academy of Management.

Tay, L. S., & Gibbons, J. L. (1998). Attitudes toward gender roles among adolescents in Singapore. *Cross-Cultural Research, 32,* 257-278.

Taylor, A. (1986, August 18). Why women managers are bailing out. *Fortune,* pp. 16-23.

Taylor, F. (1911). *The principles of scientific management.* New York: Norton.

Taylor, M. C. (1994). Impact of affirmative action on beneficiary groups: Evidence from the 1990 General Social Survey. *Basic and Applied Social Psychology, 15,* 143-178.

Taylor, P. A., Gwartney-Gibbs, P., & Farley, R. (1986). Changes in the structure of earnings inequality by race, sex, and industrial sector, 1960-1980. In R. V. Robinson (Ed.), *Research in social stratification and mobility: A research annual* (Vol. 5, pp. 105-138). Greenwich, CT: JAI.

Taylor, S. E., & Crocker, J. (1981). Schematic bases of social information processing. In E. T. Higgins, C. P. Herman, & M. P. Zanna (Eds.), *Social cognition: The Ontario Symposium* (Vol. 1). Hillsdale, NJ: Lawrence Erlbaum.

Taylor, S. E., Fiske, S. T., Etcoff, N., & Ruderman, A. (1978). The categorical and contextual bases of person memory and stereotyping. *Journal of Personality and Social Psychology, 36,* 778-793.

Tenbrunsel, A. E., Brett, J. M., Stroh, L. K., & Reilly, A. H. (1995). Dynamic and static work-family relationships. *Organization Behavior & Human Decision Processes, 63,* 233-246.

Tepper, B. J. (1995). Upward maintenance tactics in supervisory mentoring and non-mentoring relationships. *Academy of Management Journal, 38,* 1191-1205.

Tepper, B. J., Brown, S. J., & Hunt, M. D. (1993). Strength of subordinates' upward influence tactics and gender congruency effects. *Journal of Applied Social Psychology, 23,* 1903-1919.

Terborg, J. R. (1977). Women in management: A research review. *Journal of Applied Psychology, 62,* 647-664.

Terborg, J. R. (1985). Working women and stress. In T. A. Beehr & R. S. Bhagat (Eds.), *Human stress and cognition in organizations* (pp. 245-286). Chichester, UK: Wiley.

Terborg, J. R., & Ilgen, D. R. (1975). A theoretical approach to sex discrimination in traditionally masculine occupations. *Organizational Behavior and Human Performance, 13,* 352-376.

Terkel, S. (1972). *Working.* New York: Avon.

Terpstra, D. E., & Baker, D. D. (1988). Outcomes of sexual harassment charges. *Academy of Management Journal, 31*(1), 185-194.

Terpstra, D. E., & Baker, D. D. (1991). Sexual harassment at work: The psychological issues. In M. J. Davidson & J. M. Earnshaw (Eds.), *Vulnerable workers* (pp. 179-202). Chichester, UK: Wiley.

Terpstra, D. E., & Baker, D. D. (1992). Outcomes of federal court decisions on sexual harassment. *Academy of Management Journal, 35*(1), 181-190.

Terpstra, D. E., & Cook, S. E. (1985). Complainant characteristics and reported behaviors and consequences associated with formal sexual harassment charges. *Personnel Psychology, 38,* 559-574.

Thacker, R. A., & Wayne, S. J. (1995). An examination of the relationship between upward influence tactics and assessments of promotability. *Journal of Management, 21,* 739-756.

Tharenou, P., Latimer, S., & Conroy, D. (1994). How do you make it to the top? An examination of influences on women's and men's managerial advancement. *Academy of Management Journal, 37*(4), 899-931.

Thatcher, M. (1995). *Path to power.* New York: HarperCollins.

Thomas, D., & Higgins, M. (1996). Mentoring and the boundaryless career: Lessons from the minority experience. In M. B. Arthur & D. M. Rousseau (Eds.), *The boundaryless career: A new employment principle for a new organizational era* (pp. 268-281). New York: Oxford University Press.

Thomas, D. A. (1989). Mentoring and irrationality: The role of racial taboos. *Human Resource Management, 28,* 279-290.

Thomas, D. A. (1990). The impact of race on managers' experiences of developmental relationships (mentoring and sponsorship): An intra-organizational study. *Journal of Organizational Behavior, 11,* 479-491.

Thomas, D. A., & Alderfer, C. P. (1989). The influence of race on career dynamics: Theory and research on minority career experiences. In M. B. Arthur, D. T. Hall, & B. S. Lawrence (Eds.), *Handbook of career theory* (pp. 133-158). Cambridge, MA: Cambridge University Press.

Thomas, D. A., & Ely, R. J. (1996). Making differences matter: A new paradigm for managing diversity. *Harvard Business Review, 74*(5), 79-90.

Thomas, L. T., & Ganster, D. C. (1995). Impact of family-supportive work variables on work/family conflict and strain: A control perspective. *Journal of Applied Psychology, 80*(1), 6-15.

Thompson, C. E., & Carter, R. T. (1997). *Racial identity theory: Applications to individual, group, and organizational interventions.* Mahwah, NJ: Lawrence Erlbaum.

Thompson, D. E., & Gooler, L. E. (1996). Capitalizing on the benefits of diversity through workteams. In E. E. Kossek & S. A. Lobel (Eds.), *Managing diversity: Human resource strategies for transforming the workplace* (pp. 392-437). Cambridge, MA: Blackwell.

Thompson, D. E., & Thompson, T. A. (1985). Task-based performance appraisal for blue-collar jobs: Evaluation of race and sex effects. *Journal of Applied Psychology, 70,* 747-753.

Tickamyer, A., Scollay, S., Bokemeier, J., & Wood, T. (1989). Administrators' perceptions of affirmative action in higher education. In F. A. Blanchard & F. J. Crosby (Eds.), *Affirmative action in perspective* (pp. 125-138). New York: Springer-Verlag.

Tidball, M. E. (1986). Baccalaureate origins of recent natural science doctorates. *Journal of Higher Education, 57*(6), 606-620.

Tidd, K., & Lockard, J. (1978). Monetary significance of the affiliative smile: A case for reciprocal altruism. *Bulletin of the Psychonomic Society, 11,* 344-346.

Tiedje, L. B., Wortman, C. B., Downey, G., Emmons, C., Biernat, M., & Lang, R. (1990). Women with multiple roles: Role-compatibility perceptions, satisfaction, and mental health. *Journal of Marriage and the Family, 52,* 63-72.

Tiger, L. (1997, May 27). Sex in uniform. *Wall Street Journal,* p. A18.

Till, F. J. (1980). *Sexual harassment: A report on the sexual harassment of students.* Washington, DC: National Advisory Council on Women's Educational Programs.

Tilsson, T. (1996). She's the boss. *Canadian Business, 69*(11), 43-45.

Tjosvold, D., & Weicker, D. (1993). Cooperative and competitive networking by entrepreneurs: A critical incident study. *Journal of Small Business Management, 31*(1), 11-21.

Tkachencko, A. A., Koryukhina, A. V., & Matveeva, T. V. (1997). The Russian Federation. In J. Hodges-Aeberhard & C. Raskin (Eds.), *Affirmative action in the employment of ethnic minorities and persons with disabilities* (pp. 85-96). Geneva: International Labour Office.

Tolbert, P. S. (1986). Organizations and inequality: Sources of earnings differences between male and female faculty. *Sociology of Education, 59*(2), 227-336.

Tolbert, P. S., & Oberfield, A. A. (1991). Sources of organizational demography: Faculty sex ratios in colleges and universities. *Sociology of Education, 64,* 305-316.

Tolbert, P. S., Simons, T., Andrews, A. O., & Rhee, J. (1995). The effects of gender composition in academic departments on faculty turnover. *Industrial and Labor Relations Review, 48*(3), 562-579.

Tolson, A. (1977). *The limits of masculinity.* New York: Harper & Row.

Tomaskovic-Devey, D. (1993). *Gender and racial inequality at work: The sources and consequences of job segregation.* Ithaca, NY: ILR.

Tomaskovic-Devey, D. (1995). Sex composition and gendered earnings inequality: A comparison of job and occupational models. In J. A. Jacobs (Ed.), *Gender inequality at work* (pp. 23-56). Thousand Oaks, CA: Sage.

Top, T. J. (1991). Sex bias in the evaluation of performance in the scientific, artistic, and literary professions: A review. *Sex Roles, 24,* 73-106.

Tosi, H. L., & Einbender, S. W. (1985). The effects of the type and amount of information on sex discrimination research: A meta-analysis. *Academy of Management Journal, 28,* 712-723.

Tougas, F., & Beaton, A. M. (1993). Affirmative action in the work place: For better or for worse. *Applied Psychology: An International Review, 42,* 253-264.

Tougas, F., Beaton, A. M., & Veilleux, F. (1991). Why women approve of affirmative action: The study of a predictive model. *International Journal of Psychology, 26,* 761-776.

Tougas, F., & Veilleux, F. (1990). The response of men to affirmative action strategies for women: The study of a predictive model. *Canadian Journal of Behavioral Science, 22,* 424-432.

Tousignant, M., Brosseau, R., & Tremblay, L. (1987). Sex biases in mental health scales: Do women tend to report less serious symptoms and confide more than men? *Psychological Medicine, 17,* 203-215.

Townley, B. (1993). Foucault, power/knowledge, and its relevance for human resource management. *Academy of Management Review, 18,* 518-545.

Treiman, D. J., & Roos, P. A. (1983). Sex and earnings in industrial society: A nine-nation comparison. *American Journal of Sociology, 89,* 612-650.

Triandis, H. C. (1989). The self and social behavior in differing cultural contexts. *Psychological Review, 96,* 506-520.

Triandis, H. C. (1996). The psychological measurement of cultural syndromes. *American Psychologist, 51,* 407-415.

Trice, H. M., & Beyer, J. (1993). *The cultures of work organizations.* Englewood Cliffs, NJ: Prentice Hall.

Trocki, K. F., & Orioli, E. M. (1994). Gender differences in stress symptoms, stress-producing contexts, and coping strategies. In G. P. Keita & J. J. Hurrell (Eds.), *Job stress in a changing workplace* (pp. 7-22). Washington, DC: American Psychological Association.

Trompenaars, F. (1993). *Riding the waves of culture: Understanding cultural diversity in business*. London: The Economist Books.

Tsui, A. S., Egan, T., & O'Reilly, C., III. (1992). Being different: Relational demography and organizational attachment. *Administrative Science Quarterly, 37*(4), 549-579.

Tsui, A. S., & Gutek, B. A. (1984). A role set analysis of gender differences in performance, affective relationships, and career success of industrial middle managers. *Academy of Management Journal, 27*, 619-635.

Tsui, A. S., & O'Reilly, C. A., III. (1989). Beyond simple demographic effects: The importance of relational demography in superior-subordinate dyads. *Academy of Management Journal, 32*, 402-423.

Turban, D. B., & Dougherty, T. W. (1994). Role of protégé personality in receipt of mentoring and career success. *Academy of Management Journal, 37*, 688-702.

Turban, D. B., & Jones, A. P. (1988). Supervisor-subordinate similarity: Types, effects, and mechanisms. *Journal of Applied Psychology, 73*, 228-234.

Turner, C. (1993). Women's businesses in Europe—EEC initiatives. In S. Allen & C. Truman (Eds.), *Women in business—Perspectives on women entrepreneurs* (pp. 133-147). New York: Routledge.

Turner, J. C., & Giles, H. (1981). *Intergroup behavior*. New York: Blackwell.

Turner, M. E., & Pratkanis, A. R. (1994). Affirmative action as help: A review of recipient reactions to preferential selection and affirmative action. *Basic and Applied Social Psychology, 15*, 43-69.

Turner, T. (1983). What's love got to do with it. On *Private dancer* [compact disc]. Hollywood: Capitol Records.

Tversky, A., & Kahneman, D. L. (1971). Belief in the law of small numbers. *Psychological Bulletin, 76*, 105-110.

Twenge, J. M. (1997). Attitudes toward women, 1970-1995. *Psychology of Women Quarterly, 21*, 35-51.

Tyler, M., & Taylor, S. (1998). The exchange of aesthetics: Women's work and "the gift." *Gender, Work and Organization, 5*(3), 165-171.

Uchitelle, L., & Kleinfield, N. R. (1996, March 3). On the battlefields of business, millions of casualties. *New York Times*, pp. Y1, Y14-Y17.

Ulrich, D. (1997). Measuring human resources: An overview of practice and a prescription for results. *Human Resource Management, 36*(3), 303-320.

Unger, R. K. (1979). Toward a redefinition of sex and gender. *American Psychologist, 34*, 1085-1094.

Unger, R. K., & Crawford, M. (1993). Commentary: Sex and gender—The troubled relationship between terms and concepts. *Psychological Science, 4*, 122-124.

Unger, R. K., & Crawford, M. (1996). *Women and gender: A feminist perspective* (2nd ed.). New York: McGraw-Hill.

United Nations Educational, Scientific, and Cultural Organization (UNESCO). (1998). *Statistical yearbook 1998* (pp. 3-345–3-391, Table 3.12). Paris: Author.

U.S. Bureau of the Census. (1972). *Census of population and housing, 1970: Public use samples of basic records from the 1970 census: Description and technical documentation*. Washington, DC: Author.

U.S. Bureau of the Census. (1983). *Census of population and housing, 1980: Public use microdata samples technical documentation*. Washington, DC: Author.

U.S. Bureau of the Census. (1993). *Census of population and housing, 1990: Public use microdata samples: United States.* Washington, DC: Author.

U.S. Bureau of the Census. (1996). *Statistical abstract of the United States: 1996.* Washington, DC: Government Printing Office.

U.S. Bureau of the Census. (1997). *Statistical abstract of the United States: 1997.* Washington, DC: Government Printing Office.

U.S. Congressional Record, 88th Cong., 2nd Sess., 1964, Vol. 110, pt. 5, pp. 5655-7044.

U.S. Department of Commerce. (1986, July). *The state of small business: White House Conference on small business—A report to the president of the United States.* Washington, DC: Government Printing Office.

U.S. Department of Commerce. (1994). *Handbook of small business data: 1994 edition.* Washington, DC: Government Printing Office.

U.S. Department of Commerce. (1996). *SBA Office of Advocacy facts about small business—1996* [On-line]. Available: http://www.sba.gov/ADVO/stats/fact1.html

U.S. Department of Commerce. (1997a). *SBA Office of Advocacy facts about small business—1997* [On-line]. Available: http://www.sba.gov/ADVO/stats/fact1.html [1-6].

U.S. Department of Commerce, Bureau of the Census. (1997b). *Current Population Survey: Annual demographic file, 1997* [Computer file]. ICPSR version. Washington, DC: U.S. Department of Commerce, Bureau of the Census [producer]. Ann Arbor, MI: Inter-university Consortium for Political and Social Research [distributor].

U.S. Department of Commerce. (1998). *National accounts data.* Washington, DC: Bureau of Economic Analysis.

U.S. Department of Education, National Center for Education Statistics. (1994). *Digest of education statistics 1994.* Washington, DC: Government Printing Office.

U.S. Department of Education, National Center for Education Statistics. (1996). *Digest of education statistics 1996.* Washington, DC: Government Printing Office.

U.S. Department of Education, National Center for Education Statistics. (1997a). *Digest of education statistics 1997.* Washington, DC: Government Printing Office.

U.S. Department of Education, National Center for Education Statistics. (1997b). *Digest of education statistics 1997* (p. 261, Table 244, p. 308, Table 281). Washington, DC: Government Printing Office.

U.S. Department of Labor, Bureau of Labor Statistics. (1983). *Handbook of labor statistics* (pp. 44-48, Table 16). Washington, DC: Government Printing Office.

U.S. Department of Labor, Bureau of Labor Statistics. (1990). *Employment and Earnings, 37*(2), p. 29, Table A-22.

U.S. Department of Labor. (1991a). *A report on the Glass Ceiling Initiative.* Washington, DC: Author.

U.S. Department of Labor, Bureau of Labor Statistics. (1991b). *Working women: A chartbook* (p. 50, Table 18). Washington, DC: Government Printing Office.

U.S. Department of Labor. (1997a). Women in management. *Accessibility Information No. 97-3* [On-line]. Available: http://www.dol.gov/dol/wb/public/wp_pubs/wmgt97.htm.

U.S. Department of Labor, Bureau of Labor Statistics. (1997b). Labor force participation rate. In *Labor force statistics from the Current Population Survey* [On-line]. Available: Internet http://stats.bls.gov:80/sahome.html

U.S. Department of Labor, Bureau of Labor Statistics, Office of Productivity and Technology. (1997c, September). *Comparative civilian labor force statistics, ten countries, 1959-1996* [On-line]. Available FTP: 146. 142. 4. 23 Directory: pub/special.requests/ForeignLabor/flslforc.tx.

U.S. Department of Labor, Bureau of Labor Statistics. (1998a). *Employment and Earnings, 45*(1), p. 163, Table 2.

U.S. Department of Labor, Bureau of Labor Statistics. (1998b). *Employment and Earnings, 45*(9), p. 7, Table A-2, p. 27, Table A-19.

U.S. Department of Labor, Bureau of Labor Statistics. (1998c). *Employment status of the civilian population by sex and age (for May 1998)* [On-line]. Available: Internet http://stats.bls.gov/news.release/empsit.t01.html

U.S. Equal Employment Opportunity Commission. (1981). Guidelines on discrimination because of sex. In U.S. Merit Systems Protection Board (Ed.), *Sexual harassment in the workplace: Is it a problem?* Washington, DC: Government Printing Office.

U.S. Merit Systems Protection Board. (1981). *Sexual harassment in the workplace: Is it a problem?* Washington, DC: Government Printing Office.

U.S. Merit Systems Protection Board. (1988). *Sexual harassment in the federal government: An update.* Washington, DC: Government Printing Office.

U.S. Merit Systems Protection Board. (1995). *Sexual harassment in the federal workplace: Trends, progress, and continuing challenges.* Washington, DC: Government Printing Office.

U.S. Small Business Administration. (1985). *State of small business.* Washington, DC: Government Printing Office.

U.S. Small Business Administration. (1995). *The state of small business: A report to the president 1994.* Washington, DC: Government Printing Office.

U.S. Small Business Administration. (1997, April). *Women and small business—Startling new statistics* [On-line]. Available: http://www.onlinewbc.org/docs/starting/new-stats.html

United Steelworkers of America v. Weber, 443 U.S. 193 (1979).

University of California Regents v. Bakke, 438 U.S. 265 (1978).

Vaill, P. B. (1998). *Spirited leading and learning.* San Francisco: Jossey-Bass.

Valdez, R. L., & Gutek, B. A. (1987). Family roles: A help or a hindrance for working women? In B. A. Gutek & L. Larwood (Eds.), *Women's career development* (pp. 157-169). Newbury Park, CA: Sage.

Van Auken, H. E., Rittenburg, T. L., Doran, B. M., & Hsieh, S.-F. (1994). An empirical analysis of advertising by women entrepreneurs. *Journal of Small Business Management, 32*(3), 11-28.

van Knippenberg, A. F. M. (1984). Intergroup differences in group perceptions. In H. Tajfel (Ed.), *The social dimension: European developments in social psychology* (Vol. 2, pp. 560-578). Cambridge, UK: Cambridge University Press.

Van Vianen, A. E. M., & Van Schie, E. C. M. (1995). Assessment of male and female behaviour in the employment interview. *Journal of Community and Applied Social Psychology, 5,* 243-257.

Van Vianen, A. E. M., & Willemsen, T. M. (1992). The employment interview: The role of sex discrimination in the evaluation of male and female job applicants in the Netherlands. *Journal of Applied Social Psychology, 22,* 471-491.

Vardi, Y., Shrom, A., & Jacobson, D. (1980). A study of leadership beliefs of Israeli managers. *Academy of Management Journal, 23*(2), 367-374.

Varma, A., & Stroh, L. K. (1998, July). *Gender-based discrimination in performance evaluations: Evidence from male and female samples.* Paper presented at the Fifth International Conference on Advances in Management, Brayford Pool, England.

Vaz, L., & Kanekar, S. (1990). Predicted and recommended behavior of a woman as a function of her inferred helplessness in the dowry and wife-beating predicaments. *Journal of Applied Social Psychology, 20,* 751-770.

Vazquez-Nuttall, E., Romero-Garcia, I., & De Leon, B. (1987). Sex roles and perceptions of femininity and masculinity of Hispanic women. *Psychology of Women Quarterly, 11,* 409-425.

Verbrugge, L. M. (1985). Gender and health: An update on hypothesis and evidence. *Journal of Health and Social Behavior, 26,* 156-182.

Vesper, K. H. (1983). *Entrepreneurship and national policy.* Chicago: Walter E. Heller International Corp., Institute for Small Business.

Viator, R. E., & Scandura, T. A. (1991). A study of mentor-protégé relationships in large public accounting firms. *Accounting Horizons, 5,* 20-30.

Vincent, A., & Seymour, J. (1995). Profile of women mentors: A national survey. *SAM Advanced Management Journal, 60,* 4-10.

Vingerhoets, A. J. M., & Van Heck, G. L. (1990). Gender, coping and psychosomatic symptoms. *Psychological Medicine, 20,* 125-135.

Vinnicombe, S. (1985). What exactly are the differences in male and female managerial styles? *Women in Management Review, 3*(1), 13-21.

Vinnicombe, S., & Colwill, N. L. (1995). *The essence of women in management.* London: Prentice Hall.

Vitaliano, P. P., Maiuro, R. D., Russo, J., & Becker, J. (1987). Raw versus relative scores in the assessment of coping strategies. *Journal of Behavioural Medicine, 10,* 1-18.

Voydanoff, P. (1988). Work role characteristics, family structure demands, and work/family conflict. *Journal of Marriage and the Family, 50,* 749-761.

Vroom, V., & Yetton, P. (1973). *Leadership and decision making.* Pittsburgh, PA: University of Pittsburgh Press.

Wagner, D. G., & Berger, J. B. (1997). Gender and interpersonal task behaviors: Status expectation accounts. *Sociological Perspectives, 40,* 1-32.

Wagner, D. G., Ford, R. S., & Ford, T. W. (1986). Can gender inequalities be reduced? *American Sociological Review, 51,* 47-61.

Wahl, A. (Ed.). (1995). *Men's perceptions of women and management.* Stockholm: Fritzes.

Waldfogel, J. (1995). The price of motherhood: Family status and women's pay in a young British cohort. *Oxford Economic Papers, 47*(4), 584-610.

Waldfogel, J. (1997). The effect of children on women's wages. *American Sociological Review, 62,* 209-217.

Waldfogel, J. (1998). Understanding the "family gap" in pay for women with children. *Journal of Economic Perspectives, 12*(1), 137-156.

Waldron, I., & Herold, J. (1986). Employment, attitudes toward employment, and women's health. *Women and Health, 11*(1), 79-98.

Walker, B. A., & Hanson, W. C. (1992). Valuing differences at Digital Equipment Corporation. In S. E. Jackson (Ed.), *Diversity in the workplace: Human resource initiatives* (pp. 119-137). New York: Guilford.

Walker, H. A., & Fennell, M. L. (1986). Gender differences in role differentiation and organizational task performance. *Annual Review of Sociology, 12,* 255-275.

Walker, H. A., Ilardi, B. C., McMahon, A. M., & Fennell, M. L. (1996). Gender, interaction and leadership. *Social Psychology Quarterly, 59*(3), 255-272.

Wallace, M., & Kalleberg, A. L. (1981). Economic organization of firms and labor market consequences: Toward a specification of dual economy theory. In I. Berg (Ed.), *Sociological perspectives on labor markets* (pp. 77-117). New York: Academic Press.

Wallston, B. S. (1987). Social psychology of women and gender. *Journal of Applied Psychology, 17,* 1025-1050.

Walters, V. (1993). Stress, anxiety and depression: Women's accounts of their health problems. *Social Science and Medicine, 36*(4), 393-402.

Waring, M. (1988). *Counting for nothing: What men value and what women are worth.* Wellington, NZ: Allen & Unwin.

Warren, J. A., & Johnson, P. J. (1995). The impact of workplace support on work-family role strain. *Family Relations, 44,* 163-169.

Watanabe, S., Takahashi, K., & Minami, T. (1997). The emerging role of diversity and work-family values in a global context. In P. C. Earley & M. Erez (Eds.), *New perspectives on international industrial/organizational psychology* (pp. 276-318). San Francisco: New Lexington.

Watkins, D., Akande, A., Fleming, J., Ismail, M., Lefner, K., Regmi, M., Watson, S., Yu, J., Adair, J., Cheng, C., Gerong, A., McInerney, D., Mpofu, E., Singh-Sengupta, S., & Wondimu, H. (1998). Cultural dimensions, gender, and the nature of self-concept: A fourteen-country study. *International Journal of Psychology, 33,* 17-31.

Watson, C. (1988). When a woman is the boss: Dilemmas in taking charge. *Group and Organization Studies, 13,* 163-181.

Watson, W., Kumar, K., & Michaelson, L. K. (1993). Cultural diversity's impact on interaction process and performance: Comparing homogeneous and diverse task groups. *Academy of Management Journal, 36,* 590-602.

Wayne, S. J., & Kacmar, M. K. (1991). The effects of impression management on the performance appraisal process. *Organizational Behavior and Human Decision Processes, 48,* 70-88.

Wayne, S. J., Liden, R. C., & Sparrowe, R. T. (1994). Developing leader-member exchanges: The influence of gender and ingratiation. *American Behavioral Scientist, 37,* 697-714.

Weber, L. (1998). A conceptual framework for understanding race, class, gender, and sexuality. *Psychology of Women Quarterly, 22,* 13-32.

Weber, L., & Higginbotham, E. (1997). Black and White professional-managerial women's perceptions of racism and sexism in the workplace. In E. Higginbotham & M. Romero (Eds.), *Women and work: Exploring race, ethnicity, and class* (pp. 153-175). Thousand Oaks, CA: Sage.

Weeks, W. A., & Nantel, J. (1995). The effects of gender and career stage on job satisfaction and performance behavior: A case study. *Journal of Social Behavior and Personality, 10,* 273-288.

Weisman, S. R. (1986, April 11). A daughter returns to Pakistan to cry for victory. *New York Times,* p. 12.

Wellington, A. J. (1994). The male/female wage gap among Whites: 1976 and 1985. *American Sociological Review, 59*(6), 839-848.

Wellington, S. W. (1996). *Women in corporate leadership: Progress and prospects.* New York: Catalyst.

Welsh, M. C. (1979). Attitudinal measures and evaluation of males and females in leadership roles. *Psychological Reports, 45,* 19-22.

Wendelken, D. J., & Inn, A. (1981). Nonperformance influences on performance evaluations: A laboratory phenomenon? *Journal of Applied Psychology, 66,* 149-158.

West, C., & Zimmerman, D. H. (1998). Doing gender. In B. McVicker Clinchy & J. K. Norem (Eds.), *The gender and psychology reader* (pp. 104-124). New York: New York University Press.

Westman, M., & Etzion, D. (1995). Crossover of stress, strain and resources from one spouse to another. *Journal of Organizational Behavior, 16,* 169-181.

Wexley, K. N., & Pulakos, E. D. (1983). The effects of perceptual congruence and sex on subordinates' performance appraisals of their managers. *Academy of Management Journal, 26,* 666-676.

Wharton, A. S. (1992). The social construction of gender and race in organizations: A social identity and group mobilization perspective. In P. S. Tolbert & S. B. Bacharach (Eds.), *Research in the sociology of organizations* (Vol. 10, pp. 55-84). Greenwich, CT: JAI.

Wharton, A. S. (1993). The affective consequences of service work. *Work and Occupations, 20,* 205-232.

Wharton, A. S., & Baron, J. N. (1987). So happy together? The impact of gender segregation on men at work. *American Sociological Review, 52*(5), 574-587.

Wharton, A. S., & Baron, J. N. (1991). Satisfaction? The psychological impact of gender segregation on women at work. *Sociological Quarterly, 32*(3), 365-387.

Wheelan, S. A., & Verdi, A. F. (1992). Differences in male and female patterns of communication in groups: A methodological artifact? *Sex Roles, 27,* 1-15.

White, B., Cox, C., & Cooper, C. L. (1992). *Women's career development.* Oxford, UK: Basil Blackwell.

White, G. B., & White, M. J. (1994). Overevaluation and underevaluation of women job applicants: How general are the vagaries of sex bias? *Journal of Business and Psychology, 9,* 59-68.

White, M. I. (1991). *Challenging tradition: Women in Japan.* New York: Japan Society Department of Publications.

Whitely, W., Dougherty, T. W., & Dreher, G. F. (1991). Relationship of career mentoring and socioeconomic origin to managers' and professionals' early career progress. *Academy of Management Journal, 34,* 331-351.

Whyte, D. (1994). *The heart aroused: Poetry and the preservation of soul in corporate America.* New York: Currency-Doubleday.

Whyte, M. K. (1978). *The status of women in preindustrial societies.* Princeton, NJ: Princeton University Press.

Wiersma, U. J. (1990). Gender differences in job attribute preferences: Work-home role conflict and job level as mediating variables. *Journal of Occupational Psychology, 63,* 231-243.

Wiersma, U. J., & van den Berg, P. (1991). Work-home role conflict, family climate, and domestic responsibilities among men and women in dual-earner families. *Journal of Applied Social Psychology, 21,* 1207-1217.

Wiggins, J. S. (1979). A psychological taxonomy of trait-descriptive terms: The interpersonal domain. *Journal of Personality and Social Psychology, 37,* 395-412.

Wiggins, J. S. (1992). Agency and communion as conceptual coordinates for the understanding and measurement of interpersonal behavior. In W. M. Grove & C. Cicchetti (Eds.), *Thinking clearly about psychology* (pp. 89-113). Minneapolis: University of Minnesota Press.

Wightman, L. F. (1997). The threat to diversity in legal education: An empirical analysis of the consequences of abandoning race as a factor in law school admissions decisions. *New York University Law Review, 72*(1), 1-53.

Wikstrom, T., Palm Linden, K. P., & Michelson, M. (1997). Hub of events or splendid isolation: The home as a context for telework. In E. Gunnarson & U. Huws (Eds.), *Virtually free? Gender, work and spatial choice* (pp. 57-77). Stockholm: NUTEK.

Williams, C. (1992). The glass escalator: Hidden advantages for men in the female professions. *Social Problems, 39*(3), 253-267.

Williams, C. L. (1995). *Still a man's world: Men who do women's work.* Berkeley: University of California Press.

Williams, J., & Giles, H. (1978). The changing status of women in society: An intergroup perspective. In H. Tajfel (Ed.), *European monographs in social psychology* (pp. 431-440). London: Academic Press.

Williams, J. E., & Best, D. L. (1990a). *Measuring sex stereotypes: A multinational study.* Newbury Park, CA: Sage.

Williams, J. E., & Best, D. L. (1990b). *Sex and psyche: Gender and self viewed cross-culturally.* Newbury Park, CA: Sage.

Williams, J. E., & Best, D. L. (1994). Cross-cultural views of women and men. In W. J. Lonner & R. Malpass (Eds.), *Psychology and culture* (pp. 191-196). Boston: Allyn & Bacon.

Williams, K. B., Radefeld, P. S., Binning, J. F., & Sudak, J. R. (1993). When job candidates are "hard" versus "easy-to-get": Effects of candidate availability on employment decisions. *Journal of Applied Social Psychology, 23,* 169-198.

Williams, K. J., & Alliger, G. M. (1994). Role stressors, mood spillover, and perceptions of work-family conflict in employed parents. *Academy of Management Journal, 37,* 837-868.

Wilson, W. J. (1987). *The truly disadvantaged: The inner city, the underclass, and public policy.* Chicago: University of Chicago Press.

Wilson, W. J. (1996). *When work disappears: The world of the new urban poor.* New York: Knopf.

Winett, R. A., Neale, M. S., & Williams, K. R. (1982). The effects of flexible work schedules on urban families with young children: Quasi-experimental, ecological studies. *American Journal of Community Psychology, 10,* 49-64.

Winn, J., & Stewart, K. (1992). The modern entrepreneurial woman. In D. Naffziger & J. Hornsby (Eds.), *United States Association of Small Business and Entrepreneurship proceedings* (pp. 192-201). Muncie, IN: Ball State University.

Winterle, M. (1992). *Work force diversity: Corporate challenges, corporate responses* (Conference Board Report No. 1013). New York: Conference Board.

Witkowski, K., & Leicht, K. T. (1995). The effects of gender segregation, labor force participation, and family roles on the earnings of young adult workers. *Work and Occupations, 22,* 48-72.

Witteman, H. (1993). The interface between sexual harassment and organizational romance. In G. L. Kreps (Ed.), *Sexual harassment: Communication implications* (pp. 27-62). Cresskill, NJ: Hampton.

Woehr, D. J., & Roch, S. G. (1996). Context effects in performance evaluation: The impact of ratee sex and performance level on performance ratings and behavioral recall. *Organizational Behavior and Human Decision Processes, 66*, 31-41.

Wohlers, A. J., Hall, M., & London, M. (1993). Subordinate rating managers: Organizational and demographic correlates of self/subordinate agreement. *Journal of Occupational and Organizational Psychology, 66*, 263-275.

Women in American boardrooms: Through a glass, darkly. (1996, August 10). *The Economist*, pp. 50-51.

Women close the gap: Negotiating a top salary. (1997). *Management, 44*(4), 36-39. (Auckland, New Zealand)

Women workers losing out. (1997). *Worklife Report, 10, 3*, 10, 12.

Wong, P. T. P., Kettlewell, G., & Sproule, C. F. (1985). On the importance of being masculine: Sex role, attribution, and women's career achievement. *Sex Roles, 12*, 757-769.

Wood, W. (1987). Meta-analytic review of sex differences in group performance. *Psychological Bulletin, 102*, 53-71.

Wood, W., Christensen, P. N., Hebl, M. R., & Rothgerber, H. (1997). Conformity to sex-typed norms, affect, and the self-concept. *Journal of Personality and Social Psychology, 73*, 523-535.

Wood, W., & Karten, S. J. (1986). Sex differences in interaction style as a product of perceived sex differences in competence. *Journal of Personality and Social Psychology, 50*, 341-347.

Wood, W., Polek, D., & Aiken, C. (1985). Sex differences in group task performance. *Journal of Personality and Social Psychology, 48*, 63-71.

Wood, W., & Rhodes, N. (1992). Sex differences in interaction style in task groups. In C. L. Ridgeway (Ed.), *Gender, interaction, and inequality* (pp. 97-121). New York: Springer-Verlag.

Woodhall, J., Edwards, C., & Welchman, R. (1997). Organizational restructuring and the achievement of an equal opportunities culture. *Gender, Work and Organization, 4*(1), 2-12.

Woodward, A. (1993). Women in business and management—Belgium. In M. J. Davidson & C. L. Cooper (Eds.), *European women in business and management* (pp. 133-145). London: Paul Chapman.

Woolf, V. (1938). *Three guineas*. San Diego, CA: Harcourt Brace.

Wootton, B. H. (1997). Gender differences in occupational employment. *Monthly Labor Review, 120*(4), 15-24.

Workman, J. E., & Johnson, K. K. P. (1991). The role of cosmetics in attributions about sexual harassment. *Sex Roles, 24*, 759-769.

Worrall, L., & Cooper, C. L. (1997). *IM/UMIST Quality of Working Life Survey*. London: Institute of Management.

Worrell, J., & Robinson, D (1994). Reinventing analogue methods for research with women. *Psychology of Women Quarterly, 18*, 462-476.

Wortman, M. S., Jr. (1987). Entrepreneurship: An integrating typology. *Journal of Management, 13*(2), 259-279.

Wortman, M. S., Jr., & Kleis, M. (1991). Conceptual unity in research on women entrepreneurs. In J. L. Wall & L. R. Jauch (Eds.), *Academy of Management best papers proceedings* (Abstract, p. 469). Madison, WI: Omnipress.

Wosinska, W., Dabul, A. J., Whetstone-Dion, R., & Cialdini, R. B. (1996). Self-presentational responses to success in the organization: The costs and benefits of modesty. *Basic and Applied Social Psychology, 18,* 229-242.

Wright, P., Ferris, S. P., Hiller, J. S., & Kroll, M. (1995). Competitiveness through management of diversity: Effects on stock price valuation. *Academy of Management Journal, 38*(1), 272-287.

Wright, P. C., & Bean, S. A. (1993). Sexual harassment: An issue of employee effectiveness. *Journal of Managerial Psychology, 8*(2), 30-36.

Wyatt, G. E. (1992). The sociocultural context of African American and White American women's rape. *Journal of Social Issues, 48,* 77-91.

Wyatt, G. E., & Riederle, M. (1995). The prevalence and context of sexual harassment among African American and White American women. *Journal of Interpersonal Violence, 10,* 309-321.

Yakura, E. (1996). EEO law and managing diversity. In E. E. Kossek & S. A. Lobel (Eds.), *Managing diversity: Human resource strategies for transforming the workplace* (pp. 25-50). Cambridge, MA: Blackwell.

Yammarino, F. J., & Dubinsky, A. J. (1988). Employee responses: Gender- or job-related differences? *Journal of Vocational Behavior, 32,* 366-383.

Yammarino, F. J., Dubinsky, A. J., Comer, L. B., & Jolson, M. A. (1997). Women and transformational and contingent reward leadership: A multiple-levels-of-analysis perspective. *Academy of Management Journal, 40*(1), 205-222.

Yeung, A. K., & Berman, R. (1997). Adding value through human resources: Reorienting human resource measurement to drive business performance. *Human Resource Management, 36*(3), 321-336.

Yoder, J. D. (1991). Rethinking tokenism: Looking beyond numbers. *Gender & Society, 5*(1), 178-192.

Yoder, J. D. (1994). Looking beyond numbers: The effects of gender status, job prestige and occupational gender-typing on tokenism processes. *Social Psychology Quarterly, 57*(2), 150-159.

Yoder, J. D., & Aniakudo, P. (1995). The responses of African American women firefighters to gender harassment at work. *Sex Roles, 32,* 125-137.

Yoder, J. D., & Aniakudo, P. (1997). "Outsider within" the firehouse: Subordination and difference in the social interactions of African American women firefighters. *Gender & Society, 11,* 324-341.

York, K. M. (1989). Defining sexual harassment in workplaces: A policy-capturing approach. *Academy of Management Journal, 32*(4), 830-850.

Youngblood, S. A., & Chambers-Cook, K. (1984, February). Child care assistance can improve employee attitudes and behavior. *Personnel Administrator,* pp. 93-95.

Yuen, E. C., & Lim, V. (1992). Dual-earner families in Singapore: Issues and challenges. In S. Lewis, D. N. Izraeli, & H. Hootsmans (Eds.), *Dual-earner families: International perspectives* (pp. 62-79). London: Sage.

Zabalza, A., & Tzannatos, Z. (1994). The effect of Britain's anti-discrimination legislation on relative pay and employment. In P. Burstein (Ed.), *Equal employment opportunity, labor market discrimination and public policy* (pp. 329-342). New York: Walter de Gruyter.

Zabusky, S. E., & Barley, S. R. (1997). Redefining success. Ethnographic observations on the careers of technicians. In P. Osterman (Ed.), *Broken ladders: Managerial careers in the new economy.* Oxford, UK: Oxford University Press.

Zack, N. (1998). *Thinking about race.* Belmont, CA: Wadsworth.

Zapalska, A. M. (1997). A profile of woman entrepreneurs and enterprises in Poland. *Journal of Small Business Management, 35*(4), 76-82.

Zebrowitz, L. A., Tenenbaum, D. R., & Goldstein, L. H. (1991). The impact of job applicants' facial maturity, gender, and academic achievement on hiring recommendations. *Journal of Applied Social Psychology, 21,* 525-548.

Zedeck, S. (1992). Introduction: Exploring the domain of work and family concerns. In S. Zedeck (Ed.), *Work, families, and organizations* (pp. 1-32). San Francisco: Jossey-Bass.

Zenger, T. R., & Lawrence, B. S. (1989). Organizational demography: The differential effects of age and tenure distributions on technical communication. *Academy of Management Journal, 32,* 353-376.

Zinkhan, G. M., & Stoiadin, L. F. (1984). Impact of sex role stereotypes on service priority in department stores. *Journal of Applied Psychology, 69,* 691-693.

Zucker, L. G., & Rosenstein, C. (1981). Taxonomies of institutional structure: Dual economy reconsidered. *American Sociological Review, 46,* 869-884.

Name Index

Subject Index

AA. *See* Affirmative action
Academy of Management Journal (AMJ), 486, 488, 491
Academy of Management Review (AMR), 486, 488, 492
Adarand v. Pena, 434
Affirmative action (AA):
    attitudes toward, 24-25, 447-451, 452, 453-454
    court decisions, 433-434
    debate on, 429, 432, 451, 452
    earnings impact, 440
    economic effects, 436-441, 443
    future research directions, 450-451, 452
    history in United States, 430-434
    human resource management practices, 441-442
    in higher education, 436-438, 451-452, 466
    in local governments, 439
    in other countries, 434-436, 464
    in U.S. government, 332, 438-439
    minority set-aside programs, 433-434, 442-443
    mistaken beliefs about programs, 449-450
    program components, 429
    program managers, 441-442, 443
    programs ended in California and Texas, 438, 443
    requirements for federal contractors, 439-441
    results, 429-430
    selection process, 446-447
    social and psychological effects, 444-447
    stigmatization of beneficiaries, 445, 466
    strict scrutiny standard, 433-434
    See also Diversity policies
African American men. *See* Black men
African American women. *See* Black women
African Americans. *See* Blacks

Albright, Madeleine K., 239
American Association of University Women, 308
American Business Women International, 387
The American Psychologist, 484-485
AMJ. See Academy of Management Journal
AMR. See Academy of Management Review
Androgyny, 6-7, 9, 228, 354
Applicants. *See* Job applicants
Aquino, Corazon, 255, 256
Asian Americans:
    attitudes toward affirmative action, 447
    effects of affirmative action, 440
    gender stereotypes, 34
    sexual harassment of women, 277
    See also Minority individuals
Asian men, 34
Assessment centers, 169, 195
Australia:
    earnings gender gap, 104, 105
    gender bias in interviews, 155
    women in top management, 329
    women-owned businesses, 371, 383
Autonomy:
    effects on job satisfaction and family life, 402, 403
    experienced by married men, 404
Aversive racism, 448-449
Avon Corporation, 464, 470

Baby boomers, 316, 317
Beers, Charlotte, 257
Belgium:
    earnings gender gap, 105
    gender discrimination, 434-435

619

About the Editor

Gary N. Powell is Professor of Management and Ackerman Scholar at the University of Connecticut. He received his Ph.D. in organizational behavior from the University of Massachusetts. He is author of two previous books, *Women and Men in Management,* now in its second edition, and *Gender and Diversity in the Workplace: Learning Activities and Exercises,* both published by Sage. He has served as Chairperson of the Women in Management Division of the Academy of Management and has won both the Janet Chusmir Service Award for his contributions to the division and the Sage Scholarship Award for his contributions to research on gender in organizations. He has won an award for innovation in education from the Committee on Equal Opportunity for Women of the American Assembly of Collegiate Schools of Business (AACSB) and has also won the University of Connecticut President's Award for Promoting Multiculturalism. He has published over 70 articles and presented over 80 papers at professional conferences. Powell has served on the Board of Governors and as cochair of the Status of Minorities Task Force of the Academy of Management. He is a past president and fellow of the Eastern Academy of Management and has served on the editorial boards of *Academy of Management Review* and *Academy of Management Executive.* He is a former project engineer and systems analyst with General Electric, having graduated from its Manufacturing Management Program. He has provided management training and development for numerous companies, including The Implementation Partners (TIP), United Technologies–Pratt & Whitney Division, and GE-Capital, and frequently speaks on issues pertaining to gender and diversity in the workplace.

About the Contributors

Nancy J. Adler is Professor in the Faculty of Management at McGill University in Montreal, Canada. She conducts research on strategic international human resource management, global leadership, and women as global leaders and managers. She has authored more than 70 articles and produced the film *A Portable Life*. Her book *International Dimensions of Organizational Behavior* (3rd ed., 1997) has over 100,000 copies in print in English, French, Chinese, and Japanese. She has also edited the books *Women in Management Worldwide* and *Competitive Frontiers: Women Managers in a Global Economy*. In addition to her research and writing, She consults with major global companies and government organizations on projects in Asia, Europe, North and South America, and the Middle East. She is a fellow of both the Academy of Management and the Academy of International Business. She has been recognized with numerous awards, including ASTD's International Leadership Award, SIETAR's Outstanding Senior Interculturalist Award, the YWCA's Woman of Distinction Award, and the Sage Award for scholarly contributions to management. Canada has honored her as one of the country's top teachers.

Alice O. Andrews is Vice President of Research & Development at Valour, Inc., helping companies improve employee relations through real-time communication. Her primary research focus is understanding employee development and employee retention in fast-growth companies and companies undergoing major change. She received her Ph.D. in organizational behavior from the School of Industrial and Labor Relations at Cornell University.

Kathryn M. Bartol is Professor of Management and Organization at the Robert H. Smith School of Business at University of Maryland. She holds a Ph.D. from Michigan State University and a master's degree from the University of Michigan. She is past president of the Academy of Management. Her major research interests center on gender issues, compensation, performance appraisal, and information technology. She is author of several books and numerous articles in such journals as *Academy of Management Journal, Journal of Applied Psychology, Personnel Psychology, Industrial and Labor Relations Review, Academy of Management Review, Computers and Automation, MIS Quarterly, Journal of Business Research, Journal of Vocation Behavior, Journal of Occupational Psychology,* and *Employee Relations Law Journal.* She has served on the review boards of *Journal of Applied Psychology* and *Academy of Management Review* and is currently on the review board of *Human Resource Management Review.* She is a fellow of the Academy of Management, the American Psychological Association, and the American Psychological Society. She is a recipient of the Sage Scholarship Award from the Academy of Management, Gender and Diversity in Organizations Division. She has been named a University of Maryland Distinguished Scholar-Teacher and has received numerous teaching awards from the Smith School.

Susan M. Bosco is Assistant Professor in the Gobelli School of Business at Roger Williams University in Bristol, Rhode Island. She is a recent graduate of the doctoral program at the College of Business Administration at the University of Rhode Island. Her central research interest is in workplace diversity, particularly the formation of stereotypes. Diversity training implications of this process are the major areas that she is investigating. She also researches women in the workplace, especially influences on career choice. As an outgrowth of this study, she has found it interesting to review the overall state of research on gender in organizations. She has presented papers in these areas at the Eastern Academy of Management, Association for Women in Psychology, and the Institute for Behavioral and Applied Management.

Lynn Bowes-Sperry has been Assistant Professor in Management at James Madison University since 1996. She earned a Ph.D. in management from the University of Connecticut in 1996, and she has had articles accepted for publication in several journals and books, including *Journal of Management, Human Resources Management Review, Labor Law Journal, Small Group Research,* and *Group & Organization Management.* Her research focuses primarily on the topics of sexual harassment, ethical decision making and behavior, bystander intervention, and fairness in the workplace. She is a member of the

Academy of Management, Society of Human Resources Management, and International Association of Business and Society.

D. Anthony Butterfield is Professor of Management and Organizational Behavior in the Isenberg School of Management at the University of Massachusetts, Amherst. Since his days as a doctoral student in the organizational psychology program at the University of Michigan, he has been interested in leadership. His particular focus has been on gender and leadership and on leadership at the top of organizations and countries. His recent publications include articles in *Academy of Management Journal* on gender and the glass ceiling (1994) and on race and the glass ceiling (1997), both with Gary Powell. He and James Grinnell presented a paper at the 1998 Academy of Management meetings on U.S. presidential leadership. He has been tracking the U.S. presidential elections since 1980, comparing what people are looking for in a "good president" against the characteristics of the actual candidates. He has also occupied several leadership positions, including director of the doctoral program in the School of Management at UMass, Chair of the Department of Management at UMass, and President of the Eastern Academy of Management.

Linda L. Carli is Visiting Associate Professor of Psychology at Wellesley College. She received her Ph.D. in psychology from the University of Massachusetts at Amherst. Her research interests include gender differences in group interaction, communication and influence, as well as reactions to adversity and victimization. Her papers have been published in edited volumes and journals, including *Journal of Personality and Social Psychology, Psychological Bulletin,* and *Personality and Social Psychology Bulletin.* Her most recent publications include "Gender, Interpersonal Power, and Social Influence" (*Journal of Social Issues,* 1999), "Cognitive Reconstruction, Hindsight, and Reactions to Victims and Perpetrators," (*Personality and Social Psychology Bulletin,* 1999), and "Gender, Communication, and Social Influence: A Developmental Perspective," coauthored with Danuta Bukatko (in *The Developmental Social Psychology of Gender,* edited by T. Eckes & H. M. Trautner). Currently, she is involved in research examining gender effects on self-evaluation in children and adults. She has developed and conducted negotiation and conflict resolution workshops for women leaders and has also lectured for businesses and government agencies on sex discrimination and the challenges faced by professional women.

Bennett Cherry is a doctoral candidate in the Department of Management and Policy at the University of Arizona. Prior to obtaining a master's degree at the University of Arizona (1997), he was employed with the real estate firm

SENTRE Partners, where he developed strategic real estate plans for multimillion-dollar commercial properties in southern California. His research interests focus primarily on interpersonal trust. His dissertation addresses the development and consequences of trust between a manager and employee, and he has also examined individuals' justice and fairness considerations and how these relate to their expectations. He is also interested in understanding how different service delivery mechanisms affect a customer's evaluation of the service experience. Recent work in this area has focused on the trust between service provider and customer and the degree to which the two individuals know each other. He is currently developing and implementing a comprehensive performance feedback system for a large public safety department. He is a member of the Academy of Management, Society for Industrial/Organizational Psychology, Society for Human Resource Management, and the Society for Judgment & Decision Making.

Cary L. Cooper is BUPA Professor of Organizational Psychology and Health in the Manchester School of Management, and Pro-Vice-Chancellor (External Activities) of the University of Manchester Institute of Science and Technology (UMIST). He is author of more than 80 books (on occupational stress, women at work, and industrial and organizational psychology) and more than 300 scholarly articles, and he is a frequent contributor to national newspapers, TV, and radio. He is founding editor of *Journal of Organizational Behavior* and is coeditor of *Stress Medicine* and *International Journal of Management Review.* He is a fellow of the British Psychological Society, the Royal Society of Arts, the Royal Society of Medicine, and the Royal Society of Health. He is president of the British Academy of Management, a Companion of the (British) Institute of Management, and one of the first UK-based fellows of the (American) Academy of Management (having also won the 1998 Distinguished Service Award for his contribution to management science from the Academy of Management). He is editor (jointly with Chris Argyris of Harvard Business School) of the international scholarly *Blackwell Encyclopedia of Management.* He has been an adviser to the World Health Organization and ILO, and he recently published a major report for the EU's European Foundation for the Improvement of Living and Work Conditions, *Stress Prevention in the Workplace.*

Elizabeth A. Cooper is Professor of Management at the University of Rhode Island. She received her doctorate in industrial/organizational psychology from the University of Akron. She is presently on the executive board of the Gender and Diversity in Organizations Division of the Academy of Management as well as a board member of the Eastern Academy of Management. Her areas of interest include gender discrimination in the workplace, primarily in compensation; gender differences in career development; and research methods. Her work has been published in such journals as *Academy of Management Review, Journal of Applied Psychology, Human Relations,* and *Personnel Psychology.* She has recently developed an interest in the Americans with Disabilities Act and the issue of reasonable accommodations in the workplace with an emphasis on the deaf and late-deafened worker.

Marilyn J. Davidson is Professor of Managerial Psychology in the Manchester School of Management, University of Manchester Institute of Science and Technology. She is former editor of *Women in Management Review,* and associate editor of five other journals. She is author of 13 books on women at work, women in management, and occupational stress and over 100 academic journal articles. Two of her most recent books are *Shattering the Glass Ceiling: The Woman Manager* and *The Black and Ethnic Minority Woman Manager: Cracking the Concrete Ceiling* (shortlisted for the Best Management Book of the Year, 1997). She has been employed as a research consultant (predominantly in the areas of occupational stress and equal opportunity issues) for numerous organizations and government bodies. She is a chartered psychologist and a fellow of the British Psychological Society and Royal Society of Arts. Other publications include *European Women in Business and Management* (coedited with C. L. Cooper); *Women in Management: Current Research Issues* (coedited with R. Burke); and "Women and Employment," in *Psychology at Work*, edited by P. Warr.

Alice H. Eagly is Professor of Psychology at Northwestern University. Earlier, she served on the faculties of Purdue University, University of Massachusetts in Amherst, and Michigan State University and held visiting professor appointments at University of Tübingen, Harvard University, and University of Illinois. She earned her doctoral degree in social psychology from the University of Michigan. She has published widely on the psychology of attitudes, especially attitude change and attitude structure. She also specializes in the study of gender. In both of these areas, she has carried out primary research and meta-analyses of research literature. She is author of *Sex Differences in Social Behavior: A Social Role Interpretation* and (with coauthor Shelly Chaiken) *The Psychology of Attitudes,* and is also author of numerous journal articles and chapters. She is president of the Midwestern Psychological Association, past president of the Society of Personality and Social Psychology, former chair of the Board of Scientific Affairs of the American Psychological Association, and a fellow of the American Psychological Association and American Psychological Society. She has received the Donald Campbell Award for Distinguished Contribution to Social Psychology and a Citation as Distinguished Leader for Women in Psychology.

Bernardo M. Ferdman is Associate Professor in the Organizational Psychology Programs at the California School of Professional Psychology (CSPP) in San Diego, where he specializes in diversity and multiculturalism in organizations, ethnic and cultural identity, Latinos and Latinas in the workplace, and organizational development. He received his Ph.D. in Psychology from Yale University in 1987. He has published over two dozen books, articles, and book chapters, and has made more than 50 presentations at professional conferences in the areas of ethnic, cultural, and gender diversity and organizational psychology. He has conducted workshops and consulted in the areas of cultural diversity, ethnic and gender relations, Latino identity, and team building for a variety of organizations. He is editor of *A Resource Guide for Teaching and Research on Diversity* (1994) and coeditor of *Literacy Across Languages and Cultures* (1994). In 1991, he was awarded the Gordon Allport Intergroup Relations Prize by the Society for the Psychological Study of Social Issues for his paper, "The Dynamics of Ethnic Diversity in Organizations: Toward Integrative Models." He is a member of the editorial boards of *International Journal of Intercultural Relations* and of the *Interamerican Journal of Psychology,* serves as Treasurer of the Interamerican Society of Psychology, and was a committee chair for the Society for Industrial and Organizational Psychology. He is a charter fellow of the International Academy of Intercultural Research and is active in the Gender and Diversity in Organizations Division of the Academy of Management.

Sandra Fielden is Director of the Centre for Business Psychology at the Manchester School of Management, University of Manchester Institute of Science and Technology. She is responsible for the management of the center, which is involved in applied activities within the public and private sector. These activites include the conducting of stress and culture audits; the delivery of stress management courses and associated interpersonal skills training, for example, in assertiveness, time management, and team working; conducting attitude surveys; and training trainers. Research projects have included sources of stress in unemployed male and female managers, stress in hospital doctors, and identification of the needs of male and female entrepreneurs. Additional research interests cover cross-cultural work with female entrepreneurs, buyer-supplier interactions, the organizational change process in voluntary organizations, women in construction, and Health Circles. Publications include 12 academic articles, four book chapters, and two books in press. She has provided refereeing and editorial services, as well as being involved in conference organization, and has presented academic papers at conferences throughout Europe.

Sharon Foley is Assistant Professor at Richmond, the American International University in London. She earned her Ph.D. in management in 1998 from the University of Connecticut. Her dissertation topic is the effect of the perceived glass ceiling on perceptions of promotion fairness. She has published articles in *Journal of Management, Journal of Organizational Behavior,* and *Journal of Small Business Management.* Her research interests include issues related to women in management and organizational justice.

Mary Lizabeth Gatta is a doctoral candidate in sociology at Rutgers University. Her dissertation research examines the emotional balancing practices of individuals in the workplace. Specifically, she studies how restaurant servers and managers deal with their emotions in work interactions by creating and using different types of emotion scripts. She has presented her work on emotions at the American Sociological Association annual meetings, the annual conference of the Institute for the Analysis of Contemporary Society, and the Rutgers University Sociology Department Colloquium Series. She has presented her work on gender earnings at the Providence College Women's Studies Program "Celebration of Work on Gender." She also continues to work with Patricia Roos on issues related to occupational feminization and gender earnings inequality.

Mary E. Graham is Visiting Assistant Professor in the Management Science Department in the School of Business and Public Management at George Washington University. She earned her Ph.D. in 1995 from the School of Industrial and Labor Relations at Cornell University, with a concentration in human resource studies. She has published articles on gender-related pay discrimination and public policy, the introduction and effectiveness of new pay systems, and gender differences in pay satisfaction, including a forthcoming article in *Journal of Organizational Behavior* on women's and men's relative pay satisfaction. Previously, she earned her CPA in New York State and worked as a legislative aide in the U.S. House of Representatives.

Laura M. Graves is Associate Professor of Management at Clark University. She received her Ph.D. in social psychology from the University of Connecticut. She has served as chair of the Gender and Diversity in Organizations Division of the Academy of Management. Her current research focuses on multicultural work teams and the employment interview, particularly biases in interviewers' decision processes. Her work has appeared in leading academic journals, including *Academy of Management Review, Journal of Applied Psychology, Personnel*

Psychology, Journal of Organizational Behavior, Journal of Occupational and Organizational Psychology, and *Human Relations.* In addition, she has contributed chapters to several books and presented numerous papers at academic meetings. She has served as a guest editor for *Academy of Management Journal* and on its editorial board, and she is a regular reviewer for several other scholarly journals. Prior to joining the faculty at Clark, she worked in Corporate Human Resources at Aetna. She has also served on the faculty of the University of Connecticut.

Jeffrey H. Greenhaus is William A. Mackie Professorship of Commerce and Engineering and serves as Director of the Doctoral Program in Business. His research interests include work-family relationships, career management, and the management of diversity. He has published his research in such journals as *Academy of Management Journal, Academy of Management Review, Organizational Behavior and Human Decision Processes, Journal of Applied Psychology, Journal of Organizational Behavior, Personnel Psychology,* and *Journal of Vocational Behavior.* He is coauthor (with Gerard A. Callanan) of *Career Management* (third edition forthcoming) and has coedited (with Saroj Parasuraman) *Integrating Work and Family: Challenges and Choices in a Changing World* (1997). He is currently completing (with Stewart D. Friedman) *Allies or Enemies? How Choices About Work and Family Affect the Quality of Men's and Women's Lives.* He has served on the editorial review boards of *Journal of Applied Psychology, Journal of Vocational Behavior, International Journal of Career Management,* and *Lifestyle: Family and the Economy* and is former associate editor of *Journal of Vocational Behavior.*

James P. Grinnell is a doctoral candidate in the Organization Studies Program at the University of Massachusetts. In addition to gender and management research, his areas of interest in the leadership domain include charismatic leadership, as well as the relationship between macro variables and leader style.

Markus Groth is a doctoral student in management and policy at the University of Arizona. He is conducting research in organizational behavior and human resource management: the service delivery process, service interactions between employees and customers, and the link between customer service issues and human resource management practices. He is also interested in judgment and decision-making issues. His master's thesis, titled "Effects of Explanations and Waiting Duration Information on Perceptions of Service Delivery Delays," examines how certain attributes of waiting for a service delivery affect customers' reactions to the service and the wait itself. His publications include articles on attitudes toward suicide in Germans and U.S. nationals and on the perception of time pressure. He teaches undergraduate business classes and currently provides consulting services for a large public safety department. This work entails the development and implementation of a performance feedback system.

Barbara A. Gutek is McClelland Professor of Management and Policy at the University of Arizona. She spent 1992-1993 as a visiting professor at the California Institute of Technology and 1985 as a visiting scholar in Germany. She is author or editor of 10 books and over 80 articles, including *The Dynamics of Service, Women's Career Development* (coedited with Laurie Larwood), *Sex and the Workplace*, and *Women and Work: A Psychological Perspective* (co-authored with Veronica Nieva). She is a fellow in the American Psychological Association and American Psychological Society, was president of the Society for the Psychological Study of Social Issues (SPSSI), served on the board of governors of the Academy of Management, and was chair of the Women in Management Division, Academy of Management. She has been on the editorial boards of *Academy of Management Journal, Journal of Personality and Social Psychology*, and *Journal of Vocational Behavior.* In 1994, she received two awards from APA: the Division 35 Heritage Award for a "substantial and outstanding body of research on women and gender" and the Committee on Women in Leadership Award, and the Sage Scholarship Award presented by the Women in Management Division of the Academy of Management. The National Institute of Mental Health and the National Science Foundation have supported her research, which currently focuses on two areas, the changing nature of service delivery and the efficacy of the reasonable woman standard in hostile environment cases of sexual harassment. She received her Ph.D. from the University of Michigan in 1975.

Jerry A. Jacobs is Professor of Sociology and chair of the Graduate Program in Sociology at the University of Pennsylvania, where he has taught since earning his Ph.D. in sociology from Harvard University in 1983. He has studied a number of aspects of women's employment, including authority, earnings, working conditions, part-time work, and entry into male-dominated occupations. His current research projects include a study of women in higher education, funded by the Spencer Foundation, and a study of working time and work-family conflict, funded by the Sloan Foundation.

Alison M. Konrad is Associate Professor of Human Resource Administration at Temple University's Fox School of Business and Management. She received her Ph.D. in applied social psychology from Claremont Graduate University in 1987. She was a postdoctoral fellow at the Stanford University Department of Sociology for two years prior to joining Temple University. She has published several articles and book chapters on topics relevant to gender and diversity in organizations, including wage inequality, promotion discrimination, affirmative action, and workforce diversity. Her work has appeared in *Administrative Science Quarterly, Academy of Management Journal, Group & Organization Management, Human Relations, Journal of Management Inquiry,* and other publications. In 1990, 1992, and 1997, she received the Dorothy Harlow Best Paper Award from the Academy of Management's Gender and Diversity in Organizations Division. In 1996-1997, she was chair of the Gender and Diversity in Organizations Division and, in 1998, she received the division's Sage Scholarship Award. In 1997-1998, she was president of the Eastern Academy of Management. She serves on the editorial board of *Academy of Management Review* and is associate editor of *Group & Organization Management.* Current research projects focus on attitudes toward affirmative action programs, sex differences in job attribute preferences, and effects of immigration policy on organizations and individuals.

Karen Korabik is Professor in the Psychology Department at the University of Guelph in Guelph, Ontario, Canada. She received her Ph.D. in evaluative/applied psychology from St. Louis University in 1975. She is a core faculty member in both the Applied Social and the Industrial/Organizational Psychology Ph.D. programs. She was a founding member of the University of Guelph's Women's Studies Program and is currently an affiliate of the Centre for Collaborative International Development Studies and the Centre for Families, Work, and Well-being. She has been coordinator and secretary/treasurer of the Canadian Psychological Association's Section on Program Evaluation and secretary/treasurer of the Section on Social Psychology. She has also served on the board of directors of the Ontario Chapter of the Canadian Evaluation Society and is a fellow of the American Psychological Association. Her numerous publications and conference presentations include studies relating gender to person perception and impression formation; to stress, coping, and social support; to turnover and work-family conflict (with Hazel Rosin); to acculturation, leadership, conflict resolution, and managerial effectiveness (with Roya Ayman); to solidarity behavior (with Mona Abbondanza); and to interpersonal problems (with Donald McCreary). She has also written several articles on women managers in the People's Republic of China based on data collected during trips there in 1985 and 1990.

Suzan Lewis is Reader in Psychology at Manchester Metropolitan University in the United Kingdom and one of the directors of the multisite Work-Life Research Centre. Her main research interests are in work-family issues, gender, and the management of diversity. She recently coordinated a European Commission-funded five-country study of young adults' orientations to future work and family, and she is currently working on a study of the impact of economic and workplace change on the family and a project developing a work-life benchmark. She has published numerous books and articles on work, family, and gender. Recent publications include *The Work-Family Challenge: Rethinking Employment* (Sage, 1996); "Work, Family and Well-Being. Can the Law Help?" in *Legal and Criminological Psychology* (1997); "Family Friendly Policies: Organizational Change or Playing Around at the Margins?" in *Gender, Work and Organization*; and "Young Europeans' Orientations to Families and Work," in *Annals of the American Academy of Political and Social Science* (1999). She is coeditor of the international journal *Community, Work and Family*.

Frank Linnehan is Assistant Professor of Human Resources at Drexel University's LeBow College of Business. He received his Ph.D. in human resources administration from Temple University and has taught both graduate and undergraduate courses in human resources, organization behavior, compensation, leadership, and management. His research interests include affirmative action, equal employment and workforce diversity initiatives, and school-to-work transitions and workplace mentoring for high school students. He has authored or coauthored articles that have appeared in *Academy of Management Journal, Group & Organization Management, Applied Psychology: An International Journal*, and *Educational Evaluation and Policy Analysis*. Prior to receiving his Ph.D., he worked for 17 years in both line and human resource management in the financial services industry. During his 11 years with GE Capital, he held positions as a training and development specialist, HR generalist and human resources manager. At Meritor Savings Bank, he was VP-Human Resources and responsible for the employment, training, and employee relations functions.

Sharon A. Lobel is Associate Professor of Management at Seattle University. Her teaching experience includes two years at a Brazilian university. At the University of Michigan School of Business (1987-1991), she served as Visiting Assistant Professor and consultant for the Global Leadership Executive Education Program. She is Research Fellow at the Work and Family Roundtable, Boston College, whose mission is to provide leadership to shape corporate and public responses to work-life issues. As a member of the Wharton Work/Life Roundtable, she has been active in efforts to develop training materials for business schools and corporations on work-life concerns. She has served on the Research Advisory Panel at Catalyst for a study of the implementation of flexible work arrangements. She was associate editor of *Human Resource Management* and on the editorial board of *Academy of Management Journal*. She has facilitated group problem solving during many retreat weekends at Outdoor Learning. Her research focuses on the many aspects of managing diversity in organizations and has appeared in *Academy of Management Journal, Academy of Management Review,* and *Organizational Dynamics.* She has been quoted in the *Wall Street Journal, New York Times,* and *Seattle Times.* Her publications include a coedited book, *Managing Diversity: Human Resource Strategies for Transforming the Workplace.* She holds a Ph.D. from Harvard University.

Mark Maier is Associate Professor and founding chair of the Organizational Leadership Program at Chapman University, recipient of the 1998 Outstanding Leadership Program Award. He earned his Ph.D. in sociology from Cornell University, with minors in industrial and labor relations, educational psychology, and women's studies. His scholarship ranges from servant leadership to corporate masculinity to ethical decision making and has appeared in leading anthologies, management texts, and journals. He is writer-producer of the authoritative video-based instructional module *A Major Malfunction . . . : The Story Behind the Space Shuttle* Challenger *Disaster* (1992), adopted by 700 universities and corporations in 23 countries. He has received numerous awards for his teaching and scholarship, including a Woodrow Wilson Fellowship and the Fritz Roethlisbergr and Dorothy Harlow Awards. He consults and lectures widely on issues related to leadership, team development, ethics, and diversity. His clients include the U.S. Space and Missile Systems Command, the Fundación Acindar (Buenos Aires), the Federal Emergency Management Agency, Marriott Hotels, 3M, NYNEX, and Boeing. He is active in the Organizational Behavior Teaching Society and has served twice on the executive committee of the Gender and Diversity in Organizations Division of the Academy of Management.

Dorothy Perrin Moore is a Faculty Fellow and Professor of Business Administration at the Citadel, in Charleston, South Carolina. Previously an owner and operator of a small business, she is the lead author of *Women Entrepreneurs: Moving Beyond the Glass Ceiling* (Sage, 1997), nominated for a Terry Book Award in 1998. Her second book on women entrepreneurs is forthcoming. She writes a monthly-featured column on women entrepreneurs for the *Post and Courier.* She is the coauthor of two other books, one nominated for a national award, dealing with longitudinal policy and organizational changes. She serves on the editorial book review board for *Journal of Organizational Behavior.* She has served as chair of the Women in Management Division, editor of *Academy of Management Best Papers Proceedings,* vice president of the Individual Entrepreneurship Division, and vice president of the Minority and Women's Division of USASBE, on the board of the Southern Management Association, and on the editorial review boards of *Journal of Business Ethics* and *Group &*

Organization Management. She is the recipient of the Sage Janet Chusmir Service Award and the Sage Scholarship Award. In 1998, she received the Outstanding MBA Faculty Award from students at the Citadel. She holds a Ph.D. in management, organizational behavior, and human resource management from the University of South Carolina.

Saroj Parasuraman is University Distinguished Professor of Management at Drexel University. She received her Ph.D. in organizational behavior from the State University of New York at Buffalo. Formerly employed at Wayne State University, she joined Drexel as Associate Professor in 1983 and was promoted to the rank of Professor in 1989. She received the Drexel University Research Achievement Award in 1996. Her research interests focus on work-related stress, career development of women and minorities, and work-family relationships especially among dual-career partners. Her research has been widely published in such journals as *Academy of Management Journal, Journal of Organizational Behavior, Journal of Vocational Behavior, Journal of Management, Organizational Behavior and Human Decision Processes, International Journal of Man Machine Studies*, and *MIS Quarterly*. She is editor (with Jeffrey H. Greenhaus) of *Integrating Work and Family: Challenges and Choices for a Changing World*. In addition, she has also contributed several book chapters and presented numerous scholarly papers at national and international conferences. She is a member of the Academy of Management and serves on the editorial review board of *Academy of Management Journal*. She is also book review editor of the *Journal of Organizational Behavior*.

Belle Rose Ragins is Professor of Management at the University of Wisconsin–Milwaukee. Her research interests include mentoring, gender, and diversity in organizations. Her research has been published in *Academy of Management Journal, Academy of Management Review, Academy of Management Executive, Journal of Applied Psychology*, and *Psychological Bulletin*. She has received five national awards for her research, including the Sage Award for scholarly contributions to management, the American Psychological Association's Placek Award, and three Best Paper Awards from the National Academy of Management. She serves on the review boards of *Academy of Management Journal, Journal of Applied Psychology*, and *Journal of Vocational Behavior*. She was awarded the first Visiting Research Fellowship position at Catalyst, and currently serves as Research Advisor to 9-to-5, the National Association of Working Women.

Anne H. Reilly is Associate Professor in the Department of Management, School of Business Administration, Loyola University Chicago. Her educational background includes degrees in economics and finance, and she has a Ph.D. in organizational behavior from Northwestern University. Prior to her doctoral work, she worked as a commercial banking officer. Her research interests include women in management, dual-career families, and job relocation, as well as organizational change and crisis management. She has published articles on these topics in both academic and managerial journals, including *Academy of Management Journal, Journal of Applied Psychology, Strategic Management Journal, Journal of Vocational Behavior, Journal of Organizational Behavior,* and *Sloan Management Review.* She is currently working on a research project on work and family issues funded by a grant from Abbott Laboratories.

Patricia A. Roos is Professor of Sociology and Dean, Social & Behavioral Sciences, at Rutgers University. Her current research interests include occupations and professions, sociology of work, stratification, and gender. She published a comparative analysis of occupational sex segregation in 12 industrial societies: *Gender and Work: A Comparative Analysis of Industrial Societies* (1985). With Barbara Reskin, she published *Job Queues, Gender Queues: Explaining Women's Inroads Into Male Occupations* (1990), which used a queuing framework to examine the determinants and consequences of women's movement into traditionally male occupations since 1970. She continues her work with Barbara Reskin on changing occupational sex composition and on the interrelationship between occupational sex composition and earnings. She has also had a long-time interest in the gender switch that occurred in typesetting and composition, both at the turn of the century and since 1970, and has examined women's movement into sociology (with Katharine Jones) and the feminization of human resource management (with Joan Manley). She is currently working with Mary Gatta on issues related to occupational feminization and gender earnings inequality. She received her Ph.D. from the University of California, Los Angeles.

Linda K. Stroh is Professor at the Institute of Human Resources and Industrial Relations, Loyola University, Chicago. Her research focuses primarily on organizational policy affecting managers' careers, attitudes, and commitment to the organization, both domestically and internationally. Her work can be found in *Journal of Applied Psychology, Personnel Psychology, Academy of Management Journal, Strategic Management Journal, Journal of Organizational Behavior, Sloan Management Review, Journal of World Business,* and other journals. Her work has also been cited in the *Wall Street Journal, New York Times, Washington Post, Chicago Tribune, Fortune* magazine, *Newsweek, U.S. News & World Report,* and *Business Week,* among other news and popular press outlets. Her work has also been featured on the *Nightly News With Tom Brokaw.* She currently serves as the academic adviser for the International Personnel Association and has consulted with over 30 organizations regarding such issues as motivation, leadership, change management, problem solving, and global management. She also serves on the editorial review boards of *Journal of Vocational Behavior, Journal of World Business, International Journal of Organizational Analysis,* and *Journal of Applied Business Research.*

Jasmine Tata is Assistant Professor of Management at Loyola University, Chicago, where she serves on the advisory board of the Gannon Center for Women and Leadership. Her research interests lie in the areas of organizational justice, organizational communication, team management, and gender issues in organizations. She has published several articles in these areas, including recent publications in *International Journal of Intercultural Relations, Journal of Managerial Issues, Psychological Reports, Journal of Psychology,* and *Group & Organization Management.* In addition, she has presented at meetings of professional and industry associations. She received her Ph.D. from Syracuse University in 1993.

Pamela S. Tolbert is Associate Professor and Department Chair of Organizational Behavior in the School of Industrial and Labor Relations at Cornell University. Her general research interests include gender and racial inequality in organizations, processes of change in workplace institutions, and relations between professions and organizations. Currently, she is involved a study of the changes in the employment of non-tenure-track faculty by colleges and universities, and a study examining the use of work-family policies by employees. Recent publications include "Men's and Women's Definitions of 'Good' Jobs: Similarities and Differences by Age and Across Time," coauthored with Phyllis Moen in *Work and Occupations* (1998); "Institutionalization and Structuration: Studying the Links Between Action and Institution," coauthored with Stephen Barley in *Organization Studies* (1997); and "Occupations, Organizations and Boundaryless Careers," published in *Boundaryless Careers* (1996), edited by Michael Arthur and Denise Rousseau.